Parliaments and English Politics
1621–1629

Parliaments and English Politics 1621–1629

BY

CONRAD RUSSELL

CLARENDON PRESS · OXFORD
1979

Oxford University Press, Walton Street, Oxford OX2 6DP

OXFORD LONDON GLASGOW
NEW YORK TORONTO MELBOURNE WELLINGTON
IBADAN NAIROBI DAR ES SALAAM LUSAKA CAPE TOWN
KUALA LUMPUR SINGAPORE JAKARTA HONG KONG TOKYO
DELHI BOMBAY CALCUTTA MADRAS KARACHI

Published in the United States
by Oxford University Press, New York

© *Conrad Russell 1979*

British Library Cataloguing in Publication Data

Russell, Conrad, b. 1937
    Parliaments and English politics, 1621–1629.
      1. England and Wales. Parliament – History
    I. Title
    328.42´09   JN531   78-40498
    ISBN 0-19-822482-6

*Printed in Great Britain
by
Butler & Tanner Ltd
Frome and London*

Preface

IN the course of this work, I have incurred many obligations. I would like to thank the Central Research Fund of the University of London for grants towards the costs of work on the papers of the Earls of Bedford, and of microfilms of Parliamentary diaries, and the Trustees of the Bedford Settled Estates, the Trustees of the Henry E. Huntington Library and the Yale Center for Parliamentary History for permission to quote from copyright material in their possession. I owe thanks to numerous archivists for their helpfulness and courtesy, including many whose collections have not, in the event, been cited in this book. I owe particular thanks to Mr. D. L. Thomas, of the Public Record Office, and Mr. D. M. M. Shorrocks, of Somerset County Record Office. I would like to thank Professor G. E. Aylmer, Mr. J. P. Cooper, Professor F. J. Fisher, Mr. A. J. Fletcher, Professor Elizabeth Read Foster, Mr. David Hebb, and Dr. Derek Hirst, who have read all or part of this book in draft, and saved me from numerous errors: for any which remain, I am solely responsible. I would like to thank Miss Sheelagh Taylor and Mrs. Jane Passes for typing the more palimpsestic parts of my manuscript, and Mrs. Audrey Cornwall for typing the whole of the final draft. Those who have given help or advice are more than I can hope to thank, but I owe special acknowledgements to Nicholas Tyacke, Gerald Aylmer, Derek Hirst, J. N. Ball, Colin Tite, Paul Slack, David Hebb, and Richard Cust. I would also like to thank the Yale Center for Parliamentary History, and in particular Mrs. Maija J. Cole, for many kindnesses, and especially for allowing me access to the proofs of *Commons' Debates in 1628* at a very early stage.

Spelling has been modernized throughout, and some passages in Latin and French have been translated. I have endeavoured to shorten the footnotes through the use of a long list of standard abbreviations. In the case of the 1628 footnotes, the fact that some citations are from the Yale edition and some from the original manuscripts reflects the fact that the Yale text reached me after

I had finished work on the manuscripts. Since I have found no differences between my transcriptions and theirs, and since references to the folios of the originals can easily be found inside the Yale edition, I have seen no need to conduct a massive conversion operation on the footnotes. Each reference, then, is a record of where I found the passage in question.

I would like to thank my wife for contributions without which this book would never have seen the light of day. Evening after evening, she has listened to the orations of Coke and Phelips, Seymour and Alford, until they have threatened to become a Committee of the Whole House. At these vicarious assemblies, she has taken the chair with such distinction that she has always selected the right moment, and the right wording, for the putting of the question. The final structure of this book owes as much to her questions as it does to my research.

Finally, I owe special thanks to Nicholas Tyacke and the members of our Special Subject class. Some of my debts to them are acknowledged in the footnotes. The points they have discovered, argued out, and cleared up are so numerous that the only suitable way to acknowledge my debt is to ask them, collectively, to accept the dedication of this book. Like those to whom seventeenth-century books were dedicated, they should not therefore be assumed to agree with its contents. I would like to thank the Twenty-Seven Foundation for a grant towards the cost of preparing this book for publication.

Conrad Russell

July 1977

Contents

Abbreviations

Place of publication is London unless otherwise stated.

the Great Seal during the Keepership of
Lord Keeper Coventry.

C.S.P.D. Calendar of State Papers, Domestic.

C.S.P.Ven. Calendar of State Papers, Venetian.

Ec.H.R. *Economic History Review.*

E.H.R. *English Historical Review.*

Fletcher. A. J. Fletcher, *A County Community in
Peace and War: Sussex 1625–1660* (1975).

Gardiner. S. R. Gardiner, *A History of England
1603–1642*, 10 vols. (1893).

Hassell Smith. A. Hassell Smith, *County and Court:
Government and Politics in Elizabethan
Norfolk* (Oxford, 1974).

Hastings. The Hastings Journal of the Parliament
of 1621, ed. Lady de Villiers, Camden
Miscellany, vol. xx (1953).

Hirst. D. M. Hirst, *The Representative of the
People?* (Cambridge, 1975).

H.J. *Historical Journal.*

H.M.C. Historical Manuscripts Commission.

J.B.S. *Journal of British Studies.*

Keeler. Mary Frear Keeler, *The Long Parliament
1640–41: A Biographical Study of its
Members* (Philadelphia, 1954).

Knowler. W. Knowler (ed.), *Strafforde Letters*, 2
vols. (1729). All references are to vol. i.

Lords' Debates *Notes of the Debates in the House of Lords
(ed. Gardiner).* *1624 and 1626*, Camden Society, New
series, vol. xxiv (1879).

Lords' Debates *Debates in the House of Lords 1621–8*, ed.
(ed. Relf). F. H. Relf, Camden Society, Third Series,
vol. xlii (1929).

L.J. *Lords' Journals.* All references are to vol.
iii unless otherwise stated.

N.P. Sir John Eliot, *Negotium Posterorum, or
An Apology for Socrates*, 2 vols., ed.
A. B. Grosart (1881). All references are
to vol. II unless otherwise stated.

Nicholas. Edward Nicholas, *Proceedings and De-*

	bates in the House of Commons in 1620 and 1621, 2 vols. (Oxford, 1766).
Origins.	Conrad Russell (ed.), *The Origins of the English Civil War* (1973).
Phelips MSS.	Somerset Record Office, DD/PH, Phelips MSS.
P.R.O. C. 65.	Public Record Office C. 65. Parliament Rolls.
P.R.O. 31/3.	Public Record Office, French Transcripts.
R.O.	Record Office.
Ruigh.	Robert E. Ruigh, *The Parliament of 1624* (Cambridge, Mass. and Oxford, 1971).
Sackville MSS.	National Register of Archives, Sackville MSS. These MSS. are in the process of being transferred to the Kent Archive Office at Maidstone, where they are being given new catalogue numbers.
S.P.	State Papers, Public Record Office.
Statutes of the Realm.	Public Acts from the printed *Statutes of the Realm* are cited thus: *21 Jac. I c. 3*. Private Acts or Acts not printed in *Statutes of the Realm* are cited in Roman type. They may be found in House of Lords Record Office, Original Acts. In 1624 some are also enrolled on the Parliament Roll, and many which were required in legal proceedings may be found in the *Certiorari* Rolls, Public Record Office C. 89.
Supple.	B. E. Supple, *Commercial Crisis and Change in England 1600–1642* (Cambridge, 1964).
Tite.	Colin G. C. Tite, *Impeachment and Parliamentary Judicature in Early Stuart England* (1974).
T.R.H.S.	*Transactions of the Royal Historical Society.*
Wentworth Papers.	J. P. Cooper (ed.) *The Wentworth Papers, 1597–1628*, Camden Society, Fourth Series, 12 (1973).

Zaller.   Robert Zaller, *The Parliament of 1621: A*
                          Study in Constitutional Conflict (Berkeley,
                          1971).

Dates are Old Style unless otherwise stated, except that the year
is taken to begin on 1 January. The only exception is in letters by
the Earl of Holland, who used Old and New Styles indiscriminately
and without internal indication. His dates are reproduced in their
original form.

2. COMMONS' DIARIES, ETC.

1621

N.R.S.   *Commons' Debates in 1621*, ed. Wallace Note-
                          stein, Frances Helen Relf, and Hartley
                          Simpson, 7 vols. (New Haven, 1935).

Nicholas.   Edward Nicholas, *Proceedings and Debates in*
                          the House of Commons in 1620 and 1621, 2 vols.
                          (Oxford, 1766).

Hawarde.   Diary of John Hawarde, 20 Nov.–19 Dec.
                          Wiltshire Record Office, Ailesbury MSS., un-
                          numbered and unfoliated MS.

1624

Pym.   Diary of John Pym, Northants. Record Office,
                          Finch-Hatton MS. 50.

Holles.   Diary of John Holles, British Library Harleian
                          MS. 6383.

Earle.   Diary of Sir Walter Earle, British Library
                          Additional MS. 18597.

Holland, I, II.   Diary of Sir Thomas Holland, Bodleian
                          Library MS. Tanner 392 (25 February–
                          9 April) and MS. Rawlinson D. 1100 (10 April–
                          15 May).

Spring.   Diary of Sir William Spring, Harvard Univer-
                          sity Houghton Library MS. Eng. 980. Trans-
                          cript by the Yale Center for Parliamentary
                          History, generously lent by Dr. Colin G. C.
                          Tite.

Hawarde.   Diary of John Hawarde, Wiltshire Record
                          Office, Ailesbury MSS., unnumbered MS.

Jervoise. — Diary of Sir Thomas Jervoise, Jervoise MSS., Herriard Park, Hants: transcript in the possession of the Yale Center for Parliamentary History.

Rich. — Diary of Sir Nathaniel Rich, British Library Additional MS. 46191.

Dyott. — Diary of Sir Richard Dyott, Staffordshire Record Office, D.661/11/1/2.

Lowther. — Diary of Sir John Lowther, Cumberland Record Office.

Nicholas. — Diary of Edward Nicholas, Public Record Office, State Papers 14/166.

1625

1625 Debates. — *Debates in the House of Commons in 1625*, ed. S. R. Gardiner, Camden Society, New Series, vi (1873). Diary of John Pym and anonymous diary for the Oxford session.

N.P. — Sir John Eliot, *Negotium Posterorum, or An Apology for Socrates*, 2 vols., ed. A. B. Grosart (1881). All references are to vol. II unless otherwise stated.

H.o.L. — *H.M.C. Manuscripts of the House of Lords*, xi (Rough Commons' Journal for the London session).

Queen's MS. — Queen's College, Oxford, MS. 449. Anonymous diary, printed by S. R. Gardiner for the Oxford session only (another copy in British Library Additional MS. 48091). The Queen's copy is ascribed in a later hand to one William Walter.

Dyott. — Diary of Sir Richard Dyott for 5, 11, and 12 August, at end of his 1624 diary, q.v.

Rich. — Diary of Sir Nathaniel Rich for 11 and 12 August, at the beginning of his 1626 diary, q.v.

1626

Whitelocke. — Diary of Bulstrode Whitelocke, Cambridge University Library MSS. Dd 12–20, 12–21, and 12–22.

Rich.	Diary of Sir Nathaniel Rich. House of Lords Record Office, formerly in the possession of the Duke of Manchester.
Harl. 6445.	British Library Harleian MS. 6445, notes on committees by Sir John Borough.
Grosvenor.	Diary of Sir Richard Grosvenor, Trinity College, Dublin MS.E.5.17.
Lowther.	Diary of Sir John Lowther, *H.M.C. Thirteenth Report, Part 7.*

1628

1628 Debates.	*Commons' Debates in 1628*, vols. i, ii, and iii, Yale Center for Parliamentary History, ed. Robert C. Johnson, Mary Frear Keeler, Maija Jannson Cole, and William B. Bidwell (New Haven, 1977).
Stowe 366.	British Library Stowe MS. 366, anonymous newsletter of the Parliament of 1628.
Add. 36825.	British Library Additional MS. 36825. One of the MSS. of Proceedings and Debates in 1628.
Harl. 2313⎫ **Harl. 5324⎭**	British Library Harleian MSS. 2313 and 5324, anonymous diary.
Grosvenor.	Diary of Sir Richard Grosvenor, Trinity College, Dublin MSS. E.5.33–6.
Newdegate.	Diary of John Newdegate, Warwickshire Record Office.
Rich.	Notes of Sir Nathaniel Rich, Huntingdonshire Record Office, Manchester MSS. 58/5.
Lowther.	Diary of Sir John Lowther, *H.M.C. Thirteenth Report, Part 7.*

1629

1629 Debates.	*Commons' Debates for 1629*, ed. Wallace Notestein and Frances Helen Relf (Minneapolis, 1921).
Manchester MS.	House of Lords Record Office, MS. of the True Relation for 1629, containing occasional variant readings (formerly in the possession of the Duke of Manchester).

For some diaries in which the foliation is non-existent, partially invisible, or confusing, references have been given by date in the manner made familiar by Wallace Notestein. 'Rich, 23 Feb.' refers to the folios of Rich's diary covering 23 February. Where there are several diaries by the same author, references are to the diary for the Parliament under discussion, unless otherwise stated. When necessary, the year is given in parentheses thus: Rich (1624) refers to the diary of Sir Nathaniel Rich for 1624.

Note on sources

O F all the working dangers which face a historian, errors in a unique source are the hardest to take precautions against. It is then very fortunate that there are very few places indeed where it has proved necessary to rest an interpretation upon a unique source. As the work for this book has progressed, I have become more and more impressed by the consensus of the sources, rather than by their variation.

Nevertheless, the sources here used are of uneven value, and, more significantly, they are of value for different things. The Venetian Ambassador, for example, is valuable as a reporter of gossip. As a source for the statement that a rumour was being circulated, he is a good one: if the question is whether the rumour was true or false, it has to be tested, like other rumours, against other known material. The French Ambassador is similarly a source of gossip. In this role, the four French Ambassadors whose dispatches have been used at length are of very uneven value: they clearly rank in an order of merit which runs: Mende, Effiat, Blainville, Tillières. Like other ambassadors, they tend to reflect the views of their informant, who after 1625 was probably often the Earl of Holland. Among other newsletter-writers, young Conway appears to be a good guide to the private opinions of his father. Nethersole, when checked against Parliamentary diaries, emerges with credit, but the prince of newsletter-writers is undoubtedly Chamberlain. Chamberlain letters often fit the Parliamentary debates so closely that they could be footnoted sentence by sentence.

The problems presented by the purely Parliamentary sources should at once be appreciated by anyone who has ever taken lecture notes. Between the notes preserved in the diaries and the actual words spoken on the floor of either House, there is a gulf which we can never confidently cross. The extent of this gulf can be guessed at by an argument of time. If we take everything reported for a particularly well-covered day, like some of the last days before the summer recess of 1621, and compare it with the length of time the Commons were in session, we have not nearly enough material to occupy the time. Even when the maximum possible allowance is made for time taken up in other business such as the naming of committees and going to conferences, it appears unlikely that, even on the best-reported days, more than about a quarter of the words spoken in the Commons are preserved. On many days, particularly in 1626, what is preserved is likely to represent a much smaller proportion than this. In the Lords in 1628, the disproportion is even grosser: we may have three or four folios to cover debates which, with an interval for dinner, covered the time from nine in the morning to past six in the evening.

In the light of this fact, the striking thing about the Parliamentary diaries is not the extent to which they say different things, but the extent to which they say the same things. In many cases, such as those of Pym and Nicholas, the likelihood that this similarity is due to collaboration is so remote as to be negligible. Curiously, the two diarists who might have been most readily expected to collaborate, Pym and Rich, are among those whose reports differ most widely. This is because they were trying to report different things: Pym tried to record the balance of arguments on each side of a question, and Rich tried to record the balance of men. Which is the better source, then, must depend on the question being asked. The similarity of the reports cannot be explained by dependence on a hypothetical common source, since it does not only apply to those like Pym and the author of Stowe 366, who worked their rough notes up afterwards, but equally to those like Grosvenor, whose notes leave it painfully apparent that they were taken on the floor of the House. In the cases of Grosvenor and Rich, the handwriting and the spacing provide evidence on the mood of the House which cannot be reproduced even in the most perfect of editions. If the similarity of the diaries cannot be explained by collaboration or by dependence on a common source, it is necessary to explain it, either by saying they are good, or by saying they had the same faults in common. If they had the same faults in common, this would itself be significant evidence: a consensus on what were significant points would be as valuable, though in a different way, as a verbatim record of what the speakers said.

It is possible to test the diarists on occasional set-piece performances such as conferences and speeches by the Lord Keeper, for which the *Lords' Journals* commonly reproduce a text which is very full. In some cases, we know this text to be based on a script provided by the speaker. In these cases, the script is the best evidence on the speaker's mind, and the diarists the best evidence on what he actually delivered. On this test, the diarists usually appear to be capable of giving a first-class précis of the arguments of the speech. There is one significant exception to this statement: until 1628, most diarists tended to skip the bulk of the political ideas in a set-piece speech, apparently treating them as so much padding. They also conspicuously failed to provide adequate reports of Buckingham's Relation of 1624. When the diaries are compared with the script of the Relation on the Parliament Roll, it is easy to see why. Apart from the element of exhaustion, they were deterred by the lack of logical structure. Standard reporting techniques, like the standard précis, depended on picking out the structure of the argument. In a speech like this, which had no structure, they were reduced to picking out individual anecdotes. A similar fate sometimes overtook that other great rambler, Sir Edward Coke. With these exceptions, it is possible to say that most of the diaries achieved a very high standard of reporting.

For the proceedings of the Lords, the number of available sources is so small as to leave us little option but to believe them for the time being. Fortunately, such cross-checks as are possible suggest that our sources are good ones. The only significant pitfall I have found is the fact that the *Lords' Journals* do not report divisions: Lord Montagu does report them, but whether he reports them all is a question on which our sources shed no light.

For the Commons, the method followed has been to select a base text for each Parliament, which I have then collated with each other diary in turn. For 1621 and 1624, I have used Pym's diary, for reasons independent of this book. For 1625 and 1626, the selection of Pym and Whitelocke has imposed itself. For 1628, I have selected Stowe 366, rather than Proceedings and Debates, for reasons of length. I have used the process of collation to try to gain a picture of the cast of mind and interests of each individual diarist. I have thus aimed at getting some inkling of the filtering effect which happened to speeches as they passed through the mind of each individual diarist. Those who add least distinctive flavour of their own are the anonymous author (?s) of the X diary in 1621 and Spring in 1624. The others each show special strengths.

On the passage of bills, no diaries rival the *Commons' Journal*, though Pym, Holland, and to a lesser extent Lowther, are surprisingly close behind. On the contents of bills, Pym is unrivalled: the accuracy of his summary of bills for which we have a surviving text encourages us to believe his reports of those for which we have none. On personal altercations, on the other hand, Pym's impatience with time-wasting makes him a very poor reporter. A measure of this impatience may be gained through Barrington and Dyott, who became peculiarly full precisely at the moment when Pym's patience gives out. Barrington, the Nennius of Parliamentary diarists, gives a peculiarly full list of colourful words, phrases, and incidents, but is correspondingly bad at discovering the logical structure of a speech. His phrases have to be fitted with care into a framework provided by other diaries. Holles appears, when tested against the State Papers and similar sources, to have a peculiarly good ear for the echoes of court faction. Rich, an intermittent diarist, has a peculiarly sharp eye for an approaching crisis: it is hard to say whether his fellow-members would have thought it too sharp.

In comparing reports, these strengths and weaknesses of the diarists have been taken into account. So have the records of the speakers being reported. One of the discoveries resulting from the study of five Parliaments has been that on predictable topics, such as recusancy and supply, many members had a standard speech, as it were 'on tape'. In addition, I have tended, I hope justifiably, to prefer the reports which keep the speakers' inconsistencies to a minimum. Similarly, I have tended to prefer reports which make sense to reports which do not. Since these are biases, they have been kept in check, but in some measure, they must be part of an author's stock-in-trade.

I have made little use of compilations put together at a later date, such as Harleian MS. 159 or Bodleian MS. Rawlinson B. 151. These appear tolerably reliable, but if they are, it must be because of their dependence on earlier sources. I have, on the other hand, made considerable use of Sir John Eliot's *Negotium Posterorum*, which belongs to the literary genre best known as 'memoirs'. On speeches, I have used Eliot only where he seems to me not to be in conflict with Pym. His excitable cast of mind is such a good counterweight to the flat Civil Service monotone of most of Pym's diaries that it seemed plausible to suppose that using him would do something to rectify an imbalance caused by over-dependence on Pym. In addition, there are some points, like his conversation with Buckingham, the effects of the plague, and who used a written script, on which Eliot is a unique source. On many of these points, Eliot appears credible when checked against genuinely contemporary sources. On his conversations with Buckingham about the additional supply, Eliot appears particularly credible because he is, in effect, a hostile witness: the effect of his evidence runs directly counter to his own bias.

At the end of this book, it is a matter for surprise to find how rarely an argument has to rest on a unique source. Over-dependence on Whitelocke in 1626 is unavoidable, and its effects cannot be judged until further diaries are discovered. Other points quoted from a unique source are mostly ones which are implied, and certainly not contradicted, by other reports. The only conflicts among the sources which are of significance to the argument of the book concern the speeches of Weston on 27 November 1621, of Gooch on 1 March 1624, and several speeches by Sir Francis Seymour in March 1624. In these and other cases of conflict of sources, I have tried to draw attention to the conflict in a footnote.

The sources are much less satisfactory for the rather more neglected task of discovering what members were doing and thinking outside the House of Commons. Here, it could be argued that the book is distorted by excessive dependence on the large private collections amassed by Sir Robert Phelips and Sir Thomas Wentworth. Whether this is in fact the case, and if so, in what ways it affects the general argument of the book, is a point on which I look forward to enlightenment from future researchers in the field.

I

Westminster and the Wider World

I. THE STRUCTURE OF POLITICS

ALL authors, by the simple act of writing their books, run the
risk of unduly magnifying the importance of their chosen
subject. This risk is perhaps particularly acute for a Parliamentary
historian. Material already magnified becomes combustible when
further subjected to the burning glass of hindsight. It is particularly important that the author of a book on 'Parliaments and
English Politics' should not allow his book to masquerade as a
comprehensive history of English politics. In England in the
1620s, the majority of important political events took place outside
Parliament. To present these events as the background to events
in Parliament is inevitably to some extent to place them in an
a-historical context. Parliaments, if they are to be seen in perspective, should not be seen as the makers of the major historical
events of the 1620s, but as *ad hoc* gatherings of men reacting to
events taking place elsewhere. Major political decisions were
usually taken at court, and other major political events tended to
take place in the country, well away from the Palace of Westminster. To take some examples, in a balanced history of England
in the 1620s, Charles and Buckingham's trip to Madrid in 1623,
the negotiations for the marriage treaty between Charles and
Henrietta Maria, the York House Conference of 1626, Charles I's
episcopal appointments, and the assassination of Buckingham
would all deserve more prominence than any event which took
place in Parliament. Similarly, if the focus is away from Whitehall,
the trade depression of 1621–4, the plague of 1625, the effects of
war on English trade between 1625 and 1628, and county
reactions to the billeting of soldiers would all deserve more prominence than the echoes of these events which can be heard at
Westminster. Indeed, if English foreign policy is under discussion,
it must be remembered that events in Madrid, Brussels, and above
all in Paris did more to determine the course of English foreign
policy than events on the floor of either House of Parliament. In

the years between the Reformation and the Peace of Westphalia, it is rarely possible to draw a clear dividing line between foreign and domestic affairs.

A Parliamentary historian, then, runs an unusually acute risk of becoming the prisoner of his documents. As soon as Parliamentary history ceases to be treated as pure constitutional history, it loses the unifying theme which has made it appear to be a subject with frontiers. In fact, the greatest value in the study of Parliamentary history is precisely its lack of frontiers. Because a Parliament is, to some extent, a representative assembly, most matters of general concern are, at some stage, likely to find a hearing in a Parliament. The subject thus offers an unrivalled opportunity for a non-specialized approach to English history, in which the complications of foreign affairs may be seen interacting with the difficulties of Justices of the Peace or with the tribulations of the cloth industry.

Yet if Parliamentary history is seen in this way, it must also be seen, in part, as second-hand history. A Parliamentary speech then becomes a source of the same type as Clarendon's *History*: informed, but normally *ex parte*, comment on events taking place elsewhere. Few stories (not even the 'constitutional' ones like the impeachment of Buckingham or the Petition of Right) begin or end within the confines of Parliament. Stories flit through the Parliamentary debates as, in Bede's story, the sparrow flitted through the hall of King Edwin: we do not know where they come from, or where they go to. The utmost attempts to correct this defect of the Parliamentary sources cannot be entirely successful. It is possible to attempt to see Parliamentary stories in a non-Parliamentary context. Yet no mortal historian is ever likely to become equally familiar with the misdeeds of the saltpetre men at Chipping Sodbury, the fortunes of the Dartmouth fishing industry, the limits of King James I's confidence in the Duke of Buckingham, and the day-to-day fluctuations in Richelieu's relations with Marie de Medici. Since all these things influenced the course of events in Parliament, Parliamentary history must be liable to constant revision in the light of new discoveries about events elsewhere. Yet, though this approach does not produce a book which is easy to write, and may not produce a book which is easy to read, it is impossible to avoid. A more purely 'constitutional' approach constantly risks imposing categories on members of Parliament with which they were unfamiliar. It runs the risk of interpreting their intentions according to criteria which had not yet been invented.

Seventeenth-century members of Parliament lacked the opportunity to study Montesquieu. They had not yet been informed that they constituted a permanent 'legislative', whose duty was to act as a check and balance on the 'executive'.[1] Moreover, they were not merely uninstructed in the theory of the separation of powers: most of them were in a very bad position to apply the doctrine in practice. Membership of Parliament was not a profession in early seventeenth-century England, and even in a period of frequent Parliaments such as the 1620s, a Parliament was an event and not an institution. Members of Parliament spent most of their working lives outside the walls of the Palace of Westminster.[2] They were therefore likely to be influenced in their reactions to Parliamentary events, not only by what happened inside the walls of either House, but by what happened in their normal existence in their home counties, or, as they called them, their 'countries'.

At home, most members of both Houses of Parliament were part, not of the legislative, but of the executive. Most, though by no means all, held posts in their home counties which obliged them to execute laws and implement requests from the central government. Most members of Parliament held some such posts as Lord Lieutenant, Deputy Lieutenant, Justice of the Peace, Commissioner of Sewers, steward of a Crown manor, or commissioner for clearing forests or draining marshes. It is symbolic that the Stewardship of the Chiltern Hundreds was not yet incompatible with membership of the House of Commons. In these local capacities, members of Parliament had to execute, not only the commands of the Council, but also the laws they had made in their legislative capacity at Westminster. In these local capacities, they probably enjoyed both more power and more permanence than they could in the ephemeral capacity of member of Parliament.

It is therefore necessary to explain the behaviour of members of

---

[1] G. E. Aylmer, 'Place Bills and the Separation of Powers', *T.R.H.S.* (1965), 45–69.

[2] G. E. Aylmer, *The King's Servants* (1961), p. 57. Parliament was actually in session for time amounting to four and a quarter years between 1603 and 1629. These figures show that the early Stuarts called Parliament oftener, and for longer, than Queen Elizabeth. See J. E. Neale, *The Elizabethan House of Commons* (1949), p. 433. Because a Parliament is an event and not an institution, it is not a suitable subject for the rule that institutions are best studied through their own archives.

Parliament in ways which do not contradict what we know of them in their local capacities. In attempting such an explanation, we may now depend on a great body of local studies. During the past twenty years, no subject in the period has been better studied than county government and local politics. As the body of work on local government has grown, it has become increasingly clear that its findings are incompatible with many of the traditions of English Parliamentary scholarship.[1]

Studies of Parliamentary history have continued to depend on a well-worn formula, which can be traced back to Gardiner and Macaulay. Parliament is seen as a standing institution, divided, in modern fashion, into two 'sides' called 'government', and 'opposition', or, in the newer version, 'court' and 'country'. Parliamentary debates are seen as a contest for 'power' between these two sides. Where there was no separation of powers, and where the implementation of decisions depended on bargaining and compromise between the centre and the localities and within the localities, this concept of 'power', to be obtained by victories at Westminster, is unduly mechanistic.[2]

With this vocabulary of conflict comes the vocabulary of the milestone: individual events, like the questioning of the King's servants in 1610, the debate on foreign policy in 1621, or the searching of the signet office in 1626 are seized upon as milestones in the road to the future. This formula of conflict and advance is illustrated in the phrase Tanner used to describe the foreign policy debate of 1621: 'the Commons were provoked to the annexation of a new province'.[3] This teleological approach owes much to the knowledge that, thirteen years after the end of the period here described, there was a civil war.

Historians who have worked on the Parliaments of the 1620s have almost all been engaged in the traditional blood-sport of English historians, the hunt for the origins of the civil war.[4] Rarely, if ever, has this period been studied in its own right, and not as a dress rehearsal for something apparently of more long-term significance. Because the 1620s were a period of some confusion, lacking an

---

[1] T. G. Barnes, 'County Politics and a Puritan Cause Célèbre: Somerset Churchales 1633', *T.R.H.S.* (1959), 109–23.

[2] I am grateful to Mr. Timothy Miles for this point.

[3] J. R. Tanner, *Constitutional Documents of the Reign of James I* (Cambridge, 1960), p. 274.

[4] See, for example, Conrad Russell in *Origins*, pp. 91–108.

obvious shape of their own, the temptation to impose upon them a shape taken from the future becomes more acute. This means that what has given the Parliaments of early Stuart England their fame in the eyes of posterity is what they themselves regarded as their failures: the occasions when they fell into conflict with the King. To members who expected to bring some solid achievement back to their constituencies, constitutional conflicts were not a milestone towards a future they did not know: they were a failure to produce legislation for the satisfaction of the country. A Parliament which fell into constitutional conflict was sterile, or, in the contemporary word, addled.

Not only was disagreement between King and Parliament regarded by all those concerned, including King and Councillors, as a failure: it was regarded as a cause of shame and disgrace. Frequent complaints were made that England's international reputation was diminished by conflict between Crown and Parliament: the state was 'out of frame': because it was not united, it was not fulfilling its proper function, and lacked the concerted strength necessary to any successful effort in international affairs. Constitutional conflict, then, was not welcomed by members as a landmark in progress towards the Bill of Rights: it provoked the immediate question, 'What has gone wrong?'

(a) Court and Country

Our picture of a Parliament is dominated by Sir Winston Churchill's famous remark that there are only two sides to every division. In the 1620s, the division was not the central institution of Parliament. Divisions were disliked, and the putting of the question was many times postponed until the emergence of a consensus enabled resolutions to be carried without a division. When the Parliament of 1628 had been been sitting for several weeks, Sir John Coke said the Commons could regard it as matter for self-congratulation that they were yet to have their first division.[1] In the House of Lords, such divisions as did occur were not recorded in the Journals.

[1] Add. 36825, f. 139ᵛ. See also Hirst, p. 15, for a similar reluctance to admit local divisions. This was written before I had seen Mark Kishlansky. 'The Emergence of Adversary Politics', *Journal of Modern History* (Dec. 1977). Dr. Kishlansky's argument supplies a frame of reference for the points here made. I am grateful to Dr. Kishlansky for allowing me to see this article before publication.

If ideas about the proper function of a Parliament impeded
members from regarding themselves as divided into 'government'
and 'opposition', their daily local existence inhibited them even
more forcefully from accepting a division into supporters of
'court' and 'country'. Professor Zagorin, identifying the 'court'
with Montesquieu's 'executive', included in his picture of the
'court' such local officials as receivers of Crown lands, 'persons
connected with the admiralty', and stewards of royal manors. He
thereby turned into members of the 'court' such pillars of Parliamentary debate as Pym, Eliot, and Phelips. Yet, for reasons which
are not entirely clear, Professor Zagorin, while including stewards
of royal manors in the 'court', saw fit to exclude the regular
members of county government, sheriffs, Deputy Lieutenants,
and Justices of the Peace.[1] This is something of a curiosity, since
those involved in county government, more than stewards of
Crown manors, constantly depended on favour at court to do their
jobs effectively. They also depended on the court for appointment
to local government, and when appointed, continued to depend on
friends at court. In the career of a local governor, friends at court
and in the country were equally essential. Professor Barnes has
shown conclusively that the career of Sir Robert Phelips in
Somerset was dominated, not by a fruitless desire to oppose a
court to which he owed all his local offices, but by dependence on
both court and country. He needed to achieve the very unity
which was the subject of Parliamentary rhetoric and of local
necessity: to secure support at court and in the country both at the
same time.[2] The same interdependence of 'court' and 'country' is
shown in the career of Sir Thomas Wentworth. He had the same
ambitions and needed the same support: in Mr. Cooper's words,
'Wentworth's Parliamentary career should be viewed, like those
of other leaders of the Commons, in a context in which contacts
with the court, not isolation from it, were the rule.'[3] What has
been written about Phelips and Wentworth could be written, with
the few appropriate changes, for any member of Parliament
prominent in his home county or borough.

It appears, then, that we have hitherto analysed the behaviour of
members of Parliament at Westminster using analytical tools

[1] Perez Zagorin, *The Court and the Country* (1969), p. 41.
[2] Barnes, pp. 288–92.
[3] *Wentworth Papers*, p. 7.

which are incompatible with the structure of politics in the counties. The achievement of constitutional milestones like the searching of the signet office gave no satisfaction to York's desire for the dredging of the River Ouse, nor to Rye's desire for control of Dungeness lighthouse. The forming of a 'Parliamentary opposition', if it had taken place, would have made men like Wentworth and Phelips unable to do their local, and permanent, jobs. On the occasions when it did take place, it led to their dismissal from local office, a dismissal which dismayed and weakened them more than almost anything which happened to them at Westminster.

Faced with this conflict between the findings of Parliamentary research and the findings of local research, we have three possible options. We cannot dismiss the local research as wrong: its bulk, and the consistency of its main findings, have become too impressive to be ignored. We can then say that those who were elected to Westminster were untypical. This doubtless contains some truth. The fact that Sir Robert Phelips was a regular member of Parliament does not necessarily make him more typical of the Somerset gentry than his rival Sir John Poulett, who was not. Eagerness to be elected to Parliament was perhaps less universal than we have supposed, and many regular members of Parliament were distinguished from their local colleagues by their greater energy and ambition, if by nothing else. Membership of Parliament was an expensive hobby, and the cost might deter the unambitious.[1] Yet, though this explanation contains some truth, it is not sufficient. There were few if any more prominent members of Parliament than Sir Robert Phelips, and if he was disqualified by his local position from engaging happily in court–country conflict, it is likely that many others were also.

It is also possible to say, as Burghley said of the Elizabethan bishops, that 'the places alter the men': we can suppose that members arriving at Westminster, and enjoying free speech, said many things they found hard to say publicly at home. Again, the explanation has some truth. Yet freedom to criticize at Westminster did not, and was not intended to, absolve members from their responsibilities as local executive agents of the Crown. Whatever they did at Westminster, they had to go home, and, as

[1] For an example of a man reluctant to undertake the expense of being a member of Parliament, see Sir John Jackson to Wentworth, Knowler, p. 34; *Wentworth Papers*, p. 288.

subsidy commissioners or Justices of the Peace, give an account of their doings and execute their own laws.

If those two explanations are insufficient, there remains only the third: that the analytical tools hitherto used for Parliamentary history are wrong and anachronistic. This is a case I have argued elsewhere, and do not intend to elaborate here.[1] The object of this book is to reconstruct the Parliamentary history of the 1620s using a set of analytical tools which owe more to local studies than to previous Parliamentary studies. Its central contention is that the sort of men who assembled at Westminster were not widely different in character and outlook from the same men as they have become familiar to us as Justices of the Peace. The Justices of the Peace were not an opposition: they were, within certain partly self-imposed limits, loyal and hard-working servants of the Crown. Their service to the Crown, however, normally took third place behind their concern for the welfare of their countries and for their own pockets.[2] If we study Justices of the Peace, we do not find a body of men itching to take over responsibility for national government, or for the conduct of foreign affairs. We find a combination of loyalty and obstruction, of hard work and paro-chialism, of dedication and dishonesty.

Above all, they almost always put concern for their own counties above any concept of the national interest. In defending the realm against invasion, they would normally show more concern that their own county should appear with credit than that the country as a whole should be defended. In 1625, when invasion was expected in Essex, Huntingdonshire was asked to supply help, and bluntly replied that the defence of Essex was not their business. It is the contention of this book that this loyal and obstructive localism, so familiar to students of local government, was also, at least until 1628, the dominant attitude of the early Stuart House of Commons. Most members were not struggling to achieve increased national responsibilities: they were struggling to avoid them.

---

[1] Conrad Russell, 'Parliamentary History in Perspective', *History* (1976), 1–27. Many of the most significant arguments of this article are anticipated in K. M. Sharpe, 'The Intellectual and Political Activities of Sir Robert Cotton, c. 1590–1631', Oxford D.Phil. Thesis (1975). In particular, the argument of my article that the politics of this period should not be seen in 'party' terms is sustained by Dr. Sharpe's important analysis of the uses made of Sir Robert Cotton's library.   [2] Fletcher, pp. 200–5, 213, 240.

The court–country, or government–opposition, split assumed by Parliamentary historians was not only institutionally impossible. Under James and Buckingham, it was also ideologically impossible. It is not easy to be a consistent opponent of government policy unless it is clear what government policy is. Under James and Buckingham, such clarity was rarely obtainable. Both men have been frequently and justly blamed for many things, but they cannot be blamed for creating an opposition which did not exist in the England they ruled. King James lacked the political energy of his son, and was not an enthusiast for political programmes. That his inertia in the face of other men's plans was perhaps the fruit of more than mere laziness is suggested by the Venetian Ambassador's comment, at the very end of his reign, that the King 'only remains constant in his determination to do nothing'.[1] The reign of James's more determined son perhaps suggests that this desire to 'let sleeping dogs lie' had something to commend it. It is to James's credit, not to his discredit, that he came to the last year of his reign being served with equal loyalty by an Archbishop of Canterbury (Abbot) who was as nearly a puritan as most of the House of Commons, and by a Secretary of State (Sir George Calvert) who was a crypto-Catholic. King James did not allow himself to preside over an ideologically polarized country.

Buckingham, who had more energy than James, had an equal dislike of ideological polarization. While James avoided it by shunning firmly defined 'policies', Buckingham avoided it by the sheer universality of his patronage. This prevented the court from becoming a closed circle and meant that people of a remarkable variety of political and religious persuasions tended to pin their hopes for political change on Buckingham's patronage. Buckingham's monopoly of patronage created bitter resentment, especially after 1625, but this resentment had very little ideological tinge to it.[2] Buckingham the patron of Arminians was the patron of such dedicated anti-Arminians as John Preston and the Earl of Manchester. The York House conference of 1626, where official attitudes to Arminianism were debated, was not a contest between 'ins' and outs': it was a contest between rival groups of Buckingham supporters. The feud between Sir Thomas Wentworth and Sir John Saville, which dominated Yorkshire politics throughout

[1] C.S.P.Ven. 1623–5, p. 455.
[2] See below, ch. V.

the decade, was not a feud between pro- and anti-Buckingham men: it was a contest between two rival groups of would-be clients for the position of Buckingham's man in Yorkshire. Buckingham created considerable difficulties for himself by his attempt to become a hereditary favourite, descending from James to Charles, thus, by 'a kind of wonder, making favour hereditary'.[1] Yet we should perhaps ponder the verdict of the Earl of Kellie, that in handling these difficulties, he showed more sagacity than he has been given credit for.[2] Perhaps we should also wonder whether Buckingham's dominance of the court was entirely due to his homosexual relationship with the King. The appearance of a 'valido', or first minister, was a general phenomenon in many European courts at this time, and it may, even in England, have had institutional, as well as sexual, causes.[3]

The court, even while it was monopolized by Buckingham, was a far less homogeneous body than has been supposed. Above all, as Professor Elton has recently reminded us in a significant and thought-provoking article, it cannot be identified exclusively with the person of the monarch. The court was the seat of conflicting factions, whose loyalty to each other was rarely their most conspicuous characteristic. Some, if not all, of these factions tended, temporarily or permanently, to be united by commitment to common political or religious principles. There were few, if any, gentlemen in the House of Commons so eccentric that they could not find one among the many potential court patrons to share their political objectives. Since the court was a permanent centre of influence, those who could propagate their policies through court alliances were well advised to do so. Professor Elton wrote:

The Tudor court was the centre of politics not only in the sense that those seeking power needed to pursue it there, but more significantly still in the sense that the battle of politics was there fought out. None of the main solutions to the problems of the day lacked advocates within the very

---

[1] *L.J.* 596. The words are those of Sir Dudley Digges.
[2] *H.M.C. Mar and Kellie Suppl.*, p. 129.
[3] J. Lynch, *Spain under the Habsburgs*, ii, 23–30. All Professor Lynch's remarks apply to England except, significantly, that the *valido* was a member of the higher nobility. The similarities prompt the question whether the Stuarts' error may not have been the creation of this institution, but the failure to continue it after the death of Buckingham in 1628. See *C.S.P.D. 1625–49 Addenda*, vol. dxxix, no. 15.

heart of the court itself—not even peace with Rome in the 1540s or the puritan programme in the 1570s.[1]

Mutatis mutandis, the same things can be said about the court of the 1620s. Those who wanted war with Spain could logically attach themselves to the faction of the Earl of Pembroke, or, after the autumn of 1623, to that of the Duke of Buckingham. Few members of the Commons, if any, were more puritan than the lecturer John Preston, who, up to 1625, believed Buckingham to be an 'elect saint'.[2] None were more determined to reduce royal extravagance than the Lord Treasurer, Lionel Cranfield, Earl of Middlesex. No one in the Commons disliked Buckingham more than the Lord Chamberlain, the Earl of Pembroke. Few would more publicly criticize royal leniency towards recusants than George Abbot, Archbishop of Canterbury.[3] To have opposed the whole of so many-sided a court would have required a formidable feat of political gymnastics. Opposition to the views of one court faction almost automatically brought those who expressed it into agreement with another court faction. In 1625–6, even opposition to one group of Buckingham's men tended to lead to alliance with a rival group of Buckingham's men. It is hard to see how those who wished to be effective politicians could have entered into opposition to 'the court' as a whole.

Moreover, political objectives were more constructively pursued by seeking the help of a court patron than by opposing 'the court' in general. Every court patron needed, and wished for, contacts in a number of counties: like most leaders, they were willing to increase the number of their followers. Again in Professor Elton's words,

The factions in the Country linked to members of the Court: Court faction spread its net over the shires. The realm was one, and had one centre; and the situation prevailing at Court made sure that the many political divisions within that one realm and one centre should work themselves out in the ordinary context and contests of political life, without ever threatening to divide the political nation into ins and outs.[4]

---

[1] G. R. Elton, 'Tudor Government: The Points of Contact; The Court', *T.R.H.S.* (1976), 221–2, 227. This article can be applied with remarkable exactitude to a court outside the period it covers.

[2] I. Morgan, *Prince Charles's Puritan Chaplain* (1957), p. 59.

[3] *Lords' Debates* (ed. Relf) p. 6.

[4] Elton, *ubi supra*, p. 228.

These words were written of the reign of Henry VIII, but they are equally true of the age of Buckingham. The more nearly Buckingham monopolized patronage, the more his following divided into rival factions, with rival channels of access, lobbying him for rival policies. Buckingham could accommodate Preston and Laud together among his followers as easily as Henry VIII could accommodate Cranmer and Gardiner.

Moreover, it is easy to suppose that Buckingham's dominance of the court was more complete, and more secure, than it was. When Buckingham retained his power at the beginning of Charles's reign, his closest confidant Sir George Goring reported the news to the English ambassadors in France with every sign of relief. Buckingham's dominance of the court might be nearly complete, but he could never be certain it was secure until after the event. Throughout Buckingham's period of power, and especially under James, the King's ear was available to men who owed no obligation to him. The Scottish Earl of Kellie helped James in business which was to be kept secret from Buckingham, while under Charles, the Earl of Pembroke organized a public attack on the Duke, and survived.

Among the great court patrons, it was probably Pembroke, established but outgunned by the Duke within the court itself, who felt the greatest temptation to take his quarrels on to the wider stage of a Parliament. As Lord Chamberlain, and later Lord Steward, he had too powerful a position at court to be easily ignored. Yet, to secure a sufficiently powerful lobby for his views of the moment, he often needed a larger and more variegated cast than the court alone was able to provide. For this and other reasons, Pembroke established himself as one of the greatest Parliamentary patrons of the time. A conservative estimate puts his normal Parliamentary following at twenty, and in key Parliaments, such as that of 1626, it may have been considerably bigger.[1] Pembroke's faction, more than those of his rivals the Duke of Buckingham and the Earl of Arundel, shows some signs of being united by a consistent political line. The Pembroke men were

---

[1] Violet A. Rowe, 'The Influence of the Earls of Pembroke on Parliamentary Elections', *E.H.R.* (1935), 242–56. S. R. Gardiner, 'Notes by Sir James Bagg on the Parliament of 1626', *Notes and Queries* (1872), 325–6. For a fuller investigation of Pembroke and his connection, see Brian O'Farrell, 'Politician, Patron, Poet, William Herbert third Earl of Pembroke', University of California at Los Angeles, Ph.D. Thesis (1966). I am grateful to Dr. O'Farrell for permission to read and quote from his thesis.

above all consistent devotees of unity, wanting amicable relations between the King and his Parliaments, and hoping that Parliaments would accept more responsibility for improving the King's finances. It is no surprise to find that in 1635, when Edward Hyde, later Earl of Clarendon, began his political career, he did so as a Pembroke nominee.[1] The attitudes to Parliament, religion, and the law which Hyde carried into a later generation were those which were characteristic of the Pembroke connection.

In foreign affairs, the Pembroke group were anti-Spanish and pro-Dutch. They tended to be pro-French, though not so firmly that the French ambassador could take them for granted.[2] The chief House of Commons spokesman for Pembroke was Sir Benjamin Rudyerd, who gave loyal service to the house of Herbert from 1618 to 1649.[3] Like many other members of the connection, he was inherited with the title by Pembroke's brother Montgomery in 1630. Rudyerd's Parliamentary speeches are one consistent reiteration of the theme of unity between King and Parliament. On religion, Pembroke was a consistent supporter of godly Protestantism, and so long as he lived, such a cause as opposition to Arminianism could find its most powerful friends at court. On religion, as on foreign policy, there seems to have been a broad similarity of view between Pembroke and Archbishop Abbot.

These two enjoyed the confidence of some of the most vocal and effective members of the Commons. Sir James Perrott, who held a place in the admiralty through Pembroke's patronage, has as good a claim to be called a puritan as anyone in the Commons. He was one of the most heated in attacks on Catholic recusants (including his wife) and one of the very few who felt the need to show their dislike of the Mass by writing about Christ-tide instead of Christmas. He was one of those who reacted to invasion scares by combing lists of his neighbours for potential fifth columnists. Yet when Perrott was in a panic about the influence of 'popery', he did

---

[1] Coventry MSS., Grants of Offices, no. 337. On 4 Dec. 1634 Edward Hyde was granted the reversion of the office of Custos Brevium in Common Pleas, on the suit of the Earl of Pembroke. This reference only connects Clarendon with the fourth Earl, but the lukewarmness of his comments in the *History* on the fourth Earl, combined with the enthusiasm of his comments on the third Earl, suggest that the connection may go further back.

[2] For a French assessment of Pembroke, see the instructions to Blainville, 3 Sept. 1625, P.R.O. 31/3/62, p. 129.

[3] On the Pembroke–Rudyerd connection, see Sheffield City Library, Elmhirst MSS. 1360/1, 1352/2, 1351/1, Sackville MSS. ON 131, and *N.P.* ii. 69.

not denounce 'the court': he wrote to friends at court, whom he
trusted, to ask for action.[1] The case of William Coryton, one of
Buckingham's bitterest enemies, is even more interesting. He was
employed by Pembroke in 1624 in some exceptionally confidential
negotiations, and depended on Pembroke for the key Cornish
office of Vice-Warden of the Stannaries. Even after 1629, when the
King put Coryton in the Tower for his conduct in Parliament,
Pembroke insisted on keeping him in office as Vice-Warden of the
Stannaries. His case is a clear illustration of the fact that court
favour did not need to be the King's favour.[2]

In this, as in any earlier period, disputes between court factions
might become extremely bitter. In their determination to prevail,
and in the struggle for survival, contestants were often ready to
carry court faction fights into the wider theatre of Parliament.
They were prepared, as Burghley and Walsingham had been
before them, to use a Parliament as an extra lobby for a policy they
had not succeeded in getting accepted at court. As Burghley and
Walsingham had used a Parliament to help to manœuvre a reluctant
Queen Elizabeth into executing Mary Queen of Scots, so Buckingham used a Parliament to manœuvre a reluctant King James into
acquiescence in a war with Spain. Parliamentary disputes on
matters of high policy, then, were more likely to represent the
clash of rival court factions than any court–country confrontation.
The proceedings of the Lords, in particular, tended to reflect
factions at court. These struggles might be about policies, as well
as about personalities. In 1621, the Earl of Southampton's attempts
to organize attacks on Buckingham were attempts by one Privy
Councillor to attack another. In these attempts, he was probably
concerned to support the war with Spain, of which he was a consistent champion, and in which he ultimately met his death.[3] In

---

[1] S.P. 16/91/57, S.P. 14/164/46, S.P. 16/61/38, and S.P. 14/119/16.

[2] Sackville MSS. ON 245: Ruigh, p. 314n. The business in question was as
confidential as could be imagined, concerning Pembroke's tentative involvement
in Cranfield's plans to supplant Buckingham by a rival favourite. On the vice-
wardenship of the Stannaries, see *C.S.P.D. 1629–31*, vol. clxxxi, no. 47.
Coryton temporarily lost both Pembroke's favour and the vice-wardenship for
refusing to contribute to the Forced Loan, but recovered both after the Parliament of 1628. Add. 36825, f. 408ʳ.

[3] *C.S.P.D. 1619–23*, vol. cxxi, no. 136; *Cabala* (1691), I, p. 2; *C.S.P.Ven.
1619–21*, p. 52 and *1621–3*, p. 53; *H.M.C. Mar and Kellie Suppl.*, p. 100;
C.S.P.Ven. 1623–5, p. 169; Ruigh, pp. 186–7, 203; L. Stone, *Family and
Fortune* (1973), p. 230.

1624, Buckingham's attack on Cranfield, carried to its conclusion in the House of Lords, represented an attempt by the war party in the Council to override the hold which the peace party in the Council still retained on King James's favour.[1]

Impeachment in the 1620s was not a device used to secure ministerial responsibility to the Commons, but first and foremost a tool used by one Councillor to attack another. Without the safety of numbers which a Parliament provided, Councillors would rarely risk attacks on colleagues who still held the King's favour. Increasingly, then, courtiers and Councillors were finding Parliaments necessary to their own power struggles. In the words of the Commons' Remonstrance of 1626, without accusations in Parliament 'no servant to a King, perhaps no Councillor (without exposing himself to the hazard of a great enmity and prejudice) can be a means to call great officers into question'.[2] In 1626, it is possible that a majority of the Council may have been using the Parliament as an engine to lever the Duke of Buckingham out of a monopoly of their master's favour. In impeachments, perhaps more than anywhere else, the tendency to see the politics of this period as a conflict between two monolithic institutions called 'court' and 'country' has prevented us from seeing what was really happening.

In impeachments, the judges were the House of Lords. As a Parliament dominated by supply tended to put the Commons in the centre of the stage, so one dominated by impeachment tended to put the Lords at the centre of the stage. It was necessary for court magnates undertaking an impeachment to enjoy the support of such peers as Warwick, Essex, or Saye, who had connections with the court without being fully members of it. Impeachments also gave prominence to the 'discourted'—former members of the court who had been thrown out in disgrace. Men like the Earl of Bristol, a trusted Privy Councillor and ambassador of King James, disgraced by Buckingham in 1624–5, or Bishop John Williams, Lord Keeper of the Great Seal, disgraced early in Charles's reign, were among the most able and best-informed allies one Councillor could have in an attack on another.[3]

It is not easy to classify such men as members of either 'the

---

[1] Ruigh, pp. 303–44, esp. pp. 311–12.   [2] S.P. 16/24/31.
[3] I am grateful to Mr. Michael Denning for drawing my attention to the significance of discourted peers in impeachments.

court' or 'the country'. Indeed, the House of Lords as a whole is very hard to classify according to such categories. In one respect, the Crown attempted to treat the House of Lords as an extension of the court. As those temporarily in disfavour could be excluded from court, so the Crown sometimes tried to exclude them from the House of Lords, either by withholding their writs of summons, or by instructing them to send a proxy instead of attending in person. This was one of the most significant and least-noticed attacks on Parliamentary privilege during the period. It was not an attack by 'the court' on 'the country': its victims included men like the Earl of Bristol, still a Privy Councillor in 1624, the Earl of Arundel, Earl Marshal, and George Abbot, Archbishop of Canterbury.[1] Nor was it an 'opposition' which defeated this attack on Parliamentary privilege. The man who saw the long-term significance of the issue, and did most to ensure that the Crown did not have the right to withhold a writ of summons to the Lords, was Bishop Williams. He was a former Lord Keeper, who had once been in charge of denying writs to others.[2]

In the Commons, as well as the Lords, impeachments tended to become confrontations between rival factions at court. Before beginning an impeachment, it was advisable to have good intelligence between members of the two Houses. Thus, in an impeachment, members of the Commons who were clients of a great Lord acquired a peculiar importance. Clientage did not necessarily impose an obligation to follow a patron's line, unless his personal survival was at stake.[3] On many issues, the followers of Buckingham or Pembroke in the Commons did not speak with one voice. On an issue which concerned their patrons as deeply as the impeachment of Buckingham, however, they worked as teams. In the prosecution of the Duke, a key part was played by Pembroke's men in the Commons, such as Dr. Turner, Sir Robert Mansell, Rudyerd, Perrott, Coryton, and Edward Herbert. They were fought all the way by Buckingham's able team in the Commons, including Sir Robert Harley, Sir Miles Fleetwood, Sir Robert Pye,[*]

---

[1] Vernon F. Snow, *Essex The Rebel* (Lincoln, Nebraska, 1970), p. 106; S.P. 14/159/70; Phelips MSS. 212/46 (Williams to Hertford); *Cabala*, I.274, 97; Snow, op. cit., p. 154; *C.S.P.D. 1625-6*, vol. xx, no. 43.

[2] Duchy of Cornwall, True Relation of the Parliament of 1626, pp. 23-5 (Williams to the King, Feb. 1626): Huntingdon R.O., Manchester MSS. 32/5/15 (n.d. 1640: Williams to either Warwick or Manchester).

[3] See below, pp. 167-8.

[*] whose eldest daughter married Sir Robert Phelips's eldest son, but probably not until after 1629, and whose father (?), Sir Walter Pye owed his judgeship in Wales to Buckingham.

Sir Dudley Carleton, and Sir George Goring.[1] It would be a mistake to think that a solid group called 'the Commons' were united in opposition to Buckingham in 1626. Buckingham himself said in answering the Commons' charges that 'There hath been that contestation in the Commons concerning my justification that I cannot but acknowledge much favour there from many.' The closeness of a number of divisions in the Commons appears to bear him out.[2]

'The Commons' then, cannot be thought of as a separate interest, either from the court, or from the House of Lords. Many owed their seats to the nomination of such peers as Pembroke, Warwick, or Bedford, and Arundel, speaking in the Lords, once described the Commons as their younger sons. Others in the Commons needed the favour of court patrons in order to keep much of their influence in their home counties. John Hampden, a Deputy Lieutenant in Buckinghamshire, owed his position to the Lord Lieutenant, the Duke of Buckingham. Sir Francis Seymour, Deputy Lieutenant in Wiltshire, owed his office to the Lord Lieutenant, the Earl of Pembroke. Active Parliamentarians such as Sir Thomas Wentworth, Sir John Wray, Sir Francis Barrington, and Sir Gilbert Gerrard were as forward as others in the quest for court favours such as baronetcies.[3]

Some favour at court was necessary to enable the most rustic of country gentlemen to do his job in his own county. Much of the work of a county governor consisted of asking for favours from the central government, and those who do not do favours commonly do not get them. In 1628, the Deputy Lieutenants of Cornwall warned the county that they would be unwise to elect Eliot and Coryton, who were in disfavour with the King, because the knights of the shire would, when elected, have to petition for numerous favours from the court. They would want ships to defend the county against pirates and foreign invasion. They would want supplies of salt, payment of coat and conduct money for the troops they had raised, relief from the pressure of billeting, and a magazine to defend themselves against attack. All these things, they thought,

---

[1] See, in particular, the debates of 2 May in Grosvenor (1626), ff. 18–24.

[2] *L.J.* 656; *C.J.* 833, 835, 850, 852, 858. The number of divisions on major issues was a peculiarity of the Commons of 1626.

[3] Sheffield City Library, Elmhirst MSS. 1284 includes two lists of Baronets created up to 1642. In these lists, regular members of Parliament appear to be more amply represented than they are in an average commission of the peace.

would be better secured by the election of 'men of moderation' than by that of Eliot and Coryton.[1] One of the most extreme examples of a gentleman's inability to do his job in his country without some favour at court is the dismissal of Sir Thomas Wentworth from the office of Custos Rotulorum, or chairman of the bench, in Yorkshire. This dismissal, received in open court, was a 'seeming disgrace in the public face of the county'.[2] Such a disgrace did not make it easy for a man to keep his standing in his home county. It is not surprising that members of Parliament worried constantly about the need to preserve their standing and connections at court. If there is one big lack in the studies of Parliaments in the 1620s, it is the lack of studies in depth of the influence of the court, in all its multifarious forms, on the House of Commons.

Members of the Commons, even during their brief spells at Westminster, did not operate in a political vacuum. They also needed to keep up their reputation in the country, in order to preserve their claim to a hearing at court. A member who, in Mr. Cooper's illuminating phrase, 'overdrew his credit with the country' would find himself outmanoeuvred by local rivals, and unable to give effective service to his patrons at court.[3] Members of the Commons were not free agents, voting at their own whim: they were painfully aware of their need to preserve favour, both at court and in the country. Sometimes, and more frequently as the decade went on, members were forced to make temporary choices between the two. Whichever they chose, they would then have to make rapid attempts to restore their credit with the other. To ask an ambitious politician to choose between permanent allegiance to court or to country would have been to ask him to choose between alternative methods of political suicide.

Fortunately, we already possess, in Dr. Hirst's book, *The Representative of the People?*, an illuminating study of the influence of the country on the House of Commons.[4] It is necessary here to

---

[1] Add. 36825, f. 21ʳ⁻ᵛ.

[2] Knowler, p. 36.

[3] *Wentworth Papers*, p. 5. This theme is more fully developed by D. M. Hirst in 'Court, Country and Politics up to 1629' in K. M. Sharpe (ed.), *Faction and Parliament* (Oxford, 1978). I am grateful to Dr. Hirst for allowing me to see this essay before publication. Our positions have evolved first independently, and then concurrently.

[4] D. M. Hirst, *The Representative of the People?* (Cambridge, 1975), *passim*.

say a word of clarification. When Professor Zagorin spoke of 'the country', he regarded it as consisting of M.P.s themselves. When M.P.s spoke of 'the country' they did not mean themselves: they meant the electorates and neighbours to whom many of them were answerable. Their standing with them was often a vital part of their prestige. Sir Thomas Wentworth, writing about the Yorkshire election of 1620/1, used 'the country' to mean the freeholders who made up the bulk of the electorate. He was using the election to discover whether his prestige was sufficient to win a seat for Secretary Calvert as well as for himself. He expected the result would be crucial to his standing at court as well as in the country, and feared that 'the loss of it would much prejudice our estimations above'.[1]

Both inflation and the decisions of the House of Commons committee of privileges were continually enlarging the electorate, and, as Dr. Hirst has conclusively shown, many members were painfully aware of a sense of being accountable to it.[2] Wentworth succeeded in securing the election of Secretary Calvert for Yorkshire. When he came back to speak for the collection of the subsidy he had voted, he felt the need to devote much of his speech to trying to prove that the election of Calvert had been in the interests of the county as a whole.[3] In 1624, Arthur Ingram and Christopher Brooke, two M.P.s of considerable standing, felt the need to offer the town of York a lengthy justification of the number of subsidies they had voted.

The unfortunate Sir Robert Phelips appears to have left every Parliament in trouble either in the country or at court. Phelips's local misfortunes illustrate the point that the opinion of neighbours, perhaps more than of electors, was crucial to members' standing, and hence to their Parliamentary behaviour. After the Parliament of 1624, in which he had worked harmoniously with Buckingham, and helped to secure a large grant of subsidies, he was accused by a member of the rival county faction of 'lying, flattering and tale bearing', and of seeking favour so hard that he neglected other business, and of suppressing petitions the county wanted to have presented in Parliament. At the next election, in 1625, Phelips felt the need to show the Council what difficulties he was labouring under: he had one of those who had made scandalous

[1] Knowler, pp. 11–13.   [2] Hirst, pp. 178–88.
[3] *Wentworth Papers*, pp. 152–7.

speeches against him during the election called before the Council in the middle of Parliament. His rival in the county, Lord Poulett, then complained that Phelips had 'forsaken the country and was turned courtier'.[1] Sir Robert Phelips's Parliamentary career is a continual alternation between charges such as these from his county rivals, and charges from his enemies at court that he was a 'rank weed'[2] who made 'undutiful and seditious speeches'. Sir Robert's own papers suggest that he sincerely tried to give good service, both to his country and to the court, but that whenever he succeeded in satisfying one, he found himself in trouble with the other.

Protests by members of the Commons that their freedom of action was limited by the need to conciliate 'the country' have long been well known. The novelty of Dr. Hirst's contribution to the debate is not in drawing attention to their existence, but in showing that, in some cases, we may need to take them at face value. In some constituencies, notably Kent, Somerset, and Yorkshire, there existed an electorate sufficiently large, powerful, and well-informed to be capable of exerting considerable pressure on its members of Parliament. It is interesting to note how many of the active members represented, or aspired to represent, these constituencies. It is doubtful, however, whether members who talked about the reactions of 'the country' were always thinking in an electoral context. In 1624, Sir Peter Hayman complained of the burden of subsidies on 'the country', only to be brusquely reminded by his Kentish neighbour, Sir Dudley Digges, that he sat for one of the Cinque Ports, which did not pay subsidies.[3] In this case, when Hayman said 'the country' must avow what they did, he was probably thinking of his neighbours, rather than his constituents. It is difficult to be certain how much influence to ascribe to neighbours, and how much to constituents, in members' sense of being under pressure from 'the country'. In the case of the great country champion Edward Alford, it is often impossible

[1] Hirst, p. 180: Phelips MSS. 228/26 (and also Barnes, pp. 261n, 267). Phelips MSS. 216/12, 222/53. For similar difficulties suffered by Sir Edwin Sandys in Kent, see Hirst, p. 174 and Chamberlain, 6 May 1625.

[2] C.S.P.D. 1625–6, vol. x, no. 16. This unflattering phrase was applied to Phelips by Rudyerd on the occasion of his being pricked sheriff to keep him out of the Parliament of 1626. It perhaps illustrates the difficulties Phelips suffered through the lack of a good relationship with Pembroke, who was Lord Lieutenant of his county.

[3] Holles (1624), f. 109ᵛ.

to tell whether he is speaking for his neighbours in Sussex, or for his constituents in Colchester. On the occasions when it is possible to distinguish, it seems that he is more often speaking for Sussex.

Yet, whatever combination these two members may have referred to when they spoke of 'the country', there are enough unambiguous speeches to suggest that the fear of 'country' reactions could be genuine and serious. In 1628, Edward Kirton said that if the Commons voted subsidies without dealing with the grievance of billeting, 'they will not pay in the country, what we give'. Two days later, Sir Francis Seymour appeared to be facing the threat that Parliaments would become extinct if supply were not voted at once. He said that if they voted supply in these circumstances, 'We shall serve our own ends and not our country.' He was clearly capable of regarding the two as distinct. Perhaps the most unambiguous example of a genuine concern with the reactions of the public is a decision by the two Houses, on 20 June 1628, that the King's second answer to the Petition of Right should be printed in English as well as in French, 'for the better satisfaction of the vulgar'.[1] For this, or for the endless concern of Phelips or Alford with petty constituency business, there can be no explanation except the obvious one.

Members of Parliament, then, were dependent on preserving the goodwill of both court and country. They should therefore be seen as victims more often than as initiators. It is agreed that this period was one of peculiar strain in the relations between central and local government. Members of Parliament, at what Professor Elton has called 'the point of contact' between central and local government,[2] were likely to feel this strain more than most. Many, particularly Deputy Lieutenants during the war years, found their dual role as champions of the localities at the centre, and of the centre in the localities, increasingly hard to continue. Sir Robert Phelips, who denounced the Lieutenancy as the strangest engine of tyranny ever known, and a few months later accepted office as a Deputy Lieutenant, was not just indulging in a piece of opportunistic inconsistency. He was also reflecting, without much subtlety, the conflict of loyalties which was a member of Parliament's job.

[1] Hirst, p. 172; Add. 36825, f. 136^v; *L.J.* 869.
[2] G. R. Elton, 'Tudor Government: The Points of Contact: Parliament', *T.R.H.S.* (1974), 183–200.

Very rarely, instead of being exploited by country pressure, members set out to exploit it. More often, they protested, probably sincerely, that they disliked 'popularity'. At the end of the 1620s, when the conflicting pressures on many members were becoming unbearable, there are some signs of attempts to exploit public opinion. At the end of the Parliament of 1626, Whitelocke noted an order that any member of the Commons could take a copy of their final Remonstrance. One of the Sussex M.P.s was busy organizing, and paying for, the taking of copies, when Secretary Conway began a desperate and unsuccessful attempt to impound all the copies.[1] On 6 May 1628, when the debates on the Petition of Right appeared to have reached deadlock, Sir Roger North, according to one account, made the alarming proposal that they should lay aside their proposed bill on the liberty of the subject, and publish their resolutions and debates instead.[2] This proposal appears to have been more populist than most members of the Commons wanted, and no notice was taken of it. The dangers of such populist appeals were shown only a few months later, in August 1628. When the Duke of Buckingham was assassinated, his assassin was found to be carrying a copy of the Commons' Remonstrance of 1628, purchased from a Holborn scrivener, in his hat.[3] This was not what the Commons had been aiming at: this sort of popular violence was a potential threat to any gentleman. This sort of appeal to the people was the way to civil war. It was a way members during the 1620s did not wish to take. Moreover, it seems likely that this incident did them even more harm with the King than their failure to complete bills in 1621 or their generosity over subsidies in 1624 had done them with the country.

The few deliberate appeals to the people come from the end of the period here described, and would have been unthinkable at the beginning of it. The early years of Charles I were very different from the last years of James I. In the last two Parliaments of King James, the tension between central and local government which came to a head later in the decade was already there, but there was none of the sense of panic and urgency which characterized the debates of 1628. Yet, considering how much institutional and personal tension had built up by the end of the decade, it is

[1] Fletcher, p. 233; Whitelocke, 12–22, f. 60^r. S.P. 16/30/11.
[2] Stowe 366, f. 140^{r-v}; Harl. 5324, f. 32^v.
[3] C.S.P.D. 1628–9, vol. cxiv, nos. 20. 31.

remarkable how little ideological division developed during these years. Even in 1628, there was not so much an ideological gulf between court and country, as ideological gulfs within the court itself.

In a divided court, those who were temporarily outmanœuvred were often tempted to use the wider stage of a Parliament to lobby for more support for their case. It was thus that Elizabethan Councillors, for example, had encouraged Parliamentary agitation on the Queen's marriage and the succession. Yet the raising of Parliamentary support on issues of high policy was always a risky thing to do, since it laid those who did it open to a very damaging debating riposte. They could be accused of encouraging the lower orders to acquire ideas above their station. It was on this same issue of marriage and the succession that Queen Elizabeth had told the Commons that 'it is monstrous that the feet should direct the head', and had complained of 'restless heads, in whose brains the needless hammers beat with vain judgement'.[1] It was in the same vein that James in 1621, faced with a demand for war which also originated from within his own Council, replied with the same charge of social insubordination: he claimed that the Commons' petition originated from 'fiery and popular spirits of the House of Commons' wanting 'to argue and debate publicly of the matters far above their reach and capacity, tending to our high dishonour and breach of prerogative royal'.[2] It is highly improbable that either monarch was unaware that the agitation they so deplored originated from within their own Council. Yet in a society whose sense of hierarchy was always unquiet, to claim that a case originated with 'fiery and popular spirits' was usually an effective way of discrediting it.

It was not only monarchs who could use the smear of social insubordination to discredit arguments they did not like. If one faction at court called for public support, its rivals could always fall back on these charges. As anxiety grew about the balance of an unstable system of government, so it became a more damaging accusation to accuse opponents of upsetting it. In all the period, there was probably no Parliamentary manœuvre that owed more to court encouragement than the attempt to impeach the Duke of

[1] J. E. Neale, *Elizabeth I and her Parliaments*, i (1953), 150, 108.
[2] J. R. Tanner, *Constitutional Documents of the Reign of James I* (repr. 1960), 279.

Buckingham, in 1626. Yet it was still a worthwhile tactic for the author of an anonymous memorandum (possibly Sir James Bagg) to tell King Charles that the Duke's critics were 'innovators, *plebicolae* and king-haters'.[1]

It is passages of this sort which provide much of the contemporary comment on which the notion of 'the winning of the initiative by the House of Commons' has been based. To take one of the most famous examples, the memorandum composed by Lord Chancellor Ellesmere at the end of King James's first Parliament has often been quoted in a 'constitutional' context. Some of Ellesmere's comments, particularly those on the growth of Parliamentary judicature, have a strongly 'constitutional' tone. Yet these passages are only a minor part of the memorandum as a whole. The dominant theme of the memorandum is again that of innovation and social insubordination – two ideas very closely connected in many noble and gentle minds. When Ellesmere said that 'the popular state ever since the beginning of his Majesty's gracious and sweet government hath grown big and audacious', he was not just thinking of the House of Commons. His object was to raise the spectre of peasant revolt:

It was long ago observed by Livy, *vulgus aut humiliter servit aut superbe dominatur*. And it is daily found true, *plebis importunitas cedendo accenditur*. And oftentimes exhortations and persuasions, though never so wise, learned, eloquent and religious, prevail little with a heady multitude, for certain it is *malitia non instruitur sermonibus sed incenditur*. And grant wilful folly what it desireth, it will never be satisfied.

Ellesmere's object in denouncing the 'popular state' was to criticize the management of the Parliament, as much as the Parliament itself. 'If way be still given unto it (as of late hath been) it is to be doubted what the end will be.'[2] An evaluation of Ellesmere's motives in this memorandum must await an analysis, both of his objectives, and of his intended audience. Without this analysis, it is hard to take the memorandum for an objective statement of fact.

James also was capable of appealing to fear of popular disorder to overcome Parliamentary lobbying. He objected to the 1621

[1] *Cabala*, II. 226. I am grateful to Mr. Clive Hart for a valuable discussion of this document, and of many of the points discussed here.

[2] Elizabeth Read Foster, *Proceedings in Parliament 1610* (New Haven, 1966), i. 276. I would like to thank Dr. N. R. N. Tyacke for much valuable advice about this document.

petition on the execution of the recusancy laws: 'And we leave you to judge whether it be your duties, that are the representative body of our people, so to distaste them with our government; whereas by the contrary it is your duty with all your endeavours to kindle more and more a dutiful and thankful love in the people's hearts towards us for our just and gracious government.'[1] Such a line of attack, however unfair, acquired much of its force from the fact that it was one which was capable of appealing to the fears of members of Parliament themselves. It is no more necessary to take this comment at face value than it is to accept at face value the contrary, and rather more frequent, line of contemporary comment which saw Parliaments going down to eclipse: as the authors of the *Apology of the Commons* (whoever they may have been) claimed, 'The prerogatives of princes may easily and do daily grow; the privileges of the subject are at an everlasting stand.' The two common factors in these contradictory lines of comment are that they are both special pleading, and they both depend on a common fear of innovation. The key common factor, to which debaters of all sorts appealed, was the belief that the existing form of government was good, and that all attempts to innovate and change it were dangerous.[2] Accusations of 'constitutional' aims, then, do not appear in men's statements of their own motives: they appear in statements designed to discredit opponents, and such statements are notoriously untrustworthy.

In particular, the majority of statements describing the House of Commons as 'puritan' originate from untrustworthy sources. Most of them come from foreign ambassadors, particularly the Venetian Ambassador and Salvetti. Apart from the notorious difficulty of Catholics in distinguishing between different sorts of Protestant, such reporters were only too eager to convey the impression that those who pressed for the persecution of their fellow-Catholics were tarred with the brush of social revolution. Most ambassadors, moreover, were better informed about the court than they were about the House of Commons. On the whole, they were good at reporting the ebb and flow of court faction, and consequently of

---

[1] Tanner, op. cit., p. 284.

[2] For a remarkably clear example of this unanimity in disliking innovation, see Esther S. Cope and Willson H. Coates, *Proceedings of the Short Parliament of 1640*, Camden Soc., Fourth Series, 19 (1977), p. 131. The unanimity of this dislike of innovation is the more impressive for the general disagreement between those who agreed in expressing it.

English foreign policy. This was how they earned their living. However, when they report a popular puritanism of which they had been told by such men as Arundel or Cottington, their information has passed through, not one, but two distorting mirrors before reaching us. It is, then, necessary to check it very carefully against the material of the Parliamentary debates themselves.

(b) *Religion and Politics*

It is remarkable how hard it is to discover a 'puritan opposition' in the 1620s, especially in the last years of King James. Any statements about 'puritanism' are of course bedevilled by the problem of definition. If puritans be broadly defined as 'the hotter sort of Protestants', those who took their Protestantism with due seriousness, then there were a number of puritans in James's later Parliaments. There is no religious division between 'puritans' thus defined and many of the bishops. If those who sponsored legislation against Sunday football and other breaches of the Sabbath, or those who made eloquent speeches against Popish recusants be taken for 'puritans', then many of the House of Commons were puritans. If so, Richard Montagu was right in calling many of the bishops 'puritans'. The Commons' bills on these subjects were handled in the Lords by Archbishop Abbot, and normally reported fit to pass without amendment. It is a remarkable fact about the two long and busy Parliaments of 1621 and 1624 that in neither of them did any religious bill pass the Commons which failed to pass the Lords.

Puritans in this sense were in no way associated with opposition at the end of James's reign: Harley and Perrott, two of the most enthusiastic of them, were loyal followers of Buckingham and Pembroke respectively. Sir Edward Montagu is perhaps typical of a 'puritan' member in this wide sense of a man who took the established religion of the Church of England seriously. King James was prepared to tell him, before the Parliament of 1621, that 'Though you smelt a little of puritanism, yet he knew you to be honest and faithful to him; and said he heard you were a Parliament man—you must do him an errand, and he would requite you, but such a one, as I hear, as you need not be afraid of.'[1] Sir Edward

[1] *H.M.C. Buccleuch*, i. 255–6. There is no evidence on the nature of the 'errand' referred to.

Montagu had one brother who became Lord Treasurer, and another who became Dean of the Chapel Royal and Bishop of Winchester. All three had the same serious Protestantism in common, and there is no sign that it ever alienated them from the King, Buckingham, or the court. In 1626, when Buckingham needed all the friends he could find, the Montagus were among his most dependable supporters. All the Parliamentary evidence supports Mr. Fletcher's summary of the situation in Sussex:

Puritanism before 1640 was therefore a movement for zeal and godliness within the church. The Puritan gentry led a campaign to stress evangelical religion. Until the rise of Arminianism, they were not fundamentally at odds with the ecclesiastical establishment.[1]

Nor, until the rise of Arminianism, did contemporaries usually call them 'puritans'. 'Puritan' was a term of abuse, and was therefore normally reserved for those in disfavour.

For those who would employ more radical definitions of puritanism, it is hard, before 1625-6, to show that there were any puritans in the Commons at all.[2] There is no evidence in the debates to show that a single member objected to government of the church by bishops. Knightley, one of the two or three least unlikely to have done so in private, combined his puritanism with being a Buckingham client. In the regular spree in which members debated whether Oxford or Cambridge should be mentioned first in the subsidy bill, one of the arguments used for Oxford was that it was a bishop's see. Occasionally, there was an echo of old controversies. In 1626, Christopher Sherland, Recorder of Northampton, made a rare attack on the authority of the Court of High Commission, claiming it was no court of record. He was quickly answered by the more prominent member Sir Dudley Digges, who said that it was a court of record, and he was a member of it.[3] Among the most prominent members of the Commons, Sir Dudley Digges, Sir Robert Phelips, Sir Edwin Sandys, William Noy, Sir Edward Coke, and Sir Thomas Wentworth were not puritans by any possible definition. The House of Commons at the end of James's reign was then very far from being a distinctively 'puritan' body. In particular, the Parliaments of 1621 and 1624 do

---

[1] Fletcher, p. 74. See also Barnes, p. 15.
[2] On Saye, see *H.M.C. Salis.* xx. 48. P. W. Thomas, *Sir John Berkenhead* (Oxford, 1969), p. 119.
[3] Whitelocke, 12-20, f. 68ᵛ.

much to bear out Professor Elton's dictum that 'Puritanism has no continuous history'.[1]

This dictum is of course more political than theological. It is certainly possible to trace a constant religious creed through sermons and commonplace books. Yet, since the very definition of the word 'puritan' normally involves some notion of opposition to ecclesiastical authority, it is hard to call a creed 'puritan' at times when the authorities not merely failed to repress it, but even, in a large measure, shared it. If 'puritans' are defined by refusal to conform, then the meaning of 'puritanism' must necessarily vary with changes in the attitude of the ecclesiastical authorities. If 'puritanism' is thus politically defined, the ecclesiastical authorities could make and unmake 'puritans' by their own changes of policy. If, on the other hand, we try to give a constant meaning to the word 'puritan', then the correlation between 'puritanism and opposition' collapses. If we choose to search for a constant theological definition for the word 'puritan', we may take a narrow definition, or we may take a wide one. By any narrow definition, it is probably true to say that there were no puritans in the late Jacobean House of Commons: it contained no avowed opponents of episcopacy or the Prayer Book, and probably few, if any, unavowed ones. If we take a wider definition, involving such things as a desire for further reformation and the cult of the Sabbath, then 'puritanism' was an official creed, and George Abbot was, as Richard Montagu would have him, a 'puritan archbishop'. By none of these definitions is it possible to create a 'puritan opposition' in late Jacobean Parliaments.[2]

In and after 1626, there was rather more sign of religious

---

[1] G. R. Elton, *Studies in Tudor and Stuart Politics and Government* (Cambridge, 1974), ii. 160. Some supposedly 'puritan' bills were supported by lawyers with the closest connections with the Crown, simply on the ground of erastian anti-clericalism. See, for example, Sir John Finch's support for the scandalous ministers bill of 1626, Whitelocke, 12–20 f. 84ᵛ.

[2] I am grateful to Dr. Tyacke for many fascinating and inconclusive debates on this subject. It is an open question whether the word 'puritan' has become the cause of so much confusion that it should be abandoned. On changing definitions of 'puritans', see Tyacke in *Origins*, pp. 121–2, 129, 133–4, 138–9. See also P. Collinson, 'Lectures by Combination: Structures and Characteristics of Church Life in Seventeenth-Century England', *B.I.H.R.* (1975), 182–213 and W. J. Shiels, 'Religion in Provincial Towns; Innovation and Tradition', in *Church and Society in England: Henry VIII to James I*, ed. Felicity Heal and Rosemary O'Day, pp. 156–76. See also J. Sears McGee, *The Godly Man in Stuart England*, New Haven 1976.

tension. There was also then one 'puritan' in the Commons who would have been recognizable to Ben Jonson: Ignatius Jordan, member for Exeter. In 1626, he hoped to introduce the death penalty for adultery. By 1628, he had been induced to scale down his demands to a fine of 100 marks for gentlemen, and a whipping for others. Even then, he found it hard to get the House of Commons to take him seriously. Pym, whose sense of the ridiculous was not his strong point, said that he did not like the frame of the bill, but since the sin required the judgement of God on this land, they should commit it. The House burst out laughing, and shouting 'Commit it. Commit it.' Jordan was left to say that 'I did always look that this bill should find many opposers, but Mr. Speaker, this is no laughing matter'. Sir Edward Coke, who could never resist explaining a joke, said, 'But good Mr. Speaker, it is the bill not the sin which we would have committed.' This is not the reaction of a very puritanical House of Commons.[1]

Between 1625 and 1629, the religious peace of the last years of King James slowly disappeared. By 1629, the rise of Arminianism was beginning to produce a religious polarization of a sort which had been unknown since the 1580s. The crucial offence of Arminians, in the eyes of many bishops and members of Parliament, was their attack on predestination.[2] Before the rise of Arminianism, it was the normal, though not quite the official, doctrine of the Church of England that those who were saved were saved because God for reasons known only to himself had pre-destined them to eternal life. The Arminians, on the other hand, believed that a man's salvation was contingent on what he did during his life: a man who was in grace at one stage of his life might later fall from it, and start on the way which led to damnation. It must be an open question how far, before the prolonged theological education which men like Pym, Rich, and Sherland gave them in the later 1620s, members understood the full subtleties of the official predestinarian view. A study of members' wills

---

[1] Whitelocke, 12–20, f. 83ᵛ; Stowe 366, ff. 53ᵛ, 97ᵛ; Grosvenor, 22 April 1628. It is an open question whether Jordan in 1626 proposed the death penalty for adulterous ministers or for adulterers in general. I am grateful to Mr. K. V. Thomas for discussion of this question. On the uniqueness of Jordan, see also P. Collinson, 'A Magazine of Religious Patterns', *Studies in Church History*, vol. xiv (1977), ed. D. Baker, p. 239.

[2] On the nature and significance of Arminianism, see Tyacke in *Origins*, pp. 119–43 *passim*.

suggests that the point that had really captured their imagination, and which the Arminians denied, was one they had learnt from William Perkins of Cambridge, rather than from Calvin, the original fount of predestinarian orthodoxy. This was the belief that it was possible for a man to know for certain that he was one of the Elect, and therefore predestined to salvation. This previously orthodox belief was reclassified by Arminians as 'puritanism'. Sir Francis Barrington, Baronet, Knight of the Shire for Essex, and a Parliament man of long standing, made his will on 26 October 1626, after Arminianism had become a live issue, and felt the need to spell this point out with particular clarity:

> First I hold it my bounden duty to manifest and declare that all my sins (which for multitude are as the sands of the sea, or hairs of my head) are through the merits of God in Christ forgiven, and that so soon as life departeth from me my soul shall be received into eternal bliss until the day of judgement and that then when all men's bodies shall rise from the dust, mine also shall rise and then both body and soul shall with the rest of God's saints reign eternally in everlasting happiness, which no heart can conceive nor tongue utter.[1]

To challenge a conviction of this force, as the Arminians did, was a risky proceeding: to tell men like Sir Francis Barrington that they could not be sure whether they were saved or not was likely to cause some indignation.

Yet though the Arminian dispute was a bitter and important one, it was not in any sense a court–country dispute until Arminianism reached the parishes during the 1630s. In the years before 1629, it was first and foremost a dispute within the court. On the bench of bishops, George Abbot had to be suspended from his archiepiscopal functions in part because of his opposition to the new doctrine. He was supported, with equal force, by such bishops as Carleton and Coke (brother of the Secretary of State). It was not until 1626 that it could be suspected that hatred of Arminianism was incompatible with preferment to high ecclesiastical office. There was no suggestion at all, before the 1630s, that it was incompatible with preferment to high secular office. Such men as the Earl of Manchester, Lord Privy Seal, were as firm in their opposition to Arminianism as almost any of its critics in the Commons. More important, there is very little sign until June 1628 that religious grievances were yet producing that fusion with constitutional issues which made them both so explosive in

[1] P.R.O. PROB/11/154/70.

1640.[1] The anti-Arminian Earl of Manchester was, in his capacity as a lawyer, a firm champion of the prerogative. He supported the King's right to levy impositions in 1614 as firmly as he supported Buckingham in 1626, and had no notion that dislike of Arminianism turned him into a member of the 'opposition'. Though Buckingham ultimately threw his weight behind Arminianism, which was clearly the creed of King Charles, many of his Parliamentary followers were among its bitterest critics. Sir Robert Harley, for example, insisted that a condemnation of Arminianism should be put into the Remonstrance of 1628 as firmly as he argued that the Duke of Buckingham's name should be taken out of it. Conversely, the Arminian Bishop Harsnett was one of those who did much to help the Petition of Right through the House of Lords.[2]

It is also possible to wonder whether, before 1629, Arminianism was yet an issue of concern to the majority of members of the Commons. Its intense personal importance to John Pym may, with the use of hindsight, encourage us to think it roused strong emotions in more members than it did, and that they were aware of the issue sooner than they were. John Pym was exceptionally quick off the mark in seeing the potential significance of the issue in 1624. Even among the few dedicated anti-Arminians, most did not join in the attack until 1626 or 1628. It is noteworthy that in 1626, when Christopher Sherland told the House of Commons about the York House Conference, which marked the official triumph of Arminianism, he assumed that his audience would not yet have heard of it.[3] The anti-Arminians are important, partly because they include many members who were to be much more prominent in 1640, partly because they include many of the ablest members of the Commons, and partly because they include the four members (Pym, Rich, Digges, and Rudyerd) who were most eager to offer significant long-term help with the King's finances. Yet it is not

---

[1] The peculiarly heated debates of 5 and 6 June 1628 should be regarded as an exception to this statement. See below, pp. 378–382.

[2] Stowe 366, f. 223^r; Add. 36825, f. 481^r: *Lords' Debates* (ed. Relf), pp. 110, 216–17.

[3] Whitelocke, 12 20, f. 20^r. Sherland also reported the result of the conference as the opposite of what it was, although he admitted that 'rumours are spread to the contrary'. The general realization that Buckingham was entering into alliance with the Arminians cannot be easily dated before the Cambridge Chancellorship election, at the very end of the Parliament of 1626. Indeed, even this date is perhaps too early. I am grateful to Dr. Tyacke for many valuable discussions of this question.

until 1629 that Arminianism can be regarded as one of the major issues for the House of Commons as a whole.

It was not until then that it captured the attention of such middle-of-the-road men as Sir Robert Phelips, who was outraged at the notion that anyone could think him to be a puritan. Sir Walter Earle said in 1629 that in the previous session the House of Commons had been divided between those who put the issue of the liberty of the subject first, and those who put the issue of religion first. He himself, he said, had recently been converted from the first group to the second. In this, he may be typical of much mainstream opinion in the House of Commons.[1]

(c) *Desire for Office*

Up to 1628, then, dislike of Arminianism was no handicap to ambition for office, and does not seem to have prevented the most ambitious members of Parliament from hoping for office. Being a member of Parliament was not a career but at best a stepping-stone to one. Parliaments were occasional events, short-term assemblies of provincials in London. Ambitious members, then, did not normally aim at much increasing the power of so ephemeral an assembly. When they considered the prospect that assemblies of Parliament might become more regular, many found that their first reaction was not of vaulting constitutional ambition, but of alarm at the more frequent demands of subsidies they would be forced to make in the constituencies. Ambitious members, then, hoped to transfer their careers on to a more permanent stage: they hoped for office.

The ultimate constitutional ambition found among leading members was that the King should, as Sir Nathaniel Rich put it, choose an 'advised Council'.[2] On such a Council, many of them naturally hoped that they themselves or their patrons might have a substantial part to play. Almost all the really prominent members of Parliament can be shown to have had ambitions, if not for a Privy Councillorship, at least for something that would set them on the court ladder. Some, such as Sir Benjamin Rudyerd, surveyor of the Court of Wards, held such an office already.[3] Most

---

[1] *1629 Debates*, p. 18.

[2] *1625 Debates*, p. 91, *C.J.* 811. See also Digges in S.P. 16/19/107.

[3] Rudyerd hoped that on the fall of Cranfield he would be promoted to the Mastership of the Court of Wards. Keeler, p. 329.

of the others can be shown to have either hoped for office, or been seriously considered for it. One of the most frankly ambitious was Sir Dudley Digges, who was disgusted at the failure of his attempt to become a Buckingham man to bring him preferment.[1] Sir John Eliot was almost equally frank. On hearing of James's death, he told Buckingham that:

In the great desire I have unto your grace's service, nothing has more unhappied me [sic] than the want of opportunity, in which I might express the character of my heart, that only takes of your impression. The times seem therein envious to me, presenting opposition to every purpose which I make, as if misfortune were their project, I the effect.[2]

Pending such an opportunity, he assured Buckingham that he would remain 'wholly devoted to the contemplation of your excellence'. Sandys and Phelips were also expected to come into office at the beginning of Charles's reign, and in Phelips's case, such hopes had been encouraged. Sandys was being tipped for Secretary of State, by so reliable a witness as John Chamberlain, in 1625,[3] while Phelips already had behind him unsuccessful attempts to obtain the posts of Master of Requests and ambassador to the Netherlands.[4] The list of those who hoped for office should perhaps also include Sir Nathaniel Rich.[5] In the Lords, the Earl of Essex, the future Parliamentary Lord General, was tantalized with hopes of preferment for much of the period. Regarding himself as a military specialist, he seized eagerly on reports of wars as offering opportunity for preferment. All he ever obtained was membership of the Council of War to supervise the sending of a small expedition to the Palatinate.[6] The ambitions of Sir Edward Coke for the Lord Treasurership, and of Wentworth for the Presidency of the North, are well known. It seems likely that many

[1] Bodleian MS. Rawlinson A 346, f. 226ʳ. I am grateful to Dr. Hirst for this reference. Also S.P. 16/19/107. He ultimately obtained the reversion to the Mastership of the Rolls.

[2] S.P. 16/1/25. See also S.P. 16/1/69 and 16/12/95. For his attempt to transfer from the Buckingham to the Pembroke connection, S.P. 16/18/68.

[3] Phelips MSS. 219/33; Chamberlain, 23 April 1625. Phelips MSS. 216/32b.

[4] Phelips MSS. 221/18 (Phelips to 'your Grace'—probably Buckingham—before 1621); Ruigh, p. 74n.

[5] Sackville MSS. ON 1123 (Dudley Norton to Cranfield, 17 Nov. 1622, recommending Rich). *Records of the Virginia Company*, ed. S. M. Kingsbury (1935), iv. 39, 49–52 (Rich submitting a revenue project to Cranfield in March 1622/3). I am grateful to Mr. Christopher Thompson for this reference.

[6] B.L. Add. MS. 46188, f. 11ʳ; B.L. Loan MS. 23/1, ff. 174ʳ, 178–9, 190, 205 (Holland to Essex, undated).

other hopes for office were buried with men who never committed them to paper.

Other members, especially lawyers, were more successful. Both the Attorney Generals Charles employed during the 1630s, William Noy and John Bankes, had been active members of Parliament. Bankes had been particularly prominent during the attacks on martial law in the Petition of Right debates in 1628. The fact that so few of the non-legal candidates obtained office was probably not only due to their activities in Parliament: a large increase in the numbers of gentlemen, without any commensurate increase in the supply of royal patronage, necessarily produced more disappointed candidates for preferment. The same can be said of peers: the 'inflation of honours' necessarily reduced the proportion of peers who could hold such offices as Lord Lieutenant.[1]

It would be misleading to present the ambitious members, who wanted national office, as typical of the Commons as a whole. It is, however, a difficult error to avoid, since the most ambitious and the most frequent speakers are necessarily categories with a large area of overlap.[2] Some prominent members, such as Sir Francis Seymour, seem to have been content to confine their horizons to their home counties, yet even Seymour ended his career by being Chancellor of the Duchy of Lancaster twice, to Charles I during the Civil War, and to Charles II at the Restoration. Among the really prominent members, only Edward Alford fits the archetypal image of the 'country member', and even he was dependent on court favour for the business he wanted to do in his home county. He provides an interesting example of the lack of unanimity of the court, having been appointed a Deputy Lieutenant in the autumn of 1626, when his attacks on Buckingham had led to his dismissal in disgrace from the less important post of Justice of the Peace. It may be relevant that the Earl of Arundel, joint Lord Lieutenant of the county, was also in disgrace at the time for his attacks on Buckingham.[3]

---

[1] I am grateful to Mr. Paul Hughes, formerly of King's School, Taunton, for this point.

[2] I am grateful to Mr. Anthony Fletcher for this point.

[3] Fletcher, pp. 176–7. Mr. Fletcher believes that Alford owed his appointment to co-option by his fellow-Deputies, but it must at least have been approved by Arundel and Dorset. For other evidence of dealings between Alford and Arundel, see Fletcher, p. 173.

II. THE BUSINESS OF A PARLIAMENT

Members, then, did not come to Westminster to move the pieces on a constitutional chess-board. They were not in training for the civil war or for the Bill of Rights. They were, it is true, much concerned that Parliaments should continue to meet, and concerned to make each Parliament a 'Parliament of union'. Yet their greatest ambitions were not for Parliament as a body. Those who wanted to promote policies hoped to do so by converting members of the court. Digges, who wanted a drastic reduction in the numbers of the commission of the Peace, used the Parliament of 1621 as an opportunity to persuade Secretary Calvert of his case. He would doubtless have preferred the opportunity, which office would have given him, to persuade Calvert of the same case without needing the cumbersome machinery of a Parliament to do so. For Digges, the Parliament of 1621 was an opportunity to attract enough official attention to improve his chances of office.

(a) *Legislation*

Those who were unconcerned with national office were more likely to be concerned with bills for the benefit of their counties than with attempts to improve the standing of Parliament as an institution. The purpose of a successful Parliament was not to engage in constitutional conflict, but to do business. In the words of a member who was probably Sir Robert Phelips, they were occasions for the King and his people to enjoy 'a mutual and needful exchange of benefits and service'.[1] In other words, the King wanted extraordinary supply, and his subjects wanted to reform, usually by legislation, things which they thought were in need of change. As Professor Elton has stressed, a Parliament well used was meant to be an occasion, not to create conflict, but to preserve stability by providing a lawful means to satisfy legitimate demands for change.[2]

Demand for change could be intense without being concerned with an issue of great constitutional significance. For example, in 1606, there was concern about the discharge of sewage on to the banks of the Thames between London and Westminster. Because

[1] Phelips MSS. 227/16. I am grateful to Dr. Hirst for drawing this MS. to my attention. On its attribution, which is uncertain, see below, pp. 149 ff.

[2] G. R. Elton, 'Tudor Government: The Points of Contact: Parliament', *T.R.H.S.* (1974), 186–7.

the sewage lay on the foreshore under the windows of great men's houses in the Strand, there was no need to use a Parliament to bring this grievance to Councillors' attention. A Parliament was needed to remedy the abuse because the sewage was being discharged below high-tide mark, in an area not under the jurisdiction of the commissioners of Sewers. The requisite Act of Parliament was duly passed, and no more was heard of the grievance.[1] Similarly, Acts of Parliament were often wanted to settle such things as the levying of rates for building or repair of bridges. If the bridge went from one county into another, an act of Parliament could be a convenient means of sorting out the disputes about who should pay the necessary rates.

During the 1620s, Parliaments more and more established themselves in the minds of many of the public as a suitable place to transact business of this sort. At the same time, they became less and less successful at completing it. Some bills, like Sir Dudley Digges's bill for repairing the bridge in his constituency of Tewkesbury, failed because the rating disputes which had made it necessary to bring the bill to Parliament were simply reproduced in Parliament.[2] The bill was bogged down in committee, and ultimately neglected for more exciting business. Parliament's regular failures to complete legislation must in part be blamed on the revival of impeachment. Impeachment was more exciting than bills, and was a great consumer of Parliamentary time, especially in the Lords. In 1621, its effect on the legislative programme was disastrous, and in 1624 it was serious.

Yet by far the most important reason for the failure of Parliaments to complete business was that they were too successful in attracting it. Sir Francis Nethersole, in May 1624, said that there were too many private bills, and the crowd for passing them before the dissolution hindered business: 'by reason thereof there are not near so many passed as might have been, and very few of the public.'[3] The Parliamentary agenda, like the Earl of Salisbury's desk, was slowly clogged up by the increasing volume of small business

[1] *3 Jac. I c. 14.*
[2] N.R.S. iv. 307, iii. 171–2.
[3] S.P. 14/164/66. Phelips MSS. 222/108, 216/66 and 67, 228/26, 216/61, 222/100, 212/39, and other refs. For a similar volume of requests to a member in 1604, see Hassell Smith, pp. 331–2. See also Jess Stodart Flemion, 'Slow Process, Due Process and the High Court of Parliament', *H.J.* (1974), 1–16. On the attempt to impeach Williams in 1624, see below, pp. 153, 160, 187.

which came in to it. The papers of Sir Robert Phelips show that he was asked to undertake in Parliament many more pieces of business than he could complete. The papers Phelips gathered as chairman of the committee for courts of justice in 1624 suggests that Parliament was becoming a frequent place of last resort for those disappointed by verdicts in lawsuits. Phelips noted some of these petitions as not worth action, and some suitable for remedy by bill, but he took action only on those few petitions which helped in Buckingham's current attempt to impeach Lord Keeper Williams. He was also asked to remedy abuses in selection for jury service, and to help the widows of those captured by pirates in the East Indies. Sir Robert's appetite for business was inexhaustible, but even he was not able to get through most of the business which was sent to him. It was perhaps fortunate for him that he was so often able to blame his failures on premature dissolutions. This fact may explain why public confidence in Parliamentary capacity to give them relief from such things continued unabated by continual Paliamentary failures. It may explain why business continued to come to Parliament, when it might more usefully have gone to Privy Councillors instead, 'as if', as Northampton put it, 'the King slept out the sobs of his subjects, until he was awaked with the thunder bolt of a Parliament'.[1] Parliamentary success in arousing public expectation was equalled only by their failure to satisfy it.

It is difficult to be certain how much weight to give in a study of Parliaments, either to this sort of minor business, or to the progress of legislation. It did not enjoy equal importance in all Parliaments. Most historians have followed the example of Secretary Conway's son, who said, writing to Sir Dudley Carleton in 1624, that he was sure his reader would not wish to be bothered with the 'little businesses' of laws.[2] It is true that most laws concerned 'little businesses', but perhaps, if we look at Parliaments from a constituency perspective, and not simply from Westminster, some of these 'little businessses' may have concerned members and their constituents more than some of the great matters which are more familiar to us. John Angell, M.P. for Rye, unlike Conway, regarded the impeachment of Cranfield as an obstruction to the progress of legislation. He apologized to his constituency for his

[1] Hirst, p. 157.
[2] S.P. 14/163/1. He expected Carleton to hear with delight of the ruin of Lord Treasurer Cranfield.

failure to make progress with a bill to transfer control of Dungeness
lighthouse to the town of Rye (a bill vital to Rye's precarious
survival as a port), and said: 'Truly the businesses that are in the
House at this time are of so great importance and high a nature,
that these more ordinary businesses are put off from time to time
and infinitely delayed, but I make no question this Parliament will
be of so long a continuance that we shall have fit and leisurable
time to effect our desires for you.' Nine days later the Parliament
was prorogued, and the bill for Dungeness lighthouse was never
passed.[1]

One possible yardstick for judging the comparative importance,
in any Parliament, of routine legislative business and issues of high
politics is the amount of time spent in committee of the whole
House. On ordinary bills, the detailed scrutiny was given by a
select committee, and debates in the full House were not usually very
long. On an issue on which many members had strong views, both
Houses grew increasingly inclined to conduct debate in a committee of the whole House. This meant that they chose their own *ad
hoc* chairman, instead of the Speaker, and that the usual rules of
debate, which restricted each member to one speech in each debate, were suspended. Moreover, the proceedings were not on
record in the *Lords' Journal* or the *Commons' Journal*.

The committee of the whole House was seen by Notestein as
something which perhaps enabled members of the Commons to
circumvent restrictions imposed by a pro-government Speaker.[2]
This view doubtless contains some truth for the Parliament of
1604–10, during the highly partisan Speakership of Sir Edward
Phelips. It appears to contain much less truth in the 1620s, when
most Speakers preserved a remarkably high standard of judicial
impartiality. There were a few occasions when a Speaker attempted to restrict debate. The most significant are Speaker Richardson's sheltering of the referees by his 'rising unusually' in March
1621, and Sir John Finch's attempt to obey the King's command
to prevent the naming of Buckingham in June 1628.[3] There were

[1] G. G. Harris, *The Trinity House of Deptford* (1969), p. 207.
[2] W. Notestein, *The Winning of the Initiative by the House of Commons* (1924),
pp. 26, 32, 36–40. Notestein suggested this with more caution than has been
shown since. 'Was this a device developed to get rid of the Speaker? It is
impossible to say' (p. 37).
[3] N.R.S. ii. 199–202, iv. 138, vi. 45–6 and other refs. On June 1628, see below,
p. 378.

a few occasions when a committee of the whole was used to circumvent the Speaker. Mallory, in December 1621, proposed to go into committee of the whole for the debate on the Protestation, 'that we might not be troubled this day with the Speaker',[1] and in June 1628 the Speaker's ban on the naming of Buckingham was circumvented by going into committee of the whole.

Yet the striking fact about such incidents is their rarity. When they are compared with the innumerable occasions on which both Houses went into committee of the whole, it must appear very doubtful whether they can provide a sufficient, or even a significant, explanation of the use of the committee of the whole. Apart from the naming of Buckingham in 1628, the only other resolution reached in committee of the whole which would have been unlikely to be reached in an ordinary House was the decision to impeach Cranfield in 1624. This was not a piece of 'opposition', but a successful attempt by the Duke of Buckingham and his partisans to steam-roller through a measure for which there was probably not a natural majority.[2] It seems, then, that we need another explanation for the readiness to go into committee of the whole. This readiness existed in both Houses, and indeed the committee of the whole seems to have been used in the Lords (in 1606) before it was in regular use in the Commons. Professor Foster has supplied an explanation for its use in the Lords, 'not to be free of the presiding officer, but to be free of the rules of debate'.[3]

It appears that the explanation given by Professor Foster for the House of Lords also holds for the House of Commons. The chief restriction of the usual rules of debate was the rule that a member could not speak twice to the same matter. Such voluble members as Viscount Saye and Sele in the Lords and Sir Edward Coke in the Commons constantly found this rule irksome. More significantly, the use of a committee of the whole made it far easier for either House to discharge what they regarded as the proper normal

---

[1] Zaller, p. 168. Nicholas, ii. 330. Richardson, who was sitting in his first Parliament, appears to have been the most partisan of the Speakers of this period. Crew, in 1624 and 1625, was an established popular member, and was chosen for that reason. Perhaps the most successful Speaker, considering the difficulties he had to face, was Heneage Finch in 1626.

[2] See below, p. 200.

[3] Elizabeth Read Foster, 'Procedure in the House of Lords during the Early Stuart Period', *J.B.S.* (1964–5), 64–8. Professor Foster suggested that this explanation might also apply to the Commons, while adding that 'probably growing opposition to crown policy also played a part'.

function of debate: to reach a consensus. Debates were not designed, as in modern politics, to isolate the point of disagreement and put it to the vote. Formal divisions were rare, and tended to indicate, either that the issue was so contentious that members despaired of achieving a consensus, or that it was so trivial that it was not worth the time needed for a consensus to evolve. If members undertook a lengthy debate, they normally did so, like a modern committee rather than like a modern debating assembly, in order to search for common ground. As Sir Edwin Sandys put it on 20 April 1626, 'In all assemblies when men are in difference of judgement by long arguing they will be all of one opinion, if they differ not in the end.'[1] If members were to come to be all of one opinion in a contentious business, it was essential that some should be able to speak a second time, in order to say that they had changed their minds.

The classic justification for going into committee was stated, a little disingenuously in the context, by Eliot on 6 May 1628. At the crux of the Petition of Right debates, he said:

> I am for a committee which is not less but more honour for the King, 'tis but the same thing under another name, truth is best, that leads best to honour, which in this way is most open, here you may give an answer and reply, which should soonest alter a man's opinion that inclines to reason and therefore I desire that Mr. Herbert may take the chair.[2]

This speech may have been disingenuous as applied to the occasion on which it was delivered, but as a general statement of the reasons why the House of Commons went into committee of the whole, it appears to be justified. Of all types of business, the one which was most consistently debated in committee of the whole was that on which consensus was regarded as most essential: the decision how many subsidies to vote. Subsidy debates regularly continued until some of the speakers on what appeared to be the losing side were prepared to get up and say that they were converted. The 1628 subsidy debate is a classic example of this process. The debate continued, at great length, and the resolution for five subsidies was only carried when four of those speaking for a lower sum rose

---

[1] Whitelocke, 12–21, f. 143ᵛ. These conclusions dovetail with those of Mark Kishlansky, 'The Emergence of Adversary Politics', *Journal of Modern History*, vol. 49, no. 4 (1977), 617–40. I am grateful to Dr. Kishlansky for allowing me to see this important article before publication.

[2] Stowe 366, f. 139ᵛ.

in sequence to announce their conversion: Eliot, Wandesford, Phelips, and, most ungraciously, Kirton.[1] On this occasion, Eliot was right to remember that having the debate in committee of the whole had been 'not less but more honour for the King'.

The frequency with which the Houses went into committee of the whole may tend to show how often they were preoccupied with big issues, rather than with routine bills. In 1628, the Commons spent almost the whole session in committee of the whole. By contrast, in 1621 and 1624, when ordinary bills were of rather more importance, the committee of the whole was used less constantly. In 1624, the business of the breach of the treaties with Spain was debated in committee of the whole, but no one wanted to go into committee of the whole to discuss the bill to lower the rate of interest. On that bill, the need to reach consensus was not thought sufficiently pressing to justify the necessary expenditure of time. The points on which further discussion was needed, being technical, were appropriately handled in a select committee. And if the committee of the whole was not used for the bill to lower the rate of interest, *a fortiori* it was not used for the bill for Dungeness lighthouse.

Perhaps the failure of this bill may shed some light on why so little legislation passed through the Parliaments of the 1620s: the bill was purely local in its appeal. Sir Thomas Wentworth was probably no more interested in this bill than the member for Rye was interested in Wentworth's onslaughts on the man who levied illegal tolls on the Great North Road.[2] Notestein was entirely right in seeing the initiative in the legislative process passing to individual members of the House of Commons, and, to a lesser extent, of the House of Lords. For a while, this process led to a reduction in the total volume of legislation passed. There were too many bills before the Commons, and too little agreement on which were important, to permit very much progress. In 1621, no bills were presented to the King, because of premature dissolution, but the House of Commons could not blame dissolution for their own failure to complete bills while they were in session.

The first session of the 1621 Parliament lasted from February until June: ample time to permit the Commons to prepare their bills. In this time, something in the region of a hundred public

---

[1] Stowe 366, f. 50ᵛ.
[2] N.R.S. iv. 189, Stowe 366, f. 274ᵛ: Add. 36825, f. 540ʳ.

bills were tabled in the Commons, of which only nineteen completed their passage through the Commons. Another five were completed in the second session, but sent up to the Lords too late to leave the Lords time to pass them. The other bills did not, in most cases, fail because they were strongly opposed: they failed because members did not agree which bills should be at the front of the queue. At the end of April, they made an earnest attempt to range their bills in some sort of order of priority, starring those with which they most wished to make progress. However, the progress of bills between May and June shows it was not necessarily the starred bills which had advanced: it was those for which an active member could be an effective lobbyist.[1] The fate of bills in the Commons in 1621 bears out Chamberlain's remark, early in the session, that the Commons were undertaking so many businesses they could not hope to complete them all. For the small amount of legislation they achieved in the 1620s, the members of the Commons had mainly themselves to blame.

The failure of most Commons legislation during the 1620s was not primarily due to its contentious character. If a bill passed the Commons, it stood a very good chance indeed of passing the Lords, and, if there was not a premature dissolution, of receiving the royal assent. It is often hard to be certain which bills were halted by opposition in the Lords, since the Lords rarely formally rejected a bill they did not like: they allowed it to 'fall asleep'. It is thus difficult to distinguish with any certainty between bills which failed to pass the Lords because the Lords did not like them, and bills which failed in the Lords through simple lack of time. The Commons' bills the Lords appear to have held up are a short list. In 1621, they were a bill against purveyance of carts, a bill against tobacco (the subject of an unresolved conflict between some of the Virginia lobby, the pro-Spanish lobby, and the anti-smoking lobby), a bill against the transport of money, and the bills against monopolies and against hunting for concealed Crown lands. These last two were bills of some importance. They illustrate the fact that what the Lords were sensitive to in 1621 and 1624 was not ecclesiastical bills, as before and after, but bills designed to restrict the royal power of patronage, from which many of them were beneficiaries. In 1624, they stopped two Commons' bills, the bill against purveyance of carts (again) and the bill for the abbreviation of Michaelmas term.

[1] N.R.S. iv. 260–4, vii. 300–7, *L.J.* 203–4.

This last is a classic illustration of the difficulty of getting legislation through Parliament. The demand for the bill arose from the
fact that Michaelmas law term began before Quarter Day, and
therefore gentlemen were unable to be at home to supervise the
collection of their rents and the sowing of winter corn. Many of
the lawyers, including Sir Edward Coke, were induced to agree to
the bill, but it faced opposition from the City of London, much of
whose income depended on the resort of gentlemen to London. In
1601, when it was first introduced, the opposition of the City put
a stop to it. In most other Parliaments, it met little overt opposition, but, equally, never appeared to be a high enough priority to
complete its passage. The result was that a minor, sensible, administrative reform had to wait for its completion from 1601 to 1641.

In 1626 and 1628, by contrast, the bills which slept in the Lords
were mainly ecclesiastical, and, interestingly, mainly bills which
had never been moved in the Commons in 1621 or 1624. In 1626,
three ecclesiastical bills failed to complete their passage through
the Lords, the bill that clergy should not be J.P.s (though it carried
an exemption for bishops, Deans, and Vice-Chancellors), the bill
to restrict citations out of ecclesiastical courts, and the bill to
permit marriages in Lent.

One secular bill failed to complete its passage through the Lords
in 1626, the bill against secret offices and Inquisitions. This bill
must be presumed to have failed from simple lack of time, since
it had originally been sponsored by the Crown, and is unlikely to
have been seriously opposed. This is another bill which illustrates
the difficulty of carrying a minor administrative reform through
Parliament. The abuse it was designed to prevent was in the holding of Inquisitions *Post Mortem*, to discover what land belonged
to those who came into wardship. Sometimes, those in search of
wardships held these Inquisitions secretly, without giving notice
to other interested parties, and put their rivals to considerable
legal expense if they wished to challenge the findings. Sir Thomas
Wentworth is unlikely to have been alone among M.P.s in having
personally suffered from this abuse.[1] The bill to rectify it was
unlikely to face any official opposition, since it had originally
been offered in 1614, as a bill of grace, by King James himself.
However, it persistently failed to complete its passage through

[1] J. Hurstfield, *The Queen's Wards* (1958), pp. 47–9, 55: *Wentworth Papers*,
pp. 226–7.

both Houses of Parliament, and never passed into law. Secret offices were like sin: everyone was against them, and few were excited enough to take effective action about them. At least one doubted whether the bill would prove effective. In 1614, the bill seems to have been a casualty of the Commons' dispute with the King over impositions, in 1624 of the impeachment of Cranfield, and in 1626 of the impeachment of Buckingham.

In 1628, three Commons' bills slept in the Lords, the bill against citations out of ecclesiastical courts (again), the bill against scandalous ministers, and a bill to allow people to attend other parish churches instead of their own. This list of bills failing in the Lords does not suggest that much Commons' legislation was particularly contentious.

Nor is any clear pattern of confrontation suggested by the very short list of bills which received the royal veto, six bills vetoed by James in 1624, and one by Charles in 1628.[1] In 1624, James, under strong diplomatic pressure from the French, vetoed the general bill against Catholic recusants. He also vetoed a bill, popular with both Houses throughout the 1620s, to prevent Catholic recusants from evading the forfeitures prescribed by law by making their estates over to trustees. On both these bills and the bill for the Sabbath (passed by Charles in the next Parliament), James was joining issue with his Council and his bishops, as much as with the Parliament as a whole. James's other vetoes concerned more trivial bills. One was the bill for the Parliamentary representation of County Durham[2] (first moved in 1614, and passed into law in 1675), on which James commented that the Commons were too big already, and he would pass the bill if they would disenfranchise Old Sarum. Another was the alienations bill, which he said was too hastily drafted. It became law in 1625. The last was a private bill for the naturalization of a successful merchant called Philip Jacobson. James's comment on this bill was that if Jacobson were naturalized, he would cease to pay the double custom imposed on aliens. James vetoed the bill because he could not afford the loss of revenue it would entail. Charles's solitary use of the veto again concerned the bill to stop Catholic recusants evading forfeiture

---

[1] S.P. 14/167/10; B.L. Harl. MS. 159, ff. 132–6; Stowe 366, f. 288ᵛ.

[2] On this bill and its local background, see Mervyn James, *Family, Lineage and Civil Society* (Oxford, 1974), pp. 3, 166–7. He ascribes King James's decision to veto it to the influence of the Bishop, who opposed it.

through the use of trustees. Since Charles was unwilling to risk vetoing most of the legislation of the Long Parliament, he perhaps enjoys the ironic distinction of having used the royal veto more rarely than any previous English sovereign.

This very short list of Commons' legislation obstructed by the Lords or the King compares with a negligible list of Lords' legislation obstructed by the Commons, in which the only really important item is the bill for making the arms of the kingdom more serviceable in time to come. Since this bill raised the whole question of the legal authority for the militia, it is best discussed with that question. Interestingly, there is no list at all of government legislation obstructed in the Commons. Indeed, it is very doubtful whether, during the 1620s, such a thing as a 'government bill' can be identified at all.

One of the most important causes of the winning of the legislative initiative by the House of Commons, remarked in passing by Professor Elton, was the almost total disappearance of any desire by the Crown to legislate.[1] From the 1590s onwards, it became a persistent theme of opening speeches by the Lord Keeper that new laws were not wanted: there were enough already. What was wanted was some means of ensuring that the laws were executed. Perhaps the most explicit statement was by Lord Keeper Puckering in 1593:

Her Majesty further hath willed me to signify unto you, that the calling of this Parliament is not for making of any more new laws and statutes, for there are already a sufficient number both of ecclesiastical and temporal: and so many there be, that rather than to burden the subject with more to their grievance, it were fitting that an abridgement were made of those that are already. Wherefore it is her Majesty's pleasure that the time be not spent therein [2]

King James, in his opening speech to his first Parliament, told them that the Parliament had been called to consider the making of laws *and their execution*: an addition which has not received the attention it deserves.[3] Sometimes, as in 1614 and 1621, James told his Parliaments they had been called in part for the making of laws, but by this he appears to have meant only that members

[1] art. cit., *T.R.H.S.* (1974), 188.
[2] D'Ewes, *Journals of All the Parliaments* (1682), p. 458. Puckering optimistically said that the purpose of the Parliament was to reverse the decline in the yield of the subsidy.
[3] *H.M.C. Buccleuch*, iii, 78.

could spend much of their time on issues of their own choice. Members would have scanned these speeches in vain for any sign of any legislative agenda. Indeed, it is a conspicuous feature of most of James's opening speeches to his Parliaments that, apart from supply, they show little sign that he could think of any business for Parliament to do. The only measure requiring Parliamentary legislation on which James really set his heart was the union with Scotland, and after he had been forced to abandon this, he showed little desire to legislate. In James's first Parliament, in the lifetime of Robert Cecil, it is still possible to make provisional identifications of 'government' bills, and yet Robert Cecil himself was never certain how far he could safely regard even the Great Contract as a 'government' measure, enjoying the full weight of official sponsorship.

By the 1620s, under the variegated Council of James and Buckingham, the concept of a 'government' bill had lost all meaning. Even if the sponsorship of a bill can be traced to a Councillor, this need not mean that it would be supported by other Councillors, or that it would be exempt from the royal veto. Even James's 'bills of grace' of 1614 were offered more because he thought others wanted them than because he himself felt any great desire for them. Those among them which ultimately reached the statute book in 1624 mostly depended on private members to steer them through the Commons. Of the bills of the 1620s, only the Tonnage and Poundage bill, in the reign of Charles I, enjoyed the full weight of official sponsorship characteristic of a 'government bill'. In 1628, the bill which ultimately passed into law, to restrain men from sending their children to be popishly bred beyond the seas, was first recommended by Charles himself, but he put it forward more to answer fears expressed in the Commons' 1625 petition on religion than because he himself had any intense desire for it.[1] Drafts or breviates of bills in the State Papers are more often submitted by hopeful lobbyists than drafted by members of the Council. It is interesting to note that in 1624 an increasing proportion of them were printed.

A letter by Solicitor General Heath to Sir Robert Harley in 1624, dealing with a proposed tobacco bill, may serve to illustrate how official involvement in the legislative process worked. The

---

[1] This bill gave effect, in normal statutory form, to a promise formally given by Charles in answer to the Petition on Religion in 1625. See below, p. 248.

subject of tobacco was a vexed one. Members of the Virginia lobby, led by Sir Edwin Sandys, wanted a ban on imports of Spanish tobacco, in order to offer protection to colonial tobacco from Virginia. Cranfield and others were reluctant to ban Spanish tobacco, for fear that in doing so they might be construed as breaking the 1604 peace treaty with Spain. A number of obscure members hoped to take advantage of the King's known dislike of smoking in order to secure a ban on all tobacco imports. In 1622, Sir Nathaniel Rich tried to break the deadlock with a scheme to control the tobacco trade, and to increase the King's revenue, by the use of licences to control the retailing of tobacco. It was probably a variant on this scheme which was submitted to Heath in a bill 'drawn by a good member of the House'. Heath approved the scheme, and wrote to Sir Robert Harley, a private member of the Commons, asking him to approach his father-in-law, Secretary Conway, to try to secure his approval and the King's for the bill.[1] Nothing more was heard of the bill, since the Parliament was prorogued shortly after, but the method of proceeding, from a private member to the Solicitor General, to a private member, to the Secretary of State, is typical of the preparation of legislation in the 1620s.

One rare bill which might have commanded the enthusiasm of King James is a draft bill against duelling, apparently prepared for the Parliament of 1621. The bill gave authority to J.P.s to imprison those issuing challenges for duels if they were below the rank of baron, and to two Privy Councillors to imprison challengers of the rank of baron and above. Granted the intensity of James's dislike of duelling, this bill must have commanded his sympathy, if not his sponsorship.[2] Surely here is a government bill? It appears not: the bill appears to have been tabled in the Commons, but no member of James's government in the Commons helped it on even to the point of a first reading.

Almost the only active drive for official legislation during the

---

[1] S.P. 14/165/5. There is a breviate of a tobacco bill, perhaps an amended version of the 1621 bill, in Phelips MSS. 212/31. For Rich's scheme see above, p. 33, n. 5.

[2] S.P. 14/119/133. This bill gave statutory sanction to the existing procedure of the Star Chamber. It is probably the bill 'to prevent the impunities of foreign murders in some cases' which Alford, in June 1621, noted as having been tabled but not read. N.R.S. vii. 307. Duels were often fought abroad, in order not to be under the jurisdiction of English common law. That is why this draft bill proposed to make the challenge, as well as the fighting of the duel, a punishable offence.

1620s was on behalf of Prince Charles as Duke of Cornwall, and was probably managed by William Noy for the Duchy Council. By far the biggest beneficiary from private bill legislation was Prince Charles as Duke of Cornwall, yet it seems hard to consider private bills regulating the antiquated customs of the manor of Cheltenham, or digging for coal in back gardens in the manor of Macclesfield, as government bills.[1]

If the Crown did not want Parliaments for legislation, what did it want them for? Parliaments were clearly valuable as a point of contact between central and local government. They served for the mutual exchange of information, and provided more effectively than alternatives such as the Assizes for a two-way flow of information between the King and those who governed the counties for him.[2] James probably sincerely valued this function of a Parliament, and when he told the Parliament of 1621 that 'the Commons best know the state of the country and are to inform the King of the disorders that so he may show himself a just king', he probably meant what he said.[3] Many members from remote counties such as Westmorland probably never saw the King except when they attended a Parliament. However, valuable though this 'point of contact' function of a Parliament might have been, it was not alone

[1] Whatever may have been the case earlier, in the 1620s the distinction between public and private bills appears to have been based, largely arbitrarily, on the words in which the King gave the Royal Assent. See the Speaker's closing speech in 1624, Pym, f. 97ʳ. On the concept of a hybrid bill, see below, p. 275. Some of the Duchy of Cornwall Acts printed in *Statutes of the Realm* as public Acts are listed on the Parliament Roll as private Acts. The Acts on behalf of Charles as Prince of Wales and Duke of Cornwall are: *21 Jac. I c. 9* and *1 Car. I c. 2* (leases by the Duchy of Cornwall), 21 Jac. I c. 46 (jointure of Alice Dudley), 21 Jac. I c. 47 (exchange with Sir Lewis Watson, altering the boundaries of the Duchy of Cornwall), 1 Car. I c. 8 (regulating the antiquated customs of the manor of Cheltenham), 1 Car. I c. 9 (confirming a series of agreements on coal-mining and other subjects between Charles as Earl of Chester and the tenants of the manor of Macclesfield), and *3 Car. I c. 6* (confirming agreements between Charles, Prince of Wales and the tenants of the manors of Bromefield and Yale). There may also have been Duchy initiative behind *21 Jac. I c. 11*, suppressing a monopoly patent for salting fish, since it confirms a judgement given at the suit of William Noy on behalf of the Duchy Council. It is doubtful whether any of these deserve to be cast as 'government' bills. Perhaps one of the bills with the best claim to that title is the bill for making the arms of the kingdom serviceable in time to come, though it was often managed by people with no claim to membership of the 'government'.

[2] On the Assizes as a point of contact, see T. G. Barnes, *Somerset Assize Orders*, Somerset Record Society, lxv (Frome, 1959), xx–xxi, and Cockburn, pp. 8–10, 107, 153–87.

[3] N.R.S. iv. 3.

enough to justify the expensive process of holding a Parliament, with all the demands it made on the time of Councillors who were busy enough already.

(b) *Revenue and Supply*

For the Crown, the really important purpose of a Parliament was the obtaining of extraordinary supply, and, for this purpose, Parliaments proved a grievous disappointment. This was not the fault of members of Parliament in their Westminster capacity. Only once in the reign of James I, over the issue of impositions in 1614, did they attempt to make supply conditional on the redress of grievances, and that attempt was a dismal failure. On almost every other occasion up to 1626, they voted as many subsidies as were asked of them, and did so with a reasonably good grace. The Parliamentary subsidy was not obstructed at Westminster but by the collectors in the counties. All early seventeenth-century taxes were scandalously under-assessed, so much so that Sir Thomas Edmondes, speaking in Council in 1628, complained that the entire revenues of England were less than the revenues the French King derived from the single province of Normandy.[1] But if all revenues were scandalously under-assessed, the Parliamentry subsidy was more scandalously under-assessed than anything else. Members of Parliament claimed, in the subsidy Acts of 1606 and 1624, that they were voting more than had ever been voted in so short a time before. In saying so, they spoke the truth. Yet when the total yield to the Exchequer was added up, Parliamentary subsidies were more inadequate than they had ever been before. The Council regularly tried to insist that Justices of the Peace, many of whom probably had incomes of £1,000 or more, should not be assessed on an income of less than £20, but the attempt was unsuccessful. In 1621 the Somerset J.P.s replied with the usual bland evasion that all but 'some few' of them were.[2] The Lincolnshire J.P.s were more forthright: they informed the Council that their places as J.P.s were a 'daily charge' to them, and the Council could dismiss them if it wished. In other words, they were claiming a favourable subsidy assessment as the reward for their work as unpaid local governors.

[1] S.P. 16/126/94.
[2] Phelips MSS. 223/114 (draft in the hand of Sir Robert Phelips). The J.P.s ascribed the low yield of the subsidy to the shortage of coin, which they blamed on imports of Irish cattle.

Other Crown revenues fell in real terms, because assessments remained static in a period of inflation. The subsidy fell in money terms as well, and did so on a dramatic scale. Mr Fletcher says that 'the average assessment of seventy leading Sussex families between the 1540s and the 1620s dropped from sixty-one pounds to fourteen pounds'. He has also made the significant discovery that an increasing number of those who should have paid the subsidy succeeded in evading being assessed for it all. A clause in the subsidy Act of 1624 purported to put a stop to this practice, but the decline in the number of taxpayers continued unabated.[1] It was often said that the root of the trouble lay in the fact that there were too many subsidy commissioners, and each of them, in the usual manner of Tudor and Stuart local government, treated a light subsidy assessment as a way of showing favour to their friends, tenants, or dependants. William Lambarde, writing late in Elizabeth's reign, claimed that favourable assessments for subsidy, and for the militia rates which may have been based on the same valuation, had become such an abuse that they ought to be prosecuted under the medieval statutes against maintenance.[2] Since late Elizabethan days pressure had been put on members of Parliament to reform the assessment of the subsidy. A number of members, especially Rudyerd, wanted to take action about it, but the faults were too deeply ingrained in the structure of local government to be eradicated, and the more subsidies Parliaments voted, the less money each subsidy yielded. If this abuse could not be corrected, it was hard to see how Parliaments could continue to serve a useful purpose. It was an abuse which had to be corrected in the counties, not at Westminster.

Some idea of the scale of the trouble may be gained from a report laid before the Treasury Commissioners some time after 1617, and apparently largely based on papers prepared, probably

---

[1] Fletcher, pp. 203–4, 362–3; *21 Jac. I c. 33*, clause xiv. The letter from the Lincolnshire J.P.s, quoted by Mr. Fletcher, is printed *in extenso* in Joan Thirsk and J. P. Cooper, *Seventeenth-Century Economic Documents* (Oxford, 1972), pp. 608–9. It shows the difficulty of collecting subsidies during the depression. The J.P.s complained that they had tried to keep up assessments although 'rents commodities and estates' had generally fallen, and in consequence 'we were very hardly censured by the country'.

[2] Hassell Smith, p. 334. W. Lambarde, *Archeion*, ed. Charles H. MacIlwain and Paul L. Ward (Cambridge, Mass., 1957), p. 104. Assessments for subsidy. and militia rates may not have rested on the same basis in all counties. See also *C.S.P.D. 1625–49 Addenda*, vol. dxxii, no. 109.

for the Earl of Northampton, in the years after 1613.[1] This report showed James facing an ordinary deficit of £85,120 *per annum* on his peacetime expenditure. In 1606, Parliament had recognized that subsidies could be used to meet peacetime expenditure, but the figures did not suggest that subsidies, even if generously granted, were the way to solve the difficulty. A generous grant of three subsidies and six fifteenths in 1606 had yielded £453,000, and one subsidy and one fifteenth in 1610 had yielded £106,166, making a total yield from Parliamentary sources of £559,166 over some fourteen years: an average just below £40,000 a year. This figure is of course distorted by being taken from a time before the Parliaments of 1621 and 1624, but there is no calculation by which the average annual yield of subsidies under James can be made to equal the £70,000 a year James was getting from impositions when he refused to abandon them in 1614. The Parliamentary subsidies, over the first part of the reign, did not even much exceed the £418,500 raised from the sale of baronetcies, and one subsidy did not compare too badly in financial terms with the yield of £52,909 for an illegal benevolence raised after the failure of the Parliament of 1614. When the 1614 Parliament had chosen to make supply conditional on James's abandonment of impositions, it had been asking the King to undertake a very poor financial bargain. Moreover, the King's success in continuing to raise impositions without the assent of Parliament had made a vital breach in the constitutional principle that new taxes could not be raised without Parliamentary assent. There had, of course, been a number of Tudor levies of money which had not enjoyed Parliamentary sanction, but a principle can be honoured in the breach as well as in the observance. Tudor levies had never really called in question the idea that new taxes needed the assent of Parliament. Impositions, if only because a Parliament had challenged them and failed, necessarily did call it in question. If a purely financial choice were to be made, impositions, being the more buoyant source of revenue, were clearly preferable to Parliamentary subsidies.

From 1614 onwards, the survival of Parliament was periodically

[1] B.L. Add. MS. 58833, until recently in the possession of the Duke of Manchester. I am grateful to Dr. Linda Levy Peck for advice about the interpretation of this MS. Much of it appears to have been put together *c.* 1617, yet the inclusion of names of office-holders dating back as far as 1613 suggests that much of it is based on earlier drafts. Its information, whatever its correct date, appears reasonably dependable.

liable to be called into question. Sir Francis Michell, the patentee for gold and silver thread, was threatened with a Parliament by one of the people from whom he was extorting money, and in reply, 'confessed he did not expect a Parliament'.[1] In October 1620, John Chamberlain reported on a speech by Lord Chancellor Bacon that he thought it was meant to prepare the way for subsidies without Parliament. In January 1622, after the dissolution of the Parliament of 1621, the Venetian Ambassador claimed that James was threatening to have no more to do with Parliaments.[2]

Whether James said this or not, it would have been a rational opinion. It was the more justified, because the gestures of goodwill Parliaments requested in return for their subsidies also cost the King money, and further diminished the net benefit of subsidies to the Exchequer. This is a point which seems to have been made especially at the expense of the Parliament of 1624. Its legislation, especially the Monopolies Act, the Informers Act, and the Act giving security to the possessors of concealed Crown lands, deprived the Crown of sources of revenue which might have been further exploited. So did the unusually generous General Pardon at the end of the session, which was in effect an amnesty pardoning numerous old offences, including non-payment of numerous forms of revenue. James, replying to the petition of grievances at the end of the session, complained that the Parliament were trying to take from him even more parts of his revenue, such as the pretermitted custom and the revenue from wine licences, and that he could not lay them down unless given alternative sources of revenue. According to Sir Francis Nethersole, other people were talking along these lines. He reported that the bills passed were 'some of them of such importance as those of monopolies, concealments, that here wise men estimate that the subject hath more of the king in them, and the pardon, than the subsidies come to'.[3] Such an estimate, if it was made, reckoned the potential revenue from monopolies as being more buoyant than seems entirely probable, but the same reasoning was being repeated by Laud, probably in 1627, when he drew up a paper setting out the reasons for and against calling a Parliament. Laud complained that the habit of Parliaments was 'to sell

[1] C. 65/185.
[2] Chamberlain, 14 Oct. 1620. C.S.P.Ven. 1621–3, p. 207. Both Chamberlain and the Venetian Ambassador were indulging only in intelligent speculation. The point is that such speculations were being made by informed people.
[3] S.P. 14/167/10.

subsidies, and not to give them', and that 'the last Parliament of King James, they gave three subsidies, and had that from the King that was worth eight, if not ten, to be bought and sold'. The best he could find to say on the other side of the argument, in favour of a Parliament, was that though their subsidies 'will not do all that is necessary, yet it will be a good help'.[1] Laud was a biased witness, but he was right in his belief that Parliamentary revenue could only keep the King afloat if it was combined with extra-ordinary non-Parliamentary revenue. If the King were to be forced to collect extraordinary revenue from non-Parliamentary sources, whether he called Parliaments or not, it was hard to see what, in financial terms, he stood to gain from calling future Parliaments.

III. *Dominium Politicum et Regale?*[2]

What, then, were the reasons why Kings continued to call Parliaments? The answers appear to lie as much in the history of ideas as anywhere else. Englishmen brought up on Sir John Fortescue, as most of them were, had a deeply ingrained sense that there was a proper and Parliamentary way of doing things. A successful Parliament symbolized subjects' love for their King, and therefore their allegiance. The advice given to Charles by the Council before the Parliament of 1628 to abandon his revenue-raising projects and call a Parliament instead, was not justifiable in terms of strict financial arithmetic. It was justifiable only in terms of a strong preference for doing things in a proper and lawful way. As Charles himself said to the Parliament of 1628, he thought it 'the ancientest,

[1] S.P. 16/94/88. For the remarks of Cranfield, who may have been the originator of this line of reasoning, see *Debates in the House of Lords in 1621*, Camden Soc., 1st Series, no. 103 (1870), p. 104. Subsequent statements of the point seem to stick closely to Cranfield's formulation. The debatable point in this reasoning is the potential buoyancy which appears to have been ascribed to monopolies as a source of revenue. See N.R.S. iv. 173, for Heath on the mono-polies bill and the revenue from wine licences, and Towerson on the bill's threat to the charter of the Merchant Adventurers. See also N.R.S. ii. 526 for Heath's claim that the pardon prepared for 1621 would be worth three subsidies. The hypothesis that Cranfield was the originator of this line of reasoning is supported by Sir Robert Pye's attempt to refute part of it in 1624. He claimed that concealments did not bring the King the value of a quarter of a subsidy per annum, and asked to be ordered to search for the full figures. Diary of Sir Richard Dyott, Staffs. R.O. (unfoliated), 4 May 1624. See also *H.M.C. Mar and Kellie Suppl.*, pp. 203–4.

[2] See H. G. Koenigsberger, *Dominium Regale or Dominium Politicum et Regale: Monarchies and Parliaments in Early Modern Europe* (Inaugural Lecture, King's College, London, 1975), esp. pp. 9–11 and 21–3.

speediest and best way ... to give supply'. It is only the word 'speediest' in this sentence which need be regarded with much suspicion. The Lord Keeper also defended the calling of a Parliament as being the fittest way to gather the forces of a kingdom for war, because it was 'the lively representation of the wisdom, wealth and power of the whole kingdom', and because it was an outward expression of that unity to which all early seventeenth-century political thought was devoted. It represented, he said, the unity of King and kingdom, 'whom God hath joined together by an indissoluble knot which none must attempt to cut or untie [*sic*]. And let all endeavour by unity and good accord to pattern this Parliament by the best that have been that it may be a pattern to future Parliaments and may infuse into Parliaments a kind of multiplying power and faculty whereby they may be more frequent.'[1]

Respect for the rule of law was one of the strongest emotions most seventeenth-century Englishmen possessed: the rule of law the guarantee for the security of property, and, without meetings of Parliament, the rule of law was at best in question. The repeated calling of Parliaments throughout the 1620s was as much a product of sentiment as of reason, and it was a sentiment which was very deeply ingrained.[2]

Unity was also something which Councillors wanted to demonstrate during a war. Secretary Coke told the Commons of 1628 that if they gave supply, 'You shall not only make the King to subsist, but you shall advance the King's reputation in the world by the unity of his people more than any treasure.'[3] Parliament's established position in English legal thought as the ultimate source of law gave it a potential strength which was not warranted, either by the laws the Crown wanted it to pass, or by the amount of money it granted. Parliaments survived to the end of the 1620s because they were not meeting in an ideologically divided country.

Nevertheless, this sense that the survival of Parliaments was precarious was constantly with members throughout the decade.

---

[1] *L.J.* 687–8.

[2] M. A. Judson, *The Crisis of the Constitution* (Rutgers, 1949), pp. 1–107. Professor Judson rightly stressed the similarity of the political thought of her main characters. Her belief that in doing so she had demonstrated the 'meagerness of their political thought' (op. cit., p. 9) is based on the belief that the political thought was designed for a constitutional conflict. If it is taken as being designed rather to preserve unity, it appears much more to the purpose.

[3] *1628 Debates*, ii. 246.

It was this sense, probably more than anything else, which put them on the watch for attempts to do things in unparliamentary ways. It is this watchfulness which has given the Parliaments of the 1620s the appearance of encroaching on royal authority. The more they feared that Parliaments might disappear, the more things they insisted could not be done without a Parliament. The more they feared, the more they grew ready to see the shadow of 'arbitrary government' in administrative action which, under the Tudors, would only have been regarded as based on administrative convenience.[1] The more obvious it became that Parliaments did not suit the King's administrative convenience, or even his financial survival, the more ready even the most conventional members became to see the cutting of legal corners by members of the administration as part of a plan to alter the frame of government of the country.

For most people, these alarms were only the mood of a moment, but they grew from a rather more permanent knowledge that something in the government of England needed to change. This fear that an individual levy could be the beginning of a general trend was expressed particularly clearly by a Parliament man who was probably Sir Robert Phelips. He objected to a proposal to finance a war with Spain by a voluntary benevolence, saying that

This way to begin and support any great action is contrary to the custom of former times, the kings then ever having resort upon such like occasions to their people assembled in Parliament. And lastly it will be urged that this is a way of dangerous consequence, and that for a twofold respect, the first that levies of this kind will seem by use and practice to create and invest a right of property in the king in the goods of his subjects, at his own pleasure and by any pretence to be exercised, that it will procure an utter destruction of Parliaments, when one of the principal works of a Parliament may be done another way.[2]

Of all the members of the Commons, Phelips was most vocally aware of belonging to an institution whose survival was on probation. He was liable, at moments of crisis in Parliamentary affairs, to exclaim: 'I know not whether I will ever speak within these walls again', and described the meeting of Parliament in 1624 as a 'miracle', brought about, next under God, by the Prince of Wales.[3]

[1] See the material on forced loans in G. R. Elton, *The Tudor Constitution* (Cambridge, 1960), pp. 57–8.

[2] Phelips MSS. 227/16. See Coke on the patent for scouring armour: 'letters patent can lay no tax on the subject', N.R.S. iv. 231.

[3] N.R.S. iii. 347, Stowe 366, f. 218^v. Pym (1624), f. 9^r.

He regularly quoted, to James's annoyance, from the passage in the *Apology of the Commons* of 1604 which claimed that 'the rights of princes may and daily do grow; but the privileges of the subjects are at an everlasting stand'.[1] In a well-known speech, Phelips placed the threat to Parliament's survival in a European context, claiming that 'We are the last monarchy in Christendom that yet retain our original rights and constitutions.' He made this claim with some knowledge of European politics. His papers contain a number of notes on the French Estates General, and when he was learning Spanish in preparation for attachment to the English embassy in Madrid, he was advised to read Mariana's *History of Spain*.[2] It is not proved that he did so, but if he did, he would have found there a good deal of evidence to support his view that the decline of representative assemblies was a European phenomenon.

Fears of this sort were usually concentrated on questions of taxation, because it was taxation of which the King was clearly desperately in need. It is natural, under a King with so little desire to legislate as James, that the Parliamentary monopoly of legislation, though guarded, should have been guarded with rather less desperation than control of taxation. Proclamations, the obvious substitute for legislation, provoked occasional alarm, but only on occasions, such as 1610 and 1628, when alarm for the future of Parliament was already aroused for other reasons.[3] It is therefore the more interesting to find this alarm being expressed by so unlikely a man as Edward Nicholas, acting secretary to the Duke of Buckingham, and later Secretary of State to Charles I. He was

[1] N.R.S. v. 433, ii. 25, iv. 17, ii. 538. Add. 36825, f. 159ᵛ. *1629 Debates*, p. 230. Phelips MSS. 224/84 and 87.

[2] *1625 Debates*, p. 110; Phelips MSS. 219/25; 221/46 and 47; 212/48. These observations show that Phelips was most struck by the fact that the French States General did not possess legislative power, but only the power to submit petitions, which the King might 'approve, disallow or mitigate' at his pleasure. The notes show that Phelips was aware of Bodin's work, but suggest that, like many of his contemporaries, he had not absorbed any concept of sovereignty from him. On Phelips's political thought see also the conventional and largely Aristotelian collection of quotations headed *De Regimine Politico* in Phelips MSS. 221/38. For what may have appeared to Phelips an uncomfortably close parallel to French views on legislation, see James's statement in his opening speech in 1621, that he made the laws, and the Parliament merely 'advised' him on them. N.R.S. iv. 3.

[3] For examples of this occasional alarm about Proclamations, see N.R.S. iv. 484 and *1628 Debates*, ii. 137 and 252. I am grateful to Dr. Esther Cope for the opportunity to discuss the question of Proclamations with her. Rich's diary, 11 June 1628, Huntingdon R.O., Manchester MSS. 58/5.

reacting to one of the issues which did most to call Parliament's control of law into question, the persistent demands made by the French and Spanish in negotiations for Prince Charles's marriage, that the King should, as a condition of the marriage treaty, issue what was in effect a Declaration of Indulgence, suspending the penal laws against Catholic recusants. Writing to his father on the day the Parliament of 1624 was prorogued, he said:

The hopes raised by the beginning of this Parliament were much lessened; it appeared that the King was bent on ruling in his own way, by proclamations, patents, etc, and would abet the clergy against the laity, and thus gradually alter the church. His value of Protestantism is shown by his rejecting the recusant bill, merely because it would deprive him of the means of making grants to his servants.[1]

This is a particularly clear illustration of the power of anti-Catholicism as a catalyst, stirring up and amalgamating all the other fears in people's minds.[2] In Nicholas's case, it is probably also a reflection of the uncertain standing of his employer the Duke of Buckingham in the last year of James's life. There is no sign that he felt any parallel alarms either before or after this date.

The growth of constitutional fears during the 1620s is perhaps most clearly shown by changing attitudes to commitment to prison by the Privy Council. Under the Tudors, it had been frequent for the Council to commit people to prison, either for a symbolic restraint of a few days to 'cool their heels', or to allow for investigations before they were charged. In 1621, Sir William Fleetwood introduced a bill for confirmation of Magna Carta, which would have prohibited imprisonment without the preferring of a legal charge. In this bill, he allowed an exemption for commitments by the Privy Council for matters of state. Sir Edward Coke, in words which were later quoted against him, said that the King and Council legally possessed a power of commitment to prison in emergency cases. When Sir William Fleetwood reintroduced his bill, in 1624, it contained a clause giving legal sanction to warrants for imprisonment under the hands of six of the Privy Council, though the time of commitment was to be limited to ten days.[3] This clause

---

[1] C.S.P.D. 1623–5, vol. clxv, no. 61 (Edward Nicholas to his father).

[2] On anti-Catholicism as an issue in elections, see Hirst, pp. 145–53.

[3] N.R.S. v. 226, ii. 478, iv. 382. For 1624, Holland, I, f. 58, and diary of Sir John Lowther (Cumberland R.O.), f. 27. I am grateful to Professor Ruigh for drawing my attention to the existence of this diary. According to Lowther, the cause of commitment was to be expressed in writing after twenty days. Hawarde noted in his 1624 diary that 'this bill covers restraint of trade' (f. 102ᵛ).

seems to have provoked no objection in 1624. The General Pardon of 1624, passed without question as a statute, exempted from pardon those imprisoned 'by express commandment or direction of any of his Majesty's Privy Council'.[1]

Sir Edward Coke appears to have been provoked to think again in 1626, when Digges and Eliot, both managers of the impeachment of Buckingham, were arrested 'in the face of the house', while it was in open session, without any charge being preferred against them. Coke, as he later recounted, then went back to his sources, read them again, and found there was no legal warrant for commitment without charge by the Privy Council.[2] By 1628, when the King had started to imprison leading members of the House of Commons, for refusing to 'lend' him money in lieu of Parliamentary subsidies, and appeared to be holding them in prison indefinitely by refusing to prefer any charge against them, almost every member of the House of Commons, and, in the end, a majority of the House of Lords, had gone through a similar change of heart. This is the most dramatic, but far from the only, example of mounting constitutional fears whose driving force was the certain knowledge that the King needed more money than Parliament would be allowed by its electorate or the subsidy commissioners to vote to him.

It did not help, in meeting these constitutional alarms, that in 1621 it was doubtful what things necessarily had to be done by statute, and which did not. The only things for which the need for a statute was recognized without exception were the naturalization of aliens (including the children of Englishmen born abroad) and the shifting of parish boundaries.[3] For all other more important

---

[1] *21 Jac. I c. 35*, clause x.

[2] For Coke's own account of his change of mind, see *1628 Debates*, ii. 213 and n. 1621–2 is a possible date, but I have preferred 1626 for three reasons. One is the lack of any objection from Coke to the clause in Fleetwood's 1624 bill which permitted commitment by the Council. The other two are in Coke's own dating phrase: 'when I perceived some members of this House were taken in the face of this House and sent to prison, and when I was not far from that place myself'. The members arrested in 1621–2 were arrested after the House had ceased to sit: only Digges and Eliot in 1626 were arrested 'in the face of the House'. In 1626, Coke probaby stood not far from prison. After the Parliament of 1621, he was in it, and understatement is uncharacteristic of Coke.

[3] For Sir Thomas Hoby's objections to a bill, current from 1610 onwards, which would have naturalized all children of Englishmen born abroad, see Spring, 12 March 1624, and Pym, f. 27ʳ. Hoby held that naturalization could only be valid for those who proved their Protestantism by personally taking the

principles, it was alarmingly possible to find exceptions. For example, the need for Parliamentary authority to tax was, in theory, one of the most unquestioned of Parliamentary powers. Yet this principle had been undermined, since Elizabeth's days, by the proportion of taxes which were local. It was widely agreed that the Justices of the Peace in Quarter Sessions, like a Parliament, were a representative assembly of their county, and had the same legal authority to impose rates. Yet not all local rates were imposed by authority from Quarter Sessions. In particular, rates for the militia, which had normally been accepted on an emergency basis in 1588, were still imposed on the sole authority of Deputy Lieutenants. In Norfolk, there had been disputes from 1581 onwards about attempts by leading county gentlemen to levy rates for such purposes as repair of roads and harbours by the authority of royal patents alone.[1]

Charters, issued only under the Great Seal, frequently empowered corporations to impose rates on their members. In 1604, statutory authority was given to the practice of town corporations of levying rates for the relief of the plague. Yet the number of such local rates which had to be imposed made it impossible either for Parliament or for Quarter Sessions to find time to sanction them all. Many people believed that the enforcement of economic legislation by rights of search and seizure required Parliamentary authority, yet Parliaments had not the time to confer these rights as often as they were needed. Much economic legislation was enforced by companies, confining trade to their own members, enforcing apprenticeship, and exercising rights of search and seizure, and of punishing their own members. In 1604, members of Parliament had been prepared to admit that they could not confirm all such rights. In an Act for demarcation of the trades of painter and plasterer, they simply recited Elizabethan letters patent giving the right to search and punish offenders to the London Company of

---

Oaths of Allegiance and Supremacy in the presence of one of the Houses of Parliament.

[1] On disputes about military and other rates, and the authority for them, see L. O. J. Boynton, *The Elizabethan Militia* (1967), pp. 47–8, 158, 178, 223–5, 255–6, and Hassell Smith, pp. 230–1, 245, 246–7, 256, 263, 278–81 and 292–3. The character of the Quarter Sessions as a county Parliament applies to the raising of taxation. In complaints of county grievances, the task was more often discharged by the Grand Jury.

Painters, without bothering to insist that the rights were held 'by virtue of this Act'. Such a casual approach was rarer in 1621.[1]

Concern with the legal authority for enforcement of economic legislation helped to spread concern with the question of the powers which could be conferred by a royal charter. A charter, as Clare appreciated, was something conferred by royal favour, which the King could therefore, without impropriety, threaten to revoke. Corporations were therefore liable to pressure to pay money in return for their privileges. It was the City of London, not the King, which told the disputed incorporation of the Apothecaries, in 1621, that they could make none free of the City until they had paid £200 towards the benevolence for the Palatinate, but the principle was one the King could also use.[2] His attempts to raise money from the brewers and the vintners suggested that he was well aware of the fact.[3] His composition with the brewers was worth £3,300 a year. The most famous of disputed charters, that of the Merchant Adventures, involved a financial element. In 1624, the Parliamentary attack on the Merchant Adventurers grew out of an attack on the pretermitted custom, a customs duty on cloth which lacked Parliamentary sanction, and which the Merchant Adventurers had duly agreed to pay.[4] Some of the more vocal attacks on the restriction of trade by charters were thus fiscal, rather than economic, in origin.

It was also a principle of Coke's, enunciated in the Tailors of Ipswich case, that a charter could not abridge common law rights.[5]

---

[1] *1 Jac. I c.20.* See N.R.S. ii. 254 for Noy's complaint that the patent for the engrossing of wills conferred on the patentees a power to make law contrary to the Statute of York.

[2] The incorporation of the apothecaries, disputed with relentless persistence by the grocers, remained a live Parliamentary issue for most of the decade. It was still included in the grievances listed in 1624/5. For Clare, see Knowler, p. 31. For fear that incorporation tended to monopoly (expressed on the wool-carding bill of 1621) see N.R.S. ii. 68, vii. 29 ff.

[3] On the attempts to make 'compositions' with the brewers and the vintners, see N.R.S. ii. 476 and n, 480–1, Stowe 366 f. 216^r, Add. 36825, f. 433^v and Harl. 5324, ff. 54–3. On the possibility of bringing pressure to bear on companies, see also J. R. Jones, 'The Clegate Case', *E.H.R.* (1975), 265–8.

[4] The Merchant Adventurers had been allowed to lay an imposition on their members, in order to recoup a loan they had made to the King: S.P. 14/162/12. On the connection, logical and chronological, between the attack on the Merchant Adventurers in 1624 and the issue of the pretermitted custom, see J. P. Cooper, *New Cambridge Modern History*, iv. 548 and Spring, f. 212, also Pym, f. 45^v and 85^{r-v}, Dyott, 30 April. Also Supple, pp. 70–1, N.R.S. iv. 50 and n, 97–8; iii. 246.   [5] Coke, *11th Report* (1738), pp. 53–4.

In particular, he held that the right to work at the trade of a man's choice was a common law right which could not be taken away by royal charter. This ruling was a serious threat to the power of charters to impose new restrictions, and Coke and others rapidly extended its principle into other fields. Many of the rulings of the House of Commons committee of privileges widening the borough franchises were based on the principle, to which Coke helped to convert his colleagues, that a charter could not abridge existing common law rights. If it could once be proved that in any ancient time the right to vote had rested in 'the inhabitants', any borough charter purporting to restrict it to a smaller number was held *ultra vires*, and void.[1] In 1621, Crew, attacking Mompesson's patent for the licensing of inns, linked the principle of the Tailors of Ipswich case, that a grant under the Great Seal could not abridge common law rights, with his fears for the growth of possible unparliamentary legislation. He said the keeping of an inn was 'a trade or mystery, and free by the common law', and that attempts to restrict the right to keep an inn by authority of a patent were 'a novelty and an attempt to introduce a new law without the common assent of peers and Commons'. Like Phelips over taxation, he saw a principle he thought capable of general extension: 'The like novelty by example of this might be introduced to extend to carriers, millers, skippers, smiths and other trades and mysteries, which are free and no statute laws of restraint, but only that in some cases none should exercise them but that had been an apprentice seven years.'[2]

If this perception of principle was originally constitutional in inspiration, it was quickly exploited by economic vested interests. Sir Edward Coke made a magnificent guided missile to launch against an economic rival. His services seem to have been particularly in demand during the years 1621–4. These were years of severe economic depression, when attempts to restrict what trade was available were in consequence likely to be resented the more bitterly.[3] The right legal language was quickly picked up by those

---

[1] See the cases of Chippenham in 1624 and Colchester in 1628. The hostility to the restrictive power of charters in electoral and economic disputes is clearly a common hostility. It follows that in both contexts it is likely to have a common cause, which would then be legal, rather than electoral or economic. See Pym (1624), ff. 32^r, 50^v.

[2] P.R.O. C. 65/185. This is part of Crew's speech presenting the charges against Mompesson to the Lords.

[3] On the depression, see Supple, pp. 52–98.

objecting to royal grants which interfered with their trade. The London Grocers' Company was aggrieved by a new royal charter, taking apothecaries out of the control of the grocers, and setting up a new Apothecaries' Company. They said the new incorporation of the Apothecaries was against law, because it restrained grocers in their trade, by forbidding them to sell drugs, 'to the decay of many people's livings'. They not only exploited Coke's legalism by claiming that this was a restraint of trade against law, but also tried to exploit the gathering attack on Lord Chancellor Bacon for corruption, by saying darkly that he had agreed to seal the Apothecaries' charter 'upon considerations best known unto himself'. The Grocers' case against the Apothecaries was taken up by the Commons, and pursued unsuccessfully for most of the rest of the decade.[1]

The Welsh drapers, objecting to the restriction imposed on them by the Shrewsbury charter, which forced them to market their cloth through Shrewsbury, were more successful. They claimed that freedom of trade gave people employment, made them grow rich, and so enabled them to pay taxes, and they wished to be able to sell their cloth to anyone 'who lawfully by the laws and statutes of this realm may lawfully buy the same', notwithstanding any charter or grant to the contrary.[2] They obtained their wish by a statute passed in 1624. The Venetian Ambassador tactfully fostered the attack on the patent giving Sir Robert Mansell a monopoly of the glass trade, and consequently the right to ban imported glass. The London leathersellers objected to an attempt to incorporate a company of Glovers by charter, on the ground that 'they think it fit rather for Parliament than elsewhere', and warned that 'it is apparently dangerous to have such a corporation created, for that it is easy to build a monopoly upon such a foundation by the help of some by-laws and ordinances among themselves'.[3] Even an

---

[1] N.R.S. vii. 327, 82–4.

[2] *21 Jac. I c. 9:* N.R.S. vii. 73–5. See also N.R.S. ii. 318, v. 94 for Coke's ready digestion of his brief.

[3] *C.S.P.Ven. 1621–3*, p. 22. N.R.S. vii. 155. For what appear to be similar examples of exploitation of constitutional anxieties by economic lobbies, see ibid. vii. 361–2, iv. 133: vii. 364–70, v. 514. For Sandys's concern about byelaws, N.R.S. iv. 191, Pym (1624), f. 44ʳ. For Coke, N.R.S. iv. 308, iii. 172. On 26 March 1621, a bill was introduced against corporations erecting new offices or laying impositions: ibid. vi. 84. For an example of resistance to the enforcement of economic regulations which was not backed by statute, see the preamble to the Act incorporating the Hallamshire cutlers, 21 Jac. I c. 31.

attempt to raise a small toll on passing boats for the repair of Rochester bridge was once objected to on the ground that it was an attempt to impose an unlawful levy without proper authority.[1] During the depression years of 1621–4, the skilful functioning of mercantile lobbies did much to persuade members of Parliament that things were being done on the King's sole authority which ought to have been done by the authority of statute. Yet the claim of some members of Parliament that all these things should be regulated by the authority of statute would have seemed more convincing if they had shown any sign of being sufficiently expeditious to pass the necessary number of statutes. For example, in 1621, an appeal was made to Parliament by both sides in the long-standing dispute about logwood. Logwood provided a new tropical dye, which was used for the dyeing of cloth. The Dyers' Company maintained that the dye was unreliable, and should not be used. Others thought that the dye was safe under proper supervision. Since there were not enough experienced logwood dyers to erect a company, they thought that the trade should be supervised by a patentee, who would recoup himself by a share of the fines for improper and unauthorized use of logwood. In 1621, the Dyers' Company submitted a Parliamentary bill to ban the use of logwood and the patentee submitted a bill to give statutory authority to his patent. The Council, which had already suffered many years of trouble and indecision about logwood, told Parliament it would agree to whichever bill Parliament agreed to pass. Parliament, thus left with responsibility for a decision, allowed both bills to lapse at the stage of first reading in the Commons.[2] The real trouble appears to have been that the subjects requiring regulation were so multifarious that few members of the Commons, and probably few of the Lords, had the necessary interest in any given subject to ensure that a bill on it would complete its passage through both Houses. Members were claiming a power they were unable to exercise.

These mixed economic and constitutional issues rarely appear to have provided matter of the highest political drama, and do not explain the bitterness of the Parliaments of the later 1620s, in

---

[1] Pym (1624), f. 70ʳ. For a similar concern about wharfage fees, ibid., f. 69ʳ.
[2] N.R.S. vii. 404–10. After this conspicuous failure to take the initiative when invited to do so, members of Parliament were in no position to complain when they found that the logwood patent continued unchecked. S.P. 16/1/14.

which they received very little attention. What then was all the trouble about? If the Parliaments of the 1620s were not the scene of a power struggle between 'government' and 'opposition', if they were not polarized by ideological disputes, and if they were full of members who wished to preserve good relations with the court, why did they generate so much ill will?

IV. REVENUE AND ADMINISTRATION: THE FUNCTIONAL BREAKDOWN

There appear to be three important answers to this question. The first, and fundamental reason is what Professor Aylmer has called the 'functional breakdown' of English administration:[1] the straining of the links between central and local government, which meant the King was constantly unable to collect an adequate revenue. He was therefore forced to resort to methods of revenue collection which only increased the collectors' unpopularity. The second was the complex and rapid political manœuvring of the Duke of Buckingham, exploiting and discarding foreign and domestic allies as they suited his attempt to continue his power into the new reign. His very survival caused what Chamberlain called 'some heartburning' among his rivals at court,[2] and the means by which he ensured it added bewilderment to indignation. The third reason, bred from the other two, is the pressure of war on the English local administration. Because the wars of the 1620s were so unsuccessful, it is too readily forgotten that they were seriously intended, and prepared for on such a scale as to create a severe administrative burden. It was this burden of war,[3] imposed on an administration already in a state of functional breakdown by a Duke of Buckingham whose purposes, and even whose enemy, appeared unidentifiable, that brought relations between central and local government, and hence between King and Parliament, to the point of collapse. The crisis of 1626–8, like the crisis of 1640 was the result of England's administrative inability to fight a war.[4]

---

[1] *Sussex Books*, ed. W. Lamont (1976), p. 137.

[2] Chamberlain, 31 Jan. 1624, *C.S.P.Ven. 1623–5*, p. 208.

[3] See L. O. J. Boynton, *The Elizabethan Militia* (1967), pp. 245–50.

[4] The fortunate success of the defensive campaign of 1588 distracts attention from the extent to which this was a difficulty of long standing. See J. P. Cooper, *New Cambridge Modern History*, iv (1971), 531, and Geoffrey Parker, 'If the Armada Had Landed', *History* (1976), 358–68. Both the Armada campaign and

The functional breakdown of administration is now the subject of a large and excellent body of historical literature. It concerned first and foremost the problem of collecting sufficient revenue in and after a period of rapid inflation, and the interrelated difficulty of securing adequate payment for the Crown's servants. Professor Hurstfield, in his seminal book on *The Queen's Wards*, drew attention to both these difficulties. Estates valued for wardship had to be valued by local officials, often the friends of those whose estates they were valuing. They were therefore grossly under-assessed. The contemporary estimate that, in order to arrive at a correct value, an official valuation ought to be multiplied by ten appears to be approximately correct. Because estates valued for wardship were so under-assessed, they became very profitable prizes for those who were able to obtain leases of them, since they could draw far more from the estates and the body of the ward than they were bound to pay to the Exchequer. The granting of wardships therefore became a form of patronage for courtiers and Queen's servants who otherwise were unable to support their posts on salaries and fees which inflation had made laughably small.[1] Many officials felt a sense of grievance about the falling value of their legitimate incomes. Secretary Conway once complained to Lord Treasurer Middlesex that all the benefit of the Secretary's place would not defray half its cost to its holder.[2] Such remarks, of course, savour of special pleading, but it is certainly true that any early Stuart office-holder who confined himself to his strictly legitimate rewards would have been likely to find that his post was not worth the effort he bestowed upon it.

The result was a relentless pursuit of patronage, as a substitute for payment. This patronage was often at the expense of the subject: men were paid by grants allowing them to collect revenue

---

Buckingham's offensive expeditions illustrate Michael Howard's arguments that in European warfare this is a period when the advantage lay with the defensive. Michael Howard, *War in European History* (Oxford, 1976), p. 37. For a difficulty in raising troops for offensive war which would be more widely known if it dated from 1627 instead of 1587, see Hassell Smith, pp. 174–5. See also below, pp. 324–6.

[1] J. Hurstfield, *The Queen's Wards* (1958), pp. 87, 231, 273–6, 337 *passim* and other refs., and 'Political Corruption in Early Modern England', *History* (1967), 16–34.

[2] S.P. 14/162/6. Conway appears to refer to the unofficial benefits of the place, as well as to the salary. If so, his remark might be taken to belong to the history of ideas, much as to administrative history.

the Crown's administrative machinery did not enable it to collect. The use of leases in reversion of Crown lands was an example of this process. Those to whom leases in reversion were granted often did not wish to enjoy their grants: they wished the existing tenants to buy them out. They were thus able to obtain from the tenants some of the difference between the Crown's rent from the land and its economic rent. When Queen Elizabeth was unable to pay Nicholas Hilliard for making a new Great Seal, or Sir Francis Walsingham was unable to pay a secret agent whose trading career had been ruined by his detection, they gave them instead leases in reversion of Crown lands.[1] The hunt for concealed Crown lands is another example of a similar process. The Crown was unable to detect all the lands which ought to have belonged to it, and indeed mislaid some which were in its own records. It therefore granted to various patentees the right to search for concealed Crown lands, and then to 'compound' with their occupiers. The process of 'compounding' was inherently open to abuse. It involved the patentee selling out the title he had acquired on behalf of the Crown, in return for a sum of money to be fixed by negotiation. Compounding, especially in cases which might extend into expensive legal proceedings, could come perilously near blackmail. Sir Giles Mompesson, one of the most notorious of concealment patentees, found, among other things, a number of legitimate grantees of Crown land whose grants had omitted to specify that they included the dovecote. He would thus claim a dovecote in the middle of a man's property as being concealed Crown land. The opportunities for compounding which this gave to a man like Mompesson can be safely be left to the imagination.[2]

The hunt for concealed Crown lands was a subject of bitter Parliamentary complaint, and was, together with the abuse of

[1] D. L. Thomas, 'Leases in Reversion on the Crown's Lands 1558–1603', *Ec.H.R.* (1977), 67–72. I am grateful to Mr. Thomas for allowing me to read this article before publication.

[2] C. J. Kitching, 'The Quest for Concealed Crown Lands in the Reign of Elizabeth I', *T.R.H.S.* (1974), 63–78. House of Lord Main Papers, 7 July 1620 (accounts of Mompesson's concealment patent, gathered for the use of the House of Lords committee under the Earl of Southampton). Not all 'concealed' lands were deliberately hidden from the Crown, and the extent of concealments may be in part a measure of the Crown's inefficiency. For examples of concealed lands which might more properly be described as 'mislaid', see K. S. H. Wyndham, 'The Redistribution of Crown Land in Somerset by Gift, Sale and Lease', University of London Ph.D. Thesis (1976), pp. 52–5.

informers, one of the only two major abuses of the period successfully put a stop to by Parliamentry statute.[1] Yet, in complaining
of concealments and other devices to raise revenue or to reward
the King's servants, members of Parliament were complaining of
something for which much of the responsibility rested on themselves in their local capacities. Most Justices of the Peace appear
to have preferred to face the wrath of the Crown rather than the
wrath of their neighbours. If they did not adequately collect the
King's revenue, they could not be suprised if the King transferred
the task to someone else, who would get a share of the proceeds,
and therefore enforce the law for his own profit. As early as 1576,
Lord Keeper Nicholas Bacon had felt the need to warn Parliament
that if they did not execute the law more effectively in their local
capacities, the Queen would be 'driven clean contrary to her most
gracious nature and inclination to appoint and assign private men
for profit and gain's sake to see her penal laws to be executed'.[2]

If we are to believe an *ex parte* memorandum compiled in 1605
by a projector called Sir Stephen Procter,[3] local officials such as
sheriffs showed so devious an attitude to law enforcement and
revenue collection as to create a strong case for alternative methods
of revenue collection. He said, for example, that sheriffs having
process against a debtor of the King's might return that he had
land worth £25 in the county, when in fact he had land worth
£3,000 and goods worth another £3,000. He said they collected
fines from courts shortly before a Parliament, without accounting
for them to the Exchequer, so that when the fines were subsequently remitted by the General Pardon at the end of a Parliament,
sheriffs could keep them to their own use. He alleged that sheriffs
delayed accounting for fines they had collected until their term of
office was complete, and thereby succeeded in keeping them for
themselves. If any of these charges are true, they shed a curious
light on the Act of Parliament of 1624, which exempted sheriffs

[1] Kitching, art. cit., pp. 71–8. I have found no reason to dispute this verdict,
but further concealment bills were moved in 1625, 1626, and 1628. I have not
discovered their contents.

[2] Hassell Smith, p. 124.

[3] P.R.O. CREST 40/18. This memorandum is in a volume of Sir Julius
Caesar's papers recently returned to the Public Record Office from the Office
of the Crown Woods. I am grateful to Dr. Nicholas Cox and Mr. D. L. Thomas
for drawing it to my attention. It must be stressed that all Procter's statements
are special pleading in favour of his own project for the central control of
informers.

from being troubled for arrears after their final accounting in the Exchequer. It is interesting that the original draft of this Act had conferred a similar immunity on subsidy collectors, which was cut out of the final version.[1] Procter detected many similar abuses in the customs administration, such as that the best quality leather was rated for customs as if it were base leather, and escaped the customs officers because they were unable to tell the difference. The customs statistics bear him out in his claim that large amounts of tin were smuggled on shipboard without paying custom, since the total customs on the export of tin from all ports other than London amounted, at the end of Elizabeth's reign, to no more than £28 per annum.

For Procter, the answer to all these, and many other, abuses, was through the use of informers, whom he wanted to organize and supervise under the control of a special office of informers, based in London. Perhaps no issue illustrates the ambivalence of M.P.s about revenue collection and law enforcement more clearly than that of informers.[2] In their local capacities, they mostly felt an intelligible and justifiable dislike of informers, and yet, in their capacity as Westminster legislators, they still wanted their laws enforced. The 1624 Act destroyed informers' effectiveness on most issues by restricting them to local courts, where their activity could be controlled by the force of local opinion. Yet the Informers Act itself had exemption clauses allowing informers to continue their activities on issues either members or the Crown felt strongly about. They were still allowed to inform freely about recusancy, maintenance, evasion of tonnage and poundage or customs, and the illegal transport of gold, silver, munitions, wool, woolfells, or leather. In the same Parliament, the Act for free trade in Welsh cloth, in apparent contradiction to the Informers Act, provided for its enforcement by informers, and so did the Act of 1628 against pedlars and other tradesmen who travelled on the Sabbath.

[1] N.R.S. vii. 170.
[2] On informers, see M. W. Beresford, 'The Common Informer, The Penal Statutes and Economic Regulation', *Ec.H.R.* (1957), 221–38. Like Dr. Kitching, he concludes that the statute on this subject achieved the desired effect. His conclusion that this statute was part of a move away from economic regulation is true in effect, but not, so far as can be discovered from the debates, in intention. The Statute on Sheriffs' Accounts did not achieve the desired effect. See Aylmer, pp. 188–92, and also 'Studies in the Institution and Personnel of English Central Administration 1625–1642', Oxford D.Phil. Thesis (1954), pp. 654, 658–68.

An Act of 1604, against poaching, had contained a frank confession that the game laws were ineffective, because offenders lacked enough money to tempt informers to start proceedings against them.[1] An attack on informers was in part an attack on effective law enforcement.

Even when M.P.s complained of lax execution of the recusancy laws, they were in part complaining of themselves in their own local capacity. The recusancy Acts, especially that of 1606, passed after the Gunpowder Plot, gave plenty of independent scope for action to J.P.s, and it was unfair of them to blame the Crown if they failed to take advantage of it. We have perhaps missed members' share of responsibility for the failure to execute their own legislation partly because we are restricted in our thinking by the modern separation of the categories of 'legislative' and 'executive'. Those M.P.s who were also J.P.s were themselves part of the executive, and shared responsibility for any failure to execute the laws. As Sir Harbottle Grimston said in his charge to the Essex Grand Jury in 1638,

We that sit here upon the bench, and ye that stand by and are the presentors, are by his Majesty in our several places designed and appointed to be the executioners of these laws, and if they want the blessed effect of a happy reformation, or be not profitable to the common wealth for the suppression of sin and vice . . . the fault is ours, for execution does as it were *animare legem*, it quickens, animates and puts life into the law which otherwise of itself is but *littera mortua*, a dead letter.[2]

One of the subjects on which members of the Commons most conspicuously combined a Westminster enthusiasm for legislation with a local inability to execute it was that of alehouses. Between 1604 and 1628, no less than five Acts were passed against disorderly or unlicensed alehouses, yet, as Sir John Eliot ruefully admitted, the offences complained of 'were more decried than punished, as reformation is less easy than complaint'.[3] The patentees made their money from the forfeiture of alehouse-keepers' recognizances to be of good behaviour. They succeeded, as the House of Commons bitterly complained, in extracting £14 from the town of Grimsby, where a subsidy only amounted to £6. A historian may perhaps be permitted to wonder to whose discredit

[1] *1 Jac. I c. 27.*
[2] Herts. R.O., Gorhambury MS. IX A 9. I am grateful to Mrs. Julie Calnan, who discovered and identified this MS., for generously placing it at my disposal. See also below, p. 431.
[3] *N.P.* i. 126. On alehouses in their local context, see Peter Clark in Peter Clark and Paul Slack (eds.) *Crisis and Order in English Towns* (1972), pp. 140–1.

this information should redound. The patentees were denounced with particular vehemence for taking away a power which should rightfully have belonged to J.P.s When the J.P.s, as was admitted in the Commons, were often unable to make effective use of this power, their protests at having it taken away from them perhaps savour of the dog in the manger.[1]

How much emphasis is placed on this breakdown in the relations between central and local government depends in part what test of success is taken. Most leading J.P.s did work extremely hard, and found that the burden of work facing them had been a good deal increased by the flood of legislation issuing from Westminster during the Tudor period. Their sessions were becoming longer and more onerous, and, as Professor Cockburn has remarked, there is probably some truth in the picture of an overworked magistracy.[2] Nevertheless, the J.P.s succeeded, in the main, in keeping the peace in their county communities. Some critics, such as Lord Chancellor Ellesmere, claimed that when they ought to keep the peace, 'they rather make war', but these are probably not justified complaints of the body of J.P.s as a whole.[3] Where they failed, and failed catastrophically, was not in caring for their county communities, but in executing unpopular orders from the central government, especially ones commanding the raising of money or troops.

V. WAR AND SOCIETY:
PARLIAMENT, THE DUKE, AND FOREIGN AFFAIRS

It is only in the context of this curiously ambivalent relationship between M.P.s in their Westminster and local capacities that it is

[1] N.R.S. vii. 312–22, iv. 325–8.

[2] Cockburn, p. 90; Fletcher, pp. 138, 218 ff. A vivid picture of the burden placed on J.P.s by the flood of legislation issuing from Westminster in Elizabethan and early Jacobean times is given by S.P. 9/244B. This is a manuscript draft (1625–8) of an attempt to bring the standard manuals for J.P.s up to date. In addition to the bulk of statutes, the author was worried by the difficulty of discovering which statutes were repealed and which were continued. He was also worried by drafting flaws. For example, *3 Jac. I c. 12*, on the conservation of fish, failed to lay down any procedure for convicting offenders. When a J.P. guilty of a procedural irregularity was likely to face a lawsuit from an offended neighbour, such points could cause considerable anxiety.

[3] Hawarde, *Les Reportes del Cases in Camera Stellata*, ed. W. P. Baildon (1894), pp. 186–7. Cockburn (pp. 103–4) expresses some sympathy with Ellesmere's point of view, but Fletcher (p. 240) takes a more favourable view of their service to the county, if not to the central government.

possible to make any sense of Parliamentary reactions to the rapidly increasing pressure of war on county administration between 1624 and 1628.

Both in 1627–8 and in 1639–40, the failure of local government to meet the pressure of war was accentuated, though not caused, by the fact that the reasons for war were unpopular, incomprehensible, or both.[1] In 1627, for the only time for over a century, England was at war with both the great powers of Europe at the same time. Naturally, this caused some perplexity among people who wished to know for what war, and against what enemy, they were being asked to give money. Edward Kirton, in 1628, was choosing his words carefully when he complained that Buckingham 'casts the king into all kinds of wars'.[2]

Buckingham has been severely, and justly, blamed for allowing himself to be led into both these wars at once, but to cast all the blame on Buckingham is perhaps to take too insular a view of the situation. Buckingham's short-lived alliance with the French was vitiated from the start by the obstinate French insistence that Charles I's French marriage should involve all the same concessions to Catholics as had been involved in the abortive plan to marry Charles to a Spanish Princess. They appeared quite unable to understand that even Buckingham could not, at one and the same time, effectively suspend all the penal laws against Catholics, and raise from a Parliament enough supply to prosecute an offensive war. Nor did the French realize that their determination to take over from the Spaniards the position of recognized champion and protector of the English Catholics was bound to lead the English government to view them with suspicion.[3] The Anglo-French war was largely provoked by one of the most successful political gadflies of the period, the Huguenot Duke of Soubise.[4] The one man who did most to wreck the Anglo-French alliance was not Buckingham, but Soubise. The evidence is lacking, but the fear that Soubise was acting as a Spanish agent is entirely plausible.[5] For Soubise and his doings, Buckingham cannot be held to blame. Yet equally,

[1] See below, pp. 324–40.
[2] Stowe 366, f. 219r.
[3] P.R.O. 31/3/58, ff. 67r, 70v, 73–5; vol. 59, ff. 119–20, 177–80; S.P. 78/74, ff. 19, 83; C.S.P.Ven. 1623–5, pp. 435–8.
[4] P.R.O. 31/3/62, f. 145.
[5] P.R.O. 31/3/61, f. 3. Also S.P. 78/74, ff. 55, 64, 122; C.S.P.D. 1625–6, vol. vii, no. 57, vol. xi, no. 11; P.R.O. 31/3/62, ff. 146, 154.

Buckingham could not be surprised if members of Parliament found it hard to raise war fever for wars against France and Spain simultaneously. As a rallying call for war, there was nothing to compare with the invading Spaniards of 1588. With so muddled a cause, Buckingham's attempts to rouse war fever in the country were singularly unsuccessful.

This is one reason why it is now so easily forgotten that the 1620s were a war decade. Every Parliament in the decade was called because of wars or rumours of wars.[1] This is why, during the decade, there were seven sessions of five Parliaments, a frequency of meeting unknown since the reign of Mary Tudor. If Parliament in the 1620s was, in Notestein's phrase, 'a continuous performance with interruptions',[2] it is war which is responsible, and it is therefore reasonable to look to war to provide a number of the common themes which hold the period together.

In turning to war, Buckingham and Charles were putting pressure on English society and administration at their weakest point: the link between central and local government. War immediately implied an increased pressure by the central government on the counties. As Professor Barnes remarked, '*1 Charles 1* was indeed very different from *23 James 1* so far as county government was concerned. The new King's reign was marked by a quickened tempo, the cause of which was largely the government's demands on the counties' Lieutenantcy in time of war.'[3] The pressure of the war on the counties cannot simply be measured by the central government's demands for money, though those were vast enough. In 1626, there were military preparations on a scale unknown since Elizabeth. The fact that the failure of the Parliament of that year rendered all these preparations abortive did not absolve the government from demands that they should feed and clothe the sailors and soldiers they had assembled.[4] They did not succeed in doing so, but the sums they spent in the attempt were far more than they possessed. In August 1625, Secretary Coke told the

---

[1] The only possible exception is the session of 1629, but see Charles's reply to the petition for a Fast, *H.M.C. Buccleuch*, iii. 332.

[2] Wallace Notestein, *The Winning of the Initiative by the House of Commons* (1924), p. 40.

[3] Barnes, pp. 172–3. Also p. 244.

[4] L. O. J. Boynton, *The Elizabethan Militia* (1967), pp. 245–50, and 'Billeting: The Example of the Isle of Wight', *E.H.R.* (1959), 23–40. The situation in the Isle of Wight provoked vigorous protests from Hampshire members of Parliament in 1628.

Commons that the war was costing £50,000 a month on soldiers and allies, in addition to the costs of the fleet.[1] Something approaching the King's whole annual income was being spent on land forces alone. All this spending at the centre would have to be met by a mixture of Parliamentary subsidies, forced loans, borrowing, and the sale of Crown lands.

There was also a heavy burden to be raised by rates on counties. This was to pay for the impressment of troops, their billeting, coat and conduct money, powder, coastal defence against invasion, and many other things. In September 1625, the Earl of Warwick, Lord Lieutenant of Essex, and one of the enthusiastic supporters of the war, reported that the county had already been charged with between four and five thousand pounds to maintain the garrison at Harwich, and were refusing to pay any more.[2] This figure should be compared with the cost of a subsidy for Essex in 1610, which was £2,418. Warwick was not helped by the fact that the country was still in the aftermath of a severe economic depression whose worst symptom had been a shortage of coin: he reported that the county was so bare of money that borrowing was impossible. In resistance to taxation during the 1620s, the shortage of coin may perhaps deserve more prominence than it has been given.[3] In Sussex, the cost of billeting 800 men for seven months probably came to about £6,500, including the expenses of their officers, but excluding the cost of their clothing and equipment. These, moreover, were costs which were incurred at the same time as Parliamentary subsidies were being paid. Both in Sussex and in Somerset, the Deputy Lieutenants appear to have done their best to raise the sums required for the prosecution of the war, but the task was beyond them. The Earl of Dorset, Lord Lieutenant of Sussex, was justified in the foreboding he expressed to his Deputies, 'that you shall almost undergo a despairing task'.[4] Nor should the pressure of war on the counties be seen simply in terms of pounds, shillings, and pence: it should be set against the background of

[1] S.P. 16/5/14.

[2] *C.S.P.D. 1625–6*, vol. vi, nos. 76, 77, 98; vol. viii, no. 44. On the cost of a subsidy in Essex, B.L. Add. MS. 58833, f. 25ʳ.

[3] I am grateful to Professor L. M. Hill and Dr. D. M. Hirst for bringing this point to my attention. See Hirst, p. 174, Chamberlain, 6 Feb. 1621, Phelips MSS. 223/14, and particularly *1628 Debates*, ii. 304, for the report by Delbridge that some people in Devon, having no coin, were trying to pay billeting money in goods.

[4] Fletcher, pp. 200–1.

things like the entry in the Salisbury census of the poor: 'good-wife Hoskins now lieth in childbed, hath four children. Her husband was pressed for a soldier; she wanted relief', or the unpaid Irishmen at Deal who were found eating grass because they had been paid no money to buy food.[1] Such stories were familiar. In 1626, while in the middle of facing impeachment, Buckingham received a letter from Sir John Pennington, commanding the fleet, saying he could not feed his men with words, and unless money came soon, he could not long keep them together. Pennington added wearily: 'I have written so much and oft of it, I will let it rest.'[2]

Perhaps it is best to follow Sir John Pennington's example. The bulk of evidence on the pressure of the war on the counties is immense, yet necessarily distorted by the tendency for the dramatic examples to be recorded. The effect of the war on England needs more careful analysis than can be attempted here. However, it can safely be said that the burden was more than county administration could willingly carry. Even after all the pressure of raising money, the men were poorly paid, poorly trained, poorly armed, poorly clothed (or sometimes unclothed), and unable to make any effective showing against the enemy. In 1625, the war effort was handicapped as it began by one of the worst attacks of plague of the century, which meant that many areas needed most of their money to relieve their own sick and bereaved.[3] It was also handicapped, particularly in the West Country, by severe depredations from pirates based in Sallee and Algiers.[4]

It seems that the war effort was also handicapped by the fact that many respectable people, faced by starving soldiers, felt more fear and dislike for their own soldiers than they did for the enemy. In some parts of Kent, unpaid soldiers became vagrants, wandering around the country in armed bands. Sir Dudley Digges, a Kentishman, complained in Parliament in 1628 that his county were better able to defend themselves without soldiers than with them,

[1] Peter Clark and Paul Slack (eds.), *Crisis and Order in English Towns* (1972), pp. 173, 147–8.

[2] S.P. 16/24/9 and 26. It is possible, but, it is to be hoped, unnecessary to multiply such references almost indefinitely.

[3] Supple, pp. 99–114. I am grateful to Dr. Paul Slack for advice on the plague of 1625.

[4] S.P. 16/5/6 and 23; Whitelocke, 12–20, f. 57. I am grateful to Mr. David Hebb for much information on piracy, and on the fate of captives sold into slavery.

and claimed that he knew five farms in his county which had been given up for fear of soldiers.[1] Richard Knightley, from Northhamptonshire, complained that the soldiers, being papists, were only fit to die in ditches.[2] Others, such as Rich and Earle, were particularly alarmed because numbers of them were Irish.[3]

The reactions of the 1628 Parliament to these unpaid soldiers are perhaps best illustrated in their treatment of John Baber, Recorder of Wells. A party of soldiers arrived unexpectedly in Wells, and Baber billeted them by a warrant from one of the Deputy Lieutenants. Phelips, the indefatigable enemy of the Lieutenantcy until his appointment to it a few months later, decided that his duty 'to lay open the wrongs of my country' obliged him to launch a public attack on Baber. Baber was defended by the Deputy Lieutenant whose warrant he had executed, who said that the soldiers came 'with weapons by their sides, and merit in their hands from the King's service in France, and with necessity and hunger in their bellies. All we did was to make them subsist. No man will starve.' Baber rashly justified himself on grounds of necessity, rather than law. His case, in effect, was that he had no legal warrant for billeting the soldiers in Wells, but that, since they arrived there suddenly, and were clearly going to stay there whether authorised or not, he thought it best to arrange their billeting 'for the ease and relief of the town'. He said, 'They were all English, and necessity commanded me to yield to nature rather than law.'

The reactions of the Commons to this defence are summed up in the first words spoken in reply by Sir Dudley Digges: 'He does not satisfy me.' Digges said that, faced with illegal commands, he should have gone away. Littleton condemned him for 'forsaking the law', and Eliot for 'superofficiousness'. Sherland held that he was incorrigible, because a coward, and Coke that he 'hath made a warrant for fear, and forsaken his own profession'. The House finally decided that, by the exercise of 'great moderation', it should merely sequester him from membership, and not expel him.[4] What should have been done with the soldiers, who had returned from

---

[1] Peter Clark and Paul Slack (eds.), *Crisis and Order in English Towns* (1972), p. 147: *1628 Debates*, ii. 253.

[2] ibid., p. 367. [3] Add. 36825, f. 454.

[4] *1628 Debates*, ii. 254, 383–6. On the local side of this story, especially the increased local resistance to billeting after the Commons' debates on the subject, see Barnes, pp. 254–8.

a very miserable campaign at the Île de Rhé, was not explained. The reactions of the 1628 House of Commons to the soldiers sharply illustrate the difficulties of running a war with an amateur, unpaid, local government whose first loyalty was to their county and not to the country. The war was not to be won by Deputy Lieutenants who said, like Sir Thomas Wentworth, that 'when I was sought to, to join in these illegal ways, I always found means to be out of the way'.[1] The Parliamentary, as much as the local, evidence bears out the judgement of Professor Barnes: 'The institutions which were designed to create a "perfect militia", were 'too weak ever to have given satisfaction. The unmartial country squires were amateurs in the one art which is always best left to the professionals.' There were no professionals: as the Venetian Ambassador reported: 'Your serenity must not think of obtaining commanders of real worth from these parts, because there are none.'[2]

If the administrative pressure of the war was ideally designed to play on the strain which was already manifest between central and local government, the vexed question of the legal authority for the militia was ideally designed to inflame the constitutional fears which have been growing slowly since 1621. Much of the procedure of the militia, particularly the levying of military rates in the counties, had always been without secure legal authority, and protests against it go back as far as 1588. In 1601, a bill to give legal authority to the Deputy Lieutenants together with the J.P.s to impress men, levy rates, and equip their forces with modern weapons, was introduced in the Lords, and passed there after careful re-drafting by a committee including the Attorney General, Sir Edward Coke. Yet even in a time of war, with the Spanish army in Ireland, it was thrown out by the House of Commons.[3] In 1628, Sir Edward Coke was full of regret that no bill had ever been passed to give legal authority to the Lieutenantcy, but in the twenty-seven intervening years, he had made little attempt to remedy the omission.[4]

---

[1] *1628 Debates*, ii. 260.

[2] Barnes, pp. 278–9: *C.S.P.Ven. 1619–21*, p. 607. Any professionals there may have been were, like the future General Monk, in long-term employment abroad, where soldiering was more of a profession than it could ever become in an island kingdom in time of peace.

[3] L. O. J. Boynton, *The Elizabethan Militia* (1967), pp. 47–8, 69, 95, 168; Hassell Smith, pp. 292–3, 124 ff.: Fletcher, pp. 187–8.

[4] *1628 Debates*, ii. 79–81, 87–8, 281.

In 1604, the Expiring Laws Continuance Act repealed the Act of 1557 which had given the Elizabethan militia what legal justification it possessed. After that, the legal authority of the militia was uncertain. Some thought it was based on Edward I's Statute of Winchester, though the sections of that Act dealing with armour were repealed in the Expiring Laws Continuance Act of 1624. Some thought it was based on the Assize of Arms of 1181, one enterprising and careful Deputy Lieutenant succeeded in getting the authority of Quarter Sessions for his warrants, but the commonest opinion was that the Lieutenantcy and the militia rested simply on the prerogative.[1] If there was one certain recipe for disaster with a Parliament determined to maintain the need for statute law, it was setting out to fight a war with a militia based solely on the prerogative.

Yet, when the Commons were offered the opportunity to provide a partial remedy for the difficulty, in a bill for making the arms of the kingdom serviceable in time to come, they took no advantage of it. This bill would have given statutory authority to the musters, and to the finding of arms, but though it was persistently sponsored in the Lords, it never completed its passage through the Commons. In 1621, when it was debated at greatest length, it was apparently recommitted after protests from Edward Alford that it would impose too much charge on the country, and from another member that they would be bound to change their arms whenever fashions changed.[2] In 1626, when Sir Dudley Digges moved for a committee to consider this question, Spencer opposed a motion to put all the Deputy Lieutenants on the committee, on the ground that the House took no notice of Deputy Lieutenants.[3] John Selden, in one speech on impressment in 1628, appeared to be suggesting that obligation to military service should, as in the middle ages, be based on feudal tenures and the raising of retainers by indenture.[4] The Petition of Right, and the debates which led up to it, make most sense if they are seen as a resistance to attempts to put the administration on a war footing.[5] In none of the debates on the

[1] Grosvenor, 10 May 1628; Stowe 366, f. 158r.
[2] There is a breviate of what is probably the 1621 version of this bill in Phelips MSS. 222/2: N.R.S. iii. 343, ii. 405, iii. 219–21, 236–7.
[3] Whitelocke, 12–20, f. 45.
[4] 1628 Debates, ii, 279–81, 286–7, 290–1.
[5] This point emerges clearly if the Petition of Right is read as a sequel to the opening speech by Lord Keeper Coventry. It is perhaps also illustrated by the

scope of emergency power did the leading speakers in the Commons show any recognition that they were speaking in time of war. They were quite right that the Crown lacked legal authority for the money and the forces it had raised, but it lacked these things because Parliament had failed to provide them. In trying to raise the Forced Loan, Charles was not trying merely to score constitutional points, but to defend his kingdom. As he told the Parliament of 1626, when he dissolved it, he had a duty to defend his kingdom, which he could not perform unless his subjects gave him supply, 'whose readiness therein we had just reason to expect, for that we were first embarked in these wars at the earnest desire, and upon the large promises, of former Parliaments. . . . It never entering into our thoughts that by the breach of the House of Commons we should be driven to those extremities, either to break our faith with others (which we shall ever strive to keep inviolable) or to turn us to new courses, which might be grievous unto our loving people.'[1] In 1628, Sir Thomas Wentworth rightly, but vainly, reminded the Commons that if they did not pass the bills of arms and of Tonnage and Poundage they would force Charles to break the Petition of Right as soon as he had passed it.[2]

If, as historians have always believed, and as Charles I appears to have believed, these wars had been entered into largely in response to popular Parliamentary demand, the insular resistance to war in 1628 appears a gross inconsistency on the part of members of Parliament. Now that it is becoming clear that the demand for war originated from Buckingham, rather than from members of Parliament,[3] the isolationism of members in 1628 seems rather less inconsistent. A high proportion of the vocal demands for war made in 1621[4] and 1624 had been prompted by Buckingham. They came from members who hoped for his favour, and spoke in the hope of conciliating him, even if not King James. If the wars are seen as Buckingham's and Charles's wars, and not Parliament's wars, Parliamentary resistance to them in 1626 and 1628 can be

---

extent to which, after 1642, an effective war effort was to involve infringements of the Petition of Right. J. S. Morrill, *The Revolt of the Provinces* (1976), pp. 52, 65–6, 74–5, 105.

[1] S.P. 16/30/1.

[2] Stowe 366, f. 276^v: Add. 36825, ff. 542^v–543^r.

[3] Ruigh, pp. 16–42; below, pp. 145–53.

[4] On 1621, see Zaller, p. 154: the point is further developed in my article: 'The Foreign Policy Debate in the Parliament of 1621', *H.J.* (1977), 289–309.

seen as consistent with the generally local outlook of most members in 1621 and 1624. Sir Thomas Wentworth, who said in 1628 that he would 'not look further than the island we live in', had always been pro-Spanish and anti-war.[1] Clement Coke, Sir Edward's son, who infuriated the King in 1626 by saying it was better to die by a foreign enemy than to suffer at home, was probably more typical of Commons' views on foreign policy throughout the decade than he has been taken to be.[2] In the Lords, who did not have to concern themselves with constituencies, there was a sincere and consistent war party, in which men like Abbot, Manchester, Pembroke, Saye, Warwick, Southampton, and Essex were able to work happily together. In the Commons, even temporary supporters of the war had to think at the same time about constituency reactions. In 1624, Phelips, who was managing Buckingham's Parliamentary campaign for a war with Spain, at the same time tried to hamstring the war effort by placing the cost of supporting troops in the counties on the subsidies instead of on the military rates his consituents disliked.[3] In 1628, Selden committed himself to the view that the Commons should not discuss foreign affairs, because they would thereby engage themselves to support excessive expenditure.[4] The Commons never contained any large group of supporters of the war, able and willing to override the resistance offered by local taxpayers. The majority of them agreed to war in 1624 out of compliance more than out of belligerence. It was unfortunate for them that they were dependent on war for most of their opportunities to meet, and yet had to bring to their meetings demands which were incompatible with the prosecution of a war. Some members, of whom Wentworth is one, did not want to come to Westminster strongly enough to influence their views on foreign policy. For a few others, such as Phelips, Westminster was part of a way of life, and in 1624 that way of life had appeared to demand war.

Yet, even if Commons' enthusiasm for war had always been lukewarm, even what enthusiasm there had once been cooled very fast between 1624 and 1628. Some members can be shown to have changed their minds thoroughly between 1624 and 1628. Sir John Eliot, who in 1625 was welcoming the end of the 'degenerate vices

---

[1] *1628 Debates*, ii. 262. Knowler, pp. 15, 24.
[2] Whitelocke, 12–20, f. 28ᵛ.   [3] Ruigh, p. 254n.
[4] *1628 Debates*, ii. 444. For similar remarks by Eliot, see ibid., pp. 365, 401.

of a long corrupted peace', was saying in 1628 that 'looking on our late disasters I tremble to think of sending more abroad'. Eliot at least had some consistency behind his apparent change of front. Part of it appears to have been caused by a sincere concern about the misery of soldiers and sailors, which was particularly visible in his part of the West Country. Part, also, appears to have been the result of the fact that Eliot was consistently pro-French. He claimed that it had been a 'cornerstone' of Elizabethan foreign policy to remain in alliance with France, and the timing of his breach with Buckingham coincides closely with Buckingham's breach with France.[1] It is rather harder to find consistency in the foreign policy views of Sir Edward Coke: in 1624, he was claiming that England never prospered so well as when at war with Spain, and that the thought of war with Spain made him feel seven years younger. In 1628, he was saying in more cautious tones that 'a pure defensive war is a vast thing, yet in an island defensive war is the safest'.[2]

In saying this, Coke was beginning to show some strategic perception. In military history, the period was one in which the advantage tended to rest with the defensive The Armada campaign, which did most to give the English such an inflated idea of their military significance, had been a defensive operation. Even in Queen Elizabeth's Spanish wars, the offensive operations on land, in the Netherlands and in Ireland, had not been conspicuous successes. It has been a common tendency, both then and now, to throw all the blame for English military failures in the 1620s on to the very conspicuous shoulders of the Duke of Buckingham. The charge is tempting, because it contains much truth. Buckingham

[1] N.P. i. 42–5; Stowe 366, f. 212ʳ: Add. 36825, ff. 423–4. For Eliot, saying something was a cornerstone of Elizabethan policy was normally synonymous with saying he agreed with it. *1628 Debates*, ii. 247. S.P. 16/27/17, the questions asked of Eliot when he was imprisoned for his attacks on Buckingham in 1626, include the question whether he had been in conference with any foreign ambassador.

[2] S.P. 14/160/63; B.L. Add. MS. 18597, f. 74ᵛ. *1628 Debates*, ii. 250. Professor Pocock, after a study of Coke's thought, concluded that he had a mind 'as nearly insular as a human being's can be', and this judgement is confirmed by Coke's political record. It is perhaps symptomatic of Coke's insularity that when James proposed to keep him out of the Parliament of 1624 by sending him to Ireland, this supposed champion of English naval glory revealed that one of his reasons for being terrified of the proposal was that he had never been to sea. Chamberlain, 17 Jan. 1624. J. G. A. Pocock, *The Ancient Constitution and the Feudal Law* (Cambridge, 1957), p. 56.

committed a number of crass errors in the prosecution of the war. In particular, the decision to keep the troops under arms through the winter when they returned from La Rochelle in the autumn of 1627 caused a large amount of civilian resistance for no clear military purpose. Barnes has described this decision as 'idiocy', and Fletcher as 'lunatic'.[1] Yet even here, some of the blame should rest on the House of Commons, which failed to vote the money needed to pay off the troops.

Yet, just because the Duke of Buckingham's mistakes are so visible, they tend to upstage the rest of the evidence, and so distract attention from it. Charles was certainly right that in any catalogue of the reasons for English military failure in the 1620s, the failure of the House of Commons to discover any means of collecting an adequate supply has a very important place. Even if Buckingham had been a commander on the scale of Gustavus Aldolphus, he could not have mustered an effective military effort on the money available to him. Nor did it appear that, even with more goodwill, members of Parliament would have found it easy to make more money available to him. The increasing scale and complexity of warfare demanded, as Professor Howard has pointed out, considerable changes in the relationship between the State and local communities.[2] In England, those changes had not taken place, and there was a widespread desire that they should not take place. An effective war effort was incompatible with the self-governing counties which were the ideal of Stuart England. It was only in the civil war, with an enemy actually within the kingdom, that the localism of the English counties was broken down enough to make an effective war effort possible. The experience of war suggested that there was much to be said for King James's view that England was not equipped for war, and would be well advised to stay out of it. This view enjoyed more covert support in the Commons than was apparent in the early part of the decade. In matters of foreign affairs, the Commons were not seizing the initiative: they were evading it. Some of them, at least, were evading it because they realized it was beyond England's resources. Sir Edwin Sandys, on 20 April, 1626, spoke of 'the great foresight of the difficulty of the work. The better part of the business abroad may be paid by this small and not very rich island. The three

---

[1] Barnes, p. 255; Fletcher, p. 197.
[2] Michael Howard, *War in European History* (1976), pp. 55, 67–9.

subsidies and three fifteenths in regard of all the businesses in Germany etc. are as much as nothing.'[1]

It is perhaps not surprising that some members, faced by the impossibility of doing injury to a foreign enemy, should have sought for a domestic one. It was a long-standing habit among those who remembered Elizabeth's reign to think of English Catholics as a potential fifth column in support of a foreign invasion.[2] Dr. Clifton has shown that by the 1620s, this habit was often dormant in dealings with neighbours in time of peace, but could easily be stirred up by the arrival of strangers or in time of war.[3] Against this background, the billeting of Irish Catholic soldiers during an unsuccessful war was an ideal prescription for hysteria. It was a common phenomenon, particularly visible in the debates of 26 November 1621, for discussions of war to turn away into attacks on English recusants. Placed beside the inability of the English to do serious injury to their enemies, the phenomenon looks remarkably like what is now known as displacement aggression.[4] The wars, then, not merely shook English administration: they perhaps also made a big contribution to the religious tension which had been so conspicuously dormant in 1621–4.

That Parliaments were called for wars was a long-standing convention. It was continued, not only in the hope of extraordinary supply, but also in the hope of involving county administrators in the war effort. The wars had been Buckingham's wars, but after his death in the summer of 1628 the Spanish war still retained supporters in the Council, notably Pembroke, who hoped that another campaign, preceded by a happy Parliament, might enable England to recover her 'lost honour'.[5] By the winter of 1628–9, the causes of the continuation, of the war, and of the survival of Parliament, had become identified. This was an unfortunate identification for a war-weary Parliament. The session of 1629, the last of the decade, was only called because Charles still hoped, both for a legal grant of Tonnage and Poundage, and that it might still

---

[1] Whitelocke, 12–21, ff. 143–4. J. P. Cooper, *New Cambridge Modern History*, iv. 531 ff.

[2] On the habits of mind on which this practice was based, see W. Haller, *Foxe's Book of Martyrs and the Elect Nation* (1971), *passim*.

[3] Robin Clifton, 'The Fear of Popery', in *Origins*, pp. 143–67.

[4] See, for example, *C.S.P.D. 1625–6*, vol. vi, no. 41, S.P. 16/12/71 and *C.S.P.D. 1627–8*, vol. lxxxviii, no. 23.

[5] *C.S.P.D. 1628–9*, vol. cxxi, no. 66. I am grateful to Mr. Paul Fowle for this reference.

prove possible to continue the war successfully. He was disappointed in both hopes, and the decision he took in March 1629 was not
so much a decision to dispense with Parliaments, as a decision to
avoid wars. There seems to be less evidence than might have been
expected for any final decision on Charles's part to dispense with
Parliaments. Occasional rumours of a Parliament continued during
the 1630s, and two reversions were granted to the office of Clerk
of the Parliaments.

It seems that Charles had firmly decided that his father had
been right to keep England out of wars. Even after the political
tensions of the 1620s, the political temperature dropped when the
war pressure was taken off. Throughout the 1620s, the men who
had given Charles so much trouble in his Parliaments continued
to give him at least moderately loyal service in local government.
Phelips and Seymour, Earle and Hampden, Digges and Noy, and
their fellows continued to serve Charles in the counties after the
Parliamentary disputes were over. Even in 1630, England, though
a much less united country than it had been in 1620, was not a
country ripe for revolution. It was, however, a country which
could not fight. In the middle of the Thirty Years' War, it must
be an open question how long a monarchy which was unable to
fight was able to survive. It is to the credit of Charles, as well as
of the English gentry, that he managed to do so for eleven years.
In 1639–40, when war came again, it produced all the same
troubles it had produced in the 1620s, and did so in a much less
favourable political atmosphere. In England, as in Catalonia, the
political troubles of 1640 were begun by a government putting
unacceptable pressure on its subjects to try to equip itself for war.[1]
It is against this background, of a court divided on foreign policy
in a country unable to fight, that the political story of the 1620s
should be told. Perhaps there was some force in the view expressed
by Sir Robert Phelips before the Thirty Years' War had begun:

The English, having found by experience that the power to have authority
among foreigners is more safe and necessary than possessing foreign

---

[1] J. H. Elliott, 'Revolts in the Spanish Monarchy', in *Preconditions of Revolution in Early Modern Europe*, ed. Robert Forster and Jack P. Greene, pp. 122–9,
and also the remarks of Professor Mousnier, *ubi supra*, p. 131. Some of the
parallels here drawn were suggested by Professor Elliott in 'The King and the
Catalans', *Cambridge Historical Journal* (1953), 253.

dominion, they have, like the tortoise, withdrawn themselves into their own shell, from whence they do not upon slight motives sally.[1]

This was the view to which Charles I, and probably Sir Robert himself, wisely returned in 1629. It had been proved to be justified by experience.

[1] Katherine S. Van Eerde, 'The Spanish Match through an English Protestant's Eyes', *Huntington Library Quarterly* (1968–9), 65.

II

The Parliament of 1621: Business as Usual?

I. THE FIRST SESSION

IF the events of a Parliament were the interaction between the concerns of members of the court and those of members' neighbours and constituents left in the country, it was to be expected that the first session of the Parliament of 1621 should be discursive and inconclusive. The chief concerns of the members of the court were with three things which never happened, and those of the country at large with something which was not under English control. As a blueprint for a successful point of contact, this was not ideal. In the face of these difficulties, it is to the credit of those involved, including the King, that they succeeded in making the first session as harmonious as they did.

The three chief concerns of the court were with waiting for, and lobbying for or against, a war which did not happen, with watching for the development of an attack on the Duke of Buckingham which never got off the ground, and with watching eagerly for the growth of a reversionary interest which Prince Charles was too prudent, or too shy, to allow to crystallize.[1] By far the most widespread concern in the country was with what they called the 'decay of trade', which has become known to modern readers as the 'great depression', a mystifying phenomenon in which, as John Chamberlain reported, there was 'plenty of all things but money'. This physical scarcity of coin was causing a dislocation of economic life so severe that contemporaries could only compare it to the effect of war.[2] Chamberlain said many country people were offering to pay their rents in corn, or cattle, or whatever else they could find, simply for want of money. This want of money, when all other things appeared to be plentiful, defied explanation. Chamberlain,

---

[1] W. Notestein, F. H. Relf, and Hartley Simpson, *Commons' Debates in 1621*, (New Haven, 1935) iv. 119. Further references in this chapter are to this edition unless otherwise stated. Hastings, p. 16; *Lords' Debates* (ed. Relf), p. 49. In this chapter, further references to *Lords' Debates* are to this edition.
[2] Chamberlain, 10 Feb. 1621; Supple, p. 53.

claiming that 'plenty hath made us poor', admitted that 'the reason we cannot yet reach unto', and James asked the Parliament, in his opening speech, 'to search out the reasons of this scarcity of money, which neither himself nor his Council could find out'[1] As usual, those mystified by the forces of economics all seized the chance to blame their favourite scapegoats, ranging from Catholics sending out money to educate their children abroad to smokers allowing their money to be carried out of the kingdom for the import of tobacco. Sir James Perrott, who was unhappily married, put much of the blame on women coming to London and spending too much on clothes and jewellery.[2]

But if, as many of the closing speeches of the first session suggest, constituents had looked to their members of Parliament to come home with a cure for the depression,[3] they were doomed to disappointment, for we can now understand, as they could not, that the main causes of the depression were beyond English control. Professor Supple, in a definitive account, has shown that the main cause of the depression lay in a series of currency devaluations in the Baltic, which meant that silver fetched a higher price there than it did in England.[4] Hence, it was carried out to the place where it was worth most. In their attempts to deal with the depression, members of the Commons were doomed to failure. Moreover, they were being asked for supply at a time when, as Chamberlain foresaw, the shortage of coin was going to make the gathering of supply particularly difficult and unpopular.[5] Dr. Hirst has shown that constituency expectations that members should obtain relief in return for supply were growing. Many members were alarmed that the growth of these expectations was going in step with the decline of their ability to satisfy them.[6]

Nor were members of either House able to offer much assistance in the leading concerns of members of the court. Throughout the

1 Chamberlain, 9 Nov. 1620; v. 429.

2 iv. 436–7; vi. 196.

3 iii. 334 (Sir Samuel Sandys), 344 (Delbridge), 345 (Neale and Sir Edwin Sandys), 351 (Gooch), and 353 (Alford): 'All people live upon hopes, and that of this Parliament. We must not carry them home rattles.' See also Sir Edwin Sandys, iii. 374 on the inadequacy of the bills passed as relief from the depression, and iv. 104 on the danger of a Peasants' Revolt like that in Germany in 1525.

4 Supple, pp. 52–98.

5 Chamberlain, 10 Feb. 1621.

6 Hirst, pp. 169–72.

first session, they were not able, and did not try, to make any serious contribution to the leading issue of the moment, that of war or peace.[1] The unexpected calling of a Parliament, after seven years without one, made well-informed people about the court believe that James was calling it in order to announce and rally support for a war.[2] Yet though James was not averse to creating such an impression, he had not called the Parliament to announce a war. He had called it, as he honestly admitted in his opening speech, in the hope that the threat of war would fortify the efforts he was making to negotiate a successful peace.[3] As Secretary Calvert put it in his motion for supply, 'When so many swords are drawn, it is very inconvenient his Majesty's should be sheathed.'[4] Members of the Commons were being asked to give supply in order that the King could convincingly threaten to enter a war he still hoped not to be forced to join. On foreign affairs, then, members were being asked to do that most difficult of things: to wait until they were needed.

The need to wait was prolonged beyond expectation by the death of King Philip III of Spain on March 31, two months after the Parliament had assembled. In the end, Parliament was kept waiting, with nothing to contribute to the foreign affairs debate in the Council, from February until June. That members quietly, or almost quietly, submitted to this restraint on their discussions for so long must show that they did not come to Westminster in order to seize the initiative on foreign affairs. During this long period of waiting, James hoped that the depression would provide enough subjects for discussion to keep members busy. It almost did, but investigation of the depression led into questions of the restraint of trade. Discussion of the restraint of trade led members into questions of the enforcement of restrictions by patents, in which many courtiers had a vested interest. In the issue of patents, by which many countrymen were grieved, and through which ambitious men at court could hope to discredit each other, the

[1] For members' self-restraint on this subject during the first session, see my article, 'The Foreign Policy Debate in the Parliament of 1621', *H.J.*, vol. 20, no. 2 (1977), 289–309.
[2] Zaller, pp. 17 ff., S.P. 81/18/155.
[3] iv. 5, v. 427. The King said he must be provided for a war, for if he could not regain the Palatinate otherwise, he would hazard his state and the Crown, and the blood of himself and the Prince.
[4] iv. 14.

concerns of King, court, and country at last found a point of contact. In attacks on the patent for alehouses, run by two servants of Lord Treasurer Mandeville, Lionel Cranfield, the ambitious reforming Councillor who was shortly to become Lord Treasurer, could find a common cause with Edward Alford, the champion of the Sussex countrymen.

In the Council, the underlying division of opinion was on the question of peace or war. 1621 was the third year of the Thirty Years' War, when it was still at stake whether it would remain local, or turn into what it became, a European, and indeed, the first world war. There was a party on the English Council, among whom the Earl of Southampton seems to have been the most vocal, who hoped the war would spread. Others, including James, equally strongly hoped that it would not. James was not helped in his desire to avert the spread of war by the fact that his son-in-law, Frederick, Elector Palatine, had played the part of the match which lit the fuse. In 1618, Frederick had allowed himself to be drawn into a war with the Holy Roman Emperor about whether he, as elective King, or the Emperor as hereditary King, should succeed to the kingdom of Bohemia. James had no sympathy with Frederick's attempt to become King of Bohemia. The battle of the White Mountain, in the winter of 1620, when Frederick was driven out of Bohemia, caused profound dismay to many people in England, but it was of less concern to James. It was a different matter for James when the Emperor began to attack Frederick's hereditary lands in the Palatinate. For James, the crucial question here appeared to be whether Spain would help or restrain the Emperor.[1]

Spain was bound to the Emperor by the strongest ties of family and common interest, but Spanish finances were not in the healthiest state, and their far-flung empire, with its weak communications, was exceptionally vulnerable to war. In hoping that Spanish influence would be exerted towards peace, James was not hoping a vain hope. For Spain, the crucial point was that their Twelve Years' Truce with the Dutch was due to expire in April 1621. In the diplomatic background to the Parliament of 1621, the expiry of the Twelve Years' Truce was perhaps of greater importance than the Palatinate. When the Parliament began, the Dutch ambassador

---

[1] On questions to do with foreign affairs in 1621, I am grateful for the help and advice of Mr. David Hebb.

in England was busy soliciting for English assistance if war broke out at the end of the truce. James was unwilling to make promises, but hoped that Spanish fear that he might assist the Dutch would influence the Spaniards towards peace. If he did assist the Dutch, the war between Frederick and the Emperor, in Germany, and the war between the Dutch and Spain, would rapidly merge into a general European war. It was a prospect he hoped Spain might approach with reluctance. James's hopes were perhaps not misplaced during the rule of Philip III and the Duke of Uceda. They grew fainter during the new regime of Philip IV and the Count Duke of Olivares, but the character of the new regime took time to become apparent.[1]

The posture James wanted to adopt, then, was that of a regime ready, but not eager, to fight. If James was to be ready to fight, he had to have money. This is one reason why, contrary to normal practice, the motion for subsidies was introduced at the very beginning of the Parliament, before the Commons had done any business whatever. Secretary Calvert said the King desired to recover the Palatinate by treaty, 'and if he cannot get it by fair terms, he will win it by war'. Members were warned, alarmingly but realistically, that if they went to the Palatinate with a land army, a million pounds would not be enough to pay for it.[2] This motion for subsidies, coming so early in the session, naturally provoked grumbles. Members had been warned, in the opening speech by Lord Chancellor Bacon, that their actions would have an important influence on whether the King called future Parliaments, and by Calvert, in his motion for supply, that it was their task 'to procure from his Majesty the love and frequency of Parliaments'.[3] They do not appear to have felt that they had much choice about their decision to vote a grant of supply, and bowed to the inevitable with a moderately good grace. As Christopher Brooke, Recorder of York, said, King and subject were like landlord and tenant: they must pay rent. Addressed to an assembly of landlords many of whom were having difficulty collecting their rents because of the depression, the analogy had a double force.

Their chief worry appears to have been about whether they could get away with the grant with their own countries. Sir Henry

[1] J. H. Elliott, *Imperial Spain* (1963), pp. 318–22.
[2] ii. 87; iv. 57.
[3] Hastings, p. 2, iv. 56, ii. 86, v. 464.

Poole warned them not to be too bold with the countrymen's purses until they brought them something, and others said that, considering the universal want, two subsidies were as burdensome as four in former times.[1] Most members made do with the hope expressed by Coke and Crew, that because they had been generous and 'unmerchantly' with the King, he would be the more generous with them. They also agreed to two proposals by Edward Alford. One was that they should take care, in the preamble of the subsidy bill, to satisfy the subject. This was attempted by a clause declaring that the giving of subsidies at the beginning of a Parliament was not to be taken for a precedent. The other proposal was that 'the assessing to be as was usual by neighbours'.[2]

In agreeing to Alford's proposal, members of the Commons showed the adamantine resistance to the principle of honest assessment for taxation which was one of the hallmarks of the period. This resistance was shown more strikingly, because more unexpectedly, in the opposition to a bill for reforming the register of those liable to jury service. This bill, which was supported by Sir Edward Coke, provided for J.P.s to draw up, and the clerk of the peace to keep, a list of those liable to jury service, subject to a property qualification of £10. This would have met two much denounced abuses: the partisan empanelling of jurors by the sheriff, which might often alter the result of a trial, and the lack of sufficient jurors, which meant that bystanders at Assizes were liable to be called in without warning to serve on a jury. Yet the bill was bitterly opposed, especially by Sir Samuel Sandys, who thought it 'very dangerous'. He asked how the J.P.s were to assess men's liability under the property qualification: 'How shall they do it? By commission, or at random? If at random, may bring in friends, and so pack juries: if a record thereof, £10 land will be means to draw them to great charge at the subsidy.' In this speech,

---

[1] ii. 86, 91; v. 465.

[2] iv. 60, ii. 93, v. 498–9, L.J. 51. Professor Elizabeth Read Foster has now discovered a printed text of the Subsidy Act in S.P. 46/65, ff. 122–40. The Act recites that the Parliament's 'timely' resolution on subsidies, though not the sum, 'exceedeth the precedent of all former Parliaments, and which we humbly pray may be no precedent for the future'. The recital of the motives for giving, 'well knowing that the ordinary revenues of your Crown are not able to support the extraordinary expenses which the necessity of present occurrences do and may daily draw upon your Majesty', reflects the prevailing uncertainty about whether James intended war. There is no record of any ground for Alford's fear that assessment might be by some novel method.

most of the greatest difficulties of early Stuart local government were encapsulated. In spite of this opposition, the bill was sent to committee on 19 April, but it is no surprise to find that it had not emerged from committee in June. In November, at the beginning of the second session, it was still pending. Further bills introduced on this subject in the Lords enjoyed no better fortune, and throughout the decade the empanelling of jurors, like the assessment of the subsidy, remained unreformed.[1] Subject to these provisos, the Commons agreed to a grant of two subsidies (about £140,000), while declining to vote any fifteenths because these were too burdensome to the poor.

James was delighted with his success in obtaining subsidies at the beginning of the Parliament, though he had to wait from February until Easter for the bill to wend its way through three readings in each House and to receive the royal assent. When the Houses rose for Easter, he expressed his gratitude by knighting Speaker Richardson in full Parliament. As a grant towards a war which might cost a million pounds, £140,000 would not have gone very far, but only Sir Julius Caesar among the Councillors gave any hint that the King might want more. If, as is possible, James was allowing the decision for peace or war to be influenced by the size of the grant he got from the Commons, the influence would be against war.

Meanwhile, the process of preparedness for war could be assisted by two bills first introduced in the Lords, the bill of arms and the bill against the export of iron ordnance. Both of these seem to have been the subject of some division within the Council. The arms bill provided legal authority for equipping the militia with arms standardized according to the 'modern form', and was enthusiastically supported by Lord Chancellor Bacon and the Earl of Arundel, yet Lord Treasurer Mandeville said, in tones reminiscent of Edward Alford, that since the people were already so burdened with charges, and their cattle and corn fetched such a small price, the date at which this bill came into operation should be postponed. The bill passed rapidly through the Lords, and was taken over in the Commons by Sir Edward Cecil, former

---

[1] *C.J.* 582: iv. 237, iii. 19, v. 80, vii. 303, Hawarde, 20 Nov. On the abuses this bill was designed to remedy, see Hassell Smith, pp. 145, 150–1, and Cockburn, pp. 118–20, 106, 115–16 and other refs. For further bills on jurors, see *L.J.* 683, 880.

commander of the English troops in the Netherlands. There it was lost in the press of business, and never completed its passage.[1]

The demand for a ban on the export of ordinance had been a loud one in some quarters since 1601.[2] In the Lords in 1621, the bill for it rapidly received two readings, was committed in February, and was then delivered to the Lord Treasurer, who opposed it.[3] It then seems to have vanished in committee, and was not sent down to the Commons till 5 December. Such dilatoriness was unusual in the Lords, and suggests a sharp division of opinion. This impression is confirmed by the proceedings of the Commons, where Cranfield, on 30 April, asked them to prepare their own bill on the subject, only to be opposed by Secretary Calvert, who said that if the King's hands were tied he could not export to his allies, and they should leave the question in the hands of the King and the Council.[4] Like so much else in the Parliament of 1621, this bill was never completed. Since ordnance was being exported to Spain, it is perhaps not fanciful to see the tussle over this bill as involving the dispute within the Council about the question of peace or war.

Perhaps the nearest the Commons came to considering these questions in the first session was in a very lukewarm debate about freedom of speech. The question had been opened at the very beginning of the session by Perrott, who wanted to know how they could discuss supply for the Palatinate without discussing foreign affairs.[5] The issue was raised again a week later, on 12 February, when it was proposed that they should take up the case of the members imprisoned after the Parliament of 1614. Phelips, who was particularly concerned about freedom of speech as a principle (though very cautious in exercising it in practice), supported the proposal. Coke (who was still a Councillor) urged that it should be 'laid aside'. The most remarkable speeches were made by Crew and Sir Edwin Sandys. Crew said that liberty of speech would not be granted for such things as Elizabethan M.P.s were punished for, but only within the bounds of loyalty and duty. Sir Edwin

---

[1] Hastings, p. 17: iii. 343, ii. 405, iii. 219, 236–7, iv. 334, 390. See also above, p. 48n, below, pp. 222, 384 ff.

[2] J. E. Neale, *Elizabeth I and her Parliaments*, ii (1957), 419–22. N.R.N. Tyacke, 'Sir Robert Wroth and the Parliament of 1604', *B.I.H.R.* (May 1977), 120–5.

[3] *L.J.* 13, 34: Hastings, p. 10.

[4] iv. 276, ii. 333.   [5] iv. 15.

Sandys said that the Elizabethan cases of imprisoned members before 1589 were not to the point. In one of them, he said, a bill was brought in 'which would have overthrown all ecclesiastical government' (Sandys was the son of a bishop), and in the other, he said, a member had tried to raise the question of the succession for his own interest: 'and in such case reason of state is above claim of privilege'. Peter Wentworth's son Thomas, who was a member of this Parliament, did not speak.[1] Three days later, a message from the King, glossed by Secretary Calvert, induced the Commons as a whole to leave this subject aside.[2] An attempt by Sir Edward Giles to open the explosive subject of impositions was ignored.[3] This debate suggests that, given a longer period of calm, James might easily have secured acceptance of the novel limits he and Elizabeth had tried to impose on freedom of speech. It certainly does not suggest that freedom of speech as an issue of principle had the importance in February which it had acquired by December of the same year.

Having got the subsidy bill into committee, where they could debate such innocuous issues as whether Oxford or Cambridge should be mentioned first, the Commons were left free to turn their attention to the depression, as they had been invited to do in James's opening speech. Most of them were very willing to do this, but unfortunately, the subject was booby-trapped. The one subject which was even more taboo than foreign affairs was that of the King's right to levy impositions on trade, the issue which had broken up the previous Parliament. Many members, notably Alford and Delbridge of Barnstaple, believed that one of the main reasons for the decay of trade was that it was burdened with more impositions than it could support. They just managed to let this view be known without starting a constitutional debate on the King's right to levy impositions, but, in doing so, they were walking a tightrope.[4]

It was much harder to discuss the depression without running into the constitutional questions of what powers could be conferred by patents or charters. It was also very hard, in 1621, to propose enforcing machinery for any bill without causing some member to object that it set up a 'monopoly'. Even so apparently neutral a measure as the bill to conserve fish by prohibiting fishing with fine mesh nets was attacked on the ground that it set up a

[1] iv. 39–40; ii. 57–62.
[2] iv. 54–5; but see also v. 463n, ii. 84.   [3] ii. 55.   [4] iii. 373.

'monopoly'. The same objection was raised against a bill giving Trinity House power to supervise lighthouses, and against an apparently innocuous bill, sponsored by Alderman Whitson of Bristol, to extend the traditional apprenticeship system to the making of cards for wool.[1] This particular bill went ahead, but the fact that it was said to create a monopoly seems to indicate an atmosphere in which there was for a while no clear distinction between a personal monopoly and a traditional company with power to discipline its own members.[2]

Other business arising out of the depression led more directly into the labyrinth of patents. One example is the bill for free fishing, vehemently supported by West Country fishing interests, marshalled by Neale of Dartmouth and by Glanville, Recorder of Plymouth. This bill, which was vigorously prosecuted in every Parliament of the decade, and never reached the statute book, was a direct attack on Sir Ferdinando Gorges's patent for the plantation of New England. West Country fishermen fishing off Newfoundland were restrained by Gorges's patent from landing in New England to cut wood, and they claimed that they were thereby restrained from catching large quantities of fish, which they could have exported for coin. The bill was also supported by some members of the Virginia Company, led by Sir Edwin Sandys, who objected to the closing of the frontier of what he called 'north Virginia'. This bill raised in an acute form the question whether America was subject to the English Parliament, and produced an alarming declaration from Secretary Calvert that 'new conquests are to be ordered by the will of the conqueror. Virginia is not annexed to the crown of England and therefore not subject to the laws of this House.'[3] This vehement opposition may give some indication of why the bill never completed its passage.

In the attack on charters, the crucial charter was that of the Merchant Adventurers, which was examined, debated, and disputed throughout the Parliament, though no firm conclusion was ever reached about it. The Merchant Adventurers were certainly

---

[1] iv. 250; v. 283; ii. 68.

[2] See the speeches on 14 Feb. by Sir George More and Sir William Spencer, iv. 50, ii. 78. The ability to distinguish between monopolists and companies quickly revived after the Monopolies Act of 1624. See Robert Ashton, 'Conflicts of Concessionary Interest in Early Stuart England', in *Trade, Government and Economy in Pre-Industrial England: Essays Presented to F. J. Fisher*, ed. D. C. Coleman and A. H. John (1976), pp. 125–8.   [3] iii. 81–2, iv. 256.

an example of trade restrained by charter, and restrained in favour
of the big London merchants at the expense of provincial merchants. The argument in favour of the Adventurers was that the
big merchants could afford, by buying up a regular 'stint' of cloth
and, if need be, holding it before selling it, to provide a secure
purchaser of cloth, and thereby diminish unemployment. The
argument against them was that they were a London group who
shut out provincial merchants who otherwise could have played a
big part in trade. It is relevant to the debates on the Merchant
Adventurers that, as Professor Supple pointed out, in terms of
economic interests, a Parliament was a provincial assembly, in
sharp contrast to the London-based mercantile lobbies which
stood a better chance of gaining the ear of the Council between
Parliaments.[1]

If one man had a rougher ride than others in the first session of
1621, it was not one of the Councillors, but Towerson of London
and the Merchant Adventurers. For example, it was Towerson
who carried the full weight of opposing two agricultural protection
measures, the bill against the import of corn, and the bill against
the import of Irish cattle. Both bills were designed to keep up the
price received by home farmers, and it was fortunate that they
were not passed before the disastrous harvest of 1621. On the bill
against the import of corn, Alford alleged that Londoners, if
allowed, would import so much corn that they would bring the
price down till Sussex farmers were undone. Some eastern
members replied that inability to import rye from the Baltic
would further increase difficulties with the outflow of coin.[2]
Towerson retorted that London needed so much corn that, if
imports were banned, in a bad year Londoners might starve before
they were permitted again. On the Irish cattle bill, Towerson
again had to argue for the necessity for London of imports of
Irish beef, and Neale for its necessity for supplying ships.[3] Both
these bills produced interesting declarations by country gentlemen
sitting for borough seats, who said they felt bound by constituency
interest rather than their personal good. Sir Dudley Digges, a
Kentish gentleman sitting for Tewkesbury, said that the Irish
cattle bill would be for his personal benefit, but 'We must

[1] Supple, p. 71.
[2] iii. 280–3, *Nicholas*, ii. 88–9.
[3] iii. 213–15, ii. 356–7, iv. 322–3.

remember the places we serve for.' Wentworth (probably Peter Wentworth's son, M.P. for Oxford City) said that gentlemen who felt the bill was in their own particular interest should remember the corporations (*sic*) for which they served, who would benefit by the cheapness of the meat.[1] On the bill against import of corn, they were warned that 'We serve most of us for towns who may think that we have made this bill for our own profit and to their undoing.'[2] After so much time-consuming debate, it is not surprising, either that none of these bills completed their passage, or that the Commons felt bound to make an order that a member with a vested interest in the subject under discussion must declare his interest.[3]

The failure of these bills to complete their passage appears, in the main, not to be due to the Commons' inefficiency, but to their ideas about proper procedure. Most of them emerged from committee, which was the normal blocking point in the legislative process in 1621. They were then hotly debated on report stage, and, when hotly debated, were not pressed to a division, but referred back to committee. This appears, like some other Commons' proceedings, to indicate a desire to establish consensus, rather than to measure division. It was thus possible, as it often is on a modern committee, for a few determined opponents to talk a measure to a standstill without being able to muster a majority against it. In the seventeenth-century context, this made good sense. There is a point beyond which intensity of opposition to a measure indicates unwillingness to enforce it, and the enforcement of legislation was already difficult enough, without passing laws in the teeth of many of those who would have to enforce them. Thus the speed with which a measure progressed through the Commons may indicate, not how much enthusiasm it commanded, but how uncontroversial it was. The tobacco bill, the bill for free buying and selling of wools, and the bill against the import of corn probably generated more excitement than bills on the Sabbath and alehouses.[4] Yet it was the Sabbath and alehouses bills which progressed rapidly. No one was prepared to admit to being against the Sabbath except James and one reputedly Catholic

[1] iii. 215: v. 157.
[2] iv. 358.
[3] iv. 273.
[4] The tobacco bill passed the Commons, but only after prolonged delay.

member who was expelled for his pains,[1] and no gentleman at all was prepared to admit to being in favour of alehouses. There was, then, a tendency for the bills completed first to be ones which did not rouse great excitement.

This is one reason why the attempts to tackle the depression produced such small results: every bill on the subject became a matter for dispute between rival vested interests. Another reason is the intellectual inadequacy of most of the attempts to offer explanations. Two members appear to have anticipated Professor Supple in linking the depression with Baltic currency devaluations. One was Glanville, who said that 'Our money being at a greater value abroad than it is here, much is exported for gain, but no foreign coin imported, because it would be to great loss.'[2] The other, in an imperfectly reported speech, was Lionel Cranfield. Sir Edwin Sandys's committee on the decay of money did, it is true, record the loss by exchange 'because our money is better than theirs beyond sea'[3] among their explanations, but they were much more interested in explanations for which someone could be blamed. One of the favourite scapegoats was the East India Company, which was widely accused of exporting large quantities of bullion in order to pay for luxury imports. In fact, as the East India men rightly claimed, they recovered much of the bullion they took out by re-exports. They were thus able to buy much of the coin they took to the East Indies in Spain rather than England.[4] However, truth was less exciting than myth, and the East India Company duly found its way into the list of 'causes' of the decay of trade. It is hard to resist the impression that Sandys, as committee chairman, regarded it largely as a vehicle for getting through his own bill to protect Virginia tobacco against Spanish competition. Other causes, like the import of salt from France, and the sums sent over to sustain nuns in 'the College of English women at Liege',[5] carry very little conviction.

[1] For Perrott's brusque dismissal of James's message discouraging the Sabbath bill, iv. 75–6. For the reputed Catholicism of Shepherd, the only other avowed opponent of the bill, see Wilfrid R. Prest, *The Inns of Court under Elizabeth I and the Early Stuarts* (1972), p. 184.

[2] v. 3, iv. 19, vi. 17.

[3] iv. 105.

[4] K. N. Chaudhuri, 'The East India Company and the Export of Treasure in the Early Seventeenth Century', *Ec.H.R.* (1963–4), 23–38. See also p. 183 below (speech by Maurice Abbot).

[5] iv. 113.

Nevertheless, some constructive ideas did come out of the debates on the depression. One was a bill to lower the rate of interest from 10 per cent to 8 per cent. It is unfortunately impossible to discover from the Parliamentary debates who originated this bill, but it does not appear to have enjoyed the sort of support it did in 1624, when it passed into law: its slow progress to second reading suggests that no one very influential was concerned to push it forward. It received a first reading on 18 April, and a hotly contested second reading on 7 May, and then vanished into committee. It was supported by Sir Henry Poole, an obscure Gloucestershire country gentleman, and opposed by Sir Edward Montagu, on the ground that usury was sinful, by Dr. Gooch the civil lawyer, on the ground that it might lead to a flight of hot money, and as impracticable by Alderman Whitson of Bristol. Guy and Gooch feared it might interfere with mortgages already made. The nomination to the committee of all the members for London may perhaps give a clue to concern with the bill.[1]

A few members, but not nearly as many as used to be thought, hoped trade might be restored by reopening the trade to the West Indies, which would have led to conflict with Spain. Save for a very few members, such as Sir Nathaniel Rich, the West India lobby in the 1620s was not an economic interest, but an offshoot of the anti-Spanish group within the Council. Sir Henry Mainwaring, a Kentishman with seafaring interests, wanted a Navigation Act, imposing on American colonists an obligation to trade in English bottoms.[2] Perhaps the most interesting suggestion, apparently made by the farmers of the tobacco customs, and accepted by Sandys, was that re-exports should be exempt from custom, and so 'England might become a magazine to serve other nations as well as the low countries'.[3]

From the very beginning of the Parliament, business on the depression had been competing for attention and time with the much more exciting grievance of the patents. Perrott drew attention to the issue on the first full day of debate, and was referred to a select committee the next day on the motion of Edward Alford

---

[1] iv. 233; iv. 314–15, ii. 350, iii. 184, *C.J.* 611. It is noteworthy that, contrary to normal custom, the committee included some who were opposed to the body of the bill. For the type of reasoning behind the bill, see Perrott, 26 Nov., ii. 447, iv. 437, iii. 449.   [2] iv. 368.

[3] iv. 217, *C.J.* 579. For the application of this proposal to sugar by Sandys in 1624, see B.L. Add. MS. 26639, f. 6ʳ.

and Sir Edward Sackville.[1] This debate, and especially Mompesson's attempt to divert it, shows how easily debates on patents grew out of the subject of the depression.

Before the Parliament met, Chamberlain had expected the patents to provide material for constitutional conflict. He ranked them with impositions, as issues which 'are grown so grievous that of necessity they must be spoken of', while 'the prerogative on the other side is become so tender that, like a *noli me tangere*, it cannot endure to be touched'.[2] It seems that, as Chamberlain misjudged the Commons' readiness to remain silent over impositions, so he misjudged the King's willingness to redress the grievance of patents. It is true that the Council, on 14 December 1620, had refused to take any action for the reform of patents before the session, though urged by Bacon to do so. Yet, of all issues, the rewarding of royal servants was the one where the interests of the King were most likely to diverge from those of court, favourite, and Council. James was always under pressure to reward his servants: it remained to be seen what he would do if his freedom of action were increased by equally strident pressure not to reward them. Chamberlain might have been less despondent had he known that, as early as September, James had advised Bacon to consult Coke on the preparation of business for the Parliament, advice Bacon imprudently failed to take. Chamberlain might also have been more optimistic had he known that Bacon was advising the drafting of a monopolies bill, and the condemnation of many patents as contrary to the King's Book of Bounty.[3] It is a coincidence, to put it no higher, that the Book of Bounty provided the preamble for the monopolies bill ultimately steered through the Commons by Coke. When surrounded by a Parliament, James, unlike most of his Councillors, showed considerable sympathy for this bill. After Easter, the King was to grow tired of the detailed investigation of minor patents, but at no time did he object in principle to the investigation of patents in Parliament.

It takes two sides to make a constitutional conflict. Conflicts did not arise every time the House of Commons complained of a grievance. That, after all, was their proper task. Conflicts arose if members of the Commons persisted in attacking a grievance the

---

[1] iv. 15: iv. 19–20: ii. 30–1, *C.J.* 511.   [2] Chamberlain, 28 Oct. 1620.
[3] Jonathan L. Marwil, *The Trials of Counsel: Francis Bacon in 1621* (Detroit, 1976), pp. 22–3, 16, 20–1. See also p. 110 and n, below.

King wished them to leave alone. One of the most striking features of the Commons' attack on patents is the absence of any royal resistance to it, or even of any sign of royal displeasure at it. Buckingham apparently tolerated the attack on patents, finding he needed to make a virtue of necessity. James, it seems, may have done more than tolerate it. Even after the Parliament was dissolved, James looked back on the period of the attack on the patents as a happy time, when 'the House of Commons at the first, both in the manner of their supply and otherwise, showed greater love and more respect than ever any House of Commons did to us, or we think to any King before us, so we upon all their complaints have afforded them such memorable and rare examples of justice as many ages past cannot show the like'. He thought the time up to Easter had shown 'such harmony between us and our people as cannot be paralleled by any former time'.[1] This is James's description of the attack on patents and the revival of impeachment, and it is hardly a description of a constitutional conflict. When Alford and Sackville raised the issue of patents, then, they were not attacking the King. They were attacking some of his courtiers, and asking the King for his support in this attack. Some members of court and Council were against the patents: when the debate began, the King's line remained to be discovered.

Alford and Sackville's motion arose directly out of the first debate on the depression, and from consideration of a patent it was possible to blame peculiarly directly for the depression: the patent for making gold and silver thread. Since this patent involved the consumption of bullion in the manufacture, it could be used as a scapegoat for the shortage of coin. The methods of its enforcement were peculiarly scandalous even among the patents of 1621, and it therefore made a very convenient scapegoat for much else.

It also illustrates the key point about the patents of 1621: the hub of the debate was about law enforcement by, and for the benefit of, private individuals. Patents, it is true, were designed to reward the King's servants. Some, such as the monopoly of lampreys caught in the Thames, granted to the King's boatmen, were simply designed to reward his servants. Cases like the lampreys patent, though it was solemnly declared by Coke to be 'not *magni momenti*, yet *pessimi exempli*',[2] did not tend to take up much of the Commons' time. The monopolies which really

---

[1] Tanner, op. cit., p. 290   [2] v. 75.

created heat were monopolies of the right to enforce particular laws, or, still worse, to enforce non-statutory regulations like the proclamation against smoking in alehouses, enforced by the alehouse patentees. As John Crew put it, 'The greatest grief in penal laws is the putting the execution of them into private hands, whereby a rod of gold is turn'd into a rod of iron.'[1] It was because the contentious patents were a method of law enforcement that so many of the Justices of the Peace in the Commons turned on the patentees as rival agencies of local government. Whether they were ever intended for anything so constructive is an open question, but it had been clear since late in Elizabeth's reign that fears existed among country gentlemen that patents might grow into a rival system of local government.[2] In explaining the proceedings of the Commons, it is the existence of the fears, and not whether they were justified, which is important. Moreover, the charge that in some spheres patentees were supplanting J.P.s is one which appears to have survived investigation. Pembroke, chairman of the Lords' committee which investigated the patent for inns reported that the patentee 'affronted the Justices of the Peace',[3] and gave this as one of his chief grounds for condemnation. Inns, unlike alehouses, were not legally under the control of the Justices of the Peace, but that of the Justices of Assize, who were in the country for too short a time to decide which inns should be licensed. A bill was hastily prepared, and passed into law in 1624, transferring control of inns to the Justices of the Peace.

The patent giving supervision of alehouses to two private individuals, Almond and Dixon (who happened to be servants of Lord Treasurer Mandeville), attacked the power of J.P.s more directly, if not more effectively, than the patent for inns: Noy complained that 'It takes away the trust which the law reposed in Justices, and transfers it to Almon and Dixon against the intention of the law.' It seems that he was no less annoyed because he was aware that J.P.s were failing to discharge their responsibilities on alehouses: he admitted that 'We see they cannot be well ordered now, although they be under the care of so many justices.'[4] In this indignation at the transfer to others of powers they were unable to

---

[1] iv. 48. It is interesting that Pym reports only the part of this speech dealing with patents, while the report in ii. 73 covers only the part dealing with the depression and the fall in the price of wool. Crew seems to have regarded both as parts of the same subject.
[2] Hassell Smith, pp. 121–4.   [3] *L.J.* 61–2.   [4] iv. 327–8.

exercise effectively themselves, the reaction of members of the Commons shows an element of the dog in the manger. Phelips, who was distinguished by his capacity to generalize from his alarm, appears to have come nearest to thinking that patentees were an attack on the principle, as well as on the practice, of local government by J.P.s. He said that 'Whereas the King hath referred a great part of the government of this kingdom to the Justices of the Peace, this maketh a Justice of the Peace to be buffeted by a base alehousekeeper. I never knew government receive so great a wound.'[1] In addition, some patentees indulged in a good deal of extortion. The alehouse patentees appeared at Marlborough, and persuaded some people to give them a drink and to accept payment, only to prosecute those who relieved them for keeping an unlicensed alehouse.[2] Sir Giles Mompesson, patentee for inns, and ironically known as the 'lord of hosts',[3] once sent an agent posing as a benighted traveller to knock up an alehouse-keeper late at night to ask for shelter, and, when given it, prosecuted him for keeping an unlicensed inn. The Lords, on full investigation, found this particular story proved.[4]

The gold and silver thread patent also started off far-reaching legal issues. The patentees called their orders ordinances, their impositions on imported wares customs, and their meetings a court. They imprisoned people for refusing to enter into bonds not to infringe their monopoly, and Mompesson, one of the chief patentees, was said to have threatened to fill all the prisons if it were necessary to do so in order to enforce his monopoly. It was the power of imprisonment claimed by the patentees for gold and silver thread which provoked Coke to quote Magna Carta, that no man could be imprisoned except *per legem terrae*, and saying that imprisonment for breaking the by-laws of a corporation was against the law of the land.[5] They claimed the right to search, and to seize goods, and, in the words in which the charge was ultimately presented to the Lords, 'indeed they make laws and impose panalties like a court of Parliament'.[6] Many of those imprisoned by them had been released by James on the petition of the Lord

---

[1] ii. 109–10, v. 483–4. Wentworth's remarks in 1624 (Pym, 1624, ff. 81ᵛ–82ʳ) appear to repeat, with some embellishment, the contents of his diary for 1621. See also Nicholas's remarks in 1624, *C.S.P.D. 1623–5*, vol. clxv, no. 61.
[2] iii. 83–4.   [3] B.L. Harl. MS. 389, f. 19ᵛ.
[4] Gardiner, iv. 41–2: P.R.O. C. 65/185.
[5] iv. 124.   [6] P.R.O. C. 65/185.

Mayor of London, but the power of imprisonment continued unchecked. It was this patent which started the Parliamentary debate on the right to imprison, which was to culminate in the Petition of Right seven years later.

Yet in considering the story of the patents as a whole, we cannot say that right was all on one side. Some patents, like the much-abused ones for lighthouses, arose from the failure of the proper authority (in this case Trinity House) to take any appropriate action.[1] Some, like the patent for collecting the Clerk of the Market's fines, met a real administrative need in a sensible manner. The Clerk of the Market (among other duties) was responsible for raising fines for such things as the use of false weights and measures, and was bound to pay his fines into the Exchequer. The Exchequer, however, had no independent means of knowing how much the Clerk of the Market had raised in fines, and simply had to take his word for it that what he had paid in was all that he had raised. The temptation on him to defraud the Exchequer must have been considerable. In this case, the duty of the patentee was not to impose or assess fines which were partly for his own benefit. His duty was simply to watch their assessment by the Clerk of the Market, to receive them when collected, to pay a fixed rent to the Exchequer, and to keep the residue for himself.[2] In any full story of the patents, the patent for the Clerk of the Market's fines deserves a place, as well as the patent for gold and silver thread. Historians, as well as contemporaries, could heed the words of James, that we should not let the very name of a patent become a grievance.[3]

It was the desire to punish the more outrageous patentees which produced what, in the long term, was the most significant development of this session: the revival of the process which was later formalized as impeachment. It is, however, dangerously easy for those aware of the later history of impeachment to believe that the parliamentary trials of 1621 possessed the constitutional significance they were to have later. Dr. Tite, in the latest study of impeachment and Parliamentary judicature, stresses that what happened in 1621 was not an attempt to control the King's government by attacking his ministers, and that James himself 'had little grasp of the potentialities of Parliament's revived judicature'. There

[1] G. G. Harris, *The Trinity House at Deptford* (1969), pp. 153–214.
[2] vii. 341–2. By 1626, according to Harley, the Clerk of the Market had become farmer of his own fines. Whitelocke, 12–20, f. 47.   [3] iv. 109.

is even some evidence that he 'seems to have encouraged' the Lords in the most dramatic of their trials, that of Lord Chancellor Bacon.[1]

If James did not grasp the potentialities of Parliament's revived judicature, this may have been in part because, in 1621, they were not yet there. The most unchallenged of the royal prerogatives was the prerogative of mercy, and no sentence, however high the court which imposed it, was of any force unless it was executed. Execution remained with the King, as James reminded the House or Lords on 26 March. He told them he had come 'to express my readiness to put in execution (which is the life of the law) those things which ye are to sentence (for even the law itself is a dead letter without execution) for which office God hath appointed me in these kingdoms'.[2] The effusive thankfulness the Lords showed for this speech[3] suggests that they were equally well aware that their judgements were of no force unless the King would execute them. To some people, the point went home. Six weeks later, Noy spoke on the highly contentious case of Edward Floyd, in which both the Lords and the Commons claimed to act as judges. He said what mattered was not who judged him, but whether the judgement was executed: 'What court soever judges, yet the execution rests in the king.'[4] Impeachment in the 1620s cannot be seen in perspective until it is realized that it was a process which, in the last resort, could not be effective without the King's consent, however reluctant.[5] In 1621, Lord Chancellor Bacon fell and Lord Treasurer Mandeville survived, not because the Commons pursued the one more vigorously than the other (if anything, Mandeville was the more strongly attacked of the two), but because the King so willed it. Later in the decade, there was more readiness to begin impeachments without the King's consent, but even then, they could not be carried to a conclusion without it. It was not until 1679, when it was established that a royal pardon was not pleadable to an impeachment, that impeachment became a dependable weapon for securing ministerial responsibility. In the 1620s, the subject belongs, not to the history of ministerial responsibility, but to the history of court faction.[6]

It appears to have been Sir Thomas Wentworth who proposed

---

[1] Tite, pp. 131, 114n.   [2] *L.J.* 69.   [3] See below, p. 107.
[4] iii. 136, ii. 338.   [5] Ball, pp. 143, 181, 211.
[6] Dr. Tite (p. 143) observed that these trials, unlike the medieval impeachments, were not 'an open attempt to control the king's government by attacking

that the Commons should move on from a well-established procedure for investigating and condemning patents to punishing the patentees.[1] The first patentee to be punished was Sir Francis Michell, one of the patentees for alehouses. He, by rash words, presented the Commons with a welcome, if unexpected, opportunity to evade the legal complications involved in reviving Parliamentary judicature. When he appeared before the Commons to petition them on 23 February, he was unwise enough to describe the objection that he had undermined the office of a J.P. as an 'ignorant objection'. This curt dismissal of the principal grievance against him infuriated the Commons, and Sir Dudley Digges moved that he be punished in the Commons for this 'besides his other faults'.[2] He was therefore held guilty of a contempt of the House of Commons, and sentenced to be put out of the commission of the peace and sent to the Tower. Digges, the originator of the proposal to punish him for contempt, was left protesting that now, 'as justices are accounted, it is no disparagement to be put out of the Commission'. The other, original charges against Michell remained pending, and matter for further investigation. He was ultimately condemned by the Lords on the original charges. The Parliament Roll records only the judgement of the Lords, and not that of the Commons.

Sir Giles Mompesson, patentee for inns, for gold and silver thread, and for concealed Crown lands, was a more complex case. Of all the patentees of 1621, he seems to have obtained, and deserved, the greatest notoriety. Moreover, he had to be attacked with some care: he was a cousin of the Marquis of Buckingham, and Buckingham's brother Sir Edward Villiers was deeply involved in at least one of his patents, that for gold and silver thread. Partly because of the political implications of the case, and partly because Noy and Hakewill, searching for precedents in the

---

his ministers'. The point is ironically underlined by the fact that the move to punish the patentees was started by Sir Thomas Wentworth.

[1] On the rapid improvements in procedure for investigation of patents, see Elizabeth Read Foster, 'The Procedure of the House of Commons against Patents and Monopolies' in *Conflict in Stuart England*, ed. W. A. Aiken and B. D. Henning (1960), pp. 57–85.

[2] iv. 94, ii. 127–32, v. 485–6, vi. 4–5. The Commons' authority for expelling him from the Commission of the Peace was even more questionable than the authority for their other proceedings in the case, yet it was supported by the Councillor, Sir Thomas Edmondes.

Tower, appear to have found none to justify the Commons in judging anyone for offences against the state as distinct from against themselves, the Commons proposed, on Coke's motion, to refer Mompesson for judgement to the House of Lords.[1]

In so doing, they not only created a precedent of long-term significance: they also accentuated the immediate political importance of the House of Lords. Coke perceptively gave thanks for the three unities of this Parliament, 'betwixt the sovereign and us, betwixt the Lords and us, and betwixt ourselves'.[2] Exactly how the relationship between the two Houses should work during an impeachment remained in doubt for some time: in particular, who should undertake the work of preparing and presenting the prosecution case remained in doubt until 1641. Some members of the Commons, notably Pym,[3] wanted to keep the maximum possible control of the prosecution in the hands of the Commons. In practice, in 1621, most of the responsibility for investigating the charges was assumed by the Lords. The charges against Mompesson were formally presented to the Lords by the Commons at a conference, but thereafter the prosecutions were conducted by the King's counsel, with some assistance from the Attorney General. The detailed investigation took place before three Lords' committees, chaired by Pembroke (for inns), Arundel (for gold and silver thread), and by Southampton (for concealed Crown lands). It was for these committees that a veritable mountain of Mompesson's papers were gathered, annotated, and carefully studied, even after Mompesson had apparently confessed his guilt by flight. Southampton, in the concealments committee, admitted to allowing himself to be privately informed further by members of the Commons,[4] but Pembroke and Arundel's committees appear to have assumed full responsibility for their own reports. The Lords were not a judicial rubber stamp: they took their judicial responsibilities seriously, and any attempt to secure convictions before the Lords was going to depend heavily on the political attitudes of leading members of the Lords.

[1] Tite, pp. 94–8; iv. 114–17, v. 531.
[2] ii. 148.
[3] v. 340, iii. 30, *Nicholas*, i. 283.
[4] *L.J.* 46, 61–2. These private conferences were openly admitted by Southampton, without any apparent sign of disapproval. Yet they were the subject of one of the interrogatories against him after the session. Inner Temple Library, Petyt MS. 538/19. I am grateful to Dr. Tite for this reference.

Southampton, the man who took over the investigation of the concealments charge, was widely reported to be at the head of those who wished to use the Parliament to attack Buckingham,[1] while the attitude of Pembroke to Buckingham at this time seems to have been ambivalent, and that of Arundel uncertain.[2] At least it is clear that all these three wished to continue the investigation, hear witnesses on oath, and bring Mompesson to justice. So did numerous other members of the Lords, who were too powerful to ignore. Arundel and others, investigating the original charges against Michell (which were still on the file), persistently reminded the Lords that he was the Commons' prisoner, and they should be careful how they proceeded to judgement on him.[3] They thereby helped to ensure that the Michell case was not disrupted by a quarrel between the Houses.

The thankfulness of the Lords at James's speech of 26 March, allowing the execution of their judgement against Mompesson, revealed that others, some of them even more powerful, were committed to his condemnation. It was the Duke of Richmond and Lennox, a Scot whose royal blood gave him an almost unique position of independence from Buckingham, who proposed that they make every 26 March a sermon day throughout England, and Lord North moved that every year on that day the Lords should sit in their robes. Richard Neile, Bishop of Durham, wanted to express his thankfulness to Selden and Hakewill, who had searched for precedents for the Lords, by paying them. Arundel moved that there should be a general levy on the Lords to erect statues of the King *and the prince*. Buckingham immediately moved that Arundel write beyond seas to set these statues on work, thereby possibly shifting the bill to him.[4] These proceedings in the Lords clearly opened, in an acute form, the question of how much higher the investigation against Mompesson would lead. Mompesson himself was only the tip of an iceberg: behind him were Buckingham's brothers, and behind Buckingham's brothers was Buckingham

[1] *Cabala* (1691), I. 2; *C.S.P.D. 1619–23*, vol. cxxi, no. 136; *C.S.P.Ven. 1621–3*, p. 53.

[2] I am grateful to Dr. Kevin Sharpe for advice and information on Arundel.

[3] *Lords' Debates*, pp. 33, 35, *L.J.* 65, *Lords' Debates*, 34–6. Pembroke, Richmond and Lennox, Oxford, Sheffield, and Southampton were also anxious to avoid an accidental quarrel between the Houses over Michell. On the Parliament Roll, Michell's condemnation by the Lords is recorded, and his condemnation by the Commons is not.

[4] *Lords' Debates*, pp. 49–50.

himself.[1] Mompesson, on 27 February, had tried to trade testimony against his superiors for immunity.[2] Now, with the Lords so deeply involved, could the attack go any higher?

That Buckingham had enemies who resented his dominance of the court was common gossip. Southampton and Sheffield, the men most commonly mentioned in rumours to this effect, were not powerful enough to cause concern. If, however, at any moment information should emerge which so discredited Buckingham that more powerful peers, like Pembroke, Arundel, or the Duke of Richmond and Lennox, joined the attack on him, the situation could become very different. Then, the strength of Buckingham's hold on James's favour might become an open question. Moreover, all the Lords' proceedings were dominated by the presence of the colossal unknown quantity of Charles, Prince of Wales. Charles's relations with Buckingham had in the past often been bad. In 1621, they appeared, though somewhat uncertainly, to be improving. Yet Charles had thrown his weight behind the attack on Mompesson, telling Sir Edward Coke, somewhat prematurely, that he would never be weary of hearing him.[3] For a while, it was by no means impossible to imagine a court combination which would put Buckingham himself at risk.

The way upwards from Mompesson led through the referees. These were the men to whom proposed patents had been referred, for opinions on their legality and their convenience. It was an obvious question to ask on whose references so many obnoxious patents had been granted. The first proposal to attack the referees was made at the very beginning of the Parliament, by Sir Edward Sackville, a courtier whose relations with Buckingham were somewhat equivocal: he calmly informed Buckingham's man of affairs, George Goring, that he had been attending meetings called to plot against Buckingham in order to be able to report their proposals to Buckingham himself.[4] Sackville's motion lay untouched for some time, and the common opinion seems to have been Chamberlain's, that the referees were likely to be above the reach of the House.[5]

They were raised again on 15 February, immediately after the

---

[1] Buckingham's brother Sir Edward Villiers was sent abroad on a diplomatic mission. On 2 April, Buckingham found it necessary to deny that he had sent his brother abroad to escape trial in Parliament. *L.J.* 76.

[2] Chamberlain, 27 Feb. 1621, iv. 99, vi. 7. For a similar suggestion by Michell, ii. 167n.   [3] iv. 158.

[4] iv. 19–20, vii. 579.   [5] Chamberlain, 27 Feb. 1621.

vote of subsidies, by Lionel Cranfield, Master of the Wards, and were then bitterly pursued for the rest of the session by a team of three clearly acting in concert, Lionel Cranfield, Sir Francis Seymour, and William Mallory.[1] Seymour, early in 1622, was relying on the favour of the Duke of Richmond and Lennox to protect him against Buckingham's anger at his 'refractory' behaviour in Parliament,[2] but there seems to be no evidence to show whether Lennox either was aware of, or approved, his attacks on the referees. Mallory was a Yorkshire country gentleman, and nothing more can be safely said of his connections than that he did not belong to the Wentworth faction in his county.[3] He was not a frequent speaker, but was an adventurous one: he appears to be the sort of person of whom there is one in most Parliaments, whose natural habitat is where angels fear to tread. As a cat's-paw for attacks on the referees, he would have been ideal, but whether he in fact functioned as anyone's cat's-paw I have not been able to discover.

The attack on the referees raised in an actute form the question of the attitude of James. James in 1621 had to strike a difficult balance between the need to avoid oppressing his Commons and the need to reward his servants. He appears, for a while, to have positively welcomed pressure from the House of Commons, because it made this balance easier to strike. In his speeches of 10 March and 26 March, he praised his Parliament for proceeding with such moderation and love towards him, and went out of his way to accept the validity of the 'precedent' Coke offered from Alfred's reign, to prove that Parliaments used to be annual. He said that 'Never a lower house showed more respect unto their king than the Commons this Parliament have done unto me.' Above all, he was grateful to his Parliament for the freedom from suits it had brought him. James's lavish giving is commonly seen out of context, because it is considered without being seen against the background of continual begging and wheedling to which he was subjected. James's speech of 10 March, in particular, suggests that there is another side to this story. He said that suitors for patents 'have been so troublesome to me that neither my self nor those about me could rest in their beds quiet for projectors, as the

[1] iv. 59, ii. 113, ii. 121–2, vi. 7, v. 282, iv. 244, and other refs.
[2] Sackville MSS. ON 2421.
[3] I am grateful to Mr. Richard Cust for information on this point.

great back gallery, if it had a voice, could tell'. He complained bitterly that business on this subject had been brought to him even when he was in bed. He welcomed the Parliament, in part because it made it easier for him to say 'no' to some of these suits: 'I will not rest, which is no grievance, until I rid myself of a great many inutile servants, who do gain me nothing, but eat and spend my estate.'[1] However, he feared that after the Parliament all these suitors would flock back again, and therefore explicitly accepted Coke's proposal for what later became the monopolies bill; 'I am contented (as Sir Edward Coke moved) that there should be a law against these things.'[2] He gave his explicit blessing to the bill against informers, and commanded members to tell the country the bill would pass. The concealments bill, the third big bill of this Parliament, was already on offer as a bill of grace from 1614, expanded and made more generous.[3] The monopolies bill, like that other 'statutory invasion of the royal prerogative', the Act on bishops' lands of 1604,[4] was moved specifically on royal initiative, and to protect the King from the pressure of multifarious suits for favour. Thus, the resistance in the Lords to all three of these bills restricting royal bounty should be seen, not as a 'government' hardening its line against the Commons, but as a union of courtiers, facing a combined attempt by the King and Sir Edward Coke to cut off part of their source of income.[5]

In the same speech, James in effect left Bacon, Mandeville, and Buckingham to make their defence as best they could. Buckingham

---

[1] Hastings, pp. 25–7, *Lords' Debates*, pp. 13–14, *L.J.* 68–70.

[2] Hastings, p. 26. The motion by Coke, to which James was replying, had in turn been grounded on the proclamation of 1603, and on a speech by James in 1614, saying he would not have his prerogative extended to private uses. ii. 193.

[3] *C.J.* 458, iii. 64–5. The informers and concealments bills, like much of the other legislation passed in 1624, had been among the 'ten points' offered by Salisbury with the Great Contract in 1610. No less than six of these ten points were embodied in statutes in 1624. *Commons' Debates in 1610*, ed. S. R. Gardiner, Camden Series (1862), pp. 15–16.

[4] *1 Jac. I c. 3*. This Act laid down that all grants of bishops' lands, and all confirmations of such grants, were to be void. It said the King 'of his own will and motion' desired this Act, 'thereby for ever hereafter to avoid all suits and importunities for and concerning the said possessions'. See Phyllis Hembry, *The Bishops of Bath and Wells* (1967), pp. 203–4.

[5] In the informers bill, the clause most bitterly contested by the Lords was the exclusion of the King's Attorney. For Secretary Calvert's assurance of the King's support for this clause, see *Wentworth Papers*, pp. 154–5. For the exchanges between James and the Earl of Carlisle about the concealments bill in 1624, S.P. 14/167/10.

and Mandeville cast themselves on their knees before James, and offered their submissions, only to be reproved by Pembroke for speaking at a conference without leave of the House of Lords.[1] James damned the obnoxious patents by proclamation, and announced that alehouses were once again to be left to the government of the J.P.s. Yet, just because James had given so public a rebuke to his court, he had to keep the balance even, and soothe the ruffled feelings he had created. For James, the condemnation of Mompesson and his agreement to the monopolies bill should have been the end of the matter. When, nearly a month later, on 24 April, James found that many people would not trust his proclamation condemning the patents, and that Cranfield was still waiting on him asking for an investigation of the referees, his patience grew strained. He reminded the Commons that if they did not trust his proclamation, he had already agreed to the passage of an Act. He staked his influence, as he had not done in March, in defence of the referees, saying they should be careful 'not to condemn men for error in opinion if there were no corruption'. If men had been held publicly accountable for the advice they gave the King in private, that would have had the significance as a move towards ministerial responsibility which the other proceedings in 1621 lacked. It is not surprising that James defended the referees, nor that he felt the need to remind the Commons that if he went any further, 'he should not be able to reward his servants'.[2] For James, the persistence of the Commons after Easter in attacking long lists of minor patents, rather than passing bills, was both a waste of time and a nuisance. He had already shown, by dealing severely with Attorney General Yelverton, who had tried to exculpate himself by accusing Sir Edward Villiers and, by implication, Buckingham, that there was no future in any court cabal against Buckingham.

However, though James belatedly saved the referees, he was never prepared to defend any of his servants who were accused of corruption. Those who faced corruption charges were left to prove their innocence. It was then providential that, just at the moment when the attack on the referees seemed hardest to deflect, evidence of corruption came to light against one of the referees most complained of, Lord Chancellor Bacon. The story of the first

[1] *L.J.* 42.
[2] iv. 252–3, ii. 318.

bribe proved against Bacon is a curious one. The case concerned a Chancery lawsuit between two of the patentees for the issues of jurors. Bacon had received a royal letter recommending one patentee, and took a bribe from the other.[1] It would be typical of the obliquely conscientious administrative morality which distinguished Bacon, as it was later to distinguish Wentworth, if he thought that thereby he ensured his judicial impartiality. Where, if anywhere, the initiative lay in the attack on Bacon is uncertain. Dr. Tite has rightly insisted that there is no evidence of a court plot against Bacon, but equally, there is little evidence of a court attempt to save him. Dr. Field, Bishop of Llandaff, was caught up with Bacon in the same accusation, and escaped because the testimony of the witnesses against him collapsed under oath. He subsequently wrote a letter of thanks to Buckingham.[2] The lack of any such protection for Bacon is a striking contrast.

For most of the Commons, the charge against Bacon seemed too hot to handle. Two prominent members, Sir Edward Sackville and Heneage Finch, Recorder of London, spoke up in his defence.[3] Only two members of the Commons were prepared to stand forward in the attack on Bacon. One was Sir Robert Phelips, and the other was William Noy of the Duchy of Cornwall Council. Phelips had a connection with Buckingham, and, after the Parliament, wrote to another Councillor referring to 'my Lord Marq. upon whom as you know I principally rely'. However, as he showed on 2 May, by supporting a motion to exclude Buckingham's brother from the Commons pending the investigation of his patent, he was not a predictable Buckingham man. In this case, however, Goring reported to Buckingham that Phelips had handled one piece of evidence which might have reflected on Buckingham with all 'due respect' to him.[4] There is no suggestion that Phelips had offended Buckingham by his participation in the attack on Bacon. The Bacon case was sent up to the Lords on Noy's motion 'not to deliver it as a thing certain, as we did in Sir Giles Mompesson's case, but as an information'.[5] In other words, the Commons passed the buck.

In the Lords, much of the investigation into the Bacon case

[1] vii. 389, iv. 155. On Wentworth, see Aylmer, pp. 238–9, 346–7, 349.
[2] Tite, p. 118 and n. Cabala, I. 109–10.   [3] ii. 239–42.
[4] Phelips MSS. 224/82: iii. 133: vii. 579. Damport, the witness so carefully scrutinized by Goring, was the same man whose testimony collapsed against Field. See also Aylmer, p. 189.   [5] iv. 167.

appears to have been managed by Arundel, who had been bitterly offended by his attempt to make the nobility give evidence on oath in Chancery, instead of giving it on their honours, as they had done before. The committee which examined the witnesses against Bacon had a strong representation of Buckingham's enemies,[1] and in the Lords, Buckingham did at last show some signs of moving to save Bacon. The issue on which the defenders of Bacon took their stand in the Lords was curiously, but shrewdly, chosen: it was whether a Chancery decree could be reversed if a witness against Bacon proved that it had been obtained by bribery. If the answer was yes, potential witnesses against Bacon, many of whom had obtained favourable Chancery decrees from him, might disappear or change their testimony. Buckingham added the further question whether the givers of bribes could be put on oath and asked to accuse themselves. Pembroke, on the other hand, wanted to resolve that examinations taken in the Bacon case would not be used in any other, which meant that witnesses could depose against Bacon freely, without fear of the consequence to themselves. With Buckingham sided Lord Treasurer Mandeville, the Earl of Dorset, Noel, Bridgewater, Pembroke's brother the Earl of Montgomery, and the Bishop of St. Asaph. With Pembroke, and in effect against Bacon, sided Bishop Neile of Durham, Sheffield, Richmond and Lennox, Saye and Sele, North, Arundel, the Marquis of Hamilton (Earl of Cambridge in the English peerage), and, fatally, Charles, Prince of Wales. It was decided that the depositions against Bacon were not to be used in any other cause, and by this decision, Bacon's fate was probably sealed.[2] If this debate is a genuine picture of the line-up for and against Bacon, the case remains remarkably obscure, but whatever it may be, it cannot be seen as the result of a court–country confrontation.

After the Bacon case, trials continued only against comparatively unimportant men such as Sir John Bennet, who had taken bribes for probate of wills. Bennet escaped the Parliament, ironically, because the list of witnesses who could depose to his corruption was too long for the Lords to hear them, and he was subsequently

---

[1] *L.J.* 58.

[2] *L.J.* 67, *Lords' Debates*, pp. 37–9. See also Jonathan L. Marwil, *The Trials of Counsel: Francis Bacon in 1621* (Detroit, 1976), pp. 47–56. The evidence prompts the possibly fanciful hypothesis that it could have been in Buckingham's interest that the impeachment of a great officer should be attempted in the Commons, only to fail in the Lords.

condemned in Star Chamber.[1] The Commons continued to
consider complaints of injustice from individual courts, usually
the Chancery, and though they did a good deal to polish the
committee procedure for dealing with these cases, slowly became
overwhelmed by their number. Edward Alford proposed to deal
with this volume of complaints against courts by creating a Court
of Appeal, but his proposal was not taken up.[2] With these little
cases, heard by the Commons alone, the judicial activity of 1621
petered out in trivialities.

A similar fate overtook attempts at legislation. The amount of
business the Commons undertook in 1621 was far too great to be
completed, and the lack of any established leadership meant that
no agreed system of priorities could be established. In particular,
the number of committees set up was more than the most dedicated
member could handle: no man can sit on two committees which
meet simultaneously. As early as 23 February, Dr. Gooch pointed
out that some were chosen for more committees than they could
attend. The House agreed that order was to be taken for it, but it
was not.[3] On 10 March, Sir Edward Montagu made an opposite
complaint, that bills were so hastily shunted off to committee that
they did not receive a proper scrutiny in the House.[4] On 1 May,
Edward Alford complained of committees sitting while the full
House was sitting, and, on 21 April, he pointed out that they had
agreed to the simultaneous sitting of the whole House and of two
committees.[5] It was probably this difficulty in securing adequate
attendance at committees which led to the increasingly frequent
practice of resolving that all who came were to have voices, but this
too led to procedural difficulties. Earle alleged that it further
diminished attendance, because all trusted to someone else to go.
Sir Thomas Hoby raised a procedural question of some importance: he asked whether, if enough members of the House were
present to make a quorum at a committee, but they had not
been specifically named to the committee, the committee was
quorate, and able to take decisions.[6] It appears, then, that many
of the bills which were delayed in committee may have been

[1] *L.J.* 110, 112, 114, 117, 124, 133; Tite, p. 135n.
[2] iv. 193.
[3] ii. 126.
[4] iv. 141: see also iv. 44.
[5] v. 128, iii. 42. See also iii. 64 (Horsey).
[6] iv. 324-5.

delayed in committees whose membership was floating. It is not surprising, then, that bills failed to make progress.

Even the monopolies bill, which seems to have been generally agreed to have the highest priority of all, ran into drafting difficulties which could not be avoided. New administrative responsibilities were always being created, like the responsibility for administering passports introduced by the recusancy Act of 1606. These responsibilities had to rest on someone.[1] There was a widespread resistance to the creation of new offices, led by officers who considered their offices their freehold, and not to be diminished without legal authority. This resistance was encouraged by many members of Parliament, often themselves office-holders, who argued that no new office could be erected, or no new fee levied by an office-holder, without statutory sanction.[2] Yet Parliaments showed a conspicuous reluctance to create any new offices to handle the administrative responsibilities their statutes created. The only new office created by statute between 1604 and 1629 was the Garbler of Spices, created by the 1604 Act against the deceitful garbling of spices, 'to the jeopardy of his Majesty's person'.[3] Parliament, even if it had been in session continuously, could not have created a new office every time one was required.

Should the monopolies bill then contain an exemption for new offices? One of the early drafts did not, and if it remained in that form, it would risk bringing administration to a standstill. Yet if the bill allowed new offices, as the final Act of 1624 did, there was nothing to stop the King doing as Charles ultimately did, and simply circumventing the Act by calling many of his new monopolies offices. As Towerson pointed out, they faced a similar difficulty about charters and corporations. Coke, Glanville, and most of the best lawyers of both Houses were involved in the repeated conferences about the drafting of the monopolies bill, yet on these two points, of offices and corporations, however it was

[1] vii. 348.
[2] P.R.O. C. 65/185. The creation of a new office without warrant was one of the grounds on which the Lords condemned the thread patent. On the resistance to the creation of new offices, see G. E. Aylmer, 'Studies in the Institutions and Personnel of English Central Administration 1625–1642', Oxford D.Phil. Thesis (1954), pp. 655–8. Professor Aylmer noted that 'there was nothing like a pre-arranged government "line" on these questions'. I am grateful to Professor Aylmer for lending me his copy of this thesis. iv. 80 (but also iv. 294–5), iii. 1, ii. 155.
[3] *1 Jac. I c. 19.*

drafted, it must achieve either too much or too little.[1] Either it made it impossible to meet new administrative needs, or it did not make it impossible to create monopolies. The draft ultimately passed in 1624 chose the second alternative.

Apart from the big three, monopolies, informers, and concealments, the other bills which made progress, and even more those which reached the statute book in 1624, had a common theme: to shore up local jurisdiction against the shocks it had received from patentees, projectors, and informers. By the beginning of the 1624 Parliament, something of a consensus on which were the most important bills was beginning to emerge. They were bills designed to give expression to Coke's belief that J.P.s were 'the most excellent government in the Christian world'.[2] The most important of these was the bill of Supersedeas and Certioraris. This bill was designed to prevent the infliction of heavy travelling expenses on litigants, and indignity on J.P.s, by the removal of lawsuits out of local courts to central courts. It is interesting, as an anticipation of later Leveller demands, that the Commons of 1621 and 1624 were deliberately trying to reverse the centralization of legal proceedings at Westminster which had taken place during the 1590s. As Coke said, those who came to London for justice when they could have it in their counties deserved to pay for it. The Lords, who were rather more sceptical than the Commons about government by J.P.s, wanted to know how the bill provided for the punishment of a J.P. who offended in his own county.[3] With the Supersedeas bill we should classify the bill for pleading the General Issue,[4] the bill allowing J.P.s to give restitution of possession in certain cases, and the bill against troubling J.P.s in their duty with vexatious suits. These bills had to wait until 1624 to become law, because neither session of 1621 ended with the presentation of any bills to the King.

In all the welter of business, many members had lost sight of the original purpose of the Parliament, which was to make England ready in case James should wish to go to war. The summer dragged on, and no announcement about foreign policy was made.

---

[1] iv. 33–4, 160, 173, 197. See below, pp. 190–1.

[2] v. 501.

[3] *Wentworth Papers*, p. 154: iv. 374–5: W. J. Jones, *The Elizabethan Court of Chancery* (1967), pp. 375–7.

[4] This bill also goes back to Salisbury's ten points of 1610. See above, p. 110n.

Members were abruptly reminded of the issue of peace or war by the case of Edward Floyd. Floyd was a prisoner in the Fleet, and the Commons discovered his case in the course of investigating the misdemeanours of the Warden of the Fleet. This investigation was typical of the Commons of 1621: it was moved by a sincere concern for the cruelties the prisoners suffered from the Warden, and directed to an abuse badly in need of reform, but inherently unlikely to end in anything but a lot of detail and some noise. It was a great surprise when the members discovered the existence of a prisoner in the Fleet, Edward Floyd, who had rejoiced at the defeat of the King's son-in-law and daughter at the White Mountain, calling them 'goodman' and 'goodwife', terms not proper for gentry, let alone royalty. Some members appear to have seized on this case as a chance to demonstrate that their concern about the Palatinate, though dormant in response to James's wishes, was not dead. Phelips said he could wish the matter had not come into the House, but that since it had, they could not pass it over without making an example of him.[1] He later said that 'I should have been glad of a better subject and occasion to have expressed my duty to my king's children and commiserate and relieve their calamitous estate.' He added, 'If we do not punish such in time, we may cry Oh Lord, it is too late '? In this speech, he probably expressed the emotion behind the apparently hysterical reaction of the Commons to Floyd, in which, it may be noted, Buckingham's confidential friend Sir George Goring joined, proposing that Floyd should be hung with an ass's tail. The majority opinion was milder, in favour of whipping and various other mutilations. This was opposed by Sandys, on the ground that it was 'improper to whip a gentleman', only to be immediately answered by Pym: 'To whip him, . . . *quia* his gentility mistaken.'[3] In attempting to sentence Floyd themselves, the Commons nearly created a major row with the Lords and the King over the question, apparently settled, whether the Commons could judge offenders without the assistance of the Lords. In the Lords a bill against the servile punishment of whipping was read, against all precedent, three times in one day and then allowed to drop.[4] Finally, the combined weight of the King and the Lords forced the Commons to retreat. Floyd was duly punished by the King with the Lords'

---

[1] v. 117. [2] iii. 122–3. [3] v. 129–30, iii. 127.
[4] *L.J.* 137. See also 135.

advice, and the quarrel about jurisdiction left behind it only an irate entry by the Lords on the Parliament Roll.[1]

After so long a time, the Commons should not have been surprised to be told by Secretary Calvert that, now that the misunderstanding which was between King and Parliament had been happily taken away, it was time for them to go home for a summer recess. They had, after all, been at Westminster, with a short break for Easter, from 30 January to 28 May, and they were being offered at least another week to complete existing business. Those who had championed government by J.P.s so long and so vehemently could hardly take offence if James told them that the government of the country was suffering from the long absence of so many Justices of the Peace and Deputy Lieutenants, nor should they have been surprised to be told that members of the Privy Council needed more time to work than constant attendance on Parliament was allowing them. Yet this innocuous message put the Commons, as Pym's diary records with some understatement, into 'some distraction'.[2] Why was this? For some, it was because it was now at last clear that no foreign policy announcement was coming. As Edward Alford put it, 'seeing we shall have no wars',[3] they might turn their minds to details of county government. Phelips held forth on the lack of any relief for the King's daughter,[4] yet for the majority of members, the lack of any announcement of war appears to have caused less dismay than their own failure to complete any satisfactory programme of legislation. The fear appears to have been of the reaction they would meet in the country when they came home. Coke said that if they brought no laws, they would find it hard to get supply at their next meeting.[5] As Sir Edwin Sandys said, 'the eyes of all the kingdom, and hearts, are upon us. They stand expecting, and gazing, after the good we will bring them;[6] while his brother Sir Samuel said that, facing these hopes, he could hardly show his head in his country for shame.[7] Perhaps the most perceptive comment was one which appears to have been made by Sir Thomas Jermyn, that in all this time, and in their exertions, they had raised greater hopes than they could satisfy.[8]

---

[1] *L.J.* 110, P.R.O. C. 65/185; Elizabeth Read Foster, *The Painful Labour of Mr. Elsyng* (Philadelphia, 1972), p. 31. The Roll records with care that Floyd was condemned by the Lords at the suit of the King's Attorney.

[2] iv. 383.   [3] ii. 403.   [4] iv. 391–2, vi. 178, iii. 348–9.

[5] iv. 387.   [6] iii. 333.   [7] iv. 385, v. 182.

[8] iv. 410, ii. 424.

The bills which were passed did something to restore the position of J.P.s, but Phelips and Sandys were right that these bills had not much to offer ordinary freeholders.[1] To James's amazement, members decided not to present the completed bills for the royal assent, saying they would rather bring the country back no bills than bring them such an inadequate list. It is possible to appreciate the feeling which made James say this showed 'much inconstancy' in them. The most charitable, and perhaps the most perceptive, comment on the general mood was by Dudley Digges, that long sitting brings difference of opinion, and so breeds heat.[2] The Commons appear to have believed Cranfield when he answered an unspoken fear by saying that need for money would compel the King to call them together again in the autumn,[3] and decided to leave their bills till then.

Instead, on the motion of Sir James Perrott, they decided to offer something much more dramatic: a declaration that, if James should wish to go to war for the Palatinate, they would be ready to assist him. This declaration, in its conditional form, did not appear to James to be an encroachment on his prerogative: indeed, the French Ambassador said he was so pleased with it that some people thought he had a hand in drafting it himself.[4] He certainly had it translated into foreign languages, and distributed abroad. The Commons, in the words of Digges, were 'unwilling to pry into any matters of state, which they had forborne all this while'.[5] Yet they received this declaration on a wave of emotion. Delbridge offered to go to the Palatinate in person. Towerson was so overcome that he said that if the King went to war, he would be willing to give twenty or thirty subsidies, and only Edward Alford reminded him that 'that might lay on us too great an engagement'.[6] Sir Edward Coke produced the curtain-line for this scene. He broke into the prayer from the Book of Common Prayer for the delivery of the King's children, 'Almighty God, who hast promised to be a Father to thine Elect', and the House cried 'Amen, Amen'. They then adjourned for the summer.[7]

There is something theatrical about the whole scene in the Commons on 4 June, and it provides an occasion to ask what was

---

[1] iv. 397, iii. 374. See also Digges, iii. 379. [2] iii. 392. [3] v. 190.
[4] P.R.O. 31/3/55, Tillières to Puisieux, 7/17 June 1621 (unfoliated). I know no evidence in support of the French Ambassador's suspicions.
[5] iv. 415–16. [6] ii. 429; iv. 415–16. [7] iv. 417, ii. 430, v. 398.

the real strength of anti-Spanish feeling in the Commons. Did anyone really believe that Towerson would give thirty subsidies, or that Delbridge would go in person, or was there a ritual quality about these protestations? These members had mostly been children or young men during the Elizabethan war with Spain, and they had imbibed anti-Spanish feeling, and the anti-Catholicism which went with it, as a part of their mental stock-in-trade. It was, like Foxe's *Book of Martyrs*, from which so much of it was derived, something familiar to fall back on as a touchstone in time of strong emotion. There was also a serious intellectual conviction that, in the long term, no state could be stable without unity in religion. Yet for many members, the forces of neighbourhood were even stronger than the forces of religion. They believed that, in principle, no Catholic could be a loyal subject, and yet, at the same time, they knew many of their Catholic neighbours were loyal subjects.[1] The strongest force of anti-Catholicism was kept for strangers and the Irish. Most members, with some conspicuous exceptions like Sir Thomas Wentworth, had the reflex anti-Spanish feeling expressed by Delbridge and Towerson in this debate. Yet this reflex orthodoxy was again something which would not override good neighbourhood. Delbridge might or might not believe strongly enough in war with Spain to serve in person, but he certainly did not believe in war with Spain as strongly as he believed in the prosperity and harmony of Barnstaple. He might go in person, but he would not exact from out-of-work Barnstaple clothiers taxes they could not afford to pay. The disappearance of the bill of arms might have warned the Council that this House of Commons, with a few dedicated exceptions, was not in a mood to sustain a war. Sir Edward Cecil, who was in charge of the bill, took the point: 'Sorry I am that, when all Christendom is up in arms, this house should so little respect arms.'[2] It has often been pointed out that when members referred to their country, they meant their county. This fact ought to have warned us to look for a Parliament which might be anti-Spanish on principle, but whose patriotism was much too local to allow most of them to be very

[1] For a clear example of this double-take, see S.P. 14/159/28, Sir William Pelham to Conway, 12 Feb. 1624. Pelham said that though 'for my particular I love many of their persons and hate none', nevertheless no man could serve two masters, and therefore it should not be possible for a papist to be a true subject. In short, he said that 'some of my best friends are papists'.
[2] iii. 236–7.

belligerent. It would not be an exaggeration to say, in modern language, that most of them put their county before their country. If James observed the first session of this Parliament carefully, his reluctance to go to war can only have been increased.

II. THE SECOND SESSION

Time does not stand still between Parliaments, and one of the greatest dangers facing a mere Parliamentary historian is that he is compelled, by the limitations of his subject, to tell half a story. He cannot, without destroying the shape of his work, follow all the diverse concerns of those involved in Parliamentary business through the time between Parliaments. If he does not, he risks presenting something like a badly-cut film: a series of shots from a story in which the continuity has been lost. There is perhaps no session in the decade in which it is more apparent that Parliamentary history is the tip of an iceberg than it is in the second session of 1621.

It appears that the fears of many members about the reactions of their neighbours when they came home without legislation were justified. Sir Thomas Wentworth prepared a speech complaining that they might be compared to the foolish virgins in the Bible; he said they should be furnished with answers 'to such objections as they, being men wise in their own generations, ... may bluntly and shrewdly make: as thus: you have given three subsidies to be paid all in a year, which was never before, what is the reason we have not our pardon, our laws and our grievances removed? Do you delight your selves to hear one another talk, to give away our money and bring home nothing? Were you straitened of time upon your last recess, and will you still labour of the same disease?'[1] Many members, then, came back to Westminster on 20 November with a new determination to pass bills with a greater expedition than they had shown in the last session. They were fortified in this determination by the fact that the harvest of 1621 had been disastrous: the bill against the import of corn was now replaced by an equally inconclusive bill against the export of corn. The chief concern of those occupied with bills was to complete the bills of informers and of monopolies, but they also concerned themselves

---

[1] *Wentworth Papers*, p. 167. The reference to 'three subsidies' includes the extra subsidy voted on 28 Nov., and lost by dissolution.

with other issues, such as the bill against scandalous ministers, which was given a second reading on 23 November. It is typical of the secular mood of the Parliaments of 1621 and 1624 that when this bill led to a debate on the High Commission, Edward Alford's objection to it was not that it was popish or tyrannical, but that it put a burden on the country by centralizing litigation.[1] Members like Wentworth, Alford, and Glanville, who were responsive to the moods of their neighbours, were then hardly likely to want to come back to Westminster in order to be diverted into debating foreign affairs. They were much more interested in the Staplers' bill against the Merchant Adventurers,[2] or in the progress of Neale's bill for free fishing.

They had, though, to come back to Westminster to face a much more self-confident Buckingham. At the end of the first session, it was reported, correctly if prematurely, that Buckingham 'rejoices at being found Parliament-proof'.[3] Nevertheless, the investigation into the patents had come too close to him for comfort, and he seems to have picked the time between sessions to exact his revenge. Four men were put under restraint: the Earl of Southampton and his close friend Sir Edwin Sandys, the Earl of Oxford and John Selden, who, though not a member of either House, had been employed by the Lords in their search for precedents. Selden and Sandys had their studies searched, and Southampton and Sandys were induced to stay away from the second session, excusing their absence on the ground of 'ill health'. With Buckingham's other moves against his enemies, we should perhaps include the attempt, apparently led by two patentees called Lepton and Goldsmith, to get their own back on Sir Edward Coke through a series of charges to be made, apparently with semi-official encouragement, in the Star Chamber. Phelips believed that this was done 'in revenge for his service done in Parliament',[4] for Coke had been largely responsible for condemning the patents in which Lepton and Goldsmith had an interest. According to Phelips's

---

[1] iii. 433, iv. 432.

[2] *Nicholas*, ii. 192–3, iv. 435. Digges, who was in favour of depriving the Merchant Adventurers of privileges in the trade in the new draperies, but not in the old draperies, now regarded this bill as too extreme, and objected to it.

[3] Chamberlain, 19 May 1621. Chamberlain was commenting on the Yelverton case, not on any action by the Commons.

[4] iii. 438, Phelips MSS. 212/35; ii. 477, Phelips MSS. 216/74. See below, pp. 128–9.

committee report of 30 November, 'some of the best men in this kingdom were interested' in Lepton's attempt to revenge himself on Coke. Coke, unlike Southampton, had shown no evidence of a desire to attack Buckingham directly, but the sheer blundering force of Coke's attack on the patents, which he was still continuing in the second session, had uncovered many things Buckingham would have preferred not to come to light.

If the second session of 1621 is to be seen as one of confrontation, the case of Sir Edwin Sandys and the case of Lepton and Goldsmith perhaps deserve to be nearer the centre of the story than the more eye-catching debate on foreign policy.[1] It may not be a coincidence that all the members punished after the session, with the possible exception of Sir Nathaniel Rich, had been among the small list of members involved in investigating the Lepton and Goldsmith case. Nevertheless, initial reactions to these cases suggest that many members came back to Westminster as reluctant to start a privilege dispute as they were to start a foreign policy debate. In the Lords, Archbishop Abbot raised the searching of Selden's study as a breach of privilege,[2] but Southampton's so-called 'sickness' seems to have been accepted at its face value. In the Commons, Mallory persistently tried to make an issue of the absence of Sir Edwin Sandys, but his early attempts met with little encouragement. Pym noted in his diary that one of them was 'well passed over' by the House. Barrington, in his diary, noted on one of them '*quaere? quaere?*' (why? why?). Sir Thomas Wentworth prepared a powerful speech arguing that they would do no good to their liberties by raising the Sandys case, but appears to have found no need to deliver it.[3] The issue appears to have been dropped too readily for long speeches to be needed. Mallory only succeeded at his third attempt in getting messengers sent to Sandys.

If members of the Commons came back to Westminster wanting neither a foreign policy debate nor a privilege dispute, why did they find themselves, within a few weeks, involved with peculiar bitterness in both? The answers to this question appear to lie at

---

[1] On the Sandys case, see my article, 'The Examination of Mr. Mallory after the Parliament of 1621', *B.I.H.R.* (1977), 125–32. In 1628, Phelips appeared to think that the Lepton case had been one of the main causes of the dissolution: 'You remember what followed. When the House was resolved to send for him that fatal blow of the dissolution came upon us.' Stowe 366, f. 202ʳ.

[2] *L.J.* 176. [3] *Wentworth Papers*, pp. 162–5.

court, rather than in Parliamentary history, but in the absence of any satisfactory account of what was happening at court during these weeks, many of them must remain conjectural.

In part, the complexity of affairs at home reflects the complexity of affairs abroad. The Parliament had originally been put off until 8 February, but was unexpectedly recalled, at uncomfortably short notice, for 20 November. This sudden recall must have given rise to a good deal of speculation: Phelips is unlikely to have been alone in thinking that it implied 'matter of great weight'.[1] It seemed to those outside the court probable that this sudden and unexpected recall meant that the King had at last made up his mind for war. There was also diplomatic evidence to support such a conjecture. As the Parliament reassembled, the new Spanish government was increasing the size of its Atlantic fleet. Throughout the summer, speculation had centred on the probability that a decision for peace or war would follow the return of John Digby (later Earl of Bristol) from a diplomatic mission to Vienna and Madrid.[2] The decision to recall the Parliament did indeed follow hard upon the return of Digby, and was believed by the French Ambassador to be a consequence of it.[3] It seemed the more probable that war was to be announced when it was known that Digby had returned in a thoroughly irate mood. The army commanded by General Spinola, who received his commission from the Emperor, and his pay from Spain, was advancing rapidly in its invasion of the Palatinate. Moreover, the Emperor was going ahead in his plans to transfer Frederick's rights as an Elector of the Holy Roman Empire to the Duke of Bavaria. It appeared to be too late to negotiate for any peace with the Emperor.

But if, as seemed clear, war with the Emperor was to be announced, did this imply war with Spain also? Spain's twelve-year truce with the Dutch had not been renewed, and to anyone who thought in terms of general conflict, a major European war now appeared hard to avoid. There were many such people on the English Council, to whom the separation of the Spanish and Austrian branches of the House of Habsburg appeared to be splitting hairs. James subsequently maintained that, in authorizing war in the Palatinate, and consequently a debate on the supply it demanded, he had not authorized any general debate on war with

[1] C.J. 642.   [2] B.L. Harl. MS. 389, f. 42ʳ.
[3] P.R.O. 31/3/55, f. 217.

Spain.[1] It may well be that this was what James and Digby intended, but if so, they were guilty, at the least, of not making their meaning clear. To many, including Councillors, the strategic distinction later made by James appeared to be a plain impossibility. There was some point in the bewilderment of Sir Edward Giles: 'that war and peace were both propounded together. We must fight with the Spaniards in the Palatinate and be friends with them every where else.'[2] It was essential for the Commons to know what type of war they had been reassembled to support, since, until they knew what they were asked to support, they could not know how much money they must vote for it. On neither of these vital points was any clear lead forthcoming from the Councillors. Nor was it possible to get any clear lead from the King. Throughout the second session of 1621, the King, and Buckingham with him, were away at Newmarket, where James was said to have fallen ill. In the absence of both James and Buckingham, there was nowhere members of the Commons could look for really authoritative official directions: they had to feel their way, and discover by trial and error what created a favourable response and what did not.

On the first day of the new session, 20 November, there was not even an opening speech. Left to themselves, members followed the lead of Sir James Perrott, who asked for them to ensure the speedier passage of bills, and asked how they could avoid the committee bottle-necks of the previous session.[3] The opening statements, from which the Commons were to receive official direction, were made at a conference of both Houses on the second day of the session, 21 November. The three speakers at this conference were Williams, the new Lord Keeper, Digby, fresh from his embassy, and Lionel Cranfield, the new Lord Treasurer.[4] Williams, the Lord Keeper, claimed some deserved credit for the King for his suppression of thirty-seven patents after the previous session, and then told the Commons that the business of this session concerned them and not the Lords. He said bluntly that the Parliament had been called for war. 'The cause was for the maintenance of a war. Janus' temple is now opened that hath been shut these nineteen

---

[1] Tanner, op. cit., pp. 284–5. It should be noted that this point was not made in James's first letter of 3 Dec., and did not appear until his second letter of 9 Dec.

[2] iv. 438. [3] vi. 191, *C.J.* 640.

[4] During the summer recess, Mandeville was moved out of the limelight into the newly created office of Lord President of the Council.

years. The voice of Bellona is now to be harkened to and not the voice of peace.' The King, he said, wanted them to defer ordinary business till the next meeting, while allowing them to bestow on it 'such hours as may be well spared from this foreign occasion'. The Commons, then, were no longer forbidden to debate foreign affairs, but commanded to do so.[1] It was a command they showed a good deal of reluctance to obey.

What war were they asked to support? This question was left to Digby, who spoke with a good deal of ambiguity. The comment in Hawarde's diary, that 'I did not well conceive his meaning'[2] has some justification. Digby was clear that immediate war in the Palatinate was needed. He wanted urgent supply for a small force of Englishmen under Sir Horace Vere, and for a mercenary army under Count Mansfeld, both of which were in the Palatinate already. Mansfeld's army, he feared, might disband or turn the country against them by pillage if they were not immediately supplied. So far, he was clear: 'The King for a peace could descend no lower but must resolve either to abandon his children or prepare for a war.' Yet Digby did not make clear whether general war with Spain was also involved, perhaps because he himself did not know the answer. He reminded the Houses that the troops invading the Palatinate were in the pay of the King of Spain, said that the German Protestants might reunite if they saw the King 'thoroughly engaged', and said the state of religion was in great hazard, for the King of Spain now had six armies in the field.[3] If this did not invite war with Spain, at least it did nothing to discourage it. Cranfield confined himself to stating the need for money, and to answering what may have been a widespread suspicion that James intended to repeat his performance of the first session, by raising supply without declaring any war. He said that if any doubted whether the money would be employed for the purpose for which it was given, 'the House, which was so sensible of the King's honour in the case of Floyd, will give no countenance to such objections'.[4]

---

[1] iv. 423–5. Barrington (iii. 418) not only reports that there was to be war, but adds the words 'the manner he leaves to your resolution'. It is not clear whether this refers to the manner of the war or of the supply, but the two questions were so interdependent that any distinction is perhaps technical.

[2] Hawarde, 21 Nov. He believed Digby was proposing a 'public war', apparently against Spain.

[3] iv. 427–8.   [4] iv. 428.

When the Commons were back in their own House, they agreed, on the motion of Sir Robert Phelips, to defer the debate of the matter raised at this conference until the next Monday, 26 November.[1] Digges, who then opened the debate, said he had used the interval 'to clear himself at court',[2] and he is unlikely to have been the only member who did so. Meanwhile, there was time for domestic business. A bill to regulate elections was under discussion, and some anxiety was expressed about a provision in it that members should live for at least six months of the year in their constituencies.[3] It had been pointed out early in the first session that the implementation of an old statute demanding that members reside in their constituencies could result in the disqualification of the majority of the Commons.[4] Most, except those sitting for such places as Old Sarum, tried to give loyal service to their constituencies, but the idea that they should actually live there seemed rather extreme. What is perhaps reflected in this bill is the growing resistance of some constituencies to outside members, and the fear of many members of the Commons that the quest of great men for additional supplies of patronage might lay elections unduly open to 'influence'.[5] Sir Edward Sackville also showed concern for members' public reputations by moving that they deal with the abuse of protections, the device whereby members extended Parliamentary privilege to their servants. This caused no formal complaint if those involved were really servants, but some protections had been improperly given, and Lord Stafford was said to have been making an income by selling them.[6]

It was into this interval, before the foreign policy debate, that Phelips, on 24 November, dropped the case of Lepton and Goldsmith. Lepton's plan to attack Coke appears to have had some previous history, and it is not the least of the curiosities of the Floyd case that the Commons apparently got their first inkling of

---

[1] v. 401.   [2] iii. 445. See also *C.J.* 644.   [3] iv. 422, 446.

[4] iv. 22, 30, 35–6. See Ruigh, 48n, for an attempt at Chester in 1624 to use the residence qualification to exclude a Councillor. On bills to regulate elections, see Hirst, pp. 229–31.

[5] Hirst, pp. 66–70 and other refs. This fear of influence appears to be directed against great men in general, as much as against the court in particular. See the resistance of Salisbury to Pembroke's candidates for Recorder in 1623 and M.P. in 1625–6. Peter Clark and Paul Slack (eds.), *Crisis and Order in English Towns* (1972), pp. 184, 187. The depression perhaps intensified some boroughs' desire to return resident members.

[6] iv. 421, Chamberlain, 24 Nov. 1621.

its existence from a paper found in Floyd's trunk.[1] Lepton had held (and, in spite of its condemnation, was still executing) a patent giving him a monopoly of engrossing bills for lawsuits before the Council of the North. Coke, as chairman of the committee for grievances, had led with his chin by asking Lepton who drew his patent, and saying that whoever did it deserved to be hanged. Lepton said his patent had been drawn by the then Attorney General, Sir Edward Coke himself.[2] This incident may have encouraged Lepton in the idea that he might be revenged on Coke. He went into partnership with Goldsmith, whose patent for the enrolment of apprentices had also been damned, and who had been told by Coke that he was the only lawyer ever known to have been a patentee. Lepton and Goldsmith appear to have compiled a long list of misdemeanours committed by Coke in his days as a judge, and to have hoped to charge him in the Star Chamber with oppression, extortion, and various other offences. In this plan, they had secured the support necessary to gain a hearing. They were firmly backed by Lady Coke (Sir Edward was not the most happily married of men), and by Lord Haughton.[3] In addition, Phelips apparently believed, and the French Ambassador said, that they had secured the support of Buckingham.[4] In addition, rumours were circulating of a plan to send Coke to Ireland: James had been annoyed, in the first session, by the attempt of some of the Commons to complain of misgovernment in Ireland (which was, he thought, not under their jurisdiction). He seems to have regarded it as poetic justice that those who complained of the government of Ireland should be sent to remedy the complaints they had made. A plan to send Coke to Ireland, however unwelcome, could not be made matter of formal complaint, but the activities of Lepton and Goldsmith, being so plainly

---

[1] v. 359, vi. 119. Coke said Floyd had been steward to his old enemy Lord Chancellor Ellesmere. See Harl. MS. 389, f. 66^r, where it is claimed that he had also been steward to the Earl of Suffolk.

[2] Coke's discomfiture was still remembered in 1628: Stowe 366, f. 202^v.

[3] It is tempting to link Lord Haughton's involvement in attempts to charge Coke with old offences with his solitary dissent from Coke's bill for limitation of actions. *L.J.* 172.

[4] Phelips MSS. 216/74 (Phelips's text of his report of 30 Nov.). This mentions threat to send Coke into Ireland, and Lepton's claim to have secured the involvement of 'the best men in the kingdom'. For the French Ambassador's belief that Buckingham was responsible for the attacks on members, P.R.O. 31/3/55, f. 226. See also Chamberlain, 1 Dec. 1621.

aimed at revenge, could. There was truth in Phelips's comment: 'This trencheth directly to the overthrow of the liberties of the house, if the persons sentenced by the house may seek revenge even sitting the Parliament.'[1] Phelips was charged with investigating the case, and once again, as in the Mompesson case, Buckingham seems to have been left to protect a cover-up. James's first message about Lepton and Goldsmith seems to show he had known little of the case, and his later messages show that he was not prepared to countenance the use of a Star Chamber prosecution to punish Coke for his actions in Parliament. If Buckingham had indeed had such a plan, he would stand at risk if his connection with it were discovered.

The Lepton and Goldsmith case was being investigated by a committee when the Commons began their foreign policy debate, on Monday, 26 November. Sir Dudley Digges, who opened it, appears to have been one of the few wholehearted supporters of a general war in the Commons. He had the custody of many of Sir Francis Walsingham's diplomatic papers, and seems to have derived his view of foreign affairs from them. He can also be regarded as a spokesman for the war party within the Council. The same morning, his former tutor, Archbishop Abbot, was taking charge of the bill for transport of ordnance in the Lords. Its sudden waking from sleep at this time, and its delivery to Abbot, seem to confirm that it was a measure of the war party in the Council.[2] The heart of Digges's argument appears to have been that an open and general war would permit the collection of more allies than a secret one. From a former envoy to the Netherlands, the argument made sense. The fact that he was immediately supported by Rudyerd, Perrott, and Sir Miles Fleetwood would seem to suggest that the Pembroke–Abbot group in the Council had prepared in concert for this debate, and that at least one Buckingham dependent believed that there was nothing provocative in what they were saying. They were opposed by Sir Robert Phelips, who reminded them that 'the king of Spain professed to be our friend',[3] and said that want of trade rendered the country

---

[1] Phelips MSS. 212/25. This appears to be either an undelivered speech, or a full text of his very briefly reported speech of 11 Dec. (ii. 511). Phelips MSS. 216/74 (Phelips's report of 30 Nov.), P.R.O. 31/3/55, ff. 226–7, 4/14 Dec. 1621.   [2] *L.J.* 170.

[3] iv. 437–8, but see also vi. 197, where he is reported as saying we could not lose the Palatinate if Spain were our friend, and if we lost it, Spain was to be held

unfit for a war. It was Phelips who began what was to become more and more a central characteristic of the debate, the diversion of an attack on Spain into an attack on English Catholics. Secretary Calvert, the first Councillor to speak in the debate, reproved, not Digges, for talking of a general war, but Phelips, for trying to evade a subsidy.[1]

So far, there is no sign that any constitutional impropriety had been committed. Moreover, when Sir George Hastings, who spoke next, did try to talk of detailed plans for war against Spain in the Netherlands, he clearly did not catch the mood of the House, and his speech is curtly dismissed in Pym's diary in the words 'here were interposed some unseasonable motions'.[2] Glanville and Sir Thomas Wentworth wanted to get back to bills. Crew wanted to know 'against whom we are to fight', and wanted to go on with bills until the King's purpose was clear. He was in favour of a general war with Spain, but had no wish to do anything about it until the King's wishes were clear.

He was, however, the first member to mention the taboo topic of Prince Charles's marriage. James's plans to arrange a Spanish marriage for Prince Charles, while widely disliked, had been the subject of a total silence in the commons ever since February. Even now, Crew dropped the topic after one sentence, with the words 'but this is not fit for me to enter into'.[3] Digges was left to conclude the day's debate with a further plea for supply. The day's debate does not give the impression that either desire to seize the initiative in foreign affairs or desire for war with Spain was a very deep-seated emotion in the Commons. War with Spain was the more desired of the two, but even that had not been supported by many people outside the patronage of the Pembroke–Abbot group in the Council. No speaker had suggested the offering of any formal advice to the King. Even a command to debate foreign affairs had not encouraged them to attempt to direct, or even collectively advise on, the King's foreign policy.[4]

---

responsible. This has some resemblance to the wording of Goring's famous motion of 29 Nov.

[1] iv. 438–9, v. 404. Calvert would appear not to have believed the House was belligerent, since he used, as an inducement to supply, the argument that withholding it would lessen the hope of peace.

[2] iv. 439.   [3] iv. 440, vi. 198–9, *Nicholas*, ii. 215–16, v. 213.

[4] Elizabeth Read Foster, 'Petitions and the Petition of Right', *J.B.S.* (1974), 32–3.

That this was the general mood of the House was confirmed the next morning, 27 November. One single member, Serjeant Wilde, asked that the Commons should name Spain as the enemy, but he 'was quickly stopped by the dislike of the House'.[1] The silencing of Wilde is a sharp contrast to the tolerance shown to similar exuberant speeches in Elizabethan days. Neale of Dartmouth wanted war with Spain (he was one of the few members who appear to have felt under constituency pressure for it), but he too agreed with what was becoming the general mood of the House, to go on with bills until the King's will became plainer.[2] Pym and Coke also wanted to get back to bills. Since Coke's long tirade about the abuses committed by Spain is more commonly quoted in arguments that the Commons were seriously anti-Spanish than anything else, it is worth stressing that this speech was a rambling collection of memoirs, and that Coke's only formal proposal was to go back to bills.[3] Palmes, Seymour, and Sir Thomas Wentworth simply said they wanted to get back to bills, without saying anything about war, and it was Solicitor General Heath, not any private member, who introduced the idea of seizing the King of Spain's West Indian treasure.[4] Phelips, however, was still unconvinced that the King was ready for such a proposal, and said that 'they which speak for a war with Spain speak not seasonably'[5] At the end of two days' debate, this appeared to be the general mood of the Commons. They were ready to grant supply, with some reluctance, but they were not ready to offer any general advice about foreign policy.

Seen without hindsight, the debates of 26 and 27 November suggest that the anti-Spanish brigade in the Commons were neither large, powerful, nor determined. Such power as they had depended chiefly on their conciliar backing, and for this reason, if no other, they were not in a mood to propose constitutional innovation. Among the leading members, only Rich, with a proposal that any league the King might make should be confirmed by Act of Parliament, had offered any move in the direction of Parliamentary control of foreign policy. The members who appeared anti-Spanish in this debate, Digges, Perrott, Rudyerd,

---

[1] v. 214, iv. 441.
[2] vi. 215, *Nicholas*, ii. 218; iv. 441.
[3] vi. 202.   [4] ii. 455, *C.J.* 648.
[5] *C.J.* 649, iii. 469.

Crew, Rich, Pym, and Neale, consistently remained anti-Spanish. They later supported Buckingham when he too was anti-Spanish, and opposed him only when he seemed to be turning against France instead. But among them, the only ones who were able to offer the financial support needed to make a war a viable proposition were the three who, because they sat for the pocket boroughs of their patrons, did not have to depend on electorates: Rudyerd, Rich, and later Pym. There is perception in the words in which Goring reported this debate to Buckingham at Newmarket: 'I doubt not but having disported themselves they will every day more and more let his Majesty see that it was nothing but their zeal that first transported them and a desire that his Majesty might know the stream of their affection which is as great as ever was to any king and no way to cross upon his prerogative or direct him in his counsels.'[1]

The debates of 28 November supported this analysis. The Commons voted one subsidy, the second grant of the Parliament, without knowing for what purpose it was intended. Crew and Alford both protested that two grants of subsidy in a year demanded two harvests, but both nevertheless supported the grant. Yet, even while voting supply, they ignored Secretary Calvert's request that they debate the Palatinate before religion, and spent most of the day debating the question of recusancy.[2] Sir Edward Coke caught the mood of the moment by proposing that recusants, 'because they are aliens in heart', should pay double subsidy like aliens.[3] This proposal became regular practice for the rest of the decade.

After the vote of subsidy, 29 November appeared to be producing business as usual. Coke was back to the listing of patents, Neale to freedom of fishing. Five bills, for pleading the general issue, for relief of farmers of Crown land, for making estates of attained people liable to their debts, for reform of licences to alienate, and the Staplers' bill against the Merchant Adventurers, were sent up to the Lords. Even the bill for making the arms of the kingdom serviceable was briefly revived. Its revival seems to suggest a desire to please the Councillors.

The apparent peace was interrupted by Phelips's report of the case of Lepton and Goldsmith. It was this potentially emotive

[1] Zaller, p. 150.
[2] vi. 205.   [3] ii. 468.

subject[1] which in its turn was interrupted, almost on the hour of dinner, by the most significant move of the session: the motion of Sir George Goring. It was this motion which was the key event of the foreign policy discussions of the session, and Professor Zaller has proved that it was moved exactly as directed by Buckingham.[2] Goring was the first member to propose that the Commons, as a body, offer formal advice on foreign policy: he moved that 'if the King of Spain withdraw not his forces from the Palatinate and come not to the King's proposition, let us petition for war against him and we will assist him'[3] (i.e. James). Sir Robert Phelips, searching loyally for the royal line of the moment, seconded Goring, and 'confidently affirms that as the state of things are, our safety and happiness cannot be secured but by a difference with Spain'.[4] Since Phelips had, up to this moment, been the most vocal opponent of general war with Spain, his speech was taken to represent the conversion of the House. They sent Goring's proposal for a petition off to a committee, and promptly rose for their dinner.

In so doing, they had every reason to believe that they were being conciliatory. Goring's connection with Buckingham was as well known as Buckingham's with the King. Anyone who supported Goring has as good a chance as was possible in that uncertain atmosphere of saying what pleased the King. Phelips later said that he had supported this proposal for war with Spain 'not upon design or premeditation but suddenly and upon the occasion of a proposition from Sir George Goring at the rising of the house which induced me to think that something said to that purpose might conduce to his Majesty's ends'.[5]

---

[1] Rich had broadened the Lepton and Goldsmith case by attempting to link it with the case of Sir Henry Spiller. This could have involved a detailed investigation into the ways in which the recusancy laws could be allowed to remain a dead letter. S.P. 14/120/16, iv. 67, ii. 208, C.J. 652. Spiller had also been involved in searching Sandys's study during the recess. iv. 441. For the Commons' attack on Spiller in 1610 ,see Tite, pp. 72–4.   [2] Zaller, p. 152.

[3] ii. 474, v. 225. *Nicholas*, ii. 252 reports Goring's motion as in favour of a 'thorough war'.   [4] v. 225.

[5] Phelips MSS. 224/82. Like other outward letters in the Phelips MSS., this is a draft, and it cannot be proved that it was sent. Phelips thought he was in trouble for 'words of the Spanish match', not for anything said on the question of war or peace. The same point is made in Phelips MSS. 224/88. 224/87 (Phelips's preparatory notes for an examination by the Council) also dwells on the match, but not on war or peace. In his speech of 29 November, Phelips does not appear to have mentioned the match, though he did so later, on 3 December.

In the wording of Goring's motion there was a crucial clause, that *if* the King of Spain did not agree to James's terms, *then* they should support war with him.[1] There is an interesting discrepancy between the diaries' reports of Phelips's speech in support of Goring and Phelips's own reports of it. Phelips himself stressed strongly that he had spoken in the same conditional way as Goring, while the diaries report him as giving outright support for a breach with Spain.[2] It is impossible to judge certainly between these sources, but since the rest of Sir Robert's report of what happened is accurate, and since the diarists may well have been cursory in reporting the last speech before dinner, Phelips's account is perhaps to be preferred.

Goring's proposal for a petition was sent to the committee which was already in session to prepare a petition on recusancy. While it was in progress, the Commons at last completed the bill for free fishing and sent it up to the Lords. Giles and Glanville both declared, with more force than foresight, that fishing was much more important than New England.[3] When the petition came back from committee, on the morning of Monday, 3 December, it contained one clause which had not been in Goring's motion: a petition that the Prince should be 'timely and happily married to one of our own religion'. Yet though Goring had not proposed this clause, it appeared to follow logically from his motion. Goring himself described the proposal for war as 'that third point that was from my motion,' and it was reasonable to suppose that war with Spain would end plans for a Spanish marriage. Indeed, nothing expresses the entire unawareness of even the best-informed members at Westminster that they were sitting on a volcano than Goring's letter to Buckingham, written on the morning of 3 December. He said that since his last letter nothing

---

[1] I am grateful to Mr. David Hebb for persuading me of the potential significance of this conditional wording. The conditional nature of Goring's motion is clearest in *C.J.* 652 and *Nicholas*, ii. 252. Cf. p. 129n above. The interpretation here placed on the events of 29 Nov.–3 Dec. differs significantly from that in my article, 'The Foreign Policy Debate in the House of Commons in 1621', *H.J.*, vol. 20, no. 2 (1977), 289–309. Since I still regard both lines of explanation as compatible with all the known evidence, I have thought it best to let both go into print, and to leave others to choose between them. The key point of difference concerns Goring's motives, on which there is no direct evidence at all.

[2] Phelips MSS. 224/82 and 88: v. 225, vi, 213. Phelips is surely right in the stress he subsequently put on the timing of Goring's motion and his speech 'at the rising of the House'.

[3] ii. 483: also Sherfield, vi. 218.

of note had happened except the sending for Sir Edwin Sandys. He said the petition was to be debated that morning, and he thought it would be pared of anything offensive to the King 'whereof when they come to true deliberation they are most tender and sensible'. He ended casually: 'if aught of consequence happen, your lordship shall be sure to have it with all possible speed.'[1] In fact, the Commons did decide to leave the clause on the Prince's marriage in their petition to the King, but they had some ground for believing that it might be welcome to the King: as Coke later asked with some incredulity, 'Will he have wars with Spain and a marriage?'[2] To suppose James intended both at once did not make sense. If he was going to have war with Spain, then members would at last be authorized to do what they had wanted to do ever since the beginning of the Parliament, to express their dislike of the plan to make a Spanish marriage for Prince Charles.

While members at Westminster were still in blithe confidence that they were following the official line, and were encouraged in that belief by Solicitor General Heath, James at Newmarket was losing his temper. On 3 December, and therefore within twelve hours of the passage of the petition (which had not yet been presented to him), he composed an outraged letter to the Speaker.

We have heard by divers reports, to our great grief, that our distance from the Houses of Parliament caused by our indisposition of health hath emboldened some fiery and popular spirits of some of the House of Commons to argue and debate publicly of matters far above their reach and capacity, tending to our high dishonour and breach of prerogative royal.

The specific ground of James's anger was any dealing with the Prince's marriage. He also defended his right to restrain Sir Edwin Sandys, because: 'We think ourself free and able to punish any man's misdemeanours in Parliament, as well during their sitting as after'. He also told the Commons 'not to meddle with any man's particulars which have their due motion in our ordinary courts of justice'. This represented a long-standing conviction of

---

[1] B.L. Harl. MS. 1580, f. 430ʳ. On each re-reading, this letter seems harder to reconcile with any belief that Goring thought the petitioning of the King on foreign affairs was likely to be provocative. It does, however, appear possible that Goring viewed both the mentioning of the Prince's match and the case of Sir Edwin Sandys with some apprehension.

[2] ii. 505.

the King's, but in the context, it can only be taken as a reference to the case of Lepton and Goldsmith.[1]

To members who had been trying so scrupulously to follow the royal line, this royal message was a bolt from the blue. In the words of Sir Robert Phelips, he

remembreth all our proceedings this Parliament; to see whether any have deserved that, which now upon us. At the first access, the memory fresh of the late dissolution of the then Parliament, and of that which happened after; yet [we] with silence passed it over, resting upon the King's word by Mr. Secretary. [We] have never meddled with impositions (though highly concerning the subject's interest) to make this a Parliament only of union. We have broken all former precedents, in giving two subsidies at the beginning of a Parliament. In the matter of Ireland, etc. [we] forbore to proceed upon signification of the King's pleasure. That the King meriteth all this—wisheth we could do more for him [we] have given him one subsidy now more, contrary to the provision in the last Act of Subsidy. What then the cause of this soul-killing letter from his Majesty?[2]

Sir Robert's facts were right; he had indeed been conciliatory enough to be entitled to his astonishment. Can we then answer his question? What was the cause of this irate letter from the King?

Since the King, by his own account, had not yet received the Commons' petition, and indeed had not had time to do so, the 'divers reports' to which he refers must have come from somewhere else. It must be they which convinced James that the Commons had taken leave of their duty when they had not. What was the source of these 'divers reports'? Goring's letter of 3 December does not look a very convincing source of them. Goring, throughout his correspondence with Buckingham, was concerned to give a favourable impression of the Commons. He regarded them with a humorous and ironic detachment, but not with any ill will. His letter contains the information about Sir Edwin Sandys which James used that night, and Buckingham could well have used that to persuade James that the Commons were behaving badly. But nowhere in Goring's letter is the Prince's

---

[1] Tanner, op. cit., p. 279. James, while claiming that he had not restrained Sandys for Parliamentary business, nevertheless firmly asserted his right to do so. His objections to meddling with cases which should be heard in the ordinary courts of justice represented a long-standing conviction, but in the context of this session, it can only refer to the case of Lepton and Goldsmith. The imprecision of the reference, combined with James's subsequent retreat on this case, prompts the suspicion that he had been incompletely briefed.

[2] C.J. 658.

marriage explicitly mentioned. If James knew he was to be peti-
tioned on the Prince's marriage, he did not learn it from Goring.

Sir Edward Sackville, who had warned the Commons that the
petition on the Prince's marriage 'would be like the drug collo-
quintida, which being taken by the King will make him cast out
the rest', tried to persuade the Commons that James had been
informed by 'a stranger'.[1] He probably meant to cast the blame on
Gondomar, the Spanish Ambassador. According to Sir Richard
Weston, Chancellor of the Exchequer, the informant was much
nearer home: Charles, Prince of Wales. On 14 December, Weston
said the King had told him that a copy of the petition was sent
him by the Prince, 'who complained that his marriage was continually prostituted in the Lower House'.[2] If the Prince had
written to James with an entirely personal anger about the debate
on his marriage, this would help to explain the sudden outburst
of royal indignation which, it would seem, was as unexpected to
Goring as it was to Phelips. There would thus be no need to cast
Buckingham and Goring as the villains of the piece: the conditional
wording of Goring's motion makes it possible, though not necessary, to regard it as still within the terms of the King's current
foreign policy.[3] Buckingham, faced with an angry King on one
hand, and the cases of Sandys and Lepton and Goldsmith on the
other, may have been tempted to try to keep the quarrel going
when it began. He had, after all, had no reason to love this Parliament. But if it was, as Weston said, the Prince who informed
James about the debate on his marriage, it becomes possible to
understand the colossal failure in communication between Westminster and Newmarket. A very angry Prince, writing in a hurry,
could have given James the impression he received more forcibly
than any Councillor could have done without deliberate decep-
tion. This would also explain why reasonably well-informed
Councillors such as Calvert or perhaps Sir Humphrey May,
Chancellor of the Duchy of Lancaster,[4] seem to have been as

[1] ii. 487–8, 508 and n.

[2] v. 237–8, Chamberlain, 15 Dec. 1621, Ruigh, p. 12. The letter from Charles
to Buckingham, quoted by Ruigh on the same page, presents severe dating
problems. I have failed to find its MS original.

[3] I am grateful to Mr. David Hebb for persuading me of this vital point.

[4] Phelips MSS. 224/88. This is a draft letter from Phelips, addressed to 'Sr.',
reporting a conversation with 'the chanceler'. This could refer to Weston,
Chancellor of the Exchequer, or to May, Chancellor of the Duchy of Lancaster.
Since May was later described by Tomkins as Phelips's friend (Phelips MSS.

astonished by the royal reaction as anyone in the Commons. The flashpoint was not political: it was personal. This would also explain why the King's letter of 3 December says much about the match, something about Sandys, and alludes to the case of Lepton and Goldsmith, but says almost nothing about the foreign affairs debate in general.

Yet, however accidentally the issues of privilege and freedom of speech had appeared in the centre of the stage, and however reluctant James and the Commons had been to put them there, once they were there, they would not quietly go away. They were real issues. Just because most of the Commons had been so careful in practice to avoid any speech offensive to the King, they could not go further, sign on the royal dotted line, and announce that they had no right to discuss issues which did not please the King. Phelips was making a serious point when he said that if they abandoned their claim to freedom of speech, they could find they were abandoning their power to make law.[1] Even so innocuous a matter as the passing of a bill on sheriffs' accounts could involve members in listing abuses in the royal administration which powerful men did not wish to have debated.[2] Few members wanted to make the breach wider when it had happened, though Mallory may have been an exception. The King and his Parliament were supposed to be united, and if they quarrelled, they should be reconciled. As Digges put it, 'The husband and wife are to be made friends if they be fallen out.'[3] Yet Digges's image illustrates the difficulty of an accommodation, as well as the desire for one. Few members had the confidence of Sir Thomas Wentworth, protesting that their liberties could not be wrung from them by one letter,[4] or the calm of Noy, who argued that if they passed a remonstrance or a protestation to recover their liberties, they thereby acknowledged themselves out of possession.[5] Noy and Wentworth had been against war with Spain from the first, and could afford to be detached. Most of them were frightened, yet

---

219/33), he is perhaps the more probable speaker. The Chancellor, according to Phelips, 'vowed he himself, who was acquainted with the ways of court, did upon that motion believe that things were coming about and that his Majesty would have been contented to have that subject entered upon by us'. This draft was written while Phelips was in the Tower after the session.

[1] ii. 508.   [2] See Alford, 18 Dec., ii. 534, v. 241.
[3] ii. 532.   [4] *Wentworth Papers*, pp. 165–8.
[5] ii. 527.

they felt the need to make some minimum declaration of their privileges.

It is perhaps necessary to say that the constitutional power conferred on the Commons by freedom of speech has been over-rated: it was always open to the King, or the Lords, to reject what they proposed. There was much to be said for the case made by Henry Elsyng, the clerk:

And if my poor opinion may be heard, what hurt or prejudice can it be to suffer the poor Commons to have their consultations free, without check or control? They will use no unseemly terms of any man. They can do nothing of themselves; neither can they propound any thing but by way of bill or petition. If they be suffered to proceed freely, their proposition will be the sooner rejected or agreed on among themselves. If agreed on, it will be related to the Lords or to the King; and when it comes before his Majesty, it is in his power, (if the Lords stop it not) to make a full stay thereof, if he like it not. Whereas on the contrary side, to be denied liberty of speech seems very harsh unto them, and hath made them so jealous of their privileges, that they have appropriated more unto themselves than ever they claimed heretofore.[1]

From the royal point of view, it is questionable whether the issue of freedom of speech was worth the struggle devoted to it. Yet, to men like Phelips, who already believed their liberties, and Parliamentary government, were in decline, the right to freedom of speech represented an irreducible minimum, which they could not sign away.

When they said 'right', they meant the word: their privileges, they believed, were their inheritance. Liberties, like lands, were inherited from one generation to another. This was one line of reasoning that drove members' minds back to the *Apology of the Commons* of 1604, and produced from Phelips, Hakewill, and others a proposal that it should be repeated. The *Apology* also dated from a time when the Commons, again proceeding with official encouragement, had been equally badly misunderstood.[2]

Yet it seems that the introduction of the *Apology* of 1604 into the debate was one of the things which annoyed James most. For, just as the Commons could not sign on his dotted line, he could not sign on theirs. James could not accept that their privileges were their inheritance: he believed they were held by royal gift. James

---

[1] Elizabeth Read Foster, *The Painful Labour of Mr. Elsyng* (Philadelphia, 1972), 47n.
[2] N. R. N. Tyacke, 'Sir Robert Wroth and the Parliament of 1604', *B.I.H.R.* (1977), 120–5. *H.M.C. Salis.* xvi. 141–4.

had never been able to accept the body of ideas now known as belief in the 'ancient constitution'—the body of ideas with which Coke is especially associated. James had warned the Commons accordingly in his opening speech in 1621: he knew perfectly well he was taking issue with Coke when he said: 'Parliaments were instituted by monarchs, and that there were no Parliaments but in monarchies, that consequently kings and kingdoms were long before Parliaments, contrary to the fond opinion of some that thought otherwise.'[1] James believed in Parliaments, but he believed monarchies made and unmade them. The use of a cessation of business to make him say otherwise could only annoy him. That this difference in political ideas existed was something of which James and Coke had long been well aware. They had both been equally aware that they needed to work together on a variety of issues, and had tried not to thrust differences into the centre of the stage. James tried, as the Commons tried, to be conciliatory between 3 December and 19 December. Yet it caused James considerable impatience to find that, once again, members could not make ready the bill for continuance of statutes and the other business necessary for the end of a session. If the Parliament of 1621 did nothing else, it probably did more than any of James's previous Parliaments to make him doubt whether a Parliament was an efficient instrument of business. He retreated on Lepton and Goldsmith, he tried to tone down what he had said about privileges, but, however much he might try to express his willingness to continue their privileges, he did believe that it was 'antimonarchical' to claim that they were a right and inheritance, and not derived from his grace or that of his ancestors. Digges' image of the husband and wife who have fallen out was uncomfortably apt. Differences of opinion with which all parties could have lived quietly had been forced into the open, and when they were forced into the open, all the traditional compromises and silences became impossible.

The impossibility of compromise did not result from any lack of desire for it. James, in his final message of 18 December, offered to let the subsidy bill lapse. He asked the Commons only to complete the bill for continuance of statutes and the General Pardon: one administrative necessity and one concession to themselves. In the final messages, as throughout the Parliament, it is

[1] iv. 2, ii. 3, v. 425.

James and not the Commons who appears as the real enthusiast for Parliamentary initiative in legislation. James wanted to bury the hatchet, and allow the Commons to take home whatever good laws they chose to complete.

The Commons did not complete any legislation after 29 November. Nor did they make any attempt to continue a dispute on foreign policy: after the receipt of the King's first letter, there was no further suggestion that any foreign policy advice should be offered to the King at all. The Commons had not been eager to offer advice, and had done so only because they thought they had been asked to do so. Yet it was the Commons' very readiness to retreat on the practical point at issue which made it so hard for them to retreat on the theoretical point also. The final Protestation on freedom of speech was undertaken with a good deal of reluctance, and in the face of explicit opposition from Pym,[1] Sir George More, and others. They did not oppose it because they disagreed with its contents: they opposed it because they did not want to begin a fight they could not win. Many other members were so divided between desire to preserve their privileges and desire to conciliate the King that it is almost impossible to say, off the existing reports, whether they were in favour of the Protestation or not. Yet members of the Commons had retreated so far that they could retreat no further. They had abandoned their claim over Imposi tions in 1614. They had abandoned any attempt to advise the King on his foreign policy, or even to ask him what it was. If, in addition, they conceded the theoretical principle that they had no right to debate issues displeasing to the King, they would find that their institution was not merely obsolescent, but obsolete. As Hakewill said, 'The privileges of this House are the flowers of the Crown, and we shall never sit here again if they be not maintained.'[2] As Gardiner and Roskell have both pointed out, the attempt to restrict freedom of speech on principle was a new one, begun by Queen Elizabeth.[3] If these restrictions should be so far extended that members were liable to disgrace for following what

---

[1] vi. 244.   [2] ii. 533.

[3] Gardiner, iv. 255-6, J. S. Roskell, *The Commons and their Speakers 1376–1523* (Manchester, 1965), p. 51. Hakewill, the best historian in the Commons, anticipated Roskell in arguing that free speech antedated formal petitions for it. 'The prayer for this, in beginning of Parliaments, a matter of good manners: never used till of late years. Anciently, a protestation made by the Speaker in this point—1 H.4 the first prayer—fit to forbear this hereafter.' *C.J.* 667.

appeared to be the official line of the moment, Parliamentary debate could become too unsafe to be readily conducted. Having conceded all the practical points at issue, the Commons regarded their theoretical right to free speech as an irreducible minimum, which they could not abandon. They did not want to execute the right, but they could not sign it away for ever. The claims the Commons made in their final Protestation were not to debate anything novel: they were copied (correctly) from the writ of summons which James himself had allowed to pass under the Great Seal.[1] The claim that the ability to debate foreign affairs and religion was a 'right' was simply an alarmed response to an attempt to take it away from them. Later, when Coke quoted from the 1621 Protestation to support the renewed attack on Buckingham in 1628, it appeared as a document in which the Commons could take some pride. At the time, it was a powerless piece of paper, a last vain protest by a dying Parliament. James's formal removal of the Protestation from the Journals rather too heavily underlined the point. At the time, James appeared to have retained the whip hand as securely over foreign policy in 1621 as he had done over impositions in 1614. The war party in the Council, as well as in Parliament, was discredited. So far from Parliament having broken off the Spanish match, Chamberlain was reporting rumours that it was concluded. At the time the aptest epitaph on the Protestation was written by Chamberlain: 'vanae sine viribus irae, and . . . there is no disputing nor contesting with supreme authority'.[2] If anyone gained anything from the whole miserable episode, it was James. Early in November 1621, it was beginning to look as if James might be under irresistible pressure for war. The effect of the intervention of the House of Commons was to make this pressure not merely resistible, but negligible.

James did not decide till the very last moment to dissolve the Parliament. As late as 17 December, the Council were discussing excluding Sir Edward Coke, who had by now put too much strain on James's patience, from the General Pardon. In assuming there would be a general pardon, they were probably assuming that Parliament would meet again after Christmas.[3] It was not until

---

[1] P.R.O. C. 218/1. The writ of summons was no guide to the question by what right the Commons enjoyed freedom of speech. It was, however, a good guide to the subjects Parliaments before Queen Elizabeth's time had habitually debated.   [2] Chamberlain, 19 Jan. 1622. Also 4 Jan. and 22 Dec. 1621.

[3] *C.S.P.D. 1619–23*, vol. cxxiv, no. 49.

after Parliament had risen, again without completing business and without presenting bills for the royal assent, that James decided to dissolve them. In the process he threw away the second grant of subsidy, voted on 28 November, which had not yet been embodied in an act or prepared for the Royal Assent. After the Parliament, whether on James's initiative or on Buckingham's, steps were taken to punish some of the leading members. Coke, Phelips, Pym, Hakewill, and Mallory were imprisoned, Rich, Crew, Digges, and Perrott were sent to Ireland, and Sir Peter Hayman was sent to the Palatinate.[1] Phelips attempted to make his addresses to Buckingham to procure his release, and, not surprisingly, found that he was so unfortunate in his addresses to Buckingham that he decided not to trouble him further. A friendly visit from a Councillor, perhaps Sir Humphrey May, did not even get him the liberty to receive a visit from his wife and children in the Tower. He acknowledged 'want of a proportion of understanding' in what he had done in Parliament, but was not prepared to admit that he was to blame. He was finally reduced, having asked for favour in every quarter he could, to writing to Goring, calling himself Goring's 'unprofitable servant', and asking to be brought to 'trial and justice, that so I may stand or fall by the sense and censure of the laws of the kingdom the proper birthright and best protectors of the subjects thereof'. Whatever may have been privately held against him, the notes Phelips prepared for his examination by the Council suggest that, officially, he was in trouble for speaking on the Spanish match, introducing the *Apology* of 1604, helping to draft the final protestation (of which he said he was not guilty), and of trying to raise the case of Sandys and Southampton. Speaking in Parliament four years later, he remembered the Spanish match as the official issue.[2]

If it did nothing else, this imprisonment must have left Phelips with some hesitation about how far it was safe, either to follow Buckingham, or to recommend war with Spain. It must, then, have been with some trepidation that Phelips received, at the beginning of the preparations for the next Parliament, an overture from Buck-

---

[1] See my article, 'The Examination of Mr. Mallory', *B.I.H.R.* (1977), 125–32.
[2] Phelips MSS. 224/82–90, esp. 87 (Phelips's notes for his examination). *1625 Debates*, p. 81.

ingham to help him in bringing about a war with Spain. Phelips accepted this overture, but the distrust with which he did it played an important part in the history of the remainder of the decade. The fiasco of the second session of 1621 had many consequences. One of the most important for this story is that it did a great deal to increase distrust of Buckingham. In the next Parliament, when Buckingham did want war with Spain, he found that a number of people were surprisingly reluctant to believe him.

III

The Parliament of 1624: The Prince's Parliament[1]

Sir Thomas Wentworth arrived late for the Parliament of 1624. His lateness was involuntary, being due to an apparently severe illness, but it caused him no great regret. Indeed, he wondered whether to prolong it, and postpone his appearance at Westminster till after the Easter recess. Before going to Parliament, he wanted more information from the court to enable him to decide 'what I had best do'. He asked for the advice of his regular court contacts, Sir George Calvert and Sir Arthur Ingram. He also asked for a copy of the King's speech opening the session, and proposed to base his decision on them.[2] In normal times, this information would have served to give Wentworth an adequate brief to enable him to avoid giving offence. Calvert was Secretary of State, and Ingram was the close confidant of Lord Treasurer Cranfield. Together with the King's speech, their advice should have been enough. In 1624, it was not, for Wentworth's advisers themselves lacked sufficient information. Lords and Commons came to Westminster in February 1624 to face, not only the familiar obstacle race of a divided court, but a less familiar type of clash, in which, in Professor Aylmer's phrase, 'the Crown was divided against itself'.[3] On one side stood King James, on the other Charles, Prince of Wales and the Duke of Buckingham. The clash of wills between them overshadowed anything which could happen on the floor of the House of Commons. The Parliament of 1624 was not a dispute between King and Commons, or between court and country. It was a clash of generations in the royal family, which the opportunity of a Parliament allowed to spill over into public debate. As James's man the Earl of Kellie remarked shortly before the Parliament, 'It may come that the young folks shall have their world. I know not if that will be fit for your Lordship and me.'[4]

---

[1] This title was given to the Parliament by Christopher Brooke. Holles, f. 96ᵛ.
[2] *Wentworth Papers*, pp. 204–5.   [3] *E.H.R.* (1976), 131.
[4] *H.M.C. Mar and Kellie Suppl.*, p. 183 (Kellie to Mar). This report provides a sharp contrast with the enthusiasm of the younger generation in Mar's own family. Ibid. i. 123–4.

The division between James and Charles arose from James's ill-fated plan to arrange a Spanish marriage for Prince Charles. After the dissolution of the Parliament of 1621, these plans had continued at their usual stately pace. The total loss of the Palatinate had not succeeded in halting them. Though there was always a strong group in the Council which did not favour these attempts to negotiate a treaty with Spain, for much of 1622 the court was a comparatively peaceful place. Deprived of the opportunity a Parliament provided for conducting their quarrels in public, members of the court appear to have made a serious effort to make the best of each other. The future of Parliaments was uncertain. There is no need to give absolute credence to the Venetian Ambassador, who reported after the Parliament of 1621 that James had told the Council he would have no more to do with Parliaments,[1] but it was common knowledge that he had not found the second session of 1621 a good advertisement for Parliaments. Rudyerd, when he asked the Parliament of 1624 to 'cherish his Majesty's recovered inclination to Parliaments',[2] was doing no more than remind members of a distaste which was common knowledge.

What broke up the peace of the court was Charles and Buckingham's trip to Madrid. They suddenly departed from court, against James's wishes, to conduct their marriage negotiations in person, and remained in Madrid from February to October 1623. Mercifully, it is not necessary in a book on Parliaments to explain the motives for the trip to Madrid. We can still add little to the immediate comment of the Venetian Ambassador: 'The true reasons for this momentous step remain not only secret but absolutely unknown [sic]. Indeed, it is impossible to show them, since knowledge fails when there is nothing concrete.'

It is rather easier to show the consequences of the trip to Madrid. The first, the obvious consequence of a favourite's prolonged absence from court, was that his enemies began to organize themselves against him. The Venetian Ambassador, in the same dispatch, reported that 'the taking of the only Prince out of the realm or agreeing thereto is called by some, including great Lords, an act of treason for which he will have to answer one day to Parliament'.[3] Kellie, in October 1623, also reported plans to ease

---

[1] *C.S.P.Ven. 1621–3*, p. 199.
[2] Earle, f. 70ᵛ.   [3] *C.S.P.Ven. 1621–3*, p. 583; Pym, f. 10ʳ.

Buckingham out of James's favour, and said that though he was the King's man only, he would not join them. In January 1624, shortly after his return to England, the French Ambassador said Buckingham needed friends in Parliament because of the 'peu d'affection que lui porte son maistre'.[1] It is impossible, at this distance of time, to know how seriously we should take such rumours. What we can say with more confidence is that Buckingham was advised to take them seriously, and appears to have taken the advice. In September 1623, immediately before his return from Madrid, one of his confidential advisers warned him of an impending marriage alliance between the families of Lord Treasurer Cranfield, apparent leader of his new enemies, and the Earl of Southampton, who had spoken for his enemies in 1621. Buckingham was advised to make all efforts to keep friends, and to haste home 'for fear of the worst'.[2] Buckingham appears to have taken this advice seriously. Cranfield had prepared a rival homosexual favourite, who had secured James's attention, and the great men of the court, like the Earl of Pembroke, were in two minds whether to throw in their lot with this apparent new favourite. It is not surprising that when Buckingham was back in England, both Chamberlain and the Venetian Ambassador report him watching those who went in to the King 'like a sentinel'.[3]

Faced with this potentially dangerous court opposition, Buckingham survived because he was able, first to trump it, and then to split it. He trumped the opposition to him by returning from Madrid as firmly established in the favour of the Prince and future King as he had been in the favour of the old King. When he and Charles were faced by opposition, Charles was capable of threatening that, when he came to the throne, he would remember those who took part in the evil counsels' of his father.[4] This was a threat to which men like Lord Keeper Williams and the Earl of Arundel, who hoped most of their careers were still before them, could hardly be indifferent. It was sufficient to sway Pembroke, who hesitated a long time before deciding whether to back Cranfield's rival favourite for James's affections, and finally drew back because, in what appear to be his own words, 'he perceived his Grace to stand so well with the Prince'.[5]

[1] H.M.C. Mar and Kellie Suppl., p. 182; P.R.O. 31/3/58, f. 16ᵛ.
[2] Cabala, I. 230-1.   [3] C.S.P.Ven. 1623-5, pp. 208, 216.
[4] Ruigh, p. 28.   [5] Sackville MS. ON 245, Ruigh, p. 314n.

He split his court opponents by returning from Madrid a firm supporter of war with Spain. It is difficult to say whether the new policy of war with Spain was Buckingham's or the Prince's, since they both supported it with equal vehemence. What it did do was to cause consternation among Buckingham's court opponents. Since James, even after the Prince's empty-handed return from Madrid, still favoured the conclusion of a Spanish match,[1] for a short while opposition to Buckingham tended to become identified with a policy of friendship with Spain. This caused considerable dismay to men like Pembroke, in whom, as Professor Ruigh has said, hatred of Buckingham and hatred of Spain were balanced in almost exactly equal proportions.[2] For a short while Pembroke appeared to be a supporter of the Spanish match against Buckingham, causing dismay to admirers in the country who had always believed that 'the Earl favoured not the Spanish cause'.[3] During January 1624, the Prince succeeded in 'reconciling' Buckingham and Pembroke, and from then on, Pembroke allowed his hostility to Spain to beat his hostility to Buckingham by a short head, and gave wary but energetic assistance to Buckingham's plans during the Parliament.[4] Other war supporters, such as Southampton, automatically fell in with Buckingham and Charles when Buckingham and Charles adopted their policy.

The war policy split Southampton off from men like Lord Treasurer Cranfield, who, perhaps because he was aware how badly the country needed the Spanish dowry, and that it was likely to be bigger than any Parliamentary subsidies, seems to have been against war. Arundel and Williams should probably be counted, along with James, as opponents of war,[5] and the war policy made it impossible for them to continue to make common cause against Buckingham with Pembroke and Southampton.

If there was to be a war, there would have to be a Parliament, and if there were to be a Parliament, it was necessary to find some way of smoothing over the fears and distrusts which had accompanied the dissolution of the last Parliament. It has long been known that Buckingham and Charles, in managing the 1624

[1] Ruigh, pp. 18–26.   [2] Ibid., p. 262.
[3] S.P. 14/159/28, Sir William Pelham to Conway.
[4] Ruigh, pp. 176–7, 192–3 and other refs. The reconciliation was skin-deep, and in October 1624 Pembroke's brother Montgomery was again 'reconciling' the two men. B.L. Harl. MS. 1580, f. 445ʳ.
[5] Ruigh, pp. 33, 41, 141.

Parliament, made addresses to many of those who had been in most trouble after the Parliament of 1621. On 4 March 1624, shortly after the Parliament had begun, Kellie said that many of those who had troubled the last Parliament were now as much for Buckingham as they were against him.[1] Chamberlain, a few days later, said the Commons now distrusted Digges, Sandys, and Phelips because they held them for undertakers.[2] It now seems possible that Buckingham's approaches to prominent members of the previous Parliament began even before he had tried to persuade the King and Council of the case for a Parliament. In the papers of Sir Robert Phelips, there is an intriguing document entitled 'a discourse by way of dialogue betweene a Counsellor of State and a Country gentleman who served in the last assembly of the estates in the yeare 1621'.[3] This anonymous dialogue, which is corrected in Sir Robert Phelips's hand, bears what is presumably a later annotation by him: 'made in October att the returne of the Prince from Spayne by El Hombre de Marq. male dicto' (Buckingham had been raised from a Marquisate to a Dukedom in July 1623). If this document does indeed represent a dialogue between Phelips and Buckingham, the man Phelips called 'el hombre' was a likely enough man to be employed in it. He was Phelips's regular court contact, Nathaniel Tomkins, Clerk of the Prince's Council, in Buckingham's favour, and returned to the 1624 Parliament for Phelips's newly created borough of Ilchester.[4] The contents of the document confirm, on internal evidence, that it must have been drawn up within six weeks of the date Phelips ascribes to it,[5] and at all points which can be checked, the opinions stated by

---

[1] *H.M.C. Mar and Kellie Suppl.*, p. 193.

[2] Chamberlain, 20 March 1624.

[3] Phelips MSS. 227/16. I would like to thank Dr. Hirst, who discovered this document, for generously placing it at my disposal, and my wife and Mr. D. M. Shorrocks for much help in the transcription of Phelips's annotation, which remains uncertain. The attribution of this document is not beyond dispute, but its author, whoever he may have been, was clearly well acquainted with the minds and plans of both Buckingham and Phelips.

[4] Tomkins was returned for Ilchester, but ultimately chose to sit for another constituency. The other seat at Ilchester went to Sir Richard Wynne, who was secretary to the Prince, and had been with him in Spain. G. E. Aylmer, thesis cit., p. 908. On Phelips and Ilchester, see Lady de Villiers, 'Parliamentary Boroughs restored by the House of Commons', *E.H.R.* (1952), 175–202, esp. 179, 188.

[5] The plans to hold a Parliament had not yet been communicated to King or Council, and negotiations were still in progress for the Spanish match.

the Counsellor and the Gentleman coincide with those known to have been held at this time by Buckingham and Phelips.

Perhaps the main questions to be answered about this document are why, if it was authentic, it should have been drawn up, and why, having been drawn up, it should have been put into its present anonymous form. Phelips, after his unfortunate experiences in trusting Buckingham and Goring in 1621, is likely to have wanted some cut-and-dried assurance that he had not misunderstood what was proposed. Indeed, he had already shown that his reaction in such circumstances was to want to have it in writing. In December 1621, when the Commons received a message from the King permitting them to investigate the case of Lepton and Goldsmith, Phelips asked to have it in writing.[1] Faced by a second overture from Buckingham to support a demand for war with Spain, he is likely to have had the same reaction. For Buckingham, on the other hand, a written document presented problems when, as the Counsellor in the dialogue admitted, he had not yet discussed the proposed policy with either King or Council. An anonymous dialogue, a literary form to which Phelips was already addicted, was the nearest they could come to attempting to square the circle.

It is interesting that the specific undertakings the Councillor and the gentleman made in this document are all ones Buckingham and Phelips subsequently kept. The Councillor undertook to persuade the King and Council to call a Parliament, and in particular, to persuade them that a new Parliament would not begin with a big privilege dispute about the imprisonments of 1621. He undertook to attempt to break off the Spanish marriage negotiations and to bring about a war with Spain, while admitting frankly that 'his Majesty will pursue the temporizing way, and . . . till absolute necessity enforce it, he will not enter into open and public distaste with that King'. The Councillor under repeated pressure, undertook to save the gentleman harmless if he risked debating matters of state.

The gentleman, having had his arm twisted by the threat of an unparliamentary benevolence, undertook to try to procure from a future Parliament a grant of supply sufficient at least for military preparations against Spain. He undertook not to raise a dispute of principle about the issue of impositions, though making consider-

[1] N.R.S. ii. 510. The 'writing' was delivered the next day (p. 511).

able protests in doing so. It was perhaps most important to the Councillor to secure the promise he obtained that the gentleman would pass over the 1621 dissolution. In the words of the gentleman, 'I dare say they [i.e. the next Parliament] will find it work enough to deliberate and set in order the course and conduct of their future affairs, without much busying themselves to dig out of the dust the memory or trouble of past accidents, and I verily believe their affections caused by such a change (of policy) would work so powerfully with them as that they will cast upon these questions of privileges and liberties a remiss and moderate eye.' This was the point in the document which had caused the most trouble. The gentleman had entered into a vehement defence of the Parliament of 1621, most of which is a repetition of Phelips's speech of 5 December 1621. The gentleman refused, interestingly, to regard those imprisoned in 1621 as martyrs for Parliamentary liberties: 'Besides, my Lord, as it is not merely dying but the cause of death which makes the martyr, so it is not punishment which makes the offender but the offence, and when men are persuaded of the innocency of the sufferer, especially in such causes wherein themselves have an equal interest, they are more confirmed and made more constant in those ways which formerly they walked in.' The Councillor, having hotly denied having himself had any responsibility for the dissolution of 1621, threw out hints that another member of the Council had procured it. It is interesting that when the Parliament met, Phelips and Sandys, Buckingham's two closest Parliamentary allies of the day, were the two who insisted most loudly that the 1621 Parliament had been dissolved by the ill offices of Buckingham's new enemy Lionel Cranfield.[1]

It cannot be proved that these undertakings are the exact words of Buckingham and Phelips, but it can be proved that, if Chamberlain is right that there was an undertaking between Buckingham and Phelips, its terms very closely resembled these. It is also interesting that the gentleman, at one point in the dialogue, breaks into Spanish, and Phelips was one of the few prominent Parliamentarians who spoke that language. It was probably some such assurances as these which helped the Prince and Buckingham

---

[1] Holland, II, f. 12^r: Spring, 14 April. The Commons were persuaded not to blame Cranfield for the 1621 dissolution by Buckingham's most consistent enemy Sir Francis Seymour. Holland, II, f. 27^v.

to bring James and the Council round towards the decision to hold a Parliament, which appears to have been taken before December 1623.

It was still necessary to gather further support for the new policy in court, Parliament, and Council. In the Lords, the Prince was responsible for the restoration of favour to Oxford, Saye and Sele, and Hertford. Saye fell in with the Prince and Buckingham, and accepted promotion to a Viscounty. He and his circle were sincerely anti-Spanish, and his closest friends, such as Richard Knightley, seem to have tried as hard as they could to help Buckingham to his break with Spain.[1] The renewed favour of Hertford, however, did nothing to reconcile his brother Sir Francis Seymour, perhaps because Seymour, though against the Spanish match, was never a supporter of war with Spain. The Prince tried to reconcile Buckingham with another potentially useful ally, Lord Keeper Williams, but in this he was less successful: he only obtained a message to Williams from the Duke's patronage secretary, saying the Duke 'doth not seek your ruin, . . . but only will hereafter cease to study your fortune, as formerly he hath done'.[2] Digges's engagement with Buckingham cannot be dated, but we have Digges's own later word for it that it existed.[3] One by one, Buckingham's court and Parliamentary enemies were drawn into line, leaving only Lionel Cranfield exposed to the Duke's revenge.

The toughest problems in reconciliation seem to have involved Sandys and Coke, since James refused to let bygones be bygones, and made it, in effect, a condition of his agreement to a Parliament that Sandys and Coke should be sent to Ireland before it began. It was while the Prince and his friends were trying to make James abandon this determination that Sandys won the Kentish election by crying down his two opponents, one as a papist, and the other, Sir Dudley Digges, as a 'royalist'. This, Chamberlain drily remarked, 'will incense the King more towards him, which needs not'.[4]

[1] Ruigh, p. 36. *Fortescue Papers*, ed. S. R. Gardiner, Camden Series (1871), pp. 196–7.

[2] Ruigh, p. 141.

[3] Bodleian MS. Rawlinson A 346, ff. 226–7.

[4] Chamberlain, 17 Jan. 1624. I know of no other example from this date of the pejorative use of the word 'royalist'. The likeliest conjecture about its meaning would appear to be 'one who is too ready to vote subsidies'. The extent of the King's hostility to Coke and Sandys requires more explanation than is offered here.

Coke appears to have been in utter dismay at the prospect of being sent to Ireland in his old age, 'in hiberno tempore in Hiberniam',[1] and this dismay probably assisted Pembroke, Hamilton, and the Prince in bringing about the necessary reconciliation. On 31 January, only three weeks before the Parliament, Chamberlain reported that 'Sir Edwin Sandys hath made his peace, with a promise of all manner of conformity'.[2] Ironically, Sandys was the only one of Buckingham's new allies whose dependence on the favourite lasted. There is, interestingly, apparently no record of any peacemaking between Coke and Buckingham. At almost every stage of the Parliament, Coke was ready to speak alongside Buckingham's known men, Digges, Sandys, and Phelips, and appears to have been briefed on their tactical plans. There are, however, several speeches of his which indicate that his distrust of Buckingham was still on the surface. Perhaps the likeliest explanation of Coke's conduct in 1624 was that his dependence was on the Prince (he helped to manage the bill on leases in the Duchy of Cornwall)[3] but not on Buckingham. It is interesting, then, that the times when he crossed Phelips's tactical paths were to do with the abortive attack on Lord Keeper Williams, which was supported by the Duke, but not by the Prince.[4]

In the country, concern about the depression continued, and had not drastically changed since 1621. It had been joined by an increasing concern about the spread of popery, which surfaced in a number of places during the elections. In the Commons, it was expressed with vehemence by such men as Richard Dyott, member for Stafford, one of the most anti-puritan members in the whole of the Commons.[5] Two things contributed to raising this concern about popery in 1624. One was that throughout the time the Prince had spent in Spain, rumours, in large part well-founded, had been spreading that James meant, as part of the marriage treaty, to publish what would, in effect, have been a Declaration

---

[1] Stowe 366, f. 17[r].

[2] Chamberlain, 31 Jan. 1624.

[3] Pym, f. 24[r]. For the Prince's intercession on behalf of Coke, see *C.S.P.Ven. 1623–5*, p. 217.

[4] Pym, f. 7[r], Spring, 25 Feb. On the Prince's protection for Williams, see Ruigh, p. 142.

[5] Earle, f. 29[r], B.L. Harl. MS. 6799, f. 133[r]. For the remarkable 'charge' given to the voters of Cheshire by the sheriff, Sir Richard Grosvenor, see Hirst, pp. 164–5 and J. S. Morrill, *Cheshire 1630–1660* (Oxford, 1974), pp. 22–3.

of Indulgence.[1] This is what the Spaniards were asking of him, and it would have meant a full-blown suspension of the laws against Roman Catholics. Many people who were prepared to admit that some of their best friends were papists were nevertheless not prepared to admit that the principle of the country's uniformity in religion should be publicly abandoned.[2] It was in response to these fears that Charles was forced to promise, during the Parliament of 1624, that if he married a Catholic, any liberty gained by the marriage would extend only to her person—a promise noted in Pym's diary as 'worthy the memory'.[3] Such a promise was of course diplomatically impossible. France and Spain were the only countries which could supply a bride with a dowry fit to match English needs, and neither would accept a marriage treaty in which no concessions for Catholics were included.

It was also a normal reflex to identify preparations for war with attacks on recusants. One of the demands made by the gentleman in his dialogue with the Councillor was that he should be left free in Parliament to attack the spread of recusancy, and Phelips, speaking in the Commons on 1 April, said that because there was danger from abroad, they should take action against recusants at home.[4] Yet, as James had said in answering the Commons' recusancy petition of 1621, if other people executed the laws as well as himself, the problem would be much less serious.[5] The antipopish enthusiasts in the Commons persisted in demands that measures should be taken against 'justly suspected' recusants, as well as against convicted ones. The warnings of Sir Edwin Sandys, that they could not legally punish a man for being suspected, fell on deaf ears. Yet, when Phelips said that the number of convicted recusants was too small to be worth considering,[6] it is necessary to wonder whether the public protests about the need for unity in religion, passionate as they were, are the whole story.

Previous recusancy Acts, especially that of 1606, passed after

---

[1] For fears of such a declaration, see Hirst, loc. cit. For the grounds for these fears, see P.R.O. 31/3/58, ff. 67^r, 70^v and S.P. 78/74, f. 19. A draft declaration of 9 September 1623, suspending the recusancy laws, was included by Pym as an appendix to his 1624 Parliamentary diary (ff. 94–5).

[2] For the religious beliefs challenged by the Spaniards and later the French, see Russell, 'Arguments for Religious Unity in England 1530–1650', *Journal of Ecclesiastical History* (1967), 201–26.

[3] Pym, f. 51^r.   [4] Spring, 1 April 1624; Holles, f. 116^r.

[5] N.R.S. iv. 71–5, Hastings, p. 24.   [6] Holles, f. 119^v.

the Gunpowder Plot, allowed J.P.s to initiate a variety of proceedings against recusants on their own authority. With rare exceptions, of whom Sir Thomas Hoby is the most conspicuous, members of the Commons did not execute the recusancy laws in their counties with the vehemence they demanded at Westminster. They might demand the activation of the law that recusants should be disarmed, yet it was only in extreme national emergency or during a personal quarrel that they would actually use their existing authority to disarm Catholic gentlemen among their neighbours. To one brought up on John Foxe, popery was by definition foreign, and it was easy to exempt well-known neighbours from even the most vehement strictures against popery, idolatry, and the Whore of Babylon. Recusancy was yet another issue which put members of Parliament into a conflict between their central and their local capacities. At Westminster, they mostly wanted the literal enforcement of the recusancy laws. At home, most of them wanted their communities to live in reasonable harmony. They could not have both wishes.

Members, then, arrived at Westminster knowing that Buckingham and Charles were likely to press for war, that James was likely to oppose the pressure, that their countries wanted a low rate of taxation, and relief from the depression, and that, while their neighbours cried out against the Catholic threat, they equally resisted any attempts to tighten up the militia. It is no wonder that Sir Thomas Wentworth welcomed the opportunity to arrive late.

James, in his opening speech, went out of his way to be conciliatory. He invited the advice of both Houses on whether he should break the treaties (i.e. break off negotiations) with Spain about the marriage and the Palatinate. He assured them carefully that since they were invited to discuss this subject, they ran no risk of offending him by doing so. He also conceded the reading of the writ of summons which Coke had used to justify his claims to free speech in the previous Parliament. The writs said a Parliament was called 'for certain serious and urgent business touching the state and defence of the Kingdom and church of England'.[1] The wording of this writ, which Coke quoted correctly, seemed, like medieval practice, to authorize Parliamentary debates on both foreign affairs and religion. On relations with Spain, James

[1] P.R.O. C. 218/1.

said he was disappointed as if he had waked out of a dream, but said nothing on the crucial question of war. For further briefing on foreign affairs, he referred them to a 'relation' which Buckingham was to make to both Houses on the afternoon of the second full day of business, but without saying how far what Buckingham was to say enjoyed royal authorization.[1]

The new Speaker, Crew, was freshly returned from Ireland, where he had been sent in disgrace for his activities in the previous Parliament. His selection as Speaker appears to be a conciliatory gesture by Charles and Buckingham, and he was recommended for a seat by the Duchy of Cornwall.[2] He tried to make his peace by testifying eloquently to the virtues which experience had enabled him to discover in the royal government of Ireland. With his compliments, he mixed business, recommending the bills of monopolies, informers, and concealments as the three most important bills of the previous Parliament. He put in a special plea for a bill he had managed in the previous Parliament, to ease the procedural difficulties in the way of founding hospitals. His assistance probably had a lot to do with the fact that this bill reached the statute book as the first Act of this Parliament. The bill was nearly lost when Lord Russell spotted a serious flaw in its drafting *after* it had completed three readings in both Houses.[3] Without the assistance of the Speaker, it would have proved difficult to find the time to give the bill three readings in each House for the second time, and so to get it to the statute book. This measure had been introduced in 1621 as a measure for war preparedness, and it is necessary, to get the measure of what proposals for war meant, to remember that they turned members' minds to hospitals as readily as to singeing the King of Spain's beard.

Lord Keeper Williams, faced as he was by court minefields on every side, was understandably brief, confining himself to complimenting the Speaker, and giving the extremest expression ever given to the doctrine of the ancient constitution by saying that the first Parliament was when the three persons of the Trinity consulted to say *'faciamus hominem'*.[4] With this remark, the Com-

[1] Earle, f. 2ᵛ.

[2] Ruigh, pp. 59, 110, 157–8 and nn.; Duchy of Cornwall, Burgesses for Parliament 1623–4, f. 33ᵛ.

[3] *L.J.* 216, 218–19, 253, 254–5: Pym, ff. 24ʳ, 31ᵛ; *L.J.* 271.

[4] Earle, f. 10ᵛ.

mons were left on their own, with a day and a half to use as they wished before they heard Buckingham's Relation. It is instructive to see how they used it. They did not attempt to discuss foreign affairs, nor, after Sir Edward Cecil had carried a proposal for a public Fast, did they continue to discuss religion. They started passing bills with as much speed as if their lives depended on it. A list of the bills of the previous Parliament was quickly produced,[1] and they agreed on the motions of Hoby and Pym, to admit no new bills unless by special leave until all these had had a second reading. They also agreed to Pym's motion that private bills should be read before nine in the morning, to avoid obstructing the major business of the House.[2] Before Buckingham's Relation, on the afternoon of their second day, the bill against swearing had been sent to be engrossed without going through committee, amid 'general applause'.[3] The bill for the Sabbath was also engrossed without commitment, although the Recorder of London and some others objected that the bill showed a rural bias. It prevented people from gathering for festivities out of their own parish, and some members said that in small towns, this meant they could not so much as go for a walk without coming in danger of the bill.[4] Nevertheless, the rural bias of the House secured its engrossment without passing through committee. A bill for probate of wills, part of the onslaught on the centralization of litigation, had been read twice, committed, reported, and engrossed.[5] The concealments bill had been read twice, and was only sent to committee when Peter Wentworth's son Thomas insisted, in the face of Coke's vehement denials, that its text took more from the King than was intended. It ultimately came back from committee amended as Wentworth wished.[6] The bills of monopolies, supersedeas, and informers had been read a first

---

[1] C.J. 716, Earle, f. 13 ff.
[2] Hawarde, f. 10: House of Lords Record Office, Braye MS. 73, f. 5ʳ, Earle, f. 13ʳ.
[3] Holles, f. 81ʳ. The bill was moved by Alford.
[4] Pym, f. 5ᵛ, S.P. 14/159/85. Recorder Finch suggested that Londoners be granted an exemption for Moorfields, but it was not allowed.
[5] B.L. Harl. MS. 6799, f. 131ʳ⁻ᵛ.
[6] Pym, ff. 5ᵛ, 7ʳ⁻ᵛ, 31ᵛ. There was an intriguing attempt to make good come out of evil in the attempt to insert a proviso in the bill for Sir John Heigham, who had purchased a concealed rectory in order to make it presentative. The failure of this attempt is perhaps another sign of a House more interested in administrative than religious questions.

time. So had two private bills for naturalizing Philip Burlamachi, the King's biggest creditor, and his business partner, and Mr. Neale had tabled his bill for freedom of fishing. The bill to prevent recusants from evading forfeiture of their estates through uses had been read once, and the next day, was read again and engrossed without a committee stage.[1] In addition, the Commons found time to start a debate on the depression, in which Neale and Coke offered the now familiar mercantile and legal alliance. Coke complained of hindrance to freedom of trade by patents, and Neale followed him with a specific attack on the Merchant Adventurers, for restricting the sale of cloth, and on the Eastland Company, whom he held responsible for the acute shortage of masts in Dartmouth.

It is hard to resist the impression that it was with some reluctance that the Commons broke off from the passage of bills to hear Buckingham's Relation of what had passed in Madrid. Buckingham's Relation was an enormous report of the history of negotiations with Spain, which must have taken many hours to deliver. Pym records that he was given 'time of breathing' by the reading of letters, and the taking over of some points by the Prince.[2] The general message of the Relation was that both the Spaniards and some of the English ministers who had negotiated with them, were entirely untrustworthy, and negotiations should not be continued. This proposition was supported with such a wealth of detail that on the Parliament Roll, where it is engrossed as if it were a King's speech, Buckingham's Relation takes up seventeen full membranes. None of the diarists who reported Buckingham's Relation appear to have been sure of much more than that he thought Spain was a Bad Thing, and negotiations ought to be

---

[1] This list of bills is based on a conflation of C.J., Pym, Earle, Holles, and Spring. Jervoise (f. 1) also reports an attempt by Wilde to start a debate on fees in the Exchequer. The lack of a committee stage is a peculiarity of 1624, and only applies to bills carefully considered in the previous Parliament.

[2] Pym, f. 5ᵛ. P.R.O. C. 65/186. The Parliament Roll text of Buckingham's Relation is fractionally fuller than that in the Lords' Journals. The Parliament Roll has been used for formal proceedings on the breach of the treaties, partly because it is marginally the fullest account, partly because contemporaries regarded it as the authentic record, and partly because one of the most interesting procedural features of 1624 is the use of a separate Parliament Roll to record, step by step, the stages of the King's reluctant commitment to war. There are three rolls for this Parliament, one for the breach of the treaties, one for the statutes, and one for the impeachment of Cranfield. Elizabeth Read Foster, The Painful Labour of Mr. Elsyng (Philadelphia, 1972), p. 31.

broken off. Some passages, such as the hints that the Spaniards might have considered holding the Prince captive in Spain were doubtless designed to try to create war fever, but, as yet, there was no formal proposal of war: it was first necessary to break off negotiations. Buckingham had said before the Relation that any member of either House might ask him questions, but the only member who took advantage of this facility was Pembroke, with a barbed question possibly designed to establish Buckingham's share of responsibility for some of the policies he was now denouncing.[1]

When the Commons reassembled in their own House on the morning of 25 February, they were authorized to debate Buckingham's Relation, but they did not do so. They gave a first reading to the Speaker's bill for hospitals, and to Sir William Fleetwood's bill against arbitrary imprisonment contrary to Magna Carta. They gave a first reading to Neale's bill for freedom of fishing. The bill for limitation of actions, which was intended to ensure that actions of trespass and some other sorts of action should be brought within a limited period of time, was sent straight through to committee. The bill of informers was read a second time. Dr. Gooch, Vice-Chancellor of Cambridge, and Secretary Calvert, for Oxford, pleaded that the clauses directing informers to their local courts should be so re-drafted as not to threaten the privileges of the University courts. Coke replied that, because the University courts proceeded by civil and not common law, he would listen to no such amendment, so the bill was promptly engrossed[2] without passing through committee. Bills to ease the fees paid for recording land conveyances, and for the easier passing of sheriffs' accounts,[3] were read a first time. Pym, even though he was one of those who had helped to expedite procedure, was beginning to find the haste unseemly. He was rather dismayed when the bill against drunkenness was engrossed without a committee stage, although disapproval was expressed of a procedure whereby

---

[1] P.R.O. C. 65/186. On the reading of a letter from Olivares expressing objections to the match and to the treaty for the Palatinate, 'It was observed by reason of a pertinent question moved by the Lord Chamberlain that these letters were written when Porter was in Spain.' Pembroke's object could have been to establish either the Spaniards' duplicity, or Buckingham's gullibility, or both.

[2] Pym, f. 8r-v, Earle, f. 30v.

[3] Aylmer, pp. 191–2, but see also the memorandum by Sir Stephen Procter, P.R.O. CREST 40/18.

a drunkard could be convicted on the unsupported oath of his drinking companion.[1] The monopolies bill was read a second time. The procedure for committees was organized. Sir Robert Phelips moved for the Committee for Grievances to have power to send for records to summon witnesses, and to have power to hear counsel.[2] He also moved, unsuccessfully, for the Committee for Courts of Justice, of which he was chairman, to have power to set up a sub-committee to receive petitions. This appears to have been the opening move in Phelips and Buckingham's abortive attack on Williams, against whom petitions, some of them possibly solicited by Phelips, were now flooding in to the Committee for Courts of Justice. Phelips continued to make persistent attempts to get these petitions weeded out by a small sub-committee, but on this occasion he was defeated by Coke, who observed that the practice of a select committee to hear petitions had been used in ancient times, but had been abandoned for the good reason that it led to partiality.[3]

On the same day, 25 February, the attacks on recusants began. Sir John Jephson, a member of the Irish Council, and Sir Edward Cecil, later commander of the Cadiz expedition, said that two hundred determined recusants could easily destroy the Parliament, and moved for a guard.[4] This proposal was not adopted, but the Commons did adopt another proposal made by Phelips and others, that members with recusant servants should dismiss them for the duration of the Parliament. This proposal originated from an uneasy awareness that many members did not practice what they preached. A statute of 1606, for whose enforcement the Commons often asked, laid down that recusants should not come within ten miles of London without special leave. Any member who brought a recusant servant to Parliament thereby broke this statute. The motion was duly carried, but, except for an unsuccessful plea for exemption from Sir John Jephson, who said he

[1] Pym, f. 8ʳ. The offending clause was still in the bill when it reached the statute book. *21 Jac. I c. 7*, clause ii.

[2] Elizabeth Read Foster, 'The Procedure of the House of Commons against Patents and Monopolies', in *Conflict in Stuart England*, ed. W. A. Aiken and B. D. Henning (1960), pp. 57–85. Phelips seems to have been frequently associated with these improvements in committee procedure. It is tempting to compare the powers Phelips desired in committee with those he was in the habit of exercising at Quarter Sessions.

[3] B.L. Harl. MS. 6799, f. 133ʳ: Spring, 25 Feb.

[4] Spring, 26 Feb.

had an Irish Catholic servant whom he hoped to convert, we hear nothing of its enforcement.[1] It had to be left to Sir George Goring, of all unfortunate choices, to move that the Commons should defer this subject till they had handled the 'great business' of foreign affairs dealt with by Buckingham in his Relation. This time, Goring's motion had no seconder.[2] The impression is not of a House of Commons eager to seize the initiative in foreign affairs, but rather of one deferring the involvement which was asked of it until the last possible moment.

26 February was devoted to the Fast, and to the compulsory communion designed to detect concealed recusant members. When the Commons next met, on 27 February, they disposed of a subject which would remain hanging over them until it was debated: the question of privilege, raised by the imprisonments of the last Parliament. The subject was raised, significantly, by a man who was both a new member and a Buckingham client, Sir John Eliot. He suggestively took the line that the trouble had all been caused by one or two people misreporting Parliamentary proceedings to the King, and that, left to themselves, King and Commons would agree well enough.[3] According to Pym's diary, some people were afraid 'this motion would have put the House into some such heat as to disturb the great business', and Edward Alford tried to defer it to a more 'seasonable' time. Only one member tried to start a major privilege dispute, and that was Sir Francis Seymour. He moved two provocative motions, that the Protestation the King had torn out of the Journals at the end of the last Parliament should be re-entered, and that the gentlemen imprisoned after the last Parliament should declare whether it had been for Parliament business.[4] He was answered by Phelips, who said their meeting was a miracle, brought about by the Prince, that the eyes of all Christendom were on the good success of the Parliament, and, in gratitude to the Prince, they ought to lay aside 'distractions' and refer this business to a committee, 'not to

[1] Holles, f. 83r–v, Jervoise, f. 3, Spring, 25 Feb.
[2] Pym, f. 8r. Pym says Goring's motion was agreed upon, but no debate of the the 'great business' followed it.
[3] Ball, pp. 57–8, Ruigh, p. 171. For the ill will between Cranfield and Sandys, to which Eliot may have been referring, see N.R.S. iv. 399, 405–7.
[4] Pym, ff. 8v–9r, Earle, f. 31v, Holles, f. 84r. Coke's declaration that 'the liberties of Parliament are the common law' was an attempt to move the debate on to safely general ground.

meddle with matters past, but to provide nothing done might be prejudical in time to come'. If this had indeed been one of Phelips's undertakings to Buckingham, he had kept his word. Two of his fellow-sufferers, Coke and Perrott, supported him in his desire not to make an issue of what was past, and the subject was safely shunted off to a committee from which it did not emerge. Seymour, it is interesting to note, had received no support at all for his two wrecking motions, which were 'not approved of by the House'.

At this moment, Buckingham received unlooked-for confirmation of his sincerity in attacking Spain, in the form of a complaint from the Spanish Ambassador, who said that Buckingham deserved to lose his head for the things he had said about Spain in his Relation. Phelips observed that 'in the way that Buck. did now run' he expected to see many Spaniards lose their heads instead.[1] Coke, with ominous reservation, said that Buckingham did not deserve to lose his head for anything he had done since his return from Spain,[2] and the Commons as a whole resolved that Buckingham was worthy of honour and thanks. It was ordered that members could take copies of Buckingham's Relation out of the Clerk's book, and, on the motion of Solicitor General Heath, the House agreed to consider the question of the breach of the treaties next Monday, 1 March.

Even so, before taking up foreign affairs, they found time, at the Committee for Grievances that afternoon, to discuss the New England patent and its restraint on fishing, the evil and unscrupulous execution of the patents for lighthouses (which was said to have grown worse since the last Parliament),[3] and the oppressions involved in the patent for concealed tithes. It is hard to resist the impression that such subjects were nearer members' hearts, as well as nearer their homes, than the vexed question of what Charles and Buckingham had done in Madrid.

When the Commons came to take up the question of the breach of the treaties with Spain, on Monday, 1 March, the Lords had

[1] Holles, f. 86ᵛ. It is hard to tell whether Holles or Phelips was responsible for the pun.

[2] 'Sir Edw. Coke he would not speak of his going into Spain but since his return he had not deserved the loss of his head.' Pym, f. 10ʳ.

[3] Pym, f. 10ʳ, Spring, 27 Feb., G. G. Harris, *The Trinity House at Deptford*, pp. 205–6. The new complaint about the project for the Lizard lighthouse suggests the project was still on foot.

been well before them. On 29 February, Locke reported to Carleton that there had been a general cry for war in the Upper House, in which the bishops had been in the lead.[1] The contrast with 1621, when the Lords had been silent on foreign policy matters, is striking. On 27 February, the Lords began by quickly clearing Buckingham from the charges of the Spanish Ambassador, with Archbishop Abbot offering prayers of thanks to the Prince for dispersing the 'mists' which surrounded the negotiations with Spain. That afternoon, they started their debate on the breach of the treaties. Abbot, who opened the debate, still clearly feared a repetition of the fiasco of 1621. He said:

Custom of this House to be scrupulous to enter into matters of great importance until a proposition be first made to lead them thereinto. Remembered the King's speech to be advised by his people etc. This business concerns a great King that is yet in amity with our King. Therefore that we speak nothing that may be dishonourable to that great prince, but to confine them to the officers.[2]

Having, with this preamble, apparently reassured himself that he was on safe ground, he worked up to his conclusion, that past experience showed they would be 'more deceived' if they continued their negotiations with Spain. Pembroke moved that they concert their advice with the Commons.[3] Bishop Morton of Coventry and Lichfield moved to collect a list of all the disappointments the King had received in the treaties. The first two speeches apparently pressing for war came from Lord Brooke, a former Chancellor of the Exchequer, and from Neile, Bishop of Durham. Mountain, Bishop of London, offered to go and fight in person, and Lord Sheffield revived the proposal of 1621, to recover the Palatinate by a war of diversion against Spain. On 28 February, Lord Spencer joined the demand for war, and Bishop Neile compared peace between England and Spain to peace between Israel and the Ammonites—a useful reminder that strong biblical imagery was never a monopoly of puritans. Pembroke, who seems to have hedged his bets, continued to confine himself to insisting on good correspondency with the Commons. Bishop Morton thought the Spanish match a conspiracy started

[1] S.P. 14/159/94.

[2] *Lords' Debates*, ed. Gardiner, pp. 5–6. In this chapter, further references to *Lords' Debates* are to this edition.

[3] Pembroke's demands for concerted action with the Commons parallel the demands of Rudyerd and Perrott for concerted action with the Lords.

by the Pope, and gave thanks to God for giving judgement to
the Prince to discern, and Buckingham to discover, this conspiracy.
He ended with an outright call to arms. No voices were raised on
the other side.

On 1 March, the Lords went on to serious plans for war. They
set up a committee to oversee munitions, and asked Buckingham
as Lord Admiral to stay shipping. The Bishop of Bangor, and
William Laud, Bishop of St. David's, called for the disarming of
papists and the blocking up of Milford Haven. Southampton
asked for an account of the state of the Ordnance Office, which
the Master of the Ordnance promised to give 'tomorrow', Lord
Sheffield asked for every Lord Lieutenant to certify the state of
his county magazine, while Lord Russell revived the familiar
proposal to ban the export of iron ordnance.[1] If this sort of demand
for war, based on a belief that the world was divided into the
forces of light and darkness, be accounted puritanism, if it be
'puritan' to believe, as Bishop Carleton wrote to Sir Dudley
Carleton, 'that concerning the Spaniard, I never doubted but one
of these must follow: that either we must be papists as they are:
or they must be professors of the Gospel as we are: or else there
will be wars in the end',[2] then the Parliament of 1624 contained
more puritans on the bench of bishops than anywhere else in
either House. If the word 'puritan' is defined to mean those who
took their Protestantism seriously, then the bench of bishops is
the most logical place to find 'puritans'.

It is precisely this note of practical belligerence, of a sense of
impending conflict between the forces of light and the forces of
darkness, which is almost entirely lacking in the Commons'
debates of 1624. Besides the Lords' debates of 27 February to
1 March, the Commons' debates on the breach of the treaties
sound remarkably tame affairs. Outside the circle of the Prince and
the Duke only two members seem to have seen the clear-cut
conflict between good and evil which was apparent to bishops like
Morton and Abbot. One was Peter Wentworth's son Thomas,
and the other was John Pym.[3] In particular, there was very little
in the Commons of the practical readiness to prepare for war
which had been expressed by Lords like Southampton and
Sheffield. Now that Buckingham's patronage network is better

[1] *Lords' Debates*, pp. 6–16.   [2] S.P. 14/164/11.
[3] Spring, 19 March.

understood, it can be seen that demands for war coming from outside that circle and Pembroke's are conspicious by their absence. Many members were ready to agree to war, but apart from Wentworth and Pym, only Neale of Dartmouth,[1] from outside Buckingham's network, could be said to be pressing for it. We perhaps need to ask again whether, in 1624, Buckingham entered into war to satisfy the Commons, or whether the Commons entered into war to satisfy Buckingham.

It may be objected that Buckingham, whose knowledge of other people's political outlooks was exceptionally well-informed, clearly expected and believed that he had a vehemently anti-Spanish Commons to handle. It may be objected also that many anti-Spanish sentiments may have been kept quiet, either because Buckingham's and Pembroke's Parliamentary teams did all the talking that was needed, or because members were hesitant to become engulfed in an unresolved conflict between Buckingham and Charles and a still unconvinced King. Yet it should also be said that Buckingham, as Professor Ruigh has pointed out, lacked a territorial base outside London,[2] and was not as secure in his grasp of the network of loyalties that bound members to their neighbourhoods as he was of the state of faction at court. Since the pressures against war were mainly local ones, expressed in the form of resistance to taxation, Buckingham, and even more Charles, may well have underestimated them. More crucially, they may have failed to distinguish between two different senses of the words 'anti-Spanish'. Buckingham was certainly right that there was overwhelming opposition to the Spanish match. In the debates of 1 March, on the breach of the treaties, Buckingham was asking for something which was widely popular. On the other hand there was no ground for Buckingham's belief that the breach of the treaties necessarily implied war.[3] The desire to have no truck with the Spaniards did not necessarily imply a desire to fight them. The desire to break off negotiations for the marriage could as easily be based on isolationism as on belligerency, while even those who sincerely wanted a war were capable of wondering whether they really wanted it enough to press their neighbours as soldiers, or, even worse, to receive soldiers who came from other counties. If the words 'anti-Spanish' are taken to mean dislike of alliance with Spain, then the Commons throughout the decade

---

[1] Ruigh, p. 221.   [2] Ruigh, p. 68.   [3] Pym, f. 13r.

were overwhelmingly anti-Spanish. But where was the demand for war? It is with these questions in mind that we must look again at the debate on the breach of the treaties, and ask whether the war which followed was the Commons' war, or Buckingham's and the Prince's war.

It should be said that in some ways the evidence is difficult to evaluate. Much desire for war may have been muted in response to James's visible reluctance, and much hesitation was caused by doubts whether James actually intended to allow any war to break out. Members who wished to succeed in being as conciliatory as they tried to be in 1621 could well have muted their demands for war in deference to royal susceptibilities. Early in the debate on the breach of the treaties, on 1 March, a message from James, delivered by Secretary Calvert, reminded the Commons that James had not abdicated all control of policy to the Prince and Buckingham. The message said he took note that there were many petitions in the House against Lord Keeper Williams (three were delivered that morning), and that he took note that there were more to come. He commanded them to receive no more such petitions against Williams unless it were for corruption. According to Pym's diary, 'The general silence showed this to be no welcome message.'[1] Nevertheless, it succeeded in driving the attack on Williams underground. Phelips continued to labour to find evidence of corruption against him, but in all the rest of the Parliament, he only found one case, and that not to do with corruption, on which he hoped he might proceed to trial. Williams was finally cleared by vote of the Commons on the last day of the Parliament.[2] With Cranfield and Williams, as with Bacon and Mandeville in 1621, one of two threatened ministers escaped, and the other fell, because one received James's wholehearted defence, and the other did not. Once again, it was the man accused of corruption who was left to prove his innocence, and failed. If James could stop the attack on Williams, perhaps he might stop the attack on Spain also. This thought may have inhibited many prospective speakers.

Yet, if it is necessary to ask how far the debates on the breach of

---

[1] Holland, I, f. 14^v, Pym, f. 12^{r-v}, Holles, f. 87^v.

[2] Phelips MSS. 216/66, S.P. 14/164/46, S.P. 14/162/8, C.S.P.Ven. 1623–5, p. 242, C.S.P.D. 1623–5, vol. clxiii, no. 50, Holles, f. 123^v, Earle, f. 196^r. There was perhaps poetic justice in the injustice whereby Phelips, on his return to Somerset, was accused by one of Poulett's faction of suppressing petitions against Williams. Phelips MSS. 228/26.

the treaties were influenced by awareness of the views of James, it is equally necessary to ask how far they were influenced by awareness of the views of Buckingham and the Prince. This raises the whole question of how far a patron–client relationship was held to impose a common policy on those who accepted it. The normal answer appeared to be that it was only held to impose an obligation to follow a common policy on the client where the patron's personal interests were touched. A Buckingham dependant in the Commons was bound to oppose the Duke's impeachment, but he was not bound to oppose the bill to restrict purveyance of carts. In the middle ground between these two extremes, the extent to which the patron expected a common line varied according to the intensity of his involvement in the issue. On some issues, there was no suggestion of a common line at all: on others it was hoped for, but it was recognized that some with strong views on the subject would be unable to subscribe to it. Those without strong convictions, on the other hand, could easily fall in at the patron's convenience. The two demands of Buckingham and the Prince in 1624, for war with Spain and the impeachment of Cranfield, were ones to which they had committed their personal fortunes. Nevertheless, their following was not unanimous. William Noy, recommended on the Duchy of Cornwall list for Fowey, and returned on a blank indenture, is as clear a case of nomination by influence as can be imagined.[1] Nevertheless, he failed to rally to the Prince, either in the issue of war, or on the impeachment of Cranfield, which he opposed.[2] Noy's service to the Prince mainly consisted of managing the legal and Parliamentary business of the Duchy, and it is possible that he thought his obligation to the Prince extended no further. How far, then, is the demand for war with Spain explained away if it all came from clients of Buckingham and the Prince, or of Pembroke?

It is clear that their views may have been expressed in a form which was slanted towards the views of their patrons. A client, especially of so sensitive a patron as Buckingham, might be expected to stress that part of his views which was congenial to his patron. This is much more true on an issue like war with Spain in 1624, on which the Duke had staked his very survival, than it is on an issue like that of Arminianism in 1625–8, where the Duke

---

[1] Ruigh, p. 58, P.R.O. C. 219/38, pt. 1, no. 38.
[2] For Noy's defence of Cranfield, see Holles, f. 119r.

hoped to keep people guessing about his views for as long as possible. On Arminianism, a split following, each speaking according to his conscience, was a positive advantage to the Duke. On war with Spain, it was not. It is then probable that the reservations expressed by such would-be Buckingham clients as Sir John Saville ran rather deeper than the public debates suggest. Indeed, reluctance to enter into war with Spain seems to be almost the only thing on which Wentworth and Saville factions in Yorkshire were agreed. As Dr. Ball pointed out, much of the resistance to war was centred round the 'northern men' in the Parliament.[1]

Yet, when this is said, it seems that, among what might be called Buckingham's standing faction, there were a high proportion whose commitment to war with Spain was sincere, and not opportunist. Sir John Eliot, Sir Robert Harley, Sir Miles Fleetwood, and Secretary Conway are cases in point. In Conway's case, the sincerity of his commitment to war with Spain is underlined by his slow removal from the Secretaryship when the anti-Spanish policy to which he was committed was going out of favour.[2] It is less possible to be certain about the new allies of the Prince and Buckingham, the men who carried the House in 1624, Digges, Sandys, Coke, and Phelips. Among these four, Digges must count as a committed war supporter. His speech of 26 November 1621, his memorandum compiled for Charles on his accession, and his part in the impeachment of Buckingham all show Digges as anti-Spanish and pro-French.[3] It is not until the Parliament of 1628 that Digges can be seen to be really disillusioned with war. Moreover, he had been trying since 1621 to establish himself as the client of the Prince,[4] and seems to have hoped that the Prince was a likely champion of the anti-Spanish cause.

After Digges, the next on a scale of commitment was Coke. There is no doubt about the intensity of Coke's hatred of Spain. His speech of 27 November 1621 had blamed Spain for everything from the Pope to the pox. Yet that speech had ended with a proposal to go back to bills, with which Coke was much more at home. In 1624, unlike any other Parliament, Coke offered a commitment to war which was at least noisy. He claimed that

---

[1] Ball, p. 37.   [2] C.S.P.Ven. 1626–8, pp. 166, 177, 187, 214.
[3] S.P. 16/19/107: below, pp. 267, 289.   [4] S.P. 16/19/107.

England never prospered so well as when at war with Spain. Yet, when Coke said that the thought of war with Spain made him feel seven years younger, on may wonder whether there was a nostalgic element in his support for it.[1] Coke was an old Elizabethan, constantly reminiscing about the days of his youth, when England had been glorious and the identity of friends and enemies had been beyond dispute. The extent to which Coke drifted back into Elizabethan reminiscences whenever the subject of war with Spain was mentioned must raise the question whether support for war, particularly since it was so transitory, at least in any overt form, represented an attempt to live in the past or to adapt to necessity rather than to make a commitment to the present. The next time Coke made a major speech touching the subject, on 5 August 1625, the commitment to war with Spain was still there, but it was reiterated automatically and without great enthusiasm. Coke's enthusiasm had by then returned to its more regular themes, of administrative and legal reform. Coke was a supporter of war with Spain, but his support had a ritualistic quality characteristic of an old conviction unthinkingly reiterated.

The most intriguing case is that of Phelips. Up to 1618, Phelips had combined an element of isolationism with being genuinely pro-Spanish. He had served under Digby in the Madrid embassy, and still continued through the twenties both to annotate documents in Spanish, and to quote Spanish practice with approval.[2] After 1618, his reflex pro-Spanish approach, and his reflex isolationism, came into conflict with a passionate concern about the fate of the King's daughter, Elizabeth of Bohemia. Phelips was perhaps one of those who felt most strongly the sense of disgrace involved in the fact that, when Elizabeth of Bohemia was driven out of her hereditary lands in the Palatinate, it was to the charity of the Dutch, not the English, that she had to turn to relieve her destitution. Unlike ritual anti-Spaniards such as Coke, Phelips really cared about the Palatinate. After the Palatinate had come under attack, Phelips's dislike of the Spanish match was a heartfelt commitment.[3]

[1] S.P. 14/160/63; Holles, f. 97ʳ.

[2] Katherine S. Van Eerde, 'The Spanish Match through an English Protestant's Eyes', *Huntington Library Quarterly* (1968–9), 59–76.

[3] For an example of Phelips quoting Spanish practice with approval see *1625 Debates*, pp. 109–10, intriguingly, in the sentence before his famous statement that 'we are the last monarchy in Christendom that yet retain our original

Yet, though Phelips cared about the Palatinate, he cared even more about Somerset. The effect of war on his county being what it was, he could not pursue both convictions. As always with a man whose two main convictions are in conflict, Phelips could give the impression of rapid change on the subject of war: sometimes one conviction came uppermost, and sometimes the other. Phelips was the sort of man for whom the case of Edward Floyd, in 1621, had been a tailor-made opportunity to square the circle. He might say he had looked for a better opportunity to express his devotion to the King's daughter, but he never found an easier one. He did not show great enthusiasm for war either in 1621 or in 1625. His only statement giving direct support for war in 1621 had been in his speech seconding Goring's motion, when, as he said, he thought such a speech, 'might conduce to his Majesty's ends'.[1] It only took a little encouragement to turn Phelips into a supporter of war, but a man whose life was so dominated by the politics of his own county could never become a whole-hearted supporter of war. In 1624, he spoke that part of his convictions which was pleasing to the court powers he was serving at the moment.

Perhaps of these four, the most reluctant to support war was now Sandys. Unlike the other three, he had, as a member of the Virginia Company, genuine economic rivalries with Spain. Yet his concern with economic affairs, while it gave him a motive for war, also showed him powerful reasons against it. In 1621, unlike his friend Southampton, he had never appeared publicly as a war supporter. Even in 1624, he showed, in his reports from the committee of trade, that he was already worried for fear the decay and burdening of trade might 'make the people unable to support a war'. At the same time, he was more aware than most of his fellows that if they were recommending war, they must be careful not to insist on such redress of grievances as would diminish the King's revenue.[2] Sandys in 1624 was already within measurable distance of

---

rights and constitutions'. On the other hand, the failure of the Spanish match also convinced him that the Spaniards were a 'subtle, artificial, foxlike people', ibid., p. 80. Phelips's attitude to Spain is perhaps best described as a love-hate relationship.

[1] Phelips MSS. 224/82: see above, p. 133.

[2] Earle, f. 53^{r-v}, Pym, f. 19^r, Earle, f. 74^r, Pym, ff. 44^r, 46.^{v} Some of Sandys's hesitation may have been because of doubt about whether war would break out. On 22 March he said a grant of supply would follow the outbreak of a 'real war'. Pym, f. 36^v.

the Sandys of 1626, who thought that this little island was unable to support a major European war without placing an unacceptable burden on its people. If Sandys's economic realism had not restrained his belligerence, the trouble he had about subsidies with the Kentish electorate would have been enough to do so.[1] It seems a possible conclusion that Sandys gave Buckingham his support for war in 1624, with his inclination, but against his better judgement.

If we see them against this background, what impression do we get of the debates on the breach of the treaties and the granting of supply? The business of the breach of the treaties ran over a month's debates: the separate Parliament Roll devoted to the subject runs from Buckingham's Relation of 24 February to Buckingham's announcement of 24 March that messengers had been sent to Spain to break off negotiations. The Commons first considered the subject on 1 March, having already received very considerable encouragement from the example of the Lords. The debate was opened by Pembroke's client Sir Benjamin Rudyerd, in a speech which Pym's diary calls 'the mould of the resolution of the whole Parliament'.[2] Pym was right: much of Rudyerd's opening speech was ultimately incorporated in the preamble of the subsidy bill.

In asking for the breach of the treaties, Rudyerd was asking for something which, however reluctant James might be to admit it, was already to a large extent a *fait accompli*. As he pointed out, the treaty for the restitution of the Palatinate had produced effects which were the opposite of those intended: 'Since the beginning of this treaty, and most by colour of it, we have lost the Palatin[ate] altogether, and almost all our party of the religion abroad.' He did not think the Palatinate could be recovered. In words which are interesting in a man who was later in the audience at Middleton's *A Game at Chesse*, he dismissed the Palatinate as a 'lost piece'. The treaty for the marriage, as Rudyerd's extravagant praise for the Prince reminded his hearers, could not easily be continued without the Prince's consent, which was now most unlikely to be available. In spite of all the efforts of James and the Spanish ambassadors, the treaties were already dead. Parliament's help was being asked for the task of inducing James to give them

[1] Hirst, pp. 174, 144; above pp. 212–13, 223–4.
[2] Pym, f. 10ᵛ.

a formal funeral. The fact that throughout the Parliamentary debates, no one spoke openly for the continuation of the treaties may be connected with the fact that there was no practical method by which they could be continued.

But what was to happen if the treaties were broken? Rudyerd's carefully guarded opinion was that a war was 'likely to ensue'. 'If we break off the treaty, we must make good the breach, and the likeliest way is by war, which is the manlier and more English way; and though we have no war presently, yet it is fit we should presently provide as if we had one.' Yet Rudyerd did not say by which side a war would be initiated. The nearest Rudyerd came on 1 March to a formal proposal that England should begin a war was in his again carefully worded proposal that England should make an alliance with the Low Countries, and so make 'a diversion of war'.[1]

Those who expected war when they debated the breach of the treaties, then, were not necessarily supporters of war. Some of them were supporters of war, but others expected Spain to respond to the breach of the treaties by attacking England. Sir John Strangeways, one of those who spoke most practically on preparations for war, said he feared an invasion and therefore wanted a defensive war. He said: 'Necessarily if the treaties break the King of Spain is in honour engaged on a war.' This was not a voice the Commons could ignore: Strangeways was a close friend of the Earl of Bristol, the recent ambassador to Madrid, and had served with him in the Madrid embassy. Both his political record throughout the decade and his friendships suggest that he was an opponent of war when he believed that he had the choice. His desire to confine recusants, defend the sea coasts, mobilize the trained bands, and raise money through recusant forfeitures is a move for self-defence by a man who would have preferred peace, but did not believe he had the choice.[2]

For Buckingham and his team, who did want a war with Spain,

---

[1] See Phelips, *1625 Debates*, p. 81, for the view that as soon as the Prince returned from Spain 'the treaties were, in real intention, broken'. The best report of Rudyerd's speech is in Earle, ff. 33ʳ–36ᵛ. This appears to have been copied from a script. See also Spring, 1 March; Holles, f. 87ᵛ; Pym, ff. 10ᵛ–11ᵛ; Nicholas, ff. 32ᵛ–33ʳ; C.J. 722.

[2] Spring, 1 March; C.J. 723; Pym, f. 12ᵛ; Holles, f. 87ᵛ; Nicholas, f. 36ᵛ. This speech was delivered late in the morning, and it is taken out of order for the logical force of the point it makes.

but had to overcome the deep reluctance of the King, such fears were ideal supporting material. They enabled them to spread the idea that there was going to be a war, without forcing reluctant members to take sides between the King and the Prince by actively pressing for one. Sir George More, the second speaker in the debate on 1 March, reminded members of the problem of the King's attitude by asking how so wise a King came to be so long deluded, and warning them to proceed slowly.[1] Phelips, who spoke third, explicitly endorsed Rudyerd's speech, and strengthened the impression of prearrangement by referring his case for the breach of the treaties back to Buckingham's Relation. Phelips claimed that the treaties had been Spain's best army, and that they had lost 'our friends abroad, and well near ourselves at home, and almost God too'. The loss of the Palatinate he thought 'a sin, which God lay not to our charge'. For the loss of the Palatinate, he laid the blame squarely on Spain, 'the great wheel that moves the whole frame of that business'—an image which echoed Digby's speech at the conference of November 1621. Phelips made an emotional case for the breach of the treaties. Nicholas reports him as going further, and overtly proposing that England should begin a war: 'that we must resolve to make a war'. Spring, the fullest report, has him explicitly supporting Rudyerd in saying it was impossible to recover the Palatinate, and proposing a war of diversion. The *Commons' Journals* report him as proposing a 'diversive war' against Spain, but Pym and Holles, curiously, make no mention of war in reporting Phelips's speech.[2]

Sir Miles Fleetwood, another member of the Duke's team, followed Phelips, with a great wealth of religious imagery. He thought the treaties a threat to religion, reminded his hearers about 1588 and the Gunpowder Treason, and, in an image which may have disturbed James, said the Prince's return out of Spain was like Noah's dove, because it meant the flood would abate. Sir John Lowther noted that More and Fleetwood, who both used a wealth of biblical imagery, were 'long to no purpose'. Sir Francis Seymour, who followed Fleetwood, denounced papists and the

---

[1] Spring, 1 March; Rich, f. 30ᵛ; Earle, f. 36ᵛ. The fact that More was interrupted for his 'tediousness' could be in part because he was tedious, and in part because his reflections on James were touching on dangerous ground. See below, p. 174 n. 1.

[2] Spring, 1 March; Earle, f. 36ᵛ; *C.J.* 722; Pym, ff. 11ᵛ–12ʳ; Holles, f. 87ᵛ.

threat offered to religion by the treaties. Yet in Seymour, anti-popish feeling of an intense kind led, not to belligerency, but to isolationism. He complained that in Spain attempts had been made to convert the Prince to popery, and said that the treaties had been a threat to the state and to religion. Yet, beyond the breach of the treaties, Seymour's only proposals were that the recusancy laws should be enforced, and that the Spanish ambassador should be sent home. It was at this point that Sir John Eliot, yet another of the Duke's men, overtly introduced into the debate the idea that Spain might attack England. He wanted to set out the fleet 'to secure our selves', and 'to prevent the King of Spain's armado'. He was in favour of war himself, but believed Spain would start it if England did not. He believed, with an almost incredible optimism, that the forfeitures of recusants would serve to finance the fleet.[1] Pym and Serjeant Hitcham, the next two speakers, spoke simply for the breach of the treaties. Hitcham, the more unexpected speaker of the two, earned a marginal note in Spring's diary: 'well done, Mr Serjeant'.

From this point onwards, the morning's debate turned into a discussion of when they would be ready for a conference with the Lords. Sir Edward Cecil wanted speed: 'It is now time to deal with Spain, or else he will deal with us.' Coryton, Pembroke's client, and Sir Henry Mildmay, Buckingham's client, both wanted speed. Digges did not, because, though he was a war supporter, he thought the case had not yet been fully argued. Edward Alford who rapidly emerged as the most effective opponent of any move towards war or war finance, thought the business 'not yet disputed of sufficiently'.[2] Sandys, near the end of the morning's debate, thought it had wandered rather far afield. He believed they should restrict their answers to the King's question whether the treaties should be dissolved, and 'not, as yet, to meddle with the consequences'. 'When thou enterest into the presence of God, let thy words be few'.[3]

The afternoon was spent, as proposed by Digges, in further debating the question in committee of the whole House. Digges

---

[1] Lowther, f. 16; *C.J.* 722; Rich, f. 29ᵛ. I have preferred Rich's reading of the passage on the dove to Spring's. For Eliot, Spring, 1 March; Rich, f. 28ᵛ; Nicholas, f. 35ʳ; Lowther, f. 16ᵛ; Earle, f. 37ᵛ. Jervoise (1 March), in a poor report, gives a more bellicose meaning to Seymour's speech.
[2] Spring, 1 March; Earle f. 37ᵛ.
[3] *C.J.* 723; Spring, 1 March.

said they needed the opinions of common and civil lawyers, and of land and sea soldiers, and also 'country gentlemen, that could speak of the means of maintenance of wars, and the present estate of the country thereunto'.[1] Digges here introduced the practical question which was to bedevil discussion of war in 1624: if they agreed to a war, could they justify the necessary taxation in their own countries? As the debates went on, doubts on this question gained in strength, or in freedom of expression, or in both. These doubts increasingly give the impression that whatever members of the Commons might think about war in principle, in practice many of them felt unable to recommend the practical measures necessary to maintain a war. It is these debates which yield much of the best evidence for Dr. Hirst's thesis that many members felt a sense of accountability to their constituencies or to their county communities.

On the afternoon of 1 March, these doubts were still only beginning to surface. Digges, though he had first voiced them, began the afternoon's debate by saying that if they broke the treaties, 'it is probable that the necessity of a war will follow', and tried to rouse feeling for it by a narrative of the growth of the House of Austria which went back many hundred years.[2] Dr. Gooch, Vice-Chancellor of Cambridge was franker in his doubts, describing war as 'a pleasing word to men without experience', and expressed doubt whether they had provisions for one day's good service in the Palatinate. At this point, he was silenced by interruptions, presumably from the more bellicose members of the House. Sir Robert Killigrew, who had been with the Prince in Spain, replied by saying that war was not yet their business, and that they should reduce the discussion to the question whether they should break the treaties. Sir William Strode said the same. It was beginning to look as if a highly organized team of the Duke's supporters were leading the Commons into discovering that they had given support for a war before they had faced the implications of what they were doing. If men spoke against war, the Duke's supporters said they should discuss the breach of the treaties, not war. If men spoke against the burden of war supply, the Duke's supporters said

---

[1] Spring, 1 March; Pym, f. 12ᵛ. This is Digges's morning speech, not his afternoon speech.

[2] For Digges, Rich, f. 2ᵛ; Earle, f. 38ʳ. Spring, in spite of his engaging profession of distrust in his own reporting, seems to have given much the best report of this speech.

that the breach of the treaties necessarily implied war. It was a very well organized series of political manoeuvres.

Sir Edward Coke and Christopher Brooke, who gave two of the most important speeches of the afternoon, both gave an impression, which they confirmed on 11 March, of believing that war was coming because Spain would attack England. Coke said that 'the King of Spain is a great king, yet I hope we shall not fear him', and went on to collect such precedents for confidence as that England had had the precedency at the Council of Constance. Christopher Brooke, on grounds of security, emphatically supported Rudyerd's proposals for assistance to the Low Countries. Sir Thomas Jermyn, who closed the debate, again suggested that the question of war was out of their hands: 'The Spaniard will take it for injury enough that we will be no longer abused, and will not want [i.e. fail] to give us just occasions of war when we leave to treat, and so will preserve our honours for that point.'[1] Thus relieved of the responsibility for making up their minds about war, the Commons voted unanimously for the breach of the treaties. It had been a peculiarly long day, and it is possible that exhaustion played some part in the final vote. It is easy to deduce from the debates of 1 March that many members did not like Spain. It is possible to show that many of them expected that a war would follow from the breach of the treaties. Yet the debates, and the situation, were so structured that very little of their real inclinations can emerge from this day's debates. If it is to be maintained that the Commons demanded a war with Spain, the evidence used for this case must be taken from some other place than the debates of 1 March.

The Lords having already agreed to the dissolution of the treaties, a select committee of both Houses was left with the worrying task of composing a sufficiently persuasive list of reasons to set before the King. Their petition, largely drafted under the influence of Pembroke's care to secure a common statement from both Houses, was presented to James on 5 March. James's reply to this petition was equivocal and some of its apparent contradictions were due to the interlineation of James's own script with

[1] For Gooch, Spring, 1 March, Rich, f. 27ᵛ; Earle, f. 39ᵛ. For Gooch's anxiety about English military capacity in 1621, see N.R.S. iii. 343. Spring, 1 March, Earle, ff. 39ʳ–40ʳ; Rich, ff. 25ᵛ–24ᵛ, Pym, f. 13ʳ. For 11 March, see Earle, f. 74ʳ, Holles, f. 96ᵛ (Brooke), and Spring, 11 March and Holles, f. 97ᵛ (Coke). For Jermyn, Spring, 1 March.

a script Buckingham had solicitously prepared for him. The most notable deletion from Buckingham's script was a proposed promise that the King would not ask for subsidies until he was committed to war: 'that you do not desire to engage them in their gift till you be declared anent their advice'.[1]

Between 5 March and 20 March, much of the conflict between James and Buckingham narrowed down to one simple issue of time. Should the Commons first vote supply, and then James declare war, or should James declare war, and the Commons then vote supply? Buckingham was afraid, and reasonably afraid, that if James were voted supply, he would use it to pay his debts, and declare no war. James was equally reasonably afraid that if he declared war, he would get no sufficient grant of supply, and would be left committed to a war for which he could not pay. James feared that if this happened, 'I should be bound and they leap free and leave me naked and without help.'[2] It was necessary to find some way of resolving this procedural deadlock between James and Buckingham, and the way found was the appropriation of supply to the war, ultimately embodied in the subsidy act. Another supposed constitutional advance was the result, not of the initiative of the Commons, but of conflicts at court. The first known appearance of the appropriation proposal is in Buckingham's script for James's speech to both Houses, on 5 March. The appropriation proposal remained in, and was repeated unambiguously by James, together with a promise not to make peace without the advice of his Parliament.[3] But it was repeated shorn of the accompanying promise, which, for Buckingham, gave it meaning, that James would not ask for supply until he was committed to war. After 5 March, appropriation was James's proposal rather than Buckingham's The proposal for which Buckingham and the Prince's men spoke was not appropriation, but the more radical proposal of conditional subsidies, to be voted, but only paid after James's declaration of war. The Buckingham and

[1] Ruigh, 199–201, 193n.
[2] S.P. 14/163/30, James to Conway, holograph, undated. Ruigh, p. 242 assigns this letter to 4 April. This passage represents James's consistent position throughout the Parliament.
[3] Ruigh, p. 199, L.J. 251. James strengthened the wording of the appropriation clause in Buckingham's draft. At the same time, he altered Buckingham's condition, that he would not ask for subsidies until engaged in a war, into the reverse condition, that he would not engage in a war unless voted sufficient funds.

Charles group spoke either for that, or for the deferring of subsidy until after the King's declaration of war. These were the ideas sketched out by Sir Henry Mildmay, Sir Edwin Sandys, and Sir Robert Harley on 11 March, by Phelips on 13 March, by Harley and Sir Henry Vane on 19 March, and by Sandys on 20 March.[1] By then, it was being taken up outside the circle of the Prince and Buckingham, and was welcomed by Edward Alford, who was always glad of a reason to defer subsidies.

By contrast, the men who took up the King's proposal for appropriation were Lord Treasurer Cranfield in the Lords, and Sir Benjamin Rudyerd in the Commons.[2] At first, they found little response, and it was not until 19 and 20 March that Weston, Chancellor of the Exchequer, and Conway, Secretary of State, finally persuaded the Commons to accept the royal proposal for appropriation.[3] It was not a concession by the King to the Commons, but by the Commons to the King. Many of the Commons feared, as ultimately proved to be the case, that the appropriation clause of the 1624 subsidy Act would not ensure what Sandys called a 'real war'. Attempts to question the Council of War appointed under this Act failed dismally in 1625 and 1626.[4] In the long term, James had revived a medieval precedent of considerable constitutional significance, but in the short term, he outmanœuvred Buckingham's attempt to secure open war before supply was granted, and got his money in return for a scrap of paper. In return, he created a distrust of the sincerity of court desire for war which, in the next Parliament, was to haunt his son and Buckingham at the moment when they least deserved

[1] Spring, 11 March, Earle, ff. 73ʳ–75ʳ; Holland, I, ff. 46ᵛ, 51ʳ, Spring, 19 March, Earle, f. 97ʳ, C.J. 742, Holland, I, f. 69ᵛ. Alford (Holland, I, f. 63ᵛ) said the proposal of Harley and Vane for a deferred, conditional subsidy was 'not fit. Not a Parliamentary way.' Alford's proposal (Spring, 20 March) was not for a conditional subsidy, but simply for delay until the King had determined on a war, 'which is proper to sovereigns only to do'.

[2] *Lords' Debates*, p. 22, Earle, f. 73ʳ.

[3] Holles, f. 104ᵛ (Weston). Conway was also supporting appropriation when he asked the House to vote supply and 'regulate it with those reservations the King sets down'. Holles, f. 105ᵛ, Pym, f. 34ʳ. See also Edmondes, Holland, I, f. 39ʳ. James's men were not numerous in 1624. Their prominence in pressing for appropriation is therefore the more remarkable. Coke objected to Harley and Vane's proposal, because 'for a Parliament to set down nominative subsidies and not real was never heard before'. Digges then said that he had thought the proposal for a 'nominative subsidy' was a good one, but had now changed his mind.

[4] See below, pp. 223, 289. C.J. 804, S.P. 16/22/19.

such mistrust. James's outmanœuvring of Buckingham over the appropriation created much of the suspicion which marred the Parliament of 1625.

Perhaps the most interesting deletion in Buckingham's text for the King's speech of 5 March was made by Buckingham himself. His original script asked James to give the Houses thanks 'for their uniform offer of assistance in their advice'. The words 'assistance in their' were deleted: no promise of assistance had materialized, though Buckingham had clearly expected one. What Buckingham had in mind appears to have been a motion in the House of Lords on 4 March by the Earl of Southampton. This was a motion, to be presented to the joint committeee of both Houses, to declare to the King that if their motion led to the breach of the treaties they would be ready 'with our persons and our estates' to support their advice. Southampton was undoubtedly too impetuous in moving this motion: Lord Montagu noted that the Lords' committee in which Southampton had carried this proposal had delivered it to a sub-committee of the Commons before they reported it to the full House of Lords. Pembroke, Saye, and Arundel appear to have been his accomplices in this action.[1] If Southampton's motion raised procedural hackles in the Lords, it caused offence in the Commons. Pembroke, before meddling with it, might have remembered his own question to the Commons in the Floyd case: what would they have said if the Lords had moved a subsidy of their own authority?

Yet, if Southampton's motion was a procedural failure, it was also a political necessity. The Commons only voted subsidies one grant at a time, yet a war could not, once begun, be turned on and off like a tap. A King entering a war which was likely to last needed some long-term commitment to support the war from his Commons. This was why Edward III and Henry V had involved the Commons so deeply in the beginning of their French wars.[2] If the Commons were not prepared to accept something on the lines of Southampton's motion, which was not the most specific of commitments, they could not with any consistency advise the

[1] *H.M.C. Buccleuch,* iii. 231, *Lords' Debates,* p. 20. But see below, p. 287 for Montagu's readiness to follow this precedent in 1626.

[2] See E. B. Fryde, 'Parliament and the French War, 1336–1340', in *Historical Studies of the English Parliament,* ed. E. B. Fryde and Edward Miller (Cambridge, 1970), i. 242–61. Dr. Fryde's story has many resemblances to the story told in this book.

King to undertake a war. The Commons' reaction to Southampton's proposal, then, can be taken to show the comparative importance they attached to their privileges and to their constituents on the one hand, and to war on the other.

The paper written by Sandys and Pembroke, to embody Southampton's motion, was from an administrative point of view an innocuous enough document. From that point of view, it seemed like military suicide to enter on a war, which would necessarily depend largely on Parliamentary supply, without some assurance, however vague, that supply for the war would be available, and would continue beyond the first flush of enthusiasm. Southampton was asking a question to which Councillors needed to know the answer. Sir William Becher, Clerk of the Council, put the administrative point of view: 'that we by giving of our . . . advice do engage us as much as we should give an affirmative answer to the paper'.[1] For Becher, advising the breach of the treaties and supporting the paper offered by Southampton, Pembroke, and Sandys were, for practical purposes, synonymous.

Yet for many members of the Commons, Southampton's motion had raised three nightmares. One, of course, was that of privilege. Subsidies properly started from the Commons, and were not the Lords' business. Yet the examples of 1593, 1614, 1626, and the Short Parliament show that this principle could be honoured in the breach as well as in the observance, and it seems that privilege was not the main concern of most of those who opposed Southampton's motion. Coke and Glanville, the likeliest exceptions, were both lawyers. The issue touched two much deeper fears. One was that members might again be pushed into taking sides in the unresolved conflict between the King and the Prince. Glanville was not being entirely disingenuous in proposing that if the King should ask about assistance for a war, they should answer 'that we not knowing his Majesty's intentions did not presume to take the same into our consideration'.[2]

The deepest fear seems to have been that of repeating the traumatic experience of 1621, when they had raised great hopes in the country, only to return home empty-handed and without legislation, expecting, in Wentworth's phrase, to be compared to the 'foolish virgins'. Grosvenor, who had been alarmed about this

---

[1] Nicholas, f. 51ᵛ (Becher).
[2] Nicholas, f. 52ʳ; Holles, f. 93ʳ. (Glanville).

empty-handed return in 1621, was still trying to excuse himself for it in 1624, when, as sheriff, he gave a charge to the county electors of Cheshire. He said that the previous Parliament took 'indefatigable pains in finding out the causes of those growing evils and propounding remedies. But alas those great pains and care yielded not so plentiful an harvest as was expected, though they were not altogether fruitless.' The best result Grosvenor could offer from the previous Parliament was the impeachment of Bacon,[1] whereas it seems that the almost unanimous reaction of those concerned with constituencies was that what the country wanted was bills.

Edward Alford, the first man on his feet to object to Southampton's motion, at once saw the nightmare of again going home with nothing achieved: 'They should do something for the country, lest, like the last Parliament, that they gave two subsidies, and did nothing for the ease of the subject, therefore he would not have this proposition answered, for it would be a kind of engagement beforehand.' He insisted that they should first pass bills. Phelips, answering him, revealed his embarrassment by the weakness of his answer. He said they could accept the paper because it bound them only to a general, not to a particular, commitment: 'When the particulars shall be spoken he will stand as stoutly as any member of the House for the good of his country, and give with as much respect to the welfare of the kingdom.'[2] Phelips in effect conceded Alford's case. Even a man as ambitious as Phelips could not usefully pursue his career at the expense of his home power base. Phelips's usefulness to the Duke would reach its limits whenever it came into conflict with his loyalty to his Somerset neighbours. This did not make him a useful ally for the financing and organization of a war. Saville supported Alford, saying it was fit to enable the people before they charged them. Harley protested that they would delay the King's declaration, but his objection was brushed aside.[3] Wandesford said they should wait until they understood the King's demands, and good bills should come first. Mallory asked them 'not to dispose of the hopes of our country', and said that those responsible for the paper

[1] Grosvenor MSS., Cheshire R.O., 2 Feb. 1623/4. I am grateful to Dr. Derek Hirst for drawing my attention to this MS., and to Mr. Richard Cust for lending me a xerox copy of it.
[2] Holles, f. 92ᵛ; Lowther, f. 23ᵛ; Nicholas, f. 49ʳ.
[3] Nicholas, f. 49ʳ; Lowther, f. 24ᵛ.

should be put out of the House for exceeding their commission. Recorder Finch, showing more caution than in December 1621, reminded them that they did not know whether the King would have wars or not. Seymour said it was dishonourable to make war upon the promise of money. Digges and Sandys vainly tried to answer the outcry. Digges said he wished the paper had not been moved, but did not want the Spanish Ambassador to know that it had been denied. Sandys agreed that it was essential that 'good laws preceded, as was expected', yet his offer to make an addition to the paper to that effect was not enough to still the storm of criticism. Harley, for the Duke, was reduced to trying to end the discussion, moving 'that the paper may pass'.[1] It did, and with it passed the chance that King and Commons would be united in a successful war effort. At the crucial moment, members' local loyalties had proved stronger than their national ones. During a war, their aim would be, not to help win it, but to help to reduce its burden on their countries.

So Southampton's motion, to Buckingham's surprise, was passed over, and when the deputation of the Lords and Commons went to the King later on 5 March, they were unprovided with any offer of financial assistance. As Lord Montagu noted in his diary, the Commons agreed with the Lords' reasons, 'but for the matter what we would do to the king they passed it over in silence'.[2] Montagu was well aware of the procedural irregularity of Southampton's motion, and as a recent House of Commons man himself, he must have understood its implications for the Commons' privileges. Yet he had, as a supporter of war, clearly hoped it would be accepted. It was the failure of Southampton's motion which enabled James to say sincerely, and maybe truly, when he answered the deputation of both Houses on 5 March, 'Besides, I think your intentions are not to engage me in a war.'[3] If Southampton's motion had been accepted, the whole struggle between James and Buckingham over the appropriation would have been unnecessary.

In the Lords, James's refusal to commit himself to war created such anger that, on the morning of 6 March, they discussed using

---

[1] Nicholas, ff. 48^v–52^v; Lowther, ff. 23^v–24^r; Holland, I, ff. 32^r–33^r; Rich, ff. 13^v–9^v. Pym was almost completely isolated in giving wholehearted support to the paper.

[2] *H.M.C. Buccleuch*, iii. 232.   [3] P.R.O. C. 65/186: *L.J.* 251.

the procedural weapon which enraged James most: a cessation of business. Arundel even seems to have considered adjourning the House. These were procedural devices the Commons had only been reduced to twice: in the great quarrel over impositions, in 1614, and in the final quarrel on freedom of speech, in 1621. It is a measure of the intensity of the Lords' commitment to war that on 6 March they proceeded to a division on a proposal for a cessation of business, which was only lost by eleven votes.[1]

By contrast, the Commons on the morning of 6 March were a model of decorum. They completed the passage of five bills, for the Sabbath, for recusants evading forfeiture through uses, against swearing, against informers, and a bill for pleading the general issue, which was part of their drive to decentralize litigation. They gave a first reading to a bill of Coke's designed to extend benefit of clergy to women convicted of thefts of a value of less than 10s. and above 12d.[2] This meant that they would be branded instead of suffering death. They debated the charter of the East India Company, and listened patiently to a defence of the company by Maurice Abbot, brother of the Archbishop of Canterbury. He claimed that the East India Company brought in much more than it took out, and that he himself had recently brought 60 lb. weight of gold into the country. He called the company a 'nursery of treasure, and used its accounts in support of his argument.[3] The only provocative action the Commons took on 6 March concerned a bill on the purveyance of carts, which would have limited the distance for which the Crown could requisition carriage to twelve miles for carts, and eight miles for wains, and would have allowed the Justices of the Peace to fix the prices for purveyance. They knew this bill, which diminished the King's revenue, was likely to meet the same solid official opposition as it had done the previous Parliament, and nevertheless persisted with it, only to see it founder in the Lords, as it had done the Parliament before.[4] 6 March 1624 is a much more typical Commons' day than it has

---

[1] *Lords' Debates*, p. 21, *H.M.C. Buccleuch*, iii. 232. There is no record of this division in the *Lords' Journals*.

[2] All these bills were completed, and all became law except the bill against recusants evading forfeiture by uses and the Sabbath bill, which were vetoed.

[3] Pym, f. 20ᵛ.

[4] This bill was said to have originated from a Buckinghamshire Grand Jury petition. N.R.S. iv. 243, 372–4; Pym, ff. 21ʳ, 28ᵛ, Holland, I, f. 59ᵛ, Earle, f. 81ᵛ, *L.J.* 135, 177, 287, 293, 306.

been taken to be, and it shows a House which only challenged the King's interests when they conflicted with the interests of their countries. When they could, most of them were happy to leave high matters of state to the court and the House of Lords.

They continued with business of this type until 11 March, when Rudyerd and Weston again tried to lead them back to supply and the breach of the treaties. Weston, Chancellor of the Exchequer, began with a long statement of the King's expenses on foreign affairs, embassies, subsidies to the King of Denmark, payments to the small body of troops who had defended the Palatinate, and so forth. Even with a statement confining itself to foreign affairs, Weston provided enough figures to show conclusively that the King was too deeply in debt to undertake a major war without a very large grant of supply. The formal motion for supply was then left to Sir Benjamin Rudyerd, who said, with slight understatement, that 'the king hath not pressed anything unto us, but what necessarily follows upon our own premises'. He tried to reassure the Commons by saying, 'Let us not affright ourselves with an opinion of the vast charge of undertaking a great war presently', but asked that they should make some necessary provision for defence, for he feared England might be attacked. He reiterated his fourfold proposal of 1 March for strengthening the forces in the kingdom, sending out a fleet, securing Ireland, and defending the Low Countries, and repeated the offer of appropriation of supply, and asked for some members of both Houses to be named as 'a committee in the nature of a Council of war'.[1] This motion produced rather more compliance than before, because, in the words of Pym's diary, 'most men being anxious to show themselves in a plausible matter' were willing to join in, yet, as Pym said, the debate was 'not altogether without variety of expressions'.[2] Phelips and More still thought the proposal 'not seasonable', because the King's mind was not yet clear. Sir Edward Cecil, having overcome his doubts of eleven days earlier, was 'so transported with an imaginary success of the war' that he imagined himself fetching the Infanta back to England by force of arms, only to be greeted by a general shout of 'No'.[3] Old Thomas Wentworth said that now, as in Elizabethan times, there was unity between

---

[1] Earle, ff. 70ᵛ–73ʳ, Pym, f. 25ʳ⁻ᵛ.   [2] Pym, f. 25ᵛ.
[3] Holland, I, ff. 43ᵛ–47ᵛ, Pym, f. 25ᵛ, Ruigh, p. 206. Holles, f. 96ʳ, reports Sir Edward Cecil as still concerned that 'the King is unwilling to war'.

Crown and Commons, and it was based on religion. He wanted to vote money quickly, and send troops to the Low Countries. Perrott diverted this into his now familiar motion to secure the ports and remove the Jesuits. Brooke and Alford, perhaps for different reasons, maintained that they were not yet ready for this debate.[1] Coke made his big speech about the virtues of war with Spain, while Sandys wondered how to 'enable and encourage the people'. Phelips, uncertain what was happening at court, lamented, 'Whether a war or no, we know not.'[2] The debate increasingly concentrated on a general promise of assistance to the King, without any mention of a specific sum, and without any vote of subsidies until the King's policy was clearer. Conway warned them that they would not satisfy the King of the case for war without a vote of a specific sum, only to have his arguments denied by Sir John Eliot.[3] Buckingham and James were clearly still locked in their argument about whether supply or a declaration of war should come first, and the Commons were deferring any clear decision until the court wrangle was resolved.

That is why, at their next audience, on 13 March, the Houses again had to wait on the King, with a general offer of assistance, but without any specific promise of a particular sum. Archbishop Abbot, who was again made spokesman for the two Houses, thanked James warmly for showing himself sensible of the Spaniards' insincerity, but on supply, he could only say that although the King had said his treasure would not sustain a war,

We do most humbly beseech your Majesty, that neither that nor any other consideration may hinder your present resolution, for with a most cheerful and universal consent (no one disagreeing) we do with dutiful affections assure your Majesty and hereby manifest and declare, that in pursuit of our advice, upon your Majesty's declaration made to dissolve both the said treaties, (the deferring whereof may prove dangerous) we will be ready in a Parliamentary manner with our persons and abilities to assist your Majesty.

It was a fine declaration, but, made to a King heavily in debt, it was not going to finance a war. It is not surprising that James seized the chance to spell out some home truths about the policy which was being pressed on him. He said that he had not yet shown himself sensible or insensible of the Spaniards' insincerity,

---

[1] Earle, ff. 72^v–74^v, Holles, f. 97^r.   [2] Earle, ff. 74^v–75^v.
[3] Holles, f. 96^r, Pym, f. 27^r, Holland, I, f. 50^r. Eliot's objection to naming 'a certainty of subsidies' was the next day. Spring, 12 March.

and that he had not yet delivered his mind on Buckingham's Relation. 'When Jupiter speaks, he useth to join his thunder to it; and a King should not speak except he maintain it by action.' He then spelt out to the partisans of war exactly what their proposals implied: he asked for five subsidies and ten fifteenths for the war, and one subsidy and one fifteenth for himself *annually* until his debts were paid. This provoked an anguished interruption from the Prince, saying the King would ask nothing for his own needs— an assurance the Prince had been busy giving on insufficient grounds. The clerk, uncertain how to engross an interruption in a King's speech on a Parliament Roll,

⌈decided to put it inside a
│square bracket on one side
⌊of the Roll, thus.

In spite of this interruption, the King stuck to his guns. He was willing to allow the sixth subsidy to go to the war, but without six subsidies and twelve fifteenths, he was unwilling to enter into war. He repeated his promise to appropriate the supply to the war, and to allow it to be administered by treasurers appointed by the House of Commons. He repeated his promise that if there was a war, he would not make peace without the assent of Parliament, expressed his desire for the Parliament to sit long enough to make many good laws, and tried to show as conciliatory an attitude to Parliaments as he could. On only one point did he insist: if he had war, he must have money.

These remarks, it was reported, 'struck a great amazement amongst those of the committee, and put them to such a silence that there was not heard so much as one "God save the King", who put off his hat to them and went his way'. Buckingham and the Prince were aghast at this speech. The Venetian Ambassador reported that they turned pale as they heard it, and that the Prince, after his interruption, never spoke a word all day.[1] Yet, as a matter of plain fact, James's case was sound. As an assessment of the cost of a war, his figures were shown by the event to be rather an under-assessment than an over-assessment. If the Commons were not going to vote sums of this magnitude, they had to be counted as being, in terms of the practical effect of their actions, against war.

In the Lords, according to Lord Montagu, the King's answer

---

[1] Ruigh, pp. 211–12, *C.S.P.D. 1623–5*, vol. clx, no. 89, Chamberlain, 20 March 1624, *C.S.P.Ven. 1623–5*, pp. 254–6.

caused 'a great dejection'.[1] In the Commons, it was not reported to the House as a whole until 17 March. Meanwhile, the Commons gave a third reading to the bill against purveyance of carts, although Solicitor General Heath argued that it was unreasonable to make the country judges between the King and themselves.[2] They passed the bill against monopolies, engrossed the bill of licences of alienation and the bill against purveyance of carts, committed the bill for abbreviation of Michaelmas term, complained of Conciliar resistance to the free fishing bill because of what Glanville called 'an imaginary expectation of a plantation' in New England, and resolved that in the election at Winchelsea, the decree of the corporation could not alter the law.[3] Phelips produced another petition against Lord Keeper Williams, and again asked for a sub-committee of his committee for Courts of Justice. Eliot supported him with a proposal that his committee should have no dependants on it,[4] but once again Phelips was denied his sub-committee, and Williams survived. In other words, in the Commons it was business as usual.

When the King's speech was reported, on 17 March, Phelips wanted to consider it at once, and allow none to go out of town till it had been considered, but Alford and Glanville succeeded in deferring the question for another two days.[5]

Before the subsidy debate opened, on 19 March, the Venetian Ambassador claims that Buckingham had induced James to lessen his financial demands.[6] If so, James was privately committing himself to more unparliamentary taxation, since he could not, by any amount of concession to Buckingham, substantially reduce the cost of a war. Rudyerd once again opened the debate, and his speech gives some support to the Venetian Ambassador's suggestion. He did not name a number of subsidies, and said:

I believe every one in this House doth think his [Majesty's] demands to be very great, and so do I, but let us consider his Majesty doth not desire that all should be hastily levied, for he hath limited no time.[7]

---

[1] *H.M.C. Buccleuch*, iii. 234. [2] Pym, f. 28ᵛ.
[3] Holland, I, ff. 50ᵛ–53ᵛ; Pym, f. 29ʳ, 59ʳ⁻ᵛ: f. 32ʳ.
[4] Pym, f. 31ʳ, Holles, f. 102ᵛ. It is interesting that in 1624, unlike 1626, Eliot's object in proposing the exclusion of courtiers (and of lawyers) appears to have been to ensure that the committee did the will of Buckingham. Cf. Perez Zagorin, *The Court and the Country* (1969), p. 36. [5] Holles, f. 102ʳ⁻ᵛ.
[6] *C.S.P.Ven. 1623–5*, p. 255, also reported by Nethersole, who says Buckingham 'prevailed'. S.P. 81/30, f. 88. [7] Pym, f. 33ʳ.

He appeared to be hinting that part of the King's six subsidies could be deferred to a second session at Michaelmas. This impression was strengthened when Sir Henry Vane, Cofferer of the Prince's Household, said that though they should pay the full sum the King asked, part could be paid later.[1] Sir Thomas Edmondes, Treasurer of the Household, moved that they should vote £300,000 instead of any set number of subsidies. This was well below the King's demand, but it was also an early appearance of the principle by which the assessment of the subsidy was later to be reformed: the voting of a lump sum, which the counties could divide as they liked, but not reduce. Eliot said he was 'much dejected at first of his majesty's answer, but since ... resolved by the Prince his Highness' that it was impossible to satisfy the King's demands, and dangerous if they did not. He hopefully suggested a war could be financed from the profits of the Indies.[2] More wanted to follow the King 'afar off, as Peter Christ'. Alford wanted to 'look to our reputation, and do something for our countries'. Seymour declared his adamant opposition to a war in the Palatinate, because of the cost, and offered the derisory sum of two subsidies and two fifteenths.[3] Glanville feared a repetition of the last Parliament, when they had returned home with subsidies and no laws. Mallory said they were there as stewards for their countries, and not for themselves alone, and another member proposed that all those rated at under £5 in the subsidy book should be spared. Sir John Walter, of the Duchy of Cornwall Council, tried to blame God's wrath for the depression: 'God hath laid a curse on our cattle since we withdrew our hand from assisting the Protestant cause', and tried to raise the House to 'at least' four subsidies.[4]

It was soon apparent that no such sum could be obtained. Sir Thomas Belassis, from Yorkshire, asked to have a care of the poor, and vote two subsidies and two fifteenths. Sir Henry Anderson, from Durham, 'thinks the very report of subsidies is dangerous in the country', and Alford again opposed fifteenths because they were burdensome to the poor. Glanville, surprisingly, went as high as four subsidies and four fifteenths, but Peter Wentworth's son, for all his enthusiasm for war, only went to two subsidies and four

---

[1] Holles, f. 106ᵛ. The best report of this debate is in Spring, 19 March.

[2] *C.J.* 740, Holles, f. 103ᵛ.

[3] According to Spring and *C.J.* 741. Holles, f. 105ʳ and Earle, f. 95ᵛ report him as proposing the even more derisory sum of one subsidy and two fifteenths.

[4] Spring, 20 March.

fifteenths, with more if needed later. Coke observed that the King's demands came to near a million, and 'all England hath not so much'.[1]

In a House so divided, no consensus seemed likely to emerge, and Alford proposed to defer putting the question. The debate was resumed the next day, when Alford said that 'in other Parliaments they would ask their countries before they would give'.[2] As the debate continued on 20 March, a consensus slowly emerged for three subsidies and three fifteenths. They agreed, on Rich's motion, to vote the whole sum to be levied within a year,[3] and, on Seymour's motion, to charge recusants double subsidy to satisfy the country. Sandys, reporting the proceedings, said they could now ask for a 'real war'. If so, it had been entered into under protest. In the debates of 19 and 20 March, almost all members showed that their commitment to their own countries was much stronger than any commitment they might have to war. The principle of consent to taxation had proved a severe obstacle to Charles and Buckingham's plans for war. War and liberty do not easily coexist.

The joint committee of both Houses then once again had to prepare reasons to present to the King. They were encouraged when the Prince asked them, in the King's name, to omit religion from the causes of war, because he might have need of Catholic allies. One observer shrewdly reported that 'This curiousness of his Majesty in this point was the first glimpse of hope we had on Monday that his Majesty would accept of the offer made him, and declare himself thereupon.'[4] On 23 March, the joint committee once again waited on the King with their advice. This time, they were able to offer '*toward* the support of the war which is likely to ensue', 'the greatest aid which was ever granted in Parliament to be levied in so short a time'.[5] Greatest or not, the joint committee's own text shows they knew it was not enough. So did James, but he decided to make do with it. 'How far you yet declare yourselves is sufficient for the present entrance into the business, though a great deal short of what I told you it should require.' He clearly expected more if a war were begun, and thanked them for their general offers of assistance, which he said were worth more than forty subsidies. He said he was willing to break the treaties, and

[1] Earle, f. 97ᵛ.   [2] Holles, f. 110ʳ.   [3] Holles, f. 111ᵛ.
[4] S.P. 14/161/36.   [5] P.R.O. C. 65/186. Italics mine.

expected them to keep their promise to assist him. He yet again repeated his promise on appropriation, but could not resist a final word at the expense of Buckingham's Relation: 'I am sure such an account was never before given in Parliament.' He said he hoped 'at least to make a good beginning of the war, for when the end will be God knoweth'.[1] His customs, he said, would fall with the outbreak of war, but even so, he would go through with it if he had to sell jewels and all. Even then, his reputation as a peacemaker was so strong that many people did not believe he meant what he said, and the final entry on the Parliament Roll for the breach of the treaties is not James's speech, but an announcement by Buckingham that messengers had been sent to Spain to dissolve the treaty. The Roll begins with Buckingham, and ends with Buckingham. The demand for war had come from the Duke, the Prince, and the House of Lords, while the House of Commons, with a few exceptions, were almost as reluctant partners in the enterprise as King James himself. Perhaps James had judged their mood better than his son. It is natural that, in later meetings, they should have shown considerable doubt about the wars they were being asked to support, and consistent that they should have shown considerable reluctance to find enough money. In 1624, war had been forced on the House of Commons in circumstances most of its members did not understand. From that fact, most of the rest of the trouble of the decade logically followed.

On what many of them still regarded as their proper business, the passage of bills, the House of Commons showed much more alacrity than they did about matters of war and peace. They succeeded, together with the Lords, in passing, by the calculation of *Statutes of the Realm*, thirty-five public Acts and thirty-eight private Acts, or, by the calculations of the Parliament Roll, thirty-three public Acts, and forty private Acts. The passage and debating of these Acts, and of some bills which did not pass, is a subject of considerable interest in its own right. Above all, Coke's pride and joy, the Monopolies Bill, finally reached the statute book. It passed rapidly through the Commons, completing its passage on 13 March. Thereafter, as in 1621, it was debated at a long series of conferences between the two Houses. Again, part of the concern of the Lords was to defend the vested interests of those in receipt of court patronage, and part to deal with genuine difficulties in

[1] P.R.O. C. 65/186, Pym, f. 42^r.

the drafting of the bill. Sir Robert Mansell and Sir Henry Vane obtained exemptions for their monopolies of glass-making and the subpoena office respectively, to which the Commons consented only in order that the bill should pass. The Newcastle hostmen obtained an exemption on Arundel's plea that they were essential to the dredging of the Tyne, although Neile, Bishop of Durham, objected that the privileges of Newcastle were hurtful to those on the south bank of the Tyne. At a long conference on 19 April, the Lords asked a more important series of questions about the drafting of the bill. The Lord Chief Justice complained that the bill offered no definition of a monopoly, to which Coke only replied that definitions in law were most dangerous. Both points were fair ones: all definitions would cover either too much or too little. Bishop Neile underlined the difficulty by asking whether the bill would threaten his Palatine jurisdiction as Bishop of Durham. The answer was that it would not.

It was agreed in 1624, unlike 1621, that the bill should not extend to offices, so Neile's viceregal authority as Bishop of Durham, together with many more dubious offices created in the next reign, were not classified as monopolies within the meaning of the Act. The Lords also objected that it would restrain the King's prerogative in making new corporations, to which Coke replied that 'if the charter extend only to government and choice of officers, there is no abridgement, but if they shall contain any liberty of sole buying and selling, they will be within the law'. This meant that it was going to be very difficult to extend the traditional system, regulating entry to trades through apprenticeships, to new trades like sugar-refining, dyeing with logwood, or the making of tobacco-pipes. The Lords remained unhappy about the bill right up to the end of the Parliament, and were only induced to give it a rather reluctant third reading on 22 May by the personal intervention of the Prince.[1] The bills of informers and concealments, having been exhaustively debated at conferences in 1621, had more or less agreed drafts, and passed with comparatively

[1] Pym, ff. 5ʳ, 23ʳ, 28ᵛ, 52ʳ, 71ᵛ, 72ʳ, *Lords' Debates*, pp. 97–8, 101. It suffered some delay in the Lords because of the breach of the treaties and because of the need to hear witnesses and conduct conferences on the impeachment of Cranfield. *L.J.* 260–1, 267, 287, 294, 299, 335, 338, 339, 393, 394, 397, 400, 412. See also House of Lords Record Office, Original Acts, 21 Jac. I c. 3. The Act was also amended by the Lords in order not to apply to wine licences, nor to Lord Dudley's patent for making iron with coal.

little trouble. Unlike the monopolies bill, they achieved their objectives, and were perhaps the most substantial legislative achievements of the decade.

The supersedeas bill, the first of the bills designed to protect local jurisdictions, caused rather more debate in the Commons. When Coke reported it, on 23 March, one member objected that it made the J.P.s arbitrary in their own areas. This is an early sign of a slight undercurrent of reaction, just visible in 1624, against the Cokeian conviction that J.P.s were the most perfect government in the Christian world. There was rather more dispute on a proposal to amend the bill so that it should restrict transferring suits from Quarter Sessions, not only to Westminster, but to the Councils of the North and Wales, and to the Courts of the Duchy of Lancaster and the Earldom of Chester. There was, interestingly, no hint in this debate of any objection to the Councils of Wales and the North on the ground that they were prerogative courts. The objection to transferring suits to the Council of Wales came from the marcher shires, Shropshire, Herefordshire, Gloucester-shire, and Worcestershire, whose inhabitants maintained that they were not Welsh. The objection to the Council of the North was that some people had to travel 120 miles to have their cases heard at York. The Commons decided by a vote of 152 to 122 to leave these courts out of the bill, as they had been left out in 1621, and the bill passed into law without further dispute.[1]

On other bills, the resistance to the proposals for unfettered freedom of action for J.P.s was a little more powerful. An unsuccessful, and apparently ill-drafted bill for the preservation of salmon and trout was objected to on the ground that there was 'too great a scope left to the passion of Justices',[2] who would have been empowered to pull down weirs at discretion. The bill to give J.P.s control over inns, though it passed into law, was opposed by Sir George More on the ground that it gave arbitrary power to J.P.s to put down inns and so take away a man's inheritance.[3] On 21 April, a bill against removing suits out of inferior courts, which ultimately reached the statute book, was objected to on the ground that it might make J.P.s or corporations judge and party in their own cause. The part concerning corporations was answered by the point that their charters seldom gave them power in their own

---

[1] Pym, ff. 5ʳ, 23ʳ, 39ʳ⁻ᵛ, 52ʳ. See also N.R.S. iv. 117–18, 374.
[2] Pym, f. 41ʳ.   [3] Holles, f. 114ᵛ.

causes, but the point about J.P.s, according to Pym's diary, was 'left unprovided for'.[1]

Only one public bill reached the statute book which had not been debated in 1621, an Act against the Murthering of Bastard Children, which enacted that concealing the death of a bastard child was to be construed as murder, unless at least one witness could testify that the child was born dead. One bill was clearly given much higher priority than it had been given in 1621: the bill for reducing the rate of interest to 8 per cent. Much of the impetus behind the bill was probably for the reason stated in the preamble, that the shortage of coin, and consequent difficulty in borrowing money, had caused a fall in the value of land. In so overwhelmingly rural a House of Commons, this was likely to be a more widely appealing argument for the bill than the more purely mercantile arguments, and it may help to explain why support for the bill had been increased by three years of depression, during which a fall in the value of land would have become more apparent. Alderman Guy of Bristol, one of the more energetic supporters of the bill, blamed the high rate of interest for a fall in the purchase price of land from 25 to 14 years' purchase during the past seven or eight years.[2] Dr. Gooch, who appears to have been chiefly responsible for managing the bill in committee, was a convert, having been against it in 1621. Two Privy Councillors spoke on the bill: Sir John Suckling, Comptroller of the Household, reported it the last time it came back from committee. The other, Sir Humphrey May, was the only man still against it on third reading. In the second reading debate, on 6 March, it was supported by Brooke, Recorder of York, and opposed by Whistler, who thought it would make lenders call in their money, and by Glanville, who thought it would be unfortunate to lose a common 10 per cent standard to measure trade. Sir Arthur Ingram's apparent opposition to the bill suggests that it did not originate from his friend Cranfield: he thought that 'in the course of trade three parts of four are by credit: if we make a law to diminish credit we shall diminish trade'. Digges was probably for the bill, but it is only clear that he resented the commercial success of the Dutch. On the third reading, one

[1] Pym, f. 75^r.
[2] The effect of the depression on land values was a common subject of complaint in the Commons. See, for example, N.R.S. iii. 213 and Holles, f. 94^r. Also Joan Thirsk and J. P. Cooper (eds.), *Seventeenth Century Economic Documents* (Oxford, 1972), pp. 6–12.

member objected that the rate was higher in Spain, and 'it was replied that in Spain they needed not fear to be eaten out with foreign lenders because their standard was such that money will yield more profit in any place in Christendom'. It also appears that at that stage the bill contained a clause which was absent from the final draft, limiting scriveners to a rate of 5 per cent. The Lords confined themselves to adding a proviso that the bill should not 'be construed or expounded to allow the practice of usury in point of religion or conscience', and it duly passed into law. The debates, though interesting in many ways, do not tell us who initiated the Act.[1]

Sometimes, the amendment of an Act tells us something about the powers for which a statute was thought necessary. For example, the bill incorporating the Hallamshire cutlers was amended at the table because it referred to the ministering of an oath, but did not specifically confer the power to administer it 'by virtue of this Act'. A similar mention of rights of search, mentioned in, but not specifically conferred by, the Act, remained unamended.[2] One of the most interesting of the private Acts is the Act for making the Thames navigable between Burcott and Oxford, because its drafters managed to achieve some of the advantages of procedure by patent, without suffering its legal or political disadvantages. The object of the Act was to make the river navigable, in order to ship Headington stone from Bullingdon quarry, and to bring coal and fuel to the City and the University, 'where there is very great scarcity, and likely to be greater if there is nothing done'. River navigation, involving as it usually did competing county juris-dictions, was a difficult subject for the traditional methods of local government, and had often been a subject for patents. What this Act did was to give statutory authority, and restriction, to a body of eight commissioners under the Great Seal, four of them to be nominated by the University, and four by the City. They were to have power to make weirs and locks, and to dig the banks of the river and adjoining brooks and ditches. They were given authority to agree terms of compensation with those whose property was thereby damaged, and, in cases of disagreement, to refer the case

[1] Pym, ff. 14^v, 22^{r-v}, 35^r, 72^v, 73^r, 80^v, 83^v, Holles, ff. 83^v, 89^r, 94^r, Spring, 24 March. The bill was a probationer, and was continued in 1628.

[2] Pym, ff. 60^r, 78^v. 21 Jac. I c. 31. The bill was reported by Christopher Brooke, Recorder of York.

to the three nearest J.P.s who were not parties, or to the Justices of Assize. They were given statutory authority to rate the City and University, and to make orders and constitutions, and to punish their breakers. This Act allowed all the speed and ease of proceeding possible to a patentee, while at the same time securing, by the existence of statutory limits to the commissioners' powers, freedom from the extortions so often practised by patentees.[1] The bill was first moved in the Lords, where the pressure of legislative business was usually light before the bills began to come up from the Commons, and was handled by a former Vice-Chancellor, Archbishop Abbot. It passed into law without difficulty, and is a model which might have been more often followed.

Of the other private Acts, the majority concerned either naturalization or the breaking of entails. One enabling the Earl of Hertford to break an entail reveals that both he and Sir Francis Seymour were severely in debt,[2] and another, enabling Vincent Lowe Esq. to break an entail, had to be passed all over again because, through a scribal error by the clerk, the final text of the Act described him as 'of Denby in the county of Derby'.[3] An Act designed to avoid 'questions, ambiguities and doubts' by confirming the incorporation of Wadham College, Oxford, also settled a dispute they had with New College about heriots on a manor in Essex.[4] One private Act which detained the House of Lords for some time concerned one of their own number, Viscount Montagu. He needed a private Act to relieve him against a rare phenomenon, a defaulting feoffee to uses, a trustee who had continued to receive the rents after his trust was terminated. This

---

[1] 21 Jac. I c. 32, text from Parliament Roll, P.R.O. C. 65/187. In 1621, the bill had passed the Lords, and been sent down to the Commons on the inauspicious date of 7 December. For its progress in 1624, see *L.J.* 254, 257, 263, 268, 322–3.

[2] House of Lords Record Office, Original Acts, 21 Jac. I c. 39. It is interesting that in giving the Royal Assent to this Act, James commanded the clerk to enter on the dorse that his assent should not weaken the sentence given in the Queen's time on the pretended marriage of Edward, late Earl of Hertford.

[3] *L.J.* 428. In 1626, the Lords' *Journals* misrecite the *correcting* bill as 'of Denby in the county of Derby'. Ibid. 683. Lowe's first Act apparently also said '£18,000' in error for '£14,000'. Stowe 366, f. 171ʳ. Mr. Lowe finally obtained the passage of his amending Act in 1628, during the short interval after the King's second answer to the Petition of Right. Stowe 366, f. 292ᵛ, 3 Car. I cap. 13.

[4] House of Lords Record Office, Original Acts, 21 Jac. I c. 36. It is an interesting question under what circumstances an Act of Parliament was wanted to confirm the establishment of a corporation. See also 3 Car. I c. 9, confirming the incorporation of Sutton's Hospital.

Act is also an interesting example of double thinking about recusancy, for Viscount Montagu was a recusant. The use in which he was protected by this Act was precisely one of those uses made by recusants to avoid forfeiture which were prohibited by another bill which passed both Houses and was vetoed the same Parliament. It is typical of the approach to recusancy that the same practice, in the same Parliament, was prohibited in general, and protected in particular.[1]

Among the bills which did not pass, the two which generated most interest were the bill for free fishing, and the bill to prohibit arbitrary imprisonment contrary to Magna Carta. The free fishing bill, after running into the usual government opposition, was re-committed to inland members, presumably in the hope of finding some sort of acceptable compromise. It was not sent up to the Lords till 3 May, late enough for the Lords to claim the excuse of lack of time to pass it.[2] The Magna Carta bill contained, as in 1621, an exception permitting commitment to prison by six of the Privy Council, but this clause caused no debate. Instead, it was re-committed because of the objection of Dr. Duck the civil lawyer that it unduly restricted the jurisdiction of the Admiral, the Earl Marshal, and the High Commission, and therefore might not pass the Lords. Brooke of York finally reported from committee that there were many exceptions to the bill, and it could hardly be made fit. Perhaps the clue is in the report in another diary that 'this bill covers restraint of trade'. In 1621, most of the debate on this bill had concerned, not the powers of the Council, but the powers of corporations, and this may be why the Recorder of a major borough reported it unfit to pass.[3] The hostility to corporations was, however, overcome by Edward Alford, who succeeded where he had failed in 1621, in securing passage for a bill for the dredging and repair of Colchester harbour and the paving of Colchester streets. This bill had been objected to in 1621 because it empowered the unpopular corporation of Colchester to raise tolls at the custom-house, and rate the surrounding countryside in order to dredge the river.[4]

---

[1] 21 Jac. I c. 48; P.R.O. C. 89/11/76, exemplified 18 Oct. 1624.

[2] Pym, ff. 6ᵛ, 29ʳ, 58ᵛ, 83ᵛ, 87ʳ.

[3] Pym, ff. 6ᵛ, 23ʳ, 30ʳ, 43ᵛ, Holland, I, f. 58ᵛ, Hawarde, f. 102ᵛ. N.R.S. iv. 307–8, iii. 172.

[4] 21 Jac. I c. 68. N.R.S. ii. 111–12, iv. 306–7: Pym, f. 58ʳ, Holland, II, f. 21ᵛ, C.J. 697. On local distrust of Colchester Corporation, see Hirst, pp. 52, 56, 134,

Corporations also had a difficult time in the committee of privileges. Their decisions on disputed elections, largely guided by Glanville, did a great deal to widen the borough franchises. Part of this was based, as in the Chippenham case, on the Cokeian principle that a charter could not abridge a common law right. Once it accepted this principle, the committee was bound, if it could be shown evidence that the freemen had once voted, to allow them to continue to vote, notwithstanding any charter restricting the franchise to the corporation. The other principle which probably influenced the committee of privileges was the dislike of elections dominated by the 'influence' of great men.[1] This dislike was shown in the debates on the bill for the enfranchisement of County Durham, when some people feared that if Barnard Castle were given the right to return burgesses, the Prince of Wales would be given the opportunity to exercise undue influence.[2] Granted the freedom with which the Prince and the Duchy of Cornwall Council had exercised electoral influence before the Parliament, the fear was not unrealistic. However, having shut influence out with one hand, the committee of privileges let it in with the other. They accepted Coke's doctrine that a borough's power to return burgesses was a duty, not a right, and therefore that it could not lapse by lack of use. This meant that any borough which could be shown to have once returned burgesses could resume the right to do so. Sir Robert Phelips at Ilchester and Sir Thomas Wentworth at Pontefract had already exercised this right. In 1624, it was further exercised for Amersham, Wendover, Great Marlow, and Hertford. Hertford were assured by the Duchy of Cornwall Council that if they presented a petition for Parliamentary representation, the costs of their petition would be met by the Duchy.[3]

199–201. The bill empowered Colchester Corporation to raise a toll at the custom-house on vessels using the river, and specifically on colliers. The Lords added three provisos: that none but Colchester men should pay the toll unless they chose, that the privileges of the Cinque Ports should be preserved, and that the accounts of the Colchester collectors should be overseen by four Essex J.P.s. It is tempting to imagine that the Earl of Warwick had something to do with this last proviso.   [1] Hirst, pp. 232–4, 83, 77.   [2] Pym, f. 64[r].
[3] Lady de Villiers, 'Parliamentary Boroughs Restored by the House of Commons', E.H.R. (1952), 175–202, and A. J. Fletcher, 'Sir Thomas Wentworth and the Restoration of Pontefract as a Parliamentary Borough', Northern History (1971), 88–97. On the electoral influence of the Duchy of Cornwall, Ruigh, pp. 57–68 and Duchy of Cornwall, 'Burgesses for Parliament 1623–4', f. 38 and passim.

An increasing Commons' concern with University matters was shown by complaints which were to continue for several Parliaments against Dr. Anian, President of Corpus Christi College, Oxford, and by a bill, sponsored by Sir Walter Earle, to prevent simony in elections to College Fellowships.[1] This bill was designed to remedy the abuses created by the extension of the court patronage network into University posts, but it never passed into law.

As the Parliament ran on into the summer, it was increasingly occupied with this type of minor business, and, as it completed the agenda left over from 1621, it increasingly ran into its predecessor's trouble of having too many bills to be able to complete any of them. The Parliament was continued until 29 May because of the need to complete the second part of Buckingham's agenda, the impeachment of the Lord Treasurer, Lionel Cranfield, Earl of Middlesex. The committee for trade, under the chairmanship of Sir Edwin Sandys, was used as a stalking-horse to approach Cranfield. The committee of trade, while still concerned with hunting the Merchant Adventurers, were more inclined than their 1621 predecessors to centre their complaints on the overburdening of trade by impositions. This did not let the Merchant Adventurers off the hook, since they were laying an imposition on their own members to recoup the cost of recovering their charter after the Cockayne project. Sir Thomas Wentworth objected indignantly that they assumed more than the King by imposing on a native commodity within the kingdom.[2]

This concentration on impositions led on to ground more dangerous than the Merchant Adventurers. When Coke quoted the pertinent precedent from 1340 of impositions by an 'estate of merchants' overthrown by Parliament, he was, whatever he might say to the contrary, very near reopening the whole forbidden topic of the right of imposing. The Commons were again very near this subject when they investigated the so-called composition with the brewers, whereby £3,000 a year was being levied in lieu of purveyance.[3] This was the levy which Phelips, in 1621, had likened to an excise, and the comparison was alarmingly apt. It also led to

---

[1] Earle, f. 81^r, Holland, II, f. 84^r, Pym, ff. 28^r, 59^v.

[2] Pym, f. 45^{r-v}. 'Impositions by merchants themselves, and that upon native commodities. This gave them occasion to look into the state of the Merchant Adventurers.' Pym, ff. 84^v–85^v. See also Coke, Pym, f. 56^v.

[3] Pym, f. 73^{r-v}, Earle, f. 151^r.

the question of the pretermitted custom, a customs duty on cloth levied by dubious legal authority. Solicitor General Heath claimed that this custom was grounded on the statute of Tonnage and Poundage, only to have his claim completely demolished by Bankes and Berkeley, future Attorney General and high royalist judge of the Ship Money trial.[1] Serjeant Hitcham, the King's counsel, did reopen the whole right of imposing in the course of debating the pretermitted custom, and his speech was razed out of the *Commons' Journal* on the motion of Sir Thomas Wentworth.[2] Phelips and Sandys, wishing to continue the institution of Parliaments, and loyal to their undertakings to Buckingham, heroically kept themselves and the House off the general question of the right of imposing. Phelips felt compelled to draft a Protestation, recording for posterity that they had only done so 'lest it might have caused some diversion or hindrance from other endeavours that were in the present most necessary', and not because they had waived any of their rights.[3] Yet, though he felt compelled to mention the existence of this document in a speech, he took it no further, and the question of the right of imposing continued to sleep, save for one speech by Spencer, until the Tonnage and Poundage Act of 1625.

Where it was possible to release all this head of steam on impositions was where the issue touched, not the King, but the Lord Treasurer.

In his report from the committee of trade on 2 April, Sandys picked up two of these 'impositions', a 'composition' in lieu of purveyance on groceries, and an imposition on wines, for neither of which he was able to find any royal authority. Phelips, promptly on his cue, moved to deal with the referees of these impositions. Cranfield, speaking in the Lords, said there was a dangerous conspiracy against him.[4] Two days later, Cranfield's departmental subordinate, Sir Miles Fleetwood, Receiver of the Wards, charged

[1] For the identification of 'Mr. Bartlett' with Robert Berkeley, Ruigh, p. 55. On the pretermitted custom, N.R.S. vii. 425 for the Council's relief that it had not been made an issue in 1621. In 1624 it was first raised by Sir John Saville in the subsidy debate on 20 March. Holland, I, f. 69ʳ. On 13 April, Sandys claimed that the pretermitted custom in Weymouth came to more than four whole subsidies.

[2] Holles, ff. 131–2. See Pym, ff. 62ʳ⁻ᵛ, 67–9 and Spring, 13 and 15 April. Hitcham's speech was actually razed out of the Journal. Ruigh, 50n.

[3] Spring, 16 April, Phelips MSS. 216/27. This protestation is undated, but is entirely compatible with this dating. See also Phelips MSS. 227/16.

[4] Pym, f. 46ᵛ: *Lords' Debates*, p. 57.

him with the illicit use of a signature stamp in the Court of Wards, and with taking bribes. Sir Thomas Wentworth spoke up for Cranfield at the moment when it mattered most, an act of integrity which perhaps did more to lose him Buckingham's favour than any supposed misdemeanours in the next Parliament.[1] Only Noy and Sir Humphrey May had the courage to join him. Sandys promptly got the case to committee, where Buckingham's team were able to speak as often as they liked, and the committee could hear witnesses whose names Sir Miles Fleetwood had given privately to the Speaker.[2] With three such loquacious men as Coke, Sandys, and Phelips able to speak as often as they liked, there was little silence into which any defence of Cranfield could be slipped. Cranfield, in the Lords, again claimed there was a conspiracy against him, only to be challenged by Saye to name the conspirators or withdraw.[3] Since Cranfield could hardly risk publicly naming Buckingham, he was silenced. The charges against him were transmitted to the Lords by his two old enemies, Coke and Sandys, on 15 April.

The Lords, once again, did not leave the Commons sole control of the prosecution. They introduced additional charges of their own, and kept sole control of the examination of witnesses. From the transmission of the charge by the Commons, further prosecution was managed by Randall Crew, one of the King's Serjeants at Law. The Lords at least tried to be fair: Lord Russell, who had been one of Cranfield's sponsors when he took his seat as a peer, was named to the committee to take the depositions of witnesses, and attended regularly as long as there was any hope of Cranfield's acquittal. The hearing of witnesses took up most of the second part of April, and severely obstructed the legislative programme. In the Commons, there was an interesting clash of priorities between Coke and Phelips, when a crucial part of the preparation of the Cranfield case clashed with a proposed conference with the Lords on the bill of monopolies. Coke put the bill of monopolies first, and Phelips put the Cranfield case first. The House sided with Phelips.[4]

[1] Pym, ff. 48ᵛ–49ᵛ.
[2] Spring, 6 April, Pym, f. 53ʳ⁻ᵛ, Holles, ff. 118–23. The House allowed the setting up of a small sub-committee to take depositions, though Glanville reminded them that they had not allowed a similar motion for Phelips's sub-committee for courts of justice. Holles, f. 123ᵛ.
[3] *Lords' Debates*, p. 61.   [4] *C.J.* 758.

Coke at least enjoyed the prosecution of Cranfield, who was an old enemy. Secretary Conway's son commented that Coke would die if he could not help to ruin a great man once every seven years. Phelips, however, had enjoyed reasonably good relations with Cranfield,[1] and, unless he really believed Buckingham's line that Cranfield was responsible for the 1621 dissolution, seems to have joined the attack simply to conciliate Buckingham. Everything about the prosecution of Cranfield confirms the comment of the younger Dudley Carleton, that it all smelled of private grudges between Buckingham and him.[2] If Buckingham was largely responsible for the breach with Spain, he was solely responsible for the fall of Cranfield. In the final debates on the Cranfield case in the Lords, the pressure for condemnation came from Williams, Abbot, Mandeville, and Pembroke.[3] The King, in his summing-up, was so careful that Chamberlain said it was much disputed whether the King had spoken for his Lord Treasurer or against him. In fact, what James had said was that Buckingham had promoted Cranfield and assumed responsibility for him. By implication, James was saying that if Cranfield was an offender, the responsibility for the fact rested also on Buckingham.[4] After the Parliament was over, James took the chance of Buckingham's absence through illness to release Cranfield from the Tower, but during the Parliament he could do nothing.[5] Cranfield's offences were not serious by the standards of his time, and James had a case for claiming that he had not taken bribes, but only gratuities, 'pointing out the difference between the two'.[6] However, the mere fact that Cranfield had been guilty of what was technically corruption meant that James could not defend him as he had defended Williams, or as he had defended Mandeville in 1621. Yet, throughout the trial, the fear existed that the King might insist on his acquittal or his free pardon. Sir Humphrey May warned the Commons not to touch on the right of imposing in their prosecution, for this might leave Cranfield an opening 'to lay hold on the horns of the altar'.[7] It is a revealing phrase: it shows, as completely as seventeenth-

[1] S.P. 14/163/1. For Phelips's tribute to Cranfield in 1621, N.R.S. v. 518.
[2] S.P. 14/162/13.   [3] *Lords' Debates*, pp. 84–92.
[4] Chamberlain, 13 May. For a good text of James's speech, see Pym, ff. 95–6.
[5] P.R.O. 31/3/59, f. 127ᵛ (14 June); S.P. 14/167/4.
[6] *C.S.P.D. 1623–5*, vol. clxv, no. 61. Unfortunately, we appear to have no record of James's definition of the distinction between a bribe and a gratuity.
[7] Pym, f. 61ʳ.

century imagery could show, that a King's wholehearted protection was still assumed to be a cast-iron defence against an impeachment. That the King did not give that defence was partly due to the fact that the charge was one of corruption, and partly to the fact that he was fighting, very cleverly but against the odds, for control of his own court.

During the Parliament, he had partly lost that control. The Parliament of 1624 moved to a plan more than any other Parliament of the decade, and that plan was the plan of Buckingham and Charles. The timing with which, at the end of the Easter recess, the Parliament moved on from the breach of the treaties to the trial of Cranfield had the smoothness of clockwork. The Parliament of 1624 shows that, at that date, a Parliament was still an efficient instrument of business for anyone who had a programme for it, provided that members of the Commons could be reassured that the programme did not offend the King. It was a useful instrument for the political aims of Buckingham and Charles, as it was for the legislative aims of Coke. Yet the meeting of these two was a meeting of ships that pass in the night. Buckingham and his allies in the Commons had little interest in each other's business, and the temporary harmony of their purposes was largely coincidental. After the Parliament had dispersed, James, whose physical and mental strength was unimpaired,[1] slowly began to regain control of his own court. As he did so, the supposed war on which Buckingham had expended so much effort slowly degenerated into one mercenary expedition to the Palatinate. Even that expedition, when it might have contributed effectively to war against Spain by relieving the key siege of Breda, was forbidden to do so by James.[2] The Dutch envoy who began to worry about the lack of military preparations in May 1624 was a true prophet.[3] Up to James's death, for all Buckingham and Charles's belligerence, there was, in effect, no war. This fact meant that, instead of contributing to the unity of King and Parliament, the Parliament of 1624, like the Parliament of 1621, merely contributed further to a growing sense of mistrust. In 1625, when Buckingham and Charles were really

---

[1] P.R.O. 31/3/59, f. 161 and other refs. The French Ambassador was disconcerted to be woken at four in the morning to go stag-hunting.

[2] P.R.O. 31/3/60, f. 298 (11 Dec. 1624): S.P. 81/30, ff. 176–7. Buckingham induced James to countermand this order, but too late for its recall to be effective. See also Ruigh, pp. 385–97.

[3] S.P. 14/163/1.

trying to fight a war, all the mistrust which James had provoked by delaying the war until after his death broke about his successor's head. Williams, in his funeral sermon, rightly said that like King Solomon, he died in peace.[1] For the Parliament, the most appropriate verdict was that pronounced by young Conway: 'The Parliament house wants faith, and then I find no means for their salvation.'

[1] Robert Ashton, *James I by his Contemporaries* (1969), p. 20.

IV

The Parliament of 1625: The Plague and the French

I

THE Parliament of 1625, as the first Parliament of a new reign, was expected to set a pattern for much that was to come after it. It was, then, peculiarly unfortunate that the members elected to it were kept waiting in London, by a series of prorogations, from 17 May till 18 June. It is possible that, in determining the course of the Parliament, what happened during these prorogations may have been as important as anything that happened in public debate. Such a delay was an ideal preparation for the breeding of rumour and of fear. The delay was not the fault of Charles, who was eager to begin the meeting at the earliest possible opportunity. The delay was the result of the French marriage treaty begun in 1624 and not yet fully concluded when James died, in March 1625. Charles expected it to be concluded in time for a meeting of Parliament on 17 May, but it was not. The French were pressing, as a condition of this marriage treaty, for a greater measure of toleration for English Catholics than Charles could safely concede with a Parliament in session.[1] He was thus unable to assemble Parliament until his bride was secure in London.

After that, he lost no time. His new Queen, Henrietta Maria, arrived in London on 16 June, and Parliament assembled on 18 June. However, with the members already gathered in London, there was bound to be speculation about the reasons for the delay in their meeting. Some of this speculation was bound to arrive at the right conclusion: the French marriage treaty, like the Spanish, involved religious conditions which members of Parliament were likely to find objectionable.[2] Fears for the safety of religion were thus a natural result of the speculations of members kept waiting idly in London. But this period of waiting did not only put

[1] For a typical example of French pressure, *C.S.P.D. 1625–49 Addenda*, vol. dxxi, no. 8.

[2] See Locke to Carleton, 16 May, *C.S.P.D. 1625–49 Addenda*, vol. dxxi, no. 50.

members in fear for their souls: it rather more immediately put them in fear for their bodies. While members waited to discover when, if at all, they were going to meet, they had leisure to note the weekly worsening of an attack of the plague which was to become one of the worst of the century. Chamberlain noted on 14 May that because of the plague it was 'yet in suspense' whether the Parliament would meet at all. Since London was clearly the worst-affected place, it was a matter of legitimate concern to members whether they were being kept in London for a good reason, and whether the session would be concluded before the plague became devastating.

By 12 June, the Queen and her long-awaited party were on the way, but, as Chamberlain noted, 'They come in an ill time, for the sickness increaseth and is spread far and near, so that 25 parishes in this town are affected already, and this week's bill (of mortality) ariseth to 434 in all, of the plague 92; so that if God be not merciful to us, this town is likely to suffer much and be half undone. And that which makes us the more afraid is that the sickness increaseth so fast when we have had for a month together the extremest cold weather that ever I knew in this season. What are we then to look for when heats come on and fruits grow ripe?' Chamberlain's fears were not based on this number of deaths, which were insignificant compared with what they became later; his justified foreboding of a major epidemic was based on the speed with which the death rate was increasing.

Chamberlain's forebodings were shared by many members. Chamberlain noted that the delay 'makes the knights and burgesses complain that they are kept here with so much danger and expense to so little purpose, for there is no likelihood they can sit here long, if at all'. Two weeks later, with the Parliament in session, he noted that the weekly plague deaths had increased from 92 to 239. The figures increased, and continued to increase, almost in geometrical progression. Chamberlain judged the mood of the members rightly when he said that 'I fear they will prove somewhat resty.'[1] It was an unpromising beginning that the Parliament met on the day the law term was adjourned to avoid the plague. By 29 July, when the epidemic was approaching its height, Secretary Conway told his son that 'I . . . in earnest do marvel that anyone who may be called reasonable would be now in London.' He added: 'If you

---

[1] Chamberlain, 14, 21, and 28 May, 12 and 25 June.

have fear of God's justice, or the danger you may bring to your friends, get you out of London, and God bless you beyond your desert.'[1] Other members may have received similar letters from their families.

Needing to keep themselves occupied in this anxious situation, many members 'begin to mutter about matters of religion'. They knew that it was the French marriage treaty which had delayed their meeting, so suspicion and alarm had plenty to feed on. In Chamberlain's words:

> They desire to understand what hath passed in that point, and the keeping of them close makes them suspect the more; some spare not to say there that all goes backwards since this connivance in religion came in, both in our wealth, valour, honour and reputation, and that it is visibly seen that God blesses nothing we take in hand, whereas in Queen Elizabeth's time, who stood firm in God's cause all things did flourish.

It was when members sought to explain the delay in their meeting that fears for body and soul began to merge together into one. Once the fears had begun, and fastened on the French marriage negotiations, members could begin to unravel a complex web of suspicious circumstances which led them right back to the end of the previous Parliament.

The Parliament of 1624 had been promised that it would be assembled for a second session at Michaelmas. When this session failed to materialize, Sir Thomas Wentworth, writing to Secretary Calvert, had rightly concluded that the Parliament had not been reassembled for fear that it might protest against the French marriage negotiations. Wentworth was undismayed: 'For my part, I like it well, and conceive the bargain wholesome on our side, that we save three other subsidies and fifteenths. Less could not have been demanded for the dissolving of this treaty.'[2] Wentworth, though personally devout, was predominantly secular in his political outlook. It is unlikely that more theological, or more belligerent, members such as Pym and Phelips viewed the lack of a second session of the Parliament of 1624 with quite so much equanimity.

The thirteen months from the prorogation of Parliament in May 1624, to the assembly of the next Parliament, in June 1625, did not only see a change of sovereign. They also saw the beginning of the end of the long religious peace of Jacobean England. The

---

[1] *C.S.P.D. 1625–49 Addenda*, vol. dxxi, no. 121.   [2] Knowler, 24.

fears generated by the French marriage treaty, unlike those generated by the Spanish marriage treaty, could merge with the suspicions engendered by the beginnings of a doctrinal split among
English Protestants. The months of the French marriage negotiations were also the months when the rise of English Arminianism
began. Up to about 1624, disputes between English Protestants
had been muted by the knowledge that they were united in the
'fundamental points' of doctrine. By 1624 or 1625, some of the
more theologically alert members of Parliament were beginning to
appreciate that this was no longer the case. In 1624, the theologically alert members had been few: when Pym accused Richard
Montagu of Arminianism, Sir Walter Earle had supposed that he
was guilty of the more familiar heresy of Arianism.[1] In 1625, Pym
found many more members ready to join into a renewed attack on
Richard Montagu. In the atmosphere of a popery scare, the charge
of Arminianism was far more dangerous than it had been in the
comparatively calm and secular atmosphere of 1624, for it was
precisely on the 'fundamental points' which had hitherto been the
common bond of English Protestantism, the points of justification
and predestination, that the Arminians were on what their
Protestant contemporaries regarded as the wrong side. The issue
was as yet still one of minority concern in 1625, yet it deserves a
place among the issues on which the suspicions of alarmed members could feed.[2]

There seems to have been no anxiety about the religion of
Charles himself. Alarm could not be based on Charles's record,
since, in June 1625, he did not yet have a record. Indeed, as the
apparent champion of war with Spain, he looked more like a
champion of the Protestant cause than a centre of the popish
conspiracy, a King, as Sir John Davies claimed, 'like to restore the
glory of our nation by his wisdom and valour'.[3] Yet the very
invocation of the Protestant cause involved in the expectation of
war could itself feed religious suspicion. As Dr. Clifton has said,
'one of the marks of English nationalism was anti-Catholicism':[4]
when war was in the offing, an appeal to patriotism and an appeal
to anti-popery were all part of the same emotional force. Since

[1] N. R. N. Tyacke, 'Arminianism in England; Religion and Politics 1604–
1640', Oxford D.Phil. Thesis (1969), p. 168. I am grateful to Dr. Tyacke for
permission to quote from this thesis.
[2] N. R. N. Tyacke, in *Origins*, esp. pp. 119–32.
[3] *H.M.C. Hastings*, ii. 67.   [4] Robin Clifton in *Origins*, pp. 150, 157

1624, there had been war fever, but no actual war. Those who, like Bishop Carleton of Chichester, thought that in the forthcoming war all the power of the papists would be against all the power of the Protestants had nowhere to turn their energies except against English recusants. The only outlet Bishop Carleton could find for his patriotic feelings was in searching for arms at Cowdray Park, the home of his recusant neighbour Viscount Montagu.[1] Emotions of this Foxeite sort were normally called to the surface by talk of war, especially if it were against Spain.

It is not then surprising that Dr. Clifton has identified 1625, when war preparations began in earnest, as a year which produced a wave of popish plot scares comparable with those of 1588 and 1605. In normal times, the Council need not have been alarmed by the patriotic Protestantism of men like Bishop Carleton. The emotions involved were, after all, familiar as loyal and monarchist ones. Attacks on papists were identified, by a tradition which ran back through 1588 to 1534, with heightened loyalty to the Crown. Guy Fawkes, if he achieved nothing else, ensured that James, as well as Elizabeth, should benefit from this sense of heightened loyalty to the Crown.

Two things helped to make the anti-popish scare of 1625 turn a little sour. One was the continuing lack of a visible external enemy. It was a familiar part of the Foxeite tradition that the visible external enemy was to be identified with his ally the invisible internal enemy. In the absence of a visible external enemy, the hunt for invisible internal enemies was likely to be intensified. The other reason which made it likely to turn sour is that the Council were forced to obstruct it. Previous anti-popish scares had worked themselves out in a flurry of local enthusiasm for law enforcement, in which the Council had played its part. In 1625, for the first time, a major anti-popery scare coincided with court pressure for the relaxation of the recusancy laws. For the first time, then, King and Council were forced to obstruct, instead of assisting, the central patriotic convictions of their leading subjects. For this undesirable situation, the blame rested on the French. It was they who were insisting, as a necessary condition of Charles's marriage to Henrietta Maria, on the relaxation of the English recusancy laws. The fact that Charles was thereby forced to oppose the measures which most leading

[1] S.P. 14/164/10; Fletcher, p. 103.

county governors associated with war may have been an important reason why so many of them seem to have doubted whether he really intended war. When Charles had been on the throne a month, he wrote to Lord Keeper Williams telling him to send out circular letters suspending proceedings against all but the most dangerous recusants. These letters, going out almost at the same time as the writs for Charles's first Parliament, could not have gone out at a more unhelpful moment.[1]

Charles and Buckingham did not enter into this situation voluntarily: they were forced into it by the French. While the 1625 Parliament was petitioning Charles for a public declaration that the recusancy laws would be enforced, the French were threatening him with the ruin of his new marriage if he did what Parliament asked.[2] The French could not only threaten Charles with governmental wrath: they could also threaten to withhold the second half of the Queen's dowry. The first half, amounting to £120,000, came with the Queen, but a second instalment of the same size was still due. The French were able to use this as a sort of bond to force Charles to be of good behaviour. It is not surprising that traditional anti-French feelings began to come to the surface: Chamberlain said, 'It . . . would better become us to compare and dispute with such pompous kind of people in iron and steel than in gold and jewels, wherein we come not near them.'[3]

The difficulties Charles faced with the French in the first year of his reign followed logically from the contradictory promises he and Buckingham had made to Parliament and to the French in 1624. From the very beginning of the French marriage negotiations, in December 1623, the French had insisted on obtaining the same religious concessions in a marriage treaty as had been offered to the Spaniards. Charles's promise to the Parliament of 1624, that if he married a recusant, the religious liberty she would get would extend no further than her person, had been noted by Pym as 'worthy the memory', but it was noted by the French Ambassador as 'a great insult to France'. He insisted that if the recusancy laws were executed as Parliament wished the treaty would have to be broken off.[4] The French, then, were inexorably pushing Charles and Buckingham into a quarrel with Parliament. Since the war the English and the French both wanted would

---

[1] S.P. 16/2/1.
[2] P.R.O. 31/3/62, ff. 114–16.
[3] Chamberlain, 25 June 1625.
[4] P.R.O. 31/3/58, ff. 67^r, 73^r.

necessarily demand Parliamentary supply, the French were likely
to quarrel with Charles for breaking his promises on recusants
if he did conciliate Parliament, and to quarrel with him for
breaking his commitment to war if he did not conciliate them.
Either way, the Anglo-French marriage alliance appears to have
been doomed before Charles's bride had even arrived in England.

The French insisted on these impossible conditions in the
belief that, because England needed the alliance more than France,
the English would have to take whatever terms were offered.[1]
They may have been right in this belief. In terms of status, only
France and Spain could provide a good enough match to satisfy
the English sense of their own importance. Only France and
Spain could provide a large enough dowry to satisfy English
financial needs. In strategic terms, moreover, if England were
intending war against Spain, there was a strong case for securing
the friendship of the only European power of equal standing,
which was France. Moreover, if, as appeared likely for a while,
the French could be drawn into the war as well, the chances of
military success would be greatly increased. Charles and Buckingham, then, were under overwhelming pressure to conciliate the
French. Yet if they conciliated the French, they could not conciliate a Parliament. If they could not conciliate a Parliament, they
could not fight a war, and the *raison d'être* of the French alliance
was therefore likely to be destroyed by attempts to continue it.

The reasons for this unwise French insistence seem to lie in
French domestic politics, and are largely beyond the scope of this
book. It is likely that Carlisle and Conway were right in identifying
the continuing struggle between Richelieu and his opponents at
the French court as one of the reasons why the French felt bound
to continue to insist on these religious concessions.[2] James had
told them, in August 1624, that the laws were sleeping so well it
was a shame to wake them by a declaration suspending them.[3]
This was typical Jacobean advice: lazy, cynical, shrewd, and
ultimately correct. Equally typically, James decided it was not
worth making an issue of it, and agreed to the sending out of
what the French Ambassador called letters to stop the persecution
The French were well aware that they thereby prevented the
reassembly of the 1624 Parliament, and noted that Buckingham

---

[1] P.R.O. 31/3/58, f. 280.
[2] S.P. 78/74, ff. 19, 88, 58.   [3] P.R.O. 31/3/59, f. 177.

feared that a Parliament would break the marriage.[1] Charles, then
having concluded his marriage just before his first Parliament
assembled, had to fear that the marriage would break the Parliament. This alone was difficult enough as an inheritance for Charles
to bring to the throne, but in the affair of the ships for La Rochelle,
he was faced with something even more likely to provoke the
temporarily inflamed susceptibilities of his Protestant subjects.
In January 1625, the Duke of Soubise, a Huguenot nobleman,
started a rebellion by seizing the Île de Rhé, outside La Rochelle.
He did so at the very moment when French troops were moving
south to Italy, to start open war against Spain.[2] Other Huguenot
leaders, and, at first, the townsmen of La Rochelle, were said
to be unwilling to join Soubise, but they appear to have been
eventually forced to do so by the sheer impossibility of removing
the official suspicion that they intended to. The French were
reluctant to move their troops out of the country leaving an armed
Huguenot rebellion in their rear, so they asked Buckingham to
supply them with ships to repress La Rochelle. Buckingham had
promised to supply these ships, without telling James.[3]

Thus in the summer of 1625, at the very moment when the
anti-popery scare was rising to its height, the English learnt that
some of their ships were being put under foreign command, to
fight *for* papists, *against* Protestants. It was bewildering. From
the point of view of Buckingham and Charles, there were good
strategic reasons for the loan of these ships to the French, but it
is hardly surprising that these reasons proved unintelligible to
men like Sir Francis Seymour and Sir John Eliot. The method by
which Buckingham attempted to wriggle out of this commitment
is typical of his over-ingenuity. He sent the ships over to Dieppe,
with official orders to place themselves under French command. At
the same time, he sent unofficial messages to the English commander, reminding him that it was treason to hand over the
King's ships to a foreign power, and telling him to look to see
whether he had sufficient warrant.[4] In the event, the crews

[1] Ibid., ff. 228, 238, 246–7.

[2] S.P. 78/74, f. 58. *C.S.P.Ven. 1623–5*, p. 525.

[3] P.R.O. 31/3/61, f. 71, S.P. 78/74, ff. 27–9. For the seriousness of the French
military plans interrupted by Soubise, ibid., ff. 117–20.

[4] S. R. Gardiner (ed.), *Documents Illustrating the Impeachment of the Duke of
Buckingham*, Camden Series (1889), pp. 298–301 (Evidence of Edward Nicholas).
Nicholas claimed that the ships had been promised by James without the

mutinied rather than be placed under French command, and the French got the ships without the crews, a fact which was later to put difficulties in the way of their return. The English commander, who was naturally in a state of some bewilderment, was back in England in time for the second session of the 1625 Parliament. In private, even Secretary Conway rebuked Buckingham for the 'scandal' of allowing the King's ships to fight against the Protestants.[1]

It is hardly surprising, then, that in June 1625, members of Parliament assembled in an uncertain mood. Chamberlain reported that some of them were saying privately that the King had promised in the last Parliament never to contract a marriage with conditions derogatory to religion. Chamberlain hinted that many of them blamed Buckingham for this situation, and he was indeed a very visible target.[2] Charles himself, the 'prince bred in Parliaments', seems to have still been above suspicion. The mood of the opening months of Charles I's reign, from March to June 1625, was an unstable one. Immediately on Charles's accession, preparations for war at last started in earnest, and some war partisans, like the Earl of Warwick, were willing to believe in them, welcome them, and wholeheartedly participate in them. For others they came a little too long after the war promises of 1624 to carry conviction. For some, the worsening state of relations with the French may have created suspicion that war against France, rather than Spain, might be being prepared for. The new Queen could not be crowned, because the French would not agree to let her kneel before a Protestant bishop.[3] The religious anxiety this created blended with the long absence of war to produce a popular complaint that the subsidies of 1624 had been obtained on false pretences.[4] This feeling appears to have overtaken Sir Edwin Sandys at the Kentish election. He found he was losing, and made 'an oration, none of the wisest, as it is reported'. In this 'oration', he seems, judging by later reports, to have made pledges about the granting of supply. More remarkably,

knowledge of Buckingham. In the French version, the Duke was said to have made the promise without telling the King.

[1] C.S.P.D. 1625–49 Addenda, vol. dxxi, no. 118 (25 July 1625).

[2] Chamberlain, 25 June 1625. Unfortunately, Chamberlain gives neither names nor numbers.   [3] P.R.O. 31/3/62, f. 112.

[4] Whitelocke, 12–21, f. 144^r (Sir Edwin Sandys).

even though he lost the Kentish election, the Kentish electors appear to have regarded him as still bound by these promises. In 1626, a number of voters did not support him on the ground that he had 'deserted, and even betrayed, us and our freehold' by breaking the pledges he made in 1625. He and Phelips both suffered at the 1625 election for the service they had given to Buckingham in 1624, and could not serve him as freely as they had done in the previous Parliament even if they had wished to.[1]

Buckingham's undertakers of 1624 had not only faced trouble with their county electorates: they had also failed to obtain office on the accession of Charles I. In Phelips's case, this may have been because he no longer trusted Buckingham enough to accept office at his hands, but Sandys and Digges may have been disappointed.[2] Buckingham was not going to be able to manage the Parliament of 1625 as he had managed the Parliament of 1624.

Nor was the volatile mood of many members helped by events in the country before and during the Parliament. The depression, it was true, was over, and more or less disappeared from Parliamentary debates. In its place came two new menaces. One was the plague. Stuart England was used to plague, and in normal years, accepted it as one of the hazards of existence. The 1625 plague was something different. The Tuscan Ambassador reported at the beginning of August that 942 people had died in London, of whom he believed 700 had died of plague. The next week, he reported that 3,400 people had died in London and the following week that 5,000 had died. A recent work estimates that during the epidemic London lost between a fifth and an eighth of its inhabitants.[3] The death register of the parish of St. Margaret's, Westminster swelled so rapidly during the summer of 1625 that it seems unlikely that Salvetti's figures are exaggerated. It was not only Parliament which was disrupted by the plague. The law term was adjourned, London traders were forbidden to attend the Bristol fair in July, for fear they might bring the infection, and the Merchant Adventurers were so dispersed in their flight from the plague that they in effect ceased to function.[4] In these circum-

---

[1] Chamberlain, 6 May 1625; Hirst, p. 174. It is possible that Sandys's unfulfilled promises referred to the 'Phelips clause' in the 1624 subsidy Act.

[2] Bodl. MS. Rawlinson A 346, f. 227ʳ. I am grateful to Dr. Hirst for this reference.

[3] H.M.C. 11th Rep. I, pp. 26, 28. Peter Clark and Paul Slack, English Towns in Transition 1500–1700 (1976), p. 89.   [4] Supple, pp. 99–100.

stances, an invitation to attend Parliament in London, the worst-affected place was hardly likely to be congenial.

Nor did the later adjournment of Parliament to Oxford bring the relief that was expected. The Oxford City Council, during July 1625, had given orders for building cabins for lodging infected people, and for the employment of women to tend the sick and men to bury the dead. The watch were to keep out strangers 'except Parliament men and men well known'.[1] It cannot have been a reassuring atmosphere.

The plague may have exacerbated the religious tensions in Parliament. The depression had at least led interest groups to lobby against each other, but in Parliament, in sharp contrast to the Council, the only widely accepted remedy for plague was to appease the wrath of God. Phelips later regarded it as a proof of God's great mercy to the Parliament that no member died of the plague, and Towerson told the Privy Council that the only way to restore trade was to wait for God in his mercy to abate the sickness. To say members believed that appeasing the wrath of God was the practical way to cure the plague would be an exaggeration, but it would be fair to say that most believed that if there was an effective remedy, it was along these lines. In the heightened atmosphere of the summer of 1625, such lines of reasoning could appeal to people who, in the two previous Parliaments, had been much more secular in their outlook.

The Council and members of Parliament seem to have been equally alarmed by the plague, but there is an intriguing cultural difference in their reactions under stress. To members of Parliament, any possible prophylactic measures were likely to be theological, designed to avert divine wrath. The destruction of idols, the persecution of recusants, and above all a large public Fast, appeared to the most vocal members to be the least ineffective precautions they could take. To the Council, on the other hand, prophylactic measures were essentially medical, and centred on reducing the risk of contagion. Between the London and Oxford sessions, the Council itself was on the run to keep ahead of the spreading infection, but for others, their preventive measures seem to have concentrated on restricting movement out of infected areas, and on confining such dangerous tasks as burying the dead

---

[1] *Oxford Council Acts 1583–1626*, ed. H. E. Salter, *Oxford Historical Series* (1928), pp. 331–2. I am grateful to Dr. Paul Slack for this reference.

to appointed specialists. On 5 August, when the Council forbade people to gather out of their parishes to keep the Fast, for fear they might spread the infection, the alternative methods of prevention clashed head-on. This clash is symbolic of much of the incomprehension between Parliament and Council during 1625.[1]

As the plague chimed in with fears about religion, so the issue of pirates merged with concern about impositions. In 1625, the immediate concern about pirates seems to have been largely inspired by one fleet of Sallee pirates cruising off Cornwall, but the over representation of the West Country in Parliament meant that it had considerable effect on proceedings. The sight of pirates cruising unchecked off the coast of Cornwall directed hostility at the same man who was under suspicion over the treatment of the papists, the Lord Admiral, the Duke of Buckingham. The commander of the ships in Plymouth said that members of Parliament, rather than complaining, would do better to pass an Act of Parliament for a fair wind, except that he feared they could find no precedent for it.[2] However, observations like this did nothing to ease West Country alarm. When people thought of the guarding of the seas, they were reminded that Tonnage and Poundage, which was due to be granted anew at the beginning of a new reign, was supposed to be for the guarding of the seas. Tonnage and Poundage, as Digges warned Charles, was in turn likely to raise the issue of impositions. Sir James Bagg, Eliot's rival for the position of Buckingham's man in the West Country, sent Buckingham an ominous report. He said that some West Country towns had written to their members complaining of the oppression they suffered by the pirates cruising off the Lizard. This he said, 'will invite those of the Parliament to capitualte [i.e. negotiate] in passing that bill'. He advised Buckingham, to avoid the grant being held up or negotiated for, to see that the coasts were guarded before the bill came up for discussion.[3] The advice, though shrewd, came too late. Thus, Buckingham and Charles came to the Parliament of 1625 with all the cards against them. Many of the misfortunes and misunderstandings they were con-

---

[1] *A.P.C. 1625-6*, pp. 125, 98, 1423– and other refs. Add. 36825, f. 22^v.

[2] S.P. 16/5/49 (Sir Francis Stewart to Buckingham). I am grateful to Mr. David Hebb for this reference.

[3] S.P. 16/5/6: S.P. 16/19/107. Digges warned Charles that Tonnage and Poundage would raise the issue of impositions. He hoped Charles would abandon them, and raise an equivalent revenue through a new book of rates.

tending with were not their fault. Nevertheless, it must be said that in an undertaking to survive as favourite from one reign to the next, Buckingham had set out to handle more difficulties than even he could hope to overcome. He had had a good deal of bad luck, but that is something for which gamblers must be prepared.

The Parliament of 1625 lacked one necessary ingredient to an explosive Parliament: an openly divided court. For the first few months of Charles's reign, from about March to November 1625, Buckingham's dominance of the court was probably more complete than at any time before or after. The summer of 1625 was something of an interval between the two big court attacks on him, those of 1623–4, and of 1626.

Buckingham normally reacted, after surviving attacks on him, by dividing his opponents into those who were crushed, and those who had to be conciliated. In 1624, Cranfield and Bristol had been crushed. Cranfield had been impeached, and forbidden to come to court. John Digby, Earl of Bristol, appears to have caused Buckingham more alarm than any of his opponents. Bristol had continued to negotiate for the Spanish match, with James's support, after Charles and Buckingham had decided to have nothing more to do with it. This alone would have been enough to make Charles and Buckingham dislike Bristol. In addition, they appear to have feared that Bristol possessed some information, presumably gathered in Madrid, which they did not wish to have disclosed. On his return from Spain, Bristol was sent off to his house at Sherborne, and kept under what was, in effect, house arrest until the Parliament of 1626. He was ordered not to attend the Parliament of 1625, and remained at home.[1]

By contrast, Pembroke and Arundel were perhaps too thankful to find their favour continuing into the new reign to want to risk their continued favour by any overt attack on Buckingham before they had discovered what the balance of power was likely to be in the new reign. Williams was still in office as Lord Keeper when the Parliament met, but was sacked shortly after it dispersed.

Above all, Buckingham's active commitment to war with Spain split his enemies and so was still a handicap to the formation of any effective court alliance against him. Pembroke's commitment to the war made it difficult for him to oppose Buckingham while

---

[1] Bristol ultimately succeeded in obtaining leave to send a proxy, which he gave to Pembroke.

Buckingham was also committed to it. He and others at court could appreciate, as people in the counties could not, that the delay in the outbreak of war had been due to the resistance of James, and not to any insincerity in Charles and Buckingham. Almost from the day of Charles's accession, a steady series of letters were going out from the Council preparing munitions, collecting supplies of saltpetre, pressing soldiers, and fitting out ships.[1] Councillors had no doubt of the sincerity of the new King's commitment to war. It is probable that many members who had sat in the 1624 Parliament also appreciated Charles and Buckingham's difficulties. James's reluctance to agree to war had, after all, been common knowledge in the Parliament of 1624, and it is probable that many members who asked why war had not yet broken out arrived at the correct explanation. Throughout the Parliament of 1625, wholehearted supporters of the war remained supporters of Buckingham. Rudyerd, Digges, and Eliot were all allies of Buckingham in 1625, and even Sir Nathaniel Rich, according to Hacket, was 'never out of my Lord Duke's chamber and bosom'.[2] The supporters of war might not be a powerful enough group to sway the House of Commons, but they were powerful enough at court to give Buckingham the necessary protection there. The support of Rudyerd and Rich mirrors the support of Pembroke and Holland.

For the Crown, then, the assembly of the Parliament of 1625 was meant to be the signal for the war effort to move into top gear. There was no long legislative programme, and, it was hoped, no contentious business. Sir John Coke, in April, had drawn up a list of eight 'commonwealth laws'. In the event only one, that for arms, even came before the Commons. The King, who withdrew to Hampton Court shortly after the Parliament met, was well aware of the plague hazard in London, and had no desire to hazard members' lives unnecessarily. He wanted two things from the Parliament: a grant of supply commensurate with the enterprise he had undertaken, and the life grant of Tonnage and Poundage which had been made to all new kings since the fifteenth century. He appears to have wholeheartedly believed he was

[1] A.P.C. 1625–6, pp. 7 ff. Barnes, pp. 172–3, Wentworth Papers, pp. 229–30.
[2] J. N. Ball, 'Sir John Eliot at the Oxford Parliament of 1625', B.I.H.R. (1955), 127: Christopher Thompson, 'The Origins of the Parliamentary Middle Group 1625–9', T.R.H.S. (1972), 77.

doing what most of his Parliament wished, and saw no reason to expect a difficult session. It was his misfortune to meet, for the first Parliament of his reign, a House of Commons in a thoroughly querulous mood. One reason for this was that James's success in delaying the war was not as well understood in the country as it was by those with contacts at court. Most members of the Commons probably knew that Charles and Buckingham had not obtained subsidies on false pretences in 1624, but it is most unlikely that their electors had any similar knowledge. Many members of the Commons, in their capacity as subsidy commissioners, had to go back to their homes and make speeches explaining why they had voted money. A subsidy commissioner had to set out the reasons for which subsidies had been voted. It is not a fanciful hypothesis that many of them had based their explanations on the preamble of the subsidy Act, saying that the money was appropriated to a war, and that it would be accounted for to the next House of Commons. They could hardly explain the quarrel between Charles and James on the county hustings: it was, in more than one sense, not the stuff to give the troops. Phelips was facing allegations that he 'had forsaken the country and was turned courtier', and was unable to make a convincing public defence.[1] It is likely that constituency pressure contributed to the determination shown by him, Sandys, and other members to avoid making another big grant until a war was actually in progress.

In the case of Phelips, the member whose attitude to Buckingham had most conspicuously changed since 1624, there may have been another reason in operation. After the Parliament was over, Phelips drafted a letter, optimistically designed to recover the Duke's favour through an intermediary. In that letter, he indignantly denied the belief he claimed Buckingham held, that 'the Earl of Bristol and I had conspired together to do him disservice'. The denial is not altogether convincing. Bristol was Phelips's near neighbour, and former superior in the Madrid embassy, and there is at least one tenuous piece of evidence of contact between them early in 1625.[2] Conference with Bristol

[1] Hirst, p. 180: above, pp. 19–20. *C.S.P.D. 1625–49 Addenda*, vol. dxxi, no. 34.
[2] Phelips MSS. 221/12. There is no evidence to identify the intended recipient of this letter, nor that it was ever sent. Phelips MSS. 219/33 records the delivery

would explain, more easily than anything else, the patent doubt Phelips showed in 1625 about the sincerity of the King and the Duke's commitment to war. It could do much to explain the apparent intensity of his feeling that he had been hoodwinked by them in 1624.

II. THE LONDON SESSION

By the time the Parliament assembled, many members wanted nothing so much as to be allowed to go home at the earliest possible opportunity.[1] After the opening speeches, there was a marked reluctance to undertake any business which might prolong the Parliament.

The King began with suitable brevity, simply by asking for supply for the war, in which, he said, he 'was engaged by us, and we by a liberal declaration engaged ourselves, so that it would be a dishonour to him and to us not to perfect it, by yielding such supply as the greatness of the work and variety of provision did require'. This thesis, that Parliament was 'engaged' to support the war, appears to have been Charles's real conviction, and was repeated by him with increasing exasperation as the decade continued. He was supported in it by Lord Keeper Williams, who gave a description of attempts to collect allies on the continent, and of the mercenary expedition under Count Mansfield which had been sent to the Palatinate. He tried, honestly, but apparently without success, to convince the Commons that these measures had taken up almost all the subsidies voted by the previous Parliament.[2] A long oration by Crew, who was again Speaker, tried to back up this mood of loyalty to the new King. He praised Charles as 'never a stranger to Parliaments' and claimed that the last Parliament had passed more bills of grace than in Magna Carta. He gave warnings of the unpopularity of attempts to tolerate recusants, and tried to whip up enthusiasm for the war as a religious cause. He reminded the House of the curse that had been placed on Meroz because he did not come forth in the cause of the Lord, a biblical allusion likely to have been familiar to the

of a confidential letter to Phelips by Bristol's man, Gresley. See Phelips MSS. 222/53, where he again denies the Duke's belief in confidential relations between him and Bristol.

[1] Chamberlain, 12 and 25 June 1625.   [2] *1625 Debates*, pp. 1–3.

whole house. This religious patriotism was encouraged by Buck-ingham's follower Sir Miles Fleetwood, moving for a public Fast, to secure the blessing of God on the King, for the miseries of the Christian (i.e. Protestant) church overseas, for a blessing on the navy being prepared, and to avert the 'grievous visitation' of the plague.[1]

The stage was well set for a grant of supply, to be followed by an adjournment until the war was under way, and the plague finished. In spite of this skilful stage-setting, business began, to the astonishment of Eliot and other war supporters, with an 'unexpected motion' to 'decline the whole proceedings of that meeting, and petition for an adjournment to the King'. This motion might, if carried, have forced the King to conclude an immediate peace. What were the motives for this motion for the adjournment? Mallory, who moved it, said it was 'in respect of the increase of the sickness', and asked for an adjournment till Michaelmas. Should we take this reason at its face value, or should we follow Eliot's later account in believing the plague to be only the 'colour and pretext' for a motion which was moved for other reasons?[2] The plague was a good enough reason for an adjournment. If we did not know that Mallory already had a record both as a wrecker and as an opponent of the war, there would be no reason to question his motives. He received two supporters: Sir Thomas Wentworth and Sir Robert Phelips. Wentworth also was an opponent of war, and could also have regarded the motion for the adjournment as a way of preventing the war. The interesting case is that of Phelips. The reports are ambiguous on whether he proposed an adjournment to another time, or to another place. What is clear is that he did not want to vote supply and go home having nothing else. According to Pym's text, he said: 'A supply was propounded; but we ought rather to consider how we may supply the commonwealth. In the first place to look to the law of God. There was matter of fear in every part of the state. Before we think upon giving now we ought like-wise to take an account of that which was last given, and because our time cannot possibly extend to all, we should rather desire his Majesty to be referred to some other time'. After his difficulties at home, his reluctance to come home having voted supply without legislation is intelligible. There is also no reason to doubt his

[1] *1625 Debates*, p. 6; *H.o.L.*, p. 177.   [2] Ibid., p. 7; *N.P.* i. 61–2.

terror at 'the fearful increase of the sickness'. Yet Eliot was not the only person to cast doubt on his sincerity. According to Phelips himself, another member wrecked his relations with the Duke by telling him that in this speech, Phelips had attacked him in set terms.[1] It is probable that such suspicions are unjustified, yet they were natural enough. Whatever the intention of Phelips's proposals may have been, their effect, if they had succeeded, would have been to end the war to which the King and the Duke were committed.

For the time being, the motion for the adjournment was effectively set aside by a speech from Solicitor General Heath, saying they must provide for defence, and in this, the first Parliament of the new King, an immediate adjournment would cast doubt on the affection of his subjects, which must be his greatest strength. Yet, though the adjournment proposal was defeated, the desire to end the Parliament persisted. The next day, 22 June, the Commons decided not to have a committee for grievances, because they 'thought it unfit in respect of the short and dangerous time'. Coke supported this proposal, saying that the crowding of 'the meaner sort of people' to the committee would increase the risk of infection. He pointed out that the law term had already been adjourned for this reason, and said that, since it was a new reign, there were no grievances 'as yet'.[2] He proposed the course ultimately adopted, that they should petition the King for an answer to the grievances of the previous Parliament, which had been presented on the last day of the session, too late for any considered answer. Later incidents show the sincerity of concern about the plague. On 6 July, one of the members for Ipswich asked that actors, who had been forbidden to perform in London, should not be allowed to go to perform in the provinces, taking the plague with them. Rudyerd was duly sent off to convey this request to Pembroke, the Lord Chamberlain, who agreed to it. His agreement was greeted by a further proposal[3] for the sup-

---

[1] *H.o.L.*, p. 179, *1625 Debates*, p. 7, Phelips MSS. 221/12. The words which gave offence were perhaps 'there was matter of fear in every part of the state'. The words have some resemblance to those for which Cranfield chose to take offence at Sandys in 1621. Phelips does not name the fellow-member who denounced him to the Duke. It is tempting to suspect his fellow knight of the shire for Somerset. Sir John Stawell. See Barnes, p. 255, Keeler, p. 349. Mallory appears to have belonged to the Saville, rather than the Wentworth, faction in Yorkshire. Stowe 366, f. 7ʳ.

[2] *C.J.* 800, *1625 Debates*, pp. 11–12.   [3] *C.J.* 804, 807.

pression of bear-baiting, bull-baiting, and bowling alleys during the infection. Ignatius Jordan, ever the optimist about the reformation of morals, hoped to seize the occasion to suppress some of the main centres of London prostitution. The Earl of Huntingdon asked for leave to send his proxy, because the plague had spread too close to the house he had rented in London. The Lords, who had very little business in a Parliament intended only for supply, even raised a proposal to release the prisoners in London, on the ground that keeping them in prison was, in effect, giving them a death sentence. The Commons' concern about the plague did not quite extend this far, but the question raised a long debate in the House. By 8 July, according to Eliot, only about a quarter of the Commons were still attending the House, though 227 members had voted in a division on 5 July. Eliot was prone to exaggeration, but he was not exaggerating when he said that 'Divers fell down in the streets. All companies and places were suspected, which made all men willing to remove, and those of the Parliament more ready to shorten and expedite their business.'[1]

It was against this background that members were asked to raise enthusiasm for war and supply. In the Lords, the 1621 bill for making the arms of the kingdom serviceable was revived, and got as far as committee before the adjournment. In the Commons, one member revived the bill which regularly accompanied proposals for war, against the transport of ordnance. It is not surprising that neither bill was completed. On 1 July, some members of the Commons raised the thorny question of the legal authority for the militia, including the urgent questions of the authority for pressing men, and for punishing deserters. All they achieved was to get a small committee appointed to draw a bill for the next meeting.[2]

There was slightly more enthusiasm for the proposal to take the accounts of the previous subsidy, as demanded by the 1624 subsidy Act. This is a subject on which there was strong feeling in the country, and it is likely to have influenced reactions to proposals for subsidies in 1625. Phelips, on 21 June, appears to have said this should be considered before any new subsidies were

---

[1] *N.P.* i. 92–3, 84; *H.M.C. Hastings*, ii. 67. *Memorials of St. Margaret's Church Westminster*, ed. Arthur Meredith Burke (1914), pp. 537–8. The Register records 152 plague deaths in the parish during July, and 512 in August.

[2] *H.o.L.*, pp. 181, 191, 207, 199.

voted, and repeated the proposal the next day. He was supported by a Welsh member who was not a regular speaker. On 28 June, the proposal was taken up by Alford, probably looking, as usual, for means to satisfy 'the country'. On 1 July, the Commons succeeded in getting an account delivered by the Treasurers appointed by the subsidy Act of 1624. The Crown made no attempt to discourage this demand for accounts.[1] Mansfield's mercenary expedition was within the terms of the Act, and it might be hoped that the discovery that this expedition and the minimum of preparations for defence had used up almost all the subsidies would serve to educate the Commons in the financial realities of war.

If that was the Crown's hope, it was disappointed. The production of the accounts merely led to the swelling of another demand arising out of the subsidy Act of 1624. That Act had contained a clause, inserted by Sir Robert Phelips, which appeared to say that impressed troops raised in the counties should be paid, not, as before, out of local military rates, but out of the subsidies. The treasurers of the subsidy, having taken legal advice on this badly drafted clause, ignored it after 'many debates'.[2] If the clause had been implemented, the deduction of 8d. per soldier per day from the subsidies would have dramatically reduced their value. In Kent, Sir Edwin Sandys estimated the sum at stake at half a subsidy.[3] From the hearing of the accounts onwards, there was a swelling volume of protest at the ignoring of Phelips's clause in the 1624 Act. It is possible that some members, speaking as subsidy commissioners, had promised their counties that money spent on impressed troops would be repaid. Sir Thomas Wentworth said the refusal to meet counties' military rates out of the subsidies was 'quite contrary to the late last Act of subsidy', and Seymour appealed to 'the very direct words of the Act'. Alford ominously proposed to take this into consideration when they drafted the new bill of subsidy, and Sir Edwin Sandys demanded that the Council of War be called to account. On 5 July, it was reported that 'there had been complaints from divers counties, that they had sustained great charges in keeping of the pressed

[1] Sir John Coke said on 8 July that the King welcomed this desire to examine the accounts. *1625 Debates*, p. 56.

[2] Ruigh, pp. 253–4n. *C.S.P.D. 1625–49 Addenda*, vol. dxxi, no. 83.

[3] *H.o.L.*, p. 199. This may shed light on Sandys's troubles with the Kentish electorate.

soldiers, contrary to the express intention of the Act of subsidies'.[1] It was ordered that the Council of War, on receipt of certificates from the Deputy Lieutenants, should repay all the sums involved. The next day, Sandys reported 'the demands made by the country' for the repayment of this money, and the Commons resolved to defer viewing the accounts of the Treasurers of the subsidies until their next meeting, when they would, they hoped, be able to handle this question more thoroughly.[2] Meanwhile, they suspended all further disbursements under the Act. These debates give an impression that many members felt they had, to borrow Mr. Cooper's phrase, overdrawn their credit with the country.[3] The desire to satisfy local feeling was rather more intense than desire to equip the Crown to fight a war. It was an ominous atmosphere for any proposal to raise a large number of subsidies. These points, though made later, must be assumed to have been in members' minds before the motion for new subsidies was moved, and therefore to have influenced their reactions to the proposals.

On 21 June, the third day of the Parliament, Heath put the question of supply before the House, without any formal motion. Rudyerd, the next day, attempted the same sort of preparatory speech he had made in the previous Parliament, arguing that supply procured harmony between Crown and Parliament, eulogizing the new King and his devotion to Parliaments, and asking that members 'carry our selves in this first session with sweetness'.[4] Unfortunately, Rudyerd's character as a semiofficial spokesman seems to have weakened the force of his speech. No one followed him, and the comment in Eliot's account draws attention to the fact with the glee of a Buckingham man observing the failure of a Pembroke man: 'A great reputation was implied both in the learning and wisdom of the man; and as he was in use and estimation with some great ones, more was expected from him than from others, which made the satisfaction to seem less, and those that were critical to adjudge his composition more studied

---

[1] *H.o.L.*, p. 199, *1625 Debates*, p. 42. The Earl of Bedford, Lord Lieutenant of Devon, wrote 'NO' in the margin of his copy of Pym's diary against the Commons' resolution that the costs of soldiers in the counties should be chargeable to the subsidies. Bedford Estate Office, Bedford MSS., vol. 197, f. 24ᵛ. For local feeling on this issue, see Fletcher, p. 194, and S.P. 16/19/51 (D.L.s of Wiltshire to the Council). The Deputy Lieutenants of Wiltshire had paid the troops out of the subsidy in the belief that they were following 'the express words of the said Act'.   [2] *C.J.* 804.

[3] *Wentworth Papers*, p. 5.   [4] *1625 Debates*, pp. 9–11.

than exact. All men discerned in him no want of affection to be eloquent: but his expression was thought languid as the conclusion was unapt.'[1]

For the next eight days, supply was deferred, and the business of religion given priority. Supply was abruptly revived on 30 June, in an unexpected proposal by Sir Francis Seymour. He moved, as he had done in 1624, for a derisory sum: one subsidy and one fifteenth. This proposal amounted, either to disbelief in the existence of a war, or to a desire to stop any war which might be in progress. In Seymour's case, it is reasonable to construe the motion as entire opposition to war. The previous subsidies had been spent on an expedition to the Palatinate, a way of spending money Seymour in the previous Parliament had opposed with unusual frankness. His sudden attempt to secure a derisory vote of supply was probably intended both to cripple the war effort and to allow the Parliament to go home. Pym and Eliot both record that this motion was unexpected to 'courtiers', many of whom were out of the House.[2]

The task of pleading for a larger sum fell upon Rudyerd, forced for once to speak impromptu. He listed the King's engagements, to prepare the navy and to aid the Low Countries and Denmark, and reminded them of the cost of Mansfeld's expedition. He said the cost of the navy being prepared was likely to be £300,000 (between four and five subsidies), but did not make a formal motion for a set sum.[3] He received effective support only from John Maynard who moved for three subsidies, and from Sir Nicholas Sanderson, who claimed: 'Lincolnshire willing to contribute as much as may be: the most the house shall agree of.' He, unlike other members, explicitly accepted the argument that the Commons had 'engaged' the King in a war, and so were bound to sustain it.[4] One other member opposed the general inclination to defer a big grant until Michaelmas, by claiming (rightly, as it turned out) that the plague was unlikely to be over by Michaelmas, but even he only hoped to raise the House to two subsidies and four fifteenths.

[1] N.P. i. 69.
[2] 1625 Debates, p. 33, N.P. i. 75. The anonymous diarist also noted that none of the King's Council spoke. Queen's MS., f. 247ʳ.
[3] 1625 Debates, p. 30: H.o.L., pp. 196 ff.
[4] H.o.L., p. 197. The speeches of other Lincolnshire members cast some doubt on his claim to speak for the county.

On the other side was the familiar argument of the poverty of the country. Sir Edward Giles said that many of the poor had been forced to sell their necessaries to pay the last subsidies, and other members raised an attack on fifteenths, 'being very burdensome to the poorer sort, especially in towns and ancient boroughs'.[1] As in 1621, the Commons decided against fifteenths, which were not voted again.

The key speech seems to have been that made by Phelips, who agreed to two subsidies without fifteenths, saying, 'there is no cause for more, and [he] hopes no man will press for more.' Phelips was the first to deny explicitly the King's argument that they were engaged to support a war, for he said there was no war: 'There is no engagement; the promises and declarations of the last Parliament were in respect of a war: we know yet of no war nor of any enemy.' He asked again for an account of the last subsidies, and objected to subsidy being made the first work of a Parliament. He also launched into a volume of general complaint that 'the privileges of this House have been so broken, such burdens laid upon the people, that no time can come into comparison with this'.[2] This speech appears to have led the House to agree on two subsidies. Alford consented, saying that he thought the King's 'extraordinary occasions' would satisfy the country. Sandys, whose loyalty to Buckingham was less diminished than Phelips's, consented, saying they could vote more after Christmas. Sir Thomas Wentworth agreed to two subsidies, not towards the war, but as a gesture of goodwill, and added the proposal, which was accepted, that recusants should pay double. He expressed a hope that no man who wished to speak for more would be given a hearing.[2] Thus the sum was agreed to. As in 1624, the Commons' reaction to requests for war supply was a gesture of token compliance. Their grant was the bare minimum necessary to prevent the King from abandoning the war, but not enough to make its effective prosecution possible. They thus ensured that they would get the worst of both worlds.

The references in this debate to the likelihood of a new request for supply at Michaelmas or after Christmas shows that many

[1] H.o.L., p. 196, 1625 Debates, pp. 30-1.
[2] 1625 Debates, pp. 31-2: N.P. i. 76-8. 'This spell was a charm upon the courtiers, to suppress their further craving.'
[3] H.o.L., p. 197, 1625 Debates, p. 32.

members were aware that a war might make requests for subsidy so frequent as to be annual, or even twice-yearly. It is unlikely that many of them wanted to go home and justify such frequent grants of subsidies. In the subsidy debate itself, Sir Edward Coke and Sir Thomas Wentworth both expressed a desire that the King's ordinary revenues should be made able to bear a bigger proportion of his expenses. The Parliament of 1625 produced the first mentions of a proposal which was to become more frequent as the decade went on: to endow the Crown with a bigger settled revenue, so that it should not have to face Parliaments with such frequent requests for subsidies. It is intriguing that this proposal was first heard from Sir Robert Phelips, in the context of the Act of Tonnage and Poundage. On 22 June, he 'added the consideration of the new impositions and some fit provisos in this respect in the Act of Tonnage and Poundage, and how the revenue of the Crown might be supplied, being so wasted as it was unable to support public charges'.[1]

When the Commons of 1625 voted Charles Tonnage and Poundage for one year only, it has commonly been taken to have been their intention to diminish the King's revenue. In fact, it is possible that the intention of some of those involved in the decision was not to diminish the King's revenue, but to increase it. According to the anonymous diary, the intention of the House in making a one-year grant was not to deny the King Tonnage and Poundage. They remembered that in the previous Parliament the Act had been cited to justify the pretermitted custom and impositions, and wanted to draft a better-worded Act, to avoid such ambiguities.[2] The lack of time caused by the plague left them without the leisure to draft a bill of the necessary complexity. Phelips's proposal to make a grant for 'some years'[3] was designed, not to deprive the King of Tonnage and Poundage, but to leave time for a properly drafted bill.

There was much ill feeling about impositions, and Sandys

---

[1] *1625 Debates*, pp. 12–13.

[2] Queen's MS., f. 259^{r-v}, *N.P.* i. 93. For the incidents they were remembering, see above, pp. 199 and n.

[3] Phelips MSS. 216/8. This appears to be Phelips's rough notes for his speech in the Tonnage and Poundage debate of 5 July. The diaries do not permit certainty on the question whether Phelips was converted from 'some years' to one year before or after he delivered the speech, though *C.J.* 803 suggests that it may have been before.

again reverted to the impositions involved in the charge against Cranfield. He had two crucial points to make. Outport merchants could not be bound to pay impositions by the consent of London merchants, and even the consent of merchants as a body was not enough to make an imposition legal. Sandys reminded the Commons, as Coke had done in the Parliament before, of the statute of 1340, which had established that only Parliament was entitled to grant customs duties.[1] Sir Edward Coke, looking at the precedents of the same year, wanted to go further, and establish a new book of rates by Parliamentary authority.[2] The book of rates was the device whereby it was possible to make customs inflation-proof. Goods liable to poundage paid a fixed proportion per pound of value, and the function of a book of rates was to lay down the values at which goods should be rated for customs duty. A new book of rates, then, would have been more likely to increase the King's revenue than to diminish it. Yet it would have tended to establish the new constitutional principle that the valuation of goods for customs had to be done by authority of Parliament. It was thus not an attempt to diminish the Crown's revenue, but to preserve the much-battered principle that customs revenue was enjoyed by Parliamentary grant.

It is then possible that the intention of Phelips, Coke, and Sandys was not to use the Act to deprive the King of impositions, but to take up the suggestion made by James in 1610, that they should be granted by Parliamentary authority. Phelips's own words, in the rough notes for what appears to be his speech in the Tonnage and Poundage debate of 5 July, moved to grant it 'for a limited time of years. To secure in it the pretermitted custom and the other impositions.'[3] This wording is ambiguous, but, in the light of his speech of 22 June, it is as possible that he intended to use a revised bill to give Parliamentary authority to these duties as that he intended to use it to take them away.[4] It would have been the ideal proposal to enable Phelips to square the circle. Together with a new book of rates, such a proposal

---

[1] *H.o.L.*, p. 200. See pp. 194–5 (speeches of Delbridge, Phelips, and Coke) for an example of how easily debate led from impositions to Tonnage and Poundage. On books of rates and impositions, see below, p. 387.

[2] *1625 Debates*, p. 13.

[3] Phelips MSS. 216/8.

[4] For a similar proposal to confirm impositions by Act of Parliament, see the speech by Mr. Wentworth in 1626, Whitelocke, 12–20, f. 78.

would have given the Crown a larger and more secure revenue. Charles, who had no objection to Parliaments and urgently needed money, would not have rejected a secure revenue because it came by Parliamentary authority. At the same time, Phelips could have said in Somerset that he had carried a measure to secure the country against such frequent requests for supply.

If this was Phelips's intention, it was defeated by the ironic conjunction of Earle and Seymour with the Lords. Earle, who did not want a life grant of Tonnage and Poundage made until the King guarded the seas against pirates (the purpose for which the money was intended), joined with Seymour and Rolle to alter 'years' into one year, thereby introducing a much more urgent time-scale[1] The Lords, faced by a bill giving the King Tonnage and Poundage for one year only, left it to fall asleep after the first reading. Thus the King, in urgent need of Tonnage and Poundage, was forced to collect it without any Parliamentary authority at all. The result of these manœuvres by Phelips and Coke was not to preserve Parliamentary control of the customs, but almost to bring it to an end. For this disastrous muddle, the blame must be placed on the plague. It was only the plague which made a temporary bill necessary. Without it, Phelips and Coke could have drafted their bill at leisure. If they had been able to carry through the Commons a proposal giving impositions Parliamentary authority, they would have removed a standing grievance, done much to show the continuing value of Parliaments, increased the King's revenue, and shifted much of the burden of taxation off land on to trade. It would have been a considerable achievement, but it would have demanded a bill drafted and debated at greater leisure than was possible in a plague-stricken atmosphere with most members only eager to go home.

From the very beginning of the Parliament, the plague, as well as the projected war, contributed to the growing alarm felt about what seemed to be an incipient toleration of Catholic recusants. Seymour and Delbridge replied to Rudyerd's first speech of 22 June, asking members to avoid asperity, by pressing for a 'bold but mournful' petition against the toleration of papists, saying both their number and their insolency were increased.[2] A throng of members rushed to support them, one saying there was 'more

[1] 1625 Debates, pp. 43–4, C.J. 803.
[2] 1625 Debates, p. 12.

cause to fear the plague of our souls, than our bodies. The best preservative and cure the execution of the laws against Jesuits etc.'[1] Two days later, another member blamed the toleration of recusants in London for the ill success of foreign policy. 'God not the same to us that he hath been formerly goes not out with our armies: the heathen observed this to be the cause of it, when they had ill success in their affairs suffering false religions.'[2] Sir Robert Phelips was the first to voice the main ground of anxiety on this subject: 'We are not yet fallen upon the true causes of the increase of recusants and their insolency, the unfortunate treaty with Spain a great cause of it.' He appeared to be hinting that the French treaty was as much of an obstruction to the persecution of recusants as the Spanish treaty had been. His friend Sir Humphrey May answered him honestly, but not entirely reassuringly: 'Times and counsels must alter as things alter. The treaties with foreign princes of contrary religion have cast a slumber upon the laws, the king's heart as right towards religion as we would desire it: affairs of Christendom have enforced him to do as he hath, hath guided his counsels upon great reason.'[3] It is likely that this speech was meant to invite, rather than discourage, further pressure on this subject: Parliamentary pressure might serve to counterbalance the contrary pressure from the French.

Sandys reacted by moving for a committee to draft a petition showing, article by article, how to strengthen our own religion and weaken theirs'. Coke, accepting the proposal, widened it, saying, 'Where prophecy ceases, the people perish, a great part of the realm without teaching.' The petition, which was ultimately drawn by Pym and Sandys, thus covered both ways of repressing recusancy, and ways of revitalizing the Church of England by such measures as reforming the abuse of impropriations, whereby much of the tithes went to sustain lay patrons instead of preachers. There was never any likelihood that impropriations would be

---

[1] C.J. 800.

[2] H.o.L., p. 205. The speaker was 'Mr. Whitaker'. Unfortunately, as with other speeches by 'Mr. Whitaker', it is impossible to be certain whether the speaker is William Whitaker, Pym's lawyer, or Lawrence Whitaker, clerk of the Council. The fact that it is impossible to distinguish them by subject matter is significant. Only the speech for Cambridge in the 1628 subsidy debate can be identified confidently as by Lawrence Whitaker: William was an Oxford man. Stowe 366, f. 206ʳ. Dr. Tyacke takes the anti-Arminian speeches to be by Lawrence Whitaker.

[3] H.o.L., pp. 205–6.

reformed by an assembly of landowners, but other ways of encouraging godly preaching might be considered.[1]

One of these was proposed by Nathaniel Rich, who suggested that silenced ministers should be allowed to preach on all points agreeable to the doctrine and discipline of the Church of England. It was probably he who introduced the subscription bill, proposing that ministers should only be forced to subscribe to those of the Thirty-Nine Articles which had been confirmed by Act of Parliament. Rich was right that 'the like petition hath been in almost every Parliament': he was reviving a defence of moderately nonconforming ministers which had been normal up to 1610.[2] It was also, however, a concern on which the Parliaments of 1621 and 1624 had been entirely silent. In 1625, this attempt to show sympathy with puritan nonconformity seemed likely to split the House down the middle. Rudyerd immediately opposed the proposal, saying 'moderate bishops' would do it of themselves. In subsequent debates, Rudyerd was supported by Sir Robert Hatton, a Kentish steward of the Archbishop, and by Digges. Rich was supported by Hoby, and by young Crew, the Speaker's son, who argued that 'men united to the church in fundamental points' should not suffer so heavy a sentence as deprivation. Sir Henry Marten, Dean of the Arches, seeing that no consensus was likely to emerge, produced a formula to cover over the differences.[3]

One issue might have been smoothed over, but the general revival of concern about religion could not be so easily stilled. In particular, it was impossible to still the storm raised by the case of Richard Montagu the Arminian. This was raised by Henry Sherfield as an example of doctrine within the Church of England tending to popery.[4] It was then taken up, as it had been in 1624, by the member who was to make the issue his own: John Pym. Richard Montagu's central attack was on the doctrine of predestination, which Archbishop Abbot, as much as Pym, believed to

---

[1] Pym, like Rudyerd, was concerned to reform impropriations, and was put in charge of drawing a bill on the subject in 1629. *C.J.* 924. Sandys, as the son of a bishop, had a special awareness of the problem.

[2] *1625 Debates*, p. 26. *H.o.L.*, pp. 185, 190.

[3] *1625 Debates*, pp. 26, 28-9. Bedford, in his copy of Pym's diary, noted 'NO' against Rich's proposal, and also against the committee's recommendation that bishops should be empowered to charge impropriations for the maintenance of incumbents. Bedford MSS. 197, ff. 14^v, 15^r.

[4] *H.o.L.*, p. 206.

be a central point of the theology of the Church of England. The previous Parliament had referred the Montagu case to Abbot, confident of his support. Abbot, who was not equally confident of the Crown's support, had simply asked Montagu to cut out offending passages in his book. Montagu had duly made gestures of compliance, but the next Abbot heard of it was when Montagu presented him with a copy of a second book, justifying all the provocative points of the first. In 1625, Abbot was again called in, on behalf of the Commons, by a deputation led by his former pupil, Digges. He was as sympathetic as ever, but more uncertain of his power to help. It was becoming steadily clearer in 1625 that the issue of Arminianism against predestination was one which split the court and the bench of bishops down the middle. In the middle of such an intense scare about Roman Catholicism, the appearance of a serious doctrinal split within the Church of England was bound to provoke strong reaction.

It also raised the question whether the House of Commons had independent authority to take action in matters of religion, especially against a purely doctrinal offence. The committee which reported on Montagu on 7 July proposed two ways of avoiding this question. One was the way that had been used in the case of Sir Francis Michell: to punish him for contempt of the House of Commons, and leave the doctrinal question to be settled elsewhere. This was a possible line of argument: Montagu had been attacked in the previous Parliament for one offensive book, and had promptly written another repeating the offence. This could be held to be a contempt. The other was the argument that his writings 'tended to the disturbance of the church or state', and therefore that his case might be sent to the Lords for an impeachment, as involving a religious breach of the peace. The case did not create unanimity in the House of Commons. Pym, in his diary, reported that some tried 'insinuating, so far as they durst, a defence of Mr. Montagu's doctrine'.[1] Only one member, Richard Dyott, can be identified with certainty as having done this. However, Christopher Brooke of York was willing to present Montagu's petition, and Sandys to deny that he was guilty of a contempt. On the other side, Coke accepted the argument that they could censure Montagu for disturbing the peace of the church. He, Digges, and Rich supported the proposal adopted, to find him

---

[1] *1625 Debates*, pp. 51–3.

guilty of contempt, and remit him to the custody of the Serjeant till the next meeting. Only Heath, the Solicitor General, offered a direct defence of the Commons' authority in matters of doctrine, quoting the words 'pro ecclesia Anglicana' from the writ of summons to defend a claim to jurisdiction over him.[1] Heath was one of the stronger opponents of Arminianism,[2] and two days later, when Charles announced that Montagu was his servant, and therefore should be released as enjoying privilege of Parliament, Heath allowed it to be painfully clear that this was the first he had heard of Montagu being the King's servant.[3] Charles made clear in this gesture, that he was ready for a confrontation on the issue of Arminianism. Yet, at the same time, Heath, Pembroke, Archbishop Abbot, and others made so firm a commitment against Montagu that the developing confrontation remained, for several years, a struggle fought out in the first instance within the court, and between Parliaments as much as in Parliaments. Arminianism was not a court–country issue before 1629, and in 1625, most members still regarded it as merely one branch of the general attack on popery.

However, once members' religious fears were raised, a divided church gave plenty of material for fear to feed on. There can be no question of the seriousness of concern about religion in 1625. If the speeches did not prove it, the length of time spent on the subject would do so. The fact that, when they were too eager to go home to set up committees for grievances or courts of justice, members voluntarily devoted about half the time from 21 June to 11 July to religious issues must surely be evidence of genuine concern. Once raised, this concern did not go away. It should perhaps rank with the war as one of the most damning inheritances which came to Charles with his crown. Yet, though he did not create the anxiety about religion, Charles, by his defence of Montagu, helped to ensure that it would continue.

By contrast, eagerness to introduce bills appears to have been

---

[1] *C.J.* 805–6.

[2] *C.S.P.D. 1628–9*, vol. cxviii, no. 33, 7 Oct. 1628. Heath, forwarding the King's pardon to Montagu, told him he doubted whether it would be proof against Parliament, and asked him to review his book and take away things doubtful. Heath's words sound like a close paraphrase of Archbishop Abbot's advice of 1624. This could be connected with *C.S.P.D. 1628–9*, vol. cxxxv, no. 17 (7 Feb. 1629), where Heath is said to be in the King's displeasure.

[3] *1625 Debates*, p. 62, *C.J.* 807, *1625 Debates*, App., p. 153 (Locke to Carleton).

very limited in 1625, and some that were introduced, like the subscription bill and Coke's bill to reform excommunication, were offshoots of the general concern about religion. The bill of the Sabbath, another expression of the religious mood, was the first bill read. It passed rapidly through the Commons, and, in the Lords, Mandeville, although calling it the bill of 'Sunday', reported it fit to pass without amendment.[1] It at last became a statute, without any suggestion of an attempt to re-draft it to meet the points made in 1624, about its unsuitability to towns. Another bill about alehouses passed quickly, was amended by the Lords to include taverns,[2] and became a statute. So did the 1624 bill about licences to alienate, a bill mainly concerned with fees for land conveyancing. The King secured a bill regulating the habit of his tenants on the manor of Macclesfield of digging up coal in their back gardens.[3] The bills to abbreviate Michaelmas term, and to prevent simony in the Universities, were 'looked up', and progressed as far as committee.[4] The hardy perennial bill against recusants evading forfeiture by uses passed rapidly through the Commons, but did not reach the statute book.[5] The only secular bill for which the Commons showed enthusiasm, apart from the few which reached the statute book, was the bill for freedom of fishing. In the absence of Neale, Glanville steered it through the Commons, and it went to the Lords on 1 July. The Lords, proceeding at a more stately pace, sent it to committee on 11 August, the day before the final dissolution. They thus avoided the odium either of passing it or rejecting it. [6] In general, there was little enthusiasm for bills in 1625.

By about 8 July, most of the Commons hoped their work was done. The King had graciously accepted their subsidies, thereby, it was thought, indicating that he would pretend they were enough. Tonnage and Poundage would require another meeting, but few members, if any, seem to have expected that any more business

---

[1] *1625 Debates*, p. 14. It was left unamended because the King as Prince had agreed to it in the previous Parliament. *L.J.* 451. See N.R.S. iv. 337–8, ii. 397 for the Lords' alteration of the title to 'Sunday' in 1621.

[2] *L.J.* 455, 457. The bill was reported by Clare.

[3] 1 Car. I c. 9. It is typical of the way business was managed that the King's bill was reported by that quintessentially private member, Sir John Lowther.

[4] *H.o.L.*, pp. 183, 182, 192.

[5] *1625 Debates*, p. 14, *H.o.L.*, p. 192.

[6] *H.o.L.*, pp. 185, 189, 195, 199, *L.J.* 487. Mr. Snelling, burgess for Ipswich, wanted the bill to extend to all parts of the country.

would be transacted before the end of the plague. The petitions on grievances and on religion had been answered. Neither answer was entirely satisfactory, but they were good enough for Sir Edward Coke to move that they be recorded by being enrolled on the Parliament Roll. At this time, Eliot's is probably a fair summary of the mood of the House:

Their grant they saw accepted, and all things left to the discretion of the House. The business then depending was not much, new they presumed would not be received; those few questions that remained were of no great importance and most of them but formal, so as they now conceived no necessity of their presence . . . in this confidence the greater part went off.[1]

It was in this end-of-term atmosphere that members were struck 'like a lightning'[2] by Sir John Coke's motion of 8 July, for an additional vote of supply, and by his announcement of Charles's decision to adjourn the Parliament for an almost immediate further sitting at Oxford. In the attacks against Buckingham in the next Parliament, few things were looked back on with more bitterness than this decision to adjourn the Parliament, to meet on the unseasonable date of 1 August, in Oxford, where the plague had already broken out.

In all the business of the decade, none shows a more complete gulf of mutual incomprehension than the reactions to Sir John Coke's motion of 8 July for an additional grant of supply. From the point of view of many of the Commons, even those who, like Eliot, had close court connections, it was so incomprehensible that it was necessary to ascribe it to malice. To the King, and to anyone who had done the necessary financial arithmetic, it seemed the only possible alternative to the disaster his fleet experienced when it attacked Cadiz that autumn. Buckingham was telling the truth when he told Eliot that the two subsidies had been accepted 'but in respect of the affection to the King, and not for satisfaction of his business'. He was quite right that the fleet could not be kept waiting ready to sail, and paying wages daily, and that it could not be adequately equipped on the existing supply of money: 'The absence of the Commons was their own fault and error, and their neglect must not prejudice the state.' Eliot failed to dissuade the Duke from going ahead with an additional request for supply, which, as he said, was 'lodged . . . merely to be denied'.[3]

---

[1] *N.P.* i. 92–3.   [2] Ibid., p. 118.   [3] Ibid., pp. 112–13.

Sir John Coke, on 8 July, hoped to get an immediate vote of supply, or if he could not get that, at least a declaration of support, which the King could use as security to give him credit to borrow money. His case should have been persuasive.[1] His figures, £32,000 spent on Ireland, £37,000 on the navy, £47,000 on the repair of forts, £99,00 on the four English regiments in the service of the Dutch, and £62,000 on Mansfeld's mercenary expedition, showed that of the 1624 subsidies £287,000 had been spent, and only £35,000 remained. Moreover, all these figures showed what was, from a military point of view, underspending rather than overspending. Mansfeld, in particular, could have been much more successful with better logistic support. It was a clear conclusion that the two subsidies just voted, worth at the most £140,000, were not enough to sustain a year's full-scale war. He pointed out that his figures excluded the current preparation of the fleet (the fleet which went to Cadiz that autumn). On that, Charles had already spent £20,000 in the navy office, £48,000 in the ordnance office, and £45,000 on land soldiers. Charles was also committed to pay £40,000 to the King of Denmark, as a necessary subsidy to acquire an ally, and £20,000 a month to Count Mansfeld. Much of this money had been lent by Buckingham out of his own pocket. Coke rightly pointed out that two subsidies, which he optimistically calculated at £160,000, would not get the King enough money to complete such a programme. In all this, Sir John Coke rather understated than overstated his case. He said the King's ordinary revenue could contribute no more, and he could not go through with the business without further help by Parliament 'or else some new way'. It was a fair warning. Yet he was seconded only by Sir William Becher, clerk of the Council, who tried to use the ending of the depression to show the country could afford subsidies.[2]

This speech completely failed to catch the comprehension of most of the Commons, or, if Eliot is to be believed, of much of the court. It was opposed by Sir Edward Giles, whose opposition must cast doubt on his claim to be considered a war supporter, by a member from Lincolnshire, and by Littleton. Littleton cor-

[1] For Sir John Coke's speech, see Queen's MS. ff. 255ʳ–259ʳ. The anonymous diarist says the house was 'then very thin, and scarce a grand committee for number, many having gone down, and the rest expecting daily to be dismissed'. B.L. Add. MS. 48091, f. 21ʳ.

[2] *N.P.* i. 117, *1625 Debates*, p. 59.

rectly saw that Sir John Coke was giving accounts of money already spent in anticipation of the 1625 subsidies, as well as of the 1624 subsidies. He said that 'His Majesty showeth much grace to give an account before the money be paid', but said that, the House being so thin, and having given so freely so lately, this motion was moved 'very unseasonably'. On credit, he said it was 'such a merchant-like word, he knew not what to make of it'. Heath, seeing the mood of the House, despaired of the motion, and 'took care only to lay it aside quietly'.[1]

It was at the end of this day's debate that the decision was taken to adjourn the House to Oxford. The anonymous diarist was apparently as shocked as Eliot at this decision: he said 'The House generally was much amazed at it, and thought it to be strange dealing with them.' The interval between sessions, from 11 July to 1 August, was just long enough to face members with an awkward problem about where to go. Eliot, a Cornishman, said that those whose homes were remote had just time to visit their families, and then immediately take leave of them. The danger of infection in the inns, and the sight of the dead and dying in the fields and hedges, is unlikely to have contributed to a calmer mood.[2] Eliot was right in warning Buckingham that his request for additional supply stood no chance of success. Yet Buckingham was right in warning Eliot that the continuation of the war without further supply was a recipe for disaster. Neither seems to have considered the abandonment of the war, the only logical way out of the impasse. It is interesting, and perhaps matter for some thought, that Charles's ultimate decision to raise the money he needed in the form of a forced loan caused less protest than his attempt to obtain it by Parliamentary subsidies. No wonder Sir John Coke was wondering about raising money by 'some new way'. What is remarkable is that, in the face of these financial disincentives, Charles and Buckingham continued to strive so hard to reach an understanding with their Parliaments. This fact surely suggests that the tributes of Crew and Rudyerd to Charles, the Parliamentary prince, were well deserved. Only a principled belief in Parliamentary institutions can explain the effort Charles made to work them between 1625 and 1628.

[1] *N.P.* i. 117, Queen's MS., ff. 255–6 (double foliation). *1625 Debates*, p. 59.
[2] Queen's MS., f. 258ᵛ; *N.P.* i. 123–5.

III. THE OXFORD SESSION

The Oxford session of the Parliament of 1625 lasted from 1 August to 12 August. As Eliot had predicted, it produced no additional grant of supply, and ended in dissolution. As Buckingham and Sir John Coke had predicted, the failure to gain additional supply led to military defeat and disgrace. Why did the attempt to gain additional supply fail? It was not for lack of Councillors to put the King's case in the Commons. The King, pointing out that this was the first request for supply of his reign, and the fleet being prepared his first great enterprise, in effect made an issue of confidence of the motion for additional supply. He was supported by a more united court than can be seen in any other Parliamentary session of the period. The failure of the attempt to gain additional supply was not due to any lack of Councillors to put the case in the Commons. May, Edmondes, Weston, and Naunton did everything Councillors could do. They enjoyed all possible support from those with official posts or court connections. Sir Robert Heath, Solicitor General, Sir Henry Mildmay, Master of the Jewel House, and Sir Henry Marten, Dean of the Arches and Judge of the Admiralty Court all gave them the fullest support. Pembroke men like May spoke with the same voice as Buckingham men like Mildmay and Heath. For once, the clear conciliar leadership the Stuarts are reproached for not giving to their Parliaments was present in force.

Yet its only effect was to turn the session, again for the only time in the period, into a court–country confrontation. The apparently united influence of the court, supported, as Eliot conceded, by a considerable array of debating talent, was not enough to sway the Commons. Some people were converted, and Sir Roger North publicly admitted his conversion.[1] Yet, though there were unofficial supporters of a grant of supply, it was never likely that they would carry the Commons.

While this struggle for supply was being carried on, the Lords could do little but be silent spectators. Those of them who attended were gathered together for the two big conferences of both Houses, and many of them probably took part in discussions behind the scenes. Buckingham later thought that Saye, who, like Coke and

---

[1] *1625 Debates*, p. 110. North said he was in part converted by the King's answer to the petition on religion.

Phelips, had been his ally in 1624, had likewise deserted him. It would be good to know how far he was right in ascribing Phelips's change of heart to private conference with Bristol and Saye. Yet, whatever they may have done in private, the Lords had almost no business in public. In a Parliament where legislation was avoided as far as possible, petitioners were discouraged for fear they might bring infection, and no impeachment was in progress, the Lords could only wait.[1] Even the two main bills the Commons had sent to them at London, for free fishing and to prevent recusants evading forfeiture by uses, were bills on which slow proceeding was the only prudent course. The second, in particular, could have caused serious offence to the French if proceeded in, and serious offence to the Commons and many of the Council if rejected. They committed a bill for better preserving of the King's revenue, and excused the Earl of Clare because a man had died of the plague in his house.[2] As always, though, if a Parliament was solely concerned with supply, it became a Commons' Parliament.

Before the business of supply was reintroduced, the Commons were left to themselves for two days' debating, and one day's fast. In the two days of business, they committed the bill against secret offices, which was strongly supported by Coke, although Sherfield maintained it was entirely ineffectual, adding nothing to existing law except the authorization of previously unauthorized fees.[3] Apart from this, they devoted their first two days at Oxford almost entirely to religion. The first business, raised by Sir Edward Giles, was a pardon for a Jesuit, procured by Secretary Conway, and dated the day after the adjournment of the Parliament from London.[4] This immediately called royal good faith in question. If, as was widely and correctly believed, the King had given

---

[1] Phelips MSS. 221/12. Lord Montagu only managed to fill four pages with his Journal of the Lords' proceedings in 1625. Much of what he noted consisted of minor irregularities in procedure, 'but, being at Oxford, there is no precedent to be made of these small errors'. *H.M.C. Buccleuch*, iii. 250. I have not discovered the reasons for Saye's breach with Buckingham. It could reflect the views of John Preston, for whom he was executor. P.R.O. PROB 11/154; I. Morgan, *Prince Charles's Puritan Chaplain* (1957), p. 59.

[2] *L.J.* 469 The lack of business is shown in Henry Wynn's report that not more than 160 members of the Commons had attended. He also said that a commission had been made out, but not sealed, to adjourn the Parliament after four days. National Library of Wales, Wynn of Gwydir MSS. 1358 (Henry Wynn to his father, 2 August 1625). I owe this reference to the late Mr. J. P. Cooper.

[3] For Sherfield, see *1625 Debates*, p. 17.

[4] *C.J.* 809.

contradictory promises to Parliament and to the French, it would be impossible to know which he was likely to keep.[1]

The next business was the case of Richard Montagu. He had been bound over to attend the Oxford session, but excused himself on the ground that he was 'sick of the passion hypochondriacal'.[2] Sir Edward Coke took the occasion to complain of the diversity of religious books being printed, and proposed that none should be printed unless allowed by Convocation. A proposal by Coke to increase the authority of Convocation is evidence, both that his dislike of Arminianism overrode the anti-clerical prejudices of a common lawyer, and that he believed the attack on Arminianism was a defence of, not an attack on, the doctrine of the Church of England. Phelips moved to send for Montagu, and the luckless Heath was forced to claim privilege for him as the King's servant. This claim offended Alford, Seymour, and old Thomas Wentworth, who rightly pointed out that no man could commit a public offence except under colour of some public employment, and that being the King's servants had not protected a Lord Chancellor and a Lord Treasurer. Yet the King was entitled to privilege for his personal servants, and a claim of Parliamentary privilege had earlier been allowed for a Beefeater.[3]

The privilege issue symbolized the point made by Drake, that the fact that this 'so dangerous' book was printed with royal privilege 'maketh it accounted the doctrine of the church of England'.[4] The issue which held members' attention through the plague was not whether a royal chaplain was a personal servant, but whether the doctrine of Richard Montagu or the doctrine of

[1] *H.M.C. Mar and Kellie Suppl.*, p. 231. 'One thing troubles me exceedingly to hear it . . . That the King has promised all contentment to the Parliament in matters of religion, and yet they spare not to say that the Duke of Chevreuse has a contrary promise. You can not believe the alteration that is in the opinion of the world touching his Majesty.' Kellie to Mar, 26 July 1625. Others at Court disliked this pardon. Henry Wynn reported that Lord Keeper Williams disliked it, and 'it was stayed by him for three or four dayes' at the Seal. National Library of Wales, Wynn of Gwydir MSS. 1358. I owe this reference to the late Mr. J. P. Cooper.

[2] *1625 Debates*, p. 69. Montagu did not mean what he now appears to be saying in this passage. The hypochondrium, the seat of melancholy, was supposed to be an organ above the stomach. It was only when this organ was discovered to be non-existent that 'hypochondria' became established in its modern meaning. On 29 July, Montagu was too ill for the more congenial task of visiting Buckingham. *Correspondence of John Cosin*, ed. G. Ornsby, Surtees Soc., vol. lii (1868), p. 152. I am grateful to Mr. Richard Peach for this reference.

[3] *L.J.* 156.   [4] *1625 Debates*, pp. 69–71, *C.J.* 809–10.

the Archbishop of Canterbury was the doctrine of the Church of England. It was to this question, not to the legal question of the Commons' privileges, that Charles's defence of Montagu appeared to be giving the wrong answer. Coke wanted to start impeachment proceedings. He said that the words of the writ, 'pro defensione ecclesiae', dated from before the Reformation, and that though the Commons might not judge a purely doctrinal case, the Lords could, because the Bishops were there. Again, his confidence in the bishops is worth remark.

It never appeared how widespread the support for impeachment proceedings would have been. After this speech, there was only time for a complaint that Dr. Anian, complained of in the late petition of grievances, had been selected as preacher to Parliament, before the Fast and the question of supply put an end to other business. On the morning of 4 August, both Houses were summoned to attend the King in Christ Church Hall. He then staked the prestige of his office on the motion for supply by speaking to it in person. He said he knew it was a time of danger, but 'left us to consider whither was greater, the danger of the sickness or of the reputation of the kingdom'.[1] He also promised a fuller answer to the petition on religion. He was supported by Secretary Conway, and by Sir John Coke, shortly to take office as the other Secretary. Many of the Commons and some Lords were said to have taken offence that Sir John Coke, a commoner, was selected to deliver the King's pleasure in their presence.[2] However, Conway and Coke delivered a powerful defence of the need for money. By studying the points they tried to answer, we may perhaps learn why they thought the resistance to additional supply was so strong. Their chief concern was to explain the delay in the outbreak of war during the last year of James's reign. They said James had calculated the cost of a full-scale war on his own resources at £700,000 a year (an annual vote of ten subsidies). This, according to Sir John Coke, had diverted him to the 'more thrifty' course of trying to collect continental allies. They pointed out that the alliances with France, Savoy, Venice, the Low Countries, and Denmark had considerably changed the state of European politics in the past year, and that failure to send out the fleet might discourage and disperse these allies, thereby weakening England's long-term position in European politics. In the main, diplomatic documents suggest that they

[1] *1625 Debates*, p. 73.   [2] *H.M.C. Buccleuch*, iii. 250.

were speaking the truth. The main flaw in their arguments, unerringly pointed out by Sir Francis Seymour, was that if they hoped for overt help from the French, they were at least five months too late. The beginning of a Huguenot revolt had effectively ended any chance of overt French assistance, and thereby destroyed one of the purposes of the French marriage before it had even been concluded. However, to any supporter of the war, the loss of effective help from one ally was no reason for losing or exposing the others. Sir John Coke asked a fair question when he asked whether they wanted to vote supply or have the war broken off.[1] Yet the main apparent reaction to this question, from Eliot in private and Seymour in public, was a suspicion that a decision had already been taken to end the war, and that blaming Parliament for not voting supply was being used as a convenient excuse to do so.[2] Whistler asked whether the preparations in hand were so important that they mattered more than members' lives. The deep-rooted and mistaken suspicion that no war was really intended must surely be seen, as Conway and Coke saw it, as a reaction to James's delay in and resistance to the start of any open war effort since 1624.

The speech by Sir Simon Weston voices this fear very clearly:

Let us first desire to know our enemy before we agree to contribute to a war. If there be a just occasion, he deserves not the privilege of a subject that will not sacrifice both his estate and his life for the public. We have amongst us enemies to the State. Let us begin with their estates who use the means to supply foreign princes.[3]

This speech also shows how easily, especially in a situation of uncertainty, war feeling was diverted into attacks on English recusants. One of the reasons for the suspicion of Charles's intentions may have been that, to many members, fighting Spain and pardoning recusants, and even more Jesuits, looked like a contradiction in terms. Moreover, it felt like a contradiction in terms.

Seymour, who spoke next, again repeated that 'we know not our enemy', but it is unlikely that his attitude would have changed if he had known the enemy. He said he could see no reason for the meeting at Oxford 'unless some out of private ends seek to put dissension betwixt the King and his people, and gave this advice out of ignorance or malice, rather than out of any care of the

---

[1] *1625 Debates*, pp. 76–7.
[2] *N.P.* ii. 22–5; *1625 Debates*, p. 78.   [3] *1625 Debates*, pp. 77–8.

commonwealth'. It was an obvious preparation for an attack on Buckingham, and when he went on to complain that the King rewarded the undeserving, and said a King was unhappy if he rested his counsel on one or two who knew better how to flatter and beg than to give good advice, his meaning was plain. He concluded by asking 'time to do somewhat for the country' before voting supply. Seymour had always been Buckingham's most consistent enemy in the Commons, and an attack from Seymour alone could have been passed over, as it had been in 1621.

Sir Humphrey May, answering him, thought he could clear Buckingham by recounting that he had committed his personal plate and jewels to the war, and went on to explain again the need to keep together the King's allies, and the thesis that the House of Commons was engaged to support a war. Edmondes supported him with a specific motion for two subsidies and two fifteenths. They were answered by Phelips, who reminisced about his misfortunes in 1621, and then came to his fear that the French marriage treaty was having the same bad effects as the Spanish. He recalled the 1621 petition that Charles should be married to a Protestant, and said: 'What the Spanish articles were we know. Whether those with France be any better, it is doubted. There are visible articles and invisible. Those we may see, but these will be kept secret from us.' He abandoned the self-restraint he had maintained for two Parliaments about impositions, and demanded to make the Parliament the reformer of the commonwealth. According to Eliot's account, but not to Pym's, he also joined Seymour's attack on Buckingham, claiming that the meeting at Oxford was for the will and pleasure of one subject, and the King's counsels were monopolized by one man.[1] Something of a mystery is created by the fact that Phelips could support the Duke in 1624, make this

---

[1] *1625 Debates*, pp. 81–2; *N.P.* ii. 31–5. The last folio of Phelips MSS. 216/8 could be rough notes for this speech. Phelips MSS. 216/9 could be his rough notes for the final section of the speech, on reformation of domestic disorders. If so, he delivered less than was in his notes. Two folios of the notes show considerable resemblance to his words about religion as reported in *N.P.* The remaining two folios read: 'to inquire into the state of imposicions aswell in point of right as oppression and to settle that question.

To declare the yniurye done to the lybertye of the subiect aswell out of as in Parlement and to demand security for the time to come.

To complayn of the frequent and publick sale of honour, and of places of judicature where by the digniyei of this kingdom are become contemptible and the justice of the kingdome rendered saleable.

To insist constantly upon the dew and unconnived execution of all and every

speech in 1625, and then try to recover the Duke's favour when the Parliament was over. Phelips's own papers do not provide a satisfactory solution of this mystery.

It is no wonder that Weston, Chancellor of the Exchequer, who had to answer this speech, was moved to anticipate Andrew Marvell, and complain that King and Parliament, though truly parallel, could never meet. He blamed the abuses complained of by Phelips on 'long peace and dependence on deceivable treaties' under King James, and hoped that a new King might reform them by the advice of his people, but came back again to what, from the administrative point of view, was the only immediate point: supply. 'Whatsoever we do hereafter, this action must be done now.'[1]

Sir Edward Coke, the next speaker, delivered himself of what was not merely a speech: it was a major state paper, whose importance was recognized in the fact that there are more reports of it than of any other proceeding of the Parliament. He dealt with the issue of supply quickly, moving 'not to give' because 'there is no enemy yet known'. He said that even if Parliament was engaged to a war, it already voted enough to discharge its engagement, and revealingly added that 'None invades us, we have no '88.'[2] An

---

the(?) laws constituted agaynst popish priests and recusants being hys mats. naturall subiects.

An Act of Resumption and to abate the pensions now granted.'
(This possibly a later addition to the MS.)

Phelips. MSS. 216/19 is another text with some resemblance to these notes. This is a draft, with numerous additions, but not in Sir Robert's hand, of the 'Cotton' speech, printed in Eliot *N.P.* ii. 85–91, and discussed by Dr. Ball in 'Sir John Eliot at the Oxford Parliament 1625', *B.I.H.R.* (1955), 121–7. If the 'Cotton' speech was originally intended for delivery by Phelips, Phelips MSS. 216/9 could then be headings for an attempt to weave Cotton's precedents into an argument by Phelips. Both texts of the 'Cotton' speech can be dated on internal evidence after the conference of 8 August, but there is no sign that it was delivered in the House. It could have been intended for delivery by Phelips on 12 or 13 August, if the Parliament had not been dissolved. It could have found its way into Eliot's papers because Phelips, when pricked sheriff for 1626, handed his papers over to Eliot for use in the next Parliament. See Ball, p. 208. Followed as it is by an attempt to recover Buckingham's favour after the Parliament, Phelips's conduct in 1625 does not appear to make sense. The only tenable hypotheses appear to be, either that the plague put him into a state of hysteria he later regretted, or that some key parts of the evidence are missing.

[1] *1625 Debates*, pp. 83–4.

[2] P.R.O. CREST 40/18, f. 66[r]. There are reports of this speech as an addendum to the Dyott diary, and in *1625 Debates*, pp. 84–7 and 130–3. I have found it necessary to revise the order of Coke's points in an attempt to convey his argument.

offensive war was not only harder to conduct than a defensive war: it was also less likely to rouse belligerent enthusiasm or martial memories. Having disposed of the purported subject of debate, he turned to what he thought was the real subject of discussion: the reformation of the King's finances. Why were they so 'decayed' that he lacked the credit to borrow £40,000 without Parliamentary assistance? To many members, this was the real question of the Oxford session.

It was to this question that Coke's financial analysis was directed. He was stating long-held convictions, formed as a Treasury Commissioner in 1618–19, stated in the Parliament of 1621,[1] and probably shared with a number of fellow-members such as Seymour and Alford. Coke thought that Parliamentary subsidies were being asked to carry too high a proportion of the cost, and the King's ordinary revenue too little. He thought 'subsidies never given for the ordinary, but for the extraordinary, expenses of the King'. Defence against sudden invasion, aid to allies, and rewards to 'well deserving' servants he classified as ordinary expenditure, and so not to be supported by Parliamentary subsidy. The diminished dependence on subsidies Coke was proposing would have reduced the importance of Parliament, but it appeared more important to Coke that in 1381, 1489, and 1509, 'pressing the people above their abilities' by Parliamentary grant had led to rebellion. He appeared to think that the plague and the consequent cessation of trade might mean that an additional vote of supply could have the same consequences again.

His question, then, was how the King's ordinary account could be put back into balance. He believed that the fault was not in the income, but in the expenditure side of the account: 'The causes of defect not for want of income, but through the ill ordering of it.' He therefore thought the King's immediate necessity, 'in respect it hath grown by improvidence, and is not inevitable, not fit to be supplied by the House'. He thought 'the ship hath a great leak'. Instead, he wanted to start a reformation of the King's expenditure, a cutting off of pensions, an investigation of fraud in the customs, and a cutting off of the taking of 5 per cent portage money by receivers. He wanted to reform maladministration in the King's household, claiming that if 'hangbyes' were taken away, and the number of tables reduced, he could run it for £50,000.

[1] M. Prestwich, *Cranfield* (Oxford, 1966), pp. 291–2.

He wanted to cut down on new offices, claiming that the Councils of Wales and the North were superfluous. Less realistically, he believed it was possible for 'every officer to live of his office, and not to beg other things'. Perhaps only a former Attorney General and judge could believe the legitimate profits of office were sufficient to justify this remark. He was perhaps nearer the mark in quoting a precedent from Henry IV's reign that no man should beg from the Crown till it was out of debt, but he did not say how those doing such begging were to be restrained.

He believed, like Cranfield, that royal parks and forests could be made to yield much more revenue than they did. He believed a considerable increase could be achieved in the yield of the Crown lands. He thought rents could be raised by a third, or, alternatively, that anyone who held a lease of Crown land from King James would give a half-year's rent to have it confirmed by King Charles. Above all, he thought this programme of retrenchment could not be achieved without the removal of Buckingham. He thought the hunt for patronage of dubious kinds was intensified by the fact that so many of the great offices were in the hands of one man, and that 'young and unskilful' persons should not be trusted with such great offices as that of Lord Admiral, where they lacked the ability to choose competent subordinates. It was debatable then, as it is now, whether any approach to the King's financial difficulties along these lines was feasible, but at least, feasible or not, it was a carefully thought-out programme. Coke clearly gave this programme priority over the sending out of the fleet, and therefore, whatever his general feelings about Spain, must be classified in 1625 as an opponent of the war.

Heath tried both to answer Coke, and to recall the debate to the question whether the fleet should go out or not. He admitted Coke's thesis that necessity was due to improvidence, but placed the blame on King James, and asked whether it was just that King Charles should be punished for it. He tried to answer fears about the sincerity of the King's war plans by suggesting they petition the King to name the enemy, and assured them it was Spain.[1] The lack of any reaction to this proposal is significant. When Fleetwood, three days later, tried to meet the fears expressed about recusants, the offer of reassurance was immediately and eagerly taken up. When Heath offered reassurance to the vocal demand that they

[1] *1625 Debates*, pp. 87, 134.

should know their enemy before giving, he drew a response only from Sir Nathaniel Rich the next day. Rich was a well-known war supporter. The lack of any similar response from Seymour, Phelips, or Coke suggests that their protests that they did not know the enemy were being used to cover a more deep-rooted objection to the war as a whole. Alford, who followed Heath, was certainly an opponent of war, especially if it were in the Palatinate. He said, in a phrase heard repeatedly in the Oxford session, that he was 'against subsidies in reversion'. On this first day of the debate, support for supply came only from Sir George More among the ranks of unofficial members.

The next day, the debate was led aside by further complaints by Phelips and Earle about pardons for recusants drawn at the instance of the French Ambassador. Young Conway, whose father had drawn the offending pardons, was almost certainly sincere in taking this occasion to move that the House should petition the King not to hearken to foreign ambassadors. Against this background, Buckingham's client Sir Henry Mildmay led the debate back to supply, saying the House was engaged to support the war. At the same time, however, he said that the English Arminians were agents of the King of Spain, and 'little less dangerous than a foreign invasion', and blamed the plague on England's 'coldness' in religion.[1] One of the difficulties Charles led himself into in 1625 was that if he supported Arminians and war with Spain together, those who were his natural supporters in foreign affairs were his natural opponents in religion. This point was illustrated by Nathaniel Rich, who listed a 'platform' of five points. He wanted to attack idolatry, which he thought prevented the English from being successful in war, as it had prevented the Israelites. He wanted to know the enemy, that the King should use 'grave counsellors', that the King's estate should be considered at the next meeting, and that they should have an answer on impositions. The demand for 'grave counsellors' was not an overt attack on Buckingham: Rich's platform was not concerned with getting men out, but with getting men in.[2] His platform was commended by Phelips, but, because it made no clear contribution to the immedi-

---

[1] _1625 Debates_, p. 137; _C.J._ 811.

[2] _1625 Debates_, p. 91, J. N. Ball, _ubi supra_, p. 118, Christopher Thompson, 'The Origins of the Parliamentary Middle Group 1625–9', _T.R.H.S._ (1972), 78.

ate point at issue, was not debated further. The Commons gave a
second reading to a bill to put tax-collectors on oath, which suggested that someone in the House realized that they themselves,
as local administrators, were quite as open as the Duke to Coke's
strictures about the wasting of the King's revenue.[1] The House
then adjourned for the weekend.

On Monday the 8th, proceedings were opened by Sir Miles
Fleetwood, offering an olive branch from the Duke.[2] He said that
supply could be deferred until they met again, and offered a further
answer to the petition on religion. The reassurance offered on
religion was immediately taken up by Pym, and the Houses were
once again called to a conference. The King's answers to the
petition on religion were read, and were entered on the Parliament
Roll,[3] as Coke had requested. Some members hoped this gave them
the force of law. Such concessions on religion risked alienating the
French to such a point that they would refuse to pay the remainder
of the Queen's dowry. The promise of full enforcement of the
recusancy laws was a plain breach of the marriage treaty. The
willingness of Buckingham and Charles to risk a dowry worth
£120,000 for a hypothetical two subsidies and two fifteenths, worth
at most £200,000, is surely evidence that they valued good relations with Parliaments for their own sake, and not merely as a
source of money. Buckingham followed up this answer to the
petition on religion with a long, able, and in the main honest
speech on foreign affairs. He reminded the Commons of the applause they had given him in 1624, and that his own policies had
not changed in the meantime. He dwelt on the change in the
European diplomatic situation in the past year, tried to explain
King James's delays as due to diplomatic artifice, and claimed he
had followed the advice of the Council of War in preparing the
fleet. He allowed Sir John Coke to supply the information that he

---

[1] *C.J.* 811.

[2] *1625 Debates*, pp. 140–1. Eliot (*N.P.* ii. 55) confirms that Fleetwood was
speaking for the Duke. See also Ball, *ubi supra*, p. 120. The persistence of
pressure for supply, after Fleetwood's suggestion that it would be abandoned,
prompts the suspicion that Buckingham and Charles were not speaking with
one voice.

[3] The entry of the King's answers is dated 8 August on the Parliament Roll,
P.R.O. C. 65/189. See Elizabeth Read Foster, *Journal of British Studies* (1974),
40 and n, and Rich, *1625 Debates*, p. 91. 'We already expect the King's answer
for this which he desired might be in Parliament; and then it shall have the
force of a law.'

had contributed £44,000 of his own money to the fitting out of the fleet, explained (truly) that the delays before the Parliament had first met had been due to delays in the conclusion of the French marriage, and again reiterated the harmful consequences if the fleet did not go out. He gave a disingenuous answer to the anxieties about the English ships sent against La Rochelle, and an equally disingenuous defence of the French marriage, saying, in well-chosen words, that the King had been able to answer their petition on religion without breaking any *public* faith (my italics).[1] He also, interestingly, answered an objection which had not, so far as the diaries show, been voiced in the Commons: he said the cost of the war would not involve sending coin out of the kingdom, but commodities instead, and so the kingdom would not be impoverished. He was supported by a further detailed financial statement from Lord Treasurer Marlborough, showing that the King had anticipated his next year's revenue by £200,000, 'so as we are in question how to maintain him with bread and meat'.

When the Commons returned to their House, Edmondes again moved for supply in return for the King's answer on religion. He was supported by two minor members, and again opposed by Phelips. Fleetwood's suggestion that the request for supply was to be abandoned had apparently come to nothing.[2]

The next day, 10 August, Sir Richard Weston, Chancellor of the Exchequer, and Naunton, Master of the Wards, again tried to raise enthusiasm for supply. They persuaded one member to agree to one subsidy and two fifteenths. Sir Simon Weston also retracted from his previous position now that he was sure who the enemy was. He said they could avoid the precedent of two grants in one session if, instead of making a new grant, they called back their previous grant, and made an addition to it. On the other side, Delbridge remembered that it was not only the King who had to be pleased:

Heretofore we had hopes and expectations wherewith to please the country, though we gave away their money. Now there are nothing but discouragements, pardons to Jesuits, the news from Rochelle, for which town we have heretofore had public fasting; the interruption of the fishing trade, the losses by pirates; so that, whereas we returned the last time with fasting and prayer, now we may return with sackcloth and ashes.[3]

---

[1] *1625 Debates*, p. 101.
[2] *1625 Debates*, pp. 104–5, 141, *N.P.* ii. 75, *C.J.* 812.
[3] *1625 Debates*, pp. 108–9.

At least one member, faced with the panoply of official pressure, was still more afraid of his neighbours than of the Crown. Phelips, after him, tried to continue the three-man attack on the Duke of Buckingham, again trying to argue that if the King was unable to borrow such a small sum, the blame must rest on those who had advised him. He ran through precedents for the impeachment of great officers with so much thoroughness that, though he did not name the Duke, his meaning was unmistakable. He ended with a passage part of which is famous, but which needs to be seen as a whole for the remarkable *non sequitur* it contains:

We are the last monarchy in Christendom that retain our original rights and constitutions. Either his Majesty is able to set out this fleet, or it is not fit to go at all.[1]

He then asked for Sir Robert Mansell, a dissident member of the Council of War, to be heard.

Sir Humphrey May, in the face of this chilling speech, tried to put the case for supply again, only to be answered by Seymour, again pressing the attack on the Duke. He said the King's necessity had not come from want of money, since so much had already been granted, but from the fact that the money went to private men. He wanted to restore the King's fortunes by an Act of Resumption of Crown lands. When Weston tried to blame James for financial mismanagement, and offered reformation under Charles, a member reminded him that Empson and Dudley, for their offences in one reign, had been hanged in the next. The case for supply did not seem to be growing more persuasive with the passage of time. Glanville contributed two important points. One was that subsidies ought to be the last business of a Parliament, the second that it was conventional not to put supply to the question 'till it be sure to be granted'.[2] Coke, saying there had been no Dukes between the Conquest and Edward III's time, and Mansell, saying Buckingham had not followed the advice of the Council of War, concluded another day's debate.

It was clear that the debate would have to reach a conclusion soon, and that the effects of the conclusion would be considerable. The heightened drama of the last two days of the Parliament is marked by the appearance of two additional diaries, those of Rich and Dyott. The debates of 11 August began with a brief diversion caused by a series of complaints, submitted by Alderman Whitson

[1] *1625 Debates*, pp. 109–10.   [2] Ibid., p. 114.

of Bristol, against the pirates.[1] However, Sir Francis Seymour, by blaming the Lord Admiral, Buckingham, brought the debate back to the same points as before. Sir Dudley Digges, in reply, appears to have offered a hesitant defence of the Duke.[2] Coryton asked whether the advice of the Council of War had been taken, and how the country should be defended against pirates during the absence of the fleet.[3] He was followed by Alford reminding them that the 1621 subsidy Act had had a clause saying that the giving of subsidies at the beginning of a Parliament should not be taken for a precedent.[4] There were probably many members for whom the memory of their empty-handed homecoming in 1621 was an obstacle to voting supply in 1625. So was the convention, to which Alford also appealed, that the question should not be put until a consensus emerged.

There was even less sign of consensus in support of the attacks on Buckingham than there was in support of the motions for supply. On 11 August, Seymour for the first time attacked the Duke by name, and was supported by Phelips. By this stage, their attacks on Buckingham seemed to be as obviously falling on deaf ears as the Crown's requests for supply, and they were coming to seem equally repetitive. Sir Henry Marten made an able speech for supply, warning, 'Let us take heed how we discontent a prince whom we have put into a course of war.' The day's debate ended with another resolution to defer the putting of the question.[5] That night, the King decided to dissolve the Parliament.

The last day, while the commission for dissolution was being made out, began with a long row between Heath and Mansell about whether Buckingham had followed the advice of the Council of War.[6] Sherland expressed a fear that they might come to find themselves voting annual subsidies, and said that voting money in new courses was liable to cause a 'commotion' among the people. He optimistically suggested that if the laws against recusants were

---

[1] C.J. 815.

[2] The exact words of Dyott's report appear to be: 'Let us not too lightly censure t. course of state. Free not t. coasts of Sp.' Dyott's diary has been under water, and transcriptions from it are always in part conjectural.

[3] Rich, f. 1ʳ.

[4] Dyott, 11 August. Alford's words are: 'There is a proviso in t. Act not to be drawne into psident.' Only the 1621 subsidy Act had contained such a proviso.

[5] 1625 Debates, pp. 121-2.

[6] This argument is much more fully reported by Dyott than by Pym, but the additional length does not appear to add much clarity.

executed, they would all be convicted the next sessions, and then there would be enough money.[1] If there was any practicality in such a proposal, its execution depended on the J.P.s and not on the King. He in effect wrote the epitaph for the session by dismissing the attacks on Buckingham as bluntly as he had dismissed the requests for supply. 'For the calling of the actions of that great man to account who knoweth not that we can do nothing in it unless we have leave from the King? And then we may do it as well without supply as with supply.'[2] From a man who was a manager of the impeachment of Buckingham in the next Parliament, this speech demands some thought.

After this, there was only time for the drafting of a final declaration by Glanville before the arrival of Black Rod for the dissolution. With this fruitless declaration, an unsatisfactory session reached its equally fruitless conclusion. The request for an additional supply had been, as Eliot prophesied, 'lodged merely to be denied'. The session is notable, not only for this resistance to the united forces of Crown and Council, but also for what appears to be the only independent Commons' attempt to attack a great minister during the whole period. Buckingham doubted its independence, and on 15 August, the King was once again 'reconciling' him and Pembroke. Buckingham's suspicions appear to have started the quarrel.[3] Buckingham also suspected Williams, Arundel, and Abbot. For once, it appears that Buckingham's suspicions were unfounded.

If the explanation here given is correct, it is necessary to explain why Buckingham was of a contrary opinion. If the object of most members in withholding additional supply was not to bring about the fall of the Duke, but to avoid provoking their countries, and simply to go home, it is necessary to explain why not only the Duke, but a number of other commentators at court, misunderstood what was going on. In the first place, it must be said that

[1] *1625 Debates*, p. 149, Dyott, 11 August.
[2] *1625 Debates*, p. 150, *N.P.* ii. 101.
[3] *H.M.C. Mar and Kellie Suppl.*, p. 233. Buckingham was provoked by one of the French priests in the Queen's household saying that 'the Queen was resolved to take Pembroke by the hand and make a party against Buckingham, which was false indeed'. It is perhaps possible to link this remarkable piece of rumourmongering with French threats to wreck Charles's marriage if he failed to keep the religious clauses of the marriage treaty. See above, pp. 209. The task of inflaming suspicion between Buckingham and Pembroke did not require great effort.

there is no *a priori* impossibility about the idea that people at court might have misjudged the mood of the House of Commons. Indeed, if traditional accounts are to be allowed to have been based on anything at all, it must be expected that on some occasions, court comment might misjudge the Commons. The Commons seem to have been particularly liable to be misunderstood at court on those occasions on which they were most responsive to the wishes of their electorates and neighbours. Moreover, the *effect* of the withholding of additional supply was to put Buckingham's policy in ruins. It is possible that the fact that the Commons' inaction so obviously had this effect may have led some people to suppose that they intended the natural consequences of their acts.

It was not only the Duke who interpreted the Commons' behaviour in this way. Most comment interpreting the Oxford session as an attack on the Duke dates from just after the dissolution. Some of the most significant comment to this effect, because some of the earliest, comes from the Queen's Almoner, the Bishop of Mende, reporting in cipher to Cardinal Richelieu. Mende, writing on or about 8 August, records the promise to implement the recusancy laws, and adds, 'Mais quoi que Bouquingnant [*sic*] ait fait icy pour donner le change le Parlement est résolu de ne les pas prendre et de poursuivre sa ruine.' He also claimed, in a letter which presents some dating problems, to have learnt this view from Arundel and Pembroke.[1] This passage seems to suggest that Arundel and Pembroke, finding the Duke in trouble, were not above exploiting his discomfiture. It is possible that they opposed the decision to dissolve the Parliament, which appears to have been taken at a Council meeting on 11 August.[2] If they did so, they would have strengthened the general impression that the Parliament was dissolved to save the Duke. It is unlikely that Pembroke and Arundel would be averse to creating such an impression, however falsely.

However, it need not follow that what they said was true. Mende may be right in claiming that Coke, Phelips, Seymour, and Mansell

---

[1] B.L. Add. MS. 30651, f. 22^r (copy of Mende to Richelieu in cipher, received 29 August N.S.), ibid., f. 13^v. I am grateful to Dr. K. M. Sharpe for these references.

[2] Ibid., f. 27^r. Mende concluded correctly that there was now no great help to be expected from England. Pembroke and Arundel, as supporters of a French alliance, were likely to have wanted to dispel this impression.

were not the only members who wanted to attack the Duke. He said that the House wanted to do so, and these four did so 'ouvertement'.[1] Yet to concede that more than four members wanted to attack the Duke is not to concede that the Commons as a whole wanted to do so. With the exception of Coryton on 11 August, those who opposed additional supply were not those who were most responsive to guidance from Pembroke or Arundel, and Coryton was among the least predictable of Pembroke's clients. Rudyerd is a better guide to Pembroke's thinking, and Rudyerd, in November, reported the pricking of the Duke's principal critics as sheriffs in these words: 'The rank weeds of the Parliament are rooted up, so that we may make a plentiful harvest in the next: Sir Robert Phillips and six others being made sheriffs of counties.'[2] It seems that Buckingham's suspicions of Pembroke and Arundel are chronologically prior to their justification, indeed, that they had something of the quality of a self-fulfilling prophecy.[3] In bringing about this situation, it is possible that Richelieu's instructions to Mende, to widen the breach between the Duke and his critics, played a considerable part. It is, moreover, possible that Pembroke and Arundel preferred an explanation of the troubles of 1625 which gave an impression that they themselves were, in Mende's words, 'personnes puissantes dans le Parlement' to one which implied that England as a whole was militarily powerless.[4] There are, then, possible reasons why writers of newsletters at court might have given a court-centred impression of what happened at Oxford in 1625. The most conspicuous exception to the general tone of newsletters is Sir Francis Nethersole, on 9 August, who reported that the chief opponents of additional

---

[1] B.L. Add. MS. 30651, f. 22ʳ⁻ᵛ.

[2] *C.S.P.D. 1625-6*, vol. x, no. 16. Rudyerd to Nethersole, 16 Nov. 1625. The chronology of November 1625 is worth thought. This letter is before there were serious signs of an impending French war, and before there was firm news of the failure of the fleet at Cadiz. Ibid., no. 35, vol. xi, no. 32.

[3] Ingram to Wentworth, Knowler, 28. Ingram here reports the Duke's suspicions as something of which he appears to suppose Wentworth to have been previously unaware. The Earl of Clare, Arundel's ally in 1625 and one of Buckingham's foremost opponents in 1626, appears to have first thought of attacking him on the dismissal of Williams, in November 1625. *Letters of John Holles 1587-1637*, Thoroton Soc. Record Series, xxxi (1975), ed. P. R. Seddon, pp. lv–lviii. Nottingham University Library MS. Ne. C. 15, 405, ff. 116–20. I am grateful to Mr. Richard Cust for these points and the Holles references.

[4] B.L. Add. MS. 30651, f. 15ʳ (Richelieu to Ville-aux-Clercs); f. 27ᵛ (Mende to Richelieu); ibid., f. 13ʳ.

supply were 'three or four of the principal speakers who usually stand stiffest for the country, and in such a manner as they all showed a great dislike of our being called hither upon this occasion'.[1] Nethersole's account is valuable, not only because it was written before the dissolution, but also because he was the only newsletter-writer who was himself a member of Parliament. The evidence of the debates does much more to substantiate the simple negativism described by Nethersole than it does to demonstrate the high-level conspiracy feared by Buckingham.

Pembroke's first overt act of hostility to Buckingham was after the Parliament was over. On the way to visit the fleet at Plymouth, Pembroke and his brother Montgomery paid a visit to the Earl of Bristol at his home at Sherborne.[2] During the Parliament, however, there is no sufficient ground for suspecting Pembroke of fomenting the attacks on Buckingham. Among his known connections, only Mansell, who had a personal grudge because his advice was not followed, breathed any criticism against the Duke. Pembroke and Arundel almost certainly exploited the Duke's difficulties soon after the Parliament was over. Yet there is no evidence to sustain the view that they were to blame for the failure of the Parliament. Seymour, Coke, and Phelips did not have any close connection with any of the Lords Buckingham suspected. Indeed, Phelips's bad relations with Pembroke, as Lord Lieutenant of Somerset, were one of his biggest handicaps in his own county. After the Parliament was over, it was through the Duke, and not through Pembroke, that Phelips attempted the difficult task of returning to favour. Since the death of Lennox in 1624, Seymour seems to have been without any important court patron, and such few attempts as Coke made to find a patron had been addressed to Buckingham himself. It is perhaps the most significant fact about the attack on Buckingham in 1625 that two out of the four people involved had been Buckingham's allies in the previous Parliament. Coke and Phelips in 1625, as much as Bristol and Williams in 1626, should be ranked among the 'discourted'.[3] They were among those who had served the Duke, and failed to stand the pace. Sir Robert Mansell, who had relied on the confidence of James, should perhaps

[1] 1625 Debates, p. 157.

[2] H.M.C. De L'Isle and Dudley, v. 440–1. Pembroke's brother, Montgomery, appears, as usual, to have acted the part of go-between.

[3] H.M.C. Mar and Kellie Suppl., p. 233, especially the comments on Mansell.

also rank as 'discourted'. It is of course impossible to judge the strength of anti-Buckingham feeling from the debates, since many people may have thought that without court support it was wiser to stay silent. Yet it must be recorded that, for what the evidence of the debates is worth, it shows the simple reluctance to give away the country's money, the outlook of Delbridge and Alford, as much more typical of the Commons than the attacks of Coke, Seymour, and Phelips. These three, by their long and frequent speeches, perhaps managed to convince both historians and the court that they were more typical of the House of Commons than they really were. Even at court, the belief that Buckingham could be protected from the next Parliament by pricking six men as sheriffs suggests that the common court view was that the attack on him had been very narrowly based. It is perhaps significant that as late as 21 January 1626, Lord Montagu, a Buckingham man, did not foresee any attack on the Duke and thought the 1626 Parliament would produce no business sufficiently contentious to demand his attendance.[1]

If it was not out of a general hatred of the Duke, why did the Parliament of 1625 so obstinately resist the request for additional supply? It does not appear to have been in order to obtain redress of grievances. During the second session, the petition on religion was the only grievance for which the Commons as a whole asked for redress, and on 8 August this redress was granted. The Commons' continued refusal to vote additional supply was not conditional on the redress of any further grievance: it was, for the time being, absolute. An absolute refusal is more easily explained by fear of country resistance during the plague than by any grievance of the members themselves. If they wanted redress for any grievance, it was for the simple fact that they were being forced to sit in Parliament at all. Mr. Wentworth remarked, in discussing the case of Montagu, that 'though it be at no time fit to provoke the wrath of God, yet much less at this time, when we are all as it were making our wills, being already under his hand'. Glanville's final declaration, written as Black Rod approached, thanked the King for his care of their healths. The anonymous diarist glossed

[1] *H.M.C. Buccleuch*, iii. 263. I am grateful to Dr Hirst for this reference. Montagu hoped that he could stay at home because supply, which he expected to be the only business, would not be opposed in the Lords. This letter shows that as late as January 1626 it was not common knowledge that Pembroke intended to make a Parliamentary attack on the Duke.

this: 'for his care of our healths in giving us leave to depart this dangerous time'. He concluded his diary with a statement of his relief that none of them was dead. For once, the Commons were sincerely thanking the King for dissolving them.

For the mood of most members, the end of the session was the only appropriate redress. They were not attempting to defend their own pockets. Glanville claimed that during the Parliament, members collectively were spending about £7,000 a week.[1] If this estimate is correct, the sums they had spent out of their own pockets since they were first assembled in London on 17 May may have been little less than the sum they were refusing to vote to the King. Among other things, this figure reminds us of the scandalous under-assessment of the gentry for taxation. When it was proving impossible to assess J.P.s at a minimum figure of £20, it was inevitable that a disproportionate weight of taxation should fall on the lesser taxpayers. Members were no doubt sincere in their proposals that those under £5 in the subsidy book should be spared, yet these proposals were only practical if they were prepared to make a larger contribution to the subsidy themselves. Their refusal to do so seems to have been as much on grounds of status as of finance: Coke, in one interesting reflection, opposed a subsidy while saying that 'for his own part he would give £1,000 as a private man, not as a Parliament man'.[2] For what he gave as a private man, he was not accountable.

Because gentlemen assessed themselves for subsidy in a way commensurate with their status, and so bore little of the burden, they therefore increased the burden on others. They were then bound to take seriously the possible burden of the subsidy on yeomen or tradesmen. Because they normally sought service in Parliament as a way of increasing their local status, they were bound to take account of what their actions meant in their counties, as well as of what their actions meant to the King. A member of Parliament was a man of divided loyalties, to his Crown, and to his community. Neither loyalty could be discharged successfully if he failed to discharge the other. In 1625, caught between the war and the plague, in the aftermath of James's debts and of the depression, many members found these divided loyalties strained

---

[1] *1625 Debates*, pp. 70, 114, 126, 150–1. For a similar estimate of the cost to the members of the Parliament of 1626, see Whitelocke, 12–22, f. 60.

[2] *1625 Debates*, p. 115.

to breaking-point. The King was more insistent, but there is evidence to suggest that, after their exceptionally generous vote of supply in 1624, many found their countries were growing more insistent also. Of the small body of legislation passed, the Alienations Act mainly concerned gentlemen, and the Sabbath and Alehouses Acts did not make a substantial enough contribution to offer their countries in return for the amount of subsidy they were asked for. No M.P., and no J.P., liked to be faced with this conflict of loyalties. When they were faced with it, it was normal for M.P.s, as it was for J.P.s, to put their countries before the Crown. Only a more rigorous assessment of their own wealth could have saved them from the dilemma, and such a step was beneath their dignity.

On 10 August, Sir Thomas Wentworth tried to explain some of these things in a speech which was praised even by his personal enemy Sir John Eliot. He answered a proposal for the putting of the question.

May it please you to beware, Mr. Speaker; take heed how you proceed so suddenly to propound the question, the consequence is greater than I imagine by your haste you foresee: it hath ever stood with the wisdom of this House not to suffer the question to pass in these cases till all be clear and serene . . . for the manner in granting these supplies is of great import many times as the matter it self . . . That we cannot be entirely faithful to the King being the head, not having due regard to the subjects being the members nor truly liberal to his Majesty, if we appear wanton dispensers of their purses; that we should not decline from the institutions left us by our ancestors . . . except there were an evident assurance of good without all shadow to the contrary. . . . That we . . . should humbly declare unto his Majesty that this demand, being without all precedent, may be dangerous in the example, that we fear the granting thereof will be esteemed by his subjects no fair acquittal of our duties towards them, or return of their trusts reposed in us and therefore humbly to beseech him, having regard unto our credits and reputations, to take in good part our declining an absolute answer till another session, that so we may, (this session ended before Christmas) be enlightened by the beams of his grace in a free and princely pardon, as also to carry some good bills down with us to his people.[1]

He pointed out that since part of the subsidies they had voted in the first session were still uncollected, such a grant would come to the Exchequer as soon as one made then and there. If it was for this speech that Wentworth was pricked sheriff, his position was

---

[1] *Wentworth Papers*, pp. 236–9. *N.P.* ii. 92 shows that he delivered part of this speech, but it is impossible to be certain that he delivered it all. It appears to be an honest statement of his mind.

grossly misunderstood. There is every reason to believe that he spoke the truth: what the King was asking of him was simply more than he could live down when he went home. If he did more for the King than he could defend in the country, his usefulness as the King's servant would be destroyed. His references in this speech to the 'vulgar, who out of a rural and unmannerly distrust believe nothing till it come forth in print after the end of the session' suggest that he had not forgotten the disappointments of 1621. In his Rotherham speech as a subsidy commissioner, in April 1621, he had promised the passage of the bill of informers and many other bills, and, having made these promises in all good faith, was forced to come home at the end of Parliament without them. It was hardly surprising if the 'vulgar' did not believe promises until they were in print at the end of the session.

This, rather than the bitter speeches of Coke and Phelips, was probably the typical mood of members in the Oxford session. It is an overwhelmingly local mood, a mood in which the securing of bridges on the Great North Road caused more concern than the securing of the harbour at Cadiz. Wentworth's defence of old ways contained a significant exception: 'Except there was an evident assurance of good without all shadow to the contrary.' A wholehearted war supporter like Rich or Digges might have found such an assurance. Wentworth did not. When he looked at 'the troubled and cloudy face of Christendom, into which I persuade myself the sharpest sights pierce but near at hand and darkly', he did not see a case for a fleet: he saw a case for 'a well established union at home', especially in religion. The uncertainties with which English foreign and religious policy were surrounded in the summer of 1625 contributed something to this. Yet, after all the speeches at Oxford, there was little reason for doubt that the King meant to send out his fleet against Spain. The House of Commons refused him the means to do so, and must carry some of the responsibility for the consequent failure. On the maxim that reasonable men are deemed to intend the natural consequences of their acts, the Parliament of 1625 must be taken to show that the House of Commons was against the war. It was Charles and Buckingham's failure to face this central fact which produced most of the troubles of the next three years.

V

The Parliament of 1626:
The Reformation of the Duke?[1]

1.

KING Charles had told the Oxford session of the 1625 Parliament that it was better that half the fleet should perish than that it should not put to sea at all. There were persuasive diplomatic reasons for this view, involving the loss of potential allies. When the English fleet returned from Cadiz, in the autumn of 1625, nearly half of it had perished, and the diplomatic reasons for Charles's determination began to seem rather less convincing.

The outbreak of the long-heralded war with Spain was accompanied by a Forced Loan, roughly equivalent to the subsidies the Oxford Parliament had failed to vote. This loan met with some refusals, and Exeter pleaded its poverty, caused by the plague and the pirates.[2] The beginning of a serious war effort was accompanied by the usual local foot-dragging and administrative hitches. Sir Francis Seymour, in Wiltshire, wanted disciplinary action against constables who took bribes to release pressed men.[3] Rather more seriously, the Deputy Lieutenants of Wiltshire tried to invoke the 'Phelips clause' in the 1624 subsidy Act, to recover money they had paid to Mansfeld's soldiers while in a 'dangerous mutiny', as they thought the express words of the Act directed. They said if this were done, they would then 'hope to be able to draw from our countrymen greater payments, when occasion shall require the same for the public good'.[4]

However, in 1625 this local foot-dragging was not yet on a serious enough scale to be a significant handicap to the war effort. There was more cause for alarm about the effect of the war on trade. The part of the cloth industry which had escaped most

[1] Grosvenor, ff. 21–2.
[2] *C.S.P.D. 1625–6*, vol. ix, no. 68, reported by Lord Russell, Lord Lieutenant of Devon. See Supple, p. 101.
[3] S.P. 16/4/125.
[4] S.P. 16/19/51. On the 'Phelips clause', see above, pp. 213n, 223, 224n, 260.

lightly from the depression of 1621-4 was the new draperies, and this was the part which was hit most heavily by the outbreak of war with Spain. The new draperies, lighter cloths made of fine wool, were suitable for warm climates, and were often exported to Spain and the Mediterranean. The embargo on trade with Spain, in December 1625, and the risks in passing the Straits of Gibraltar during war, caused particular dislocation in areas like Essex and Devon, which depended heavily on the new draperies.[1] Those very areas where religious sympathy with the war was strong were the same ones where it caused most economic dislocation. This may be one reason why the embargo on trade with Spain was lifted in the middle of the impeachment of Buckingham.[2]

It was not only the Spanish trade which was disrupted in 1625-6. The outbreak of war involved the issuing of letters of marque, authorizing their bearers to seize at sea any enemy goods or ships carrying military cargoes to the enemy. Such activities invited, and received, retaliation from the effective privateers based on Dunkirk. The Eastland and Levant Companies formed convoys for protection against piracy, but local trades such as Yarmouth fishing and the coal trade between Newcastle and London suffered severely. More seriously, indiscriminate seizures inflamed the growing hostility between England and France. Some of the ships seized were taken with some notional justification. The *St Peter* of Le Havre (commonly known as Newhaven), one of those about which there was most dispute, contained, among many such innocuous things as wool, a small number of rapier blades bound for Spain.[3] For other seizures, such as those of ships going to La Rochelle for salt, there was no excuse.

When the French responded, in an escalating series of retaliatory embargoes, the French trade came to be as disrupted as the Spanish and the wine trade as dislocated as the trade in the new draperies. A large part of the ill feeling expressed in the Parliament of 1626 arose from the effect of French embargoes on the wine trade.

These things alone would have done so much to diminish the popularity of the war, but there is nothing which decreases the

---

[1] Supple, pp. 102, 104-5, 153-62.
[2] H. G. Koenigsberger, *Estates and Revolutions* (Cornell, 1971), p. 104: *A.P.C. 1625-6*, p. 441. See Peter Clark and Paul Slack, *English Towns in Transition 1500-1700* (1976), p. 51 for the effect of the war on the trade of Bristol and Exeter.
[3] S.P. 16/6/120.

popularity of wars so easily as defeat. The defeat suffered by the English fleet sent, in traditional manner, to Cadiz discredited the war effort at the very beginning. Rudyerd said that when the troops reached the walls, they found they had neither pickaxes to begin the work of attacking them, nor food to continue it, and so were forced to leave the town for impregnable. Rudyerd said: 'Thus have we provoked a powerful enemy, without weakening him, and that which might have heartened our party by an effectual engagement, I fear will weaken it by an unadvised miscarriage.' The inquest on the defeat began at once. Chamberlain reported on 19 January 1626, that the troops blamed Edward Cecil, the commander, calling him 'Viscount Sit-Still', but that most people blamed the Duke of Buckingham.[1] It is not the purpose here to join in this inquest, but it must be said, without exonerating the Duke, that some share of the responsibility must rest on the House of Commons. What had happened was precisely what Charles had warned the Oxford session would be the consequence if they did not vote money. However mismanaged the Cadiz expedition may have been, the chief weakness about it and the rest of the English war effort was that it was disastrously under-financed. In addition to the lack of Parliamentary subsidies, the yield of the customs was said by the farmers to have fallen by £5,041 because of war and plague.[2] This also was something of which James had given warning to the 1624 House of Commons. The arrival of the first half of the French portion was not enough to make good the financial shortfall, and even attempts to mortgage the Crown jewels lost more in dignity than they gained in money. By January 1626, some of the captains at Plymouth were forced by lack of pay to pawn their arms, and, by April, the troops there were threatening, if not clothed, to march on London, 'to show their nakedness'.[3] Sir John Coke, the new Secretary of State, was furthering plans for a West India Company, to conduct what would in effect be a private enterprise war.[4] It was hard to see, without large further revenues, what other sort of war was open to the English.

---

[1] S.P. 16/11/32; Chamberlain, 19 Jan. 1626.

[2] C.S.P.D. 1625–6, vol. xiv, no. 3. Sir John Wolstenholme to the King. The statement is ex parte, but credible.

[3] C.S.P.D. 1625–6, vol. xix, no 66: S.P. 16/24/26.

[4] S.P. 16/1/59. See also Christopher Thompson, 'The Origins of the Parliamentary Middle Group 1625–9', T.R.H.S. (1972), 80, and the enthusiastic comments of Rudyerd, S.P. 16/24/48.

After the plague and the depression, the war was breaking out at a time when England was least able to afford it. It was also breaking out, as a result of diplomatic moves nearly two years old, at precisely the moment when it ceased to be relevant to England's diplomatic preoccupations. The Palatinate and Breda were lost and the cause for which Charles and Buckingham had intended to fight in 1624 had gone by default. Yet Buckingham had, since 1623, been surrounding himself with supporters of a Spanish war, and in 1626 he was, in patronage terms, the chief champion of the Protestant cause. This fact probably did much to diminish his freedom of manœuvre. His dependence on his clients, the Secretaries, Conway and Sir John Coke, Holland, Carlisle, Manchester, Montagu, Harley, and Mildmay may have done much to bind him to the cause of continuing war with Spain. Yet, at the very same time as Buckingham had most carefully surrounded himself with anti-Spanish and pro-French clients, he found he was facing diplomatic breakdown and the prospect of war, not with Spain, but with France. It was this diplomatic breakdown between England and France which provided the key to the Parliament of 1626. At the very moment when Charles and Buckingham had staked their honour and their good faith on a war with Spain, they found themselves looking forward to a war with France. Salvetti, the Tuscan Ambassador, foresaw war between England and France by November 1625, and Rudyerd foresaw it by New Year's Eve.[1] The French blamed this drift to war on the Duke of Buckingham, and therefore accompanied it with an intense diplomatic offensive against Buckingham at the English court. With the creation of a Queen's household, Buckingham faced for the first time an independent centre of patronage within the English court. When, at the same time, the French were inciting Pembroke and Arundel to join in plans for his impeachment,[2] it is not surprising that Buckingham felt the need to control this independent power base. His attempts to do so, by providing further breaches of the marriage treaty, simply further inflamed the quarrels with the French.

The bad relations with the French began, as always, with the question of the English Catholics. The French rightly regarded Charles's promises to the Parliament of 1625 as a breach of the marriage treaty, and when enforcement of the penal laws began again, the French complained that many Catholics were 'forced

---

[1] *H.M.C. 11th Report I*, pp. 37–8: S.P. 16/12/93.　　[2] *Cabala*, I. 296.

to declare themselves Spanish'. At this rather delicate moment, there arrived a new ambassador, Blainville, who was still remembered in 1628 for his tactlessness and his willingness to foment quarrels in England.[1] Yet the English were exaggerating, or deceiving themselves, when they claimed that Blainville could be blamed for all the trouble. The key to Anglo-French relations in 1625–6 is in a sentence in Blainville's instructions, that questions of the Queen's household must not be divided from those of religion. With the French attempting to make the Queen's household a focal point for English Catholicism, and Parliament pressing for the suppression of Catholics, Buckingham had every excuse for doing what he doubtless wished to do anyway: attempting to place his family and dependants in the Queen's household. In November 1625, forty of the Queen's household were sent home, and the French were enabled to complain of another breach of the marriage treaty. Blainville was instructed to remind Buckingham that an express provision of the marriage treaty excluded all non-Catholics from the Queen's service. By this time, the French were convinced that their difficulties in securing toleration for the English Catholics were entirely the fault of the Duke of Buckingham, and that his person was their sole cause of complaint. It was at the beginning of October 1625 that the English began to react to this remorseless French pressure by trying to make a parallel issue of the treatment of the French Huguenots.[2]

At first, the intention of Charles was probably simply to draw a parallel, such as had been frequently drawn by James, between the two cases. The principle to which he appealed, which he hoped the example of the Huguenots would bring home to the French, was simply that it was not good that one prince should intervene in another's differences with his subjects.[3] Unfortunately, Blainville interpreted the raising of the question of the Huguenots as a direct threat, and warned the French Secretary to take measures against it.

It was at this stage, with his usual theatrical timing, that the Huguenot Duke of Soubise again intervened in the story. He had been holding out in the Île d'Oleron, off La Rochelle, since January, and had been appealing for Charles's help since May. On 1/11 October, the same day on which Charles introduced the

---

[1] P.R.O. 31/3/62, f. 133. Stowe 366, f. 13ᵛ.
[2] P.R.O. 31/3/62, ff. 125, 134, 145.   [3] Ibid., ff. 145, 156.

question of the Huguenots into his negotiations with the French Ambassador, Soubise was defeated at the Île d'Oleron, and fled for refuge to England. Blainville at once suspected the worst. In fact, Charles had no great wish to help Soubise, and sent him out of the way to stay in the country. His host, curiously, was Phelips's great local rival, Sir John Poulett. Yet, however little Charles might want to help Soubise, he was bound to resent an attempt by the French to seize his ships in Falmouth harbour: Blainville was informed that it was an act of war to take a ship in an English port.[1]

However, the French did not desist. On 26 November, Sir John Eliot, Vice-Admiral of Cornwall, reported to Conway that he feared a fight between the French and Soubise's ships in Fowey harbour. His fears were not exaggerated: in December, the mayor and justices of Penryn sent a bewildered report of a fight between Soubise's men and the French in their harbour.[2]

In reply, Charles said he would resent threats to Soubise as if to his own subjects, and the Deputy Lieutenants of Cornwall were instructed to mobilize the trained bands to defend Soubise.[3] If the English did not want to help the Huguenots before these incidents, they had now been provoked enough to wish to do so.

The presence of Soubise, an exile for the cause of religion, was enough to give a further spur to pan-Protestant sentiment. The obvious place to which to direct this sentiment was the demand for the return of the ships lent to the French for use against La Rochelle. On New Year's Eve 1625, Rudyerd reported that ambassadors were being sent to demand the recall of these ships, 'and if they be denied, we are to take a forcible course'.[4] This was the brink of war. Charles, by this time, did not only hold the French guilty of fighting in English harbours: he held them guilty of coming between him and his wife. He said everyone should be master in his own house, and in future, he would appoint as many English as he pleased to the Queen's household. He sent a long complaint against Blainville: that he never talked without threats, that he embittered the spirit of his wife against him, and those of her servants, that he hindered her household from living

[1] Ibid., f. 154; S.P. 16/7/57.
[2] C.S.P.D. 1625-6, vol. x, no. 35; S.P. 16/12/47.
[3] C.S.P.D. 1625-6, vol. xi, no. 11.
[4] S.P. 16/12/93.

'comme il était convenable', and that the Ambassador went particularly out of his way to displease Buckingham, 'qui lui était une personne si cher et si utile'.[1]

Richelieu was indifferent to these English threats, having now formed a more accurate assessment of English military prowess. He told the Venetian Ambassador to Paris that he 'cannot bring himself to believe that the English will do much. . . . He says the King is poor without the help of Parliament, and that will never meet because of Buckingham, who very nearly came to grief through the last one.'[2] However, if Richelieu and Charles could view the prospect of an Anglo-French war with equanimity, Pembroke and Arundel could not. War with France and Spain simultaneously, when England already lacked the resources to fight Spain with foreign assistance, was an alarming prospect. During the summer of 1625, Pembroke had done all he could to prevent the outbreak of quarrels between England and France.[3] If the French were now making the removal of Buckingham a condition of continued peace, the opportunity to attack his old enemy was too good to be missed.

It is hard to be certain when the attacks by Pembroke and Arundel on Buckingham began. In November 1625, Buckingham believed they had been behind the attacks on him during the Parliament of 1625, but there is little independent evidence to support this. It is possible, indeed, that one of the French techniques for provoking Pembroke and Arundel to attack Buckingham was inflaming suspicion by rumouring that they were already doing so.[4] By March 1626, Holland was reporting to the King that the French appeared to have intelligence with some of Buckingham's principal enemies.[5] His suspicions seem to be justified: the Bishop of Mende, the Queen's Almoner and Richelieu's nephew, admitted to leading Arundel to suppose the Queen supported the impeachment of Buckingham. He also admitted to a 'secret understanding' with seven or eight of Buckingham's principal opponents in the Lords.[6] Meanwhile, Blainville hinted that he had been in touch with members of the Commons about the

---

[1] P.R.O. 31/3/63, ff. 5–8.
[2] C.S.P. Ven. 1625–6, p. 245.
[3] See, for example, S.P. 16/4/134, Pembroke to Pennington, 28 July 1625.
[4] Knowler. p. 28; H.M.C. Mar and Kellie Suppl., p. 233. Ingram, who said the Duke was 'possessed' by this conviction, appears not to have shared it.
[5] Cabala, I. 231.   [6] P.R.O. 31/3/63, ff. 73, 61.

St. Peter, the French ship whose seizure had become a symbolic focus for the maritime disputes between England and France.[1] Buckingham, then, came to the Parliament of 1626 facing a powerful court conspiracy whose centre was in the Queen's household. He came, moreover, in an impossible political situation. He could not avoid a Parliament: the Spanish war, in which he and Charles had invested too much political capital to draw back, could not be sustained without one. Even if there had been an immediate peace, a Parliament would probably have still been necessary, to raise the money to meet arrears of pay already owed to sailors and soldiers under arms. Yet the very measures he had to take to survive a Parliament were the same ones which would further widen his breach with the French. Parliament wanted peace with the French, and yet at the same time wanted measures against recusants which probably implied war with the French. Both parties were asking him for incompatible things.

It is instructive, in the light of the change in Anglo-French relations, and the state of the court, since 1625, to see who, among the Commons, supported Buckingham in 1625 and opposed him in 1626. The conspicuous examples are Eliot and Digges. Both were firmly pro-French, and in Parliament both concentrated much of their attention on the case of the *St. Peter*, so zealously pursued by the French Ambassador. It was a natural suspicion which prompted the Council, interrogating Eliot towards the end of the Parliament, to ask him what conference or correspondence he had had with any foreign ambassador or agent.[2] Rich, another

---

[1] Ibid., f. 39. Blainville's words are not conclusive: '[Votre Majesté] se souviendra ... que le Parlement d'Angleterre sur la crainte de tomber en mauvaise intelligence avec Elle [sc. Votre Majesté] s'estoit résolu de donner contentement aux marchands François dont les biens sont arrestées a la Tour de Londres et mesmes de rechercher les autheurs du peu de justice qu'ils ont receu jusques icy pour leur faire cognoistre qu'ils n'approuvent nullement les conseils qui tendent à desobliger la France.' He then adds that, over the case of the *St. Peter*, this investigation had reached as far as Buckingham. Nowhere in this letter does Blainville say in so many words that he had encouraged the Commons to pursue the case, but he is so closely concerned in it that it would be surprising if he had not. Blainville au Roi, 7/17 March 1626. It was on this case that Carleton, recently returned from an embassy to Paris, warned the Commons not to be led astray by the practice of foreign ambassadors. *C.J.* 853.

[2] S.P.16/27/17. Eliot was still entertaining Secretary Conway's son for the Christmas holidays while trying to transfer his allegiance to Pembroke. S.P. 16/12/95 and S.P. 16/18/68. The evidence tends to support Bagg's summary that Eliot was 'in a distraction how to divide himself betwixt your Grace and the

supporter of Buckingham in 1625 and his opponent in 1626, was also conspicuously pro-French, but in his case, it is possible that the growth of Arminianism was an even bigger influence than the growth of Anglo-French hostility. Rudyerd and Coryton swung against Buckingham together with their patron, Pembroke. Other members may have been saying in public what they had thought in private in the previous Parliament. Sandys, on the other hand, remained Buckingham's ally in 1626, and even had to depend on him to find a seat.

When the writs for the Parliament had gone out, in December 1625, both Anglo-French relations and Buckingham's relations with the rest of the court had been less deeply soured than they were when the Parliament met, in February 1626. Buckingham clearly hoped that he could count on facing only the same enemies he had faced in 1625. This was why he reasoned that he could protect himself by having six former members pricked as sheriffs. Coke, Seymour, and Phelips, the only three (apart from Mansell) who had attacked him directly in 1625, were obvious choices. Sir Guy Palmes, whose allusion to Empson and Dudley in the previous Parliament had been most uncomfortable, was another. Alford was an obvious candidate because of his negative approach to the war, but the sixth, Sir Thomas Wentworth, was a surprise. It is possible that he suffered more for his defence of Cranfield in 1624 than for anything he had said in 1625.[1] Wentworth and Seymour were ably replaced by their understudies, Wandesford and Kirton. Even when these men had been pricked sheriffs, it cost some effort to keep them out. Coke appeared before the Council demanding amendments to the sheriff's oath. He succeeded in obtaining the abolition of the oath to extirpate Lollardy in his county, but the clause saying the sheriff should remain in his county was left in. Someone drew in the margin a large hand, pointing to this clause.[2] Charles and Buckingham paid attention

Earl of Pembroke', S. R. Gardiner, 'Notes by Sir James Bagg on the Parliament of 1626', *Notes and Queries* (1872), pp. 325–6.

[1] Buckingham's hostility to Wentworth appears to go too far back to be explained by Wentworth's conduct in the Parliament of 1625. Eliot reported that in the Yorkshire election dispute in 1625 the majority of 'the courtiers' voted against Wentworth. *N.P.* ii. 103.

[2] S.P. 16/11/20. See *C.S.P.D. 1625–5*, vol. xix, nos. 95 and 96 for a proposal to revive the statute which required that burgesses should be resident in their constituencies.

to the composition of the upper House also. At the beginning of the Parliament Earls were being created, whom Rudyerd wryly described as 'cardinals to carry the consistory, if there be occasion'.[1]

However, these preparations were not enough. The court conspiracy against Buckingham was too powerful to be suppressed. Moreover, it could join hands with a large body of feeling in the Commons. For once, Buckingham's heterogeneous enemies could combine. The quarrel with France united the anti-Spanish Pembroke and the mildly pro-Spanish Arundel in opposition to it. It also enabled the supporters of peace, such as Bristol and Williams, to emerge from obscurity and join forces with war champions like Pembroke and Saye. In the Commons, they could combine with impoverished cloth merchants, embargoed wine merchants, members from provincial ports complaining about pirates, Deputy Lieutenants weary of pressing soldiers, and a host of other provincial discontents. In the attack on Buckingham in 1626, as in the attack on the patents in 1621, the concerns of court and country found a point of contact.

II

The writs for the Parliament of 1626 went out as soon as the collection of the subsidies of 1625 was completed. The Parliament met in time of open war, and Charles called it solely in order to obtain supply. The House of Commons were unwilling to vote supply unless they could impeach the Duke of Buckingham, insisting, for the first time since 1614, on redress of grievances before supply. Charles was unwilling to accept supply on these terms, and, there being no further work for the Parliament to do, it was dissolved. If this summary is correct, as in broad essentials it appears to be, the agenda sounds a rather short one.

It thus becomes the major difficulty in explaining the Parliament of 1626 to show why it was the longest session of the decade. Parliament met on 6 February, and remained in session, with two short recesses for Easter and Whitsun, until 15 June. If this short agenda is an adequate summary of the business of the Parliament, how was all this time consumed? We have had several discussions of why the Parliament of 1626 was dissolved in June, but, in

[1] S.P. 16/20/23.

seventeenth-century idiom, we are not ripe for the question. We cannot understand why the Parliament was dissolved in June unless we can understand why it was not dissolved in March, April, or May. In the words of Richard Montagu, writing on 20 April, 'I confess I marvel the Parliament holdeth so long and that they thus dawdle out the King with doing nothing.'[1] When Charles kept this aggressive Parliament in session for so long, what was he waiting for?

It is obvious, and tempting, to give the short answer, 'supply'. It is true that Charles's financial needs had become desperate even by the somewhat remarkable standards of the later 1620s. When Sir John Coke, now Secretary of State, made a full financial statement on 21 March, he showed that the King had current commitments for the war amounting to £1,067,211, all to be met within the next year, and most of them within the next eight months. He put the cost of the Cadiz expedition and the next fleet at £420,854, most of it still to be met. There were treaty commitments to pay the King of Denmark £30,000 a month for eight months, Count Mansfeld £20,000 a month, and the Netherlands £8,900 a month for the same period of time. Forty ships were ready at Plymouth, with men wasting wages until the King could afford to victual the ships to put them to sea. The guard of the coasts was costing £10,000 a month, which was rather less than was needed. It is typical of the financial awareness of the early seventeenth-century Commons that many of the items in Coke's statement are hard to report properly because of the random distribution of noughts in the figures reported in the diaries: Sir John Burroughes added two extra noughts into the grand total. With commitments of this size, an intense desire for supply is intelligible.[2]

Yet to explain the continuance of the Parliament by Charles's desire for supply is to create as many problems as we answer. Did Charles believe that the Commons would back down and vote supply without any action against Buckingham? It appears improbable. It is possible, if not entirely probable, that the King was misled by an ambiguity later pointed out by Sir Nathaniel Rich.[3]

---

[1] *Correspondence of John Cosin*, ed. G. Ornsby, Surtees Soc., vol. lii (1868), p. 89.
[2] Diary of Bulstrode Whitelocke [Cambridge University Library MSS. Dd 12–20, 12–21, and 12–22], 12–20, ff. 77–80. In this chapter, further references are to this diary unless otherwise stated. Harl. 6445, ff. 38–40. For what appears to be the correct text of Secretary Coke's statement, see *C.S.P.D. 1625–49 Addenda*, vol. dxxi, no. 181.   [3] 12–22, f. 55ᵛ.

When members of the Commons demanded redress of grievances before supply, it is now, with hindsight, possible to see that 'grievances' normally meant the Duke of Buckingham. It is possible that it took Charles some effort to absorb the fact that the mere existence of his chief minister was now the main grievance. If the Commons' demand had been redress of the items reported by the committee of grievances, many of these were things Charles could have granted. On two of them, impositions and the pretermitted custom, Charles could make no concession without reciprocal concession from the Commons. On the other things reported from the committee for grievances, there would have been much more room for manœuvre. Gorges's patent for New England, the abuse of begging briefs, the surveyorship of sea coals, the fees of the customers, purveyance of hawksmeat, the abuses of the aulnagers, the use of recognizances for fish days, a patent to examine witnesses in the Court of Exchequer of Chester, the patent for salt, the misbehaviour of Dr Anian, President of Corpus, Oxford, or even the privileges of the Merchant Adventurers were not issues on which it was worth risking the survival of the kingdom, or even of its first minister.[1]

It is highly unlikely that Charles hoped to get off so lightly from the Parliament of 1626. Whatever he expected its resolution to be, he eventually allowed the attack on the Duke of Buckingham to go forward. On 29 April,

Mr. Chancellor of the Exchequer [Weston] delivereth a message from his Majesty; that having given way to the enquiry about the Duke of Buckingham, and hearing there is new matter intended to be brought in; in respect of the season of the year, and the affairs of the state, desireth, the House therein will avoid all loss of time; and leaveth them to their own way, either by presenting the [blank in original] to himself, or to the Lords.[2]

Charles permitted the Commons to attack Buckingham. Why did he do this? It would be unwise to be too cynical about the explanation given by Weston on 12 June: 'The King hath given way to many of our proceedings which he did at first forbid with a mind willing to be in league with his people.'[3] The feeling expressed by

---

[1] 12–22, ff. 28–30. In this list of grievances, only impositions, Tonnage and Poundage, and the pretermitted custom are issues of weight. The others are described in an account in the State Papers, probably in the hand of Sir Robert Heath, as 'more friendly' grievances. S. P. 16/30/3.

[2] C.J. 851.   [3] 12–22, f. 55ʳ.

Weston, that it was neither right nor proper that the King and his people should be divided, was very strong both in the Council and in the House of Lords. In wartime, the double meaning of the word 'league' used by Weston is unlikely to have been accidental: With Charles's debts, and the danger from abroad, both at such a high point, the consequences of an angry dissolution were alarming to think about. Even if Charles might have ridden it out, the consequences were ones which respectable Buckingham supporters like the Earl of Manchester, who enjoyed popularity among the gentlemen of their home counties, found painful to think about.

Yet granted that there was a strong case against a dissolution, how could Charles have hoped the contest would be resolved? It here becomes relevant that Dr. Tite has shown that the procedure later formalized as 'impeachment' was, in the early 1620s, considerably less precise than it subsequently became. What Dr. Tite calls 'Parliamentary judicature' could take a variety of forms, leading to a variety of conclusions. Indeed, Dr. Tite concludes that the impeachment of the Duke of Buckingham became the first of the Parliamentary trials of the 1620s which can, without inaccuracy, be described as an 'impeachment'.[1] If, then, an 'impeachment', with the Commons as prosecutors and the Lords as judges, was a concept too precise for most members except Selden, it becomes a question exactly *what* Charles thought he had allowed to go forward. In this context, it is worth looking at the exact words of Weston's message of 29 April, which said the King had given way to the *inquiry about* the Duke of Buckingham, not to the charge against him. There is no concession here to the central demand made by Sir John Eliot, the Duke's loudest accuser: 'We but desire that he may come to his trial.'[2] There is, then, a fundamental ambiguity about what Charles thought he had agreed to, and what the Commons thought he had consented to. It is necessary, as a result of Dr. Tite's work, to dismiss any preconceived idea that he had agreed to a recognizable procedure called 'an

[1] Tite. *passim* and pp. 194–8. Dr. Tite is probably right in suggesting that for Selden, impeachment was intended to have the advantage of enabling the Commons to maintain their own suit. However, as Pym had foreseen in his speech of 20 April 1621, the Commons did not have this power until they had control of the 'inquisition of the fact': until they had control over the examination of witnesses. They lacked this control in 1626, whether proceeding by impeachment or otherwise.

[2] 12–22, f. 54ᵛ.

impeachment': procedure in Parliamentray trials and accusations was still being worked out day by day.

It is, then, necessary to examine the Parliament of 1626 with an eye to its chronology. Approached chronologically, its proceedings divide into three phases. In the first, from the assembly of the Parliament on 6 February to the decision to charge the Duke of Buckingham before voting supply, on 27 March, the focus is on the House of Commons. Here, the slow proceeding is easily explained by the Commons' alarm at their own temerity: they were, as Rudyerd told Nethersole on 19 March, discussing points so dangerous that they dared not discuss them freely among themselves.[1] Even if they were being strongly encouraged from within the court, or, as the next sentence of Rudyerd's letter could be taken to hint, by the French Ambassador, an attack on a man of the Duke of Buckingham's standing was not to be lightly undertaken. That the Commons should have spent seven weeks feeling their way to such a charge is not remarkable: what is more remarkable is that they were not firmly and conclusively warned off before they had made it.

The second phase of the Parliament runs from 29 March to 2 May. On 29 March the King apparently unambiguously forbade the attack on Buckingham. He did not dissolve the Parliament when his prohibition was ignored. On 29 April, he allowed the attack on the Duke to go forward, and on 2 May, the Commons decided to present their charges to the Lords. Explanations of the length of the Parliament must explain why it was not dissolved during this second phase.

It is the length of this second phase which is the real chronological peculiarity of the Parliament, and the King's objectives during it which are its main mystery. The public record of Parliamentary proceedings during this second phase is not always helpul. It seems probable that the focus of activity was then at court, and that the evidence now available to us is only the tip of an iceberg. In the third phase, from the Commons' decision to present their charges to the Lords, on 2 May, to the dissolution on 15 June, the focus of activity shifts to the Lords. There is probably no other period in the Parliaments of the 1620s when proceedings were so entirely dominated by the Lords, and during this last phase, Parliamentary history must be taken to be the

[1] S.P. 16/23/30.

history of the House of Lords. To understand why events unfolded as they did, it is necessary to examine these three phases in sequence.

The opening speech was made by the new Lord Keeper, Sir Thomas Coventry. It suggests that the Crown had learnt from the experience of 1621 and 1625 that many members found it difficult to return home at the end of a Parliament having voted supply but passed no laws. The opening speech, remarkably, contained no mention of supply, and said the Parliament had been called for the making of good laws. This was not an announcement of a government legislative programme: some bills, such as that for reforming secret outlawries, may have enjoyed some official sponsorship,[1] but when Coventry said the Parliament had been called for the making of good laws, he was inviting members of both Houses to take the initiative and provide their own legislative agenda. He did, it is true, warn the Houses what a misery it would be if the kingdom should want Parliaments, but if this was a threat, it was very gently delivered, and no more than the facts of the case demanded. Coventry also stressed, with some justification, the devotion to Parliaments shown by Charles as Prince, and his 'daily access' to Parliaments while he was Prince.[2] On his record to date, this stress on Charles's devotion to Parliamentary institutions was justifiable. The necessity to make these statements arose simply from the overwhelming urgency of the need to provide Charles with more revenue.

It was this need which provided the subject of the first bills read in both Houses. In the Lords, the first two bills were veterans. One was a bill 'for the better preserving of his Majesty's revenues', which passed the Lords quickly, and was sent to committee in the Commons on 7 March. It did not emerge.[3] The other was the familiar bill for making the arms of the kingdom more serviceable in time to come. This bill, in time of war, had become more urgent than ever: both up-to-date equipment for soldiers and some legal basis for its provision were things not easily dispensed with in wartime. The Lords pushed this through a committee to which all Lords Lieutenant were appointed, and sent it down to the

---

[1] There are notes on the bill against secret outlawries in S.P. 16/21/1.

[2] *Lords' Debates* (ed. Gardiner), p. 108. In this chapter, further references to *Lords' Debates* are to this edition unless otherwise stated. *L.J.* 493.

[3] *L.J.* 496, 502.

Commons.[1] The bill remained in committee from 25 March to 9 June, when it was reported by old Mr. Wentworth, a lonely war supporter in this Parliament. He said the bill had encountered 'many difficulties', and asked for it to be referred back to a committee of the whole House.[2] No more was heard of it, and once again an opportunity was lost to save the militia from its dependence on the prerogative. The first bill in the Commons was the bill begun in 1625, for accounting on oath for public rates and taxes. This bill provided for the imprisonment of those who refused to take the oath. It was sent to committee on 11 February, but never emerged.[3]

A similar fate overtook a Lords' bill for the restraint of apparel, which was designed, both to preserve social status by making, people dress according to their rank, and to provide protection for the domestic clothing industry. In the Lords, it was first reported by Clare, who said it was a good bill but imperfectly drafted, and a new bill should be drawn. The new bill was reported in the Lords on 15 April, and passed in the teeth of a spirited defence of the lace-makers by Dorset. In the Commons, it was reported a first time on 25 April by Noy, who wanted to know whether it applied to foreigners. The Commons, showing a sensitivity which was common in 1626 to what is now called a hybrid bill, resolved to hear counsel from the wire-drawers and the silkmen, whose business was seriously affected, before proceeding further. On 25 May, the bill was again reported by Noy, who admitted its adverse effect on some trades, but compared it with the effect of the Protestant settlement of 1559 on 'holy water shops' and other sellers of the impedimenta of Catholic worship. He said that the incidental evil was one which must be borne for the sake of the greater good. Nevertheless, nothing more was heard of the bill. The apparel bill, like many of the 1621 bills, illustrates the difficulty of passing economic legislation while allowing a hearing to all the competing vested interests involved.[4]

Other bills showed more sign of prospering, but even so, the progress of the most popular bills was slow. The pattern of busi-

---

[1] *L.J.* 501–2; *Lords' Debates*, p. 116. Wallingford and Clare wanted the bill amended to punish those who borrowed horses and arms for musters.

[2] 12–20, ff. 45ʳ, 59ʳ, 61ʳ, 88ʳ; *C.J.* 869.

[3] *C.J.* 816; Rich, 10 Feb.; 12–20, f. 94.

[4] *L.J.* 549; *Lords' Debates*, p. 141; 12–21, ff. 165ᵛ, 179ʳ; 12–22, f. 27ᵛ. On the background to this bill, see N. B. Harte, 'State Control of Dress and Social

ness on bills is like that of 1621, when progress was slow because there was no agreement on priorities, rather than like that of 1624, when bills before Parliament for a second time had been debated long enough to allow some order of priorities to emerge. The first four bills were sent from the Commons to the Lords on 7 March, a month after the Parliament began. One was the familiar bill against recusants evading forfeiture through uses. This passed rapidly through the Lords, being reported by Saye six days after it was sent up, and agreed to. We can only guess whether, if bills had been presented to the King at the end of the Parliament, Charles would have supported this bill, as he had done in 1624, or vetoed it, as he did in 1628.[1] The second was the now familiar bill for free fishing, which, remarkably, also passed the Lords under the care of Buckingham's friend, the Earl of Westmorland.[2] The third bill was to confirm the incorporation of Sutton's Hospital. It is interesting that legislation was thought necessary on this subject, since the incorporation had already been confirmed by all twelve judges in Exchequer Chamber. It must have been wanted badly, since this bill was preferred in every Parliament from 1621 until it became a statute in 1628. It was not resisted by the Lords, who simply added two provisos to confirm leases in Charterhouse Yard held by Lord North and Lady Maidstone.[3] The fourth was a routine private bill empowering a man to sell some land.

The second list of bills did not come up to the Lords from the Commons until 21 April.[4] These included a bill against travelling on the Sabbath, which was approved by the Lords, and became law in the next Parliament. Another was a bill against citations out of ecclesiastical courts, in which, to their subsequent embarrassment, the Commons tried to restrict the practice of citing people

---

Change in Pre-Industrial England', in *Trade, Government and Economy in Pre-Industrial England: Essays Presented to F. J. Fisher*, ed. D. C. Coleman and A. H. John (1976), pp. 132–65.

[1] *L.J.* 525; Ruigh, p. 241.   [2] *L.J.* 526.

[3] 12–20, ff. 41ᵛ, 80ʳ; *L.J.* 536; 3 Car. I c.9. The provisos remained in the final Act. The Act recounts that legislation was needed because Sutton's heir was trying to overthrow the incorporation, but does not say why he should have had any hope of succeeding in the face of an Exchequer Chamber judgement.

[4] *L.J.* 567 The list includes the bill against the transport of wool, which had been noted as ready for the Lords on 20 March. 12–20, f. 62ʳ. Compared with other bills which originated during the depression, this one showed an unusual vitality after the depression was over. See *C.J.* 927.

to appear before ecclesiastical courts because there was a 'common fame' that they had committed an offence.[1] This and a bill to prevent clergymen from being J.P.s were examples of a drift back towards religious bills which had not been moved in the Parliaments of 1621 and 1624. Neither passed the Lords. The bill against clergy being J.P.s should probably be regarded as an anticlerical measure rather than as a puritan measure. It allowed exemptions for bishops and the Vic-Chancellors of the Universities, and was amended in committee to allow a further exemption for Deans.[2] The fourth bill, which also made no progress in the Lords, was for the better venting of kersies. It probably grew out of a proposal, made by the committee of trade in 1624, to restrict, without abolishing, the privileges of the Merchant Adventurers.

The growing concern with ecclesiastical issues was also apparent in a bill against the *Ex Officio* Oath, in an attack by Jordan and Harley on the idolatrous monument of Cheapside Cross, and in the case of Sir Robert Howard. Howard had been excommunicated (for adultery with Sir Edward Coke's daughter) while privileged as a member of the 1624 Parliament.[3] He had been returned in 1626 while still excommunicate, and, in a rare exception, was allowed to take his seat without receiving the compulsory communion.[4] John Selden pointed out that Howard's excommunication was the greater excommunication, which drew the lesser excommunication on all who kept him company, so that the whole Parliament was excommunicate: 'this is a great indignity to this House'.[5]

Some of the economic bills, such as the hotly disputed bill against the export of wool, had been put on the Parliamentary agenda during the depression. Others, such as two bills against increase of cottages, one 'in cities, boroughs, towns corporate and market towns', and the other in the neighbourhood of London, may have reflected a concern with overcrowding heightened by the

[1] 12–20, ff. 55ᵛ, 34ᵛ, 64ʳ; 12–21, ff. 136–7. Mr Wentworth attempted to draw a distinction between fame, which was majority suspicion, and rumour, which was minority suspicion.

[2] 12–20, ff. 41ʳ, 32ᵛ, 44ʳ, 64ʳ, 88ʳ. Selden supported the bill on the ground that the clergy should not give judgements of blood, and an anonymous member on the less fundamentalist ground that a clergyman had become a J.P. without achieving the minimum qualification of holding land worth £20 p.a. in the county.

[3] C.J. 821; C.J. 858; 12–21, f. 183ʳ. Grosvenor, f. 59.
[4] C.J. 821.   [5] Rich, 17 Feb.

plague.[1] An election bill was proposed, which would have revived the residence qualification, and forbidden canvassing.[2] The secret offices bill was ventilated again, as was a bill to prohibit the abuse whereby those with friends in the Exchequer could employ the administrative machinery of the Exchequer to collect their debts by the legal fiction of assigning them to the King. Bills against 'temporal simony' and the purchase of judicial places for money reflected increasing concern with administrative malpractice.[3] Among all these bills, only the bill for scandalous ministers, transferring jurisdiction over a number of offences from the ecclesiastical to the lay courts, caused much contention. It is interesting that it was Harley, one of Buckingham's leading defenders, who led the support for this bill, while Digges, one of the managers of Buckingham's impeachment, led the opposition to it.[4] Similarly, the bill against recusant uses had been reported by Buckingham's client, Mr. Clark.[5] There was growing evidence of religious enthusiasm in the Parliament of 1626, but it shows no clear correlation with opposition to Buckingham.

For the first three weeks of its sitting, the House of Commons was concerned with business as usual. Sir John Eliot, on 10 February, had made a preliminary effort to turn attention to the Duke of Buckingham. He was supported in this by Sir Edward Coke's son Clement, but the House as a whole showed no inclination to take his proposals up. From 10 February until 21 February, it looked as if the Commons, as in 1625, had no more inclination to take up the attack on the Duke of Buckingham than they had to take up proposals for supply. Left to themselves, they might have continued with their bills.

They were led back slowly towards the question of the Duke by the petitions of the French merchants and the wine merchants. Both were taking part in a depressed trade. Bateman of London said the plague had knocked the bottom out of the wine trade, and the grievance of impositions, eating into profit margins, was still with them. Losses by war and losses by piracy had made their life

---

[1] 12–20, ff. 82ᵛ, 67ᵛ.   [2] Hirst, p. 230; 12–20, f. 87ᵛ.

[3] 12–20, f. 85ᵛ. The Speaker refused to read the bill of 'temporal simony' on the ground that he had been brought no brief or breviate of it beforehand. The resemblance of the idea to Sherland's speech presenting the articles of impeachment against the Duke prompts a suspicion as to both the author and purpose of the bill.

[4] 12–20, ff. 84ᵛ–83ᵛ.   [5] 12–20, f. 55ᵛ.

harder, and a series of seizures of their goods in France had brought their patience to an end. These seizures were commonly thought to have been started by the business of the ship *St. Peter* of Newhaven (alias Le Harve), which had been arrested in England on suspicion of carrying goods to Spain. It had been released on the orders of the Court of Admiralty, and then re-arrested on the order of the Duke of Buckingham, the Lord Admiral.

The French merchants may have been slightly surprised by the limited sympathy they at first got for their complaint about impositions. Delbridge and Spencer were ready to pursue the issue, but Digges said they should not take from the King when expected to help him, and old Mr. Wentworth, remarkably, seemed to be willing to legalize impositions by Act of Parliament.[1] They met a great deal more sympathy in their complaints about the seizure of the *St. Peter*, which were immediately taken up with enthusiasm by Sir John Eliot.

Dr. Ball, in his study of the Parliamentary career of Sir John Eliot, has drawn attention to the inadequacy of the *St. Peter* case as the basis for any legal charge against the Duke.[2] The Duke's stay of the *St. Peter* could be regarded as high-handed, rather than illegal, and moreover, he was able to justify himself on the ground that he had acted by the King's personal command. It is hard to resist the impression that the significance of the *St. Peter* case was not in any illegality involved, but in the light it shed on the Duke's foreign policy. England was already at war with Spain: the *St. Peter* case showed that England was in danger of finding itself at war with France also. This danger was foreseen by Salvetti on 26 January/6 February, and it appears to have been in the mind of Rudyerd when he claimed, on 24 February, that 'this kingdom was never so much endangered without conquest'.[3] If Eliot's object in the *St. Peter* case was to draw attention to the danger of war with France, his concentration on it seems the more intelligible. He set the issue off with a long report on 22 February, in which

[1] Rich, 15 Feb.; 12–20, ff. 85ᵛ, 78ᵛ–79ᵛ. Wentworth repeated much of his 1610 speech, including the quotation from Sir John Fortescue, but now seems to have believed that the only way to preserve England's status as *dominium politicum et regale* was to give the King Parliamentary authority to collect the money he was going to collect anyway. He also stressed that the new King was 'not an imposer'. His proposal to merge the committee of trade and the committee of grievances was rejected.

[2] Ball, pp. 174–5.

[3] *H.M.C. 11th Rep. I*, p. 43; Rich, 24 Feb.

he complained that 'Frenchmen respected our justice till Christmas almost'.[1] In this phrase, he showed that the timing of his own breach with Buckingham did not merely coincide in fact with Buckingham's breach with France, but also coincided with when he believed Buckingham's breach with France to have taken place. The immediate official comment on Eliot's speech was by Sir Humphrey May, another Pembroke man, who said that Eliot reported truly the proceedings of the Council table—hardly a comment calculated to silence discussion of the issue. May then sturdily repeated the official defence of the Duke, to the effect that the embargo on English goods in France was not the result of the *St. Peter* case.[2] Other members argued that it was unwise to pursue this case too far, in order not to encourage the French to claim they had done justly in seizing English goods.[3] Attempts were also made to cast the blame on Sir Henry Marten, judge of the Court of Admiralty, who, being present, defended himself vigorously.

As the *St. Peter* case developed, it became increasingly clear that those involved in pushing it forward were an alliance of Pembroke men and West Countrymen. Eliot, Coryton, and Long probably spoke in the Pembroke interest, and Delbridge, Matthews, and perhaps Sir John Strangeways, knight of the shire for Dorset, spoke for West Country merchants.[4] It was one of the Pembroke men, Lord Cavendish, who first named the Duke, in the debate on 22 February. He complained that, 'The French complain much of our Admiral, which breeds a great hate by them to us.' In the light of the French Ambassador's close interest in this case, it is hard not to give weight to Cavendish's offer to read a letter from a factor in France, or to his claim that he had three French merchants at the door ready to explain the truth of the business.[5] It was in a later debate of the same case that Carleton claimed that the French Ambassador 'did mortally hate' the Duke, and urged

---

[1] 12–20, ff. 75ᵛ–74ᵛ; Rich, 22 Feb. Buckingham's client Clarke reacted to the attacks on the Duke by denying hotly that there was any further risk of a breach with France. Gardiner, vi, 68–9.   [2] 12–20, f. 74ᵛ; Rich, 22 Feb.
[3] Rich, 22 and 24 Feb. Sir Henry Mainwaring and Sir John Finch put this argument most strongly.
[4] Strangeways had been with Bristol in Spain. His daughter was married to Sir Lewis Dives, Bristol's stepson and another effective opponent of the Duke. Keeler, p. 353.
[5] 12–20, f. 72ᵛ; C.J. 823. The term 'French merchants' is ambiguous. Cavendish succeeded to the Earldom of Devonshire on 6 March, and took his seat in the Lords in time to have his own charges presented to him. C.J. 831.

the House not 'to be carried away with the practice of foreign ambassadors'.[1]

If this interpretation of the *St. Peter* case is correct, it was perhaps the object of Eliot and the other Pembroke men to use it to frighten the Duke out of a French war, not to drive him out of office. It would lend credence to this interpretation that the attack on the Duke over the *St. Peter* was supported, at least by implication, by one of the Privy Councillors, Sir Thomas Edmondes, who, according to the French Ambassador, 'est tout Français'.[2]

To achieve the diplomatic effect which the French required, the investigation into the *St. Peter* case needed to be backed at least by the threat of a prosecution against the Duke.[3] On 23 February, the Commons interrogated the Lieutenant of the Tower, in order to determine the Duke's share of responsibility for the stay of the *St. Peter*. Only Selden and Coryton appear to have been satisfied that the interrogation gave sufficient justification for further proceedings.[4] The next day, 24 February, the Duke's opponents attempted to broaden the issues against him. Christopher Wandesford, one of the members given a chance to show their talents by the absence of those pricked as sheriffs, demanded a settlement of the question of impositions. Mansell, who probably owed his return to this Parliament to Pembroke,[5] suggested an investigation into the Cadiz voyage, while Eliot held forth more generally on military and naval misgovernment. Harley, for the

---

[1] Grosvenor, ff. 8, 18; *C.J.* 853.

[2] 12–20, f. 71ᵛ; P.R.O. 31/3/62, f. 107 (Effiat au Roi, 6/16 May 1625).

[3] Rich, 23 Feb.

[4] Rich, 23 Feb. Littleton and Newberry, both later firm opponents of the Duke, were unwilling to proceed on the *St. Peter* case.

[5] S. R. Gardiner, 'Notes by Sir James Bagg on the Parliament of 1626', *Notes and Queries* (1872), p. 325. The accuracy of Bagg's information seems to be sustained by the Parliamentary debates. He is also exactly accurate in his description of the blank indenture on which Sir Robert Mansell was returned for Lostwithiel. P.R.O. C. 219/40, pt. ii, no. 284. Among the managers of the Duke's impeachment, Edward Herbert at Downton and Selden at Great Bedwin were also returned on blank indentures. Evelyn, another of the Duke's most active critics, sat for Pembroke's home borough of Wilton. Arundel's connection has so far been less studied than Pembroke's, but it appears to have included John Selden in the Commons and the Earl of Clare in the Lords. K. M. Sharpe, 'The Intellectual and Political Activities of Sir Robert Cotton, *c* 1590–1631', Oxford D.Phil. Thesis (1975), pp. 123, 227. *Letters of John Holles 1587–1637*, Thoroton Soc. Record Series, xxxi (1975), ed. P. R. Seddon, p. lix, Nottingham University Library MS. Ne. C. 15, 405, f. 121. I am grateful to Dr Sharpe for permission to quote from his thesis, and Mr. Richard Cust for the Holles references.

Duke, asked in vain that they should not dispute of errors past. He was answered by Kirton, steward of the Duke's enemy the Earl of Hertford,[1] who said they should consider errors before they considered supply. Digges, who took a surprisingly long time to commit himself to the attack on Buckingham, wanted to consider supply first, but the mood of the House was not with him. Sir John Saville, who enjoyed the Duke's support in Yorkshire, asked 'that the honourable persons near the chair should lead us in the way, and the right way',[2] but received no answer. It is hard to resist the impression that, at this stage, the Councillors' commitment to discouraging an attack on the Duke was less than total.

If the Commons were to insist, as they appeared to be doing, on redress of grievance before supply, they would find, as they had done before, that the subsidies they had to offer were not of sufficient value to purchase any substantial redress of grievances. This is perhaps why some of their members had proposals, to which Dr. Ball has drawn our attention, to 'settle the King's estate'.[3] The plan was, as Spencer put it in 1628, to 'dower' the King: to make a substantial permanent addition to his ordinary revenue, in addition to voting him supply for his immediate necessities. Sir John Eliot, in his speech of 24 February, said that if the King's ancient revenues were not fit, they should make them so, but at the same time produced a series of precedents, stretching back to the case of Hubert de Burgh in Henry III's reign, in which grants of taxation had been made conditional on the punishment of a minister who had wasted the King's estate. His meaning was plain: a new settlement of the King's ordinary revenue was to be made conditional on the punishment of the Duke of Buckingham.[4] He was immediately supported by Pym and Rich. Weston, Chancellor of the Exchequer, answered this debate, not by rebuking the Commons for their presumption, but by saying, 'It is the King's desire that we should enter into the consideration of his revenue. He [Weston] will be ready to give an account of the King's estate when the King shall give him leave.' He asked leave to report the day's proceedings to the King, which was granted. The prompt-

---

[1] On the Kirton–Seymour connection, see Keeler, pp. 241–2.

[2] 12–20, f. 65ᵛ.

[3] Ball, pp. 18, 134–8. Contrast the treatment of Eliot's speech in Russell (ed.), *Origins*, p. 269n. Further study of the debates has convinced me that Dr. Ball's interpretation is right, and mine wrong. See, particularly, S.P. 16/24/48.

[4] For Spencer, *1628 Debates*, ii. 269. 12–20, ff. 67ᵛ–66ᵛ; Rich, 24 Feb.

ness of Weston's response, and even more his confident statement
of the King's opinion about a proposal which had only just been
made, encourages the suspicion that he and Eliot were speaking
by prearrangement, and that the King was at least willing to learn
what the Commons thought was the price of the Duke. The whole
scheme seems to bear the distinctive stamp of Pembroke.

Throughout the decade, there were some members who wanted
a permanent improvement of the King's ordinary revenue. What
is distinctive about the 1626 proposals is that support for them
was not confined to the regular revenue reformers, Pym, Digges,
Rich, and Rudyerd. At least nineteen members publicly declared
their support for some form of settlement of the King's estate, and
some of them were well outside the circle of those who normally
supported such proposals. Perhaps the most unexpected members
of the list are Delbridge, Coryton, Hoby, Saville, Goodwin of
Goodwin v. *Fortescue*, and old Thomas Wentworth.[1] If these proposals had been more seriously investigated, this support might
well have diminished. Any concrete proposals about how the
money was to be raised would have alienated the support of some
members who favoured different methods. Conversely, however,
the prospect of some action on Buckingham could have attracted
support from some who in the event remained silent. Only trial
would have made it possible to say whether there was majority
support in the Commons for any such proposals, but whether it
was a majority or not, the range of support or token support is
impressive.

The most widely canvassed proposal was the one Sir Edward
Coke had advanced in the previous Parliament, for a Tonnage and
Poundage bill which would settle impositions and increase the
King's revenue through a new book of rates. Eliot and others also
favoured an Act of Resumption of Crown lands, a proposal which
gained such wide currency that Wandesford and Sir Thomas
Wentworth, in 1628, discussed whether it should be regarded as a
reason against purchasing former Crown lands.[2] There was also

---

[1] 12–20, f. 81ᵛ (Delbridge); Grosvenor, ff. 36–7 (Coryton); 12–20, f. 83ᵛ
(Hoby); 12–20 ff. 62ᵛ, 30ᵛ (Saville); Rich, 15 Feb. (Goodwin), and 12–20, f. 77ᵛ
(Wentworth). The support of some of these members was distinctly lukewarm,
and Bankes, the future Attorney General, regarded the proposals as a way of
averting the increasingly feared prospect of annual subsidies. 12–20, f. 28ᵛ.

[2] 12–20, f. 77ᵛ (Wentworth), f. 66ᵛ (Eliot); Grosvenor, ff. 36–7 (Coryton);
L.J. 613 (Pym); *Wentworth Papers*, p. 300; P.R.O. 31/3/64, f. 118ᵛ.

talk of reforming the administration of recusancy fines, cutting down on pensions, and reforming the management of the King's parks and forests.[1] Perhaps the most interesting proposal was for the revival of the Great Contract of 1610. This was advanced by Sir Nicholas Sanders, who said that in order to avoid having to pay the King annual subsidies, they should give him support as well as supply. It was also advanced by Sir John Saville, who had opposed it in 1610, but now said that if it had been passed then, it would by this time have brought in more than two million pounds. Saville, after the Parliament was over, was given a chance to give practical expression to his support for the Contract. He was given a commission to compound with men in Yorkshire who held their land by feudal tenures, and to find out what they would pay to be quit of the obligation to wardship.[2]

The King, however, appears to have insisted on an immediate grant of supply before any such negotiations were begun.[3] If we want to look for reasons why he might have done so, it is hard to find them better set out than in the Commons' speeches. The complaints of failure to guard the coasts against piracy had grown to an outcry. A Welsh member said it was now unsafe to sail from Glamorgan to Somerset.[4] There were said to be 2,000 Englishmen captured and in slavery at Algiers, above 2,000 in Sallee, and 2,500 English and Scottish prisoners at Dunkirk.[5] Soldiers under arms also had to be paid. Sir John Saville said there were 3,000 men within ten miles of his house, and if they did not have relief, they

[1] There is a summary of what appears to be a draft committee report on this subject in the manuscript True Relation of the 1626 Parliament in the Duchy of Cornwall office (ff. 90ᵛ–91ʳ).

[2] See *H.M.C. Hastings*, ii. 69, where the Commons are said to be considering 'supply and support'. *Lowther*, p. 4 (I am grateful to Mr. Christopher Thompson for this reference); 12–21, ff. 158–9. Meautys, Bacon's former sercetary, objected that this mutual selling of wants was 'displeasing to the King and to Almighty God'. For further support for the Contract, see 12–21, f. 162ʳ; Grosvenor, ff. 36–7, and Duchy of Cornwall True Relation, ff. 90ᵛ–91ʳ. Saville's commission is in Birmingham Reference Library, Coventry MSS., Commissions, no. 8. It covers socage in chief, and offers freedom from licences to alienate, as well as from wardship.

[3] 12–20, f. 82ʳ.   [4] Rich, 16 Feb.

[5] 12–20, ff. 59ᵛ, 56ᵛ; Harl. 6445, f. 9ᵛ; Rich, 27 Feb. The estimates, which are slightly on the large side, were made by Matthews (Algiers), Delbridge (Sallee), and Sir Henry Anderson (Dunkirk). The Dunkirk figure includes Scots. The Dunkirk prisoners, unlike those at Algiers and Sallee, were not slaves, but they also required ransom. I am grateful to Mr. David Hebb for much guidance on these matters.

would take it where they could get it. A member for Dover claimed
that on the Cadiz expedition, 200 mariners from Dover had sailed
and only four returned, while from Dorset thirty were said to have
returned out of 500.[1] These might have been thought to be more
persuasive arguments for supply than any the King could advance,
but they were not so interpreted, and while supply remained in
abeyance, other business remained in abeyance also.

In trying to give priority for supply before discussing the Duke
of Buckingham or a revenue settlement, Charles appears to have
enjoyed majority support in the House of Lords, where support
for the war was still much stronger than it was in the Commons.
In the first phase of the Parliament of 1626, the Lords were
primarily concerned with securing a full attendance of their members. As the Commons were anxious about the attempt to deprive
them of members by making them sheriffs, so the Lords were
anxious about the attempt of Charles to deprive them of the services
of Bristol and Williams by denying them their writs of summons.
The chairman of their committee of privileges was Hertford, who
himself had recent experience of being denied his writ, and whose
brother was excluded from the Commons as a sheriff. Williams,
after half-hearted attempts by Buckingham to offer charges against
him, succeeded in obtaining his writ, and took his seat on 23
March.[2] Buckingham's deadly enemy Bristol was a rather harder
case. On 30 March the Lords' committee of privileges reported
that 'no precedent being found that any writ of summons hath
been detained from any peer that is capable of sitting in the House
of Parliament; and considering withal how far it may trench into
the right of every member of this House, whether sitting by
ancient right of inheritance, or by patent to have their writs detained', they would beseech the King to send a writ of summons
to Bristol and to any other peers who had been denied one, unless
they were disabled by judgement of Parliament or other legal
judgement.[3] It was as part of a continuing drive to secure a full
attendance that the Lords, on 25 February, resolved to restrict the
number of proxies any one Lord could hold to two. This resolution
was clearly a gesture of hostility to Buckingham, and was so
recognized by Chamberlain. The list of speakers also shows clearly
that the clash was between Buckingham's supporters and his

[1] 12–20, f. 60ᵛ; Harl. 6445, f. 5ᵛ.
[2] L.J. 538, 532; H.M.C. Buccleuch, iii. 269, 277.   [3] L.J. 544.

opponents. Buckingham himself opposed the order, while his known enemies such as Arundel supported it. Pembroke, according to Chamberlain, made a superb gesture of indifference by casting four proxy votes on each side: unfortunately, the House of Lords Proxy Book only shows Pembroke enjoying five proxies. Saye's fear that 'the whole House may be enclosed in two or three, and their voices, with certain pieces of parchment' expresses a fear which was probably general among the nobility, that the rise of Buckingham and a few others was a threat to the privileges of their order as a whole.[1] It was the same feeling which had made Spencer claim in 1621 that it was against the orders of the House to describe any of their members as 'great lords', for they were all peers.[2]

There is no need to disbelieve the Venetian Ambassador when he says that the vote on the proxies encouraged the Commons in their desire to attack the Duke.[3] The Duke enjoyed thirteen proxies, and the hostility to him expressed in this motion is plain. However, as a contribution to a possible impeachment of Buckingham, the vote on the proxies was more symbolic than real. In the first place, Buckingham's opponents Pembroke and Arundel enjoyed between them nearly as many proxies as he did, and they could probably be less confident than the Duke that their proxies, if redistributed, would go to other Lords on the same side. In the event, Buckingham gave up his proxies, apparently as a voluntary gesture to forestall criticism, and of thirteen whose redistribution is recorded at least ten went to men who were his known and dependable supporters.[4]

This touchiness of the Lords about their privileges was much

---

[1] *Lords' Debates*, pp. 113–15; *H.M.C. Buccleuch*, iii. 268; *L.J.* 507; Chamberlain, 7 March 1626. The House of Lords Proxy Book also credits the Duke with 13 proxies, while Chamberlain allows him only 11.

[2] *Lords' Debates* (ed. Relf), pp.–19–20. The peer reproved for speaking of 'great Lords' was Pembroke.

[3] Tite, p. 181.

[4] House of Lords Record Office, Proxy Book, 1626. The proxies of Chichester, Tunbridge, and Teynsham went to Buckingham's father-in-law, Rutland, that of Cumberland to his brother-in-law, Denbigh, Bath's to Dorset, Robartes's to Dorset, Eure's to Holland, Noel's to Manchester, and St. John of Basing's to Marlborough. Only Northumberland's proxy, which went to Percy, Darcy, and Meynell's, which went to Mansfield, and that of Mansfield, who appears to have attended in person, went outside Buckingham's immediate circle. Arundel lost one proxy, that of Lord Petre, to North, and Pembroke appears to have kept all his proxies.

heightened on 5 March, when Buckingham's opponent the Earl of Arundel was sequestered from the Council and imprisoned in the Tower. His alleged offence was allowing his son to marry without permission into the royal family. It is true that there were numerous precedents for regarding this as a criminal offence, but unfortunately for Charles, he never succeeded in inducing the Lords to believe that Arundel was really imprisoned because of his son's marriage.[1] The general opinion appears to have been that he was imprisoned because of his hostility to Buckingham. The fact that, except for a week's liberty at the end of the Parliament, he remained under suspended sentence of house arrest until the Parliament of 1628 would appear to confirm contemporaries' interpretation.[2]

However, strongly though the Lords might feel about Arundel's arrest, they could not forget that there was a war on. On 6 March, the day after Arundel's arrest, Lord Montagu said that according to their writ, they were called to consider the defence of the realm, and had sat a month without touching it. He therefore suggested that they should use the precedent of the Earl of Southampton's intervention in 1624 to justify reminding the Commons of the need for money. Coming from a veteran House of Commons man, who had been dubious about Southampton's motion at the time when it moved, this is an impressive motion.[3] It was immediately seconded by Warwick, and broadened by the Duke into a proposal for a committee for the defence of the realm. The Lords were thus enabled to bend their collective energies to practical questions like how to guard the sea between London and Newcastle in time to reopen the Newcastle coal trade before the mines flooded. When Neile, Bishop of Durham, alleged that if the mines were closed for a month, they would be flooded, never to be recovered, he was explicitly putting the Commons under pressure to vote supply.[4]

This pressure had been begun at a conference of the two Houses on 7 March, where the chief part had been given to Pembroke.

[1] M. L. Bush, 'The Tudors and the Royal Race', *History* (1970), 37–48. Perhaps the best comment on the Arundel case is Bush's on the case of Sir Thomas Seymour: 'It was yet another charge to bring against a magnate who had proved himself to be an unequivocal nuisance to the government' (p. 46).

[2] On the Arundel case, see Vernon F. Snow, *Essex the Rebel* (Lincoln, Nebraska, 1970), pp. 154–7.

[3] *H.M.C. Buccleuch*, iii. 273–3; *Lords' Debates*, pp. 121–2. For Montagu's reservations about Southampton's motion when it was moved, see above, p. 179.

[4] *Lords' Debates*, p. 137.

It was an embarrassing commission for Pembroke: he had to choose, neither for the first time nor for the last, between his hatred of Buckingham and his hatred of Spain. He gave the appearance of giving priority to his hatred of Spain, and, according to Lord Montagu, who was a Buckingham supporter, 'performed his trust very nobly'. He reminded the Commons that failure to pay the subsidies promised to the King of Denmark would lead to his withdrawal from the war, thereby threatening the Low Countries, said that Buckingham had contributed over £60,000 of his own money for the war, and put heavy stress on the need to preserve the alliance with France.[1]

Pembroke's speech at the conference of 7 March was a ministerial performance, and not necessarily a guide to his real convictions. On the other hand, it has a remarkable resemblance to Rudyerd's speech of 23 March, in which he followed Sir John Coke's financial statement with a motion for supply:

We are bound to make good our former protestations etc. Notwithstanding some sly objections that we are not bound by a former parl. engagement. Other parl. led the k. invited him besought him to these actions. All Christendom 2 great factions, with the Pope, against the Pope.[2]

From this point on, his comments on the need to preserve the alliance with the King of Denmark come near straight repetition of Pembroke's speech of 7 March. No proposal for supply resulted, because such men as Delbridge fell back on the proposals to settle the King's estate as a substitute for supply. Rudyerd's formula that before the end of the Parliament they would give the King enough 'to make him safe at home and feared abroad'[3] was never achieved. Yet if this represents a consistent Pembroke–Rudyerd position, it means that room for compromise between Pembroke and Buckingham existed. It means that the basis existed for a negotiated settlement between Pembroke and Buckingham in terms of peace with France and war with Spain. Coryton's statement, right at the end of the Parliament, that it would do much good if the King would proclaim open war with Spain, would become central.[4] Pembroke, then, would be facing the same problem which faced Pym in 1640–1: how to get the House of Commons to finance

[1] H.M.C. Buccleuch, iii. 273; Lords' Debates, p. 122; Harl. 6445, ff. 22–5.
[2] 12–20, f. 80^v.
[3] 12–20, ff. 41^r–42^r.
[4] 12–22, f. 53^v.

a settlement which could not exist until they had already financed it.[1]

Pembroke may have found the House of Commons uninterested in his war, but they were more willing to help him to put pressure on the Duke. They were diverted by attempts to interrogate the Council of War set up under the 1624 subsidy Act, which were unsuccessful, but the question whether the Council of War's advice had been followed led naturally on to another, more congenial to Pembroke: was it good for the state that all things should be guided by the Duke's 'single counsel'? Long, Turner,[2] Coryton, and Eliot, all Pembroke men, were prominent in putting this question. As Eliot put it on 10 March, there was little reason to give 'while affairs are not guided with the public counsel'.[3] One of the best ways of cutting Buckingham down to size would be the elevation of the official Privy Council—one possible reason why its members showed so little enthusiasm to stop the attacks on the Duke. As the case of the *St. Peter* ran into difficulties, this increasingly came to seem the most promising line of attack on the Duke. On 11 March, the Commons decided, by a majority of six, not to take the case of the *St. Peter* further for the time being.[4] Eliot and Digges, the enthusiasts for the French alliance, were tellers for the minority.

Immediately this case was dropped, another Pembroke man stepped into the breach: Dr. Turner. Turner offered six queries, which provided the agenda for Commons' proceedings against Buckingham right down to the drafting of articles of impeachment in May. He asked whether, by common fame, the general cause of evils in the kingdom was the Lord Admiral, whether his being Admiral was the cause of the King's loss of his control of the Channel, whether unreasonable gifts to the Duke and his kindred were the cause of impairing the King's revenue, whether the multiplicity of offices held by the Duke and his dependants was the cause of the ill government of the kingdom, whether recusants were increased because his mother and father-in-law were known

---

[1] See below, pp. 300–2 for the debate on Carleton's report of his mission to France.

[2] For further evidence on the Turner–Pembroke connection, see Keeler, pp. 367–8. Turner also witnessed a codicil to the will of Lord Cavendish, Earl of Devonshire, the first man to name the Duke. P.R.O. PROB 11/154, f. 38.

[3] 12–20, f. 29ᵛ. The most famous speech on this subject was that of Sir William Walter. 12–20, f. 63; S.P. 16/23/37.   [4] *C.J.* 835.

papists, whether he was a cause of scandal through sale of offices, and whether his being Lord Admiral was the cause of the ill success of the Cadiz action.[1] It was a comprehensive charge, made the harder to rebut because it was cast in interrogative form. From then on, as the Lord Keeper put it on 29 March, 'Your committees have walked in the steps of Turner.'[2] This was the plain and literal truth. The King complained of Turner, and rashly asked the Commons to investigate his conduct. The committee, under the chairmanship of Christopher Wandesford, adopted the brilliant procedural stroke of transforming the investigation of the King's complaint against Turner into the investigation of whether Turner's charges were justified. The committee could thus continue to prepare the case against Buckingham while appearing to obey the King's commands.[3]

The committee duly investigated misemployment of revenue, engrossing of offices, and the sending of ships to La Rochelle. Harley, for the Duke, interestingly attempted to isolate this grievance from the others and send it on alone, perhaps hoping that its investigation would diminish the pro-French mood of the Commons.[4] In all this, there was no sign of any willingness to prosecute the war. Weston was entitled to his comment that the Commons showed more mind to stir up anger at home than to resist it from abroad. The introduction of the Tonnage and Poundage bill, which a number of members had been prepared to pass at the beginning of the session, merely produced a resolution that impositions were one of the causes of the evils of the kingdom. Almost in the same breath, members complained of failures to supply convoys for merchant ships.[5] Pym and Hoby employed the recusancy issue, about which they cared profoundly, to attack the Lord President of the North, Lord Scrope, who was married to the Duke's sister-in-law. Pym and one of the Yorkshire members inspired a search of the signet office, to see whether a pardon issued for priests was genuine. A Dorset member complained of

---

[1] For the text of Turner's queries, see S.P. 16/22/71. This exploitation of the interrogative form was a technique often used by Pembroke.
[2] 12–21, f. 104ᵛ.
[3] Wandesford's reports of 25 March and 28 April are in S.P. 16/23/68, together with some later notes which may have been taken by Eliot. This paper may have been taken when Eliot's study was searched in May.
[4] 12–20, f. 58ᵛ.
[5] 12–20, ff. 62ᵛ–63ᵛ.

the coasts being guarded by soldiers, saying the soldiers were dangerous, and not to be kept there.[1]

Apart from occasional diversions, such as a bill for the preservation of salmon, reported by Coryton,[2] this agenda took up all the time from 11 March to 27 March. On 27 March, the Commons at last resolved to consider supply. They decided to vote three subsidies and three-fifteenths, about a third of the King's military commitments for that year. At the same time, they decided, on the strength of Eliot's regular series of precedents, not to embody this grant of supply in a bill until their grievances were redressed. In this context, there was no legitimate room for doubt that supply was being made conditional on the fall of Buckingham, nor that the supply being offered on these uninviting terms was so small that it would force the King to raise substantial unparliamentary taxation as well. The next day, Weston delivered a message from the King that he wanted to address both Houses at Whitehall, and in the meantime, all proceedings were to cease. The Commons had made their challenge, and it had been taken up.

III

On 29 March, at Whitehall, the King ordered the Commons to stop their attack on Buckingham. He apparently nailed his colours to the mast in defence of the Duke. The Lord Keeper claimed that though Turner's speech was apparently aimed at the Duke, it was really intended to wound the honour and government of the King and of his father. He said the King would not tolerate such proceedings against the meanest of his servants, and said the King accused the Commons of trying to 'pull out of his bosom' those who were closest to him. He then said that the King had commanded him to pay tribute to the sincerity and the caution of the Duke's proceedings, 'and therefore his Majesty cannot believe that the aim is at the Duke of Buckingham, but . . . your proceedings do expressly wound the honour and government of himself and of his father'. He therefore delivered the King's 'express and final command' to cease this 'unparliamentary inquisition'. He objected to conditional supply, and said that the delayed supply, so far from being enough to make the King 'safe at home and feared abroad'

---

[1] 12–20, f. 90ᵛ. On the search of the Signet Office, see f. 76ᵛ.
[2] C.J. 842, 12–20, f. 89ᵛ. The bill was re-committed, and got away.

was so small 'as contrariwise it exposeth him to danger and dis-
tress'. He said the King could endure no longer delay, and that
unless the Commons voted further supply, without condition
direct or indirect, before Saturday next they would be dissolved.
Charles himself ended the performance by reminding them
of their share of responsibility for the outbreak of the war. 'You
may remember that in the time of my blessed father then you did
with your counsels and your actions persuade both my father and
me to break the treaties', though some seed of doubt appears in
Charles's next words: 'I confess I was your instrument.' He concluded: 'Remember that Parliaments are altogether in my power
for the calling, sitting, and continuance of them, therefore as I
find the fruits of them either good or evil, they are to continue or
not to be.'[1] For the first time, the King, in public, had called the
survival of Parliaments into question. When he compared his
obligations, and his needs, with the sum on conditional offer from
the Commons, it was hard to see how he could do less. Even if
there had been no Buckingham to consider, fighting an effective
war on three subsidies and three-fifteenths would have been a
plain impossibility. These speeches were an impressive performance, but this public commitment to the Duke would have stood
a better chance of silencing his critics if it had come rather earlier
in the Parliament. Both the wording and the timing of his message
gave the impression that the small number of subsidies resolved
on was as great a cause of offence as the attack on the Duke. Charles
took up this uncompromising stance on 29 March, only to retreat
from it on 29 April. What happened during the intervening month?

The Commons did not retreat in the face of this show of authority. The next day, Eliot was chiefly concerned to vindicate the
Commons from the charge that their proceedings, being based on
common fame, were 'unparliamentary'. Later on 30 March, the
Commons were summoned to the Lords, and treated to a long
self-exculpation by Buckingham, who protested his devotion to
the war with Spain, his belief in the French alliance, that he had
never done anything by single counsel, and that 'in all the world
I have not £5,000 *per annum*'.[2] He finally told them that the King
gave them leave to proceed with their grievances. It is here that
the ambiguity of the word 'grievances' is crucial. It was possible

---

[1] The text of the King's and Lord Keeper's speeches is taken from Whitelocke's fair reports, 12–21, ff. 103–7.   [2] 12–21, ff. 114–15.

to believe or pretend to believe, that this speech meant that Buckingham intended to stand trial and be acquitted. The gesture would be in character, but anyone who believed Charles would permit him to make it was equally likely to believe Buckingham's statement about his income. Most of the rest of the week was devoted to a Remonstrance defending the Commons against the charge of unparliamentary proceedings. Buckingham was named in the Remonstrance, in spite of a protest by Weston, who said that Buckingham had been named in the hope that they would not name him back again.[1] The Remonstrance was presented to the King on 4 April, and he said he would give no answer to it. The Parliament then adjourned for Easter. In spite of the King's ultimatum, it had voted no further supply.[2]

This is the point at which a dissolution might reasonably have been expected. The King had staked his authority in defence of Buckingham, and been met only by a Remonstrance which named the Duke again. It might have been supposed that this was the real point of confrontation.

Yet it was the day after the adjournment for Easter that Rudyerd wrote to Nethersole to say that 'The storms of this Parliament have been very high, but I hope they now well are overblown.' At first sight, this comment, at this date, does not appear to make sense. The charges against Buckingham were still there, and so was the King's opposition to them. What then had changed? It is perhaps a good start to look at the remainder of Rudyerd's letter. He sent Nethersole the speech of 'a friend' (possibly his own speech of 23 March), to assure him the Palatinate was not forgotten in Parliament. He said the Commons were giving as much as could possibly be granted in a year. 'Besides, they intend to make his Majesty an orderly warrantable revenue too, proportionable to his ordinary charge.' He added 'the greatest of all', a West India Company, to be regulated and established by Act of Parliament, thereby to settle and secure against the intrusion of any powerful hand, 'so that the subject shall make war against the King of Spain, and his Majesty shall have no more to do at sea, but to defend the coasts'.[3] This proposal, which was in fact the first

[1] 12–21, f. 121ᵛ. Whitelocke's report on Weston's protest is laconic: 'sed non allocatur'.
[2] The Commons resolved to vote a fourth subsidy nearly a month later, on 26 April. 12–21, f. 163ᵛ. A suggestion that methods of assessment should be improved was rejected.   [3] S.P. 16/24/48.

business after the recess, had been introduced by Digges as a way
of financing the war without burdening poor men's purses with
subsidies.[1] It would have the advantage for war partisans of
ensuring that war with Spain was beyond Buckingham's power
to stop, and the further advantage of diminishing his control over
its conduct. From Pembroke's point of view, it was a scheme
which had much to commend it. Meanwhile, Blainville, the de-
tested French Ambassador, was dismissed, and negotiations to
preserve peace with France were being conducted, with some
apparent success, by Sir Dudley Carleton in Paris.

That some sort of compromise had been considered during these
weeks is clear from the speeches of the Duke's partisans on 2 May,
when the Commons finally decided to transmit their charges to
the Lords. When Weston, on 29 April, announced a reversal of
policy and said the King gave the Commons leave to proceed, he
had apparently not intended that Buckingham should be brought
to trial before the Lords. On 2 May, Sir William Becher, clerk of
the Council, said, 'Though the King gave us leave to proceed
against the Duke, yet rather in general to reform hereafter
than upon his particular.' Sir George Goring said that if they
presented formal charges, 'We are upon a great rock. By this
course, we aim at one of two ends, either to remove him or to
reform him.' For the second, he said, the grievance would reform
itself. Harley assured the Commons that if they 'ask reformation
of this gent.' the King would cast the eye of love upon them.
Clearly, these three well-informed partisans of the Duke had
believed a compromise had been worked out.[2] It is perhaps in this
context that we should see the insistence of Harley and Sir Robert
Pye that the charges should be presented to the King and not the
Lords.[3] Since no negotiations for any such compromise have
survived on paper, we can only attempt to surmise what its main
elements may have been, and what may have been the reasons for
its failure.

The existence of negotiations was remarked upon in passing by
the French and Venetian Ambassadors, but, except for one casual

---

[1] 12–20, f. 45^v (14 March).   [2] Grosvenor. ff. 21–2.

[3] 12–21, f. 173^v. The key speeches in favour of going to the Lords were made
by Long and by Bristol's friend Strangeways. Sir John Finch's plea that the
Duke should first be allowed to clear himself of Bristol's charge, so that the
House could show 'that they delight reformation more than ruine' was rejected.
f. 174^v; Grosvenor f. 23.

allusion by Mende, dated after 9 May, to the possibility of Buckingham giving up offices, there is no hint of what they may have contained.[1] There is, then, only one way of looking for the outlines of a possible compromise: that is to look at the public demands of the Duke's critics, and to consider what concessions might have satisfied them, while sufficiently saving the face of the King and the Duke.

It is remarkable, when we look at the public attacks on the Duke, how little sign there is of any ideological gulf dividing him from his critics. The *St. Peter* case had shown the one policy issue on which Pembroke was unwilling to yield: that there should be no French war. This, however, was a demand to which Buckingham and Charles had no objection in principle, if means could be found to achieve it. The heart of the case against the Duke is to be found in Dr. Turner's queries, and in the material produced in support of them.

In Turner's queries, grievances against the Duke took a form which should be familiar to students of medieval baronial crises. The complaints can be grouped under three heads: monopoly of counsel, monopoly of patronage, and inefficient discharge of his duties. These were the sort of complaints which would be met, not by major changes of policy, but by a reshuffle among the great officers, and by increasing the standing and independence of those newly appointed. For the King to take the advice of a Privy Council which he had himself appointed could hardly be regarded as an intolerable sacrifice of principle. Beyond this, Turner's queries concentrate on two themes. One is 'the impairing of the King's revenue', by unreasonable gifts to the Duke and his kindred. This was again a familiar feature of medieval baronial complaints against favourites. A traditional remedy for this grievance would be the appointment of a Lord Treasurer who was not the Duke's partisan, and the allowing to him of a considerable say in the disposal of patronage. There would have been no trouble about dismissing Marlborough, the existing Lord Treasurer, who was more than ready to resign on grounds of old age. The sympathy shown to the Commons' revenue proposals by Weston, Chancellor

---

[1] P.R.O. 31/3/63, f. 63ᵛ. The Bishop of Mende, Richelieu's nephew and the Queen's Almoner, took over as acting French Ambassador on the departure of Blainville. Mende's objective seems to have been to widen the breach between King and Parliament, rather than to help one side. *C.S.P.Ven. 1625–6*, p. 390.

of the Exchequer, prompts a suspicion as to who such a Lord Treasurer might have been. Weston appears to have been an Arundel man,[1] and his appointment could have done something to reconcile Arundel to a settlement which, based as it was on the continuation of the Spanish war, had little to offer to his views on foreign policy. The other central grievance expressed by Turner was 'the Duke being Admiral', and more specifically 'the Duke staying at home being Admiral'. There was, significantly, no public attack on the Duke's tenure of Court and Bedchamber offices, the real seat of his power, but there was a widespread feeling, encapsulated by Pym, that he held 'offices not in their nature to be joined'. In time of war, the case for having a Lord Admiral whose other duties did not tie him constantly to the court was a strong one. The Duke could have resigned the Lord Admiralship while retaining the dominant position at court which was the real centre of his power.

Moreover, a suitable candidate for the position of Lord Admiral was to hand, though no evidence survives that he was considered. He was the Earl of Warwick. Warwick's credentials as a seaman, which were the first thing being asked of a Lord Admiral, were beyond dispute, and he was deeply involved in preparing his own private fleet to contribute to a naval war against Spain. His vehement pro-French sympathies could have helped to reassure Pembroke and Richelieu that the navy would not be used for anti-French provocation at sea, while his brother Holland, who was one of the Duke's closest friends at the time, could have warmly recommended the appointment to the Duke. His speech of 6 March, seconding Lord Montagu's motion to ask the Commons for supply for the war, showed that he was prepared to put the prosecution of the war above the prosecution of the Duke.[2] He thus subscribed to what was the central point of all the Buckingham–Pembroke reconciliations of the decade.[3]

The object of this reconstruction is not to suggest that these

---

[1] M. C. V. Alexander, *My Lord Treasurer* (Chapel Hill, 1975), pp. 12, 39, 121, 173–5. The feebleness of Marlborough's signature indicates his readiness for retirement.

[2] *H.M.C. Buccleuch*, iii. 272; 12–20, f 56[r].

[3] If any such scheme was considered, it seems highly unlikely that it was mentioned to Warwick. In the debate on the West India Company on 14 April, Sir Nathaniel Rich, who was deeply in Warwick's confidence, insisted that the Company should not pay the Lord Admiral's tenths. 12–21, f. 129[v].

were actually the changes contemplated: on that point the evidence is missing. Its object is to show that the gulf between Pembroke and Buckingham was not a gulf of principle, and therefore could have been bridged by alterations of men rather than of measures. It is, in particular, designed to show that the case against the Duke had been put forward in a way which did not make a compromise impossible. Only two ideological issues emerged from the charges. One was the Duke's patronage of recusants, which was made the subject of one of Turner's queries. Turner, significantly, put this in the context of the Duke's mother and father-in-law being known papists. He thereby put it in its correct proportion, as being, not a pure issue of religion, but another symptom of the Duke's readiness to patronize all his kindred, whether suitable or unsuitable. The removal of one officer, Lord Scrope, President of the North and husband of the Duke's sister-in-law, would have been a necessary sacrifice on this front.[1] It is perhaps in this context that we should place a remarkable petition from Wentworth to Conway, dated January 1626, asking for the Presidency of the North, and saying he would think nothing of the office unless he could receive it with a 'special obligation to the Duke'.[2] For Pembroke himself, his promotion to Lord Steward, which was concluded immediately after the Parliament, was being rumoured by John Chamberlain before it.[3] It is perhaps significant, in the context of such proposals, that the 'Cotton' speech, prepared for the Parliament of 1625, draws a long contrast between Buckingham and the Earl of Somerset, which is strongly in Somerset's favour.[4] The chief point of contrast was that in Somerset's day 'all things of moment were carried by public debate at the Council table'. If Buckingham had retained a position on the scale of Somerset's, he could not be said to have been 'pulled out of his Majesty's bosom'. It is surely interesting that Buckingham's leading critics said nothing to close such a line of retreat.

The one ideological obstacle to a compromise was the issue of

[1] *H.M.C. 12th Report 4*, p. 477 for Lady Scrope's recognition that her husband's removal was one of the things the Duke's critics were demanding.
[2] *C.S.P.D. 1625–6*, vol. xviii, no 110.   [3] Chamberlain, 19 Jan. 1626.
[4] *N.P.* ii. 85–6; Phelips MSS. 216/19. The comparison is more explicit in Phelips's text than in Eliot's and carries the addition: 'as some members of this House can testify from his own charge unto them'. The Eliot text says that under Somerset 'all things of moment carried by *public counsel*' (Eliot's phrase of 1626), while the Phelips text makes the more explicit assertion that 'all things of moment were carried by public debate at the Council Table'. See above, 243n.

Arminianism, but this still appears to have been a minority issue. Buckingham's commitment to Arminianism, at York House in February 1626, was too recent, and too little publicized, to have yet created a major issue for most people. A few people felt very strongly indeed about it, and Sherland, in presenting the articles of impeachment to the Lords, accused the Duke of being 'the principal patron and supporter of a semi-pelagian, semi-popish faction, dangerous to the church and state, lately set on foot among us'. It is perhaps significant that Buckingham answered this accusation by saying, perfectly correctly, that 'this he had no charge to accuse me of from the Commons'. It was, as yet, the accusation of a few people, and not of the whole Commons.[1]

It seems probable that the issue was discussed between Buckingham and Pembroke. On 22 April, Rudyerd wrote another newsletter to Nethersole, in which he still appeared to believe that a compromise might work. He said, 'I hope we have ridden out all our storms, for his Majesty hath given us leave to proceed with our grievances, and as he hath already shown himself a good master, so he will now express himself to be a good king, which is his greater part.' In this letter, he made an interestingly ambiguous statement about Arminianism. 'My Lord Chamberlain in his opinion doth not think it fit his Majesty should stand neutral towards the Arminians, lest he should give them too much countenance, and make the Prince of Orange more confident and obstinate than otherwise he could be.'[2] At about the same time, Richard Montagu feared that Buckingham was about to abandon him.[3] Perhaps the possible lines of a resolution of this question were hinted at in the Commons when Pym reported the case of Richard Montagu on 17 April. Perrott, Pembroke's supporter, proposed to send the case to the learned divines, and not to the Lords as an impeachment. Harley, Buckingham's supporter and a passionate opponent of Arminianism, proposed to entreat the King that there should be no more writing in this case until he had heard what the Commons had to say.[4] This seemed to leave

---

[1] *L.J.* 611; *Lords' Debates*, p. 193.   [2] S.P. 16/25/46.
[3] *Correspondence of John Cosin*, ed. G. Ornsby, Surtees Soc., vol. lii (1868), p. 89.
[4] 12–21, ff. 135ᵛ–136ʳ. On 12 June, Fanshawe said he was 'glad to hear that the Arminians shall be by proclamation cried down', 12–22, f. 52ᵛ. Wherever Fanshawe heard this version of the 1626 Proclamation, he did not hear it in the House of Commons.

open a retreat to the *status quo ante* of 1623, when the episcopal bench had included some Arminians, as well as some doctrinal Calvinists, and a decent silence among the Arminians had made it possible to avoid the imposition of strict uniformity. There is every reason to believe that Pembroke and Buckingham, if not Charles or Pym, would have found such a compromise entirely tolerable.

If there were such good grounds for a compromise settlement, why was it not achieved? What happened between 6 April and 2 May, which forced the case of Buckingham to come before the Lords as an issue presented for public trial? If a compromise was being worked out, why did so many people fail to accept it? And when the compromise failed, why did the King still allow the Parliament to remain in session?

These questions call for a detailed scrutiny of the debates after Easter. On 13 April, when the recess ended, the Commons were innocuously occupied with the bill for continuance of statutes. Discussion of whether shipwrights were within the statute of Artificers, of which laws on apparel were in force, and whether to continue 13 Elizabeth, allowing purveyors in some cases to take victuals within five miles of Oxford or Cambridge, sounded like business as usual.[1] Something more immediate in its implications was introduced on the second day after the recess, with Digges's proposal for setting up a West India Company. This proposal had figured prominently in Rudyerd's letter of 6 April. It was modelled on the Dutch West India Company, and involved the raising of £200,000 per annum by private investment for the creation of a company which would carry on a private enterprise naval war against the Spanish Indies. It is significant that Digges had first floated this proposal, on 14 March, by saying that 'a subsidy burthens poor men'. Here was a way of tapping the under-assessed wealth of the gentry, by inviting them to invest voluntarily and for their own profit in the prosecution of a Spanish war. Rudyerd, repeating the words of his financial offer at the beginning of the Parliament, said that this was intended to make the King 'safe at home and feared abroad'. Pym, one of the real enthusiasts for a Spanish war, joined into the proposal that the preservation of this company should be made an article of a peace treaty, and Delbridge, the enthusiast for the outports, proposed

[1] 12–21, ff. 127–8, 132ᵛ.

that its members should be free in all companies whatsoever.[1] At first glance, this debate gives the impression of a universal enthusiasm, but this impression is rapidly diminished if we ask who did not take part in it. The speakers were the traditional enthusiasts for a Spanish war, Digges, Rudyerd, Mansell, Earle, Rich, Pym, Delbridge, and, it is interesting to note, Glanville. There was a deafening silence from those among the Duke's critics who were not public supporters of the Spanish war, from those for whom Arundel and Bristol, rather than Pembroke, were their likely champions. Among the Duke's most vehement critics, Wandesford, Selden, Strangeways, and Kirton had nothing to say. There is no reason to believe that the creation of such a company would have met any of their resentments, or discouraged them from prosecuting the Duke. Even among the war supporters, Eliot's silence was sufficiently unusual to be regarded as ominous.

Any fears his silence might have provoked were justified by the debates of 18 and 19 April. On 18 April, Sir Dudley Carleton made his report of his embassy to France. The possible significance of this embassy is suggested by Weston's report that Carleton had been employed 'for the satisfaction of the House'; Carleton in fact brought back a remarkably successful story of negotiation completed, but if the fears expressed in the *St. Peter* case were to be stilled, it was essential that this report should carry conviction. Carleton reported that the ships used against Rochelle were to come home as soon as mariners could be paid to sail them, that the Huguenots would have peace, and that 'we have it by commission under the King of France's hand' that the merchants should have their seized goods restored to them. Even more encouragingly for war supporters such as Pembroke, Carleton reported that 'the French King is ready to join with his Majesty in the affairs of Germany': in other words, the war could be continued with the vital asset of a French alliance.[2] To achieve this end, it was necessary that the English should 'really show themselves': that they should make some concrete contribution to the war against Spain. Thus, in bringing back apparent peace with France, Carleton merely brought back the question of immediate supply. In removing one obstacle to a compromise, he had merely drawn

---

[1] 12–21, ff. 128ᵛ–131ᵛ; 12–20, f. 45ʳ: Christopher Thompson, 'The Origins of the Politics of the Parliamentary Middle Group 1625–1629', *T.R.H.S.* (1972), 80–1.   [2] 12–21, f. 137ʳ.

attention to another. At once Eliot was on his feet to say that he did not believe Carleton's report. He said a similar agreement with the French had been reported to the Parliament at Oxford.[1] That the Parliament's failure to provide supply might have contributed to the agreement's ill success does not seem to have occurred to him. More significantly, Digges, Carleton's former junior at the Hague embassy, was unwilling to believe his report. This was the occasion on which Digges denounced his old friend as a 'stranger in Israel,' and said that all of these negotiations gave too much power to one subject. If there was a compromise, Digges did not appear to want to participate in it.[2] He had been slow to commit himself to the attack on the Duke, but having done so he seems to have been reluctant to draw back. Events after the Parliament suggest that lesser men were more at risk than Pembroke if the Duke survived. Having committed themselves to an attack on the Duke, men like Digges and Eliot were more at risk than Pembroke if it did not succeeed. In any likely compromise, they would be more vulnerable than men of the standing of Pembroke.

In these circumstances, May and Weston had an uphill task in attempting to move again for immediate supply.[3] Weston was entirely right to warn the Commons that the lack of a supply 'proportionable to the great actions whereupon we have engaged him will force him to new counsels', but the rightness of Weston's arithmetic did not add to the persuasiveness of his speech. Sandys attempted to put the case for supply, while aware, as ever, of the limitations of English resources, but Eliot repeated that 'the whole kingdom suffers under the too great power of man', and Digges proposed to lay aside all other business until the question of the Duke was disposed of.[4] It was proving harder to call the

---

[1] 12–21, ff. 137ʳ– 138ᵛ; *C.J.* 846. On French pressure for English intervention with a land force in Europe, see S.P. 78/77, ff. 211ᵛ, 238ᵛ, 308ᵛ. Secretary Coke believed the cost of such a plan made it impossible.

[2] 12–21, ff. 137ʳ–138ᵛ, 142ʳ–143ᵛ, 137ʳ. It is possibly Eliot's rejection of Carleton's report of his French embassy to which Carleton alluded on 17 May, when he said he had been 'bitterly offended by Sir John Eliot, by a declamation made by him against me'. 12–22, f. 16

[3] 12–21, f. 142ʳ. Weston's 'new counsels' speech is perhaps even more interesting than the later, and more famous, speech to the same effect by Carleton. Its timing, in the context of proposals to revive the war, underlines the theme that war and Parliament were not easily combined.

[4] 12–21, ff. 143ʳ–144ᵛ.

Commons off than it had been to call them in, and impossible to induce them to vote supply. This, again, might have seemed a logical moment for a dissolution. After 20 April, what did the King hope to obtain from the Parliament? Why did he still think it worth keeping it in session?

A few hours before these speeches, an event had happened which may have done much to call out the latent distrust of Buckingham which Digges and Eliot already felt. On 19 April Edward Kirton, the Earl of Hertford's steward, introduced the case of the Earl of Bristol into the Commons. Kirton presented to the Commons Bristol's charge that Buckingham had been responsible for the loss of the Palatinate, and offered Bristol's servant Gresley as a witness to the charge.[1] Kirton thus offered the Bristol case as a tailor-made opportunity for those members who did not regard a Spanish war as a substitute for the Duke's removal, and, at the same time, called in doubt the Duke's anti-Spanish credentials in the eyes of war supporters like Digges and Eliot. On 22 April, when the Commons debated whether common fame was a sufficient ground to accuse the Duke, one of the key contributions was made by Littleton. He, together with Noy, was named to the Lords by Bristol twelve days later as one of his counsel.[2] In the week from 22 April to 29 April, men like Selden, Strangeways, Wandesford, and Kirton, who were not war supporters, made much of the running against the Duke.

On 29 April, they received further reinforcement from a petition submitted to the Commons by Bristol's son, George Digby.[3] Digby was not officially a party to his father's case, but claimed that he was entitled to petition the Commons because he did not want to inherit a 'tainted honour'. He accused Buckingham of conspiring with Gondomar to carry the Prince to Spain, of encouraging the Spaniards to hope for the Prince's conversion to popery, and of winning the support of the 1624 Parliament by a false relation. On 4 May, Bristol's partisans produced a further witness to show that the Duke had adored the Host in Spain.[4]

---

[1] 12–21, ff. 140–1.
[2] *Lords' Debates*, p. 176.   [3] 12–21, ff. 170^v–172^r.
[4] 12–21, ff. 187–9. The extent to which Bristol could undercut the position Buckingham had built up with the House of Commons is suggested by Selden's proposal of 9 June to send for the 1624 Parliament Roll to see how far the Duke had abused the Houses in his Relation of the negotiations with Spain. 12–22, f. 50^v, S.P. 16/30/3.

In encouraging the Commons to persist with public charges against the Duke, the fact that Bristol had accused him of treason before the Lords played a crucial part. For Bristol ensured that, in some form, the Duke's conduct must be liable to a public hearing.

IV

Immediately after the introduction of the Bristol case, the Commons revived their own complaint against the Duke about the stay of the *St. Peter*. Matthews of Dartmouth, one of the merchant members concerned, complained of a further stay of English ships in France, and Eliot again attempted to induce the Commons to blame the French embargoes against English shipping on the Duke's handling of the *St. Peter* case.[1] This time, the Duke received a much stronger official defence than he had done at the beginning of the Parliament. Sir Humphrey May said the King took responsibility for the act, while Carleton argued passionately that the *St. Peter* was not the reason why English ships were embargoed in France. He put the blame for the pursuing of the case on the French Ambassador, who, he said, 'did mortally hate' the Duke. He was particularly concerned by the weakening of the English negotiating position if the condemned themselves: they would then be prevented from saying that the French had done them injustice. In the face of this official discouragement, Eliot, Long, Earle, Pym, and Digges persisted in demanding to have the *St. Peter* voted a grievance. No consensus seemed likely to emerge, and the issue was put to the vote. The House, which had previously voted by a majority of 6 to lay the issue aside, now voted it a grievance by a majority of 37.[2]

The quickening of the pace continued on the next day, 2 May. On that day, Bristol avowed his son's petition to the Commons.[3] The Commons then debated whether to send their charges against the Duke to the King or to the Lords. Sir John Finch, one of the Duke's keenest defenders, tried to induce the Commons to defer their charge until the Duke had answered Bristol's charge, only to be answered by Sir Lewis Dives that Bristol had given authority for the laying of his charge before the Commons. Goring, Becher, Harley, Pye, and interestingly, Pembroke's client Coryton

[1] *C.J.* 851; 12–21, f. 170.
[2] 12–21, ff. 169–70; Grosvenor, ff. 5–8.   [3] S.P. 16/30/3.

spoke in favour of going to the King, which the first three saw as the way to 'the reformation of the Duke'. Long, also a Pembroke man, disingenuously answered that they should go to the Lords because the business would be 'too tedious' for the King. Digges spoke for going to the Lords, and so did Bristol's former junior in the Madrid embassy, Sir John Strangeways. The House resolved accordingly.[1]

From 2 May onwards, the Commons were climbing on the back of the Bristol case in order to secure a hearing for their own charges. Yet, though the Bristol case emboldened them by ensuring that they would enjoy powerful and informed support in the Lords, it also raised the stakes. The King's commitment against Bristol was so painfully apparent that Commons' complaints in support of Bristol would incur the King's certain wrath. By gaining more Lords' support, the Commons also faced severe royal displeasure. Some members appear to have appreciated this fact.

The only weapons the Commons still possessed were the uncompleted bills of subsidy and of Tonnage and Poundage. The subsidies had now been increased to four, and the Tonnage and Poundage bill was still in committee, whence it was ultimately reported by Noy on 5 June. In addition, the proposals to increase the King's estate were revived on 4 May, when they were supported by Drake, Perrott, Bish, and Eliot.[2] The Pembroke men evidently still hoped that some part of the Duke's power was for sale:[3] as Rudyerd said on 5 May, 'I cannot believe that the King will do so dishonourably as to take our money and refuse our justice.'[4]

On 8 and 10 May, the Commons presented their charges to the Lords, with great eloquence and at great length.[5] Digges offered a preamble. The first three articles, concerning engrossing and purchasing of offices, were presented by Pembroke's kinsman Sir Edward Herbert. The complaints of the Duke's purchasing of offices were concentrated on the offices of Lord Admiral and Lord Warden of the Cinque Ports. The charges on the Duke's failure to guard the narrow seas and on the *St. Peter* were managed

---

[1] 12–21, ff. 173–4. [2] Grosvenor, ff. 36–8.
[3] *C.J.* 855; 12–21, f. 178. [4] 12–21, f. 179ᵛ.
[5] The correct order of speeches was established by Tite, p. 198n. See also Duchy of Cornwall True Relation, f. 89ʳ⁻ᵛ.

by Selden, the extortion of money from the East India Company and the case of the ships at La Rochelle by Glanville. The sale of honours and of places of judicature were managed by Christopher Sherland, in place of Edward Whitby, who had fallen ill. The charge that the Duke had exhausted the King's revenue by exorbitant grants for his kindred and others was managed by Pym, and Wandesford undertook the dangerous charge about the unauthorized giving of medicine to James on his death-bed. Sir John Eliot concluded the proceedings by an 'aggravation'. To modern historians, this has always appeared the central attack on the Duke, but it was not obviously so to contemporaries. In the State Papers, there is a three-folio calendar of the main events of the Parliament, apparently compiled by a well-informed partisan of the Duke. In general, this account presents the proceedings of the Commons in a provocative light, and it has missed very little.[1] It is therefore striking that the only incident recorded in this account under 8 May is that the Commons asked for the commitment of the Duke on Digby and Bristol's charge. The fact that the Commons presented articles of impeachment against the Duke to the Lords nowhere receives a mention. Its author was much concerned about the sending for Parliament Roll of 1624, and about the revival of the grievance of impositions on 24 May (though he noted that it was accompanied by 'divers other grievances which were friendly'). Of all the main events of the Parliament, only the Commons' impeachment of the Duke goes unrecorded by him.

This sense of priorities is intelligible. Once the Commons had transmitted their charges to the Lords, they had shot their bolt: since they had no control over the examination of witnesses, they could not ensure that their case would receive a hearing. Nor could they prevent the King from dissolving the Parliament whenever he chose. If the King was only refraining from dissolution in order to secure the condemnation of Bristol, then the priority given to the Bristol case is well-judged: it was the

---

[1] S.P. 16/30/3. This account is probably in the hand of Sir Robert Heath. In fact, sequestration was moved by Kirton and resolved on 8 May, and a further proposal to ask for the Duke's commitment was carried in a division on 9 May. The vote against the Duke was now by 225 to 106: the majority against him appeared to have increased since 29 April from 37 to 106. The numbers voting, 333 in the first division and 331 in the second remained, remarkably constant.

only thing which kept the Parliament in being. The Commons, then, had little significant new business after 10 May. They had, though, a good deal of drama. On 11 May the King imprisoned Digges and Eliot for their speeches to the Lords on the impeachment. The particular ground of offence was the presentation of the charge that Buckingham was responsible for the death of James, in which both of them contrived, perhaps unwittingly, to give the impression that they regarded Charles as an accessory. Charles's wrath at this charge is natural, and he did what he did not dare do in the case of the five members: he arrested them in open Parliament, in the face of the House.[1] It is hardly surprising that the next morning the Commons had a 'sad face', and 'sat long silent, no man offering to speak'. When the Speaker tried to say he was sorry,[2] 'the house cry sit down'. The silence was ultimately broken by Sir Dudley Carleton, who made a long official statement claiming that the members had exceeded their instructions, and then added what appeared to be a personal plea for the survival of Parliaments. He said that 'This manner of Parliaments hath been altered by new counsels.' These 'new counsels' he thought had destroyed the prosperity of other countries along with their liberty: 'In this house and kingdom we look like men; in other places they look rather like ghosts than men.' He warned the Commons that a 'tumultuary liberty' might bring such new counsels upon them. It was a fair warning, almost certainly delivered in the sincere hope that Parliaments would continue, but the only result was to divert the Commons' wrath from the King to Carleton himself. Lowther noted: 'This speech exceedingly disliked, though I see not the cause. Somebody much to blame for it.'[3] Wandesford anticipated Oscar Wilde by saying they might lose one member but to lose two was 'more than ordinary',[4] and the debate rambled on till it was rescued from incipient chaos by Pym. He proposed that the members of both Houses should be asked to take a protestation that Digges and Eliot did not speak the words of which the King complained. Thirty-six Lords, as well as the Commons, took this Protestation,[5] and in

---

[1] Grosvenor, f. 77.   [2] Grosvenor, f. 78; 12–22, f. 8.
[3] 12–22, f. 9; Rich, 12 May; *Lowther*, p. 23.   [4] Grosvenor, f. 86.
[5] *L.J.* 627; *H.M.C. Buccleuch*, iii. 292. Lord Montagu said only six or eight Lords did not make the Protestation as intended. See *Lords' Debates*, 196–200 for the debate on the Protestation. Some Lords took it in equivocal forms. The outright refusers appear to have been Scrope, Laud, Neile, Bridgewater,

the face of this impressive list of compurgators, the King was forced to retreat. Digges and Eliot were duly released, and Dudley Carleton was raised out of the firing-line to the House of Lords, together with some other Buckingham supporters.

From the return of Eliot, on 20 May, until early June, there was little business. The Whitsun recess, together with the usual decision not to sit on Ascension Day, lost some time. Some bills went forward, such as the apparel bill, the subscription bill, and the bill to allow marriages in Lent. The bill for the abbreviation of Michaelmas term was read a first time, and Jordan's bill against adultery was re-committed. For a short while, there was the illusion of business as usual. The apparent quiet was broken on 3 June, when Kirton and Long complained of the creation of new peers. Long also complained that Arundel and Williams were being kept away from the House of Lords.[1] The most explosive new issue, Buckingham's candidature for the Chancellorship of Cambridge University, was introduced by the Bristol partisan Sir John Strangeways. The point of this issue was not the importance of the Chancellorship: Dr. Eden claimed that a Chancellor did not have much power, and no one argued with him, though those concerned with Arminian books easily could have done. The issue was symbolic. It implied a public commitment by the King, not only to Buckingham's retention of his existing offices, but to his acquisition of another. For Pym and Hoby, it was even worse to discover that in a contested election, Buckingham was the candidate of an Arminian faction. Overt Arminian support for Buckingham at this critical juncture had an effect almost like that of river capture, in which the stronger or swifter stream draws the other into its own course: by supporting him, they bound him more closely to their cause, and turned their opponents more bitterly against him. For the first time, the opposition to Buckingham was coming to have an ideological flavour which had been lacking in March, April, and May.[2] The Commons were not left to continue in this atmosphere long: on 9 June, they were interrupted by a letter from the King giving for the second time his 'last and final admonition' not to delay supply. He said the bill must pass by the end of next week, or he would be forced to

---

Holland, Carlisle, Buckingham, and Dorset, whose integrity as a reporter was in question.
[1] 12–22, f. 33ᵛ.   [2] 12–22, ff. 33, 37, 40.

take 'other resolutions'—a phrase perilously close to the 'new counsels' which had given so much offence when mentioned by Carleton. It is possible to explain the King's timing in many ways connected with the progress of the Parliament, but it is perhaps more appropriate to explain it in terms of the progress of the campaigning season. Moreover, it was nearly the end of the Parliamentary season, and, after 1625, Charles was unlikely to risk the unpopularity involved in prolonging a Parliament into the summer.

On 12 June, then, the Duke's much-tried Parliamentary team made a last effort to persuade the Commons to vote subsidies.[1] It can hardly be supposed that they had much hope of success, but there was little to be lost by the attempt. Sir Henry Poole and Sir Richard Weston first moved a subsidy, Sir Thomas Fanshawe followed by saying that if the King had required subsidies for his own occasions, he would not have supported them, but they were needed for the wars, in which religion was at stake. He was supported by Sir Edwin Sandys, Sir Robert Pye, Sir Humphrey May, Sir George Goring, Sir John Coke, Richard Spencer, Mr. Carvile, and Sir Robert Mansell, whose belligerence would seem to have triumphed over his hatred of the Duke. On the other side, Browne said the country would blame them if they gave away 'the people's money', without redress. He was supported by Newberry, Coryton, Kirton, Wandesford, Littleton, Long, Eliot, Digges, and Sir Thomas Hoby. As in the final supply debate in 1614, no clear majority seemed to emerge. Weston and Sandys made one final attempt to argue that the 'reformation' of the Duke would follow a grant of supply, but other members were no longer interested in these proposals. The crux of the debate was in the final exchange between Sir Robert Pye and Sir Nathaniel Rich. Pye wanted the question put for supply, and Rich wanted to complete a remonstrance before considering supply. It is unfortunately not clear whether a voice vote was taken, or whether a formula was patched up which avoided the putting of the question, but the upshot was that there was no proceeding with supply, and the remonstrance continued. If the Parliament had been kept in session in the hope of supply from the Commons, its usefulness was now at an end. In what had become a confrontation on whether supply should be granted without any action on the Duke, neither side was prepared

[1] 12–22, ff. 52–6.

to move first. The next morning, Sir John Eliot moved the regular end of-session motion for a collection for the clerks and officers of the House.[1] On 14 June, the remonstrance was presented to the King, who said he would give his answer the next morning. The next morning, he dissolved the Parliament.

If the final six weeks of the session are to be explained in terms of the actions of the Commons, then the key event is the failure to obtain supply on 12 June. It seems improbable that the King had kept the Parliament in session for a hope of supply which was extremely faint. The attacks on his honour by Digges and Eliot had not been pleasant, and the revival of complaint about impositions was ominous. For the King, it was a thoroughly unpleasant six weeks. He had no solid benefit to show for it, and it was never likely that he would have. It seems unlikely that he kept the Parliament in session simply in order to allow the Commons to go on talking. Perhaps, then, an attempt to search for the reasons why the King kept the Parliament in session should turn not to the House of Commons but to the House of Lords. In the Lords, events moved slowly: as Eliot complained: 'That there is a hesitation with the Lords it is too true.'

V

It was the Earl of Bristol's case, and not the Commons' impeachment, which dominated all the Lords' discussion of the Duke of Buckingham. The Bristol case was one in which the Commons were not in any official sense involved, and the Lords were not answerable to the Commons for their conduct of it. Bristol had been a bitter enemy of Buckingham ever since Buckingham and Charles's trip to Madrid, when he had been permanent ambassador in Madrid. During their stay in Madrid, both Buckingham and Charles appear to have quarrelled bitterly with Bristol, and when Bristol returned from Madrid, during the Parliament of 1624, he was in effect put under house arrest before he could appear at court and tell his story of what happened at Madrid. From 1624 to 1626, Bristol had remained at his house at Sherborne, constantly petitioning for a hearing which he never got.

It was then Bristol's desire to recover his liberty which led him to put his case in front of the House of Lords, in the form of a

[1] 12–22, f. 56ᵛ.

petition for his writ of summons and for the right to attend, and a petition to be heard as the Duke's accuser. He said he was being kept from Parliament and the King, 'lest he should discover many crimes concerning the said Duke'. He asked for a hearing, 'and this, he is most confident, will not be denied, since the high court of Parliament never refuseth to hear the poorest subject seeking for redress of wrong: nor the accusation against any, be he never so powerful'.[1] Among Bristol's charges against the Duke, there were only two which Lord Montagu regarded as being of any moment: that he had tried to convert the Prince to popery, and that for that end he had conspired with Spain and the Pope to take him to Madrid.[2] Such a charge could not be made without reflecting an implied discredit on Charles, and Montagu noted that Bristol's original petition 'cast very foul aspersions against the Duke in abuses towards the late and this King'. Whether because the King's honour had been touched, or simply because Bristol had been too much of a threat for too long, Charles and Buckingham decided not to respond to Bristol's charges by trying to hush them up, but by summoning him before the House of Lords as a delinquent. On 21 April, a message from the King was delivered to the House of Lords, saying that Bristol's petition was so devoid of duty that the King had great cause to punish it. The King said he thought the Lords knew that Bristol had been restrained for matter of state, and asked for Bristol to be sent for as a delinquent to answer for his offences in Spain and since.[3] The King was responding to Bristol's attempt to bring Buckingham to trial by attempting to bring Bristol to trial. He appears to have hoped that the Lords would condemn Bristol, as they had condemned Yelverton in 1621, without investigating his counter-charges against the Duke. From 21 April onwards, it was therefore the King, the Duke, and the Attorney General, rather than the House of Commons, who were pressing the House of Lords for a public hearing of questions which came to involve Buckingham's conduct in office. This alone was enough to torpedo any plans for a compromise settlement. The Lords were not prepared to condemn a member of their own order without hearing him in his own defence, and Bristol's defence consisted of the prosecution of Buckingham. It was thus the King himself who

---

[1] *L.J.* 563; *H.M.C. Buccleuch*, iii. 284, *C.S.P.D. 1625–6*, vol. xxv, no. 32.
[2] *H.M.C. Buccleuch*, iii. 279.   [3] *L.J.* 567; S.P. 16/25/41.

was forced by Bristol's intervention to abandon any compromise by which the charges against Buckingham would not have come before the Lords. From 21 April onwards, the King's chief reason for continuing the Parliament was his desire to secure a public condemnation of Bristol.

The Lords appear to have viewed the task which was thus thrust upon them with some distaste. When Bristol was at the Lords' bar on 1 May, Lord Montagu noted that 'in his departure he was very violent and earnest with the House to consider of their own privileges, and, turning to the bishops, besought them to look unto it because the Duke would have altered all the course of religion'.[1] In addition to the distaste caused by the palpable personal ill will between Buckingham and Bristol, the Lords were being asked to hear witnesses about many matters of high policy, touching the King very closely, which would normally have been kept confidential. On 16 May, the Earl of Clare wrote to the Earl of Exeter: 'This business of reciprocal accusation between these two Lords was ill begun for either of them, for their own defence discovers the mysteries of state, which I fear will turn little to the honour of the dead, or the living King, for now comes all abroad, instructions, letters, directions, etc.' On 14 June, when Bristol was at last allowed to begin to produce his proofs, he was given leave to produce letters containing state secrets, and yet asked to keep them secret until he was forced to use them in the course of his defence.[2] In handling the Bristol case, the Lords were being asked to sit in judgement on something which was potentially damaging to royal authority, and also on a case in which the bad blood between the parties was a painful cause of embarrassment. The Lords were a court. In such a case, seventeenth-century courts often hoped for the parties to settle out of court.

Many attempts have been made to classify the Lords of 1626 in terms of whether they were for or against Buckingham.[3] While

---

[1] *H.M.C. Buccleuch*, iii. 283.

[2] *Letters of John Holles 1587–1637*. Thoroton Soc. Record Series, xxxi (1975), ed. P.R. Seddon, p. lx; Nottingham University Library MS. Ne. C. 15, 405, f. 144. I am grateful to Mr. Richard Cust for this reference. *Lords' Debates*, pp. 228–229. It was proposed that any parts of depositions by 'strangers' which might turn out not to be material should be burnt.

[3] There is one contemporary classification of the Lords for an unstated purpose, ascribed by the Editor of the *Calendar of State Papers* to Laud: S.P. 16/20/36. This classifies most of the Lords by the symbols +, −, and O. It is possible that this is a survey of the Lords' likely voting intentions on the Duke,

it is true that the Lords were divided between Buckingham's supporters, his opponents, and the uncommitted, it does not follow that their views on this question were necessarily their top priority. For almost all the Lords, four other things mattered more. The first was the preservation of the privileges of their House and of their order. The second was the desire to prevent sharp practice, and ensure, as far as possible, fair play for all parties. The third was the desire to avoid the fearful consequences of an angry dissolution in time of war. The fourth was the desire to restrict, so far as they could, the use of their House as a laundry for the washing of the court's dirty linen. It is against this background that we should see both the slowness of the Lords' proceedings in 1626 and their intense concentration on points of procedure.

The Lords' privileges and standing were potentially threatened by the power of Buckingham on one hand, and by the aggressive tactlessness of the Commons on the other.[1] But the biggest threat to their privileges was the imprisonment of the Earl of Arundel. If any compromise settlement was to satisfy the Lords, the release of Arundel would have to be one of its conditions. The Venetian Ambassador commented: 'The most unfortunate circumstances for Arundel is the enmity of the Duke, against whom he has expressed himself very openly and forcibly in Parliament.'[2] The Venetian Ambassador was probably referring to Arundel's speech in the proxies debate, when he sided firmly against the Duke. The Lords, however, waited ten days after his arrest on 4 March before raising the case in public. It was then raised in the most circumspect manner by the Earl of Lincoln, who 'moved we to proceed, as no offence to the King, nor breach of the Lords' privileges'. He was immediately answered by the Lord Keeper, claiming that he was speaking by the King's command. He said Arundel was committed by the King for a misdemeanour

---

since Mende reported that such a survey had been taken, and had been met with many dishonest answers from those who did not wish the Parliament to be dissolved. P.R.O. 31/3/63, f. 61. However, the presence of Suffolk, Salisbury, Exeter, Montgomery, and Montagu in what would otherwise appear to be the anti-Buckingham camp raises the possibility that it is really a survey of likely voting intentions on the Bristol case.

[1] As in the Commons' misguided attempt, at the beginning of March, to send for the Duke without asking leave of the Lords.

[2] *C.S.P.Ven. 1625-6*, pp. 358-9.

personal to himself, which had no relation to the Parliament. This message, resolutely staking the King's authority on the imprisonment of Arundel, seems to have caused some dismay. In Lord Montagu's words, the message 'caused a great silence for a while, yet after some pause, it was spoken of two and two, and that every man might be the freer to speak *pro et con*, the House was put into a committee'.[1] Bridgewater, Carlisle, and Manchester tried to defend the King's action, while Saye complained that this might be extended further against the Lords' privileges. The committee of privileges was ordered to search for precedents. The business was debated again the next day, when the precedent produced by the Earl of Manchester was denied by Clare. Saye wanted 'mediation, if the offence will bear it', to enable Arundel to sit during the Parliament. Bishops Harsnett of Norwich and Morton of Coventry and Lichfield wanted to petition the King in such a way as to avoid offending him, while the Lord Steward, the Earl of Worcester, wanted the rather blunter instrument of a Protestation.

The general mood of the House was plainly in favour of Arundel's release, but against a direct challenge to the King. Only Laud struck a discordant note, in a speech using the precedent of Peter Wentworth to justify imprisonment of members for what they did in Parliament. In this, one of the most foolish speeches of a long career, Laud not only undercut the King's defence that Arundel was not imprisoned for what he had done in Parliament. He also, in comparing the Earl Marshal of England to an obstreperous member of the House of Commons confirmed what were precisely the Lords' worst fears about the incident.[2] In spite of this provocation, the Lords decided by the narrowest possible majority not to go into committee to pursue the matter further. The voting was 34 for the committee, 31 against it, with proxy votes completing a majority against.[3] However, in spite of another message from the King, the Lords did not decide to let the matter drop. They decided, in spite of an attempt by Buckingham to end the issue, to defer it and reserve the right to raise it again. They resolved, on Dorset's motion, 'to suspend the decision of it as

[1] *Lords' Debates*, p. 126; *H.M.C. Buccleuch*, iii. 274.
[2] *Lords' Debates*, p. 128.
[3] *H.M.C. Buccleuch*, iii. 274. The absence of this and other divisions reported by Lord Montagu from the *Lords' Journals* suggests that the Journals made a practice of not reporting divisions.

now'. It was this resolution which was to become the signature tune of the Lords of 1626.

The Lords left the case there until 5 April, the day before the Easter recess. On that day, Hertford reported from the committee of privileges that all five Lords who had granted their proxies to Arundel had lost their votes, and that 'viewing the precedents they find none that a peer of this House can be committed in Parliament time without judgement of his peers'.[1] This report produced a long and disorderly debate about whether the committee of privileges, by raising the issue, had broken the order of 15 March, to defer the case. The Lords again resolved to defer the case, by a vote of 37 to 29, but also accepted a motion that the King's counsel should show their precedents, which were to be reported to the House after the recess. This motion was moved jointly by Buckingham's supporter Westmorland and his opponent Clare: it was becoming increasingly clear that, on procedural questions, the Lords were not going to react on party lines.[2] It was a typical Lords' move to leave the task of preparing a report on the issue during the recess to a balanced committee including the Duke and some of his leading critics.

It was this committee which reported on 18 April, shortly after the Easter recess. Manchester, reporting from this committee, was unable to show any precedent for Arundel's imprisonment. Hertford, from the committee of privileges, reported to the same effect, and added ominously that the Commons had an interest in the presence of all the Lords.[3] Saye took the opportunity to move that the question be put, and it was agreed *nem. con.* that it was a breach of privilege for any Lord to be imprisoned during the Parliament, except for treason, felony, or refusing to give surety for the peace. It was further resolved, on Devonshire's motion, that this should be entered in the clerk's book, and that a committee should prepare a Remonstrance to present to the King. On 19 April, the Remonstrance was reported by the Earl of Manchester, and it was agreed that the whole House should present it to the King.

This decision was taken immediately after the reading of Bristol's petition, on 19 April. The Bristol case thus came before a House in which the feeling that the Lords' privileges were not

---

[1] *Lords' Debates*, p. 139; *L.J.* 552.
[2] *Lords' Debates*, p. 140. This division is also not reported in the *Lords' Journals*.   [3] *Lords' Debates*, pp. 142–3; *L.J.* 558.

being respected stretched far beyond the ranks of Buckingham's normal opponents. Yet, while the Lords were a worried House, they also wanted to be conciliatory to the King. On 21 April, when the King demanded justice against Bristol, it was Buckingham's bitter opponent Saye who moved that the Lord Keeper and some others should wait on the King to give him thanks, and to offer the assurance of the peers that they would respect his honour.[1] The desire to be careful of the King's honour, like the desire to preserve the Lords' privileges, stretched right across the political spectrum of the Lords. The next vital question was raised, in typically interrogative manner, by Pembroke. He wanted to know in what manner Bristol should be sent for. Bristol wanted to come as a prosecutor, and the King wanted him to come as a delinquent. Bristol, as he later put it, wanted the King to sit on his throne of justice, impartial in a private quarrel between the Duke and himself. The Duke and the King wanted Bristol summoned as a delinquent to answer a charge in which the King was both accuser and witness. This was the background to the long, worried, and inconclusive debate conducted on 29 April, about whether the summons to Bristol to attend allowed him to take his seat. The House was clearly divided, but Buckingham might have taken warning from the fact that such natural supporters of authority as the Earl of Dorset wanted Bristol to be allowed to take his seat.[2] The Lords wanted to conciliate the King, but they were most reluctant to deprive Bristol of his right to a hearing. He could not have a fair trial unless he were allowed to tell his side of the story, and since his side of the story consisted of accusations against Buckingham, he would have to be allowed a hearing, not only as accused, but as accuser.

The proceedings in the Commons on the previous day, 28 April, gave warning of how dangerous such a hearing could become. On that day, Wandesford reported from committee a charge that Buckingham had caused James's death by the unauthorized application of medicine during his last illness. In the hands of the Commons, this was a charge of manslaughter, of what Wandesford called a 'transcendent presumption'.[3] In the hands of Bristol,

---

[1] *Lords' Debates*, p. 145.   [2] *Lords' Debates*, p. 151
[3] *C.J.* 850–1. It is perhaps not fanciful to connect this charge with Charles's insistence, seven years later, when Wandesford was appointed Master of the Rolls in Ireland, that his appointment should last no longer than Wentworth's Lord Deputyship. Coventry MSS., Grants of Offices, no. 244.

speaking before the Lords on 1 May, it became a charge of murder. In the eyes of the Lord Keeper and the Attorney General, Bristol was before the Lords on 1 May to be charged with high treason. Yet it was Bristol's accusation against Buckingham which made the day's big news. He said that, ever since his return from Spain, he had tried to be heard by King James, and that in the end James promised to hear him, and then died: 'He promised it: I pray God it did him no hurt.' Bristol called Pembroke to witness to the existence of King James's promise.[1] What, in the Commons' hands, had simply appeared to be another case of Buckingham believing he had a competence he lacked, now became a charge of deliberate murder, designed to prevent James from hearing what Bristol had to reveal. Since Charles had been present at the time when Buckingham was alleged to have performed this unauthorized administration of medicine, the Lords risked finding that they were investigating a charge against the King of being accessory to the murder of his father.

The French Ambassador, indeed, suggested that this was why the murder charge was offered at all.[2] The common opinion seems to have been that of Sir Humphrey May, that it added to the bulk, but not the weight, of the charge.[3] Yet, as the French Ambassador pointed out, the effect of making Charles an accessory was to give him an interest in procuring a full hearing for the charges, in order to procure his own exoneration. Yet, if this was its object, the charge boomeranged. It certainly gave Charles an interest in having a full hearing, but at the same time, it effectively deterred the Lords from conducting one. A loyal House of Lords, holding their places, like the King, by the hereditary principle, could not give a hearing to charges against the King of being an accomplice in the murder of his father. Bristol himself seems to have felt that he had overreached himself: on 6 May, when he was before the Lords again, he 'craved pardon for earnest speeches the other day'.

Lord Montagu, on 2 May, noted that he thought the major part of the Lords were against Bristol, but not inclined to take the case further.[4] They had resolved on 1 May that the King's charge

[1] *Lords' Debates*, p. 154; *L.J.* 577.

[2] Tite, p. 192n; P.R.O. 31/3/63, f. 61; *C.S.P.Ven. 1625–6*, p. 432

[3] 12–21, ff. 166–7.

[4] *H.M.C. Buccleuch*, iii. 284; *Lords' Debates*, p. 172. Two years later, rumours were still being spread that the Duke had poisoned James with Charles's connivance. *C.S.P.D. 1628–9*, vol. cxix, no. 54.

should not be allowed to hinder Bristol's testimony against the Duke, yet, even while reserving the right to hear Bristol, they took no steps to do so. Even the attempt by Carlisle, to accuse Bristol of a breach of the Lords' privileges by putting his charge before the Commons, did not shake the Lords out of their firm stance of judicial impartiality.[1] Dorset complained that while the Lords were considering whether the matter was too confidential to be communicated, 'he hath strewen papers of it elsewhere'. Yet Spencer and Clare pointed out that the Lords could have no more right to take notice of the Commons' proceedings, of which they only knew by common fame, than the Commons had to take notice of the Lords' proceedings. The Earl of Bridgewater, one of Buckingham's firmer supporters, moved next business, and Buckingham himself, who was usually sensitive to the Lords' sense of fairness, moved that Bristol should not be asked about this until he had heard his charge, and answered it, 'lest it disturb him in his answers'. At the same time, the Lords firmly rejected an attempt by Buckingham's partisans to allow the clerk of the Crown in King's Bench to be present, which would have allowed King's Bench to continue the case if Parliament were dissolved. They also resolved to make yet another attempt to secure the attendance of the Earl of Arundel.[2]

Between 4 and 8 May, the Lords were engaged in handling three related procedural questions: whether Bristol should be allowed counsel, whether he was accused of treason (he was, but the Lords persistently refused to take cognizance of the fact,) and whether the King's testimony as a witness could be received. The last question was referred to the judges, who, after a week's delay, refused to answer it.[3] The morning of 8 May began with a message from the King, saying that the use of counsel by those accused of treason was against 'an ancient fundamental law of his kingdom', and that Bristol should not be allowed it.[4] The Lords refused to be cowed by this message. Pembroke, coming into the open on this case for the first time, said they could not settle this until it was decided whether it was treason that Bristol was accused of, and that in the mean time, they should consider what to do about the King's message. Saye capped Pembroke, saying he agreed, 'and

[1] *Lords' Debates*, pp. 163–6.
[2] *L.J.* 581–2; *Lords' Debates*, pp. 165–6, 171–2.
[3] *Lords' Debates*, p. 191.   [4] *Lords' Debates*, p. 178.

to be allowed counsel in the mean time'. Much is concealed in the next two words of the report: 'not settled'. The Lords then debated the use of the King's testimony, and then returned again to a further debate on Bristol's claim to counsel. It was at this point, at the end of a long and tiring morning on a hot day, that a message came from the Commons asking the Lords to hear the Commons' charges against the Duke. Buckingham, who was throughout careful to avoid giving the impression of stifling investigation, asked for the charges to be heard quickly, and the Lords agreed to hear them that afternoon. Buckingham was given leave to be present, but refused leave to speak. Lord Montagu's report does much to tell us the mood in which the Lords came to this meeting:

To avoid the great thronging, and keeping the Lords out of their places, which commonly the Commons did at such great meetings, it was ordered that all the Lords should come in first, and place themselves, and the doors to be kept shut, and then the Commons to come in, which was done. [The Commons] pressed much to come in with the Lords, but were all kept back.

The Lords then listened for the whole afternoon to the Commons' lengthiest orators, until, at six in the evening, they were 'wearied with the heat, being thronged', and adjourned, interrupting the Commons in full flow.[1]

The next morning, Buckingham again asked for a speedy meeting with the Commons to hear the rest of the charges. The Commons replied, to the irritation of some Lords, that they wanted to defer the business, and it was agreed that it should be heard at eight the next morning.[2] Accordingly, on 10 May, the remainder of the Commons' charges were heard.

On 11 May, the King came to the Lords in person, and offered the Duke a general clearance, He said: 'Touching the accusations against him, I can be a witness to clear him in every one.' Buckingham followed, in typical style, delivering what Montagu called 'a fine speech, . . . The effect I do not remember.' The Lords seem to have accepted the finality of this, and Saye, one of Buckingham's strongest opponents, immediately said: 'I suppose this business is settled, and therefore speak touching that of the Earl of Arundel.'[3] From then on, there was no sign that any proceedings were

---

[1] *H.M.C. Buccleuch*, iii. 287–8. [2] *Lords' Debates*, p. 184.
[3] *H.M.C. Buccleuch*, iii. 291; *Lords' Debates*, pp. 188–9.

going to take place on the Commons' charges against Buckingham. The Lords directed that Buckingham's answer should be put in after the Whitsun recess. Nearly a month later, on 9 June, the Commons asked for a copy of the Duke's answer, and to be allowed to send up proofs. The Lords resolved that they would answer 'with all convenient speed', and apparently intended the ambiguities which a modern reader might see in their choice of adjective. Having delayed proceedings in order to amend the Duke's answer on La Rochelle, they said on 10 June that the Commons might send up their proofs to be examined.[1] No witnesses were sent up, and, in sharp contrast to the Bacon and Cranfield cases, no Lords' committee was ever named to take the examination of witnesses. The fact that the Lords, and not the Commons, retained control over the management of the witnesses on an impeachment was now crucial. If the Lords delayed, there was no procedural device open to the Commons except the vain one of requesting the Duke's commitment to prison on Bristol's charge. If the Lords refused to proceed on the Commons' charge, the Commons could do nothing in the world to make them proceed.

The Commons' charge did not go forward because the King did not wish it. The Bristol case was a different matter, because the King and the Duke did wish it to go forward. Yet even there, the Lords showed a remarkable reluctance to hear the first witness. The continued restraint of Arundel contributed something to this reluctance. The Lords felt the more strongly about this after Digges and Eliot had been imprisoned for reflecting on the King's honour during the presentation of the charges against Buckingham. The Commons succeeded in securing their release, thereby strengthening feelings among the Lords that if the Commons could obtain release of their imprisoned members, they should be able to do so too.[2] Yet the Lords' debates on the case of Digges and Eliot showed quite how difficult it would be to hear Bristol's case, even if they wished to do so. Digges and Eliot had been imprisoned for their remarks on the murder charge, which Bristol had made in a stronger form than the Commons. Saye and Montagu both thought that the Lords' loyalties were impugned by the suggestion that they had even listened to such speeches, while Elsyng noted in perplexity: 'Query how far I shall enter these

---

[1] *Lords' Debates*, pp. 220-1.
[2] Duchy of Cornwall True Relation, f. 175 (17 May).

protestations, and the occasion thereof.'[1] If they could not even hear the charges mentioned, it was hard to see how they would give a proper hearing to the Bristol case.

On 26 May, when the Lords resolved on a week's cessation of business, they did so because of the continued imprisonment of Arundel. Yet their continued reluctance to hear any witnesses on the Bristol case suggests that their concern about Arundel may have been in part an excuse, even if a highly congenial one. When the Lords reassembled, on 2 June, Arundel had still not been released, and they resolved that they would undertake no other business till he was released. Charles told the Lords that by Wednesday week, the fourteenth of June, he would either show cause for the imprisonment of Arundel, or release him. The fact that Charles gave the same deadline in his 'last and final admonition' to the Commons on supply, and that he kept it, suggests that he had fixed a time beyond which he would not allow the Parliament to drag on fruitlessly. He was having no more success in obtaining the condemnation of Bristol from the Lords then he was in obtaining supply from the Commons. The next day, 3 June, the Houses adjourned for the Whitsun recess.

When they reassembled, on 8 June, Arundel had been released, and came to the House, but his presence did not make the Lords much more eager to take action against Bristol. If Bristol wished to stress how embarrassing proceedings could become, he could not have done it better than he did on his appearance at the bar on 8 June. He said that he was 'not permitted to defend my innocency, for that will lay dishonour on the King'. He then offered 'to show somewhat to 2 or 3 Lords rather than openly'.[2] The Lords resolved to adjourn till the next day, leaving the Attorney General, who had his witnesses ready, complaining, 'The house will not sit then for the witnesses to be sworn.'[3] On 9 June, the first witnesses were at last sworn, though their depositions were not taken till 13 June. If Charles had any lingering hope of securing Bristol's condemnation, it would have been dispelled by a procedural decision on 13 June. Bristol protested that the examinations of his witnesses should not be taken by the King's counsel, because he did not trust their impartiality. The Lords granted this request, and appointed three Masters in Chancery to take the depositions of

---

[1] *Lords' Debates*, p. 196; *H.M.C. Buccleuch*, iii. 292.
[2] *Lords' Debates*, pp. 216–17.   [3] *Lords' Debates*, p. 219.

Bristol's witnesses, and to be sworn to keep them secret.[1] In this gesture, the Lords finally made it clear that they were no more willing to condemn Bristol on the King's charge than they were to condemn Buckingham on the Commons' charge. In the face of the tangled and sometimes malicious evidence before them, the only course compatible with judicial impartiality was to give no judgement, and hope that the good sense of the parties would bring them back to a compromise which had once seemed to be within reach. The next day, Charles decided to dissolve the Parliament.

On the morning of 15 June, the Lords knew that the decision for dissolution had been taken. Lord Montagu asked that the whole House should move the King to pause, 'for that it may be of the most dangerous consequence'. He noted that 'this motion was well approved of, and seconded by divers Lords', and Manchester, Pembroke, Carlisle, and Holland were sent to inform the King that the Lords wished to see him.[2] The King refused to receive them, and sent back a message that 'his wound is not from your Lordships, but from the Commons'.[3] The Lords' declaration, asking the King not to dissolve the Parliament among such 'great and apparent dangers both at home and abroad,' still survives in the draft the King refused to receive. They were right that dissolution merely changed the problems, and did not remove them, for, as Secretary Conway told the committee for defence on 10 June, 'though there be no money, yet the realm must be maintained'.[4] The dissolution of Parliament left the King at war abroad, and in dispute with his subjects at home. The dissolution led logically to the Forced Loan. It was an unhappy position for a country at war. It was one which Buckingham and Pembroke, according to their lights, had each striven to avoid: they were both responsible

---

[1] *Lords' Debates*, pp. 226–7; *L.J.* 676. I would like to thank Mr. Michael Denning for drawing my attention to this important evidence.

[2] *Lords' Debates*, p. 231; *H.M.C. Buccleuch*, iii. 302. The Venetian Ambassador noted that the Lords received the dissolution with dismay; 'A general murmur sounded through the House'. *C.S.P.Ven 1625–6*, p. 452.

[3] As late as 14 June, Viscount Grandison, a member of the Council of War, still hoped, both that a dissolution could be avoided, and that the Commons could be induced to vote supply. S.P. 16/29/82. S.P. 16/30/1 and 2 are the House of Lords' petition and a draft reply from the King. It is unlikely to be the King's draft, but in the priority it gives to the task of defending the kingdom, and to the Commons' duty to maintain that task under their supposed engagement of 1624, it is probably a faithful reflection of Charles's mind.

[4] *Lords' Debates*, p. 223.

members of a government which had to preserve the country. Their attempts to arrive at a workable settlement had been destroyed, first by the distrust of Digges and Eliot, second by the existence of a large body of feeling in the Commons which was more keen to prosecute the Duke than to prosecute the war, and third, by the undiplomatic intervention of the Earl of Bristol. Not for the last time, it had proved easier to call in the Commons as critics of an unpopular minister than it was to call them off when they had served the purpose of those who first called them in. What had been intended as an attempt at the reformation of the Duke had instead nearly led to the destruction of the country. If there was one clear lesson to be learnt from the Parliament of 1626, it was that until England had solved its difficulties at home, and created a financial system adequate to the purpose, it could not enter into any major European war. To attempt, as Buckingham and Pembroke had done, to use war as a solution for financial troubles at home was to put the cart before the horse.

VI

The Parliament of 1628:
War and the Petition of Right

I

'THEY wish for war against heaven and earth, but lack the means to make it against anyone.'[1] This comment by an unofficial French agent is an apt summary of the mood of Buckingham and Charles between the Parliaments of 1626 and 1628. The failure of the Parliament seems to have done nothing to quench the martial ardour of the King, who was concerned about his reputation for good faith in the eyes of his allies. Even more, he was rightly concerned about the diminution of his own and his country's military reputation. The Duke may have hoped that a great military exploit could do something to recover for him the popularity he had so much enjoyed in 1624.

The military preparations of the years 1626-8 were undertaken on a greater scale (and at greater cost) than anything since 1588, yet, even with the most dedicated effort by many of the people involved, the results ranged from the laughable to the lamentable. The French agent reported on the horse that he had never seen 'semblable canaille à cheval', and the more measured researches of Professor Barnes do not encourage us to dispute his verdict.[2] The French agent was undoubtedly right in laying the central blame on lack of money. An expedition could not sail until ships and equipment were ready, and lack of money often delayed their setting forth. Every delay in an expedition's departure increased the period for which wages had to be paid to the temporary levies raised for it. Lack of money was thus a continual cause of extra expense.

[1] P.R.O. 31/3/65, f. 31. Dumolin to D'Herbault, 3 Apr. 1627. After the expulsion of Mende and the Queen's French attendants during the summer of 1626 and a brief visit by Bassompierre, there was no accredited French ambassador in England. Dumolin reported unofficially to the French government from December 1626 until the fleet sailed for La Rochelle, in July 1627.
[2] Ibid., f. 61ʳ. See also Barnes, pp. 251-2 and Fletcher, pp. 185-6.

Yet, when this is said, it is possible to wonder whether English military failures during these years reveal rather deeper flaws in the structure of administration. Perhaps the Duke's belief that there was nothing wrong some Parliamentary subsidies would not put right was as naïve as Eliot's belief that there was nothing wrong the removal of the Duke would not put right. For, when we look for scapegoats for English failures, they are harder to find than at first appears. S. R. Gardiner stressed the military gallantry shown by the Duke at La Rochelle, and laid much of the blame for his failure on the absence of adequate supplies or reinforcements from England.[1] The lack of money and equipment in England was the result of the failure of local administrators to place sufficiently harsh pressure on their countrymen. Many countrymen were naturally reluctant to incur heavy taxation or overseas service in a cause of which they probably understood little. Yet to blame local administration is perhaps also to look too easily for scapegoats. Mr. Fletcher has recently stressed how much effort Deputy Lieutenants put into unpopular and unpaid work among their friends and neighbours: 'In fact', he concludes, 'the Deputies were indefatigable. But it was hard for them to square their duty to the King with their concern for the good of the county community.'[2]

Here Mr. Fletcher pinpoints the central difficulty of the English war effort: a successful war could not readily be combined with the local self-government which was the tradition of the English counties. Deputy Lieutenants, like Justices of the Peace, depended for their claim to obedience on retaining trust among those they governed: in the cause of sending their countrymen into battle, those who did the King adequate service risked forfeiting their countrymen's trust. In Somerset, where the Deputies had to face continual harassment from Sir Robert Phelips, as well as 'the opposition of the county at large to all things military,' Professor Barnes suggests that their attempts to do their duty, while inadequate from the King's point of view, were sufficiently determined to do long-term injury to the reputation of their office. 'The odium incurred by their actions in 1627 and 1628 remained

[1] Gardiner, vi. 172–84. Gardiner's judgements on these years are often more measured than later summaries of them.
[2] Fletcher, pp. 185, 201. His remarks are only intended to apply to Sussex, but the county, though more than usually harmonious, was not unique.

attached to their office and to their persons with consequent injury to their usefulness.' In 1588, with an enemy visibly attempting to invade the kingdom, it had been barely possible for local governors to combine serious military preparations with retaining the trust essential to their office. In 1626–8, for an offensive war, it was not possible. The government of the counties through their own leading residents had to remain in some sense government by consent. In Somerset, with Sir Robert Phelips saying that the Deputies' attempts to billet soldiers had 'dangerously undermined the fabric of the government of England', a few anti-billeting riots during the Parliament of 1628 became more serious than the Deputies could control. Their scale was not large: yet they had to be taken as a warning. If the habit of obedience to the country governors were to disappear, their power would disintegrate.[1]

It was no longer possible to raise or equip large armies by indenture, and the English government's lack of resources meant that Protector Somerset's brief experiments with foreign mercenaries were not continued. Elizabeth and James had tried to avoid the sending of large-scale expeditions abroad.[2] In 1626–8, then, the compatibility of county self-government with large-scale conscript warfare overseas was perhaps being seriously tested for the first time. Tudor and Stuart local governors had to owe their first loyalty to their local communities. In the age of gunpowder, an effective army probably needed to be based on a more centralized administration than England had to offer. Except under Oliver Cromwell, whose régime, resting as it did on a standing army, profoundly altered the balance between the centre and the localities, the English fought no effective land war on the Continent between the development of gunpowder and the campaigns of the Duke of Marlborough. In England, as much as in continental countries, the development of armies capable of fighting on the new scale was not possible without a profound shift in the relations between central and local government. The shift which ultimately occurred in England was very different from that which occurred in, for example, Brandenburg-Prussia, but it was

---

[1] Barnes, pp. 263, 258, 257, and other refs.

[2] When they had done so, they had not been conspicuously successful. Elizabeth's expeditions to Le Havre, the Netherlands, Lisbon, and Ireland do not rank prominently in the list of English martial achievements. Nor, indeed, do Henry VIII's campaigns in France.

equally indispensable.[1] Until it had occurred, the gulf between local governors doing their job adequately by their own standards and the appearance of an adequate army in the field was too big to be bridged. Since, in the early years of the reign of Charles I, such a shift was not desired, and indeed its possibility was barely comprehended, it is perhaps unduly parochial to blame the failure of the English war effort on the Duke of Buckingham, or even on Sir John Eliot and Sir Robert Phelips. There is much food for thought in the words with which Professor Barnes began his chapter on the Somerset militia: 'This chapter is not intended to show why the men of Somerset would not fight to the death for the King in 1640. It is intended to show why, even if they had the will to fight, they could not have fought effectively.'[2]

In June 1626, the Council of War thought the country was in danger of invasion. Attempts to convey the sincerity of this fear to the country at large were conspicuously unsuccessful. Yet, together with the plain fact of political deadlock, it may well have helped to induce Buckingham and Pembroke to bury the hatchet when the Parliament of 1626 was dissolved. Pembroke was promoted to the office of Lord Steward, while his brother Montgomery replaced him as Lord Chamberlain. At the same time, 'to gain the Lord Chamberlain's faction',[3] as the Venetian Ambassador reported, a marriage was arranged between Buckingham's daughter and Pembroke's nephew and heir. Clare, in a very bitter letter to Saye, said Pembroke was 'peradventure better satisfied in this new alliance, the same was done to undo the better part: I wish therefore it had been sooner, ere a Parliament, ere the whole kingdom had been a party'. This marriage contract, making the Herbert family fortunes dependent on a dowry from Buckingham which was yet to be paid, appears to have marked the final reconciliation between Buckingham and Pembroke. The Herberts were too much indebted to risk losing a portion of £20,000, to be paid in two instalments six and eight years later. At the same time, the contracting parties realized that, in arranging a marriage between two children of seven and eight, it was advisable to make some

[1] Michael Howard, *War in European History* (1976), pp. 68–9. See also p. 55.
[2] Barnes, p. 244.
[3] *C.S.P. Ven. 1625–6*, pp. 512, 515. Sheffield City Library, Elmhirst MSS. 1352/4. *Letters of John Holles 1587–1637*, Thoroton Soc. Record Series, xxxi (1975), ed. P. R. Seddon, p. lxiii. Nottingham University Library, MS. Ne. C. 15, 405, f. 170. I am grateful to Mr. Richard Cust for this reference.

arrangement for their possible refusal to consummate the marriage when of age. They provided that if the Lord should refuse the lady, 'it being a great dishonour to the lady', the penalty was to be £30,000, but if the lady refused him, 'which can be no dishonour to the Lord', the penalty was to be only £20,000. From the conclusion of this contract onwards, the impeachment of Buckingham ceased to be a serious possibility.

Others, who lacked Pembroke's power to take cover, were less fortunate. The Earl of Arundel remained under suspended sentence of house arrest, and yet, interestingly, remained in office as Lord Lieutenant of Norfolk and Sussex. Bristol, after a spell in the Tower, was allowed to return to what was, in effect, house arrest at his home at Sherborne. Lower down the social scale, Buckingham's critics were more dispensable than Pembroke, or even Arundel, and twenty-two gentlemen and two lords were dismissed from the Commissions of the Peace.[1] The list included Eliot (who also lost his office of Vice-Admiral), Mansell, Digges, Sir Thomas Wentworth, Wandesford, Strangeways, Phelips, Seymour, and Alford. Seymour and Alford,[2] however, continued to function as Deputy Lieutenants. Their position, in disgrace and opponents of the war, and yet essential to its prosecution, is typical of the ambiguities of early Stuart administration. When Seymour, together with his fellow-Deputies, wrote to desire the direction of Pembroke, the Lord Lieutenant, because their countrymen began generally to refuse to pay billeting rates, he merely provides an unusually vivid illustration of what is meant by saying that the early Stuart administration system was unsuited to the conduct of a major war. Seymour, like Wentworth, Digges, or or Phelips, believed he owed loyalty, both to his county, and to his King. His attempt to serve two masters was none the less sincere for being inherently self-contradictory.

It did not help the war effort that its cause was probably even more obscure to contemporaries than it should, by this time, have become to the reader. Some observers expected Buckingham

---

[1] Phelips MSS. 229/34 (I am grateful to Mr. Allen Croessmann for this reference), Coventry MSS., Commissions of the Peace, no. 15. See also R. P. Cust, 'A Supposed *Liber Pacis* of 1626', *B.I.H.R.* (forthcoming).

[2] Fletcher, pp. 176–7; S.P. 16/94/22. In the Parliament, Seymour placed much of the blame for the Forced Loan on gentlemen who feared the loss of their places as Deputy Lieutenants or J.P.s if they did not forward the service. Harl. 5324, f. 48[v].

to press for peace with Spain after the failure of the Parliament of 1626, but he did not do so. The reasons can only be conjectured, but it is possible that he wanted to keep open the possibility of another Parliament, in which he could attempt to revive his alliances of 1624.[1] At the same time, attempts to avoid a war with France were growing more obviously fruitless. Pembroke, in spite of his reconciliation with Buckingham, complained 'confidentially' to the Venetian Ambassador 'that never will an instance be found of a rupture, should it occur, between two sovereigns and kinsmen upon such slight grounds'.[2]

Yet, slight or not, the grounds of quarrel proved surprisingly difficult to remove. French insistence on the observance of the letter of the marriage treaty was incompatible with Charles's desire to be master in his own house. French suspicions were constantly inflamed by the presence in England of the Duke of Soubise, who was said to have demonstrated his influence by persuading Charles to make his host, Sir John Poulett, a baron.[3] The existence of La Rochelle was a constant appeal to pan-Protestant sentiment, and English desire to recover the ships they had lent to the French was also spurred on by the fact that they were needed for other things. The French perhaps made the less effort to heal the breach because they could observe, in the misfortunes of the King of Denmark, the uselessness of England as a continental ally. The King of Denmark had entered the war on promises of English assistance which the failure of the Parliament had made impossible to fulfil. In spite of repeated promises that he would be helped 'sometime', the money was not there, and his forces ultimately went down to defeat. The English did not merely lack the money to pay allies: by 1628, they even lacked the money to pay Conway's salary as Secretary of State, and Conway had to threaten to 'seek it by other means'.[4]

The drift to war between England and France accelerated during the winter of 1626-7, with a series of seizures of ships,

[1] Coventry opened the Parliament of 1628 with a very traditional denunciation of the ambitions of the House of Austria, though the fleet being prepared at the time was to sail against France.

[2] *C.S.P. Ven. 1625-6*, p. 583.

[3] P.R.O. 31/3/65, f. 8^r; Coventry MSS., Commissions, no. 19; *H.M.C. 11th Rep. I*, pp. 89, 102; B.L. Harl. MS. 7010, f. 19^v.

[4] *C.S.P.D. 1628-9*, vol. xcvi, no. 41. Conway to Lord Treasurer Marlborough, 18 March 1628.

including a seizure of all the English wine ships in Bordeaux. The French agent reported that 'this would spoil their Christmas'.[1] By the campaigning season of 1627, it was France, not Spain, that was the enemy.

The fleet gathered for the summer of 1627 was sent out to give relief, which was apparently not particularly welcome, to La Rochelle. This was an ambitious plan for amphibious operations, and implied military preparations on a grand scale: 1,000 men were pressed for service at La Rochelle from Somerset alone. The Deputies, in spite of another quarrel with Sir Robert Phelips, succeeded in getting the men out of the county with their numbers nearly up to strength. It was the return of the survivors which brought tension in Somerset to the point of the unendurable.[2] Except from Felton, the Duke's assassin, we possess few comments by ordinary soldiers and sailors on the La Rochelle expedition. If we had them, it is unlikely that they would be flattering. It was an offensive expedition which illustrates as clearly as any campaign of the period Professor Howard's thesis that in European warfare this was a period when the advantage was with the defensive. Navigation into and out of the harbour of La Rochelle is controlled by the two islands of Rhé and Oleron, and the Duke and Soubise calculated correctly that it was impossible to give effective naval assistance to La Rochelle without control of one of these islands. The island chosen was the Île de Rhé, commanded by a particularly strong fort. The walls of this fort were sufficiently proof against bombardment from the sea. The Duke succeeded in landing a large party of soldiers in the face of the French army, though he did so at considerable loss. The fort was then invested on all sides. However, the landward side of the fort was as immune to English bombardment as the seaward side, and the ground was too rocky to permit the making of mines. The English were thus forced to attempt a blockade, aiming at starving the fort into surrender. It was precisely this type of warfare, in which the ultimate weapon was time, which gave the biggest advantage to the side with the longest purse. It was therefore precisely the sort of warfare the English were least equipped to conduct, and which was likely to put the severest strain on the administration at home, for the least possible reward. The English landed on the Île de Rhé on 10 July 1627. On 30 October they re-embarked, suffering severe losses in the face of

---

[1] P.R.O. 31/3/64, f. 172. [2] Barnes, pp. 254–5.

French attacks as they made their way back to their ships. Less, and perhaps much less, than half the English force returned to Plymouth and Portsmouth. Insupportable casualties, and insupportable costs, had been incurred for no achievement whatsoever. It is questionable whether better generalship could have achieved more. The plan was one only a country inexperienced in European land warfare would have been likely to attempt. Somehow, all this activity had to be paid for. The fleet of 1626, which had been assembled but had not sailed, had to paid for as well as the fleet of 1627. There were plans to send out a third fleet in the summer of 1628, so the Crown had somehow to find the money for three fleets, as well as all the miscellaneous expenses of powder, artillery, armour, rigging, shot, siege engines, and the other impedimenta of war. During the years 1627–8 almost every possibility for revenue raising, however obscure, was explored. The need was visibly urgent: in 1626 the Duke's coach had been smashed by rioting sailors, and it had only proved possible to quieten them with 'a little money from the mint'. In March 1628, another sailors' mutiny in front of the Duke's house was quietened by an issue of money.[1] These issues of money merely encouraged other unpaid sailors to come for more. Against these massive demands, such petty pieces of antiquarianism as a commision to compound for villein tenures in Cornwall appeared to be a drop in the ocean.[2]

Two substantial sources of funds were used. One was the Crown lands. The Crown adopted Sir Edward Coke's suggestion of 1625 that those who already held leases of Crown lands would be prepared to pay large entry fines to have their leases confirmed at existing rents. However, this method of fund-raising was subject to a law of diminishing returns: those who paid to have their leases lengthened to ninety-nine years were unlikely to pay again to have them lengthened further.[3] In addition, the Crown preserved its precarious credit with the City by involving it in the last major sale of Crown lands by the monarchy: the Ditchfield Grant of 1627–8.[4] However, this also was a once-for-all measure. It perhaps

---

[1] *C.S.P. Ven. 1625–6*, p. 587; *H.M.C. 11th Rep. I*, p. 140.

[2] Coventry MSS., Commissions, no. 73. This case is nine years later than what has previously been said to be the last known appearance of villeinage in English law. Russell, *The Crisis of Parliaments* (Oxford, 1971), p. 13.

[3] Coventry MSS., Grants of Leases, nos. 1–30.

[4] On the Ditchfield Grant, see Robert Ashton, 'Charles I and the City', in *Essays in the Economic and Social History of Tudor and Stuart England*, ed.

shows the scale of Charles's difficulties that the capital value of the *whole* of the Crown lands would have done little more than meet his current expenditure during 1627-8.[1] After the Ditch-field Grant, the Crown lands were no longer a significant source of income. Their diminution is highlighted by the Receivers' Accounts, which continued to be kept in volumes of unchanging size. As the 1620s continued, a steadily increasing proportion of each page became blank.[2]

The other substantial source of money was the Forced Loan.[3] In its original version, this had been intended to be a benevolence, and attempts to levy it began immediately after the Parliament of 1626. The original attempt was too blatantly designed to collect the money Parliament had refused to meet with very much success.

By the winter, the Council had changed the name of what they were requesting to a Loan. It is doubtful whether many people supposed the Loan would ever be repaid, but the request for a Loan was less overtly an assault on the principle of Parliamentary taxation than the benevolence had been. Lord Montagu could reflect that the King had promised not to turn it into a precedent, and that he owed obedience to the King by the law of God. Besides, as his brother Manchester reminded him, they did not want Northamptonshire to be behind other counties.[4] Phelips was in some confusion about the Loan. We possess the advice he received from his Court correspondent Nathaniel Tomkins,[5] but,

---

F. J. Fisher (Cambridge, 1961), p. 161 and n. The majority of this money was assigned to paying Crown creditors, over £158,000 for an old loan, and £120,000 for a new one. Like other financial expedients, it fell well short of what was required. See also Ashton, *The Crown and the Money Market* (Oxford 1960), pp. 39-40.

[1] This conclusion is conjectural. The annual value of the Crown lands in 1603 was £88,000. At twenty years' purchase, on which the Crown might perhaps have improved, they would have fetched £1,936,000. It is improbable that improvements in yield since 1603 had exceeded losses by sales. In 1626, Sir John Coke had said the Crown was short of £1,067,000. Since then, there was the cost of the La Rochelle campaign to be met, as well as the repayment of existing debts. It can at least be said that the sale of all the Crown lands would not have left a large surplus after debts had been repaid.

[2] P.R.O. L.R. 7/116-20.

[3] I am grateful to Dr. Derek Hirst and Mr. Richard Cust for allowing me to read unpublished papers on the Forced Loan.

[4] *H.M.C. Buccleuch*, i. 264-5. I am grateful to Mr. Richard Cust for this reference.

[5] Phelips MSS. 219/35. I am grateful to Mr. Allen Croessmann for this reference.

unfortunately, do not know what action he took on it. Tomkins said that he had tried, through the intermediacy of the Earl of Holland, to recover favour for Phelips at Court, but that Phelips would have to do the King some service before he could succeed. He thought that if the Loan succeeded 'we may forget what the word Parliament means', yet his assessment of 'what I would do were I Sir Robert Phelips' is based purely on self-interest. 'I should not in this case judge the middle way a good way. If you deny handsomely and fairly and are not a leader of those who shall refuse you will hardly be held a master among them: if you do not avowedly declare yourself to advance the work you shall have no thanks from the King. You who best know the constitution of your country can best advise your self which course to take.' Among the leaders of county society, including peers and former members of the Commons, there were a number of people sufficiently determined to refuse the Loan to face imprisonment, or, in the case of the peers, removal from local office. Both for the Crown and for the refusers, such a conflict could only be temporary: the Crown could no more dispense permanently with the services of Sir Thomas Wentworth in Yorkshire than Wentworth could hold his position in Yorkshire if in permanent disfavour with the Crown. In Staffordshire, Essex's replacement as Lord Lieutenant, the Earl of Monmouth, wrote him an apologetic letter. He said he hoped that Essex would not take his accepting the office as a personal affront, and that Essex might soon recover favour and receive it back again.[1]

This letter seems to illustrate that both loan collectors and loan refusers did not think that the sort of pressure on county government involved in collecting the Forced Loan could be regularly repeated.[2] Somehow, means would have to be found for an accommodation. Men like Digges, who appear to have collected the Loan,[3] wanted to recover local favour, while men like Wentworth,

---

[1] B.L. Add. MS. 46188, f. 102. Monmouth said the Lieutenantcy had been imposed on him 'very strangely, and upon my credit much against my will'. He said he was a mere stranger in the shire, with neither acquaintance nor lands in it.

[2] The Earl of Banbury, in Berkshire, engaged himself, if the Loan were paid, not to ask for any such levy again. Gardiner, vi. 227.

[3] The statement of Tomkins (Phelips MSS. 219/35) that Digges advanced the Loan appears to be supported by the renewal of payment of his pension. S.P. 16/126/82. For the argument that Digges refused the Forced Loan, see Peter Clark, *Religion, Politics and Society in Kent 1500–1640* (Hassocks, 1977),

who refused it, wanted to recover court favour. Neither was dispensable. In many cases, of which those of Wentworth and Eliot are the most obvious, the decision whether to help to collect the Loan was a short-term decision, reflecting as much men's relationship with their local rivals as their long-term views on the government of England. The dilemma created by the Loan was particularly acute for the holders of the already overburdened office of Deputy Lieutenant, since they were saddled with the task of collecting it. It perhaps reveals the Crown's long-term dependence on the leaders of county society that Sir Thomas Wentworth and John Hampden remained in office as Deputy Lieutenants while in prison for refusing to collect the Loan.[1] For others, such as Phelips, the Loan and the war appeared to be elevating the Deputy Lieutenants to a position approaching that of provincial governors. One administrative reformer submitted a project to extend the authority of Deputy Lieutenants, to make it cover towns, where he said the citizens had little understanding of martial matters, and to extend their functions beyond the military ones. He even wanted to put them in charge of what sounds like a forerunner of the Book of Orders.[2] It is against this background that the hostility of the Parliament of 1628 to Deputy Lieutenants should be seen. Yet to members of Parliament like Sir Edward Giles, Edward Alford, or Sir Francis Seymour, who were Deputy Lieutenants themselves, this did not appear to be a real danger. Their real fear was that they would become too unpopular, both personally and officially, to remain able to govern their counties.

This tug of war between central and local loyalties, which in these years tormented Deputy Lieutenants even more than it tormented members of Parliament, was an ordeal which was a privilege of the leaders of county society. For those of less distinction, the Forced Loan appears to have often been just another disagreeable and, in the end, inevitable demand for money.

---

p. 345 and n. The likeliest resolution of this contradiction appears to be that Digges first refused the Forced Loan, and then paid it. I am grateful to Mr. Richard Cust for advice on this point.

[1] The evidence that Wentworth was a Deputy Lieutenant is from one of his speeches in the Parliament of 1628. See above, p. 76. The right to appoint and dismiss Deputy Lieutenants was normally the property of the Lord Lieutenant, not of the Crown.

[2] S.P. 16/89/17.

In many counties, the sums demanded were smaller than those being raised for such local taxes as billeting rates, and the legal basis of both levies was equally questionable. In Essex, where some disruption had been caused by trade embargoes which interfered with trade in the new draperies, there were numerous refusers in small towns. In other parts of the country, refusal seems to have been largely a luxury for the gentry. Even among the gentry, many simply wanted to dispose of the issue. In Yorkshire, Christopher Wandesford reported 'every man praying that the safe shelter of collectorship may cover and protect him' (itself a comment which says volumes about early Stuart taxation), and that there was 'no man I met with more sensible of the right we have than my neighbour was when he only enquired for the *quota pars* of Richmondshire'.[1] Even with some allowance for exaggeration, remarks like these as much deserve a place among reactions to the Loan as the perhaps equally exaggerated protests in Parliament. Moreover, it should not be forgotten that some of the leading protesters against the Loan in Parliament had, like Digges, helped to collect it. In immediate financial terms, it brought in the money, though slowly and laboriously. The ultimate yield was £264,000, against £275,000 for the five subsidies of 1628.[2] However, even people like Dorset, Lord Lieutenant of Sussex, were later prepared to describe it as an experiment which should not be repeated.[3] It threatened a co-operation between King and county gentry for which no substitute existed, and for which no substitute was desired.

The most serious flashpoint of these years, though, appears not to have been the Loan: the most serious flashpoints, if later Parliamentary debates are any guide, were the Five Knights' case, and the issue of billeting. The Five Knights' case arose out of the Forced Loan, but soon acquired an importance in many people's minds which far transcended that of the Loan. The case arose out of an attempt to sue a Habeas Corpus by five knights who had been imprisoned for refusal to pay the Loan. In reply to the Habeas Corpus, the King's Attorney had to produce the prisoners in court, and show cause why they had been imprisoned. The five

[1] *Wentworth Papers*, pp. 276, 278.

[2] Robert Ashton, *The Crown and the Money Market* (Oxford, 1960), pp. 39, 41. The yield was still far lower than the King's needs.

[3] *Lords' Debates* (ed. Relf), p. 176n. In this chapter, further references to *Lords' Debates* are to this edition unless otherwise stated.

knights presumably hoped that he would return that they had been committed to prison for refusal to pay the Loan, and that they would therefore be able to test the legality of the Loan in a court of law. Instead, he returned that they had been imprisoned 'per speciale mandatum domini regis'—by the King's special command. The court, in its official capacity, was shown no other reason why these men had been imprisoned. What was meant to be a test case on the Loan thus became, to the judges' great embarrassment, a test case on the King's prerogative power to imprison those who had offended him without showing any cause. The judges, according to their own later account of the case, gave no judgement on this issue, and simply remanded the prisoners in custody pending a possible further hearing. According to Selden, however, the remand was entered in the King's Bench records in the same form as if a judgement had been given against them. Moreover, from the prisoners' point of view, the question whether the judges had adjourned the case or given judgement against them was of somewhat academic interest: in either case, they remained in prison, and the law had failed to give them deliverance. It was this complete failure to secure a legal remedy which caused so much alarm to those who assembled in Parliament in 1628.

Why did this arbitrary imprisonment create so much alarm? Why was it that, unlike the many previous arbitrary imprisonments recorded in this book, it created a widespread fear that the rule of law was in danger? Part of the answer must be that, unlike previous arbitrary imprisonments, it was tested in a court, and not remedied. Part must be that the new threats of 'new counsels' made since 1626 had contributed to a growing atmosphere of constitutional alarm: the members who assembled in 1628 had a sharper eye for illegalites than those who had met in 1626. For some lawyers, notably Sir Edward Coke, the honour of their own profession was at stake. The King's overt claim to imprison on discretion threatened the centre of Coke's legal ideal: the freedom to live by settled and known rules of law.

Yet it is perhaps more important than any of these things that in the winter of 1627–8 the King had a large body of troops under arms. They might be unpaid and mutinous, and they might be unfit to stand against a continental enemy, yet they would have been more than fit to overawe a Justice of the Peace, or even, if needed, a Justice of the King's Bench. The big difference between

1627–8 and any previous occasion when the King had attempted arbitrary imprisonment was that he had these troops to hand. If he wished to set up an 'arbitrary government', he had possible means of enforcing his will. If he wished to adopt 'new counsels', and free himself from financial constraints by regularly levying taxes without consent, he now possessed the force without which the attempt could not be made. In fact, neither Charles nor his Council had any such intention, as the very assembly of the Parliament testifies. There were a few, very few, occasions when the threat of troops was used, either to influence an election or to secure compliance with some other order.

Few, and often trivial, though they were, these occasions appear to have been enough to trigger off an outburst of fear which neither the Five Knights' case nor the soldiers alone could have explained. In the minds of men like Coke and Digges, it was the fusion of the two which produced a nightmare of alarming proportions.

In the fear of soldiers, billeting had become the symbolic issue. Not merely was it one of the most expensive of all the war demands: it also, in the most literal sense, brought the war home to people. In threatening recalcitrants, the threat to billet troops in their houses could easily be made, since the troops, after all, had to be billeted somewhere. Sir Edward Coke and Phelips, falling back on Sir John Fortescue, robustly insisted that no one could be compelled to take soldiers but inns, and they were to be paid for them, but Fortescue's picture belonged to a vanished age of warfare. The impact of billeting was very uneven, being naturally more severe near the ports of Plymouth and Portsmouth, where the soldiers were landed. In those areas, the effect could be alarming: *inter arma silent leges*: it is not surprising that people with soldiers forcibly billeted in their houses thought the rule of law was in danger. The Recorder of Taunton, in Parliament, claimed that 'our houses are our castles', and that soldiers coming into men's houses by force was a violation of the laws.[1]

It was a real point of doubt whether the soldiers could be effectively kept under the control of a civilian local government. Sir William Fleetwood, author of two previous bills to confirm Magna Carta, was told he had no jurisdiction over soldiers, and replied that if that was so, he wished to resign his office as a J.P. In the Lords in 1628, Saye complained of a similar case in

---

[1] Barnes, pp. 256–8; Stowe 366, f. 10ᵛ. *1628 Debates*, ii. 254, 264.

Banbury, where 'the soldiers apprehended that they were not to be governed but by their own officers'. Saye got a ruling from the Lord Keeper in full Parliament that soldiers 'are not to governed by a distinct law but by the law of the kingdom and charge them to live orderly according to law'. Such a charge, however, was easier to give than to enforce.[1]

It was becoming equally difficult to deal with some of the disorders which grew up around the soldiers. The Deputy Lieutenants of Essex asked for a commission of martial law because many people were refusing to receive soldiers. In Cheshire, Sir George Booth reported that he and Sir William Brereton wanted power to discipline servants and tenants bearing arms under them. At Eton, the Provost and Fellows reported that the soldiers and the scholars 'do not well comport'. In many places, local autonomy was necessarily threatened by the presence of soldiers. Commissions of martial law appeared necessary to many of those actually responsible for disciplining a body of soldiers who may, by this time, have been in a state of some bitterness. Yet to those who were already alarmed about the rule of law, martial law commissions merely seemed to show that county autonomy, as well as personal liberty, was threatened. The rule of law was an ideal which meant many things to early Stuart gentlemen. It meant certainty, security in their property and inheritances, and perhaps as much as anything else, the liberty of counties to govern themselves by the authority of their own Quarter Sessions. In a gentleman's daily existence, Quarter Sessions was perhaps a more important, because more permanent, symbol of the rule of law than Parliament.[2] There is no evidence at all that anyone in authority in London *wished* to threaten the authority of Quarter Sessions, yet the mere presence of soldiers was a threat to it. Authority is necessarily threatened by disorders it cannot control.

There was more sympathy for these local, and legal, fears

---

[1] *C.S.P.D. 1627–8*, vol. xcii, no. 69; *Lords' Debates*, pp. 75, 77. On the difficulties experienced in billeting soldiers in Essex, see G. E. Aylmer, 'St. Patrick's Day 1628 in Witham, Essex', *Past and Present*, no. 61 (1973), 139–48. The Deputy Lieutenants reported that men were refusing to receive soldiers into their houses, and asked for a commission of martial law. It is possible that these points were connected.

[2] Hassell Smith, pp. 246–7, also pp. 131–2, 230–1, 240, 259–60, 281. The disputes described by Dr. Hassell Smith suggest that the Armada war had begun to breed arguments with some resemblance to those of 1628. It is also worth noting that these disputes began the political education of Sir Edward Coke.

among the Council than has often been allowed for, just as there was more desire among Loan refusers to recover Conciliar favour than has been allowed for.[1] Between November 1627 and January 1628 there was a vigorous debate in the Council about what to do next. A long series of revenue projects, including ones for Ship Money and for what later became known as an Excise, got as far as the drawing-board stage. Sir Thomas Edmondes pointed out that the whole revenues of England were less than those the French King got from the province of Normandy alone, yet he said he had 'learnt by what has passed at this Board that it is dangerous to put any of these things in practice, without either the consent of a Parliament, or the hope of gaining the conformity and submission of the people thereunto'.[2]

A few tantalizing pieces are all that can now be reconstructed of the Conciliar debate on whether to call another Parliament. It seems that Weston may have advised withdrawal from the war, the only practical way of ending the difficulties. A memorandum by Laud, which probably dates from this time, was slanted against the calling of a Parliament.[3] His most telling point was that however much a Parliament voted, it could not be enough for the business in hand. He also feared 'that they will fall upon church business which (*in the way they have gone*) is not fit for them' (my italics). Rous and Rudyerd were perhaps right in their fear that Arminians were coming to feel a vested interest in the avoidance of Parliaments. Laud's summary of the arguments on the other side is cursory: the two main ones are 'that the king and the people may peace [?] again and the kingdom not endangered by this division,' and 'that the sight of this union at home will do much good to the affairs abroad'.

Perhaps the Conciliar case for a Parliament is set out most tellingly in the speech with which Lord Keeper Coventry opened the Parliament when it met. Above all, a Parliament was the proper way of doing things: 'a way most pleasing to the English, which brings forth many pardons and causes good kings to refrain their

[1] See, for example, an attempt by Sir Peter Hayman to recover the favour of Buckingham. *C.S.P.D. 1628–9*, vol. xci, no. 63.
[2] S.P. 16/126/44 (undated). This memorandum is placed by the *Calendar of State Papers* in the winter of 1628–9, but December 1627 or January 1628 is perhaps a more likely date. Internal evidence is not conclusive. See *A.P.C. 1627–8*, pp. 202–3. I am grateful to Professor G. E. Aylmer for this reference.
[3] Gardiner, vi. 225; S.P. 16/94/88.

prerogatives and this way best unites with his Majesty's own disposition'. A Parliament was 'a lively representation of the wisdom, wealth and power of the whole kingdom', and they should join together to repel attempts by their enemies. 'Besides, just and good kings finding the love of their people and the readiness of their supplies may the better forbear the use of their prerogatives and moderate the rigour of their laws towards their subjects.'[1] The Council, and perhaps its lawyer members in particular, were not immune from the sentiments felt by members of the Commons. They were not adherents of despotism or of Realpolitik, but people who preferred the King to rule in the traditional way, according to law, and with the goodwill of his subjects. They were not setting out to convert the King to 'new counsels', but to operate the traditional forms for as long as they were able. Provided only that the soldiers could be paid, most of the Councillors were as attached to the ideal of the rule of law as almost any speakers in the Commons. They too had estates, and neighbours, and posterities. They had not persuaded the King to release the loan refusers and call a Parliament simply in order to seek a confrontation with it. In their ideals of good government, men like Sir John Coke, May, Edmondes, Coventry, and Manchester did not differ much from leading members of the House of Commons.

The area of disagreement in 1628 was not about what was the right way of doing things: it was about the question what alternatives should be turned to when things went wrong. It was on that question that the Councillors could not help seeing things from an administrative point of view. From this point of view, they were well aware of the danger to the future of Parliaments posed by any possible refusal of supply. The letter in which Sir

---

[1] Stowe 366, f. 3ᵛ; *L.J.* 688; Duchy of Cornwall True Relation, f. 3ʳ. K. M. Sharpe, 'The Intellectual and Political Activities of Sir Robert Cotton, *c.* 1590–1631', Oxford D.Phil. Thesis (1975), pp. 221–2, B.L. Lansdowne MS. 254 (Cotton to the Council, 27 Jan. 1627/8), ff. 261ᵛ–263ʳ. Cotton thought that for defence preparations, 'There is requisite two things, money and affections, for they cannot be properly severed.' He thought that further attempts to collect taxes without Parliamentary assent would force them to depend on 'the humour of the headless multitude'. I am grateful to Dr. Sharpe for permission to quote from his thesis. See *1628 Debates*, ii. 3–9 and G. R. Elton, 'The Business of the House', *Times Literary Supplement*, 24 June 1977. The version of the Lord Keeper's speech engrossed on the Parliament Roll, and printed in the *Lords' Journals*, shows a sufficiently close resemblance to MSS. 4–13 of *Proceedings and Debates* to support the Yale Editors' hypothesis that this text was compiled with assistance from inside the Clerk's Office. *1628 Debates*, i. 17–19.

Humphrey May told Sir Thomas Wentworth he was to be set at liberty gives vent to his impatience on this subject:

Sir, Yesternight out of more grace and favour than all you refractory fools can deserve, his Majesty gave order for a general releasement out of your several confinements. I call you fools, as well for the damage you have done to yourselves, as for the interest of our posterities that may suffer by your ill example. Do not construe this course as an argument of a Parliament at hand, for I protest faithfully it is very far from it.[1]

This letter was sent a month before the Council finally persuaded the King to agree to the summons of a parliament. It is a thoroughly undiplomatic performance. It is worth remembering, though, that its impatient style is one we now remember as characteristic of its recipient, rather than of its sender.

II

Every Parliament of the 1620s assembled in a different mood, and with different concerns, from the one which met before it. The chief catalyst of change was war, and since most of the pressure of war on the English counties had happened between 1626 and 1628, it is to be expected that the change between these Parliaments is greater than between any other two of the decade. In the Parliament of 1628, any such enthusiasm for war as there may have been was dead: only Sir Francis Nethersole, agent for Elizabeth of Bohemia, tried as part of his professional duty to carry it on.[2] Charles, on the other hand, was still determined on war. La Rochelle, which had not been eager to see the English in 1627, was desperate for their assistance in 1628. Charles's use of La Rochelle as a thorn in France's side had helped to convince Richelieu that the independence of the town must be ended. Since November 1627, the harbour of La Rochelle had been closed, and Richelieu's troops were slowly starving the townsmen to death. To Charles, who rightly believed that the Rochellois were suffering for the (very limited) assistance they had given him the previous year, it was matter of urgency, on grounds of humanity and on grounds of honour, to raise the siege. When Parliament met, on 17 March, the fleet at Plymouth was expected to sail on the

---

[1] *Wentworth Papers*, pp. 282–3, 27 Dec. 1627. The letter is an interesting contrast with a much more soothing message from Dorset, yet it was Dorset, not May, who revealed that the word 'refractory' had been used by the King. Cf. May, Stowe 366, f. 235ʳ.

[2] *C.S.P.D. 1628–9*, vol. ci, no. 54.

twenty-sixth. Yet it could not sail without money. Thus Charles came to the Parliament of 1628 in such unseemly haste for money that Hakewill once said, with some excuse, that he was sure the King would prefer four subsidies on Friday to five on Monday.[1] In these circumstances, he was kept waiting three months for the subsidies he was eventually voted. Such men as Delbridge had previously spoken warmly of prayer and fasting for La Rochelle, but, in 1628, it appeared to cause them no concern that the liberties of La Rochelle were an almost certain casualty of an attempt to preserve the liberties of England. The French war was mentioned by Rudyerd and Phelips, only in order to object to its very existence. As Rudyerd asked, 'Is it a small matter that we have provoked two mighty enemies and not hurt them, and made them friends to themselves to agree to destroy us?'[2]

Yet, in sharp contrast to 1626, Rudyerd's attempt to make an issue of the French war was not followed up. Over and over again, members said they were not concerned about foreign enemies; they cared about events at home. When, in the subsidy debates, questions arose about the purposes for which the money was wanted, Eliot, recounting the ill fortune of previous foreign expeditions, said: 'Those things quail me so much that I dare not think of any putting forth again.'[3] He added that their ancestors had left foreign wars alone. Selden said that 'In Parliament the Commons ever decline to advise to foreign wars, for it is an engagement to them.'[4] Secretary Coke's attempt to induce members to consider a series of 'propositions' on foreign affairs met almost no success, and in the subsidy debates, most speakers confined themselves to expressing a longing to get the soldiers out of their counties.[5] In political, as in intellectual terms, it was the most insular of an insular series of Parliaments.

[1] Stowe 366, f. 48^r.

[2] Stowe 366, f. 10^r. On this speech, see G. R. Elton, *ubi supra*, and *1628 Debates*, ii. 72. Rudyerd was in the habit of using a written script (*N.P.* i. 75, 69). It is, then, not an implausible hypothesis that Newdegate and Stowe 366 represent notes taken on what he said in the House (*1628 Debates*, i. 21), and MSS. 4–13 of Proceedings and Debates represent copies taken from his script. If Rudyerd in the legal sense 'published' his script by depositing it in the Clerk's Office, it would then become a matter for debate which version should be regarded as the more 'authentic' record.

[3] Stowe 366, f. 38^{r-v}; Add. 36825, ff. 118–19.

[4] Add. 36825, f. 135^v.

[5] e.g. Delbridge (Stowe 366, f. 44^v), Wilde (ibid., f. 54^r), and Rich (Harl. 2313, f. 39^r). Rich feared that the soldiers would mutiny.

Not only were members not making an issue of foreign affairs: they were not being led by court divisions. In 1626, Conciliar leadership for the attack on Buckingham had meant that it was never quite without the cynical, unideological atmosphere of high power politics. In 1628, this atmosphere was missing. So was the attempt, which came with it, to attack the Duke of Buckingham. It has commonly been thought that there was a meeting, before the Parliament assembled, at which some of its leaders agreed not to attack the Duke. No documentary proof of this meeting can now be produced, but events suggest that it probably took place. The new Pembroke–Buckingham alliance held, and Rudyerd made it clear early in the Parliament that the Herbert forces would no longer be at the disposal of any attack on the Duke.[1] Without them, such an attack had no chance of success. Some members, of whom Seymour, Eliot, and Selden are the most likely, probably still wished to attack the Duke if they could, and Coke, when quoting precedents which recited that the King was acting with the advice of his 'Earls, Barons, etc.', took a mischievous pleasure in adding: 'There were no Dukes then.'[2]

However, even for Buckingham's bitterest enemies, it is unlikely that the hope of impeaching him would at first have been very high on their list of priorities, even if they had had full freedom of action. During the administration of the war, so many things they had believed to be among their liberties had been overidden in the course of the war effort that the key question now appeared to be what sort of government existed in England: was it still, in spite of the war, what Fortescue called a *dominium politicum et regale*, in which the King could not make laws or raise taxes without the assent of Parliaments, or was it being slowly driven by the inexorable necessities of war towards some form of arbitrary government?[3] It does not seem that at the beginning of the Parliament many of them thought Charles *wanted* to set up any form of arbitrary government, but they could see that, as Sir Humphrey May said, necessity had been a pressing counsellor in late years, and, 'I hope he is upon his departure.'[4]

If they wished to restore their liberties, it was necessity, rather than the Duke, who needed to be banished from the King's

[1] Stowe 366, f. 10[r].   [2] *1628 Debates*, iii. 497, iii. 105.
[3] See Phelips, Stowe 366, f. 20[r–v].
[4] *1628 Debates*, iii. 453.

counsels. There were two ways of banishing necessity: one, favoured by the Councillors and by Rudyerd, was to vote the King enough money to remove necessity. To others, such as Seymour, this savoured of giving under compulsion, especially if it were done before anything were done to confirm the threatened liberties. They therefore fell back on the second way of trying to banish necessity. They attempted to establish, by weight of legal argument, that necessity was no justification for administrative action which could not be warranted by the rule of law. As Sir Edward Coke said, to what end was it to give, if they must give again on compulsion? Before they gave, they must know what was their own to give.[1] The result was that the whole Parliament was spent on a comprehensive and eloquent vindication of the ideal of the rule of law. In the eyes of later readers, from John Lilburne down to the present day, this vindication appears magnificent. Yet, though no members of the Commons appear to have given any weight to the fact, what they were debating was civil liberties in time of war. Under those circumstances, their deliberations deserve the verdict: 'C'est magnifique, mais ce n'est pas la guerre.'

This Parliament, then, was the first of the decade which came to Westminster with the conscious and deliberate aim of vindicating English liberties. Other Parliaments had been concerned with particular liberties: they had been concerned with the liberty of the brewers not to pay purveyance, with the liberty of the Turkey merchants not to pay the imposition on currants, and with the liberty of innkeepers to pursue their trade without interference by Sir Giles Mompesson. What makes the Parliament of 1628 an intellectual watershed is their concern with all these liberties, seen collectively and as a body. It was the Parliament of 1628 which first saw these liberties as collectively threatened by a threat to the ideal which held them all together, the ideal of the rule of law. In seeing this threat, and in desiring to avoid it, all the members, court and country, official and unofficial, were united. It was Sir John Coke, Secretary of State, who introduced into the Parliament an idea which was to have a long later history: 'Our liberties are our birthright: unity confirms them.'[2]

In seeking the renewal of their liberties, the Commons showed

---

[1] Stowe 366, f. 11ʳ.
[2] Stowe 366, f. 13ᵛ. For an earlier example of the idea of the birthright, see Phelips MSS. 244/90 (1622). It goes back to the Protestation of 1621.

a unity of purpose unknown in any other Parliament of the 1620s. To an extent unknown even in 1626, the Parliament of 1628 was a one-issue Parliament. Instead of a multiplicity of small items of business jostling for priority, there was now one theme to which all members agreed to give priority. There was, if anything, even less interest in the passage of bills than there had been during the plague of 1625: some were handled while the House was filling up in the mornings, and some were handled during April, because 'the labour of liberties is now with the Lords',[1] and time had to be filled in while the Lords deliberated. At no stage between their assembly on 17 March and the King's final answer to the Petition of Right, on 7 June, did the Commons give priority to any other business. Other matters were neglected, and grand committees concerned with other matters almost ceased to function. Noy once reported that no one had appeared at the committee for continuance of statues but himself. Noy, Pym from the committee of religion, and Digges from the committee of trade all complained that they were unable to secure an adequate attendance at their committees.[2] A House of Commons which would, for three months, neglect religion, trade, and legislation in order to stick to one issue was showing a purposefulness which had not been seen for a long time.

Even among breaches of liberties, there was a remarkable degree of unanimity in concentrating on the four which ultimately found their way into the Petition of Right: the Forced Loan, arbitrary imprisonment, billeting of soldiers, and the use of martial law. There were two other issues a body of members wanted to pursue. One was impositions, introduced by petitions from the wine merchants and the Turkey merchants. Alford and Delbridge would have liked this issue to have a place together with the four main issues. Phelips, whose concern with impositions was well established, wanted to discuss the issue. Yet, when Alford wanted to put illegal collection of Tonnage and Poundage into the Petition of Right, it was Phelips who overruled him, saying that only the 'murdering grievances' should go in.[3] An issue which could override impositions in the mind of Phelips must have been serious indeed. Even Sir Edward Coke was content to ask only that

---

[1] Wandesford, 22 April. Add. 36825, f. 216ʳ.
[2] Stowe 366, ff. 54ᵛ, 105ʳ, 173ᵛ, 119ʳ, 175ʳ, 200ʳ, 203ʳ.
[3] Add. 36825, f. 291ʳ.

Charles should not introduce any new impositions: 'We know the King's wants to be great, and so never questioned this revenue. Shall this moderation of ours bring in these new impositions?'[1]

The other peripheral issue which concerned a number of members was that of Arminianism. To Pym and Sherland, liberties were as much threatened by what they saw as the incipient disappearance of true religion in England as they were by billeting or the Five Knights' case. In trying to make a central issue out of Arminianism, they had the co-operation of a few intensely concerned members. Richard Knightley, Henry Sherfield of Salisbury, and Buckingham's men Sir Henry Mildmay and Sir Robert Harley would have supported making Arminianism one of the leading issues of the Parliament. It was Harley who introduced the proposal, of which much more was to be heard in 1629, to rule out Arminianism by confirming Archbishop Whitgift's Lambeth Articles. Yet concern about Arminianism was very far from universal. Sir Edward Coke, for example, did not have even the limited sympathy for proceedings on this issue that he had for proceedings on impositions. When Mildmay, Harley, and Sherfield started an attack on one of the leading Arminian clergymen, Dr. Jackson, Coke intervened in Jackson's defence, saying he was learned and honest [2] Pym made some progress on this issue, but only by working in select committees, leaving the full House to concentrate on issues of more universal appeal.

One reason for this remarkable unanimity on their agenda was that there was probably an equally remarkable sameness about the complaints members were receiving from their countries. Unlike previous country grievances, the effects of the war, in various forms, were nation-wide. Some other grievances, such as the patents of 1621, had affected many areas, but there was not the same uniformity about them that there was about the effects of war in 1628. There is an interesting difference of emphasis between the complaints members made on their own account and those they reported as made in their countries. The one issue which concerned most members more than any other was that of arbitrary imprisonment, but the issue that was most widely said to be complained of in the country was that of billeting. This, it is true, was chiefly a grievance of the south and south-west of the country,

1 Add. 36825, f. 332r.
2 Add. 36825, ff. 52–3, further reported by Newdegate.

but these were also the areas which were most heavily over-represented in Parliament.

Other issues, such as the Forced Loan, impressment of soldiers, or the levying of militia rates and coat and conduct money, affected all the country. Edward Alford, from Sussex, said his countrymen had been asked for four or five payments of coat and conduct money, and that without relief from this, they would hardly be able to pay the subsidy. Mr Fletcher's conclusions suggest that Alford much exaggerated the cost of coat and conduct money (unless he confused it with the much heavier rates for billeting), but that he did not exaggerate local resistance to it.[1] Crew, from Northamptonshire, said it was essential that, when the country said: 'You have given five subsidies', they should be able to reply, 'But we have eased you of soldiers.' Digges claimed, stretching the limits of legal memory, that in East Kent men had been terrified 'before, at, nor since' the Conquest (sic), 'and the best of us all are scarce safe in our houses'.[2]

At the beginning of the Parliament, and indeed up to Easter, it appeared that in asking for a confirmation of their liberties, members of the Commons were beating on an open door. The Councillors made no attempt to deny that many of the methods of government used during the past two years had been illegal, and seemed as eager as most private members for some sort of confirmation of liberties to show that this extraordinary period was at an end. Secretary Coke said on 2 April that the cause of calling this Parliament had been the 'desire to fall to regular courses'.[3] On 3 April, he delivered an encouraging message from the King. By this time, the King was well able to discover what the grievances were, yet he led the Commons to have every hope that they would get a favourable answer to them: 'Our grievances he will hear with a pious and princely care, and professes he will never command slaves, but freemen.' 'For their grievances says he let them go on in God's name. Why should any man hinder them?'[4] On 1 May, speaking on his own behalf, Secretary Coke was even more explicit: 'We speak out of sense of our suffering. We desire this breach to be made up. We hear no defence of that which was done, confessed to be unlegal. Consider the time—when wants time of action: a young king newly come to his crown: in war. The

[1] Stowe 366, f. 71^r; Fletcher, p. 195.   [2] Stowe 366, ff. 40^r, 59^v.
[3] Stowe 366, f. 37^v.   [4] Stowe 366, f. 41^{r-v}.

King was desirous to come out of the extraordinary way, and called this Parliament to bring us into the old way.'[1] With this much official encouragement, it should have been possible to obtain a confirmation of liberties which said, in a way acceptable to all parties, that the traditional forms were going to be restored. Why, when so much of what they were saying was acceptable to the King and Council, were the House of Commons so determined to express their demands in a form which proved unacceptable to the King and Council?

Part of the reason must be that it was so plainly impossible for things to return to normal during a war. When the Commons voted five subsidies, which were to be embodied in a bill when the grievances were redressed, the King, even in the midst of his gratitude, plainly admitted they were not enough: they were about a quarter of what he needed. There was some excuse for the fear of Sir John Strangeways, that, having given subsidies, they would be forced to give loans as well after the Parliament.[2] Since the Commons were not voting enough to enable the King to do without arbitrary taxation, they were bound to expect him to continue it.

Yet distrust of the King was not the only reason, and perhaps not even the main reason why the Commons in this Parliament asserted the ideal of the rule of law in so inflexible a form. At the beginning of the Parliament, some of members' suspicion was fastened on something more far-reaching than the King's mood: some of the initial distrust was directed at the common law itself. Most English gentlemen had taken it for granted that the law guaranteed them certain liberties, above all that of security in their property. While they were secure in this belief, they were prepared to admit certain exceptions, which, while they might offend against the practice of the rule of law, were not taken to offend against its principle. As the veteran Sir Thomas Hoby reminded the Commons, when the Elizabethan traitor Francis Babington had been arrested, there had been no objection to the fact that he was held without trial or charge while his accomplices were rounded up. Similarly, there had been no application for a Habeas Corpus on behalf of Guy Fawkes.

What happened after the Five Knights' case was that a fear

---

[1] *1628 Debates*, iii. 195. Grosvenor's appears to be the best report of this speech.   [2] Newdegate, i. f. 32.

began that the common law had allowed so many of these discretionary exceptions that it had ceased to be any safe rule. If a
residual discretionary power in the King were used, not merely to
imprison Guy Fawkes, but to imprison Justices of the Peace and
Deputy Lieutenants, then a law which allowed such a power was
no safe guarantee of liberty: the law on which they had depended for so long might be turning out to offer an illusory security.
Sir Robert Phelips remembered that in test cases before the common law judges, things had not gone as he would have wished:
'We have had three judgements of late times, all exceeding one
another in prejudice.' The first two he mentioned were Calvin's
case and Bate's case, and the third that in the Five Knights' case:

I can live, although another (without title) be put to live with me. Nay,
I can live though I pay excises and impositions for more than I do, but to
have my liberty (which is the soul of my life) taken from me by power,
and to be pent up in a gaol without remedy by law, and to be so adjudged
(shall I perish in gaol) O improvident ancestors! O unwise forefathers!
to be so curious in providing for the quiet possession of our lands, and the
liberties of Parliament, and to neglect our persons and bodies, and to let
them lie in prison, and that, *durante beneplacito*, remediless. If this be law,
what do we talk of our liberties?[1]

It was not of the King or Council that Phelips was complaining in
this passage: it was of a ruling by the common law judges in open
court. He was not the only man to find that his confidence in the
law as a ground of security was weakened by the Five Knights'
case. The Earl of Clare, writing privately to Wentworth a week
before the writs went out for a Parliament, was more explicit:

Son Wentworth, God be thanked your string is lengthened at the last. For
I cannot term you, nor myself, a freeman, when law hath no protection
for us; for this diseased body our councillors have left us and the disease
still strengtheneth upon us. Neither do the lawyers, the physicians for
this subject, heal us any whit, for *meum* or *tuum* between common persons
they crow in every corner, but when the question transcends between
the head and the body, they are crestfallen and have nothing to say and
if accidentally something of them be heard and show themself in the
lawn [sic], they only beray the place and leave the matter worse than
they found it; witness the late *Habeas Corpus*.[2]

On many occasions, speakers in the Commons admitted that their
real question was not whether the King would agree to rule by
law, but what the law was. To discover that a phrase as central as

[1] *1628 Debates*, ii. 63; Add. 36825, ff. 38–9.
[2] *Wentworth Papers*, pp. 287–8.

lex terrae, the law of the land, was, as Sir Roger North put it on 6 May, 'an unfolded riddle' to which no clear meaning could be assigned was a cause for alarm about the law, rather than about the King.[1] Eliot, asking 'Where is law? Where is *meum et tuum*? It is fallen into the chaos of a higher power', was expressing a fear which went deeper than fear of the King.[2] It was a fear that the common law was too uncertain to provide for the security of the subjects. Pym, on 6 May, bluntly drew attention to the fact that the key issue was that they and the Council did not agree what the law was: 'If they were not persuaded of the lawfulness of these commitments, I think they would not do it.'[3]

The problem, then, was not just to re-establish trust in the King: it was to re-establish trust in the certainty of the common law.

To some extent, then, the exceptional dominance of lawyers in the Parliament of 1628 is deceptive: they were speaking for the justification of their own subject and their own profession. For all the trust Stuart gentlemen had felt in the law, distrust for its practitioners was never very far away from their minds. The Earl of Bedford, in his commonplace book, noted with strong approval an occasion when the Roman Republic was said to have banished all its lawyers.[4] In the Parliament, this hostility showed up in a speech made by Goodwin on a bill to exempt the four marcher shires from the jurisdiction of the Council of Wales. He said the benefit of it would come only to some gentlemen who happened to have practice in Westminster Hall. He said that, 'In Westminster a man be gone thrice to the West Indies before their suits be determined: nay, a man may grow old, and yet his suits but young. The 10th part of expenses in any courts here shall end a suit there.'[5] Clare's letter suggested that this type of hostility, with which lawyers were familiar, was now invading the one area in which men had depended upon them: their ability, by their technicalities, to erect a secure bulwark for preservation of liberty

---

[1] *1628 Debates*, iii. 280.   [2] *1628 Debates*, ii. 57.

[3] Grosvenor, 6 May, 1628; Harl. 5324, f. 31ᵛ.

[4] Bedford MSS., vol. XI. i, p. 25. Bedford also wrote 'that common lawyers want nothing of the office of King but the name, and are perpetual dictators—an office which the Romans could not hold above six months'. He noted an Italian proverb that 'the devil makes his Christmas pies of lawyers' tongues and clerks' fingers'. The comparison with the clergy, like Clare's with physicians, may shed some light on lay resentment of lawyers.

[5] *1628 Debates*, iii. 423.

and property. If men were to lose faith in the ability of the law to do that, lawyers would be in a bad way indeed.

Men like Coke, then, had more than one cause at stake when they spoke to try to prove the certainty of the common law. When he repeated one of his favourite maxims, *misera servitus est ubi jus est vagum et incognitum* (wretched is the slavery where law is wandering or unknown) he was facing many of his personal nightmares at once. He was facing a private fear that he would be unable to know what the law was, a professional fear that the reputation of his subject would be shattered, and a public fear that the restraints on arbitrary power in which he had always trusted might turn out not to be there. Selden, who had been counsel on the losing side in the Five Knights' case, drew attention to this anti-lawyer feeling: 'I have spoken for my fee in this case already, and now I speak to discharge a duty to my country.'[1] These may have been among the reasons which led Sir Edward Coke to claim such absoluteness for the common law. Speaking at a conference with the Lords, 'I replied that we desired to leave nothing to constructions and we sought to keep away all uncertainty from posterity.'[2] The trouble, after the Five Knights' case, was that the law was thought to have left too much trust in the King. It was then possible, either to restore trust in the King, by a general confirmation of the laws such as the Councillors wanted, or to restore trust in the common law by asserting that, rather than allowing such discretion to the King, it gave rules to him. It is perhaps not surprising that, faced by this choice, Coke, Selden, and their fellow-lawyers chose to restore trust in the common law. Their success, whether complete or partial, was far-reaching in its effects, but it precluded any workable settlement with the King.

It also led to the beginnings of a political theory, to a growing cult of the rule of law as an ideal which could stand beside the religious ideals of John Foxe. In the process, however, it led to the exposure of many of the jurisprudential difficulties facing the English common law. The common law is a law based, as Hobbes would have it, on what 'the lawyers, who only use this false measure of justice, barbarously call . . . a precedent':[3] it is built up out of particular cases, and therefore does not readily receive a concept of sovereignty. Concepts of liberty drawn from the com-

[1] Stowe 366, f. 23ᵛ.   [2] Stowe 366, f. 176ʳ.
[3] T. Hobbes, *Leviathan*, pt. I, ch. xi.

mon law are therefore likely to be made up of a set of particular points, of a Burkeian series of 'liberties'. As Sir Edward Coke said, 'Franchise is a French word, and in Latin it is liberty. In Magna Carta, *nullus imprisonetur* nor put out of his liberty or franchise.'[1] A liberty based on the common law will be a series of franchises, particular liberties, and immunities granted or adjudged on particular occasions. Such an approach to liberty leads easily to the identification of liberty with property, and of liberties with inheritances. As the Petition of Right itself said, it was designed to confirm the liberties the subjects had inherited. Liberties, like title-deeds, were traced back to an original grant, in this case mainly to Magna Carta.

This was very suitable to the members, since the sort of liberty it confirmed was the sort they hoped to enjoy. Yet the common law faced two serious difficulties in the way of any attempt to base a general theory of liberty and trial by due process of law upon it. In the first place, its own precedents were too various, and too particular. For every precedent which was produced to one effect, a precedent might be produced which appeared to make to the opposite effect. Until the writing and publication of Coke's *Institutes*, the common law lacked any adequate general body of principles which could be used as an analytical tool to handle large and miscellaneous bodies of precedents. As Coke himself said, when faced with a contrary precedent from a judgement of his own, this precedent should be ignored because it was 'under age': it was less than twenty-one years old.[2] Coke himself later explained convincingly how, on fuller study of the law, he had been led to change his mind. Yet, however much this may enhance respect for Coke as a scholar, it does nothing for the authority of the common law as a whole. How, unless by a general body of legal principles, should men choose between the authority of a precedent from the early Coke and one from the later Coke? A law based on precedent must, for all Coke's insistence to the contrary, run the risk of lacking certainty. It is noteworthy how much Selden and Littleton, who were in charge of the management of precedents, retreated from an authority based on precedent towards one based on statute. As Selden told the Lords on 7 April, 'Precedents, my Lords, are good media or proofs, of illustration

---

[1] *1628 Debates*, ii. 64.
[2] Stowe 366, f. 32[r].

or confirmation, when they agree with the express law; but they can never be proof enough to overthrow any one law.'[1] Selden, as he examined the material he was handling, was driven inexorably back upon the supremacy of statute. By 19 April, he had been drawn into a fully formulated theory of Parliamentary sovereignty, involving the claim that Parliament could enact whatever they chose. He said: 'The same power that established the common law must establish martial law, and were it established here by Act of Parliament, it would be most lawful, for so it might be made death to rise before nine a clock.'[2]

In asking for the power which established the common law, Selden was asking precisely the question Coke found it hardest to answer, for in Coke's ancient constitution theory, as followed by Pym or Digges, there was no such power. Coke claimed that Magna Carta was a source of authority, and that all statutes against Magna Carta were void.[3] Yet the tendency in Coke towards erecting Magna Carta to the status of a constitution was one he never carried through to a conclusion: even the famous phrase 'Magna Carta is such a fellow he will have no sovereign' appears to read correctly 'Magna Carta is such a fellow he will have no saving'.[4] It is easy to see, in the face of Selden's questions, why Coke should have resisted the temptation to erect Magna Carta into a constitution. If Magna Carta were a constitution, then its framers would be constitution-makers, and Coke would have introduced the one thing he could not abide: a sovereign authority of higher authority than the laws. *Oportet neminem esse sapientiorem legibus*: no man should be wiser than the laws. No man, then, could be one of the original makers of the common law. Indeed, in Coke's

---

[1] *L.J.* 722. As Phelips put it, precedents were the servants to Acts of Parliament. Stowe 366, f. 34ʳ.

[2] Harl. 2313, ff. 54–3.

[3] *L.J.* 730. See J. G. A. Pocock, *The Ancient Constitution and the Feudal Law* (Cambridge, 1956).

[4] The reading 'sovereign' is commonly quoted from Rushworth. Grosvenor (20 May) reads 'saving', and the Editors of *1628 Debates*, after collation of manuscripts, have taken a reading of 'saving' for the Proceedings and Debates also. Since Coke immediately goes on to say that Magna Carta has been 33 times confirmed without a saving, there is at least as much logical probability in the reading 'saving' as in the reading 'sovereign'. In another speech on the same day, Coke said that 'What is warranted by law is lawful: what is not warranted by law is unlawful.' This sentence is a good illustration of the complete rejection of legal *adiaphora* which Coke was attempting in 1628. *1628 Debates*, iii. 501.

view, there were no such things as original makers of the common law: he believed 'the grounds of the common law are grounded upon the law of God'.[1]

For Coke and his followers, then, the common law had no original founder: it had existed from time immemorial, had been embodied in Magna Carta, and confirmed again each time breaches of Magna Carta made a confirmation necessary. The origins of the common law therefore could not be discovered: they were lost in the mists of antiquity. This left Coke painfully vulnerable to a civilian lawyer with a formulated concept of sovereignty. For example, it was agreed in the Commons that martial law was only legal in armies in time of war. Coke admitted that it was difficult to define a time of war, or to say how many men made an army. Sir Henry Marten, the civilian, said that since the King made peace and war, his was the authority which could say whether a time of war existed. To this Coke replied: 'Let us go to our rules and hold ourself to our law as Ulysses to his ship, and not hear any siren's song.'[2] It also left Coke painfully vulnerable to the proposition suggested by the Lords on 25 April, that the King had a 'royal prerogative, intrinsical to his sovereignty and betrusted him withal from God for the common safety of the whole people and not for their destruction'. It was the whole object of Coke's exercise to show that the common law could control, or, as he put it, admeasure such a prerogative. This claim was very different from the claim made in 1610, that the common law laid down the limits within which the prerogative could operate.

Yet he had no answer to this proposed Lords' saving except to say it was contrary to Magna Carta. He saw all the possible gravity of the Lords' saving, in a way the Lords themselves probably had not: 'It is meant that intrinsical prerogative is not bounded by any law, or by any law qualified. We must admit this intrinsical prerogative an exempt prerogative, and so all our laws are out. And this intrinsical prerogative is entrusted him by God, and then it is due by divine right, and then no law can take it away. Then it follows for defence etc. if his Majesty shall "find cause" to commit, he may.' This was a better summary of the Lords' case for a

---

[1] Harl. 2313, f. 16ᵛ. For support for Coke's rejection of any notion that the common law had original makers, see Sir Leslie Scarman, *English Law: The New Dimension* (1975), pp. 1–3.

[2] *1628 Debates*, iii. 307, 315.

residual power of imprisonment to be left in the Crown than the Lords could make, but his only reply was, '*Nolumus leges Angliae mutare*. I would never yield to alter Magna Carta.'[1]

To control a power which, in the eyes of some of the Lords, antedated Magna Carta and had survived it, Magna Carta was not a sufficient authority. To control a prerogative which Coke could not prove had not survived Magna Carta, some higher authority was necessary. The King out of Parliament could only be controlled by a higher authority, and this could only be, as Selden would have it, the King in Parliament. Between 3 May and 22 May, it became increasingly clear that what the Commons were asking was not a confirmation of Magna Carta or of the existing law: it was a new legislative enactment, giving statutory force to their own interpretation of Magna Carta and the six statutes confirming it. Thus, little by little, what was meant to be an attempt to secure the King's confirmation of an immemorial and unchanging common law became an attempt to secure a new statute, in which a reluctant King was to be persuaded to agree to give legislative force to the Commons' interpretation of existing statutes. On 6 May, Littleton made the revealing comment on the proposal to confirm the existing laws that even the best lawyers would not be able to extract the Commons' resolutions out of Magna Carta and the six statutes confirming it, on which the Commons had insisted, unless they had followed the proceedings of the House.[2] In fact, whatever Coke might say to the contrary, the existing common law had proved not to be certain.

That is why the Commons were determined, in the face of the King's opposition, to use a new statute to enforce new legislative restrictions on the King out of Parliament. Thus it was that, for the first time in the 1620s, Parliamentary proceedings came to be dominated by a contest between the King and the Commons about the nature and limits of supreme authority. Digges perceptively compared their proceedings to the debate at the Council of Basle 'whether the Pope be above the church or the church above the Pope, so now there is a doubt whether the law be above the King or the King above the law'. Wentworth might protest that 'I trust no question shall ever stir whether the king be above the law or

---

[1] *1628 Debates*, iii. 95. I would like to thank Mr. Richard Radway for drawing my attention to this difference between the ideas of 1628 and the ideas of 1610.
[2] *1628 Debates*, iii. 280, 291–2.

the law be above the King, neither does it', but the question did stir, and was not easily stilled.[1] It stirred, for the first time in the 1620s, because Coke and his colleagues were unable, without recourse to the legislative authority of the King in Parliament, to show the ground and authority for their interpretation of an immemorial and unchanging common law. Their difficulties were well shown by Digges on 7 April, opening what he rightly called the 'cloudy part' of the Commons' case in their first big conference with the Lords. He set out the Cokeian doctrine of the ancient constitution, as eloquently as Coke ever did. He said he was defending 'laws so ancient, as that the Saxons' days notwithstanding the ruins and injury of times, continued the same constantly'. He traced them back to the laws of Ethelbert of Kent. He said that, in confirming them, 'St. Edward received those laws, did not give them. And ever since him, William the Conqueror and his successors, kings of England, are sworn to them. Now with these laws of our Saxon kings, the modern laws do concur.' Yet, in this magnificent picture of the ancient constitution, Digges revealed, by an ill-chosen metaphor, that he could show no authority by which these things were made law. In the course of an image which was designed to compare the Commons' precedent-hunters to King Josiah and the high priest, he said 'they found (he could not say a book of our law, but) the main and fundamental points of law, neglected and broken'. Digges's metaphor had simply shown up the fact that, unlike King Josiah, he lacked an authoritative source. In claiming that 'the laws of England were grounded upon reason more ancient than books', he issued an open invitation to the development, not of law, but of speculative political ideas.[2]

This invitation was taken up. Speculation about the ultimate source of law led to speculation about the ultimate source of civil authority. Some people, including Pym,[3] seemed to suggest that authority was founded on an original contract between King and people. Rudyerd and Mason, in a significantly modified version of ancient constitution theory, thought that William had ruled by right of conquest, but in Magna Carta, the King had voluntarily restored to his people the right to be ruled by their ancient laws.

---

[1] Stowe 366, f. 111^{r-v}.   [2] *L.J.* 718.
[3] See Pym's speech on the impeachment of Manwaring. J. Rushworth, *Historical Collections* (1659), i. 596, 602.

By contrast, Sir John Coke, Secretary of State, even while saying that 'we all hold the common law our inheritance that doth preserve us', produced some dramatically different reflections on the origins of civil power. In debating the authority for martial law, he said: 'We are in the government of a state. The martial law touches kings highly. It is their very original. They are God's captains and leaders of his people. The name of kings is sacred, and the foundation of the commonwealth depends on them.'[1] It is probable that this idea owed more to the words of Samuel in the Old Testament than to any theory of conquest, but the divergence now appearing between him and his namesake Sir Edward Coke is striking. As recently as the beginning of the Parliament, five weeks before this speech, they had appeared to hold closely similar positions. Their divergence had appeared in the crucible of the Parliamentary debates.

For those who accepted it, there was room behind the façade of Sir Edward Coke's ancient constitution for a large growth of political ideas. One of the key points in the Commons' thought was the distinction between rule over freemen and rule over villeins. As Sir Edward Coke said, 'No man can be imprisoned upon will and pleasure of any, but he that is bond and a villein; for that and to tallage him high and low are proper to villeins. Now . . . the species are convertible; whosoever is a bondman may be imprisoned upon will and pleasure, and whosoever may be imprisoned upon will and pleasure is a bondman.'[2] Selden, with typical attention to his sources, added recusants, Jews, and madmen along with villeins.[3] In ruling over free subjects, the King must not imprison them without a cause shown, to which they could make a legal answer. 'According to the law of the land', in the words of Magna Carta, they translated as 'by due process of law', involving a writ, asserting a cause, to which those accused might make answer. Though the King was supreme, he must exercise his power in the proper channels: he could only imprison a man by using the correct legal procedure, through a writ: 'He could not imprison by word of mouth: and the reason, because the party hath no remedy; for the law leaves every man a remedy of causeless imprisonment.'[4]

---

[1] *1628 Debates*, iii. 31; 1 Samuel, chapter 8.
[2] *L.J.* 729. The question of villeinage was not entirely antiquarian: see above p. 330.   [3] Stowe 366, f. 39ᵛ.   [4] *L.J.* 731.

With this idea of inherited liberties, handed down from generation to generation, broken, but confirmed and renewed every time they were broken, there came many others. A link was enunciated between liberty and prosperity: in the words of Sir Nathaniel Rich, 'No propriety, no industry; no industry, all beggars, no propriety, no valour, no valour, all in confusion.'[1] In Littleton's words, to reduce men to the status of villeins 'takes away industry, valour and justice, which concerns only *meum* and *tuum*, and besides, it brings a confusion of all estates'.[2] With this came the line of argument suggested by a reading of Sir John Fortescue, that there was a distinctive quality of liberty enjoyed by the English, whose fruits were shown up in their prosperity. This line of argument had been started by Sir Dudley Carleton[3] in his 'new counsels' speech of 1626, and the man who did most to continue it in 1628 was Carleton's former ambassadorial assistant, Digges.[4] He said that strangers admired our liberty, and that 'The king that is not tied to the laws is a king of slaves. I have been in employment abroad: for the propriety of goods and of liberty see the misery of the contrary in other nations.' In this speech Digges was referring to his embassy to Russia, rather than to his embassy to the Netherlands. This comparison was doubtless highly flattering to a country whose arms had just been so humiliated at the hands of the arbitrary power of France.

The same intellectual nationalism showed up in the resistance to all foreign parallels, and to foreign laws, particularly to the civil law. When Sir Francis Nethersole said that martial law was allowed in the Low Countries, Ball replied: 'What the civil law or practice of the Low Countries is, nothing to us: . . . the lords said *nolumus leges Angliae mutare.*' He said (rightly) that it had been resolved in 11 Richard II that the kingdom was not governed by the civil law. In the same debate, Sir Edward Coke objected to an attempt by Sir Henry Marten to base the martial law on civil law, and to say that the common law did not enjoy a legal monopoly in England: 'The civilian talks of conveniency. God keep us to the discretion of our common law. The civilian says both laws may stand together: as well may the judge and soldier sit both

---

[1] Stowe 366, f. 21r.   [2] Harl. 2313, f. 28r.

[3] Add. 36825, f. 69v. For Carleton, see J. P. Kenyon, *The Stuart Constitution* (Cambridge, 1966), pp. 50–1. Carleton, when he made the speech quoted, had just returned from France.

[4] Add. 36825, f. 43r.

together on the bench.' It was an essential part of Sir Edward Coke's case that 'two laws will never stand together in England', and 'there is no law like ours: to talk of foreign law is but a foreign speech'. 'No other state is like this: we are *divisos ab orbe Britannos.*' 'We have a national appropriate law to this kingdom. If you tell me of other laws, you are gone.' The reader is reminded of the recent reflection of Sir Leslie Scarman, that the common law, while having many things to learn from the civil law, is remarkably resistant to any process of merging with other legal traditions.[1]

Yet it is possible that the intensity of hostility to the civil law was not merely a fear of the will of the prince having the force of law, but, at least occasionally, a case of protesting too much. There was probably no member in the Commons who felt more hostility to the civil law than John Selden, yet even he, in his first major speech on martial law, on 15 April, conceded some unexpected points. He conceded that martial law had a proper place in an army in time of war.

As the canon and civil law we have from Rome and out of the Empire, so is this martial law out of the law of the Emperor. In the title of the civil law they have titles *de re militari*. Those laws were at the pleasure of the Emperor or general of the army. And there is no certain *leges militares*. As in the empire they had *leges militares*, so have we our martial law, which is according to the pleasure of the kings of England: at divers times divers laws.[2]

Perhaps, even after the Parliament had been in session for a month, confidence in the total adequacy of the common law was less complete than the impression given by some of the speeches would lead us to suppose.

It is in the debates on martial law that we see what is perhaps the main reason why this Parliament is so different from what had gone before: the presence of armed force under the King's command. There is no need to follow Sir Robert Phelips in claiming that 'We now little differ from the course in Turkey, where the Janissary sets his halberd there he is master without resistance.'[3] Phelips was well aware that the troops at Charles's disposal were not

---

[1] Grosvenor, 18 April; Stowe 366, f. 92ʳ; *1628 Debates*, ii. 555; Stowe 366 f. 16ᵛ; Add. 36825, f. 58ʳ. Sir Leslie Scarman, *English Law: The New Dimension* (1975), pp. 9–10.

[2] *1628 Debates*, ii. 463. Cf. Littleton, iii. 487.

[3] Stowe 366, f. 10ᵛ. *1628 Debates* (ii. 69) reads 'Janissaryes'. The final 's' is uncertain.

Janissaries. It is perhaps easier to follow him in believing that Deputy Lieutenants, with power to raise money by warrants, were 'the great practical power to subdue English liberty'.[1] It is only necessary to remember that Phelips accepted appointment as a Deputy Lieutenant in September 1628. The martial law commissions, as Mason pointed out on 15 April, not only gave authority over people other than soldiers: they also joined captains with local gentlemen in the government of the army. Where soldiers were billeted in private houses, it was impossible that two laws should live in the same house. Martial law commissions created a real possibility that soldiers would be used to interfere with the most cherished of all English liberties: the autonomy of county government. The hub of the Commons' objection to martial law was best stated by Strode on 22 April. He asked whether martial law was now being extended to gentlemen. 'If a soldier wrong me, I must complain to a martial court, and am then subject to that court. Moved that all matters between countrymen and soldier to be ordered by commission of oyer: and between soldier and soldier by martial law.' The objection was not to the existence of martial law: it was to the possibility of using it to govern civilians. This was a possibility which had been made real by the fact of billeting: soldiers, subject to martial law, might bring that law, like the plague, into the houses where they were placed.[2]

Almost all the elements in the debates of 1628 can be found, in isolation, somewhere in earlier Parliaments. What is new in 1628 is, first the obsessive concentration on issues of liberties, and second, the merging together of so many concerns about liberty all at the same time. What brought all these concerns together was the centralization, and the finance, required by organizing a war effort. Among the collection of legal maxims, perhaps the one which best explains the fears of the Commons in 1628 is *inter arma silent leges*: amidst arms the laws are silent. The converse is also true: *inter leges silent arma*. And though most of the other things the Parliament of 1628 contended for were not achieved, they did at least succeed in putting an end to the King's war effort.

[1] Stowe 366, f. 40ʳ.
[2] *1628 Debates*, iii. 32, 28. See above, p. 337 and n.

III

Until Easter, King and Commons of 1628 appear to have been happily unaware that they were heading for a confrontation. The Commons had voted five subsidies, a sum which, inadequate as it was, was the largest the King could possibly have hoped for. In return, it was clear that they expected some form of confirmation of their liberties, to be made before the subsidy bill was complete. They had been encouraged in this desire by Councillors, and not discouraged from it by the King. The King's need for subsidies was too urgent to give him much room for manœuvre. He could not, without fear of mutiny, attempt to disband his soldiers and sailors without paying them, and he could not, without fear of paralysing civil authority, keep most of them under arms much longer. Moreover, another fleet was waiting at Portsmouth, while the King daily hoped to go to it. At La Rochelle, where the townsmen, while waiting for relief, were dying of starvation, the urgency appeared even greater than it did to the King. If any reminder of the urgency of money was needed, it was provided by the appearance, at the door of the House of Lords on 21 April, of a group of mariners whose pay was fifteen months in arrears. They 'denied they have raised any tumults, but it is in their power'. Finally, after an assurance from Buckingham that they would be paid 'this week', '*exeunt*, promising to pacify their fellows'.[1]

In these circumstances, it is not surprising to find that there was some connection in Charles's mind between the discovery that the Commons' demands were cast in an unpalatable form and the discovery that they were cast in a form which would take a long time. On 10 April, Charles told the Houses, to the indignation of the Commons, that shortage of time did not permit an Easter recess. An attempt to hasten supply on Good Friday produced the cynical reply from Alford that they should 'leave it, with this excuse, to serve God'.[2] Sir Thomas Wentworth, saying they must remember both the trust they owed to their countries and the duty they owed to their King, agreed to Sir Edward Coke's motion to fix the time of payment of subsidies, but persuaded the Committee not to report the decision to the full House until there was a bill for their liberties. On Good Friday, 11 April, then, the Commons resolved in principle to pay five subsidies in a year, but took no

---

[1] *Lords' Debates*, pp. 123–4.   [2] Add. 36825, f. 163ᵛ.

action on the resolution. The subsidy bill was to wait for the confirmation of their liberties.

The next day, Secretary Coke delivered an angry message from the King calling for haste. It was in glossing this message that Secretary Coke said the King was becoming alarmed by the constitutional implications of what the Commons were demanding:

I must with grief tell you, it is conceived as this House spares not to trench upon abuses of power, so it spares not power itself, a power by which we are all supported. He [the King] likes well to hear complaints of any abuse whatsoever, and not to except against his regal power, but the abuse of it.[1]

This was the first of many messages in which it was conveyed that the King now thought that the essentials of his power were under attack. As these exchanges went on, it emerged that King and Commons intended very different things by a confirmation of the laws. For the King, and for his Councillors, a confirmation was first and foremost a symbolic act: a sign that the King meant to return to what Secretary Coke called 'regular courses'. Above all, it meant to the Councillors a decision to continue calling Parliaments. They saw no incompatibility between Parliaments and prerogatives.[2] And the survival of Parliaments was now in very considerable doubt, a doubt which the inadequacy of the five subsidies in the pipeline might well reinforce.[3] For King and Councillors, then, a confirmation of liberties was not to be a legislative enactment, but a declaration of intent.

Such a declaration of intent would commit them to a gamble on future Parliamentary supply. Should the gamble fail, they might well find they were again in need of powers they were willing and happy to abandon if they could afford to do so. The King was willing to confirm the existing law, including Magna Carta and the six supporting statutes cited by the Commons, but he was not willing to allow the making of anything he took to be new law. He was willing to give way on the question of Forced Loans, and committed himself, in his letter of 12 May, not to imprison for refusal of loans in future. The power the King would not abandon was the power of imprisonment. In the same letter, the King made it clear that he believed he had a residual power

[1] *1628 Debates*, ii. 434.
[2] Harl. 5324, f. 45ᵛ (1 May) when Secretary Coke said that, whatever Parliament resolved, his Councillor's oath bound him in some cases to commit without showing cause.
[3] See Hakewill, Stowe 366, f. 124ʳ.

of imprisonment which was above the law and could not be controlled by it:[1]

We find it still insisted on, that in no case whatsoever, though they should
never so nearly concern matters of state and government, we or our Privy
Council have power to commit a man without the cause shown, whereas
it often happens that should the cause be shown the service itself would
thereby be destroyed and defeated. And [that] the cause alleged must be
such as may be determined by our judges of our courts at Westminster
in a legal and ordinary way of justice, whereas the cause may be such as
those judges have no capacity of judicature nor rules of law to direct and
guide their judgements in causes of that transcendent nature, which
happening so often, the very intermitting of the constant rules of government for so many ages within this kingdom practised would soon dissolve
the very frame and foundation of our monarchy. . . . Without overthrow
of sovereignty we cannot suffer this power to be impeached. Notwithstanding to clear our conscience and just intentions, we publish that it
is not in our heart, nor will we ever extend our regal power (lent unto us
from God) beyond that just rule of moderation in any thing which shall
be contrary to our laws and customs, wherein the safety of our peoples
shall be our only aim.

In this passage, Charles denied, as categorically as was possible,
Sir Edward Coke's doctrine of a prerogative limited by the rule
of law. He was claiming what Sir Humphrey May said was something not in Parliament's power to take away: a power which had not
been conferred by the law, and could not be controlled by the law.[2]

It is at this point that it begins to become clear that the King,
under the stress of events, and the Commons, under Sir Edward
Coke's guidance, were coming to attach two different meanings
to the word 'prerogative'. The Commons repeatedly declared that
they did not intend to diminish the King's prerogative, and, according to the meaning they attached to the word 'prerogative',
these declarations were sincere. Hakewill said on 20 May that the
Commons did not intend to diminish the King's prerogative,
because, on the matters covered by the Petition of Right, he had
none.[3] The Commons recognized that the King had a specific list
of 'prerogatives' as itemized by Sir Thomas Smith which were
conferred and 'admeasured' by law. The King could make war
and peace, he could pardon offenders, he could grant letters of
denization to aliens, and he could strike coin. The King had these
prerogatives because he was granted them by law. Even where

---

[1] Stowe 366, f. 161ᵛ. *1628 Debates*, iii. 372.
[2] *1628 Debates*, iii. 533.   [3] Stowe 366, f. 179ᵛ; Grosvenor, 20 May.

they were granted by common law, they could be limited by Act of Parliament. Coke claimed that the powers of coining and of pardon had been so limited.[1] The law, in Coke's picture, then became the ultimate source of authority. As Bracton would have it, law makes the King: *attribuat rex legi quod lex ei; dominium enim et imperium exerceri sine lege non potest.*

Though Coke was the chief inspirer of this doctrine which made law the ultimate source of authority, he was far from its sole adherent. Bankes, known to history as the Attorney General in charge of the Ship Money case, said that 'Subjects have their rights and kings their prerogative, yet the ocean hath banks, and common law limits prerogative.'[2] Glanville, at the conference of 23 May, divided statutes into those prohibiting *mala prohibita* (things merely illegal) and *mala in se* (inherently evil). In the first case, statutes allowed the King a trust, regulated by law, to grant dispensations from statutes. In the second case, he said no such exemptions were allowed. The statutes under discussion, he said, were declaring 'an inherent right and interest of liberty and free-dom, in the subjects of this realm, as their birth-right and inheri-tance, descendable to their heirs and posterity, statutes incorporate into the body of the common law, over which (with reverence be it spoken) there is no trust reposed in the King's sovereign power, or prerogative royal, to enable him to dispense with them, or take from his subjects that birth-right and inheritance which they have in their liberties, by virtue of the common law and these statutes'. Such a trust, he said, in a successor of a different temper, 'might enable him to alter the whole frame and fabric of the common-wealth and so dissolve that government whereby this kingdom hath flourished for so many years and ages'.[3]

Thanks to the efforts of Coke, Glanville, and their colleagues, this body of ideas has gone down to history as the belief of 'the common lawyers'. In 1628, it was very far from clear that 'the common lawyers' outside the House of Commons were agreed on this interpretation of the common law and of its relationship to the prerogative. In particular, the lawyers were not agreed in their interpretation of Magna Carta, that no man should be imprisoned, except *per legem terrae*, by the law of the land. Attorney General Heath pointed out many times that this phrase, while accepted on all hands, shed no light on the question what the law of the land

---

[1] *L.J.* 761.   [2] Stowe 366, f. 85ᵛ.   [3] *L.J.* 815.

was. Since all but one of the statutes relied on by the Commons were worded as more or less plain confirmations of Magna Carta, they then shed no light on the question whether imprisonment by the King's special command was or was not part of the law of the land. As Heath said, 'Inference. If Magna Carta not clear, the rest make it more obscure.'[1] To attempt to prove something to be the law of the land simply by quoting phrases saying men could only be imprisoned according to the law of the land was, as Heath said, *petitio principii.*[2]

Heath, it must be allowed, was speaking to a brief. However, he was not an uncritical speaker to his briefs, and since he subsequently lost office rather than support Ship Money, it is at least possible that he believed the case he developed. The contrast with his handling of the uncongenial case of Richard Montagu is certainly marked. Moreover, Heath's case was supported by the judges, led by Chief Justice Whitelocke. Whitelocke, as in 1610, showed signs of having a concept of sovereignty, but seemed less disposed than he had been in 1610 to repose sovereignty in the King in Parliament. Whitelocke, when consulted by the Lords in his official capacity, asked, 'Is there not a trust to be put in the sovereign power to restrain liberty?', or, according to another text, 'A sovereign power rests in all commonwealths. Is there not a trust to be reposed in a sovereign power to restrain a prisoner for some convenient time?'[3] Whitelocke believed that the common law judges possessed an ultimate power of controlling the King's exercise of such a trust, but that it was not to be used lightly, wantonly, or unadvisedly. He said that he had never read of any such case in which the party had been immediately discharged *rege inconsulto*, and that therefore the judges had adjourned the case: 'If we had delivered him presently, it had been precipitate, and not to be revoked.' In other words, Whitelocke believed that, though the judges might ultimately control the King's power to commit people to prison by his special command, they should, because the King was trusted with the government of the country, exercise such a power only with the greatest hesitation.

With either Heath or Whitelocke all the common lawyers attending the Lords were agreed. Chief Justice Hyde exposed the fallacy in the Commons' use of Magna Carta: he said: 'They

---

[1] Huntington Library, Ellesmere MS. 7785, f. 17. [2] *L.J.* 746.
[3] Ellesmere MS. 7785–6, f. 29; *Lords' Debates*, p. 100.

may commit by that statute, but not commit illegally.'[1] Manchester, a former Lord Chief Justice, firmly claimed that the King had a prerogative to imprison without cause shown, and that such a prerogative was recognized by law. The law entrusted the King with such a power: 'This trust is the fundamental law of the Crown. True, that state is happy, where nothing is left to discretion, yet in all places, a latitude is left to the Crown. And *salus populi suprema lex* will restrain the King. Bracton. *Nemo de factis regis presumat disputare*, yet here is a remedy, vizt. petition. . . . After, statutes are, that the subject is not to be imprisoned at the suggestion of a subject without a cause shown. But for a commitment by the King, no law book against it.'[2] Sir Edward Coke no more enjoyed a monoply of Bracton than he enjoyed a monopoly of the common law. Marlborough, another former Lord Chief Justice in the Lords, agreed with Manchester. Manchester, moreover, was not stating a sudden opinion: he had held in 1614, when still a member of the Commons, that the King had power, by a *non obstante* clause in a grant, to dispense with Magna Carta itself.[3] It was Coke, not Manchester, who had changed his mind since 1614. Lord Keeper Coventry developed an argument with a respectable history when he argued: 'If you weaken the proceedings of the Council Board, you weaken the law. *Sacrum iudicium*, if any with force and arms etc. to arrest them; but if they cannot arrest them, then to complain to the King and his Council, etc. Here appears the King might proceed, and not by process of law, for they were too strong for those process. The King must add his strength.'[4] The cause of law enforcement itself depended on the power of the King and Council to proceed arbitrarily against those so powerful the law could not touch them. In an argument which was essentially about the imprisonment of men who were leaders of their counties, Justices of the Peace and Deputy Lieutenants, the point might appear to have a certain uncomfortable relevance.

Whatever the actual state of the law may have been, the normal practice of county government did not accord with Sir Edward Coke's view of the rule of law. This was pointed out by the Earl of Northampton, who asked about the Commons' case: 'If I give

[1] *Lords' Debates*, p. 107; Ellesmere MS. 7787, f. 4.
[2] *Lords' Debates*, 127.
[3] *C.J.* 469.   [4] *Lords' Debates*, p. 128.

my voice to it, where is the training of men, musters etc.?'[1] Some
people may have believed that they could find a statutory or
common law foundation for the militia, but mustering and militia
training were regularly enforced by those who believed they had
no warrant for doing so but the prerogative. In this context, it was
possible to imagine that the spreading of Coke's doctrine that
nothing could be enforced without clear legal authority could have
a dangerously undermining effect on authority. The Earl of
Dorset, on 24 May, said: 'Yesterday, in the King's Bench a man
was returned for refusing to contribute to the musters (upon a
Habeas Corpus). Answered, because there is no law for it. So you
see the King's prerogative is necessary.'[2] It was hard to see how a
House of Commons whose members had, for twenty-four years,
allowed and assisted the militia to continue without giving it any
secure legal basis could dispute this argument.

This argument from the practice of county government was one
of those to which Attorney General Heath appealed at the conference of 17 April. He argued that the words of Magna Carta,
'according to the law of the land', could not be, as the Commons
wished, translated as 'due process of law'.

Then could not a constable, which is the lowest and yet the ancientest
officer to the Crown for these causes, nor a Justice of the Peace (but in
these cases only where there is a precise statute to warrant him) commit
one to prison, or set a knave in the stocks, for a just suspicion, nay, if he
were taken with the manner, unless the fact were first presented or found
by a jury. My Lords and gentlemen, for I speak to those of whom I am
sure the greatest part are persons of authority in your countries, I appeal
to you all, whether, if this be held for a direction, I may not truly say,
in hoc erravimus omnes.[3]

Heath was right that those in positions of authority had regularly committed people to prison on grounds which were in effect
either of suspicion, or of contempt. Yet, in the unideological
atmosphere of the pre-Caroline age, they had not been forced to
answer the question Coke and the Commons were now asking:
'By what authority doest thou these things?' Heath quoted popish
traitors of the reign of Elizabeth, held in prison without charge
while their ringleaders were yet to be arrested. He quoted farmers
in time of famine compelled to bring out their corn to sell at a
reasonable price: 'Is there any law to order or compel this? Yet is

[1] *Lords' Debates*, p. 130.
[2] *Lords' Debates*, p. 203.   [3] *L.J.* 754.

not this fit to be done?' For the first time, Heath and his colleagues were asked to produce an authority for these discretionary exercises of power, not to cover a particular instance, but to make a general rule capable of standing its ground against Coke's rule of law.

Heath and Charles replied by citing the only authority who could undoubtedly not be controlled by the rule of law: God. In Heath's words:

> But the true answer for these and the like cases is, this is not contrary to the laws. God has trusted the King with governing the whole. He hath therefore trusted him with ordering of the parts; and there are many cases, of infinite importance to the subject, and of undoubted trust, wherein notwithstanding it was never questioned by a subject of the King why he did thus or thus. As the King is trusted with the coins and monies of the kingdom, of his absolute power, he may abase, he may enhance them; he may turn our gold and silver money into brass or base money, and in one instant undo his people thereby. The answer is, he will not do it: he is trusted.[1]

Heath was right that in any commonwealth there is some residual discretion left to the highest authority to vary the strict rules of law in particular cases. It was in invoking God as the source of the trust thus committed to the King that new arguments were being joined. Sir Edward Coke recognized that he was being trumped by this invocation of a power derived from God. He objected to the Lords' first drafting of this idea: 'Entrusted "from God". Then it is *jure divino. Nullo jure humano dirimi potest.*'[2] It cannot be limited by any human law. This was the ground on which men like Sir Humphrey May said that the King's discretionary power was one which no law could take away.[3] From this, it might have been a short step to go on to say that, rather than the law making the King, the King made the law. This step was not taken by the King's supporters in 1628, who were law-abiding men. Yet its possibility was what made men like Glanville believe that allowing the King the illimitable discretionary power he was claiming could lead to the alteration of the form of government in England. For the first time in this story, divine right has become an issue. For the first time, divine right is here used not as a general declaration of the legitimacy of authority, but as a specific sanction for specific and disputed powers. Moreover, the invocation of a trust from God as a warrant for specific acts produced the immediate and obvious riposte. Mason, on 22 May, said: 'The next word is "trusted", which is very ambiguous, whether it be meant trusted by God only, as a conqueror, or by the people also, as kings which are to govern by laws *ex pacto*. In this point I will not presume to adventure further.'[1] Mason might prudently not adventure further, but once the question had been opened what was the ultimate source of civil authority, it proved a Pandora's box, which was not easily closed.

This was the question which had been thrown open by the Commons' original quest for certainty in the common law. They could only achieve the degree of certainty needed to resume trust in the common law as a protector of their liberties by reaffirming the common law so stridently that it admitted of no exceptions. The Commons had the choice, either of restoring trust in the common law, or of restoring trust in the King. Under the leadership of common lawyers, they chose to restore trust in the certainty of the common law. The King, unfortunately, took all the distrust to be of himself, and therefore took personal offence at the Commons' demand for a new explanation of the law. When he offered, on 3 May, to secure the Commons from their 'needless fears' by confirming Magna Carta and the six statutes without addition or explanation, he had not fully identified the fears the Commons had in mind. The Lord Keeper asked on 5 May why they needed an explanation if they trusted the King. Secretary Coke might protest on 6 May that a report would fly into the world that the people would not trust the King, but the debate of 6 May shows that it was not only the King in whom trust needed to be restored: as Eliot said, 'All the question is what the law is.'[2] That question would not be answered by a bare confirmation. The distrust of lawyers expressed by Clare before the Parliament would not be dispelled by a repetition of apparently ambiguous rules. Sir Edward Coke, using the idea of divine right in a very different sense from Charles, acknowledged the King to be God's lieutenant, but asked, 'What is the law of the realm?' It was not a question on which he found uncertainty tolerable.[3] Or, in the more dangerous version offered by Pym, what did the King think the law was?[4] 'If he understood the laws, he would not err.' More than a bare confirmation would be needed to satisfy the Commons.

---

[1] *1628 Debates*, iii. 529.   [2] *1628 Debates*, iii. 272.
[3] Add. 36825, ff. 288ᵛ–289ʳ.   [4] Harl. 5324, f. 31ᵛ; Grosvenor, 6 May.

Yet a bare confirmation was all the King would agree to. It was to meet this deadlock, in which the King would not proceed with any new legislation, and the Commons would not proceed without it, that Sir Edward Coke produced the idea of a Petition of Right. This was to be couched as a petition for existing liberties, which could be precisely recounted. The King's answer, in full Parliament, could then be enrolled on the Parliament Roll, and remain as matter of record. It was a method of proceeding which had been tentatively explored with the 1625 Petition of Religion. It was a deliberately antiquarian attempt to revert to an older method of legislation. Hakewill, as a good legal historian, expressed misgivings. He thought that legislation had once been by petition and answer, but had not been so for two hundred years. He thought it had been abandoned for the good reason that the law had to be collected out of the words of the King's answer.[1] Hakewill's misgivings were to be justified by the King's first answer to the Petition, if not by the second. For the moment, however, Coke's apparent relief from deadlock was seized on so eagerly that all such doubts were forgotten.

The Commons, then, were committed after 6 May to proceeding by Petition of Right. Yet the Commons alone could not proceed by Petition of Right: if the Petition were to have the force of law, it had to come from both Houses of Parliament. As Wentworth said, 'Unless the Lords co-operate with us, the stamp is cut off that gives a value to the action.' Without the Lords' assent, the Commons' text might be kept in a study, but it would never be a record.[2] So, once again, a profoundly reluctant House of Lords was being pushed into a position of arbiter between King and Commons. This time, the dispute was one they could not quietly leave to go away: the King was as insistent as the Commons in pressing for an early decision. The Lords had to give an answer. It was not a task they found congenial. Most of them could see the force of the arguments on both sides, and many probably agreed with the remark Sir Thomas Wentworth attributed to the Earl of Dorset, that the dispute was between just liberty and just prerogative.[3] The Lords had been possessed of the Commons' case on the key point of arbitrary imprisonment since the conference of

---

[1] *1628 Debates*, iii. 290, 284.
[2] *1628 Debates*, iii. 559.
[3] Harl. 2313, f. 57ᵛ; *1628 Debates*, iii. 55 and n.

7 April. On that issue, they showed what had been their two conspicuous characteristics in 1626: a stately rate of progress, and a scrupulous concern for correct procedure. When the conference of 7 April was reported, the report was greeted, according to the clerk, with 'profound silence'.[1] It was then Saye, the Commons' strongest ally in the Lords, who moved for the King's counsel to have time to prepare a case on the other side; 'Not to cast clouds. Let us clearly see what is the truth of this business.'[2] Dorset, one of the Commons' strongest opponents, followed this with an equally scrupulous motion to see the originals of records cited, and not to rely on copies. Devonshire, another of the strongest supporters of the Commons' case, made the gloss: if anything was not spoken of for the King, the records would bring it out. As in 1626, the Lords did not proceed on partisan lines.

The Lords then heard the Attorney General, and heard the judges. On 17 April, they conducted another long conference with the Commons. It was not until 22 April that they proceeded to a serious debate on the case the Commons had laid before them. On 22 April, Bristol, whose record may have made him anxious, asked to be assured of freedom of speech.[3] They then proceeded to a remarkably open-minded debate. Saye, opening the debate, conceded, as none of the Commons would publicly do, that there had to be room for reason of state. He argued, however, that it was better to have the law, rather than the reason of state, clearly affirmed. 'Reason of state in times of necessity etc. but not to rule the law nor leave a gap. But we are now to consider of the ancient liberties used in the best times of our kings. Better have the law to be positive and absolute, than the reason of state: for the law will in cases of necessity yield to reasons of state, *prout* in cases of fire, forts, etc. to pull down houses and build on the owners' grounds, etc. But will you not make the law absolute, but leave the King power to pull down houses etc. at all times.'[4] Saye was the first to make the point since made by Dr. Ball, that any formal saving of the King's discretionary power in response to the Commons' case would be a big change, in that it would give a clear legal recognition to a power which had previously only existed on sufferance.[5] Arundel, the next speaker, bluntly expressed the fact that con-

[1] *Lords' Debates*, p. 84.
[2] Ellesmere MS. 7785, f. 15.
[3] Ellesmere MS. 7785, f. 26.
[4] *Lords' Debates*, p. 124.
[5] Ball, pp. 266–7.

ventional wisdom was on both sides. '1. By law the king cannot commit without a cause expressed. 2. And yet it is inherent to the King's prerogative to commit without a cause expressed in some cases.' It should be noted that Arundel was still under a suspended sentence of house arrest, and had not sued a Habeas Corpus. Pembroke asked why the Commons so often pressed for recusants to be committed on suspicion, 'suspicion being no legal cause for their commitments'. Dorset said the King had been and would be trusted, 'whether we will or no'. Bristol, another Lord with experience of the subject, conceded the distinction the King drew between his legal and his regal power: he admitted that the King had a power not bound by rules of law.[1] He thought they could reaffirm the law without depriving the King of his discretionary power of imprisonment: 'So the law to be positive, yet reason will admit of exceptions necessary for the King's prerogative.' From a man of Bristol's experience, such a defence of 'exceptions' must be taken seriously. Dorset claimed that the King could not commit for any cause triable at the common law, but for reason of state he might. The King, he said, had a right to *lex terrae* for matters of state. Clare and Saye defended the Commons' case, and Arundel and Bishop Harsnett opposed an attempt by Buckingham to force a vote. Buckingham reminded the Lords that the King was unlikely to agree to the Commons' formal case, and the debate ended in a request for a further conference. The one area of common ground through the whole House was the desire for 'accommodation': the Lords, as politicians, wanted to achieve a compromise.

Unfortunately, of all arguments, perhaps the hardest to bring to a compromise is one about the ultimate source of authority. The difficulty is particularly acute if neither contending party will accept any ambiguity. This appears even more clearly after 9 May, when the Petition of Right was brought up to the Lords, and read twice. The result was 'profound silence', ultimately broken by a motion from Archbishop Abbot to read it a third time. Pembroke and Dorset were then galvanized into moving to 'sweeten the manner' of the petition for the King. Their choice of words reveals the extent to which their concern was with the politics, not with the law, behind the issue.[2] The Lords' concern with the political issues of the moment became even more acute after the reading of

[1] *Lords' Debates*, pp. 125–7; Ellesmere MS. 7787, f. 28.
[2] *Lords' Debates*, pp. 148–9.

the King's letter of 12 May, in which he said that he would not suffer his power to be impeached. Once again, Charles had nailed his colours to the mast, and staked his authority in defence of a position he was to prove unable to maintain. Pembroke and Buckingham then spoke, in very similar phrases, to propose that they should urge the Commons to bring the Petition within the compass of the King's letter. Further attempts to reach a resolution by conference were unavailing, and on 14 May, Buckingham prematurely proposed that, since the Commons would not compromise, they should not confer further.[1] A week later, this motion might have succeeded, but, moved when it was, it simply provoked another long debate.

On 15 May, Arundel was the first to put the case for a compromise with the Commons. 'The nobility extracted from the Commons. Our younger children revert to the Commons again.'[2] Williams, seeing the danger involved in his proposal for adding a saving to the Petition, said it should make no new affirmation of the prerogative, nor place any new negative restriction on it. The ambition, though laudable, was unfortunately impossible. Archbishop Abbot again supported the Petition, saying: 'By the word of God, no man punished but a reason given, from Genesis to Revelation etc, and cited them. To imitate God herein.' He added that the late imprisonments had done good neither to the King nor to the people, and he hoped never to see the like again. Dorset suggested that the King had power for the good of the commonwealth, but not for its hurt. The House adjourned without any conclusion.

On 16 May, the Lords did not debate the issue in public. On 17 May, the debate was opened by Williams, offering a draft of a saving. He was followed by Arundel, who expressed the sense of the House pithily. 'We all agree on the ground, to preserve the prerogative, some [sc. so?] that it be tacite intended, and moderately used.'[3] The difficulty was to find a form of words which ensured in a watertight legal form that the prerogative should be 'moderately used'. Dorset also had similar hopes: he did not intend a saving of the prerogative to be a justification for resuming the methods of government which had recently been used. 'I do not think it will fall into the breast of any honest man so far to reserve

---

[1] *Lords' Debates*, p. 158.   [2] *Lords' Debates*, pp. 166–7.
[3] *Lords' Debates*, p. 170.

sovereignty of power to the King that a man may again suffer in the kind before complained of. I should think it would clear the addition much if instead of due regard were put in intention.'[1] In fact, no such formula could be achieved: it was an attempt to give legal formulation to a compromise which was intended to be essentially political.

The form of words ultimately adopted for the Lords' proposed saving, to be added to the Petition of Right, was proposed by Weston.[2] He wished to add that they left entire that sovereign power wherewith the King was entrusted for the safety, and not for the destruction, of his people. As a political device to save the King's face, these words might have passed muster. As a declaration of the law, they were either valueless, or a contradiction of the whole Petition. No one supported them in the Commons except those speaking to an official brief, and in the conference of 23 May, the Commons' spokesmen, Glanville and Marten, made legal mincemeat of Weston's proposed saving. The conference justified the doubts which had been expressed by Conway and Paget on 20 May. Conway doubted 'whether power of sovereignty can be expressed in a Parliamentary [i.e. legal] way'.[3] Paget, speaking in his family tradition, suggested that if, as Weston claimed, the prerogative was inseparable from the Crown, their debate was unnecessary. 'The King cannot divest himself of his prerogatives more than he can of his Crown. If nothing that we can add to this Petition can add or weaken the prerogative, no need of addition.' It was a line of reasoning of which Charles was later to be glad enough, but its cynicism was too old-fashioned for the day's debate, and it was ignored. On 24 May, after the Commons had demolished the Lords' proposed saving, they had to begin all over again.[4] This time, it was Arundel and Bristol who led the demand to concur with the Commons. Dorset passionately objected that the Petition would give monarchy a greater blow than any enemy from beyond the seas, and Buckingham unwisely protested that he would rather have been impeached than concede to this Petition. Saye proposed, if the Petition were thrown out, to enter his Protestation in the Journal against its rejection. Clare, following Paget, proposed that they join with the Commons, because 'no

---

[1] *Lords' Debates*, p. 176n.   [2] *Lords' Debates*, p. 177.
[3] Ellesmere MS. 7788, ff. 9–10; *Lords' Debates*, p. 186.
[4] *Lords' Debates*, pp. 199–204.

law can hinder what is necessary to be done for the safety of us all etc.'. Essex proposed to reconcile Buckingham and Saye, which was duly done. By then, 'the Lords were hungry, and some went to dinner it being very late, and others went away etc.'.[1] True to their style as politicians, the Lords reached their final decision behind the scenes. The next day was a Sunday, and when the Lords met again on Monday the twenty-sixth, the Lord Keeper resumed the debate by proposing that they join with the Commons, with no other proviso but a request that the Commons pass a law for regulating the Lieutenantcy.[2] Charles had lost the support of his House of Lords, in spite of a large amount of intellectual sympathy for his case. It should be noted that the two Lords whose conversion turned the debate, Arundel and Bristol, were themselves both victims of arbitrary imprisonment. What is remarkable is not their final conversion to the Commons' case, but the fact that they resisted it for so long. This is perhaps suggestive of its intellectual novelty. The Lords learnt much in the way of political ideas in 1628, but they did not experience the intellectual crucible of the Commons' debating chamber. Charles's defeat in the House of Lords, which in the short term was the key event of 1628, was not an intellectual defeat. It was the price he paid for a simple political failure to maintain good relations with his nobility.

The Lords' assent to the full, unembroidered version of the Petition of Right appears to have briefly convinced most of the Commons that the King's assent would follow. Sir Edward Coke claimed to be almost dead for joy,[3] and thereafter, as the temperature dropped, there was a rapid return to business as usual. Coke said they must do something about a bill for Deputy Lieutenants, and Phelips that they must do something about Tonnage and Poundage. In fact, the Commons turned to more congenial business. They heard complaints against the saltpetre men, who had been digging under churches. They listened to a Yorkshire complaint of the revival of Lepton's patent (condemned in 1621) for engrossing bills in the Court of the Council of the North, and duly condemned it. They listened to Cornish complaints from Sir John Eliot, who objected to the administration of the Stannary Court

---

[1] *Lords' Debates*, p. 204. The unusual length of the Lords' sittings is a mark of the importance of the occasion. On 20 May, well before the end of the debate, Bridgewater noted a complaint by Bristol that it was already six o'clock in the evening. Ellesmere MS. 7788, f. 8.

[2] *Lords' Debates*, p. 205.   [3] Stowe 366, f. 192ᵛ.

by his local rival Sir Reginald Mohun, now a baron. Eliot said he was raising money in the Stannary Parliament, and holding pleas of life and limb in the Stannary Court.[1] Pym obtained approval for the start of what was in effect an impeachment proceeding against Roger Manwaring, a clergyman who had claimed that the Forced Loan was due by the law of God. In an interesting procedural innovation, Pym did as he had proposed on 20 April 1621, and kept the handling of the witnesses under his control, and not that of the Lords.[2] He succeeded, after a speech which was a lucid distillation of much of the political thought of the Commons of 1628, in obtaining Manwaring's condemnation. Archbishop Abbot, who appears to have been as angry with Manwaring as Pym, roundly rebuked him for using the text from Psalm 82, which said that Kings were Gods, to justify arbitrary taxation and to exempt the King from the rule of law.[3] Abbot said the text warranted no such thing. Read in context, it sustains Abbot's objection. The case of Manwaring, whose sermons had contained some remarkably novel and high-flown political ideas, is one of the landmarks in the process whereby religious and constitutional fears were fused into one common terror of 'alteration of government'. It should, though, be noted in passing, both that there is no evidence that Manwaring was an Arminian, and that Pym had been something of a one-man band in forcing the case through the Commons.

When the subsidy bill was revived, there was rather more widespread interest in a proposal by Mallory and Phelips that holders of Scottish and Irish peerages, and also English Baronets, should have a minimum assessment laid down for them in the subsidy.[4] The proposal for Englishmen holding Scottish and Irish peerages caused no dispute. The Baronets, who were always well represented in Parliament, were a more contentious case. Selden

---

[1] Stowe 366, f. 195ʳ; Add. 36825, f. 489ʳ. It may be suspected that Pembroke's replacement of Coryton by Mohun as Vice-Warden of the Stannaries had something to do with this first appearance of Parliamentary complaints against the Stannary Court. The complaints were presented by Eliot.

[2] Add. 36825, f. 510ᵛ, reports the Lord Keeper, pronouncing judgement against Manwaring, saying he 'hath been impeached'. For Pym's speech of 20 April 1621, see above, p. 106. On the witnesses, see House of Lords Braye MSS. i, f. 67.

[3] For Abbot, see *L.J.* 853. An extract from Pym's speech is printed in J. P. Kenyon, *The Stuart Constitution* (1966), pp. 16–18. I hope to discuss the numerous contemporary texts of this speech elsewhere.

[4] Stowe 366, ff. 199–200.

supported the proposal, saying that men were normally raised in the subsidy when they became gentlemen or were made Knights. Sir John Wray and Sir John Scudamore, Baronets, were also agreeable. Sir Thomas Wentworth, Baronet, was less agreeable: 'We are good subjects to the King, no aliens, such as have done as good service as most of you could desire. I beseech you to forbear to set this brand upon us.' Again, it appears clearly that a high subsidy assessment was taken as a mark of ill favour. A more serious objection was raised by Whitby: 'Take heed you open not a new gap, to proceed by degrees to other taxes upon honour, as knights, Esquires etc.' In other words, the proposal might be the beginning of a move towards honest assessment of the subsidy. The proposal was laid aside, and later dropped when Whitby's objections were supported by Hakewill.[1]

After this business was laid aside, there was only one leaf of the subsidy bill left to be read, and the Commons had no wish to conclude the bill before the King had answered the Petition of Right. It is, then, at least tempting to interpret the exceptionally long debate on whether Oxford or Cambridge should be mentioned first as a delaying tactic. It is, however, worth noting that the author of one account ascribes the delay to the fact that the Solicitor General, who was in the Chair, was from Cambridge. Cambridge being in a minority, he was reluctant to put the question.[2] The debate did produce one remarkable intervention from Sir Nathaniel Rich. It had been a generally accepted convention of these debates that victory went to those proving the superior antiquity of their University: the virtue of antiquity was not questioned. It is then rather surprising to find Rich, as a Cambridge man, saying that Oxford could only claim priority of 'age and decrepitude'.[3] Meanwhile, the Lords were busy investigating a dispute between a Lord Lieutenant and a local gentleman about the provision of 'snapsacks' for the militia. In the context of the case, the gentleman's much-quoted declaration that he cared not for any Lord except the Lord of Hosts might be part, not of a declining respect for the aristocracy, but of a declining respect for the militia.[4]

[1] Add. 36825, f. 469r; Grosvenor, 10 June.
[2] Stowe 366, ff. 204v ff.
[3] Stowe 366, f. 205v; Grosvenor, 31 May.
[4] Lords' Debates, pp. 198–9, 204, 211. L. Stone, The Crisis of the Aristocracy (Oxford, 1965), p. 265. See also ibid., p. 747.

On 2 June, this agreeable atmosphere of normal business was brought to an abrupt end by the delivery, in full Parliament, of the King's first answer to the Petition of Right. The exact words of the King's answer were:

The King willeth that right be done according to the laws and customs of the realm, and that the statutes be put in due execution, that the subject may have no just cause to complain of any wrong or oppressions contrary to their rights and just liberties, to the preservation whereof he holds himself in conscience as well obliged as of his prerogative.[1]

This was not a satisfactory answer. In the first place, as Williams in the Lords and Pym in the Commons pointed out, it was not an answer to the Petition, nor to any part of it.[2] In the second place, it was clear, on the previous history of the session, that this was only the bare confirmation, without any addition or explanation of the laws, which the King had from the first said was all he would offer. In the face of both Houses, Charles stood his ground. The Commons were not going to complete a subsidy bill in return for this answer. When the Commons turned to consider the answer, a long silence was broken by Eliot, moving for a Remonstrance.[3] Further silence could only be broken by Eliot's willingness to speak again. An attempt by Sir Humphrey May to interrupt him was brusquely overruled.[4]

In the Lords, there was equal dismay, but less volubility about its expression. Bristol began a public demand for a Remonstrance, protesting, with only slight exaggeration, that 'the whole Christian world is enemy to us'.[5] Arundel, in a soothing intervention, suggested that, rather than passing a Remonstrance, they should allow the Lord Keeper to deliver to the King 'the sense of the House in general'. The 'sense of the House in general', as recorded in the *Lords' Journals*, bears some resemblance to Bristol's speech, including the fear of danger to the kingdom if the Parliament should be dissolved without a happy conclusion in time of war.[6] True to their traditions, the Lords began, through their Privy

---

[1] Stowe 366, f. 211–12.
[2] *Lords' Debates*, p. 217; *Lowther*, p. 39; Add. 36825, f. 449ᵛ; *1628 Debates* iv, 127.
[3] Newdegate, ii, f. 73ʳ.
[4] Stowe 366, f. 212ᵛ. Wallace Notestein, *The Winning of the Initiative by the House of Commons* (1924), p. 29n. The words at which May rose to interrupt were that the course of English foreign policy was 'such as will rather be thought a conception from Spain than from us'. It was an exceptional reaction to a Privy Councillor on an exceptional day's debate.
[5] *Lords' Debates*, p. 214.   [6] *L.J.* 839.

Councillor members, a behind-the-scenes search for a compromise, in reply to which Charles, on 6 June, thanked them for not
drawing a Remonstrance 'though it were in your hearts', and
hinted that this gesture of compromise might meet with some
reciprocal action.

The Lords' attempts to arrange a compromise were speedy, but
they were not speedy enough to prevent outbursts in the Commons
which produced the ugliest Parliamentary scenes before 1640.
They took about two days to absorb the full measure of the
significance of the King's first answer. A message from the King
on 4 June, that he intended to stick to his answer to the Petition
of Right, and would end the session on the 11th, did not end the
debate, as the King hoped, but poured oil on the flames. If the
Parliament were to be dissolved in anger, with no subsidies voted,
members had nothing more to gain by moderation. A further
message on 5 June, forbidding attacks on the state, government,
or ministers, had the same effect. They could speak all the fears
which had been in their minds, and more which were only just
occurring to them.[1] Phelips said that he would rather have lost
wife and children than received this message. He said that if they
could not proceed with a Remonstrance, there was nothing more
to do but to go home and pray. Eliot began to talk of vindicating
the King's honour when he was stopped by the Speaker, who
appeared to think he was about to name Buckingham. For the
first time in the session, a situation existed for which Buckingham
made a convenient scapegoat. The general points involved in the
Petition of Right, which could not easily be blamed on one man,
had been hammered out. What was now at stake was the King's
failure to give a satisfactory answer. That could be blamed on one
man, and as Eliot suggested, it was better if that one man were
not the King.

The Speaker's command from the King not to name Buckingham did not stem the flood long. Digges proposed to sit in silence,
since they were so miserable they did not know what to do, and
Seymour, seconding him, suggested that the silence should be confirmed by order. Rich, on the other hand, said that they had a duty
to their country to speak. He said they should think of those for
whom they served, and regard silence as a breach of their duty to
the country.

[1] Stowe 366, ff. 218–20.

Pym seconded Rich in proposing to go on with the Remonstrance, moving that the doors be locked and no one should go out, on pain of being sent to the Tower.[1] The Remonstrance debate of 1628 was under way. For once, Sir Robert Phelips appeared to be being realistic in saying: 'I fear it is the last time that I shall ever speak in this House': an angry dissolution, without supply, would force Charles to further unparliamentary methods of taxation. However inadequate these methods were, they could not be much more inadequate than the subsidies Charles had as yet failed to obtain after so much effort. Even if the gulf between King and Commons were bridgeable, it was, from Charles's point of view, a real question whether it was worth the effort to bridge it. It is only in the context of the overwhelming pressure on Charles to raise unparliamentary sources of finance that the terrors of the Remonstrance debate can make sense.

The first stage of the debate, the naming of Buckingham, was begun by Sir Edward Coke. After Coke came most of the Duke's familiar enemies. Mansell said he would do his duty, Coryton specifically attacked him as Admiral, Kirton complained that he cast the King into all kinds of wars, and Selden proposed to demand judgement from the Lords on the charge of the previous Parliament.[2] Coke defended their right to debate this subject by calling for a reading of the Protestation of 1621.

So far, there was nothing startlingly novel in the debate: the same people were saying the same things as in 1626. There was something more novel in the manner of presenting the charge that Buckingham was threatening the ruin of religion. Sherland had more backing than in 1626 for raising the subject of Arminianism: 'Why are Arminians that have sought the ruin of the Low Countries allowed here? They run in a string with the papists and flatter greatness to oppress the subject.'[3] Here is a new intellectual link: the connection of alteration of religion with alteration of government. Those who wish to alter religion wish to alter govern-

---

[1] Stowe 366, f. 218ᵛ. It is not clear what method of exit Pym was envisaging. See Rushworth, i. 609–10 for a report that Pym was in tears when he delivered this speech.

[2] The fullest report of this debate is in Stowe 366, ff. 219ʳ–220ᵛ. See also Add. 36825, ff. 440 ff.

[3] Stowe 366, f. 219ʳ. Lowther, p. 37 reports Sherland adding at this point in his speech that the journey (to La Rochelle) was Spanish in effect if not in conception. Also 1628 Debates iv, 132.

ment, in order to protect themselves from questioning: those who wish to alter government provoke quarrels with Parliaments by supporting those who would alter religion. Knightley, accusing Buckingham of treason for granting letters of marque to papists, and Hampden, saying religion was likely to be altered by the Duke's means, followed where Sherland led.[1] Hampden said that the alteration of religion and the alteration of government amounted to 'no less than the subversion of the whole state'. It is here, in the debates of 5 and 6 June, that the notion of a 'popish and malignant party', which was later to hold the Grand Remonstrance together, was born.

The fears were fortified by the fear of soldiers which throughout distinguished the Parliaments of 1628 and 1640 from other early Stuart Parliaments. Eliot was too good a classical scholar to be unaware of the allusion when he said that 'praetorian bands' were drawn near the City, and Valentine explicitly said Buckingham could 'now set soldiers to cut our throats'.[2] Buckingham (or Charles) was now suspected of planning nothing less than an armed *coup d'état*.

In the middle of this debate, the House, which was in committee of the whole, had reluctantly agreed to let the Speaker go to see the King. He returned, and asked the House to suspend the debate till the next day, which it did. On 6 June, the Speaker repeated a message from the King against attacking his ministers, but this time saying nothing to the effect that his answer to the Petition of Right was final. The King also stressed his desire for another meeting of Parliament in the near future. Rudyerd followed this by asking that, since the King's answer to the Petition of Right 'admits various constructions', they should move him for a 'full and satisfactory' answer to it.[3] It was clearly an inspired motion. Unfortunately, it came twenty-four hours too late to do any good.

---

[1] Stowe 366, f. 220ᵛ. Grosvenor (5 June) reports Knightley as repeating Bristol's charge that Buckingham was responsible for the loss of the Palatinate. For Hampden, see Newdegate, iii, f. 3ᵛ, Stowe 366, f. 220ᵛ (*bis*). For the intellectual roots of this type of argument, see Robin Clifton, 'Fear of Popery', in *Origins*, pp. 155–6. The use of this type of Protestant nationalism against the Crown, instead of for it, is a landmark of the greatest importance.

[2] Add. 36825, f. 444ʳ⁻ᵛ; Grosvenor, 5 June; Stowe 366, f. 220ᵛ. Mr. Cox, on 6 June, said: 'Burlemack hath had licence to carry out ordinance, and to bring in ordinance to kill us.' Add. 36825, f. 454ʳ. This is a good example of the illogical fusion of fears which was taking place. See also Valentine, *Lowther*, p. 37.   [3] Stowe 366, f. 222ʳ; Grosvenor, 6 June.

Phelips insisted that they had shown too much moderation already, and the Remonstrance debate swept on.[1]

The chance for a second answer seemed about to be missed when Alford said that if they did not ask for a new answer, they might be taken to be satisfied with the existing answer, and Sir Peter Hayman said that they could not go home without a good answer to the Petition. Perrott supported the attempt to get a new answer, and it was, surprisingly, Harley who called instead for the heads of the Remonstrance, and again linked alteration of religion and alteration of government.[2] His speech illustrates one of the distinctive features of this debate. Almost all the group of godly Protestant Buckingham men, the group who had been associated with John Preston, were now loudly supporting the Remonstrance, and expressing fears of a link between Arminianism and popery and arbitrary government. Harley, Hampden, Knightley (and, if we take him for Lawrence Whitaker) Whitaker, who feared attack by the papists in Drury Lane, belonged to this group.

With these religious fears were introduced the fear of a body of German horse. These were to be brought to England, according to May, for foreign service as soon as there was money; but according to Knightley, to act as a 'garrison'. Giles and Kirton produced a commission of February 1628, to consider ways of raising money, which, on their gloss, has been dubbed the 'excise commission', though the word excise does not appear in it. Phelips blamed idolatry for English defeats in war, and Hoby complained of the number of recusant Lords Lieutenant and Deputy Lieutenants. The task of weaving these fears together into a coherent fabric of terror was undertaken by Rich, Pym, and Knightley. It was Pym who introduced fear of the Irish into the debate. He said

---

[1] Grosvenor: Add. 36825, f. 448ᵛ ff.

[2] Diary of Sir Nathaniel Rich, Huntingdon R.O., Manchester MSS. 58/5. Only the early part of this debate is reported in Stowe 366, ff. 222–3. The fullest report of this day's debates is in Add. 36825, ff. 448ᵛ–465ᵛ. The reports by Grosvenor and Rich, the religious enthusiasts, capture in their very confusion the mood which had overtaken the House. It is ironic that Dalbier, the commander of these much-feared German horse, later served under Essex at Edgehill. According to Rich, Henry Sherfield, another religious enthusiast, even succeeded in identifying the commission on fees as part of a project for alteration of government. The 'heads' in Rich's diary appear not to be a part of any member's speech. They are perhaps Rich's own list of headings to be used in the drafting of the Remonstrance. I am grateful to Mrs. Maija J. Cole and the Yale Center for Parliamentary History for help and advice on these notes. The 'heads' are possibly designed for Rich's report of 11 June; *1628 Debates* iv, 170.

the state of religion in Ireland amounted to 'little less than a toleration', and that many companies of soldiers there were commanded by recusants. He immediately linked this with seizures of merchants' goods. Rich said that 'now when religion is in peril it is dangerous to instruct the Irish in arms', and Earle suggested that Irish soldiers in Kent were well placed to assist an invasion from the Archduchess's dominions in Flanders. Strangeways linked the fear of German horse to the fear of martial law, and Rich linked the fear of the Irish to the fear of excise. The most comprehensive weaving together of these terrors was in the 'heads' listed by Rich, which began with the preferment of Arminians, linked that to 'the often abortions of Parliaments', and tied both up with 'the lodging of soldiers within the bowels of the kingdom to impoverish it'. This in turn he linked with favour to Manwaring, the turning out of office-holders in the country who were 'faithful', and with the sending for German horse and foreigners ill affected in religion. Eliot followed Rich's laconic report 'Praetorian bands some strange mist lies hid under these pretences. The D. Somerset accused of high treason, for drawing in foreign horse.' After this apocalyptic vision, Charles's second answer to the Petition of Right, late the next day, appeared something of an anticlimax. Two points emerged from the debates of 6 June. One was that the House of Commons was much more capable of concerted action in an atmosphere of grand crisis than when they were each attending to their diverse pieces of local business: it took a crisis to give the Commons a common purpose. The other point was that once fears of this magnitude had been raised, they would not easily vanish: by the end of 6 June, it was certain that a new answer to the Petition of Right would come too late to stop the Remonstrance.

On the morning of 7 June, attempts to arrange a second answer to the Petition were well organized in both Houses. Sir Edward Coke and Digges, who had not joined in the previous day's debate on plots to 'change the government', began the debate with more traditional complaints about the transport of ordnance. As Eliot, always ready to leap on the nearest bandwaggon, began to produce more fears about the purpose of the German horse, a message came from the Lords to ask the Commons to join them in asking the King for a new answer to the Petition of Right. While Sir Edward Coke went up to answer the Lords, Pym, prompt on his cue, moved to name a committee to draw the preamble to the subsidy bill.[1] In the Lords, Harsnett, Bishop of Norwich had started the motion to ask the King for 'such an answer as may flow fully to the Petition'. Oxford, Hertford, and Arundel had joined in pressing for a speedy conference with the Commons, and a tendency on the part of Bristol to dwell on the unsatisfactory character of the King's first answer had been successfully diverted. Buckingham and Saye jointly arranged to proceed, not by taking notice of what the Commons had done, nor by inviting them to petition the King to change his answer in the face of his explicit refusal to do so, but by saying the Lords intended to petition, and asking whether the Commons intended to join.[2] Even at this moment, the Lords were true to their procedural, non-partisan approach to difficult questions. Those who had spoken in the Commons on 6 June might have noted that the speakers included one Arminian (Harsnett), and one suspected papist (Arundel). One manuscript even includes Bishop Laud among the Lords proposing to petition for a new answer. 7 June 1628 appeared to be a triumphant day for the Lords' political approach.

The King, having been manœuvred into the right position, pronounced the words of assent to a private bill: 'soit droit fait comme est désiré'. With the aid of these words, the Petition of Right was enrolled on the Parliament Roll, where it is placed among the statutes with the number '1' beside it. At the same time, Charles warned his hearers that he meant no more by this than he had meant by his first answer: 'knowing . . . that you neither mean nor can hurt my prerogative'. Charles had given an assent in which a measure of equivocation was involved.[3] At least it may be said that he had given his hearers fair warning that he was doing so, and the House of Commons chose to be deceived. He concluded with a warning that 'I have done my part, wherefore if this Parliament have not a happy conclusion the sin is yours: I am free of it'. These words should perhaps be read as a warning to Parliamentary supporters on the Council, as much as to the House of Commons.

When the Commons were back in their own House, they allowed themselves a moment of light-heartedness, and perhaps of light-headedness. Sir Edward Coke, discussing the royal words of

---

[1] Stowe 366, f. 225ʳ.   [2] *Lords' Debates*, p. 217 and n.
[3] Stowe 366, f. 228ʳ: see below, pp. 388n, 401–2.

assent, which he said had no shadow of ambiguity, had to break off to say, 'Laugh not at my French, gentlemen, for I have gotten as much by it as some of you.'[1] When they met again, on Monday, 9 June, the Commons had to set about doing their part. Rich listed the agenda as supply, the Remonstrance, Tonnage and Poundage, and the continuance of statutes. Wandesford and Alford wanted to proceed first on the bill of arms, to give legal authority to the Lieutenantcy. It was an unpromising beginning when the Commons followed the lead of Eliot, and decided, in spite of the King's second answer, to proceed first with their Remonstrance. The Remonstrance occupied most of 11 June, and Rich then showed that for him, at least, the fear that there was a connection between alteration of religion and alteration of government had not disappeared.[2] Most of the day, however, was spent on a long discussion of whether to name the Duke of Buckingham. Long, Coryton, Kirton, and Sir Edward Coke led the attack on him, while the Pembroke men, Rudyerd and Perrott were on the other side. Rudyerd opposed naming him, and Perrott said the Duke should resign some, but not all, of his offices, because, 'We desire rather his reformation than his ruin.'[3] From 10 June to 17 June, the Remonstrance took most of the Commons' time, and even the subsidy bill was not sent up to the Lords until 16 June. Everyone wanted their own grievance inserted: Long successfully secured the naming of Neile and Laud for Arminianism, and Alford and Selden unsuccessfully tried to secure the inclusion of proclamations.[4] Digges secured the inclusion of lengthy complaints about the decay of shipping and loss of sailors by death or desertion. Others complained of the state of the forts, saying it was impossible to fire a gun in Sandown Castle without shaking it so badly that it fell down. The contrast with the French fort on the Île de Rhé was painful. Here, as in so many other things, the Commons were raising matters of which Charles was well aware, and on which they would have been better occupied in providing remedies than in offering complaints. They rehearsed again almost all the contents of the Petition of Right. On the one hand, they reproached Charles with illegally raising money, and on the other, reproached him for not spending money they had failed to provide. It is possible to understand the irritation in the answer

---

[1] Stowe 366, f. 225ᵛ.   [2] Stowe 366, ff. 235ʳ–236ᵛ (Rich's report).
[3] Add. 36825, f. 481ʳ.   [4] Stowe 366, f. 248ᵛ; Grosvenor, 11 June.

Charles gave to the Remonstrance when it was presented to him on 17 June: 'Now I see you are fallen upon points of state which belongs to me to understand better than you, and I must tell you that you do not understand so much as I thought you had done.'[1] Charles then 'gave the Duke his hand to kiss before us all'. It was growing increasingly clear that the Commons were better at representing popular grievances, which many of them thought was their proper job, than they were at taking any constructive action to remedy those grievances.

If the Commons wished to take advantage of the opportunity to resume 'regular courses' offered by the King's second answer to the Petition of Right, there were two bills they had to pass, the bill of Tonnage and Poundage and the bill of arms. If they wished Charles to observe the rule of law, they had to provide him with sufficient legal authority for those things he had to do in order to defend the kingdom. If they failed to provide him with this authority, it would be an irrelevance and an impertinence to offer him remonstrances about the inadequacy of the kingdom's defences, or to reproach him for failing to observe a law which did not empower him to do what they themselves recognized as his duty. Pym and Wentworth, who were already recognizable as the two leading natural administrators in the Commons, both saw this clearly. On 21 June, Pym moved 'that the King may not lose Tonnage and Poundage, nor yet take it against law', and asked for proceeding on the bill of arms. Wentworth asked the same, saying: 'It is our duty and wisdom to give all encouragement to his Majesty to serve our liberties without prejudice to his revenue.' Otherwise, he said, 'we shall put an impossibility upon his Majesty'.[2] The King could not be expected to manage without arms, or without the main part of his revenue, in time of war. If he was to do all things legally, he must be provided with legal means to do them. It seems that no members of the Commons wanted to put an end to the militia, but if they did not give the militia legal authority, they forced Charles to choose between putting an end to it and abandoning the attempt he had undertaken to rule according to strict rules of law.

In these circumstances, it is instructive to trace the fate of these two bills. Both were technical, and presented considerable drafting

[1] Stowe 366, f. 256ʳ⁻ᵛ. *C.S.P.D. 1625–49 Addenda*, vol. dxxviii, no 78.
[2] Stowe 366, f. 276ʳ⁻ᵛ; Add. 36825, ff. 542–3, Grosvenor, 21 June.

difficulties. The difficulties, however, were not insuperable, and the Commons had known since the beginning of the session that if any satisfactory conclusion were to be reached, these bills would have to be completed. They had already investigated both subjects, but, having identified the difficulties, had proceeded no further. Hakewill, on 9 June, said they would have difficulty in drafting the bill of arms in time, and they could not include in it such local matters as Edward Alford's complaint of the difficulty of forcing men to watch beacons to give warning of an invasion.[1] On the afternoon of 10 June, the committee discussed some of the rating difficulties involved, and listened to the commissions of array of 5 Henry IV as a possible precedent. They resolved that it would be impossible to draft a proper bill in the time available, and that the best they could do was to draft a short provisional Act to last until the next session.[2] On 13 June, Ball reported a draft which was given a first reading. Coryton objected that it allowed too much to discretion, and Mallory chose this occasion to repeat the complaint of German horse, and of English horse being moved to Hounslow: 'What might become of our government, God knows.'[3] The upshot was that the bill was deferred till nine the next morning. The Commons then headed off on complaints against the so-called Excise Commission. The next morning, they were busy with recusants, Arminians, and Manwaring, and did not give the bill its appointed second reading. Apart from Pym's speech of 21 June, urging that the bill be revived, nothing more was heard of the bill before the session ended on 26 June. It can only be supposed that, whatever had been said during the debates on the Petition of Right, most of the House of Commons were not sufficiently dismayed by a militia based on the prerogative to attempt to do anything about it. The bill of arms had not been defeated, nor even choked by difficulties: it had died of neglect.

Tonnage and Poundage was at least in a rather more forward state on 7 June. The bill had been read a first time on 2 April, and a second on 4 April. Coke had then objected that the bill was retroactive, legalizing Tonnage and Poundage since 1625.[4] It thereby deprived the Commons of any opportunity to punish

---

[1] Add. 36825, f. 463ʳ.   [2] Grosvenor, 10 June; Stowe 366, f. 233ᵛ.
[3] C.J. 912; Stowe 366, ff. 244–5.
[4] Harl. 2313, f. 31ᵛ. The version read on 4 April did not legalize the pretermitted custom (f. 31ʳ).

those who had illegally collected it since then. On 9 April, it was reported in an amended form by Bankes. It was then agreed that, as part of the bill, Parliament should authorize a new book of rates, and proposed to accept James's offer of 1610 to trade his right of imposing for a Parliamentary confirmation of existing impositions.[1] On 11 April, Sir Edward Coke said the bill was delayed because the rates were not agreed upon, and it was resolved that the customers should be sent for. Nothing more was then heard of it until Digges, on 4 June, lamented the lack of any proceeding on it.[2] On 9 June, Strangeways and Eliot said the House should go ahead with it, and on 13 June, it was referred to a select committee to consider what was fit to be done. Mallory chose the occasion to complain of a new book of rates.[3] On 19 June, the committee reported that it was impossible to perfect the bill in the time available, and that they should pass a short bill to last until the next session. Auditor Sawyer of the Exchequer revealed the true source of the difficulty: in all the time since Bate's case, so much confusion had arisen that they could not tell what was custom and what was imposition. Dawes, from the customers, said that six weeks was the shortest time in which it was possible to make a new book of rates.[4]

Faced with the impossibility of proceeding, the Commons vented their anger by deciding to punish Auditor Sawyer for working on a new book of rates without the explicit command of the Commons. They expelled him from membership, sent him to the Tower, and judged him unfit to sit in the Commons in future. On 24 June, they listened to Alford asking them to sort out the mixture between Tonnage and Poundage and impositions, to Sir Edward Coke saying it could not be done without a book of rates, and to Long saying they could not grant 'we know not what'. Bankes, from the chair, then proposed to leave Tonnage and Poundage till the next session, and that the King should take none till then. Instead, they resolved to send the King a Remonstrance, reproaching him, both for taking Tonnage and Poundage, and for

[1] Add. 36825, f. 153^{r-v}, Newdegate, i, f. 88^r.
[2] Stowe 366, f. 69^r. Coke said it was a misconception to suppose 'there is nothing done in it because it may be thought the house hath no mind to it'.
[3] Stowe 366, f. 217^{r-v}; Add. 36825, f. 462^r, Grosvenor, 9 June; Add. 36825, f. 485^r, Grosvenor, 13 June.
[4] Stowe 366, f. 275^{r-v}; Add. 36825, ff. 540^r–541^v, Grosvenor, 19 June.

not guarding the narrow seas.[1] Having laid aside this worrying business, the Commons settled down to hear Coke and Selden deploying the full weight of their legal learning on the question of the intestacy of bastards. Sir John Lowther commented: 'I never heard the like.'[2] Charles, perhaps naturally, decided to end the session a little early rather than receive a Remonstrance reproaching him for taking Tonnage and Poundage.[3] If this was to be a sample of the House of Commons' sense of responsibility, the case for continuing Parliaments was going to be increasingly difficult to argue.

Taken as a whole, the Parliament of 1628 perhaps suggests that the Commons had been a little too successful in establishing themselves as representatives of the people. They had always had to strike a balance between doing the King's business and doing the country's business, and their survival had depended on their ability to combine the two. In 1628, they had succeeded in doing the country's business. The unanimity of country complaints had done much to hold the Commons together: as Marten said at the conference on 23 May, they were regularly receiving letters, till their pockets were stuffed full of complaints against the soldiers. The French war, which had been Eliot's first subject of complaint on 3 June, had few, if any, Parliamentary supporters. While it was still continuing, the task of returning home and explaining that they had legalized many of the burdens of which their countrymen complained could have been an uncongenial one. Many members had become so well schooled in the presentation of complaint that the provision of remedy did not come nearly so naturally to them. The saltpetre patent, for example, called on much more familiar reflexes than the bill of arms. By establishing their usefulness to the country, members were coming to destroy their usefulness to the King.

In both cases, they had their reward. The session of 1628 probably went a long way towards persuading Charles that Parlia-

[1] Stowe 366, ff. 282ʳ–284ᵛ, Add. 36825, ff. 552ᵛ–556ʳ.

[2] *Lowther*, p. 56. He was commenting on Coke's belief that a bastard had 'no hereditary blood'. *1628 Debates* iv, 462–4, 476.

[3] Stowe 366, f. 288ʳ. Charles protested at 'false interpretation' of the Petition of Right, insisted that he had granted no new liberties but merely confirmed the old, and that a Parliament could not hurt his prerogative. He again insisted on what seems to have been, for him, one of the key points of the debate: that the proper interpreters of the law were not the House of Commons, but the judges.

ments were not worth continuing. Yet at the same time, and through the same things, the session did much to convince members of the public at large that Parliaments were their proper champions. There had never been a better-reported session of Parliament. Above all, the manuscript Proceedings and Debates represent a newly developed form in Parliamentary reporting. They are not made up of the usual abbreviated jottings of a diary, designed for the author and perhaps for a few friends. They are full accounts, in grammatical and consecutive prose, of most of the main speeches. Such a form of report had been attempted before, but never on this scale or this standard. It was much easier for the public to follow than any diary, and much more informative, and provocative, than the normal newsletter. It was not printed, but survives in numerous manuscript copies. In addition, some big set-piece performances, such as the speeches of Glanville and Marten on 23 May, designed to reject the Lords' saving to the Petition, were printed. Highly polished arguments about the profoundest questions of authority were thus made available to the public at large. The public seems to have been duly appreciative. The passing of the Petition of Right was celebrated by numerous bonfires.[1] In the long term, it is possible that these bonfires were more important than the event they were meant to celebrate.

---

[1] Stowe 366, f. 247^r. Richard Montagu, at Windsor, took a discontented kick at one of these bonfires, and said those making it would answer for it. The men thus threatened promptly complained to the House of Commons.

VII

The Death of Buckingham and the Session of 1629

I

CHARLES had promised the Parliament of 1628 that it would be recalled for another session. When the session of 1628 ended, then, he did not dissolve the Parliament: he prorogued it. It thus remained available to be reassembled, at short notice and without fresh elections, whenever the moment appeared suitable. The date to which it was at first prorogued was 20 October 1628, but prorogations could be, and often were, extended without any difficulty. Fresh subsidies could not be expected before March 1629, when the last of the subsidies voted in 1628 would be collected. However, Phelips and others had frequently said that they would not think Parliaments were understood until they were called when there was no need for subsidies. A King who wished to make a last determined effort to establish a working relationship with a Parliament might, then, call one when there was no prospect of money.

Even if there were no prospect of money, there was certainly need of money. A list of anticipations of revenue, drawn up in July 1628, showed that the King had anticipated his income by £276,113. 5s. 3d.—a sum fractionally greater than all the Parliamentary subsidies which had just been voted.[1] It is, then, not surprising that the ending of the Parliamentary session was almost immediately followed by moves for the ending of the war. On 31 July, Sir Francis Nethersole told Conway that he must report the rumours of peace with Spain to his employer, Elizabeth of Bohemia.[2] The rumours were well founded: an unofficial emissary had just been sent off with peace proposals to the Duke of Olivares.[3] The time was a propitious one to negotiate peace, since the inter-

---

[1] *C.S.P.D. 1628–9*, vol. cx, no. 21.

[2] *C.S.P.D. 1628–9*, vol. cxi, no. 44.

[3] A. J. Loomie, 'Olivares, The English Catholics and the Peace of 1630', *Revue Belge de Philologie et d'Histoire*, vol. xlvii (1969), no. 4, pp. 1156–7. I am grateful to Professor J. H. Elliott for drawing my attention to this article.

national situation turned as much in England's favour in 1628 as it had been against England during 1627. In 1627, France and Spain had been temporarily enjoying friendship, and a Spanish fleet had actually been sent to help the French at La Rochelle. In January 1628, the war of the Mantuan succession had begun, and France and Spain were again occupied in fighting each other in Italy. This meant that an invasion scare which had been real enough in 1627 had receded. It also meant that France and Spain, being now sufficiently occupied with fighting each other, would both be glad to be relieved of the minor irritation of a war with England.

Before Charles and Buckingham could consider a general peace, however, they had to deal with one question they regarded as a matter of honour: that of La Rochelle. The town was under siege in part, at least, because it had furnished Charles and Buckingham with their excuse for intervention in French affairs in 1627. It was holding out, in part, at least, because it hoped for relief from England, though those not under arms were now reduced to eating grass, roots, boiled leather, and occasional shellfish.[1] It is easy to see how Charles and Buckingham might have felt that their reputation demanded that they relieve La Rochelle before making any general peace. A fleet was already assembled at Portsmouth, waiting for the subsidies which had been so long in coming. Buckingham paused only to secure his base at court before heading for the fleet.

This time, the two men Buckingham selected as in need of conciliation were Arundel and Bristol. On 23 June, while the Parliament was still sitting, an order had been given to pay the arrears of a pension granted to Bristol by King James.[2] Arundel was admitted to kiss the King's hand at the Duke's house, and his prospective influence was increased when his friend and former client Weston was appointed Lord Treasurer.[3] Arundel, unlike Bristol, had recovered Charles's favour as well as Buckingham's, and was restored to the Council in November. Another Howard came back into office when Buckingham voluntarily resigned the Lord Wardenship of the Cinque Ports in favour of Suffolk.

Buckingham might succeed in reshuffling his potential opponents at court but he was less successful in handling popular hostility.

[1] Gardiner, vi. 342. [2] C.S.P.D. 1628-9, vol. cviii, no. 1.
[3] C.S.P.D.Ven. 1628-9, pp. 168-9, 213.

At the end of June, his astrologer Dr. Lambe was torn to pieces by a crowd in a London street. The Venetian Ambassador noted that 'the example is very perilous'.[1] It was: when Buckingham reached Portsmouth, he was approached by one Felton, a naval Lieutenant who was the latest in a procession of sailors appearing tumultuously before Buckingham to receive their pay. Felton did not receive his pay, but, according to one account, got a kick instead.[2] He then stabbed the Duke, who died almost instantly. A long search for Felton's accomplices failed to produce any, and Felton himself claimed that the Parliament's Remonstrance was the only cause of his actions.[3] The Duke's death appears to have met with almost universal satisfaction, and, in some places, with embarrassingly obvious signs of celebration. So many offices were vacated that it would be surprising if there were not some covert celebration at court, as well as in the country. The one person whose reaction remained entirely private is Charles: he refused to admit anyone into his chamber for two days after the murder.[4] For a long time, he took little or no counsel on the major decisions facing him. This is why it is so hard for us, as it was for the Councillors, to assess the drift of English policy at this time. Carleton reported that the King directed affairs, leaving only the execution to others.[5] Charles received advice, but he did not discuss it, and which way his mind was moving on issues of policy was a matter of conjecture even for those closest to him.

The only clear clue was from his appointments. In religion, these had already shown a strong movement towards Arminianism, emphasized by the appointment of Richard Montagu as Bishop of Chichester on 4 July. Others got the message: by September, the Earl of Norwich said almost the whole world was turned Arminian.[6] If this strong tide towards Arminianism were to continue, it would be taken as an argument that the King was not likely to reassemble his Parliament. Shortly after Buckingham's murder, Parliament was further prorogued from October to January, but the court was in such disarray that it could not be expected to hold a Parliament in October: the further prorogation was not taken as evidence for or against an ultimate reassembly.

[1] *C.S.P.Ven. 1628-9*, p, 157.   [2] *Wentworth Papers*, p. 303.
[3] *C.S.P.D. 1628-9*, vol. cxvi, no. 101.   [4] *C.S.P.Ven. 1628-9*, p. 283.
[5] *C.S.P.D. 1628-9*, vol. cxvii, no. 83.
[6] *C.S.P.D. 1628-9*, vol. cxvi, no 11.

The fleet sailed in spite of Buckingham's death and in spite of the armed rescue of some pressed sailors, and duly failed.

On the other hand, some of Charles's other appointments suggested a move towards peace. The preferment of Weston, Arundel, and Cottington argued peace with Spain, and the preferment of Holland as Chancellor of Canbridge and Constable of Winsor Castle argued peace with France. Even more, Charles's new-found devotion to his wife argued peace with France if, as Goring put it, it could be secured without filling the Queen's household with 'a fresh supply of French'.[1] In October, the fall of La Rochelle, where between fourteen and fifteen thousand people were said to have died of starvation,[2] removed the last real obstacle to peace with France. The ending of the war would be likely to be generally popular, since the Venetian Ambassador was probably right that the country was weary of it, because of loss of trade. He was certainly also right that Parliament had 'never thought of the common cause, the affairs of the nation absorbing all their attention'.[3] In Parliament, only a few members would be likely to feel any regret at the ending of the Spanish war, and none at the ending of the French war. The disbanding of the soldiers and sailors, in the third week of November, was another sign that Charles was thinking of peace. At least, the country was to be spared another winter's billeting, and with the disappearance of the soldiers, the political temperature might be expected to drop. In the same week, the Venetian Ambassador commented on Arundel's recall to the Council, and said that he and Weston were 'downright Englishmen, who care little for foreign affairs, following the example of King James, and would willingly make peace with everybody'. He thought Weston's suspected Catholicism might put him off Parliaments, and that he would endeavour to make ends meet by cutting off the cause of expenditure.[4]

Among Charles's appointments, only that of Carleton as Secretary of State appeared to point towards the continuation of the war. During November and December, when men were speculating on whether Parliament would be reassembled, the causes of Parliament and of the war appeared to be identified. Pembroke, who, even more than Buckingham, had been the consistent champion of war throughout the period, still hoped

[1] C.S.P.D. 1628–9, vol. cxxiii, no. 8.   [2] B.L. Harl. MS. 7010, f. 91ʳ.
[3] C.S.P.Ven. 1628–9, pp. 358, 557.   [4] C.S.P.Ven. 1628–9, p. 394.

both for war and for a new session of Parliament. Carleton was also in favour both of the war and of the Parliament. He wrote a report to Carlisle on 30 September which is probably our best summary of the debates on whether to hold the Parliament: writing before the decision to prorogue it until January had been taken, he said:

Whether the Parliament will hold at the appointed time is not resolved, but it being a subject of much discourse, though many are of opinion the present opportunity is not to be let slip of a presumed desire the Parliament will have to make it appear their former distempers were rather personal than real, yet others wish time may be taken till the next spring at least, and in the mean time a settled form of government should work better effects than may be premised upon any assurance. It imports more than anything else that the next meeting may be without the late disorders.

Hearing, as he finished the letter, of the decision to prorogue Parliament till January, he added: 'The bitterness in men's minds requires time to take it away, and the medicine of a constant and settled government is like to be applied.'[1] Goring, on 22 December, thought the cooling-off period had not been long enough, and feared that the evil spirits were not all laid.[2] The Venetian Ambassador thought that the decision whether to continue the Spanish war had, in effect, been left contingent on the Parliament. He said that if the Parliament should prove recalcitrant, the English would 'shut up shop' and devote themselves to home affairs.[3]

It was an open question, then, what a Parliament, if it should assemble, could be asked to do. Charles did not want it to discuss Arminianism, and tried to protect himself by measures to round up London recusants, and by a temporary reconciliation with Archbishop Abbot. If a Parliament was not to discuss religion, and was not likely to encourage the war whose supporters provided the main pressure for its assembly, what was it to do? Charles appears to have given his mind to this question, and the 1629 session is the only one of the decade for which there appears to be a 'legislative programme'. This, though, is perhaps a rather grandiose title for the 'memorial of Acts sent by the King unto the Lower House, to be drawn against the next session'.[4] J.P.s were to be discouraged from leaving their countries and dwelling in

---

[1] C.S.P.D. 1628–9, vol. cxvii, no. 83.
[2] C.S.P.D. 1628–9, vol. cxxiii, no. 8.
[3] C.S.P.Ven. 1628–9, pp. 431–2.
[4] S.P. 16/124/10.

London, whereby hospitality was decayed. Fish days and the watch were not duly kept. Legislation was wanted against disorder in alehouses, new buildings and inmates (i.e. multi-occupation), against erecting of cottages on wastes, and against maintainers of pirates. An Act was wanted for preservation of timber and wood, and others against spending of silver and gold in gilding swords and against seditious books. He wanted the profession of attorneys regulated, and only the skillful allowed, and restriction of liberty given in prisons after execution. Only two proposals seemed substantial. One was a possible new source of revenue, the rating of lawyers' fees. Another memorandum had proposed that rich lawyers should be taxed at a fortieth on their annual earnings.[1] One item is noted laconically as 'the fees of Serjeants and officers'. It is impossible to tell whether this is a proposal to extend a similar system of taxation on fees, or whether it is an attempt to give statutory backing to some of the work of the Commission on Fees. Apart from these two, the others are all minor proposals, and were mostly done by proclamation during the 1630s. If this were all the Parliament was to have to do, it would go even less far than the bills of grace of 1614 to distract them from issues Charles did not want to have discussed. This list suggests, as strongly as almost any document, that by this time Charles had very little use for Parliaments. The one thing a Parliament could give him was a legal grant of Tonnage and Poundage. Yet, though there was some active resistance to the payment of Tonnage and Poundage after the Parliamentary session of 1628, this soon petered out, because few merchants could afford to continue it. To refuse to pay customs meant to cease to trade. If a legal grant of Tonnage and Poundage was the only reason Charles had for calling the Parliamentary session of 1629, he may have called it out of inertia. He may have called it in order to keep his word, given in 1628. It is, however, most probable that he called the session because, like other prominent Englishmen of his day, he had a strong attachment to the proper, traditional, and legal way of doing things. A successful Parliament was a symbol, both of subjects' affection for their King, and of their allegiance. If Charles was still a believer in Parliamentary ways of doing things, the assembly of 1629 needs little explanation. Anyone who wishes to maintain that Charles was a natural enemy to Parliaments

[1] S.P. 16/126/47.

must produce a better explanation of the recall of Parliament in 1629 than has yet been heard.

II

The achievements of the Parliament of 1628 had been in the realm of the history of ideas: they did little to alter the immediate realities of power politics. In May and June 1628, members of Parliament might reasonably have thought themselves to be of some importance in the commonwealth. The idea was a heady one, and the disillusion from it therefore proved the more painful. The discovery made by members in 1629 that they had, if anything, less power to get their own way than before, and, indeed, that for a clergyman to be complained of by the Parliament was probably the shortest road to preferment, was therefore the more bitterly disillusioning. In the 1628 Remonstrance, the Commons had named two bishops as being justly suspected of unsound and Arminian opinions. These two, Neile and Laud, had been made members of the Privy Council. They had impeached Roger Manwaring for his belief that taxes were due by the law of God, and for his belief that the King's sovereign power could not be controlled by law. They came back to Westminster, on 20 January 1629, to find that Manwaring, though duly sentenced by the House of Lords, had been pardoned, preferred, and made a royal chaplain. Auditor Sawyer, who had been sent to the Tower in the closing weeks of the 1628 Parliament, had been released immediately it was over. Moreover, the King had paid his fees.[1] Perhaps worst of all, Richard Montagu, who had been being denounced by the Commons since the end of James's reign, had been made a bishop, succeeding to the see of one of his strongest theological opponents. It was not surprising that Littleton concluded: 'You see the affronts by books, by preaching, by rumours, by being daily served with process, that are put upon us, that we are become but a mere scarecrow'.[2] If Parliamentary censures could be so systematically ignored, it was natural that members should begin to ask whether they served any useful purpose. As

[1] C.S.P.D. 1628-9, vol. cviii, nos. 28, 30. Sawyer, along with two of the Deputy Lieutenants of Cornwall, was released on the day the Parliament was prorogued.

[2] 1629 Debates, p. 57. (Further references are to this edition unless otherwise stated.) For a fuller account of the main issues of this session, see Christopher Thompson, in Kevin Sharpe (ed.) Faction And Parliament (Oxford 1978) pp. 245-84.

Phelips said, when facing what he took to be another refusal by the common law judges to enforce the rule of law: (it is) 'to no purpose to sit here if these things be put upon us'. The cult of the rule of law, which had been the centrepiece of the ideology of 1628, was useless if the judges' interpretation of the law did not coincide in the main material points with that of the House of Commons. Faced with another case, this time concerning the laws against popish priests, in which he thought the judges had plainly failed to enforce the rule of law, Phelips was reduced to complaining that: 'If the judges give us not better satisfaction, they themselves will be parties.'[1]

This sense that a Parliament's words made no difference to what happened did not only produce widespread disillusion: it also produced a more negativist and obstructive House of Commons than had been seen for a very long time, They met, in fact, in the chararacteristic mood of men facing redundancy, Why had the heady hopes of 1628 evaporated so quickly? It had always been the justification of Parliaments that they provided a point of contact between the King and the country: the job of a member of Parliament was to discharge a dual loyalty, to his King and to his local community. By the winter of 1628–9, this dual loyalty was becoming almost impossible to discharge, and, as Sir Thomas Wentworth had warned in 1625, if it ever became impossible for members of Parliament to combine these dual loyalties, their usefulness, both to the King and to the country, would be at an end.[2] The King had not received much benefit from the Parliament of 1628. He had, it is true, received five subsidies, but these had been so little, and more important, so late, that it was questionable whether they had been worth the sacrifice to his dignity involved in the Petition of Right debates. In the short term, the King in 1628 had had no choice about it, because the urgency of the need to pay armed soldiers could not be denied. In 1629, with the soldiers disbanded, he could think at leisure about whether this contentious body was really the best means of getting supply. In his declaration justifying the dissolution of 1629, Charles recorded his view of the Parliament of 1628, and it deserves a hearing. He stressed, first, the urgency of his need for supply, because of the state of the reformed churches abroad, and because of 'the distressed extremities of our uncle, the King of Denmark,

---

[1] p. 90: Manchester MS. f. 25ᵛ: also p. 55.   [2] See above, pp. 258–9.

chased out of a great part of his dominions'. He said that the Commons had at first appeared to appreciate the urgency of this need for supply:

But before it was brought to any perfection, they were diverted by a multitude of questions, raised amongst them, touching their liberties and privileges, and by other long disputes, that the bill did not pass in a long time; and by that delay, our affairs were put into a far worse case than at the first; our foreign actions, then in hand, being disgraced and ruined for want of timely help.

As a strategic assessment of the foreign policy consequences of the Parliament of 1628, this was hard to dispute. In addition, they had tried to claim binding force for their own interpretation of the rule of law: 'Young lawyers sitting there, take upon them to decry the opinions of the judges; and some have not doubted to maintain that the resolutions of that House must bind the judges, a thing never heard of in ages past.' In taking the view that the judges were a more authoritative guide to the meaning of the law than the lawyers of the House of Commons, Charles had adopted a position which was at least intelligible. In order to justify facing such a House, 'blasting our government, as we are unwilling to remember', Charles needed some solid benefits.[1]

It appeared significant to Charles that the assessment of the subsidy, so far from being reformed, as Rudyerd and others had wished, was actually worse in 1628 than it had ever been before. The yield of a subsidy fell from £70,000 in 1624 to £55,000, subjecting Charles to a total loss, in a grant of five subsidies, of £75,000 simply by under-assessment. Charles blamed this on the unreasonableness of the House of Commons:

And their spirit, infused into many of the commissioners and assessors in the country, hath returned up the subsidies in such a scanty proportion, as is infinitely short, not only of our great occasions, but of the precedents of former subsidies, and of the intention of all well affected men in the House.

To members of the Commons, facing electorates already indignant at the sums they had paid out for billeting and other military charges, the influence had appeared to be the other way. Kirton and Seymour had both expressed the fear that a grant not accompanied by substantial concessions would simply not be paid.[2] In the event, members were able to use the Petition of Right to

---

[1] J. Rushworth, *Historical Collections* (1659), i, appendix, pp. 1–10.
[2] See above, p. 21.

justify themselves at home, but there was a feeling among them that visits by the subsidy commissioners since 1621 had been more frequent than they could easily justify. At the very end of the Parliament of 1628, Digges had revived his proposals to increase the King's ordinary revenue, 'so as his Majesty may be eased, and subsidies less sought after to the grievance of the subject.'[1] It is an arresting phrase: if even Parliamentary subsidies were going to be accounted a 'grievance' in the country, it was hard to see what members could offer to meet the King's needs. Many of them appreciated that he must look for further sources of revenue. At the end of the 1628 session, they noticed with justifiable alarm that the General Pardon offered (but unprecedently rejected) at the end of the session did not pardon those liable to fines for distraint of knighthood.[2] The pressure on the King to finance himself by unparliamentary means was approaching the irresistible.

But if members could not offer any adequate supply to the King, what could they offer to the country? Their apparent success as champions of the country in 1628 had been based on the Petition of Right, yet the Petition itself rested most insecurely on the interpretation Charles chose to give it. As Secretary Coke had warned them before the event, there was no use in making a law if the King were not willing to execute that law. Indeed, the King had been forced into enunciating positions which made it appear that no Parliamentary statute could be a substantial gain for the country. If he really held, as he had suggested, that he enjoyed an ultimate discretionary prerogative which no statute could tie, members who went home and told their countries that they had won concessions through statutes, or even through impeachments, were taking part in a charade. The number of unreformed grievances, complained of but never remedied, which littered the road of Parliamentary progress since 1604 could only serve to underline the point. Dungeness lighthouse was as dangerous as ever, illegal tolls were still levied on the Great North Road, the patent for issues of jurors, condemned in 1606, was still being used, Even Sir Giles Mompesson, though degraded from his knighthood and

---

[1] Stowe 366, f. 276^r.
[2] Stowe 366, f. 287^r. Rushworth, *ubi supra*, p. 2. Nethersole claimed that the pardon had been refused in order not to free the Duke from a possible revival of the charges of 1626. *C.S.P.D. 1628–9*, vol. cviii, no. 52.

banished, was back in England and again being referred to as
'Sir Giles'.[1] It was vital to members of Parliament that the blame
for this continued list of failures should be placed on someone
else, and not on themselves. In 1626, when Hoby asked that they
search through Petitions of Grievances back to 1604, in order to
find out what had been remedied, he was raising a most uncomfortable question.

This list of failures was heavily underlined by the preferment
of Neile, Laud, Montagu, and Manwaring during the recess
between the sessions of 1628 and 1629. In approaching such an
offensive list of preferments, the House of Commons came back to
Westminster with a smaller amount of bargaining power than they
had enjoyed in any other session. Supply could not be voted
before March, when the last of the 1628 subsidies was to be
collected. If there were to be any supply in 1629, it would have to
come, in the traditional fashion, at the end of the session, and
not in the fashion which had become normal since 1621, at its
beginning. The one thing Charles wanted in 1629 was a Parliamentary grant of Tonnage and Poundage. This was a revenue he
already enjoyed, and he was asking for Parliamentary confirmation
out of goodwill, not out of need. The number of merchants
refusing to pay Tonnage and Poundage because it had not been
granted by Parliament was small, and diminishing. A resolution
to refuse customs duties could, in the end, only be sustained by
abandonment of trade, which few merchants wished to do. Moreover, it was dangerously easy to meet any attempt to bargain about
Tonnage and Poundage by claiming, as Secretary Coke ultimately
did, that the King, having possession, must be supposed to have
a right.[2] Any attempt to bargain about Tonnage and Poundage
was almost certain to be self-defeating. The 1629 Commons, as
they saw it, were assembled simply in order to provide a rubber
stamp for what they took to be an illegal Act. The consequence of
refusal might be the redundancy of Parliament. In terms of
political good sense, the case for a quick and uncontentious confirmation of Tonnage and Poundage was overwhelming. It was,
though, hard to see how men like Phelips, Eliot, and Selden

---

[1] *C.S.P.D. 1628–9*, vol. cxvii, no. 94. Contrast S.P. 14/159/21 (8 Feb. 1623/4,
in which 'Giles Mompesson' (not Esquire) was told to leave the country within
five days.
[2] p. 230.

could combine this with the preservation of their self-respect. It was even harder to see what explanation for a quick grant of Tonnage and Poundage they could have offered to merchants like Rolle or Chambers, who had refused Tonnage and Poundage because the draft Remonstrance of 1628 had asked them to do so, and had suffered heavily in the process. If any settlement were reached, it would have to be one of its conditions that there should be no victimization of tax refusers.

If there was any chance of a satisfactory conclusion of the session, the events of its first few days would have much reduced it. There was less time to be spent on ritual opening business in a new session than in a new Parliament. There was no new Speaker to elect, and very few elections to discuss. A writ had to be issued for a new election for Yorkshire, to replace Sir Thomas Wentworth, who had been raised to the peerage and to the Presidency of the Council of the North. Excuses had to be accepted from another prominent absentee: Sir Edward Coke, whose 'great age' was held to excuse his absence.[1] What effect Coke's absence had on the session of 1629 is a matter for conjecture, but it can safely be supposed that it was considerable.

In particular, they lacked Coke's guidance in dealing with the first item of serious business, the printing of the Petition of Right. The 1628 Parliament had arranged, by agreement of both Houses, that the Petition of Right and the King's second answer should be printed. This had duly been done, and an impression of 1,500 copies, with the King's second answer, had been printed while Parliament was in session. The day after Parliament rose, the Attorney General told the printer that, by the King's command, this edition was to be 'made waste paper'. Instead, the Petition was printed with the answer of 2 June, the answer that in Eliot's words 'never gave any satisfaction'. With this answer, the King printed his speech of 7 June, saying that his second answer conceded no more than the first, and that a Parliament could not hurt his prerogative. He also included his speech of 26 June, at the closing of the session, warning against 'false constructions' of the Petition of Right, and in particular, stressing that it did not prohibit the levying of Tonnage and Poundage.

In this publicly circulated manifesto, Charles appeared to withdraw all the concession he had made between 2 June and 7

[1] C.J. 921.

June.[1] The apparent certainty of the rule of law, which appeared to have been enshrined in the second answer, had evaporated in favour of the uncertainties of a discretionary, and therefore unpredictable, dispensing power. Liberties, instead of resting on a secure foundation of law, again rested on the King's gracious willingness to execute the law. Members were right back to the terrors which had possessed them on 5 and 6 June. Moreover, the extent to which the 1628 House had erected 'liberties' into one indivisible whole meant that the threat which was seen in an individual illegal act was now much greater than it had been before. Pym, who was later to be one of the few non-Councillor members to propose directly that the Commons should vote Tonnage and Poundage, heroically proposed that this issue should be deferred till the House were fuller.[2] He was overruled by Eliot and Selden, who procured the setting up of a committee to investigate violations of the Petition of Right since the last meeting. It was an unpromising beginning: as Charles said on 24 January: 'The order made on Wednesday last might have made me startle, there being some show to suspect that you had given yourselves the liberty to be enquirers after complaints, the words of your order being somewhat largely penned.'[3] In other words, Charles thought Eliot and Selden were trying to make trouble. It was becoming painfully clear that he and the members were living in two different worlds, speaking a different language about different things.

On 22 January, the question of the King's right to levy Tonnage and Poundage was transformed into a dispute about Parliamentary privilege. The farmers of the customs had continued to take leases of the contentious duties, and had continued to take proceedings against those who refused to pay. Very shortly before the Parliament, they had, 'through some great error', as Sir Humphrey May put it,[4] seized the goods of a merchant member of Parliament, John Rolle. Rolle had pleaded Parliamentary privilege, only to be told by one of the customs officers that even if the whole Parliament were involved in his person, they would still seize his goods. It was in the demand to punish these customs officers for

---

[1] Elizabeth Read Foster, 'Printing the Petition of Right', *Huntington Library Quarterly*, vol. xxxviii, no. 1 (Nov. 1974), 81–3.

[2] pp. 4–5. See also pp. 156–7, 222–3.

[3] p. 11. [4] pp. 187, 136.

their breach of privilege that the session was to peter out into futility. It was on this issue that Littleton complained that 'we are become but a mere scarecrow' if they allowed the offence to pass unpunished. Yet, as Sir Humphrey May pointed out, the King could not be expected to allow the punishment of his officers for obeying his commands. As he said, 'God forbid that it is delinquency to obey the King's command.' If it were, 'The king might think *actum est de imperio*, that he should be no more obeyed.'[1] Above all, the dispute underlined the fact that the King was already in possession of the duties he was asking Parliament to grant. The subject invited what it got: a long speech on a point of principle from Sir Robert Phelips: 'If we suffer the liberty of this House out of fear or compliment to be abused we give a wound to the happiness of this kingdom.'[2]

The King, who seems to have been determined either to reach good relations with his Parliament or to show that his failure to do so was not his fault, immediately intervened. He told both Houses that the best way to settle these disputes was by passing a Tonnage and Poundage bill. He said he did not claim Tonnage and Poundage by hereditary prerogative, but by the gift of his people.[3] He said that his speech at the end of the previous session had been meant to show his necessity, not his right, and that he had accepted their professions that they wanted the time, not the will, to pass it. According to Lord Montagu, this speech was thought to have given great satisfaction.[4] However, even if Montagu was right that it appeared pleasing to the Commons, it did not remove the issue of privilege. This swiftly became apparent in the next day's proceedings, those of 26 January. After a brief diversion to handle a complaint about export of corn and ordnance to Spain, the day's key business began when Secretary Coke offered the bill of Tonnage and Poundage, with a commendation in the King's name. Eliot objected to the bill because it did not settle the issue of impositions, and Selden introduced the novel doctrine that it was against the liberties of the House for a subsidy bill to come in by the King's recommendation or, according to Lowther, argued the more credible case that it was not normal to introduce a bill for subsidies before the subject had been debated. Digges and Harley

[1] p. 157.   [2] p. 158. Also pp. 157, 224, *Lowther*, p. 73.
[3] p. 7.
[4] *H.M.C. Buccleuch*, iii. 331.

tried to put the case for the bill, but Phelips said it should not be passed until the liberties of the House were righted.[1]

It was at this moment that Pym's stepbrother, Francis Rous, chose to introduce the issue of Arminianism, now a matter of much more general concern than it had been in any previous Parliament. The leaders of the attack on Arminianism were the same members as before: Pym, Rich, Sherland, Harley, and Mildmay. What is new is not the intensity of their concern: it is the extent to which they had induced more secular members such as Phelips, Eliot, Kirton, and Earle to share it. For the first time in 1629, the Commons as a whole regarded the growth of Arminianism as a conspiracy to alter the doctrine of the Church of England. It is tempting to attempt to divide the 1629 Commons into those who gave priority to Arminianism, and those who gave priority to the privilege issue. It is possible to make such a division with confidence for four members, Pym and Rich, who put Arminianism first, and Eliot and Selden, who put the privilege issue first. For the weathercock members, like Phelips, it is impossible to make this distinction, because they saw the issues as too closely connected.

The key to the nightmares of 5 and 6 June had been the belief that a design existed to bring about alteration of religion and alteration of government, both as part of one common programme. It was this nightmare which the growth of Arminianism served to perpetuate. There was nothing irrational about the central belief of the 1629 Commons, that Arminians wished to avoid Parliaments because they thought Parliaments would attempt to persecute them. The point was underlined by the fact that Montagu and Cosin, together with the two clerical champions of the Forced Loan, Manwaring and Sibthorpe, had fortified themselves against the Parliament by obtaining pardons under the Great Seal. These pardons had been passed through the intervention of the Arminians' chief patron, Neile, Bishop of Winchester. That Arminians had cause to fear the success of Parliaments was clear enough. It seemed a logical deduction from this fact to suppose that Arminians were likely to be adherents of 'new counsels', involving rule without any Parliaments. Laud's memorandum of 1627/8, on whether a Parliament should be summoned, suggests that, so far, the Commons' reasoning was justified.[2]

---

[1] pp. 108–9. *Lowther*, p. 62.
[2] See above, p. 338.

Many Arminians, with the conspicious exception of Harsnett, Bishop of Norwich, perhaps did hope that Parliaments would become obsolete.

It was then possible to suppose that Arminians were deliberately conspiring to wreck the Parliament, in order to protect themselves. Phelips said on the privilege dispute: 'I conceive this to be a bone thrown in by them, that have drawn a cloud over our sun, our religion, to divert or interrupt us in the prosecution of them.'[1] For Phelips, the conclusion followed that the survival of Arminianism and the survival of Parliament were mutually exclusive: 'If we find not those that throw these stones upon us, it is in vain to sit here.'[2] Eliot agreed that the privilege dispute had been provoked to prevent an investigation into religion: 'The ground of this I conceive to proceed from those who would take us off the matter of religion.'[3] Sir Henry Mildmay, who as Buckingham's former client, and Master of the Jewel House, was not ignorant of events at court, said, 'We all know how many there are who watch for occasion to breed distraction betwixt the King and his Parliaments.'[4] Sir Walter Earle, in an important speech on 27 January, said that in the previous session, he had been one of those who wanted to give priority to their liberties, and 'postpone the business of religion'. In this session, he said he had changed his mind: 'As for the passing of bills, settling of revenues and the like, without settling religion I must confess I have no heart unto it: take away my religion, you take away my life, and not only mine, but the life of the whole state and kingdom. For I dare boldly say, never was there (in point of subsistence) a more near connection between the matter of religion and matter of state in any kingdom in the world than there is in this kingdom at this day.'[5]

Sir Walter Earle's view that he had no heart for bills seems to have been general. It is noteworthy that among the uncompleted bills of 1628, religious bills, almost alone, were reintroduced in 1629. The only bill which got as far as engrossing was the bill against recusants evading forfeiture by uses, vetoed in the previous session. It was followed by a bill for the maintenance of the

---

[1] p. 55.
[2] I have followed the reading 'stones' in the Manchester True Relation (House of Lords R.O.), f. 15ᵛ, rather than the reading 'scornes' taken by Notestein and Relf, op. cit., p. 55. A thrower of stones may remain invisible, and stones are more readily thrown than scorns.
[3] p. 186   [4] p. 188.   [5] pp. 18–19.

ministry, a bill to permit marriages in Lent, Jordan's bill against adultery, a bill to reform impropriations, the bill against simony in the Universities, a bill against clergy J.P.s, and the bill against citations out of ecclesiastical courts. Only seven public bills reached committee. They were the bills for liberty to hear preaching, against begging forfeitures before attainder, against buying judicial places, on recusants' leases, for the increase of trade, to confirm the plantation of Bermuda, and against simony in Colleges and Halls. Only the bill on recusants' leases progressed as far as engrossing. Even the bill for free fishing, which had passed the Commons in every previous session, did not progress as far as a first reading. Such an atmosphere of concentration on religion had not been known in any previous Parliament of the decade. The decision, on 27 January, that religion was to be given priority over other business, seems to have reflected the mood of the House as a whole.[1]

From 27 January onwards, then, Charles was faced with a double obstacle to a vote of Tonnage and Poundage. He not only had to remove the stumbling-block of the privilege dispute: he also had to face a determined attempt, led by Pym and Rich, to make the granting of Tonnage and Poundage conditional on his abandonment of Arminianism. Charles reacted with some indignation to the introduction of this issue, saying he had expected rather thanks than a Remonstrance. However he did not dissolve the Parliament. After 27 January, there was no prospect of the Parliament's success, and Charles's willingness to keep it in session is perhaps the biggest unexplained mystery about it.

It must be doubtful whether Pym and Rich believed they could force Charles to abandon Arminianism by threatening to refuse to grant a revenue he already enjoyed. By 1629, however, the issue went too deep for this type of calculation. It is possible that Pym and Rich cared more about the abolition of Arminianism than they did about the survival of Parliament. For them, and for their friends, the popish menace they had been brought up to fear all their lives had now moved from Rome and Madrid to Whitehall. More secular members thought that false religion could explain English disgrace in war. Phelips wanted a fast, 'to divert God's wrath, to bring God into our counsels before our armies', while Sir Francis Seymour thought that 'If God fight not

[1] p. 21.

our battles, the help of man is in vain. . . . the cause hereof is in our defects, and the same is idolatry and popery.'[1]

For Phelips and Seymour, fear for religion did not mean quite what it meant for Pym and Rich. When Phelips and Seymour spoke of fears for religion, they usually placed them directly in the context of the war. False religion, for them, was to be dreaded because it led to disaster and defeat. Their ultimate nightmare seems to have been, not so much of hell-fire, as of a Spanish army, aided by a domestic fifth column, marching across Wiltshire and Somerset. This fear, unlike the more theological fears of Pym, Rich, Knightley, or Harley, could be removed by the making of peace. Seymour and Phelips, then, though apparently as intense in their religious alarm as the others, were less settled in it. It makes sense that they did not become irreconcilable during the 1630s, for the chief root of their fears had by then been removed.

Francis Rous, whose speech is heavily and approvingly underlined by Bedford in his copy of the True Relation, saw something more permanent at stake than a few military defeats:

I desire that it may be considered, how the sea of Rome doth eat into our religion, and fret into the banks and walls of it, the laws and statutes of this realm. . . . I desire that we may look into the very belly and bowels of this Trojan horse to see if there be not men in it, ready to open the gates, to Romish tyranny and Spanish monarchy; for an Arminian is the spawn of a Papist. . . . And if there come the warmth of favour upon him, you shall see him turn into one of those frogs, that arise out of the bottomless pit.

These, he said, were the same people who had attempted the taking away of their goods, for the devil, 'when he meant to take away Job's religion, he began first at his goods'. 'Either they think thereby to set a distaste between prince and people, or to find out some other way of supply to avoid or break Parliaments, that so they may break in upon our religion and bring in their own errors.' In Rous's mind, the effects of insolvency had become a new decking for the Whore of Babylon.[2]

It was not only Rous who was now thinking like this: Sherland said that

They creep into the ears of his Majesty, and suggest, that those that oppose them, do oppose his Majesty, and so they put him upon designs that stand not with public liberty, that he may command what he listeth

---

[1] pp. 109–10, p. 14: Manchester MS., f. 6ʳ.
[2] pp. 12–13: Manchester MS., ff. 3–4.

and do what he pleaseth with life, goods and religion. And so they involve all true hearted English men and Christians [*sic*] under the name of Puritans, and involve our master's quarrel with theirs, which is treason in the highest degree and quality.[1]

Earle, similarly, thought an English Protestant would have no chance of living a freeman and not a slave, if popery and Arminianism were allowed to bring in Spanish tyranny.[2]

If members were in this mood, there was no point in a search for compromise: no common ground existed. The Lords, interestingly, were not publicly involved in any search for compromise in 1629, but went quietly on with their own business. Little of that business was dramatic. On 31 January, they sent down four bills to the Commons: a bill for the preservation of the King's revenues, a bill for the increase of trade, a bill to clarify privilege of Parliament, and a bill for the naturalization of Lady Strange. The bill for the increase of trade, which was designed to clarify the use of bonds and bills of exchange, got as far as a second reading in the Commons.[3] After that, the Lords debated a bill on apparel, one of the apparently contentious issues in the Lords in the later 1620s. The bill was carried by 36 votes to 31, and a call for the proxy votes confirmed the original division.[4] They also drew up a long protest against the fact that English subjects holding Scottish and Irish Viscounties were allowed to take precedence over English Barons.

The key issue being a supply bill, they were not in a good position to intervene in the Commons' proceedings, so the Lords were forced to remain helpless spectators during the session of 1629. As always, a session dominated by supply became a Commons' session. The Lords might relieve their feelings by ordering the Mayor and Aldermen of London to search for 'sophisticated, artificial and falsified wines' brought in from France,[5] but they could make no contribution to the vital issues. They were not even consulted by the Commons about the issue of Arminianism, perhaps fortunately for themselves, since a number of their own members were deeply involved on both sides. The Lords' capacity for patching up compromises had been exhausted in 1626 and 1628. They were never consulted by the Commons about their next task, that of formulating the doctrines of the

---

[1] pp. 15–16: Manchester MS., f. 6^v.
[2] pp. 18–19.   [3] *C.J.* 928–9.
[4] *H.M.C. Buccleuch*, iii. 340.   [5] *L.J.* iv. 39.

Church of England with such authority that Arminianism should be clearly excluded.

The problem of authority in doctrine was an awkward one for the Commons. Like the Five Knights' case, it involved a question of interpretation where the Commons thought there should be no room for interpretation. As in law they were incredulous of the interpretations of the judges, so in the matter of Arminianism they were incredulous of the interpretations of some of the bishops. Eliot, much though he honoured the order of bishops, and many of the existing bishops, found his faith in the bishops as interpreters of doctrine much shaken by the appointment of Montagu, whom he claimed to regard as no true bishop. He accepted the authority of the Thirty-Nine Articles, but distrusted Montagu and his colleagues as interpreters of them:

Mark the ground of our religion, it is contained in the body of these articles; if there be any difference in opinion concerning the sense and interpretation, the bishops and clergy in convocation have power admitted them to do any thing that shall concern the countenance and maintenance of the truth professed, which truth being contained in these articles, and these articles being different in the sense, so as if there be any dispute about it, it is in them to order which way they please. And for ought I know. Popery and Arminianism may be in a sense introduced by them, and then it must be received.

Eliot, like many Protestants, did not take kindly to the idea of interpretation in theological matters: he thought truth should be obvious and plain, and not standing in need of interpretation by a human, and therefore potentially popish, authority. 'Shall posterity think that we have enjoyed our religion four score years almost, and are now doubtful of the sense? God forbid.' For a Protestant, it was hard to admit human authority over divine truth: 'The truth which we profess is not man's, but God's. And God forbid, man should be made judge of that truth.'[1] Yet, just as the rule of law could not be enshrined as an ideal without giving someone power to interpret the law, so the truth of God could not be enshrined as an ideal without giving someone power to decide what was the truth of God. Just as the 1628 House had been driven towards giving legal force to Parliamentary interpretation of the law, the 1629 House was driven towards wishing to give legal authority to Parliamentary interpretation of religion. Eliot concluded: 'I desire (to the end to avoid confusion and distractions)

[1] pp. 24–8.

that we may go presently to the ground of our religion, and lay that down for rule, on which all others rest; then, when that is done it will be time to take into consideration the breakers of and offenders against this rule.'[1] As Eliot, Rudyerd, Pym, and many others had always said, the structure of authority they had enjoyed, with a King and a Parliament working together, could only continue if it rested on an agreed religion. If there were not an agreed religion, somewhere there would have to be lodged an arbitrary power to decide what the true religion was.[2]

In this respect, Arminianism was a graver threat to English political thought and practice than popery: popery might be countenanced, but nobody claimed that popery was the doctrine of the Church of England. What was dangerous about the Arminians was that they did claim, to the bewilderment of many members, that theirs was the doctrine of the Church of England. The Commons wished to look no farther than the Thirty-Nine Articles for a condemnation of Arminianism. This was safe enough, for whatever doctrine of authority might be used, the Thirty-Nine Articles were authoritative on points of doctrine. They had been drafted in Convocation, proclaimed by the Crown, and, in all the disputed points, confirmed by statute. Unfortunately, as Digges reminded the Commons, 'It seems the Arminians do all agree on the articles, but the difference is on the sense of it.'[3] The Arminians' refusal to accept that their doctrine was condemned by the Thirty-Nine Articles created an alarming problem of interpretation.

The problem, then, was of deciding which was the authoritative sense of the Thirty-Nine Articles. Rudyerd, like Henry VIII in a similar situation, wanted to fall back on the Universities, and persuaded the Commons to send to them for a list of occasions on which they had condemned Arminianism.[4] Pym, in his first report from the Committee of Religion, attempted to repose an authoritative interpretation of the Thirty-Nine Articles on a constant tradition of the Church of England. He began the task of com-

---

[1] p. 28: Manchester MS., f. 5ᵛ.

[2] Conrad Russell, 'Arguments for Religious Unity in England 1530–1650', *Journal of Ecclesiastical History* (1967), 205–11, 217–22.

[3] p. 122. Digges, revealingly, thought that the danger could be averted if bishops in their dioceses were free to put down those who taught against the 'orthodox' sense of the articles. *Lowther*, p. 64.

[4] p. 137: *C.J.* 930.

posing what seemed to be a list of Church of England Fathers, in which he included Wycliffe, Bucer, Peter Martyr, Cranmer, Ridley, and King James I. It is noteworthy that he now omitted Calvin, Beza, Perkins, and Whitaker, who had been in his original list of writers of 'our side' in 1625–6. He was trying as hard as he could to find a list of Church of England Fathers which could command general acceptance. He also relied on semi-official formularies of faith as guides to the exposition of the Thirty-Nine Articles: these included the Catechism of Edward VI's reign, the Lambeth Articles, and the Irish articles of 1615. Pym was right in his interpretation of all these works, but he was still short of a doctrine of authority.

This authority he ultimately had to find in Parliament:

And howsoever it is alleged that the Parliament are not judges in matters of faith, yet ought they to know the established and fundamental truths and the contraries unto them for Parliaments have confirmed Acts of General Councils, which have not been received until they have been so authorized, and Parliaments have enacted laws for trial of heretics by jury.[1]

Ironically, his prize example of a Parliament assuming authority in doctrine was the Act of Attainder of Thomas Cromwell, condemning him for 'countenancing of heretics'. Undoubtedly he was right that in that case 'no court can meet with this mischief but Courts of Parliament'. No other court had the authority to pronounce that the men Cromwell favoured were heretics. Convocation, Pym said, could not be the residual seat of authority in doctrine, for it was a provincial synod: there were two convocations, for Canterbury and York, and they might reach different conclusions. Inexorably, he was driven back on Parliamentary authority, 'the judgement of the Parliament being the judgement of the king and of the three estates of the whole kingdom'.

Yet for Selden, Littleton, and Coryton, Pym was insufficiently fundamentalist in his approach to Parliamentary authority. They would not allow the Lambeth Articles, because they were not authorized by any 'public authority of England', nor acts of Convocation unless they enjoyed the 'assent of the state'—i.e. the authority of an Act of Parliament.[2] This cultivation of the authority of Parliament was no doubt very pleasant for those who took part in it, but it was going on while it seemed ever more questionable that Parliaments could continue. The use of ideas to make

[1] pp. 20–1.   [2] pp. 119–20, 121–2, *Lowther*, p. 68.

themselves indispensable would only be effective if they could convert the King to those ideas, and there is no sign at all that they succeeded in doing this. For the King, this debate appears to have been no more than a distasteful preliminary to a possible vote of Tonnage and Poundage. Members' awareness of the risk of irate action by the King shows through their brave words in the exceptional frequency with which they resolved to lock the doors, presumably to prevent the carrying of messages to the King which might lead to the dissolution or to the arrest of some of their members.

Some members were aware that they lacked the power to indulge in a confrontation. Rudyerd, on 23 February, warned the House that 'I am sorry we should be so greedy to punish others as thereby to endanger to punish ourselves . . . our sentence (against the customers) will be but *brutum fulmen*: how shall we be assured to have time to put it in execution?' Sir Thomas Barrington, writing to his mother, was similarly aware of the Commons' lack of power to achieve their objectives. He used the parallel of a shipwrecked man, who should rather try to save his best goods than lose the most precious by trying to save all. He thought Charles's terms should be accepted: 'Princes should in policy have some time and way left to evade, when point of honour is in competition: if they acknowledge their acts past illegal, and their ministers confess it, and plead ignorance, I know not why it were not better to take reasonable satisfaction for the rest, and declare our right to posterity by a law, and the errors past, than of labouring to punish more, to let fall the end of our desires in that and all.'[1] Barrington, like Pym, would have settled for the terms offered in Charles's speech of 24 January. Unlike Pym, he did not say so on the floor of the House. There, the kamikaze strategy of Eliot and Selden prevailed, and led to the consequences which Barrington foresaw.

On 10 February, the Commons reverted from the issue of Arminianism to the privilege case, and resolved to send the Sheriff of London to the tower for abusing the committee before which he had been called to answer. By 12 February, it was Sir Humphrey May, and not just Phelips, who was saying 'I know not whether I shall have liberty to speak or you hear any more'.[2] He and his Conciliar colleagues had a very difficult Parliament: for

---

[1] p. 235. *H.M.C. Seventh Report*, p. 544.   [2] p. 61.

the first time, there was a settled hostility to Privy Councillors and royal servants, illustrated in Eliot's mischievous proposal to take proceedings against Attorney General Heath for drawing pardons for Arminians.[1] Heath, who was already in trouble with the King for warning Montagu that his pardon might not be sufficient, might have echoed the complaint of Secretary Coke, that he 'goeth in a slippery way between his Majesty and his people'. In reply, Eliot proposed to expel Secretary Coke from the House.[2] Coke and May, and perhaps Edmondes, were doing everything humanly possible to preserve Parliaments, but are unlikely to have found that their enthusiasm for their task was increased by speeches such as this. One by one, the House of Commons was busy alienating its natural friends.

The sort of distrust of the King's servants shown in 1629 had occasional precedents, but these occasional precedents had concerned individual members, rather than the House as a whole. In 1625, for example, Edward Alford, one of the few archetypal country members, had objected to having one of the King's servants in the chair at a committee of the whole. The House appeared to feel that he was making a needless fuss, and overruled him.[3] Eliot, for his own immediate purposes, had created some such precedents himself. Yet though it is possible to find individual examples which foreshadow the 1629 attitude towards Privy Councillors, as a general phenomenon, it was new. Never before, unless perhaps in the debate over the Attorney General's membership in 1614, had such a sense of division been part of the settled mood of the House. Because it was now part of the settled mood of the House, attempts to achieve consensus by debate were vain. In early Stuart England, a House of Commons with two sides could not function. When, for the first time, two settled sides appeared, dissolution was the only procedural recourse left.

On 19 February, Pym, Digges, and Rich made a last attempt to divert the Commons from their determination to punish the customs officers before doing any other business. Pym moved to forbear a debate of the question, saying the liberties of the House were inferior to the liberty of the kingdom, and by comparison

---

[1] pp. 131, 176.
[2] p. 121. Eliot's proposal to expel Secretary Coke rested on a complex piece of wilful misunderstanding.
[3] *1625 Debates*, p. 16.

with the subjects' settled possession of their goods, 'the privilege of this House is but a mean matter'.[1] Such unparliamentary language was an unwise piece of debating, and was vehemently castigated by Sir John Eliot. Eliot carried the House in resolving that no other business should be undertaken before the punishment of the customs officers. From this point, it was hard to see how further proceedings were possible. Sir Robert Phelips once again, as at so many previous crises, quoted the *Apology* of 1604: 'How easily we see the prerogative of princes thrive, when the liberties of subjects are at a stand.'[2] This time, Phelips's cries of 'wolf' were justified: it was the end of the road. There was nothing the King wanted enough from his Parliament to induce him to accept any more disagreeable behaviour. For anyone who was already inclined to see Parliament as a negative, irresponsible, obstructionist, and vindictive body, the Parliament of 1629 could do nothing but strengthen them in their opinions. Burgess, Vicar of Witney, who had been before the Parliament of 1628 for composing a vehemently anti-puritan catechism, was called before the Commons at this time for complaining that he had been in the company of 'Parliamentary hell-hounds and Puritans'.[3] It is likely that he spoke for others: for the first time in 1629, the explosive fusion of puritanism (by the Arminians' new definition) and opposition had become a fact. However much the King and his Councillors might be attached to Parliamentary institutions, if a Parliament should turn into an opposition, it would lose its usefulness to all concerned. There was no room for a 'formed opposition' in seventeenth-century England, and if a Parliament attempted to fill that role, it would have power to bring about nothing but its own demise. Between June 1628 and February 1629, there is an exact coincidence between the rise of Parliamentary opposition and the decline of Parliamentary power. Such power as Parliaments had enjoyed was persuasive, not coercive. In the capacity of an opposition, they were useless; they did not carry enough guns.

On 25 February, according to the compiler of the True Relation, there was much talk of dissolving the Parliament. Surprisingly, the King did not dissolve it, but announced an adjournment till 2 March. According to the Venetian Ambassador, the interval

---

[1] pp. 156–7, 222–3. [2] p. 230.
[3] *C.J.* 931–2.

was used to look for a settlement: 'During the interval a compromise was covertly negotiated, but the leaders persisted in the punishment of those who levied the duties.'[1] When the Houses reassembled on 2 March, the compiler of the Manchester True Relation believed it was 'plainly apparent' that Charles intended a dissolution, but it is possible that he had jumped the gun. All Charles was ready to announce was a further adjournment to the 10 March.[2] According to the Venetian Ambassador, the Council was sharply divided: he said there was a 'large party' led by Lord Keeper Coventry, in favour of gentleness, while Lord Treasurer Weston and others, 'seeing themselves in danger', were in favour of dissolution.

Sir John Eliot and a group of his friends appear to have believed that there was no further useful purpose to be served by trying to persuade the King, and instead planned for 2 March a demonstration whose object was the potentially revolutionary one of appealing over the King's head to the country at large. Members of this group arrived early at the House, and occupied the seats next to the Chair, which were normally reserved for Privy Councillors.[3] When the House assembled, Eliot moved to have a declaration read, 'which he flung down upon the floor'. The Speaker's attempt to rise, and end the sitting, was restrained by Valentine and Holles holding him down in his chair. Strode, one of Eliot's allies, plainly admitted the propaganda purpose of the exercise: 'that we go not out like sheep scattered, but to testify to the world that we have a care of their safety and religion'.[4] Unfortunately, the attempt to read Eliot's paper was frustrated by the refusal of the Speaker to put the question. Sir Peter Hayman, showing the localism characteristic of much of the Parliaments of the period, found the first thought which came to mind was that he was sorry it was a fellow Kentish man who was plucking up their liberties by the roots. Digges, who had changed less in the past year than most other members, raised a solitary voice in favour of adjourning. Finally, Eliot succeeded in obtaining the reading of his paper. It was an attack on 'new counsels': 'The safety of the king cannot but be in the safety of his people'. He attacked popery and Arminianism,

---

[1] C.S.P.Ven. 1628–9, p. 579.
[2] Manchester MS., f. 30ᵛ: pp. 101n, 102n.
[3] I. H. C. Fraser, 'The Agitation in the Commons March 1629', B.I.H.R. (1957), 86–95.
[4] pp. 240, 252 ff.

and attacked two ministers by name: Bishop Neile and Lord Treasurer Weston. Weston, as a suspected Catholic, was singled out as an agent of the popish conspiracy: he was said to have deliberately weakened shipping 'to make this land fit for invasion'.[1] Of all charges levelled in the 1629 Parliament, this is the most startling. The depth of incomprehension recalls Weston's own complaint, in 1625, that King and Parliament were like parallel lines, which could never meet.

Eliot followed this declaration with three resolutions, which declared favourers of Arminianism, and collectors *or payers* of Tonnage and Poundage to be capital enemies of King and kingdom. It was an invitation to the public at large to make up for the powerlessness of their representatives at Westminster by instituting a taxpayers' strike. It was a genuine act of opposition: an attempt to appeal to public opinion to bring pressure to coerce the King to change his policy. In thinking that such an act of opposition was practical politics in 1629, Eliot, Selden, and their friends were suffering from delusions of grandeur. In the policy of seventeenth-century England, there were only two places for a leader of the opposition. One was at the head of a rebel army, and the other was in the Tower. Eliot neither enjoyed nor wished for the support of any army, and was promptly taken to the Tower. His attempt to obtain release by suing a Habeas Corpus was, in spite of the Petition of Right, unsuccessful. It is typical of the misunderstanding characteristic of the whole story that the decision to dissolve the Parliament against which Eliot was protesting on 2 March had not yet been taken. The Parliament was not dissolved until 10 March, and it was Eliot himself who made it impossible for Charles to avoid a dissolution. The end of an epoch is perhaps symbolized in one of the final exchanges between Strode and Speaker Finch. Strode, trying to get Finch to read Eliot's declaration, told him he was either the House's servant or the King's servant. Finch replied: 'It doth not make me to be none of your servant because I am the King's servant.'[2] In 1621, 1625, or even 1626, such a dual loyalty would have been too obvious to create comment. When it became impossible, regular meetings of Parliament became impossible also. The Parliament of 1629 brought about its own destruction.

[1] p. 241.   [2] p. 241.

VIII

Conclusion

THE one conspicuous success of Parliaments during this period was their success in getting themselves recognized as 'the representative of the people'. On the whole, members of both Houses of Parliament tended, in their public contributions, to mirror what was going on elsewhere. Much Parliamentary business originated in the country, and much originated at the court. With the possible exception of the 1629 privilege dispute, almost none of it originated by spontaneous combustion at Westminster. The implications of this fact for traditional 'constitutional history' are perhaps more far-reaching than has yet been pointed out. For it means that the difficulties of the early Stuarts were not, in the first instance, difficulties with their Parliaments: they were difficulties which were reflected in their Parliaments. In trying to explain, in purely Parliamentary terms, why Charles I had a difficult reign, we are asking the wrong question: we are mistaking the symptom for the disease.

The early Stuarts suffered from plenty of genuine difficulties. Above all, they suffered from an inadequate revenue, and from a local government unsuited to the task of making that revenue adequate. They consequently suffered from the lack of satisfactory methods of giving adequate rewards to their servants. They suffered, as almost all rulers of the period did, from the difficulty of preserving religious unity during the century after the Reformation. They suffered further from the vocal belief that division in religion was dangerous, a belief it was awkward to accommodate in a country where religion could no longer be made uniform. As a man electioneering against Sir John Holland on the ground of his wife's recusancy once put it, 'There are too many religions in Holland.'[1] The coexistence in one country of recusants and Foxeites was always likely to be difficult.

The early Stuarts also suffered severely from the lack of any

[1] Clive Holmes, *The Eastern Association in the English Civil War* (Cambridge, 1974), p. 25.

adequate means of warfare. A country which depended on voluntary unpaid local governors to turn their neighbours into a conscript army was always likely to be at a military disadvantage against seasoned Spanish tercios. The disadvantage was only underlined if memories of Crécy and Agincourt ensured a continued insistence on proper training in archery in an age of firearms. Revenue, local government, patronage, religion, and war were the areas of difficulty for Charles I. They are a fairly comprehensive list, but to credit his Parliaments with *creating* any of these difficulties is to magnify their importance beyond the bounds of the credible. Even in the area of revenue, where Parliaments could most easily be held responsible, it seems that the ultimate responsibility should rest, not on Parliaments, but on local government. The under-assessment of the subsidies voted in 1628 sharply underlined the point that there was no use in getting a Parliament to vote money if the existing system of local government was not adequate to bring it into the Exchequer. Even in the Restoration financial settlement, the Hearth Tax, which depended on the traditional machinery of local government, was a disappointment. The most successful part of the Restoration financial settlement was the Excise, originally invented by Pym during the Long Parliament. The success of the Excise was largely due to changing methods of collection. The Excise Commissioners, in stark contrast to early Stuart J.P.s, were forbidden to serve in their home counties.[1] It was, then, not a shift in relations between Crown and Parliament which made the biggest contribution to solving the Stuarts' financial problems, but a shift in the balance between the centre and the localities. This shift was expressed, not primarily in relations between Crown and Parliament, but in new methods of administration.

If the Stuarts' Parliaments were not the cause, but the consequence, of their difficulties, it becomes more necessary than ever to stress that a Parliamentary history is not a history of England. Parliaments were a mirror of what went on elsewhere: a history written from a mirror is likely to be written at best backwards, and at worst, through the looking-glass. However, even if Parliaments are peripheral to the Stuarts' real difficulties, they are a good indicator of political tension. If they are used in this way,

---

[1] G. G. Chandaman, *The English Public Revenue 1660–1688* (Oxford, 1975), pp. 73–4, 89–94, and other refs.

they show up a great difference between the beginning and the end of this period.

There has been a tendency to treat the 1620s as a homogeneous period, and to assume that it is possible to generalize about the political mood of the whole decade. This is not the case. The mood and the atmosphere of 1621–4 is completely different from that of 1626–8. Statements which can be happily made about one part of the period are likely to be inapplicable to the other. It is possible to employ hindsight within the 1620s: the Protestation of 1621, for example, appears from the vantage-point of 1628 to have a significance which was not apparent at the time. This retroactive significance of many of the supposed milestones of the decade is useful to an understanding of its end. For example, it contributes to the understanding of 2 March 1629, to know that the House of Commons' right to adjourn itself had been claimed by Phelips and Alford in 1621.[1] However, this fact is not a significant part of the history of 1621.

In general, the story of 1621 and 1624 suggests that not very much was wrong with relations between Crown and Parliament. Evidence of administrative difficulties was plentiful, but in their attempts to handle these difficulties, James and his Parliaments achieved a remarkable degree of harmony. It is hard to believe that any members of Parliament, in June 1628, would not have cheerfully settled for a return to June 1621. Even more, in March 1628 they would have settled with enthusiasm for a return to March 1621. Beside 1628, the scale of the difficulties of 1621 appears minuscule. Above all, the absence of religious and political polarization in the later part of the reign of James is one of the most striking facts about it. Without the ingredient of religious fear, mixtures of political trouble rarely became dangerous. In the last years of King James, members of both houses of Parliament enjoyed an unusual confidence that the fundamentals of religion were secure. They might worry that a recusant minority was not rooted out with sufficient enthusiasm, but under James, these fears never became hysterical. The general confidence in freedom to preach the Gospel in a Protestant church seems to have been at a higher point in the last years of James than it was under either Elizabeth or Charles. With this confidence came a

---

[1] N.R.S. iv. 417, ii. 430, and other refs: J. E. Neale, *Elizabeth I and Her Parliaments*, ii (1957), p. 155.

general fall in the political temperature. James, at the end of his reign, was still ruling over a united country. When Pym, in 1629, tried to include King James in a list of 'Fathers of the Church', it seems likely that he was not indulging in an uncharacteristic piece of courtliness: he was expressing a sincere trust in James's religious dependability. He was, after all, only saying much the same things as were being said from the other side of the new religious fence by Bishop Neile.[1]

The fears of 5 and 6 June 1628, when former Buckingham clients like Hampden and Harley feared 'no less than the subversion of the whole state' would have been unimaginable under James. The fear for the extinction of Parliaments existed under James, but even to so dedicated a Parliamentarian as Phelips, the fear of extinction of Parliaments did not become a matter for apocalyptic terror until it was regarded as a cloak for the alteration of religion. The fears of Earle, in 1629, that he was on the way to seeing the introduction of Romish tyranny and Spanish monarchy, belong to a world which was in some ways closer to 1640 than to 1621. Both the fear for the disappearance of the rule of law, in 1628, and the fear for the subversion of religion, in 1628–9, come from a much more frightened and angry house of Commons than had been known under James: they belong to a much less safe world.

This rapid change of political mood has been one of the most striking findings of this book. Correspondingly, one of its biggest unanswered questions has been how far this change is a change from James to Charles, and how far it is a change from peace to war. It is at least clear that the political reputation of James I is due for some revision.[2] Whatever his personal faults may have been, he cannot be blamed for things he never allowed to go wrong. He was not efficient in the management of money, though even on that subject, he never reached so parlous a state as Charles in 1627–8. On foreign affairs and religion, James should be given credit for a considerable measure of success. His foreign policy shows a considerable resemblance to Queen Elizabeth's: like her, he appreciated that the country could not afford war, and tried to

---

[1] *1629 Debates*, pp. 139, 193; 144, 203–5. It is noteworthy that Neile's remarks were drawn to the Commons' attention by the maiden speech of Oliver Cromwell.

[2] For a striking exercise in such revision, see R. C. Munden, 'James I and the Growth of Mutual Distrust: King, Commons and Reform 1603–4' in K. M. Sharpe (ed.), *Faction and Politics* (Oxford 1978).

keep out of it as long as possible. Like her, he tried to use the threat of military intervention, backed up by small token forces like that taken by Sir Horace Vere to the Palatinate, as a lever to induce Spain to keep the peace. Like her, he kept his diplomatic intentions obscure, even to his own ministers. Whatever is regarded as successful and prudent policy in one ruler should be so regarded in the other.

On religious matters, James should perhaps be regarded as more successful than Queen Elizabeth. Elizabeth had no Parliament which was free of trouble about religion, but James enjoyed two. At no time after 1559 is it harder to make the traditional correlation between 'puritanism and opposition' than it is in 1621–4. If any family can be seen representing a continuous 'puritan opposition', it is the Wentworths of Lillingstone Lovell, whose Parliamentary service runs in an almost unbroken sequence of three generations from the mid-Elizabethan period to the Rump. Yet even Thomas Wentworth, in 1621–4, was not complaining about the state of the Church of England. Ten years of the regime of Archbishop Abbot appear to have convinced him that the church was not in danger, and, in sharp contrast to 1614, his crusading mentality emerged only in his comments on Spain and on recusants. Moreover, James achieved this sense of safety among the hotter sort of Protestants without oppressing his other subjects. He did it while running so latitudinarian a church that there was room for some covert Arminians on the bench of bishops. To enjoy the religious confidence of Pym and old Thomas Wentworth simultaneously with that of Andrewes and Overall was no mean achievement. It was managed by running a genuinely latitudinarian Church of England, the sort of church symbolized by the man who attended James on his death-bed, Lord Keeper Williams. It is perhaps significant that in 1641–2, those who thought they might restore piece by restoring a latitudinarian church looked again to James's men. Williams and Ussher.

In his handling of the monopolies issue in 1621, and in balancing the conflicting pressures from his Parliament and his servants, James showed a considerable degree of political skill. Like Elizabeth, James was a hard king to serve, because he believed in keeping his options open. Perhaps, in handling his Parliaments, he was as successful as Queen Elizabeth, or even more so. His speech of 26 March 1621, like Elizabeth's of 1601, was referred to at the time as worthy to be written in letters of gold. To make the comparison fairly, it is essential to look at the remainder of the quotation from which the phrase 'golden speech' originated: it was proposed that Elizabeth's speech be written in letters of gold, 'lest it be . . . not so happily effected'.[1] It was not: of all the attempts to suppress monopolies, almost the only one which even approached success was that made by James and Cecil in 1603.[2] James, it is true, was more ready than Elizabeth to resort to the ultimate weapon of dissolution in handling his Parliaments, but at the same time, he was ready to keep them in session for very much longer than Elizabeth had ever done. James, like Sir Robert Walpole, was not glamorous, but like Sir Robert Walpole, he achieved a high degree of political stability.

The disappearance of this stability immediately after his death is so rapid that it is tempting to blame much of it on the personality of Charles. Charles, unlike James, suffered from energy. It is perhaps worth thought that both the energetic Stuarts lost their thrones, while both the lazy ones died in their beds. With an inadequate administrative machinery, those who put least pressure on it are likely to suffer least misfortune. In a country slowly learning to live with the permanent fact of religious and political division, those who believe in letting sleeping dogs lie are likely to do better than those who wish to define the point of issue. The Book of Orders is perhaps typical of both the best and the worst of Charles's regime: the sincere good intentions, combined with an unjustified faith in his system of local government. Charles's energy certainly disturbed the political equilibrium. While it was disturbed, the effect of Charles's Arminianism, at least on some people, was devasting. However, it should be pointed out that Charles's Arminianism can only be held to flaw his general political judgement by those who believe religion should give way to politics. Neither Charles nor his critics were among this number.

Though some people were alienated by Charles's Arminianism, more widespread difficulties were caused by Charles's belief that the Parliament of 1624 meant what it said about undertaking a war. The depth of incomprehension which grew up between Charles and his early Parliaments arose from Charles's pardonable

[1] Sir Symonds D'Ewes, *Journals of All the Parliaments* (1682), p. 656.
[2] N. R. N. Tyacke, 'Sir Robert Wroth and the Parliament of 1604', *B.I.H.R.* (May 1977), 120–5.

belief that if they said they wanted him to fight a war, they would assist him to finance it. This was what drove him to a point where he had to threaten publicly to do without Parliaments, and had to levy the Forced Loan. Until 1629, Charles showed no more hostility to Parliaments than was necessary to fighting a war he could not safely lose. Indeed, the patience he showed with the negativism and obstructionism of the Parliaments of 1626 and 1628 deserves more remark than it has normally been given. Charles, as much as James, wanted to be known as a King who could get on with his Parliaments, and devoted a surprising amount of time and patience to attempting to succeed.

Except for his introduction of Arminianism, he made few catastrophic errors. He suffered for a number of tactical errors, usually involving the staking of his authority on positions he was unable to maintain. His decision to speak in person in favour of the additional supply of 1625 is a typical example: the ultimate and inevitable failure discredited Charles's authority more than if the demand had come only from his Councillors. Both over the impeachment of Buckingham and over the Petition of Right, he made the political error of saying 'never' and then retreating. Yet most of his difficulties resulted, not from these tactical errors, but from his attempt to give priority to foreign over domestic issues. In time of war, this was a natural enough error, but it did not commend itself to insular Parliaments. Charles's Declaration of 1629 gives a clear picture of how irritating the domestic pre-occupations of the Parliament of 1628 appeared to a King whose mind was fixed on questions of grand strategy. It was on these questions that Charles failed, mainly because his Parliaments were not interested in them. The political difficulties of the early years of his reign, then, appear to be first and foremost, not the difficulties of a bad King, but the difficulties of a nation reluctantly at war.

Ultimately, the truth or falsehood of this statement must be tested by further study of the 1630s. Charles and the war came so hard on each other's heels that their effects are hard to disentangle. An attempt to disentangle them must be based on a study, which has not been attempted here, of Charles at peace. In particular, we need to know more of the attitude of leading county gentry to Charles during the 1630s. Did the Remonstrance debate of 1628 illustrate an alienation deep enough to last unbroken till 1640, or did it indicate a wartime panic which slowly subsided with the return of peace?[1] This question need not have a general answer. Apart from Sir Robert Harley, the members who generated most heat in this debate were the nucleus of the future Providence Company. It is perhaps possible to assume that these members were fundamentally disillusioned with Charles's regime. Yet even in these extreme cases, it is necessary to remember that John Hampden continued to serve as a Deputy Lieutenant, and John Pym as Receiver of Crown lands, enclosure commissioner, and so forth.

For other, less theological, members the absence of a Parliament and the absence of a war probably meant a bigger drop in the political temperature. Their mood in 1628–9 may more easily be regarded as a mood of the moment. In comparing the mood of Parliament in 1628–9 with the mood of the country at large, we should not forget to allow for the effects of constant sitting in a large, overcrowded, and over-excited assembly. This is perhaps particularly important in 1628, when the members acquired, through their unanimity and their long sitting, an exceptionally strong sense of corporate identity. Some hint of how far this changed their aspirations may perhaps be got from comparing the Petition of Right with the much less ambitious proposals offered by Sir Edward Coke at the beginning of the Parliament. At first, the summit of Coke's ambition was to pass a subsidy bill retrospectively legalizing the Forced Loan, and to restrict commitment by the Council to the respectfully long period of two months.[2] The overheated atmosphere in which the Petition of Right was passed was one which was unlikely to survive eleven years of the humdrum business of being a J.P. settling bastardy cases and dealing with militia defaulters.

Certainly the best-documented and best-studied of the leading members, Sir Robert Phelips, appears to have rapidly recovered from the intense alarm he was showing in 1628–9. By 1631, Phelips was busy as usual, in charge of collecting the knighthood fines in Somerset.[3] He seems to have been able to accommodate himself to the rise of Arminianism, and perhaps found it the

---

[1] On one member who was deeply alienated, see Peter Clarke on the diary of Thomas Scott, *H.J.* (1978). I am grateful to Dr. Clarke for allowing me to see this article before publication. It describes an obscure and occasional member who suspected more prominent members, such as Digges, of being tainted with 'Dukism'.

[2] *1628 Debates*, ii, pp. 65, 74: 45.   [3] P.R.O.E. 407/35.

easier because his rival, Lord Poulett, found it difficult. In 1637, he even offered Laud an unsolicited letter, congratulating him on his success in dealing with those 'lunatics', Burton, Bastwick, and Prynne. Although Phelips appears to have expected another Parliament, he seems to have benefited from the lack of one: in Professor Barnes's words, 'the absence of Parliament increased the potency of Phelips's bid for supremacy'.[1] It permitted him to concentrate his energies. Such tasks as collecting the knighthood fines were perhaps easier because he did not face an electorate which would wish to instruct him to protest at his own activities. Phelips in the 1630s perhaps served his county's interests more effectively for the fact that he was able to use his discretion about when it was expedient to do so.

This perhaps suggests that, even if Parliaments did not create the difficulties of the early Stuarts, their meetings, and even more the elections for them, may have done something to worsen difficulties. A forum of complaint for grievances is only useful if there is some prospect of those grievances being remedied. The years without a Parliament, then, were something of an Indian summer of Phelips's career. Such evidence as we have suggests that Pym may be more nearly unique than Phelips. Other leading members accommodated themselves to the regime of the 1630s. Sir Francis Seymour served as a Deputy Lieutenant and as an enclosure commissioner.[2] Sir Dudley Digges, in 1630, at last received the preferment he had awaited for so long. When it came, it was only a reversion to the Mastership of the Rolls, but he lived long enough to enjoy it before his death in 1639. If preferments are any guide, the lawyers who so distinguished themselves in the Petition of Right debates do not appear to have been profoundly alienated from the regime. Edward Littleton, who took the chair in the Petition of Right debates, was the man who took the Great Seal to York in 1642. He therefore gave visible embodiment, at a crucial moment, to Charles's claim that he, as much as the Long Parliament, stood for the rule of law. Hakewill became Solicitor General to Queen Henrietta Maria, Noy and Bankes in turn became Attorney General, Mason became Recorder of London, and Edward Herbert became Solicitor General.

[1] Phelips MSS. 221/20. Barnes, p. 292.
[2] J. Hurstfield, *Freedom, Corruption and Government in Elizabethan England* (1973), p. 240.

He therefore enjoyed the distinction of managing both the impeachment of Buckingham and the impeachment of the Five Members. Even John Selden, though he did not get office, became a friend of Archbishop Laud, who found him his seat in the Long Parliament.

The fortunes of surviving members of Parliament, then, do not suggest that Charles was facing a profoundly alienated country before the outbreak of the Scottish troubles in 1637. In peacetime, his regime was perhaps stronger than has been thought. There are two vital tests of a regime's ability to survive. One is its solvency, and the other is the willingness of its local governors to serve it. By both these tests, it is arguable that Charles was in a stronger position in 1637 than he was in 1627. It is then at least a tenable hypothesis that his difficulties in 1627–9 owed more to administrative incapacity for war than to the political difficulties of a polarized country.

It seems, then, unlikely to be a coincidence that both the crisis of 1640 and the crisis of 1642 arose from pressure for wars, one against Scotland, and the other against Ireland. At this stage, it is perhaps permissible to break the self-denying ordinance which has been observed throughout this book, and to ask what light its conclusions shed on the crises of 1640 and of 1642. It should not be forgotten that, as Professor Elton has pointed out, these are two separate crises: in one, we have to explain the unity of the political nation, and in the other, we have to explain its division.[1]

In the first place, it now appears possible to say that the civil war was undoubtedly not the culmination of a struggle for power between King and Parliament. Whatever may have happened in 1640–2, up to 1629, Parliaments had little power, and showed little desire to increase what they had. At the beginning of the Spanish war, in 1625–6, there was a prospect that the power of Parliament might increase, and the prospect was unwelcome to many members. Alford, Sherland, and Bankes feared it might mean the nightmare of annual subsidies, and Coke, Eliot, and Digges thought that the King's ordinary revenue ought to bear a bigger share of the cost of war, and Parliament ought to bear less. When faced with the opportunity to increase the power of Parliament, many leading members not merely failed to take the

[1] G. R. Elton, 'A High Road to Civil War?', in *Essays in Honour of Garrett Mattingley*, ed. Charles H. Carter (1966), pp. 325 ff.

opportunity, but actively rejected it. Ironically, as the story of the 1624 appropriation shows, Charles and Buckingham were more eager to increase the power of Parliament than most members of the House of Commons. This should not cause too much surprise once we understand the proper function of a Parliament. A Parliament was a body for making complaints. Like other pressure groups and lobbies, it found power unwelcome because with power came responsibility. Organizations responsible for making protests on behalf of those they represent may find the acquisition of responsibility a crucial handicap. For the same reason, those in authority may wish to thrust responsibility on them: as responsibility grows, the power of protest diminishes. A House of Commons which had taken the share of responsibility for the war that Buckingham and Pembroke wanted it to take would have been fatally handicapped in passing on its constituents' complaints about billeting, military mismanagement, and failure to pay the troops. If they had accepted Southampton's motion in 1624, the House of Commons might have found that they were no longer the organizers, but the victims, of these complaints. Pym, Rich, and Rudyerd, who did want to increase the power of the House of Commons, were a lonely group whose freedom of action was dependent on their lack of responsibility to an electorate. In the Short Parliament of 1640, as in 1625–8, one of the forces helping to provoke a crisis was the refusal of the House of Commons to assume responsibility for a war. By 1640, their refusal was clothed in a respectable collection of political excuses. At bottom, the problem was still the same as in 1628. The administration was in trouble because of the House of Commons' refusal to accept responsibility. When called to provide remedies for military defeat, the House of Commons washed its hands of the task. Similarly, in 1641, the Long Parliament abolished Ship Money. It then entreated Charles to send out a fleet against the very pirates Ship Money was levied to suppress.

Nor can the civil war be seen as the legacy of divisions within either House of Parliament. The traditional view that Sir Thomas Wentworth 'changed sides' rests on the hypothesis that the sides of 1640 or of 1642 show some continuity with divisions of opinion in the 1620s. This appears not to be the case. In the first place, it is necessary to remember that in the eleven years between 1629 and 1640, and even more in the thirteen years until 1642, a very large proportion of the leading members died. The deaths of Buckingham, Pembroke, Manchester, Southampton, and Carlisle changed much in the House of Lords. In the House of Commons, those who died before 1642 include Sir Edward Coke, Phelips, Digges, Sandys, Rich, Knightley, Crew, Eliot, Carleton, and Alford. To a greater extent than has been recognized, the generation who experienced the civil war were not the generation who served in the Parliaments of the 1620s. Even more, their leaders were not the same generation.

Nor is it possible among the survivors to make very obvious correlations between political behaviour in the 1620s and allegiance in 1642. If any two members of the Commons during the 1620s deserve the title of 'opposition members,' it is those two persistent wreckers, Sir Francis Seymour and William Mallory. Yet in 1642, both of them proved to be royalists. If any one man in the Commons of 1628 established himself as a defender of the prerogative, it was Charles's loyal servant, Secretary Coke. Yet in 1642 Secretary Coke appears to have been a Parliamentarian.[1] Cases like these can be multiplied, and they are hard to reconcile with the belief that the Parliamentarians of 1642 were the residuary legatees of a 'Parliamentary opposition' of the 1620s.

The occasion when the Commons, if not the Lords, were most obviously divided into two 'sides' was the impeachment of Buckingham. On this occasion, a cursory investigation of those who were prominent enough to place their position beyond doubt prompts the interesting suspicion that there may actually have been more future Parliamentarians among Buckingham's supporters than among his opponents.[2] This fact does seem to underline the point that though Buckingham may have divided the court by his excessive prominence, he did prevent it from being ideologically polarized.

[1] A. J. Fletcher, 'Petitioning and the Outbreak of the Civil War in Derbyshire', *Derbyshire Archaeological Journal* (1973), 38. The evidence, which is not conclusive, shows Sir John Coke reproving his neutralist son for his reluctance to execute the Militia Ordinance.

[2] Evidence on allegiance in the civil war is taken from either M. F. Keeler, *Members of the Long Parliament* or G. E. Aylmer, *The King's Servants*, unless otherwise stated. In the cases of those, such as Arundel and Holland, who changed sides during the war, the initial allegiance has been used here. For Grosvenor, see J. S. Morrill, *Cheshire 1630–1660*, p. 208, and for Coryton, Mary Coate, *Cornwall During the Great Civil War* (Oxford, 1933), pp. 207–9 and other refs.

The issue of Arminianism, unlike the impeachment of Buckingham, shows some correlation between attitudes in the 1620s and allegiance in 1642. It is here possible to aim at more precision than can be attempted with Buckingham's supporters, since we are able to depend on the work of Dr. Tyacke, who has now established a list of thirty anti-Arminian speakers in the Commons. Among these thirty, sixteen were dead before 1642, a fact which underlines Dr. Tyacke's observation that the majority of them had left University before 1600.[1] Among the survivors, Parliamentarians outnumber royalists by two to one.

There is an even more impressive correlation between Parliamentarianism and support for the Spanish war. There is an almost equally clear correlation between royalism and opposition to the war. I have identified twenty-six members of the two Houses as supporters of the war, and fourteen as opponents of it. These statistics underline the correlation between the more belligerent and the more vocal. Among the supporters of the war, there are thirteen Parliamentarians or neutrals with Parliamentarian sympathies, nine dead, one royalist, one neutral, and one uncertain. Among the opponents of the war, there are two Parliamentarians, seven royalists, and five dead. The two Parliamentarians, Arundel and Selden, are of a peculiarly unideological cast of mind. Perhaps the most striking feature in this sample is the differential rate of deaths between the supporters and the opponents of war. This serves to underline the picture of the Parliamentarians as an ageing group, holding fast to old-fashioned Elizabethan reflexes. It is also striking to notice how much the war supporters and the anti-Arminians are the same people. Many of them were men with an ideological approach to politics, who regarded foreign policy as subsidiary to religion. Most of them were men with a vivid conviction that popery, whether it was in Madrid or in Whitehall, was antichristian, and must be opposed. In the context of the House of Commons as a whole, they are a vocal minority.

Indeed, perhaps the most striking fact about these statistics as a whole is how far they are statistics about a vocal minority. The rank and file of the county gentry, who made up what Sir Dudley

[1] N. R. N. Tyacke, thesis cit., p. 168. I am very grateful to Dr. Tyacke for permission to use his revised and corrected list of anti-Arminian speakers. Information on their allegiance in the civil war is my own.

Carleton called the 'silent majority' of the House of Commons,[1] do not appear in them. The sample is too small to be statistically significant, and this may be the most significant fact about it. If the activities of these people are to be regarded as responsible for the civil war, it would indeed underline Professor Aylmer's conclusion that 'two dynamic minorities . . . made the Civil War'.[2]

But was the civil war made by men, or by events? Dr. Morrill has recently stressed the strength of neutralist conviction in the provinces in 1642. Many law-abiding people, receiving the Militia Ordinance and the Commission of Array both together, wanted to obey at once. They were both commands by lawful authorities. In the words of the Devon petition of July 1642, 'In how hard a condition are we, whilst a twofold obedience, like twins in the womb, strives to be born to both.' Dr. Morrill illustrates this obstinate, and localist, neutralism, from the commonplace book of William Davenport, whom he takes as typical of the 'silent majority' in the provinces. In Dr. Morrill's words, 'Davenport resented royal policies, but he does not appear to have articulated this resentment within a radical framework of reference, or into any intellectual or idealized mould whatsoever. It is a crucial distinction which separates him, and, I suspect, a majority of his peers, from men like Pym and Hampden.'[3] To Dr. Morrill, the findings of local and Parliamentary research on 1642 appear to be out of line with each other.

Yet it is possible that, in 1642, as in the 1620s, the apparent divergence between local and Parliamentary research merely means that Parliamentary history needs to be revised to bring it into line with local history. Davenport's reactions in the 1620s are not profoundly different from those of such men as Edward Alford. It is possible that Sir Dudley Carleton was right that Parliament, too, had its 'silent majority'. It is true that our sample of prominent members shows an under-representation of neutrals. Yet even among the prominent members, there may be many who, like Rudyerd, might have preferred to pass for neutrals.[4] It was the misfortune of those who were members of Parliament in 1642 that their position made it harder for them than for almost anyone else

    [1] Whitelocke, 12–22, f. 8ᵛ.   [2] G. E. Aylmer, thesis cit., p. 980.
    [3] J. S. Morrill, *The Revolt of the Provinces* (1976), p. 42, and 'William Davenport and the "Silent Majority" in Early Stuart England', *Journal of the Chester Archaeological Society* (1975), 122.
    [4] Aylmer, pp. 381–2.

to pass through the civil war under the cloak of neutrality. The fact that many of them were forced to take sides cannot be regarded as sufficient evidence to prove that they wanted to take sides. Even in the Long Parliament, the would-be neutralist Sir John Potts may well be more typical than John Pym.[1] Even the prominent members, on closer investigation, often come to seem less like puritan revolutionaries than they appear at a distance. Sir Harbottle Grimston, knight of the shire for Essex in the Short Parliament, is perhaps as typical as anyone of the 'puritan opposition' of 1640. Yet even he turns out, eighteen months earlier, to have been charging the Essex Grand Jury to ensure the prosecution of those who failed to use the Prayer Book.[2]

If there was as little support for war in 1642 as the researches of Dr. Morrill and Mr. Fletcher would suggest, why was there a war at all? It will be interesting to see whether future work on 1640 and 1642 sustains what has been the central theme of this book: the country experienced political crises because it was unable to fight a foreign war. It appears that this theme might make sense of the unity of the political nation in 1640. The Short Parliament, like the Parliament of 1628, could be seen as registering the protests of local governors at the trials and tribulations of preparing a force for war. That the war was overwhelmingly unpopular merely made the task of protest easier. Those responsible for preparing a force for war would have been likely to protest anyway: their system of local government was inadequate for the task. The system of local government by Justices of the Peace and Deputy Lieutenants, depending on prominent local gentlemen to

---

[1] Holmes, op. cit., pp. 57–63 and other refs.
[2] Herts R.O., Gorhambury MSS. IX A 9, Grimston's charge to the Grand Jury at Chelmsford, Easter 1638. I am grateful to Mrs. Julie Calnan, who discovered and identified this MS., for generously placing it at my disposal. Grimston said: 'The first thing I shall commend to your cares, is the true worship of God in his church, in the order of our divine service, and in the manner of the administration of the sacraments, as they are settled by divers excellent statutes, made against those that refuse to use the Common Prayers, or to administer the Sacraments according to the book of Common Prayer, or that speak in derogation of it.' Having given a lengthy charge on recusants, including recusant wives, he continued: 'And besides these foreign opposites of the peace of our church there be some domestical which are brought up and nourished here in our own bosoms, and these are the Brownists that deny our church, and the king's supremacy over it, and that refuse to communicate with us, or submit themselves unto his Majesty's ecclesiastical laws, these are by the statute of 35 of the Queen to be abjured.'

enforce the will of the central government, was unsuited to a conscript militia. Conscripts are not easily collected by those who have to retain their trust. Nor are they easily collected by those who, in the words of the Deputy Lieutenants of Shropshire, have 'a persuasive, but no compulsive, power'.[1]

This may be a sufficient explanation for the collapse of the English regime in the face of the Scots. Yet it was not the Scottish war which produced the final crisis leading to the English civil war. It was the Irish rebellion. The Irish rebellion created a second demand for an army within eighteen months. It was a demand the King and the country were in no position to meet, yet it came in the name of a cause which appealed to the strongest belligerent reflexes in England. A popish Irish enemy was, to the ideologically committed, even more terrifyingly antichristian than a popish Spanish enemy. Yet, against this most terrifying of enemies, England was unable to fight.

It was at this stage, when the English were unable to fight the foreign popish enemy, that some of them became ready to fight against his domestic fifth column where they could find it. It was at this stage, when the King could not suppress the Irish rebellion, that anti-popery, the traditional driving force of English patriotism, was, for some, transformed from a force for loyalty to the Crown into a force for loyalty to the Parliament. It is perhaps here that Parliament's success in winning trust among the electorate during the 1620s became crucial to the outbreak of the civil war. Without this trust, it is doubtful whether so many people would have looked to Parliament to suppress the 'popish and malignant party' in England. It was in this search for the 'popish and malignant party' that the force of anti-popery was turned so far inwards that it engulfed the court itself. Thus it was that, in Dr. Clifton's words, 'the emotions which under Elizabeth had unified and strengthened the nation against foreign attack were now turned inwards and helped to shatter it'.[2] Even in passing the Militia Ordinance, members of Parliament were reacting, rather than initiating. They were reacting, in a state of panic, to the fact that the King was unable to fight, and that some of them would not have trusted him to do so if he could. In the Militia Ordinance, the breakdown of local government and the fear of popery were for the first time welded together into a common theme. It was

---

[1] Russell (ed.), *Origins*, p. 109.   [2] Ibid., p. 167.

that theme which made the Long Parliament begin to raise troops.

The efficient cause of the civil war was Parliament's demand that local officers should execute the Militia Ordinance. It was the reluctant choice between Parliament's Militia Ordinance and the King's Commission of Array, which forced men, sadly, and often unwittingly, to choose sides. A decision to execute the Militia Ordinance normally made a man a Parliamentarian. In asking why men decided to execute the Militia Ordinance, it is important to remember exactly what it said:

Whereas there hath been of late a most dangerous and desperate design upon the House of Commons, which we have just cause to believe to be an effect of the bloody counsels of Papists and other ill-affected persons, who have already raised a rebellion in the kingdom of Ireland; and by reason of many discoveries we cannot but fear they will proceed not only to stir up the like rebellion and insurrections in this kingdom of England, but also to back them with forces from abroad. For the safety therefore of his Majesty's person, the Parliament and kingdom in time of imminent danger: it is ordained by the Lords and Commons now in Parliament assembled that Henry Earl of Holland shall be Lieutenant of the county of Berks. . . .[1]

When bewildered local governors wondered whether to obey these words or not, it is possible that some of them may have believed they meant exactly what they said.

[1] S. R. Gardiner, *Constitutional Documents of the Puritan Revolution* (Oxford, 1889), pp. 245–6. See J. S. Morrill, *The Revolt of the Provinces* (1976), p. 142. (Lady Eure to Sir Ralph Verney) 'My Lord of Holland is generalled, which puts me in the most comfort that we shall have peace' (24 June 1642).

Appendix

Political Views in the 1620s and Allegiance in the Civil War

SOME SUPPORTERS AND OPPONENTS OF THE DUKE OF
BUCKINGHAM IN 1626, AND THEIR ALLEGIANCE IN
THE CIVIL WAR

Pro-Buckingham
Sir Robert Heath R.
Sir John Coke P.
Sir Edwin Sandys d.
Sir Robert Harley P.
Sir George Goring R.
Sir Henry Mildmay P.
Sir Robert Pye PN.
Sir Miles Fleetwood d.
Sir William Becher RN.
Laurence Whitaker P.
Sir Henry Vane P.
Sir Dudley Carleton d.
Lord Conway d.
Sir Henry Poole d.
Lord Montagu R.
Lord Kimbolton (second Earl of
  Manchester) P.
Sir John Hippisley P.
Edward Nicholas R.
Earl of Holland P.
Sir John Finch R.
William Laud R.

Anti-Buckingham
Sir Robert Phelips d.
Sir Edward Coke d.
Sir Dudley Digges d.
Sir John Eliot d.
Sir Nathaniel Rich d.
Sir Benjamin Rudyerd P.
William Coryton R.
Edward Littleton R.
John Selden P.
Sir Thomas Wentworth d.
Christopher Wandesford R.
Earl of Aruhdel P.
Viscount Saye and Sele P.
Sir Edward Herbert R.
John Glanville R.
Christopher Sherland d.
Edward Whitby d.
Walter Long P.
Sir Robert Mansell N.
Sir Walter Earle P.
Lord Cavendish d.
Edward Kirton R.
Sir Francis Seymour R.
Earl of Hertford R.
John Evelyn P.
Dr. Samuel Turner RN.
Sir Thomas Hoby d.
Earl of Bristol R.
John Digby R.
John Pym P.

P. = Parliamentarian.   R. = Royalist.   N. = Neutral.   d. = dead.
For men who changed sides, the first allegiance has been taken.

ANTI-ARMINIAN SPEAKERS IN THE COMMONS AND
THEIR ALLEGIANCE IN THE CIVIL WAR

John Pym P.
Mr. Thomas Wentworth d.
Sir Heneage Finch d.
Laurence Whitaker P.[1]
Francis Drake d.
Sir George More d.
Sir Robert More d.
Henry Sherfield d.
Christopher Sherland d.
Sir Thomas Fanshaw d.
Sir Robert Harley P.
Sir Henry Mildmay P.
Sir Nathaniel Rich d.
Richard Knightley d.
Walter Long P.
Sir Francis Annesley (Lord Mountnorris) ?N.
Francis Rous P.
Edward Kirton R.
Sir Robert Phelips d.
Sir Walter Earle P.
Sir Benjamin Rudyerd P.
Sir John Eliot d.
William Coryton R.
Sir Thomas Hoby d.
Sir Francis Seymour R.
Sir James Perrott d.
Sir Dudley Digges d.
Henry Waller ?
Sir Miles Fleetwood d.
Sir Richard Grosvenor R.

ATTITUDES TO THE SPANISH WAR AND ALLEGIANCE

For the War	Against the War
Pym P.	Bristol R.
Rich d.	Arundel P.
Digges d.	Selden P.
Rudyerd P.	Mallory R.
Wilde P.	Sir Francis Seymour R.
Neale ?	Sir Thomas Wentworth d.

[1] William Whitaker, the alternative speaker, was also a Parliamentarian.

For the War	*Against the War*
Delbridge ?	Wandesford R.
Eliot d.	Kirton R.
Mansell N.	Sir John Strangeways R.
Saye P.	Sir John Saville d.
Warwick P.	Littleton R.
Essex P.	Noy d.
Southampton d.	Gooch d.
Mr. Thomas Wentworth d.	Alford d.
Earle P.	
Coryton R.	
Crew d.	
Sir Henry Mildmay P.	
Lawrence (?) Whitaker P.[1]	
Sir Robert Harley P.	
Sir Miles Fleetwood d.	
Sir John Coke P.	
Sir James Perrott d.	
Sir Francis Nethersole PN.	
Sir Thomas Roe PN.	
Holland (Earl of) P.	

---

[1] William Whitaker was also an anti-Arminian and a Parliamentarian.

Index

n, 239, 255, 269, 280n, 285, 302–3, 327, 370, 373, 374 and n, 377, 380n, 383, 391, App.

Bristol case (1626), 302–322 *passim*

Brooke, Christopher, 19, 89, 145n, 185, 193, 194n, 196, 232

Brooke, Fulke Greville first Lord, 163

Browne, ? George, 308

Brownists, 431n

Bucer, Martin, 411

Buckingham, George Villiers first Marquis and Duke of:
patronage of, xxi, 9–12, 33, 122–3, 128, 144, 149ff, 164–5, 167–8, 173–4, 263, 338n
and James I, 57, 100, 107–8, 110–11, 146–7
and Charles I, 145–6, 147, 216, 323, 385, 391
and foreign affairs, 71–3, 78–82, 148–53, 158–9, 163, 164–6, 190, 210–11, 263, 323
and religion, 31n, 307
and Parliaments, 133, 136, 137, 143–4, 148–53, 164–6, 235–7, 243–6, 250, 252–6, 378–80, 384, 399n
speeches etc. in Parliament, xix, 107, 110 11, 113, 138 9, 248 9, 371, 372, 373, 374
other references, 38, 238–9, 262, 326
impeachment of, 267–322 *passim*
articles of impeachment of, 304–5
death of, 392

Buckinghamshire, 17. See also Fleetwood, Sir William

Building, restrictions on, 395

Burlamachi, Philip, 158, 380n

Burgess, Richard, 413

Burroughes, Sir John, 270

Burton, Henry, 425

Bye-laws, 62 and n, 102

Cadiz (Spain), 260, 262, 270, 281, 285

Caesar, Sir Julius, 91

Calvert, Sir George, 9, 19, 20, 35, 87, 89, 92, 93, 94, 110n, 118, 130 and n, 132, 137, 145, 159, 166

Calvin, John, 411

Cambridge University, Chancellorship election (1626), 31n, 307. See also Universities

Carleton, Sir Dudley, 16–17, 37, 280–1, 294, 300–1, 303, 306, 357, 392, 393–4, 428, 429–30, App.

Carleton, Dudley, the younger, 201

Carleton, George, Bp., 30, 164, 208

Carlisle, James Hay first Earl of, 306n, 313, 317, 321, 394, 428

Carvile, John, 308

Cavendish, Lord, see Devonshire, Earl of

Cecil, Sir Edward, first Viscount Wimbledon, 120, 157, 160, 184 and n, 262

Cecil, Sir Robert, first Earl of Salisbury, 46, 110n, 116n, 422

Cecil, William, see Salisbury, second Earl of.

Chamberlain, John, xvii, 33, 42, 52, 64, 85–6, 99, 108, 142, 147, 149, 152, 205, 262

Chambers, Richard, 401

Chancery, court of, 114

Charles I, King, 422–3
and Duke of Buckingham, 10, 12, 248n, 268–9, 269–74, 290, 306, 310, 318, 378, 385, 391, 392
and Parliaments, 44–5, 53–4, 78, 219, 234n, 234–5, 238, 241, 248, 259, 268 9, 269 74, 290, 306, 307–8, 310, 318, 321 and n, 340–1, 360–3, 372, 378, 380, 383, 385, 388, 394–6, 397–8, 400, 402, 403, 406, 414–5
and foreign affairs, 78, 219, 238, 240n, 248, 264–5, 323, 391, 393, 397–8
and religion, 240n, 241, 248, 392, 394, 400, 406, 413
and law, 340, 360–3, 367, 372, 383, 388n, 398, 399, 401, 425
as Prince of Wales, 48, 55, 85, 107, 108, 113, 137, 145, 146–53 *passim* 158, 167, 186, 191, 197
other references, 315n, 391, 392, 393

Charters, 59–64 *passim*, 94–5, 115–16, 191, 192–3, 195 and n, 196–7 and n, 198

Cheapside Cross, 277

Chester, 127n
Earldom of, 192
Exchequer of, 271
county of, 181, 337